THE
WISDEN
BOOK OF TEST CRICKET
2009–2014

THE
WISDEN
BOOK OF TEST CRICKET
2009–2014

Sixth edition, Volume 4

Edited by
STEVEN LYNCH

BLOOMSBURY
LONDON · NEW DELHI · NEW YORK · SYDNEY

John Wisden & Co Ltd
An imprint of Bloomsbury Publishing Plc

50 Bedford Square
London
WC1B 3DP
UK

1385 Broadway
New York
NY 10018
USA

www.bloomsbury.com

WISDEN and the wood-engraving device are trademarks of John Wisden & Company Ltd,
a subsidiary of Bloomsbury Publishing Plc

First published 2015

www.wisden.com
www.wisdenrecords.com
Follow Wisden on Twitter @WisdenAlmanack
and on Facebook at Wisden Sports

British Library Cataloguing-in-Publication Data
A catalogue record for this book is available from the British Library.

ISBN: HB: 978-1-4729-1333-3
ePub: 978-1-4729-1334-0

2 4 6 8 10 9 7 5 3 1

Typeset in 7.75pt Times New Roman by Deanta Global Publishing Services, Chennai, India
Printed and bound in Great Britain by CPI Group (UK) Ltd, Croydon CR0 4YY

To find out more about our authors and books visit www.wisden.com.
Here you will find extracts, author interviews, details of forthcoming
events and the option to sign up for our newsletters.

Contents

Preface and Acknowledgements

This book follows on from the previous editions of *The Wisden Book of Test Cricket*, the most recent of which were published in 2009. Since then, over 200 Test matches have been played, taking the total number well over 2,100. This volume fills the gap, with scorecards of all the Tests played since the 2009 English season, up to the end of the 2014 one.

The scorecards are taken directly from *Wisden Cricketers' Almanack*, so are laid out slightly differently to the earliest volumes. The match reports are often edited versions of *Wisden's* own accounts, and include the Almanack's traditional mix of informative comment, facts and figures – and, occasionally, fun. The information given includes close-of-play scores, changes of batting and bowling order in the second innings, details of substitute catchers, the identity of umpires (including the TV one) and referees – and the number of matches in which they have officiated – plus the winners of Man of the Match awards, while the fall-of-wicket information includes the identity of the outgoing batsman.

Test career records are given at the back of the book, as well as an Index showing in which matches a particular player appeared. A range of other records can be found on the wisden.com website, which is regularly updated.

Each match has a reference number to show its overall position, and its place in that particular series. This volume, for example, includes the 2,000th Test match ever played – England v India at Lord's (appropriately enough) in 2011. Its full reference number is "Test No. 2000/100 (E912, I452)". This indicates that it was the 2,000th Test match overall, and the 100th between England and India; furthermore, it was England's 912th Test and India's 452nd.

The overall numbers are arranged chronologically by series – so all the Tests of a particular series appear together and in numerical sequence, even if a match started in another country before the end of the series in question.

Many people gave invaluable assistance in compiling this latest volume. Christopher Lane at Wisden had the original idea for an update, while my colleagues Lawrence Booth, Hugh Chevallier, Harriet Monkhouse and James Coyne were always helpful, and didn't seem to mind that I was occasionally diverted from helping to produce next year's Almanack by having my nose stuck in previous editions. Charlotte Atyeo and Jane Lawes at Bloomsbury saw the project through, while the typesetters Deanta Global Publishing Services dealt capably with the demanding layout. Philip Bailey produced the Test Career Records and the Index with his customary accuracy and speed, while Julian Flanders assisted with the proofreading. And at home, my partner Inese was a great help, while my two young sons Daniel and Mark showed welcome signs of being interested in cricket's constant churn of statistics – and how to play the game they commemorate.

Finally, a great many people contributed to the accuracy of the original facts and figures in *Wisden*, and they are acknowledged in appropriate annual editions of the Almanack.

STEVEN LYNCH
October 2014

INDIA v SRI LANKA 2009–10 (1st Test)

At Sardar Patel Stadium, Motera, Ahmedabad, on 16, 17, 18, 19, 20 November, 2009.
Toss: India.   Result: MATCH DRAWN.
Debuts: none.
Man of the Match: D. P. M. D. Jayawardene.

A result seemed certain when Sri Lanka took four wickets inside the first hour, led by some probing left-arm swing from Welegedara, a last-minute inclusion after injuries to others. But the pitch remained hard as granite, and Dravid led the recovery with an uncharacteristically attacking innings. He collected 110 of his 177 in boundaries, passing 11,000 runs in the process. He was out without addition next morning, and the tail soon folded. Sri Lanka then ran up a mammoth 760, the highest in a Test in India. After Dilshan and Sangakkara laid a strong platform, Mahela Jayawardene showed amazing focus. He reached his sixth Test double-century, passed 9,000 runs, and added 351 with his namesake Prasanna, a new sixth-wicket record, eclipsing 346 by Australians Jack Fingleton and Don Bradman against England at Melbourne in 1936–37. Leg-spinner Mishra became only the sixth Indian to concede 200 runs in a Test innings. Sri Lanka possibly missed the chance of victory when they failed to accelerate on the third evening and the fourth morning. They eventually left themselves 135 overs to bowl India out again, but encountered solid resistance. Tendulkar's century was the 43rd of a Test career that had begun 20 years and one day before this match started. Muralitharan went wicketless in an innings in which he bowled 20 overs for the first time since December 1999 at Harare. Ultimately the dead pitch was the only winner: Sunil Gavaskar felt the groundsman could work on Gujarat's roads, so flat was it.

India

G. Gambhir b Welagedara	1	– c Prasad b Herath	114
V. Sehwag lbw b Welagedara	16	– c Mathews b Herath	51
R. Dravid b Welagedara	177	– lbw b Welagedara	38
S. R. Tendulkar b Welagedara	4	– (5) not out	100
V. V. S. Laxman b Prasad	0	– (6) not out	51
Yuvraj Singh c Dilshan b Muralitharan	68		
*†M. S. Dhoni c H. A. P. W. Jayawardene b Prasad	110		
Harbhajan Singh b Muralitharan	22		
Zaheer Khan lbw b Herath	12		
A. Mishra not out	7	– (4) c Dilshan b Mathews	24
I. Sharma st H. A. P. W. Jayawardene b Muralitharan	0		
B 2, l-b 2, w 1, n-b 4	9	B 12, l-b 9, w 2, n-b 11	34
(104.5 overs)	426	(4 wkts, 129 overs)	412

1/14 (1) 2/27 (2) 3/31 (4) 4/32 (5) 5/157 (6) 6/381 (7)   1/81 (2) 2/169 (3) 3/209 (4) 4/275 (1)
7/389 (3) 8/414 (9) 9/426 (8) 10/426 (11)

Welagedara 22–4–87–4; Prasad 22–1–106–2; Mathews 12–1–50–0; Muralitharan 25.5–4–97–3; Herath 22–2–79–1; Dilshan 1–0–3–0. *Second Innings*—Welagedara 21–1–76–1; Prasad 13–0–56–0; Herath 40–6–97–2; Muralitharan 38–6–124–0; Mathews 15–6–29–1; Dilshan 1–0–2–0; Paranavitana 1–0–7–0.

Sri Lanka

T. M. Dilshan c Dravid b Zaheer Khan	112
N. T. Paranavitana c Dhoni b Sharma	35
*K. C. Sangakkara c Tendulkar b Zaheer Khan	31
D. P. M. D. Jayawardene b Mishra	275
T. T. Samaraweera c Yuvraj Singh b Sharma	70
A. D. Mathews c Gambhir b Harbhajan Singh	17
†H. A. P. W. Jayawardene not out	154
K. T. G. D. Prasad c Mishra b Harbhajan Singh	21
B 5, l-b 16, w 4, n-b 20	45
(7 wkts dec, 202.4 overs)	760

1/74 (2) 2/189 (1) 3/194 (3) 4/332 (5)
5/375 (6) 6/726 (4) 7/760 (8)

H. M. R. K. B. Herath, M. Muralitharan and U. W. M. B. C. A. Welagedara did not bat.

Zaheer Khan 36–6–109–2; Sharma 33–0–135–2; Harbhajan Singh 48.4–4–189–2; Mishra 58–6–203–1; Yuvraj Singh 16–1–64–0; Tendulkar 7–0–20–0; Sehwag 4–1–19–0.

Umpires: D. J. Harper *(Australia)* (86) and A. L. Hill *(New Zealand)* (12).
Third umpire: A. M. Saheba *(India)*. Referee: J. J. Crowe *(New Zealand)* (36).

Close of play: First day, India 385–6 (Dravid 177, Harbhajan Singh 2); Second day, Sri Lanka 275–3 (D. P. M. D. Jayawardene 36, Samaraweera 45); Third day, Sri Lanka 591–5 (D. P. M. D. Jayawardene 204, H. A. P. W. Jayawardene 84); Fourth day, India 190–2 (Gambhir 74, Mishra 12).

INDIA v SRI LANKA 2009–10 (2nd Test)

At Green Park, Kanpur, on 24, 25, 26, 27 November, 2009.
Toss: India.   Result: INDIA WON BY AN INNINGS AND 144 RUNS.
Debuts: India – P. P. Ojha.
Man of the Match: S. Sreesanth.

By the end of the first day, India had scored more runs than in one day of a Test before. By the end of the second, Gambhir (after completing his fourth century in as many matches) was confident there could be only one winner. And by the end of the third Sreesanth had virtually ensured the win, forcing the follow-on. An hour after lunch on the fourth day, India completed their 100th Test victory. Sehwag – dropped by the wicketkeeper in the first over – started the torture for Sri Lanka. After 11 overs India were 31 without loss, but by lunch they had added a further 100, with 73 plundered from nine overs of spin. When Sehwag departed in the 42nd over, to a brilliant diving catch at extra cover by Dilshan, India already had 233. Dravid added another hundred to his Ahmedabad blitz; the only blot was that the last six wickets fell for only 29. Herath, who dared to flight the ball, was rewarded with his first overseas five-for. Sri Lanka were immediately in trouble: Dilshan top-edged the first ball, a harmless leg-side loosener, and Pragyan Ojha at mid-on took the catch from his first possible delivery in a Test. Sreesanth – whose previous Test, 19 months before, was also at Kanpur – capped a successful return with two spectacular spells. Samaraweera resisted spiritedly in the follow-on, but India were soon eying their next goal – reaching No. 1 in the world rankings. For that, they needed to win the Third Test.

India

G. Gambhir c and b Muralitharan	167
V. Sehwag c Dilshan b Muralitharan	131
R. Dravid run out	144
S. R. Tendulkar c Samaraweera b Mendis	40
V. V. S. Laxman c Dilshan b Herath	63
Yuvraj Singh c Sangakkara b Mendis	67
*†M. S. Dhoni b Herath	4
Harbhajan Singh b Herath	5
Zaheer Khan c D. P. M. D. Jayawardene b Herath	1
S. Sreesanth lbw b Herath	0
P. P. Ojha not out	1
B 4, l-b 11, n-b 4	19
(154 overs)	642

1/233 (2) 2/370 (1) 3/464 (4) 4/511 (3) 5/613 (5)
6/619 (7) 7/639 (8) 8/641 (6) 9/641 (9) 10/642 (10)

Welagedara 26–4–103–0; Mathews 17–2–49–0; Herath 33–2–121–5; Mendis 38–3–162–2; Muralitharan 37–0–175–2; Dilshan 3–0–17–0.

Sri Lanka

T. M. Dilshan c Ojha b Zaheer Khan	0	– (2) c Dhoni b Sreesanth	11
N. T. Paranavitana c Dhoni b Sreesanth	38	– (1) lbw b Sehwag	20
*K. C. Sangakkara b Sreesanth	44	– b Harbhajan Singh	11
D. P. M. D. Jayawardene c Tendulkar b Ojha	47	– run out	10
T. T. Samaraweera b Sreesanth	2	– not out	78
A. D. Mathews b Harbhajan Singh	13	– c Dravid b Zaheer Khan	15
†H. A. P. W. Jayawardene c Dhoni b Sreesanth	39	– b Harbhajan Singh	29
H. M. R. K. B. Herath b Sreesanth	11	– lbw b Harbhajan Singh	13
M. Muralitharan lbw b Ojha	6	– b Ojha	29
U. W. M. B. C. A. Welagedara lbw b Harbhajan Singh	7	– (11) c and b Ojha	4
B. A. W. Mendis not out	6	– (10) lbw b Yuvraj Singh	27
B 9, l-b 2, n-b 5	16	B 7, l-b 1, n-b 14	22
(84 overs)	229	(65.3 overs)	269

1/0 (1) 2/82 (2) 3/101 (3) 4/111 (5) 5/134 (6) 6/194 (7)   1/13 (2) 2/37 (1) 3/54 (4) 4/54 (3) 5/79 (6)
7/204 (4) 8/216 (8) 9/219 (9) 10/229 (10)   6/140 (7) 7/154 (8) 8/191 (9) 9/264 (10) 10/269 (11)

Zaheer Khan 17–5–51–1; Sreesanth 22–4–75–5; Harbhajan Singh 21–5–54–2; Ojha 23–12–37–2; Yuvraj Singh 1–0–1–0. *Second Innings*—Zaheer Khan 11–0–63–1; Sreesanth 11–4–47–1; Harbhajan Singh 22–2–98–3; Sehwag 3–0–4–1; Ojha 15.3–4–36–2; Tendulkar 1–0–6–0; Yuvraj Singh 2–0–7–1.

Umpires: A. L. Hill *(New Zealand)* (13) and N. J. Llong *(England)* (7).
Third umpire: S. S. Hazare *(India)*. Referee: J. J. Crowe *(New Zealand)* (37).

Close of play: First day, India 417–2 (Dravid 85, Tendulkar 20); Second day, Sri Lanka 66–1 (Paranavitana 30, Sangakkara 30); Third day, Sri Lanka 57–4 (Samaraweera 1, Mathews 2).

INDIA v SRI LANKA 2009–10 (3rd Test)

At Brabourne Stadium, Mumbai, on 2, 3, 4, 5, 6 December, 2009.
Toss: Sri Lanka. Result: INDIA WON BY AN INNINGS AND 24 RUNS.
Debuts: none.
Man of the Match: V. Sehwag. Man of the Series: V. Sehwag.

Sri Lanka tried everything they could to avert Hurricane Sehwag, but were swept aside for the second time in a fortnight. Sehwag started slowly, but soon took off, Usain Bolt-style: he fell just short of becoming the first to make three Test triple-hundreds. Uniquely, he was involved in double-century stands for the first two wickets for the second time (also against South Africa at Chennai in 2007–08). The pitch for the Brabourne Stadium's first Test since February 1973 turned from the start, so Muralitharan and Herath had favourable conditions … but they were rendered impotent. Sehwag hurried from 184 to 202 in five balls from Kulasekara, with four of his eventual 40 fours (there were also seven sixes), and had 284 as India again broke their daily run-record, with 443 from just 79 overs. "It was one of those days you needed 20 fielders out there," said Sri Lanka's coach Trevor Bayliss. But after adding only nine next morning, Sehwag scooped a simple return catch, having faced 254 balls in 366 minutes. Dhoni, who hit six sixes himself, declared at India's highest total, beating 705 for seven at Sydney in 2003–04. Sri Lanka had started strongly but, not helped by Dilshan being wrongly given out twice (the new Decision Review System was not in use in this series), eventually succumbed to another innings defeat, which put India on top of the Test rankings for the first time since their introduction in 2003. Gambhir missed the match to attend his sister's wedding.

Sri Lanka

N. T. Paranavitana c Dravid b Harbhajan Singh	53 – lbw b Sreesanth	54
T. M. Dilshan c Vijay b Harbhajan Singh	109 – lbw b Harbhajan Singh	16
*K. C. Sangakkara c Dhoni b Ojha	18 – c Dhoni b Zaheer Khan	137
D. P. M. D. Jayawardene c Sehwag b Sreesanth	29 – c Dhoni b Zaheer Khan	12
T. T. Samaraweera c Vijay b Harbhajan Singh	1 – c Laxman b Zaheer Khan	0
A. D. Mathews run out	99 – c Dhoni b Ojha	5
†H. A. P. W. Jayawardene c Harbhajan Singh b Ojha	43 – lbw b Ojha	32
K. M. D. N. Kulasekara c Dhoni b Zaheer Khan	12 – c Laxman b Zaheer Khan	19
H. M. R. K. B. Herath c Dravid b Harbhajan Singh	1 – c Ojha b Zaheer Khan	3
M. Muralitharan not out	4 – c Dhoni b Harbhajan Singh	14
U. W. M. B. C. A. Welegadara lbw b Ojha	8 – not out	0
B 4, l-b 6, w 2, n-b 4	16	B 12, l-b 1, w 1, n-b 3	17
(94.4 overs)	393	(100.4 overs)	309

1/93 (1) 2/128 (3) 3/187 (4) 4/188 (5) 5/262 (2)   1/29 (2) 2/119 (1) 3/135 (4) 4/137 (5) 5/144 (6)
6/329 (7) 7/359 (8) 8/362 (9) 9/379 (6) 10/393 (11)   6/208 (7) 7/278 (3) 8/282 (9) 9/307 (8) 10/309 (10)

Zaheer Khan 19–2–70–1; Sreesanth 16–1–82–1; Harbhajan Singh 32–3–112–4; Ojha 23.4–1–101–3; Yuvraj Singh 4–0–18–0. *Second Innings*—Harbhajan Singh 34.4–5–80–2; Ojha 23–4–84–2; Zaheer Khan 21–5–72–5; Sreesanth 13–4–36–1; Sehwag 9–2–24–0.

India

M. Vijay lbw b Herath	87
V. Sehwag c and b Muralitharan	293
R. Dravid c H. A. P. W. Jayawardene b Welagedara	74
S. R. Tendulkar b Kulasekara	53
V. V. S. Laxman c Kulasekara b Muralitharan	62
Yuvraj Singh c Mathews b Herath	23
*†M. S. Dhoni not out	100
Harbhajan Singh b Muralitharan	1
Zaheer Khan c Kulasekara b Muralitharan	7
S. Sreesanth lbw b Herath	8
P. P. Ojha not out	5
L-b 3, n-b 10	13
(9 wkts dec, 163.3 overs)	726

1/221 (1) 2/458 (2) 3/487 (3) 4/558 (4) 5/591 (5)
6/610 (6) 7/615 (8) 8/647 (9) 9/670 (10)

Welegadara 30–3–131–1; Kulasekara 20–1–105–1; Herath 53.3–2–240–3; Muralitharan 51–4–195–4; Mathews 6–0–36–0; Dilshan 3–0–16–0.

Umpires: D. J. Harper *(Australia)* (87) and N. J. Llong *(England)* (8).
Third umpire: S. K. Tarapore *(India)*. Referee: J. J. Crowe *(New Zealand)* (38).

Close of play: First day, Sri Lanka 366–8 (Mathews 86, Muralitharan 0); Second day, India 443–1 (Sehwag 284, Dravid 62); Third day, Sri Lanka 11–0 (Paranavitana 8, Dilshan 3); Fourth day, Sri Lanka 274–6 (Sangakkara 133, Kulasekara 9).

NEW ZEALAND v PAKISTAN 2009–10 (1st Test)

At University Oval, Dunedin, on 24, 25, 26, 27, 28 November, 2009.
Toss: Pakistan.   Result: NEW ZEALAND WON BY 32 RUNS.
Debuts: Pakistan – Umar Akmal.
Man of the Match: S. E. Bond.

From the first ball, which bowled McIntosh, there was always something happening on a bowler-friendly pitch in what was, in theory at least, a home series for Pakistan (security worries forced the switch). Guptill and Taylor added 117, then Vettori grafted nearly four hours for 99, putting on 164 with McCullum, reprieved by the third umpire after being given lbw to Mohammad Asif, who did well in his first Test back after a drug suspension. Pakistan fielded poorly, and were not immune from batting problems either. Martin removed both openers, then Bond grabbed three wickets in ten balls, including Mohammad Yousuf, another rehabilitated Indian Cricket League returnee. But Umar Akmal, 19, hit his first ball to the third-man boundary, and became the 11th Pakistani to make a Test-debut century (the second in five months, after Fawad Alam). He raced to his hundred with four, six and four in four balls from O'Brien. His brother Kamran was evidently overwhelmed, falling next over after a stand of 176 in three hours. Runs in the bank proved vital, as New Zealand collapsed again: Pakistan had 91 overs to score 251. Bond reduced them to 24 for three, but Yousuf and Umar Akmal resisted (only K. S. Ranjitsinhji, with 216 for England v Australia at Manchester in 1896, made more runs on debut in a losing cause), before New Zealand won with 15 overs left on an exciting final day. Bond finished with eight wickets – but sadly it was to be his Test swansong.

New Zealand

T. G. McIntosh b Mohammad Aamer	0	– (2) lbw b Mohammad Asif	31
M. J. Guptill c Fawad Alam b Mohammad Aamer	60	– (1) b Mohammad Aamer	0
D. R. Flynn c Kamran Akmal b Mohammad Asif	8	– lbw b Mohammad Aamer	0
L. R. P. L. Taylor c Imran Farhat b Saeed Ajmal	94	– run out	59
P. G. Fulton b Mohammad Asif	29	– lbw b Umar Gul	0
G. D. Elliott c Kamran Akmal b Mohammad Asif	8	– c Kamran Akmal b Umar Gul	25
†B. B. McCullum b Umar Gul	78	– c Kamran Akmal b Mohammad Asif	0
*D. L. Vettori c Kamran Akmal b Umar Gul	99	– c Fawad Alam b Mohammad Asif	8
S. E. Bond c Kamran Akmal b Mohammad Asif	22	– b Mohammad Asif	7
I. E. O'Brien not out	13	– lbw b Umar Gul	4
C. S. Martin lbw b Saeed Ajmal	0	– not out	1
L-b 14, w 1, n-b 3	18	B 4, l-b 5, w 1, n-b 3, p 5	18
(131.5 overs)	429	(67 overs)	153

1/0 (1) 2/27 (3) 3/144 (2) 4/192 (4) 5/210 (5) 6/211 (6)
7/375 (7) 8/402 (8) 9/428 (9) 10/429 (11)

1/0 (1) 2/0 (3) 3/87 (4) 4/91 (5) 5/112 (2) 6/115 (7)
7/123 (8) 8/143 (9) 9/150 (10) 10/153 (6)

Mohammad Aamer 24–3–87–2; Mohammad Asif 34–6–108–4; Umar Gul 36–10–129–2; Saeed Ajmal 37.5–10–91–2. *Second Innings*—Mohammad Aamer 16–7–29–2; Mohammad Asif 20–6–43–4; Umar Gul 14–3–41–3; Saeed Ajmal 17–5–26–0.

Pakistan

Khurram Manzoor b Martin	6	– c McCullum b Bond	4
Imran Farhat lbw b Martin	22	– c McIntosh b Martin	1
Fawad Alam c McCullum b Bond	29	– c Fulton b Bond	5
*Mohammad Yousuf c and b Bond	17	– c McCullum b Martin	41
Umar Akmal c Fulton b Bond	129	– c and b Bond	75
Shoaib Malik b Bond	2	– c McCullum b O'Brien	32
†Kamran Akmal c Taylor b Vettori	82	– lbw b O'Brien	27
Mohammad Aamer c Vettori b Bond	26	– c and b Vettori	15
Umar Gul lbw b Vettori	6	– c Vettori b O'Brien	4
Mohammad Asif c McIntosh b Martin	10	– c Taylor b Vettori	0
Saeed Ajmal not out	1	– not out	1
N-b 2	2	B 9, l-b 1, w 2, n-b 1	13
(96.5 overs)	332	(76 overs)	218

1/11 (1) 2/43 (2) 3/74 (4) 4/79 (3) 5/85 (6) 6/261 (7)
7/293 (5) 8/302 (9) 9/320 (10) 10/332 (8)

1/4 (1) 2/6 (2) 3/24 (3) 4/95 (4) 5/161 (6) 6/195 (5)
7/197 (7) 8/203 (9) 9/213 (10) 10/218 (8)

Bond 27.5–4–107–5; Martin 21–8–63–3; O'Brien 21–3–98–0; Vettori 27–7–64–2. *Second Innings*—Bond 21–5–46–3; Martin 16–4–45–2; O'Brien 23–3–63–3; Vettori 14–1–51–2; Elliott 2–0–3–0.

Umpires: B. R. Doctrove *(West Indies)* (26) and S. J. A. Taufel *(Australia)* (60).
Third umpire: R. E. Koertzen *(South Africa)*. Referee: A. G. Hurst *(Australia)* (34).

Close of play: First day, New Zealand 276–6 (McCullum 25, Vettori 40); Second day, New Zealand 404–8 (Bond 8, O'Brien 2); Third day, Pakistan 307–8 (Mohammad Aamer 12, Mohammad Asif 0); Fourth day, New Zealand 147–8 (Eliot 20, O'Brien 4).

NEW ZEALAND v PAKISTAN 2009–10 (2nd Test)

At Basin Reserve, Wellington, on 3, 4, 5, 6 December, 2009.
Toss: New Zealand.   Result: PAKISTAN WON BY 141 RUNS.
Debuts: none.
Man of the Match: Mohammad Asif.

Before the 50th Test at the Basin Reserve, New Zealand suffered a severe blow when an abdominal strain forced Shane Bond to withdraw: not long afterwards he announced his retirement from Test cricket. After a delayed start, Pakistan's new opening pair put on 60, but then three wickets fell in four overs, including Mohammad Yousuf for a second-ball duck. Again, the Akmal brothers did the most productive scoring, though this time not in tandem. Umar smashed 46 in 48 balls, and Kamran 70 in 85, although he survived two reviews of lbw decisions, before both fell to the recalled Tuffey. Locals chortled when Yousuf proclaimed himself satisfied with 264 – but he was even happier after the second day, as New Zealand batted abysmally: all out for 99, with eight men contributing 13 runs between them against bowling that was accurate but hardly deadly. Yousuf returned to No. 3 in the second innings, and made 83 in 283 minutes before he was lbw on review. Umar Akmal wafted, knowing he had the freedom of a substantial lead, to make 52 from 33 balls. The final six wickets fell for 29, but New Zealand's target was an improbable 405. Mohammad Asif again led the way with the ball, taking five wickets, and only Taylor – who narrowly missed a century for the second match running – and Vettori batted with anything like the required purpose. Once again, New Zealand had been unable to build on the advantage of winning the first Test of a series.

Pakistan

Imran Farhat c Taylor b Vettori	32	– c Fulton b O'Brien	35
Salman Butt c Tuffey b O'Brien	29	– c Taylor b O'Brien	18
Umar Akmal b Tuffey	46	– (5) c Vettori b Martin	52
*Mohammad Yousuf lbw b Vettori	0	– (3) lbw b Martin	83
Misbah-ul-Haq lbw b Vettori	21	– (4) c McCullum b O'Brien	33
Shoaib Malik c Vettori b Tuffey	9	– c McCullum b Elliott	3
†Kamran Akmal c Vettori b Tuffey	70	– c McCullum b Elliott	0
Mohammad Aamer c Taylor b O'Brien	21	– c Guptill b Martin	9
Umar Gul c O'Brien b Tuffey	31	– c Fulton b O'Brien	1
Mohammad Asif c and b Vettori	4	– (11) not out	0
Danish Kaneria not out	0	– (10) c Taylor b Martin	0
W 1	1	B 4, l-b 1	5
(88.2 overs)	264	(86.3 overs)	239

1/60 (2) 2/66 (1) 3/66 (4) 4/119 (3) 5/131 (6) 6/156 (5) 7/193 (8) 8/257 (7) 9/264 (10) 10/264 (9)

1/49 (2) 2/54 (1) 3/131 (4) 4/197 (5) 5/210 (6) 6/210 (7) 7/230 (8) 8/239 (3) 9/239 (10) 10/239 (9)

Martin 20–2–64–0; Tuffey 23.2–5–64–4; O'Brien 23–4–78–2; Vettori 22–6–58–4. *Second Innings*—Martin 19–4–52–4; Tuffey 16–3–45–0; Vettori 25–11–63–0; O'Brien 21.3–4–66–4; Elliott 5–1–8–2.

New Zealand

T. G. McIntosh c Salman Butt b Mohammad Asif	4	– (2) lbw b Mohammad Asif	2
M. J. Guptill c Kamran Akmal b Mohammad Aamer	0	– (1) b Mohammad Asif	15
D. R. Flynn lbw b Mohammad Asif	29	– c Kamran Akmal b Mohammad Asif	20
L. R. P. L. Taylor b Umar Gul	30	– c Misbah-ul-Haq b Mohammad Aamer	97
P. G. Fulton lbw b Umar Gul	0	– c Kamran Akmal b Mohammad Aamer	13
G. D. Elliott c and b Danish Kaneria	20	– b Danish Kaneria	6
†B. B. McCullum c Shoaib Malik b Mohammad Asif	0	– c Kamran Akmal b Danish Kaneria	24
*D. L. Vettori c Misbah-ul-Haq b Danish Kaneria	6	– c Umar Akmal b Mohammad Asif	40
D. R. Tuffey c Mohammad Yousuf b Mohammad Asif	3	– lbw b Danish Kaneria	3
I. E. O'Brien c Imran Farhat b Danish Kaneria	0	– c Shoaib Malik b Mohammad Asif	31
C. S. Martin not out	0	– not out	0
L-b 7	7	B 6, l-b 6	12
(36.5 overs)	99	(82.5 overs)	263

1/1 (2) 2/5 (1) 3/48 (4) 4/52 (5) 5/85 (3) 6/85 (7) 7/95 (6) 8/96 (8) 9/96 (10) 10/99 (9)

1/4 (2) 2/36 (1) 3/37 (3) 4/80 (5) 5/108 (6) 6/186 (4) 7/206 (7) 8/212 (9) 9/252 (8) 10/263 (10)

Mohammad Aamer 11–2–25–1; Mohammad Asif 12.5–2–40–4; Umar Gul 7–2–21–2; Danish Kaneria 6–2–6–3. *Second Innings*—Mohammad Aamer 16–3–64–2; Mohammad Asif 23.5–9–67–5; Danish Kaneria 31–6–74–3; Umar Gul 11–2–41–0; Shoaib Malik 1–0–5–0.

Umpires: R. E. Koertzen *(South Africa)* (102) and S. J. A. Taufel *(Australia)* (61).
Third umpire: B. R. Doctrove *(West Indies)*. Referee: A. G. Hurst *(Australia)* (35).

Close of play: First day, Pakistan 161–6 (Kamran Akmal 21, Mohammad Aamer 2); Second day, Pakistan 64–2 (Mohammad Yousuf 10, Misbah-ul-Haq 1); Third day, New Zealand 70–3 (Taylor 15, Fulton 12).

NEW ZEALAND v PAKISTAN 2009–10 (3rd Test)

At McLean Park, Napier, on 11, 12, 13, 14, 15 December, 2009.
Toss: Pakistan.   Result: MATCH DRAWN.
Debuts: New Zealand – B-J. Watling.
Man of the Match: D. L. Vettori.

A dramatic, dogged, exciting match ended when heavy rain stalled New Zealand's victory charge at 90 without loss, with another 118 runs needed from 24 overs. Rather than start with his power-hitters, Vettori had bravely retained the dogged McIntosh and the novice Barrie-Jon Watling to start the chase. They started carefully – six runs from five overs – then stepped up to 35 from ten before Danish Kaneria applied the brakes. But Watling's inventiveness put New Zealand in pole position… and then the heavens opened. Because the threat of terrorism had forced them to play what should have been a home series on opposition soil, Pakistan had asked that the Tests start at noon so viewers back home could switch on at 4am rather than 2.30. The number of overs should have been unaffected, but it had been a sunny morning, so without the change New Zealand might well have won before the rain arrived. The early exchanges had seen Imran Farhat carry his bat after a burst of four for three in five overs from O'Brien, playing his final Test before retirement. Later the recalled Tuffey took four wickets, all caught behind. New Zealand were again rescued by Vettori, who promoted himself to No. 6: he put on 176 with McCullum, and went on to his fifth Test century while Tuffey biffed eight fours and two sixes. Kaneria finished with seven wickets from 53 overs. Pakistan batted steadily, taking their lead past 200 despite three wickets from Guptill's very occasional off-spin.

Pakistan

Imran Farhat not out	117	– c and b Guptill		61
Salman Butt b Southee	9	– c and b Guptill		66
Faisal Iqbal c Guptill b O'Brien	6	– c Taylor b Martin		67
*Mohammad Yousuf c McIntosh b O'Brien	0	– c McCullum b O'Brien		89
Umar Akmal c Guptill b O'Brien	0	– c McCullum b Southee		77
Misbah-ul-Haq c McCullum b O'Brien	0	– st McCullum b Vettori		7
†Kamran Akmal c Guptill b Martin	22	– not out		56
Mohammad Aamer c McCullum b Tuffey	23	– c Martin b Vettori		7
Umar Gul c McCullum b Tuffey	24	– c Flynn b O'Brien		0
Mohammad Asif c McCullum b Tuffey	0	– (11) lbw b Guptill		0
Danish Kaneria c McCullum b Tuffey	16	– (10) c McCullum b Southee		11
L-b 2, n-b 4	6	B 3, l-b 2, w 1, n-b 3, p 5		14
(64.3 overs)	223	(193.2 overs)		455

1/14 (2) 2/39 (3) 3/43 (4) 4/51 (5) 5/51 (6) 6/90 (7)
7/159 (8) 8/194 (9) 9/194 (10) 10/223 (11)

1/129 (2) 2/146 (1) 3/274 (3) 4/333 (4) 5/361 (6)
6/397 (5) 7/421 (8) 8/423 (9) 9/449 (10) 10/455 (11)

Martin 9–0–37–1; Southee 17–4–62–1; O'Brien 15–5–35–4; Tuffey 15.3–4–52–4; Vettori 8–0–35–0. *Second Innings*—Martin 32–6–82–1; Southee 31–8–64–2; O'Brien 40–6–108–2; Tuffey 21–2–61–0; Vettori 56–25–93–2; Guptill 13.2–2–37–3.

New Zealand

T. G. McIntosh c Kamran Akmal b Danish Kaneria	74	– not out		23
B. J. Watling c Umar Akmal b Mohammad Asif	18	– not out		60
M. J. Guptill lbw b Danish Kaneria	13			
L. R. P. L. Taylor c Mohammad Yousuf b Danish Kaneria	21			
D. R. Flynn c Kamran Akmal b Danish Kaneria	5			
*D. L. Vettori c Umar Akmal b Mohammad Asif	134			
†B. B. McCullum c Faisal Iqbal b Umar Gul	89			
D. R. Tuffey not out	80			
T. G. Southee lbw b Danish Kaneria	0			
I. E. O'Brien st Kamran Akmal b Danish Kaneria	19			
C. S. Martin lbw b Danish Kaneria	0			
B 8, l-b 4, w 2, n-b 4	18	B 2, l-b 1, n-b 4		7
(139 overs)	471	(no wkt, 19 overs)		90

1/60 (2) 2/82 (3) 3/118 (4) 4/136 (1) 5/145 (5) 6/321 (7)
7/408 (6) 8/409 (9) 9/471 (10) 10/471 (11)

Mohammad Aamer 22–6–74–0; Mohammad Asif 31–10–103–2; Umar Gul 33–5–114–1; Danish Kaneria 53–10–168–7. *Second Innings*—Mohammad Asif 5–0–15–0; Mohammad Aamer 6–1–27–0; Danish Kaneria 5–0–21–0; Umar Gul 3–0–24–0.

Umpires: B. R. Doctrove *(West Indies)* (27) and R. E. Koertzen *(South Africa)* (103).
Third umpire: S. J. A. Taufel *(Australia)*. A. G. Hurst *(Australia)* (36).

Close of play: First day, New Zealand 47–0 (McIntosh 31, Watling 13); Second day, New Zealand 346–6 (Vettori 100, Tuffey 13); Third day, Pakistan 128–0 (Imran Farhat 55, Salman Butt 66); Fourth day, Pakistan 347–4 (Umar Akmal 48, Misbah-ul-Haq 4).

AUSTRALIA v WEST INDIES 2009–10 (1st Test)

At Woolloongabba, Brisbane, on 26, 27, 28 November, 2009.
Toss: Australia.   Result: AUSTRALIA WON BY AN INNINGS AND 65 RUNS.
Debuts: West Indies – A. B. Barath, R. Rampaul.
Man of the Match: B. W. Hilfenhaus.

Australia were seeking redemption after Ashes defeat in England, while West Indies, back almost to full strength after a contracts dispute led to a replacement team losing to Bangladesh, were simply looking to be competitive. Australia recalled off-spinner Hauritz, who duly produced his finest performance in his eighth Test, spread over more than five years, clipping a maiden half-century and taking five cheap wickets. Hilfenhaus shrugged off knee tendinitis to collect five wickets, while Hussey had an even rarer success, taking his second Test wicket when Bravo hooked a very medium-paced bouncer. Travis Dowlin, a survivor of the Bangladesh shambles, was a revelation with a fighting 62, but the real find was the Trinidadian Adrian Barath: just 19, he was only the ninth teenager to score a century on Test debut, following Pakistan's Umar Akmal by a day or two. He was the youngest West Indian to score a Test century, beating George Headley (1929–30) by a year, and only the fifth batsman to hit the only century of a Test his side lost by an innings. Ponting enforced the follow-on for only the third time in his 62-match tenure (there had been seven further occasions when he had declined to do so; an eighth followed at Perth), whereupon his bowlers scythed through some feeble batting. The innings victory was Australia's ninth consecutive win against West Indies at home, equalling their record against anyone, and their 16th win in 21 Tests at Brisbane since losing to West Indies in 1988–89.

Australia

S. R. Watson lbw b Taylor	0
S. M. Katich c Ramdin b Bravo	92
*R. T. Ponting c Ramdin b Roach	55
M. E. K. Hussey c and b Benn	66
M. J. Clarke c Gayle b Bravo	41
M. J. North c Ramdin b Bravo	79
†B. J. Haddin c Ramdin b Rampaul	38
M. G. Johnson c Ramdin b Benn	7
N. M. Hauritz not out	50
P. M. Siddle not out	20
B 2, l-b 9, w 1, n-b 20	32
(8 wkts dec, 135 overs)	480

1/0 (1) 2/126 (3) 3/200 (2) 4/253 (4) 5/287 (5)
6/371 (7) 7/386 (8) 8/444 (6)

B. W. Hilfenhaus did not bat.

Taylor 9–2–43–1; Roach 25–4–76–1; Rampaul 26–3–110–1; Bravo 32–4–118–3; Benn 34–5–86–2; Gayle 9–0–36–0.

West Indies

*C. H. Gayle lbw b Hilfenhaus	31	– lbw b Hilfenhaus	1
A. Barath c Watson b Johnson	15	– lbw b Watson	104
T. M. Dowlin c Watson b Hauritz	62	– b Hilfenhaus	4
S. Chanderpaul lbw b Siddle	2	– c Katich b Hilfenhaus	2
D. J. Bravo c Watson b Johnson	0	– c Hilfenhaus b Hussey	23
B. P. Nash c Haddin b Watson	18	– lbw b Hauritz	7
†D. Ramdin c North b Johnson	54	– c Haddin b Hauritz	16
S. J. Benn c Siddle b Hilfenhaus	28	– (9) not out	15
J. E. Taylor c Katich b Hauritz	8	– (8) c Hilfenhaus b Watson	0
K. A. J. Roach c Clarke b Hauritz	0	– c Hussey b Siddle	5
R. Rampaul not out	1	– c Haddin b Johnson	0
B 1, l-b 3, n-b 5	9	L-b 4, n-b 6	10
(63 overs)	228	(52.1 overs)	187

1/49 (1) 2/49 (2) 3/58 (4) 4/63 (5) 5/96 (6) 6/174 (7)   1/6 (1) 2/18 (3) 3/39 (4) 4/105 (5) 5/141 (6)
7/212 (8) 8/221 (9) 9/221 (10) 10/228 (3)   6/154 (2) 7/158 (8) 8/170 (7) 9/187 (10) 10/187 (11)

Hilfenhaus 16–6–50–2; Siddle 13–4–51–1; Johnson 19–4–75–3; Watson 9–0–31–1; Hauritz 6–3–17–3. *Second Innings*—Hilfenhaus 7–3–20–3; Siddle 10–3–41–1; Johnson 9.1–1–35–1; Watson 10–0–44–2; Hauritz 14–1–40–2; Hussey 2–0–3–1.

Umpires: Asad Rauf *(Pakistan)* (27) and I. J. Gould *(England)* (7).
Third umpire: M. R. Benson *(England)*. Referee: B. C. Broad *(England)* (36).

Close of play: First day, Australia 322–5 (North 42, Haddin 9); Second day, West Indies 134–5 (Dowlin 40, Ramdin 22).

AUSTRALIA v WEST INDIES 2009–10 (2nd Test)

At Adelaide Oval on 4, 5, 6, 7, 8 December, 2009.
Toss: West Indies.   Result: MATCH DRAWN.
Debuts: none.
Man of the Match: C. H. Gayle.

What a difference a week makes. Reeling from a three-day shellacking that gave rise to "Worst Indies" headlines, the tourists outplayed their recent conquerors. Sarwan (injured for Brisbane) helped stabilise West Indies' first innings, before Chanderpaul's four-hour 62 ended controversially when third umpire Asad Rauf gave him out on referral, claiming "common sense" enabled him to deduce the faintest of edges despite the technology being unable to pick one up. On-field umpire Mark Benson withdrew that night, pleading illness, and flew home to England, inciting speculation that his decision was driven by Rauf's overrule. Bravo glided to his third Test century, helped by 92 from the former Queenslander Nash, as West Indies reached 451. Australia went close in reply, although the batsmen continued their new-found habit of passing 50 without reaching 100. Watson made it to 96 before losing his middle stump attempting to heave the boundary that would have completed his maiden Test century. Soon Gayle entered the fray. He found allies who hung around while he resisted his natural attacking instincts, en route to a splendid chanceless 165 out of 317. He batted through the 441-minute innings, saw off 285 deliveries and ten partners, and struck 16 fours and a six. Only three other West Indian openers had carried their bats – Desmond Haynes (three times), Conrad Hunte and Frank Worrell. Gayle might perhaps have declared earlier, instead continuing well into the last day for a lead of 329. Australia were rarely troubled, although Bravo jangled nerves with three quick wickets.

West Indies

*C. H. Gayle c Haddin b Bollinger	26	– not out	165
A. Barath c Hussey b Bollinger	3	– run out	17
R. R. Sarwan c Clarke b Johnson	28	– c Haddin b Johnson	7
S. Chanderpaul c Haddin b Watson	62	– lbw b Bollinger	27
B. P. Nash b Johnson	92	– b Watson	24
D. J. Bravo b Hauritz	104	– c Hauritz b Johnson	22
†D. Ramdin b Watson	4	– b Johnson	0
D. J. G. Sammy lbw b Siddle	44	– c Ponting b Bollinger	10
S. J. Benn lbw b Hauritz	17	– c Siddle b Johnson	5
K. A. J. Roach c Haddin b Johnson	2	– (11) c Ponting b Bollinger	8
R. Rampaul not out	40	– (10) b Johnson	14
B 5, l-b 14, w 5, n-b 5	29	B 8, l-b 3, w 1, n-b 6	18
(124.1 overs)	451	(99.5 overs)	317

1/26 (2) 2/39 (1) 3/84 (3) 4/235 (4) 5/239 (7)   1/45 (2) 2/61 (3) 3/133 (4) 4/194 (5) 5/251 (6)
6/273 (6) 7/336 (8) 8/380 (9) 9/383 (10) 10/451 (5)   6/251 (7) 7/277 (8) 8/284 (9) 9/302 (10) 10/317 (11)

Bollinger 25–3–67–2; Siddle 25–6–92–1; Johnson 26.1–3–105–3; Hauritz 36–5–111–2; Watson 12–2–57–2. *Second Innings*—Johnson 22–1–103–5; Bollinger 17.5–3–50–3; Hauritz 27–4–68–0; Siddle 8–2–28–0; North 14–2–42–0; Watson 11–5–15–1.

Australia

S. R. Watson b Benn	96	– c Bravo b Sammy	48
S. M. Katich c Barath b Benn	80	– c Barath b Bravo	21
*R. T. Ponting c Bravo b Roach	36	– b Rampaul	20
M. E. K. Hussey c Ramdin b Roach	41	– c Ramdin b Bravo	29
M. J. Clarke c Sarwan b Benn	71	– not out	61
M. J. North c Bravo b Benn	16	– c Sarwan b Bravo	2
†B. J. Haddin not out	55	– not out	21
M. G. Johnson c Gayle b Sammy	7		
N. M. Hauritz c Ramdin b Roach	17		
P. M. Siddle c Bravo b Benn	0		
D. E. Bollinger run out	0		
L-b 2, n-b 18	20	B 1, l-b 2, n-b 7	10
(131.1 overs)	439	(5 wkts, 76 overs)	212

1/174 (1) 2/193 (2) 3/233 (3) 4/312 (4) 5/353 (6)   1/33 (2) 2/68 (3) 3/114 (1) 4/133 (4) 5/139 (6)
6/370 (5) 7/377 (8) 8/418 (9) 9/419 (10) 10/439 (11)

Roach 25.1–3–93–3; Rampaul 14–1–52–0; Bravo 12–1–43–0; Sammy 18–2–79–1; Benn 53–8–155–5; Gayle 9–1–15–0. *Second Innings*—Roach 16–3–66–0; Rampaul 9–2–22–1; Benn 27–10–51–0; Bravo 15–4–37–3; Gayle 3–1–8–0; Sammy 5–0–21–1; Barath 1–0–4–0.

Umpires: M. R. Benson *(England)* (27) and I. J. Gould *(England)* (8).
Third umpire: Asad Rauf *(Pakistan)*. Referee: B. C. Broad *(England)* (37).
Asad Rauf (28) replaced Benson from the second day; B. N. J. Oxenford *(Australia)* took over as third umpire.

Close of play: First day, West Indies 336–6 (Nash 44, Sammy 44); Second day, Australia 174–0 (Watson 96, Katich 71); Third day, West Indies 23–0 (Barath 10, Gayle 12); Fourth day, West Indies 284–8 (Gayle 155, Rampaul 0).

AUSTRALIA v WEST INDIES 2009–10 (3rd Test)

At W. A. C. A. Ground, Perth, on 16, 17, 18, 19, 20 December, 2009.
Toss: Australia.   Result: AUSTRALIA WON BY 35 RUNS.
Debuts: Australia – C. J. McKay. West Indies – G. C. Tonge.
Man of the Match: C. H. Gayle. Man of the Series: C. H. Gayle.

Having played the tortoise with such solidity at Adelaide, Gayle released the hare the following week. His 70-ball assault meant he reached three figures one delivery faster than Roy Fredericks's famously furious century at the WACA in 1975–76. Yet for all the drama of Gayle's remarkable innings – which included six sixes, one of them on to the roof of the five-storey Lillee–Marsh Stand – the fact that his team ran Australia so close was overshadowed by a series of ugly confrontations. Four players were disciplined: Benn was banned for two one-day internationals, while Johnson, Haddin and Watson were fined. Roach relished the conditions, producing some dynamic high-speed bowling that raised questions about Ponting's longevity (he retired hurt for the first time in his career when a bumper slammed into his left elbow). Australia declared at 520, Katich suffering his second Test dismissal for 99, and West Indies fell 208 short (Ponting again waived the follow-on). But Gayle's rampage seemingly inspired his bowlers: Australia were rattled by Roach's pace and Bravo's late swing. West Indies required 359 for their sixth victory at Perth, but the absence of Chanderpaul (who damaged a finger at Adelaide) proved crucial. Deonarine and Nash added 128, then Benn and Roach hoicked effectively. The game had a dramatic finale, with the players waiting in the middle for several minutes while the last wicket was upheld on Asad Rauf's review, despite no evidence to support Billy Bowden's decision that Roach had feathered a catch behind.

Australia

S. R. Watson c Ramdin b Roach	89	– lbw b Tonge 30
S. M. Katich c Roach b Benn	99	– b Rampaul 10
*R. T. Ponting retired hurt	23	– (9) c Dowlin b Roach 2
M. E. K. Hussey c Ramdin b Rampaul	82	– c Dowlin b Benn 17
M. J. Clarke c Gayle b Deonarine	11	– (3) c Ramdin b Bravo 25
M. J. North c and b Deonarine	68	– (5) c Ramdin b Bravo 1
†B. J. Haddin c Ramdin b Roach	88	– (6) c Bravo b Benn 23
M. G. Johnson c Benn b Bravo	35	– (7) c Nash b Bravo 5
N. M. Hauritz not out	2	– (8) c Sarwan b Bravo 11
C. J. McKay (did not bat)		– c Deonarine b Benn 10
D. E. Bollinger (did not bat)		– not out 2
B 4, l-b 2, w 1, n-b 16	23	B 9, l-b 2, w 1, n-b 2 14
(7 wkts dec, 130.4 overs)	520	(51.3 overs) 150

1/132 (1) 2/260 (2) 3/277 (5) 4/355 (4) 5/444 (6)
6/510 (7) 7/520 (8)

1/15 (2) 2/66 (1) 3/81 (3) 4/89 (4) 5/109 (5)
6/117 (6) 7/125 (7) 8/134 (9) 9/146 (10) 10/150 (8)

In the first innings R. T. Ponting retired hurt at 175–1.

Roach 22–2–104–2; Rampaul 22–6–85–1; Tonge 18–1–85–0; Bravo 17.4–1–79–1; Benn 28–4–87–1; Deonarine 23–4–74–2. *Second Innings*—Roach 6–0–18–1; Rampaul 6–1–21–1; Tonge 10–2–28–1; Deonarine 1–0–1–0; Bravo 17.3–6–42–4; Benn 11–2–29–3.

West Indies

*C. H. Gayle c Watson b Bollinger	102	– c Haddin b Watson 21
T. M. Dowlin c Hussey b Johnson	55	– c Clarke b Bollinger 22
R. R. Sarwan c Hussey b Bollinger	42	– c Haddin b Hauritz 11
N. Deonarine c Watson b Johnson	18	– b Watson 82
B. P. Nash c Clarke b Hauritz	44	– b Bollinger 65
D. J. Bravo c Haddin b Bollinger	26	– c Hussey b Johnson 1
†D. Ramdin b Bollinger	8	– b McKay 14
S. J. Benn c Haddin b Hauritz	3	– c sub (T. P. Doropoulos) b Johnson 33
R. Rampaul c Haddin b Hauritz	0	– c McKay b Johnson 10
K. A. J. Roach not out	0	– c Haddin b Bollinger 17
G. C. Tonge c Haddin b Bollinger	2	– not out 23
L-b 5, w 1, n-b 6	12	B 9, l-b 9, w 1, n-b 5 24
(81 overs)	312	(94.3 overs) 323

1/136 (1) 2/175 (2) 3/214 (3) 4/239 (4) 5/285 (6)
6/295 (5) 7/310 (8) 8/310 (9) 9/310 (7) 10/312 (11)

1/35 (2) 2/52 (1) 3/68 (3) 4/196 (4) 5/197 (6)
6/231 (7) 7/245 (5) 8/279 (8) 9/279 (9) 10/323 (10)

Bollinger 20–3–70–5; Johnson 18–3–92–2; McKay 14–3–45–0; Hauritz 17–1–66–3; Watson 12–3–34–0. *Second Innings*—Bollinger 20.3–3–71–3; Johnson 16–5–67–3; McKay 14–2–56–1; Watson 14–5–30–2; Hauritz 23–7–61–1; North 7–1–20–0.

Umpires: B. F. Bowden *(New Zealand)* (57) and I. J. Gould *(England)* (9).
Third umpire: Asad Rauf *(Pakistan)*. Referee: B. C. Broad *(England)* (38).

Close of play: First day, Australia 339–3 (Hussey 81, North 23); Second day, West Indies 214–2 (Sarwan 42, Deonarine 10); Third day, Australia 137–8 (Hauritz 11, McKay 1); Fourth day, West Indies 308–9 (Roach 13, Tonge 12).

SOUTH AFRICA v ENGLAND 2009–10 (1st Test)

At Centurion Park, Pretoria, on 16, 17, 18, 19, 20 December, 2009.
Toss: England.   Result: MATCH DRAWN.
Debuts: South Africa – F. de Wet.
Man of the Match: G. P. Swann.

For the second time in five months, England's last-wicket pair saved a Test amid high drama but, unlike the opening Ashes Test at Cardiff in July, when James Anderson and Monty Panesar defied the odds to conclude a prolonged rearguard, this time it was more a tail-between-the-legs escape after an embarrassing collapse. Kallis's 32nd Test century propped up South Africa's first innings, then Swann reduced the deficit with an exuberant 81 from 85 balls. He had earlier taken his 50th Test wicket, a record 33 of them left-handers. South Africa then slipped to 46 for four, a lead of just 108, but Amla – whose seventh Test century took more than five hours – led a recovery. Any target over 300 on a dry, slow, cracked pitch would probably have been beyond England, but 364 in 96 overs was never likely. Early on the final morning England were 27 for three, but Pietersen and Trott – two converted South Africans – made the surface look pristine in a stand of 145 and, more pertinently, 43 overs, until Pietersen ran himself out after tea. The 29-year-old debutant Friedel de Wet then grabbed three for 11 with the second new ball, as five wickets tumbled in 11 overs. Collingwood produced a smaller version of his Cardiff blockade with 26 from 99 balls, but was unable to prevent last man Onions from facing a dozen torturous deliveries, including the final six from Ntini, the fifth South African to play 100 Tests. But Onions survived with some aplomb.

South Africa

*G. C. Smith c Prior b Broad	0	– (2) b Onions	12
A. G. Prince c Collingwood b Swann	45	– (1) b Anderson	0
H. M. Amla c Collingwood b Onions	19	– (4) b Anderson	100
J. H. Kallis c Collingwood b Anderson	120	– (5) c Cook b Broad	4
A. B. de Villiers c Cook b Swann	32	– (6) c Bell b Broad	64
J-P. Duminy c Collingwood b Swann	56	– (7) lbw b Anderson	11
†M. V. Boucher c Cook b Swann	49	– (8) not out	63
M. Morkel c Prior b Onions	13	– (9) not out	22
P. L. Harris b Onions	38	– (3) b Anderson	11
F. de Wet lbw b Swann	20		
M. Ntini not out	4		
B 2, l-b 15, w 5	22	L-b 10, w 4	14
(153.2 overs)	418	(7 wkts dec, 85.5 overs)	301

1/1 (1) 2/51 (3) 3/93 (2) 4/159 (5) 5/283 (4) 6/316 (6) 7/341 (8) 8/377 (7) 9/414 (9) 10/418 (10)
1/2 (1) 2/20 (3) 3/34 (2) 4/46 (5) 5/165 (6) 6/191 (7) 7/266 (4)

Anderson 37–9–104–1; Broad 32–8–74–1; Onions 30–5–86–3; Swann 45.2–10–110–5; Collingwood 7–1–18–0; Trott 2–0–9–0. *Second Innings*—Anderson 20.5–1–73–4; Onions 16–3–50–1; Broad 16–5–58–2; Swann 27–3–91–0; Collingwood 6–1–19–0.

England

*A. J. Strauss b Ntini	46	– c Boucher b Morkel	1
A. N. Cook c Boucher b de Wet	15	– c Smith b Harris	12
I. J. L. Trott b Harris	28	– (4) c de Villiers b de Wet	69
K. P. Pietersen b Morkel	40	– (5) run out	81
P. D. Collingwood c Kallis b Harris	50	– (6) not out	26
I. R. Bell b Harris	5	– (7) c Boucher b de Wet	2
†M. J. Prior c de Wet b Harris	4	– (8) c Boucher b de Wet	0
S. C. J. Broad lbw b Duminy	17	– (9) c Boucher b Harris	0
G. P. Swann c Smith b Harris	85	– (10) lbw b Morkel	2
J. M. Anderson c Morkel b Ntini	29	– (3) c Boucher b de Wet	10
G. Onions not out	4	– not out	1
B 8, l-b 8, w 5, n-b 12	33	B 10, l-b 3, n-b 11	24
(104 overs)	356	(9 wkts, 96 overs)	228

1/25 (2) 2/98 (1) 3/119 (3) 4/168 (4) 5/189 (6) 6/211 (7) 7/221 (5) 8/242 (8) 9/348 (10) 10/356 (9)
1/5 (1) 2/16 (3) 3/27 (2) 4/172 (5) 5/205 (4) 6/207 (7) 7/208 (8) 8/209 (9) 9/218 (10)

Ntini 23–4–78–2; de Wet 20–3–72–1; Morkel 21–0–60–1; Harris 37–10–123–5; Duminy 3–0–7–1. *Second Innings*—Ntini 18–7–41–0; Morkel 18–3–46–2; Harris 26–11–51–2; de Wet 23–8–55–4; Duminy 8–2–17–0; Kallis 3–1–5–0.

Umpires: Aleem Dar *(Pakistan)* (58) and S. J. Davis *(Australia)* (20).
Third umpire: A. M. Saheba *(India)*. Referee: R. S. Mahanama *(Sri Lanka)* (25).

Close of play: First day, South Africa 262–4 (Kallis 112, Duminy 38); Second day, England 88–1 (Strauss 44, Trott 18); Third day, South Africa 9–1 (Smith 6, Harris 2); Fourth day, England 11–1 (Cook 4, Anderson 6).

SOUTH AFRICA v ENGLAND 2009–10 (2nd Test)

At Kingsmead, Durban, on 26, 27, 28, 29, 30 December, 2009.
Toss: South Africa.   Result: ENGLAND WON BY AN INNINGS AND 98 RUNS.
Debuts: none.
Man of the Match: G. P. Swann.

As they had done in the preceding Ashes series, England bounced back from near-defeat in the First Test to record a convincing victory in the Second. It was the first time Smith had lost a Test by an innings, and his side also lost any hopes of regaining the No. 1 Test ranking they had held the previous month. Smith could neither deny the excellence of England's batsmen – Cook and Bell collected their tenth and ninth Test centuries respectively – nor ignore his own side's capitulation for just 133 in exactly 50 overs to finish the game. Another five-for by Swann earned him successive match awards to complete a remarkable year. Things had looked very different when Smith and Kallis were motoring along on the first afternoon, but both fell within seven overs of tea, and the eventual 343 was soon put into perspective. Cook, with just one half-century in 11 innings, ground his way to the most disciplined hundred of his career to date, practically ignoring anything outside off stump. Then Broad stepped in: finding early reverse swing, he hit the top of Kallis's off stump with no shot offered, soon trapped de Villiers lbw as the ball zeroed in towards off stump – again, no shot was attempted – and the next ball clattered into Duminy's stumps via the inside edge after he thought about playing a shot then decided against it. Fifteen balls, one run, three wickets, and not a shot in sight… the game was as good as up.

South Africa

*G. C. Smith run out	75	– (2) lbw b Swann	22
A. G. Prince c Swann b Anderson	2	– (1) c Bell b Swann	16
H. M. Amla lbw b Broad	2	– b Swann	6
J. H. Kallis c Collingwood b Swann	75	– b Broad	3
A. B. de Villiers c Prior b Broad	50	– lbw b Broad	2
J-P. Duminy lbw b Onions	4	– b Broad	0
†M. V. Boucher lbw b Swann	39	– c Prior b Broad	29
M. Morkel lbw b Swann	23	– lbw b Swann	15
P. L. Harris lbw b Swann	2	– c Broad b Anderson	36
D. W. Steyn c Prior b Anderson	47	– lbw b Swann	3
M. Ntini not out	6	– not out	1
B 1, l-b 17	18		
(108.3 overs)	343	(50 overs)	133

1/3 (2) 2/10 (3) 3/160 (4) 4/166 (1) 5/170 (6)
6/233 (7) 7/269 (5) 8/280 (9) 9/285 (8) 10/343 (10)

1/27 (1) 2/37 (3) 3/40 (4) 4/44 (5) 5/44 (6)
6/50 (2) 7/86 (8) 8/108 (7) 9/129 (9) 10/133 (10)

Anderson 23.3–4–75–2; Onions 23–6–62–1; Broad 20–6–44–2; Swann 35–3–110–4; Trott 4–0–19–0; Pietersen 2–0–7–0; Collingwood 1–0–8–0. *Second Innings*—Anderson 8–2–24–1; Onions 4–1–12–0; Swann 21–3–54–5; Broad 17–3–43–4.

England

*A. J. Strauss b Morkel	54
A. N. Cook c Kallis b Morkel	118
I. J. L. Trott c Boucher b Morkel	18
K. P. Pietersen lbw b Harris	31
P. D. Collingwood c Boucher b Duminy	91
I. R. Bell c Boucher b Steyn	140
†M. J. Prior b Duminy	60
S. C. J. Broad c Kallis b Duminy	20
G. P. Swann c Prince b Steyn	22
J. M. Anderson not out	1
G. Onions not out	2
L-b 10, w 6, n-b 1	17
(9 wkts dec, 170 overs)	574

1/71 (1) 2/104 (3) 3/155 (4) 4/297 (2) 5/365 (5)
6/477 (7) 7/536 (8) 8/564 (9) 9/568 (6)

Steyn 34–6–94–2; Ntini 29–4–114–0; Morkel 31–6–78–3; Kallis 14–1–43–0; Harris 38–4–146–1; Duminy 24–1–89–3.

Umpires: Aleem Dar *(Pakistan)* (59) and A. M. Saheba *(India)* (3).
Third umpire: S. J. Davis *(Australia)*. Referee: R. S. Mahanama *(Sri Lanka)* (26).

Close of play: First day, South Africa 175–5 (de Villiers 8, Boucher 1); Second day, England 103–1 (Cook 31, Trott 17); Third day, England 386–5 (Bell 55, Prior 11); Fourth day, South Africa 76–6 (Boucher 20, Morkel 7).

SOUTH AFRICA v ENGLAND 2009–10 (3rd Test)

At Newlands, Cape Town, on 3, 4, 5, 6, 7 January, 2010.
Toss: England.   Result: MATCH DRAWN.
Debuts: none.
Man of the Match: G. C. Smith.

A dramatic match ended when, for the second time in the series, Graham Onions survived the last over to salvage a draw. The last day was remarkably similar to the First Test's: England appeared to have made the game safe before collapsing in the final session. This time they had five wickets left at tea, but the last-wicket pair came together with 17 balls remaining, 11 of which Onions blocked out – all from Morkel. Collingwood, reprieved by the third umpire after being given out caught first ball off the hip, produced another trademark rearguard: 40 from 188 balls. His sixth-wicket stand of 112 in 57 overs with Bell appeared to have saved the match, for only 13 overs remained when Collingwood was out. But Prior and Broad were caught at short leg, then Bell steered his 213th ball to first slip. South Africa scented victory, but Onions was again unshiftable. An entranced final-day crowd of 14,364 took the total to 79,375, a Newlands record. Earlier Kallis had batted immaculately for his third hundred in successive Tests against England on his home ground, his sixth there in all. In the second innings, on a boiling third day, Smith (four of whose 25 fours came in one Trott over) and Amla put on 230 for the second wicket, another Newlands record, beating 172 by Eddie Barlow and Tony Pithey against England in 1964–65. Some ill-feeling was generated mid-match when the South Africans hinted that England's bowlers had been tampering with the ball.

South Africa

*G. C. Smith c Prior b Anderson	30	– (2) c Collingwood b Onions	183
A. G. Prince c Prior b Anderson	0	– (1) lbw b Swann	15
H. M. Amla lbw b Onions	14	– c Cook b Swann	95
J. H. Kallis c Prior b Onions	108	– c Prior b Anderson	46
A. B. de Villiers c Strauss b Swann	36	– c Broad b Anderson	34
J-P. Duminy c Prior b Swann	0	– c Prior b Anderson	36
†M. V. Boucher lbw b Broad	51	– c Bell b Swann	15
D. W. Steyn c Trott b Anderson	26	– not out	1
M. Morkel c Swann b Anderson	0		
P. L. Harris not out	10		
F. de Wet lbw b Anderson	0		
B 1, l-b 13, w 1, n-b 1	16	B 8, l-b 7, n-b 2, p 5	22
(86.1 overs)	291	(7 wkts dec, 111.2 overs)	447

1/1 (2) 2/46 (3) 3/51 (1) 4/127 (5) 5/127 (6)   1/31 (1) 2/261 (3) 3/346 (2) 4/376 (4)
6/216 (7) 7/280 (4) 8/280 (8) 9/281 (9) 10/291 (11)   5/401 (5) 6/442 (7) 7/447 (6)

Anderson 21.1–1–63–5; Onions 20–4–69–2; Broad 19–6–54–1; Swann 22–1–74–2; Pietersen 4–0–17–0. *Second Innings*—Anderson 22.2–1–98–3; Onions 22–4–87–1; Swann 37–5–127–3; Broad 22–4–79–0; Pietersen 3–0–6–0; Trott 5–0–30–0.

England

*A. J. Strauss c Boucher b Morkel	2	– c Amla b Harris	45
A. N. Cook c Prince b Morkel	65	– c Boucher b de Wet	55
I. J. L. Trott b Steyn	20	– b Steyn	42
K. P. Pietersen c and b Steyn	0	– lbw b Steyn	6
P. D. Collingwood lbw b Morkel	19	– (6) c Kallis b Duminy	40
I. R. Bell c Duminy b Kallis	48	– (7) c Smith b Morkel	78
†M. J. Prior b Steyn	76	– (8) c de Villiers b Duminy	4
S. C. J. Broad b Steyn	25	– (9) c de Villiers b Harris	0
G. P. Swann c Smith b Morkel	5	– (10) not out	10
J. M. Anderson c Smith b Morkel	0	– (5) c Prince b Harris	9
G. Onions not out	4	– not out	0
L-b 6, w 2, n-b 1	9	B 1, l-b 4, w 1, n-b 1	7
(88 overs)	273	(9 wkts, 141 overs)	296

1/2 (1) 2/36 (3) 3/36 (4) 4/73 (5) 5/133 (2) 6/174 (6)   1/101 (2) 2/107 (1) 3/129 (4) 4/153 (5)
7/225 (8) 8/241 (9) 9/241 (10) 10/273 (7)   5/160 (3) 6/272 (6) 7/278 (8) 8/286 (9) 9/290 (7)

Morkel 22–4–75–5; de Wet 16–3–36–0; Steyn 22–5–74–4; Kallis 14–2–27–1; Harris 9–0–39–0; Duminy 5–0–16–0. *Second Innings*—Morkel 28–9–51–1; Steyn 35–11–74–2; de Wet 12–5–23–1; Harris 40–14–85–3; Kallis 14–4–28–0; Duminy 12–3–30–2.

Umpires: D. J. Harper *(Australia)* (88) and A. L. Hill *(New Zealand)* (14).
Third umpire: Aleem Dar *(Pakistan)*. Referee: R. S. Mahanama *(Sri Lanka)* (27).

Close of play: First day, South Africa 279–6 (Kallis 108, Steyn 26); Second day, England 241–7 (Prior 52, Swann 5); Third day, South Africa 312–2 (Smith 162, Kallis 20); Fourth day, England 132–3 (Trott 24, Anderson 0).

SOUTH AFRICA v ENGLAND 2009–10 (4th Test)

At The Wanderers, Johannesburg, on 14, 15, 16, 17 January, 2010.
Toss: England.   Result: SOUTH AFRICA WON BY AN INNINGS AND 74 RUNS.
Debuts: South Africa – R. McLaren, W. D. Parnell.
Men of the Match: M. Morkel and D. W. Steyn. Men of the Series: M. V. Boucher and G. P. Swann.

South Africa squared the series – and retained the Basil D'Oliveira Trophy – with an emphatic performance, winning in around two and a half days of playing time. England were pulverised as surely as if they had been a welterweight contesting a heavyweight bout. The key difference was in pace bowling: Morkel and Steyn shared 14 wickets as England were twice bowled out for under 200, neither innings lasting more than 50 overs. The problems began straight away: Strauss turned Steyn's first ball off his hip, and was brilliantly and instinctively caught by Amla at short leg. It was the 28th time a batsman had fallen to the opening delivery of a Test, but the first for England since Stan Worthington in the 1936–37 Ashes series. When South Africa batted there was another marvellous hundred from Smith, although England were convinced he was caught behind off Sidebottom when 15. The edge was heard by all and sundry… except the onfield umpire, Tony Hill, and the third official, Daryl Harper: England were unamused at suggestions that the sound on Harper's TV monitor had been turned down. Then, at 242 for five – with the lead 62 – Harper overturned a decision against de Villiers off Swann, despite minimal evidence to contradict the on-field umpire who thought he had gloved an attempted sweep to leg slip. De Villiers survived to add 120 with Boucher as South Africa waltzed to 423, then England lost three wickets on the third evening. Next day only Collingwood showed much fight.

England

*A. J. Strauss c Amla b Steyn	0	– lbw b Parnell	22
A. N. Cook lbw b Morkel	21	– c Smith b Morkel	1
I. J. L. Trott lbw b Morkel	5	– c de Villiers b Steyn	8
K. P. Pietersen c Parnell b Morkel	7	– c Boucher b Parnell	12
P. D. Collingwood c Duminy b McLaren	47	– c Morkel b Duminy	71
I. R. Bell b Steyn	35	– c Kallis b Morkel	5
†M. J. Prior c Boucher b Steyn	14	– c Smith b Morkel	0
S. C. J. Broad c Morkel b Kallis	13	– c Boucher b Morkel	1
G. P. Swann c Boucher b Steyn	27	– c de Villiers b Steyn	20
R. J. Sidebottom c Boucher b Steyn	0	– b Duminy	15
J. M. Anderson not out	6	– not out	1
L-b 2, w 3	5	L-b 6, w 1, n-b 6	13
(47.5 overs)	180	(42.5 overs)	169

1/0 (1) 2/7 (3) 3/32 (4) 4/39 (2) 5/115 (5) 6/133 (6)
7/136 (7) 8/148 (8) 9/155 (10) 10/180 (9)

1/6 (2) 2/21 (3) 3/48 (1) 4/84 (4) 5/103 (6) 6/103 (7)
7/104 (8) 8/134 (9) 9/154 (5) 10/169 (10)

Steyn 13.5–1–51–5; Morkel 11–1–39–3; McLaren 10–3–30–1; Parnell 3–0–18–0; Kallis 10–3–40–1. *Second Innings*—Steyn 14–1–64–2; Morkel 16–5–59–4; Parnell 8–1–17–2; McLaren 3–1–13–0; Duminy 1.5–0–10–2.

South Africa

*G. C. Smith c Strauss b Sidebottom	105
A. G. Prince c Swann b Broad	19
H. M. Amla c Prior b Broad	75
J. H. Kallis c Anderson b Sidebottom	7
A. B. de Villiers c Collingwood b Broad	58
J-P. Duminy c Collingwood b Swann	7
†M. V. Boucher c Trott b Swann	95
R. McLaren not out	33
D. W. Steyn not out	1
B 8, l-b 9, w 5, n-b 1	23
(7 wkts dec, 119 overs)	423

1/36 (2) 2/201 (1) 3/217 (3) 4/217 (4) 5/235 (6)
6/355 (5) 7/419 (7)

M. Morkel and W. D. Parnell did not bat.

Anderson 30–4–111–0; Sidebottom 31–6–98–2; Broad 29–4–83–3; Swann 23–0–93–2; Collingwood 6–1–21–0.

Umpires: S. J. Davis *(Australia)* (21) and A. L. Hill *(New Zealand)* (15).
Third umpire: D. J. Harper *(Australia)*. Referee: R. S. Mahanama *(Sri Lanka)* (28).

Close of play: First day, South Africa 29–0 (Smith 12, Prince 15); Second day, South Africa 215–2 (Amla 73, Kallis 7); Third day, England 48–3 (Pietersen 9, Collingwood 0).

AUSTRALIA v PAKISTAN 2009–10 (1st Test)

At Melbourne Cricket Ground on 26, 27, 28, 29, 30 December, 2009.
Toss: Australia.   Result: AUSTRALIA WON BY 170 RUNS.
Debuts: none.
Man of the Match: S. R. Watson.

Australia's most complete bowling performance of 2009 produced a comfortable win, although Pakistan could take encouragement from the efforts of two daring teenagers, Mohammad Aamer and Umar Akmal. Umar Gul was omitted because of poor recent form: his replacement, Abdur Rauf, dropped Watson at backward point on 99 to hand him his long-awaited maiden Test hundred, also ending an Australian century drought after 20 unconverted fifties since the Fifth Ashes Test in August. Rauf's match was otherwise unexceptional, and afterwards he was sent back to Lahore. His lapse was part of a wider malaise among Pakistan's fielders. They set the tone for a clumsy series when they dropped both openers during a stand of 182, which laid the foundations for a big first-innings total. Ponting declared with fewer runs than he'd ever closed at before, to give his bowlers more time. Pakistan's reply was unremarkable apart from a cameo from Umar, who took 19 off a Siddle over not long after ducking into one of his bouncers. Australia built on a lead of 196, and this time Watson did get that elusive hundred, although 17-year-old Mohammad Aamer sliced through the middle order to become the youngest to take a five-for in a Test. Johnson's brilliant first over on the final day ended Pakistan's slim hopes: Umar again edged a ball angled across him, and Misbah-ul-Haq went the same way next delivery. Hauritz sacrificed accuracy for more aggressive lines, and was rewarded with his first five-for – in first-class cricket as well as Tests.

Australia

S. R. Watson run out	93	– not out ... 120
S. M. Katich c Salman Butt b Mohammad Asif	98	– c Kamran Akmal b Mohammad Asif ... 2
*R. T. Ponting c Misbah-ul-Haq b Mohammad Asif	57	– c Salman Butt b Mohammad Aamer ... 12
M. E. K. Hussey lbw b Saeed Ajmal	82	– lbw b Mohammad Aamer ... 4
N. M. Hauritz lbw b Abdur Rauf	75	– (9) st Kamran Akmal b Saeed Ajmal ... 8
M. J. Clarke not out	28	– (5) c Kamran Akmal b Mohammad Aamer ... 37
M. J. North (did not bat)		– (6) b Mohammad Aamer ... 8
†B. J. Haddin (did not bat)		– (7) c Kamran Akmal b Mohammad Aamer ... 0
M. G. Johnson (did not bat)		– (8) run out ... 22
B 2, l-b 12, n-b 7	21	L-b 2, w 3, n-b 7 ... 12
(5 wkts dec, 128 overs)	454	(8 wkts dec, 73.1 overs) ... 225

1/182 (1) 2/233 (2) 3/291 (3) 4/382 (4) 5/454 (5)

1/15 (2) 2/32 (3) 3/40 (4) 4/143 (5) 5/161 (6)
6/161 (7) 7/198 (8) 8/225 (9)

P. M. Siddle and D. E. Bollinger did not bat.

Mohammad Asif 27–5–86–2; Mohammad Aamer 27–7–101–0; Abdur Rauf 23–4–86–1; Saeed Ajmal 46–3–150–1; Imran Farhat 5–0–17–0. *Second Innings*—Mohammad Asif 16–3–38–1; Mohammad Aamer 24–6–79–5; Saeed Ajmal 23.1–1–73–1; Abdur Rauf 10–3–33–0.

Pakistan

Imran Farhat lbw b Johnson	9	– lbw b Bollinger ... 12
Salman Butt lbw b Watson	45	– lbw b Johnson ... 33
Faisal Iqbal c Clarke b Hauritz	15	– b Hauritz ... 48
*Mohammad Yousuf c Haddin b Siddle	22	– c Katich b Hauritz ... 61
Umar Akmal c Ponting b Johnson	51	– c Haddin b Johnson ... 27
Mohammad Aamer c North b Bollinger	15	– (8) c Katich b Hauritz ... 0
Misbah-ul-Haq not out	65	– (6) c Haddin b Johnson ... 0
†Kamran Akmal c Haddin b Bollinger	12	– (7) st Haddin b Hauritz ... 30
Abdur Rauf c North b Bollinger	3	– b Bollinger ... 5
Mohammad Asif c Watson b Siddle	0	– (11) not out ... 1
Saeed Ajmal b Johnson	4	– (10) c Watson b Hauritz ... 10
B 4, l-b 3, w 1, n-b 9	17	B 13, l-b 4, w 2, n-b 5 ... 24
(99 overs)	258	(72 overs) ... 251

1/26 (1) 2/59 (3) 3/84 (2) 4/109 (4) 5/159 (5) 6/203 (6)
7/215 (8) 8/219 (9) 9/220 (10) 10/258 (11)

1/18 (1) 2/80 (2) 3/116 (3) 4/171 (5) 5/171 (6)
6/214 (7) 7/214 (8) 8/221 (9) 9/250 (4) 10/251 (10)

Bollinger 20–6–50–3; Siddle 24–7–77–2; Hauritz 20–3–58–1; Johnson 22–10–36–3; Watson 13–3–30–1. *Second Innings*—Bollinger 15–5–42–3; Siddle 13–5–32–0; Hauritz 24–4–101–5; Johnson 18–6–46–3; Katich 2–0–13–0.

Umpires: B. R. Doctrove *(West Indies)* (28) and R. E. Koertzen *(South Africa)* (104).
Third umpire: E. A. R. de Silva *(Sri Lanka)*. Referee: R. S. Madugalle *(Sri Lanka)* (113).

Close of play: First day, Australia 305–3 (Hussey 37, Hauritz 5); Second day, Pakistan 109–4 (Umar Akmal 10, Mohammad Aamer 0); Third day, Australia 111–3 (Watson 64, Clarke 21); Fourth day, Pakistan 170–3 (Mohammad Yousuf 45, Umar Akmal 27).

AUSTRALIA v PAKISTAN 2009–10 (2nd Test)

At Sydney Cricket Ground on 3, 4, 5, 6 January, 2010.
Toss: Australia.   Result: AUSTRALIA WON BY 36 RUNS.
Debuts: none.
Man of the Match: M. E. K. Hussey.

When Pakistan took a first-innings lead of 206, they should have been safe from defeat: only five times previously had any team overturned such a deficit to win a Test, and Pakistan's classy seam attack (admittedly lacking Mohammad Aamer with a groin strain) was brimming with confidence after despatching Australia for 127 inside 45 overs in the first innings, their lowest total at home since 1996. Mohammad Asif's rare ability to move the ball both ways off the seam earned him a career-best six for 41. Actually the lead should have been even bigger: Pakistan were cruising at 205 for two, but the rest of the batting seemed to forget they were playing a Test – two were caught on the boundary – and they were all out for 333. Still, when Australia dipped to 257 for eight in the second innings, only 49 ahead, it looked all over bar the shouting. But wicketkeeper Kamran Akmal fluffed four simple chances: three of them from Hussey ("he said 'Sorry mate' three times," lamented the suffering bowler Danish Kaneria), which allowed him to reach only the second hundred in his last 22 Tests. Siddle also survived an easy chance during a stand of 123, which gave Australia something to bowl at. Then Johnson and Hauritz – who claimed another five-for despite losing his thumbnail taking a sizzling return catch from the shell-shocked captain Mohammad Yousuf – bundled Pakistan out for 139. Sadly, later developments in England ensured that the fixing spotlight fell on this match too.

Australia

S. R. Watson c Kamran Akmal b Mohammad Sami	6	– c Faisal Iqbal b Umar Gul		97
P. J. Hughes c Faisal Iqbal b Mohammad Sami	0	– c and b Danish Kaneria		37
*R. T. Ponting c Umar Gul b Mohammad Sami	0	– c Faisal Iqbal b Umar Gul		11
M. E. K. Hussey c Misbah-ul-Haq b Mohammad Asif	28	– not out		134
M. J. Clarke b Mohammad Asif	3	– lbw b Mohammad Asif		21
M. J. North c Kamran Akmal b Mohammad Asif	10	– c Faisal Iqbal b Danish Kaneria		2
†B. J. Haddin c Mohammad Yousuf b Mohammad Asif	6	– lbw b Danish Kaneria		15
M. G. Johnson c Imran Farhat b Mohammad Asif	38	– b Danish Kaneria		3
N. M. Hauritz b Mohammad Asif	21	– c Misbah-ul-Haq b Umar Gul		4
P. M. Siddle not out	1	– c Misbah-ul-Haq b Mohammad Asif		38
D. E. Bollinger b Umar Gul	9	– b Danish Kaneria		0
B 1, l-b 2, w 1, n-b 1	5	B 6, l-b 5, w 3, n-b 5		19
(44.2 overs)	127	(125.4 overs)		381

1/2 (2) 2/2 (3) 3/10 (1) 4/36 (5) 5/51 (4) 6/51 (6)
7/62 (7) 8/106 (9) 9/117 (8) 10/127 (11)

1/105 (2) 2/144 (3) 3/159 (1) 4/217 (5) 5/226 (6)
6/246 (7) 7/252 (8) 8/257 (9) 9/380 (10) 10/381 (11)

Mohammad Asif 20–6–41–6; Mohammad Sami 12–4–27–3; Umar Gul 10.2–0–38–1; Danish Kaneria 2–0–18–0. *Second Innings*—Mohammad Asif 27–8–53–2; Mohammad Sami 19.5–4–74–0; Umar Gul 28–4–83–3; Danish Kaneria 47.5–3–151–5; Imran Farhat 3–0–9–0.

Pakistan

Imran Farhat c Haddin b Hauritz	53	– c Johnson b Bollinger		22
Salman Butt c Haddin b Johnson	71	– c Haddin b Johnson		21
Faisal Iqbal c Watson b Siddle	27	– c Haddin b Johnson		7
*Mohammad Yousuf c Haddin b Johnson	46	– c and b Hauritz		19
Umar Akmal lbw b Bollinger	49	– c Johnson b Bollinger		49
Misbah-ul-Haq c Haddin b Bollinger	11	– c Hussey b Hauritz		0
†Kamran Akmal c Watson b Bollinger	14	– c Haddin b Johnson		11
Mohammad Sami c Haddin b Watson	13	– c Haddin b Hauritz		2
Umar Gul c Bollinger b Watson	12	– c Siddle b Hauritz		6
Danish Kaneria c Hussey b Bollinger	4	– c Watson b Hauritz		0
Mohammad Asif not out	0	– not out		0
B 2, l-b 16, w 5, n-b 10	33	W 1, n-b 1		2
(96.5 overs)	333	(38 overs)		139

1/109 (1) 2/144 (2) 3/205 (3) 4/237 (4) 5/277 (5)
6/286 (6) 7/295 (7) 8/323 (9) 9/331 (8) 10/333 (10)

1/34 (1) 2/50 (3) 3/51 (2) 4/77 (4) 5/77 (6)
6/103 (7) 7/133 (8) 8/133 (5) 9/135 (10) 10/139 (9)

Bollinger 21.5–5–72–4; Siddle 22–4–62–1; Johnson 20–2–64–2; Watson 17–4–40–2; Hauritz 16–3–77–1. *Second Innings*—Bollinger 12–3–32–2; Siddle 4–1–27–0; Hauritz 12–1–53–5; Johnson 10–2–27–3.

Umpires: E. A. R. de Silva *(Sri Lanka)* (42) and B. R. Doctrove *(West Indies)* (29).
Third umpire: R. E. Koertzen *(South Africa)*. Referee: R. S. Madugalle *(Sri Lanka)* (114).

Close of play: First day, Pakistan 14–0 (Imran Farhat 9, Salman Butt 3); Second day, Pakistan 331–9 (Danish Kaneria 2, Mohammad Asif 0); Third day, Australia 286–8 (Hussey 73, Siddle 10).

AUSTRALIA v PAKISTAN 2009–10 (3rd Test)

At Bellerive Oval, Hobart, on 14, 15, 16, 17, 18 January, 2010.
Toss: Australia.   Result: AUSTRALIA WON BY 231 RUNS.
Debuts: Pakistan – Sarfraz Ahmed.
Man of the Match: R. T. Ponting. Man of the Series: S. R. Watson.

Pakistan made four changes after their implosion at Sydney, including flying in a new wicketkeeper, Sarfraz Ahmed, to replace Kamran Akmal (who, as a member of the tour selection committee, initially refused to concede his place). But their fielding woes continued: Mohammad Aamer dropped Ponting at deep backward square before he had scored, and he ended a run of poor form by extending his 39th Test century into a magnificent 209, his fifth double. Ponting and Clarke, who returned to form himself with 166, put on 352: only Bradman and Ponsford, with 388 at Leeds in 1934, had a larger fourth-wicket stand for Australia. By the end of the second day the contrast between the triumphant Australian captain and his despairing counterpart could not have been more pronounced: Mohammad Yousuf stood with hands on hips in disbelief and glared at Salman Butt after the first of two diabolical run-outs that robbed Pakistan of their most gifted batsmen. Butt thought it safest to stay in the middle and seek redemption with 102. Katich's rarely seen chinaman instigated a dramatic collapse, but a defiant last-wicket stand changed Ponting's mind about a follow-on. Still, only the Hobart weather threatened Australia's clean sweep after a fluent 100 from Katich helped stretch the advantage to 437. Watson, bowling from stump to stump with dangerous reverse swing, then accounted for Yousuf and Umar Akmal, and the rain held off long enough for Hauritz to live up to his new-found reputation as a fourth-innings finisher.

Australia

S. R. Watson c Imran Farhat b Umar Gul	29	– c Mohammad Yousuf b Mohammad Aamer..	1
S. M. Katich lbw b Mohammad Asif	11	– c Shoaib Malik b Danish Kaneria	100
*R. T. Ponting c Mohammad Yousuf b Mohammad Aamer...	209	– c Sarfraz Ahmed b Shoaib Malik	89
M. E. K. Hussey c Sarfraz Ahmed b Mohammad Aamer	6	– not out	13
M. J. Clarke b Danish Kaneria	166		
M. J. North c Sarfraz Ahmed b Mohammad Asif	21		
†B. J. Haddin c Umar Gul b Danish Kaneria	41	– (5) run out	8
M. G. Johnson c Sarfraz Ahmed b Danish Kaneria	8	– (6) c Imran Farhat b Shoaib Malik	0
N. M. Hauritz not out	12		
B 1, l-b 3, w 5, n-b 7	16	B 4, l-b 4	8
(8 wkts dec, 142.5 overs)	519	(5 wkts dec, 48.4 overs)	219

1/28 (2) 2/52 (1) 3/71 (4) 4/423 (5) 5/443 (3) 6/498 (7)
7/499 (6) 8/519 (8)

1/1 (1) 2/192 (2) 3/202 (3) 4/213 (5)
5/219 (6)

P. M. Siddle and D. E. Bollinger did not bat.

Mohammad Asif 36–8–104–2; Mohammad Aamer 31–7–97–2; Umar Gul 25–4–98–1; Danish Kaneria 42.5–2–189–3; Shoaib Malik 8–0–27–0. *Second Innings*—Mohammad Asif 9–0–48–0; Mohammad Aamer 12–2–46–1; Umar Gul 10–0–45–0; Danish Kaneria 14–2–56–1; Shoaib Malik 3.4–0–16–2.

Pakistan

Imran Farhat c Haddin b Siddle	38	– c Haddin b Siddle	14
Salman Butt c Clarke b Katich	102	– b Bollinger	8
Khurram Manzoor c Ponting b Siddle	0	– c Haddin b Hauritz	77
*Mohammad Yousuf run out	7	– lbw b Watson	23
Umar Akmal run out	8	– lbw b Watson	15
Shoaib Malik c Bollinger b Hauritz	58	– c Haddin b Siddle	19
†Sarfraz Ahmed c Clarke b Katich	1	– c Clarke b Hauritz	5
Mohammad Aamer c Watson b Katich	4	– not out	30
Umar Gul not out	38	– c Clarke b Hauritz	0
Danish Kaneria c Ponting b Hauritz	8	– (11) b Siddle	1
Mohammad Asif c Hussey b Hauritz	29	– (10) b Johnson	0
B 2, l-b 2, w 2, n-b 2	8	B 10, l-b 3, n-b 1	14
(105.4 overs)	301	(86.2 overs)	206

1/63 (1) 2/63 (3) 3/74 (4) 4/84 (5) 5/213 (2) 6/215 (7)
7/219 (6) 8/227 (8) 9/248 (10) 10/301 (11)

1/11 (2) 2/29 (1) 3/61 (4) 4/83 (5) 5/104 (6)
6/123 (7) 7/189 (3) 8/191 (9) 9/192 (10) 10/206 (11)

Bollinger 15–6–35–0; Siddle 20–8–39–2; Johnson 20–2–76–0; Hauritz 33.4–9–96–3; Watson 7–2–17–0; Katich 10–3–34–3. *Second Innings*—Bollinger 13–4–31–1; Siddle 15.2–7–25–3; Johnson 21–4–59–1; Watson 17–4–38–2; Hauritz 17–6–30–3; Katich 3–1–10–0.

Umpires: E. A. R. de Silva *(Sri Lanka)* (43) and R. E. Koertzen *(South Africa)* (105).
Third umpire: B. R. Doctrove *(West Indies)*. Referee: R. S. Madugalle *(Sri Lanka)* (115).

Close of play: First day, Australia 302–3 (Ponting 137, Clarke 111); Second day, Pakistan 94–4 (Salman Butt 34, Shoaib Malik 4); Third day, Australia 59–1 (Katich 33, Ponting 25); Fourth day, Pakistan 103–4 (Khurram Manzoor 23, Shoaib Malik 18).

BANGLADESH v INDIA 2009–10 (1st Test)

At Zohur Ahmed Chowdhury Stadium *(formerly the Bir Shresthra Shahid Rahul Amin Stadium, and before that the Divisional Stadium)*, Chittagong, on 17, 18, 19, 20, 21 January, 2010.
Toss: Bangladesh.   Result: INDIA WON BY 113 RUNS.
Debuts: Bangladesh – Shafiul Islam.
Man of the Match: S. R. Tendulkar.

India's acting-captain Sehwag (Dhoni had back trouble) said Bangladesh were an "ordinary" side not capable of taking 20 wickets: they hit back by putting India in and shooting them out for 243. Sehwag declared eight down in the second innings, maybe to avoid the embarrassment of eating his words – but by then victory was all but assured, as India led by 415. Only one run separated the sides on first innings, after both suffered similar collapses. But India's mighty batting was never likely to misfire twice: Gambhir led way with his fifth hundred in consecutive Tests, matching Jacques Kallis and Mohammad Yousuf; only Don Bradman ever managed six in six. Gambhir was dropped at short leg when 55, by Imrul Kayes, who also missed Tendulkar (at first slip) at 16: he went on to his 44th Test hundred, becoming the first to 13,000 runs, in a record 266th innings (beating Allan Border's 265). Shahadat Hossain and Shakib Al Hasan were the 52nd pair to claim five-fors in the same Test innings. Mushfiqur Rahim rescued Bangladesh's first innings, sharing a seventh-wicket stand of 108 with Mahmudullah, and he did it again in the second: only 62 when the ninth wicket fell, he hammered 39 from his next 28 balls to complete a maiden Test century. Debutant fast bowler Shafiul Islam did little with the ball, but got off the mark in both innings with sixes off Mishra: he was the first player whose first two scoring shots in Test cricket were sixes.

India

G. Gambhir c Mushfiqur Rahim b Shahadat Hossain ...	23	– c Shahriar Nafees b Shafiul Islam	116
*V. Sehwag c Tamim Iqbal b Shakib Al Hasan	52	– c Raqibul Hasan b Shakib Al Hasan	45
R. Dravid b Shahadat Hossain	4	– (4) run out	24
S. R. Tendulkar not out	105	– (5) lbw b Rubel Hossain	16
V. V. S. Laxman st Mushfiqur Rahim b Shakib Al Hasan...	7	– (6) not out	69
Yuvraj Singh c Rubel Hossain b Shakib Al Hasan	12	– (7) c Mohammad Ashraful b Shahadat Hossain..	25
†K. D. Karthik c Raqibul Hasan b Shahadat Hossain....	0	– (8) c Rubel Hossain b Mahmudullah	27
A. Mishra lbw b Shahadat Hossain	14	– (3) c Tamim Iqbal b Mahmudullah	50
Zaheer Khan c Raqibul Hasan b Shakib Al Hasan	11	– b Shakib Al Hasan	20
I. Sharma c Mushfiqur Rahim b Shahadat Hossain	1	– not out	7
S. Sreesanth c Imrul Kayes b Shakib Al Hasan	1		
B 1, l-b 6, w 1, n-b 5	13	B 1, l-b 5, w 3, n-b 5	14
(70.5 overs)	243	(8 wkts dec, 87 overs)	413

1/79 (2) 2/79 (1) 3/85 (3) 4/107 (5) 5/149 (6) 6/150 (7)   1/90 (2) 2/188 (3) 3/233 (1) 4/245 (4) 5/272 (5)
7/182 (8) 8/209 (9) 9/230 (10) 10/243 (11)   6/313 (7) 7/362 (8) 8/394 (9)

Shafiul Islam 9–1–41–0; Shahadat Hossain 18–2–71–5; Rubel Hossain 10–0–40–0; Shakib Al Hasan 29.5–10–62–5; Mahmudullah 3–0–17–0; Mohammad Ashraful 1–0–5–0. *Second Innings*—Shafiul Islam 15–0–87–1; Shahadat Hossain 16–1–53–1; Rubel Hossain 15–0–94–1; Shakib Al Hasan 27–2–112–2; Mahmudullah 13–0–52–2; Mohammad Ashraful 1–0–9–0.

Bangladesh

Tamim Iqbal b Zaheer Khan	31	– c Dravid b Sehwag	52
Imrul Kayes lbw b Zaheer Khan	23	– c Karthik b Zaheer Khan	1
Shahriar Nafees c Laxman b Sharma	4	– c Sehwag b Sharma	21
Mohammad Ashraful c Dravid b Sharma	2	– c Dravid b Sharma	27
Raqibul Hasan c Karthik b Sreesanth	17	– lbw b Sharma	13
*Shakib Al Hasan c Sehwag b Zaheer Khan	17	– c Sehwag b Mishra	17
†Mushfiqur Rahim c Sehwag b Mishra	44	– c sub (P. P. Ojha) b Mishra	101
Mahmudullah c Karthik b Sreesanth	69	– c Karthik b Zaheer Khan	20
Shahadat Hossain c Yuvraj Singh b Mishra	11	– b Mishra	24
Shafiul Islam c Yuvraj Singh b Mishra	6	– c and b Mishra	8
Rubel Hossain not out	0	– not out	4
B 4, l-b 1, w 1, n-b 12	18	B 4, l-b 3, n-b 6	13
(65.2 overs)	242	(75.2 overs)	301

1/53 (2) 2/58 (3) 3/58 (1) 4/68 (4) 5/89 (6) 6/98 (5)   1/8 (2) 2/47 (3) 3/79 (4) 4/97 (5) 5/135 (1)
7/206 (7) 8/228 (9) 9/235 (8) 10/242 (10)   6/145 (6) 7/170 (8) 8/230 (9) 9/258 (10) 10/301 (7)

Zaheer Khan 20–4–54–3; Sreesanth 11–1–55–2; Sharma 13–3–47–2; Mishra 16.2–2–66–3; Yuvraj Singh 5–1–15–0. *Second Innings*—Zaheer Khan 20–5–90–2; Sreesanth 12.2–0–53–0; Sharma 15–4–48–3; Mishra 22.2–3–92–4; Sehwag 4–1–7–1; Yuvraj Singh 1.4–1–4–0.

Umpires: B. F. Bowden *(New Zealand)* (58) and M. Erasmus *(South Africa)* (1).
Third umpire: Enamul Haque, sen. *(Bangladesh)*. Referee: A. J. Pycroft *(Zimbabwe)* (7).

Close of play: First day, India 213–8 (Tendulkar 76, Sharma 1); Second day, Bangladesh 59–3 (Mohammad Ashraful 0, Raqibul Hasan 1); Third day, India 122–1 (Gambhir 47, Mishra 24); Fourth day, Bangladesh 67–2 (Tamim Iqbal 23, Mohammad Ashraful 16).

BANGLADESH v INDIA 2009–10 (2nd Test)

At Shere Bangla National Stadium, Mirpur, Dhaka, on 24, 25, 26, 27 January, 2010.
Toss: Bangladesh.   Result: INDIA WON BY TEN WICKETS.
Debuts: none.
Man of the Match: Zaheer Khan. Man of the Series: Zaheer Khan.

Some destructive reverse swing from Zaheer Khan inspired India to their fifth successive series victory, a national record. He scuppered a promising position for Bangladesh: only 21 behind at 290 for three, they fancied giving India a testing chase – but after the spinners broke through, Zaheer, who had spent most of the morning in a back-brace, grabbed three wickets in four balls, finishing with Test-best figures and his first ten-for. Bangladesh lost six for 14: India needed only two to win, and didn't have to play a shot – the second ball went for two byes. Bangladesh struggled from the start, losing five wickets on the opening morning. Mahmudullah averted disaster, but was stranded four short of a deserved century. Bangladesh's fielding woes continued: Tendulkar, dropped at 27 and 53, was again the main beneficiary. He and Dravid both went on to centuries, and shared a stand of 222 – a record 17th hundred partnership between two batsmen in Tests, beating Greenidge/Haynes and Hayden/Ponting – before Shahadat Hossain's bouncer broke it, and Dravid's jaw. Gambhir's run of centuries in successive Tests was also ended by a bumper, although he had the consolation of emulating Viv Richards with fifties in 11 consecutive matches. Dhoni declared 311 ahead, but Tamim fought back, reaching his hundred from 101 balls (beating Mushfiqur's previous week as Bangladesh's fastest in Tests). He and Junaid Siddique added 200, a national record. But Zaheer removed both of them late on the third evening, and finished the job the following day.

Bangladesh

Tamim Iqbal b Zaheer Khan	0	– c Dhoni b Zaheer Khan	151
Imrul Kayes c Dhoni b Sharma	0	– c sub (K. D. Karthik) b Zaheer Khan	5
Junaid Siddique c Dhoni b Zaheer Khan	7	– c Dhoni b Zaheer Khan	55
Mohammad Ashraful st Dhoni b Ojha	39	– (5) c Dhoni b Ojha	25
Raqibul Hasan c Dravid b Sharma	4	– (6) b Zaheer Khan	5
*Shakib Al Hasan c Dhoni b Zaheer Khan	34	– (7) c Gambhir b Ojha	7
†Mushfiqur Rahim lbw b Sharma	30	– (8) not out	10
Mahmudullah not out	96	– (9) c Vijay b Zaheer Khan	0
Shahadat Hossain st Dhoni b Ojha	8	– (4) c sub (A. Mishra) b Harbhajan Singh	40
Shafiul Islam c Dravid b Sharma	9	– b Zaheer Khan	0
Rubel Hossain b Harbhajan Singh	4	– b Zaheer Khan	0
L-b 2	2	B 7, l-b 5, w 2	14
(73.5 overs)	233	(90.3 overs)	312

1/0 (2) 2/4 (1) 3/13 (3) 4/44 (5) 5/51 (4) 6/106 (7)
7/127 (6) 8/155 (9) 9/213 (10) 10/233 (11)

1/19 (2) 2/219 (3) 3/222 (1) 4/290 (4) 5/291 (5)
6/301 (7) 7/304 (6) 8/304 (9) 9/304 (10) 10/312 (11)

Zaheer Khan 19–3–62–3; Sharma 18–3–66–4; Ojha 16–1–49–2; Harbhajan Singh 18.5–3–48–1; Yuvraj Singh 2–0–6–0. *Second Innings*—Zaheer Khan 20.3–2–87–7; Sharma 15–2–50–0; Harbhajan Singh 26–7–75–1; Ojha 22–4–77–2; Sehwag 7–2–11–0.

India

G. Gambhir c Mushfiqur Rahim b Shafiul Islam	68	– (2) not out	0
V. Sehwag c Mushfiqur Rahim b Shahadat Hossain	56	– (1) not out	0
R. Dravid retired hurt	111		
S. R. Tendulkar c Imrul Kayes b Shakib Al Hasan	143		
M. Vijay c Mahmudullah b Shakib Al Hasan	30		
*†M. S. Dhoni st Mushfiqur Rahim b Raqibul Hasan	89		
Harbhajan Singh c Mushfiqur Rahim b Shafiul Islam	13		
Zaheer Khan c Shahadat Hossain b Shafiul Islam	0		
I. Sharma c Mushfiqur Rahim b Mohammad Ashraful	13		
P. P. Ojha not out	1		
B 3, l-b 6, w 1, n-b 10	20	B 2	2
(8 wkts dec, 133 overs)	544	(no wkt, 0.2 overs)	2

1/103 (2) 2/146 (1) 3/421 (4) 4/436 (5) 5/459 (7)
6/467 (8) 7/518 (9) 8/544 (6)

Yuvraj Singh did not bat (wrist injury). *In the first innings Dravid retired hurt at 368–2.*

Shafiul Islam 23–1–86–3; Shahadat Hossain 22–2–91–1; Rubel Hossain 28–1–115–0; Shakib Al Hasan 34–3–118–2; Mohammad Ashraful 9–0–38–1; Mahmudullah 15–0–78–0; Junaid Siddique 1–0–9–0; Raqibul Hasan 1–1–0–1. *Second Innings*—Shakib Al Hasan 0.2–0–0–0.

Umpires: B. F. Bowden *(New Zealand)* (59) and M. Erasmus *(South Africa)* (2).
Third umpire: Sharfuddoula *(Bangladesh)*. Referee: A. J. Pycroft *(Zimbabwe)* (8).

Close of play: First day, India 69–0 (Gambhir 26, Sehwag 41); Second day, India 459–5 (Dhoni 22); Third day, Bangladesh 228–3 (Shahadat Hossain 2, Mohammad Ashraful 2).

INDIA v SOUTH AFRICA 2009–10 (1st Test)

At Vidarbha C. A. Stadium, Jamtha, Nagpur, on 6, 7, 8, 9 February, 2010.
Toss: South Africa.   Result: SOUTH AFRICA WON BY AN INNINGS AND SIX RUNS.
Debuts: India – S. Badrinath, W. P. Saha.
Man of the Match: H. M. Amla.

After India reached No. 1 in the ICC rankings late in 2009, it became apparent that they did not have enough Tests scheduled for 2010 to stay there, so two were added to what had originally been a one-day series. But South Africa upset the calculations with a stunning victory. India were without Dravid (broken cheekbone), Laxman (finger) and Yuvraj Singh (wrist): when Rohit Sharma twisted an ankle in the warm-ups, reserve wicketkeeper Wriddhaman Saha had to play as a batsman. Zaheer Khan claimed two early wickets, but Kallis settled in for his 34th Test century (joint third on the all-time list at the time, behind only Ponting and Tendulkar), eventually putting on 340 with Amla – South Africa's best for any wicket against India, and the fifth-highest in any Test there. In all Amla batted for 675 minutes, the second-longest innings for South Africa after Gary Kirsten's 878-minute marathon against England at Durban in 1999–2000, and their highest against India (beating de Villiers' 217 not out at Ahmedabad in 2007–08). Although Sehwag applied himself well – receiving valuable support from Subramaniam Badrinath, another debutant – he fell shortly after reaching three figures. Steyn then swept away the tail with five for three in 22 balls, finishing with career-best figures, and India were soon in trouble in the follow-on. Tendulkar reached 50 for the 100th time in Tests, and went on to his 46th hundred, but once he unluckily dragged on an attempted sweep, it was really only a matter of time.

South Africa

*G. C. Smith b Zaheer Khan		6
A. G. Prince c Dhoni b Zaheer Khan		0
H. M. Amla not out		253
J. H. Kallis c Vijay b Harbhajan Singh		173
A. B. de Villiers c Badrinath b Sehwag		53
J-P. Duminy lbw b Harbhajan Singh		9
†M. V. Boucher c Mishra b Zaheer Khan		39
D. W. Steyn not out		0
B 8, l-b 8, n-b 9		25
(6 wkts dec, 176 overs)		558

1/5 (2) 2/6 (1) 3/346 (4) 4/454 (5) 5/476 (6) 6/554 (7)

W. D. Parnell, P. L. Harris and M. Morkel did not bat.

Zaheer Khan 31–7–96–3; Sharma 28–4–85–0; Harbhajan Singh 46–1–166–2; Mishra 53–5–140–0; Sehwag 18–1–55–1.

India

G. Gambhir c Boucher b Morkel	12	– b Morkel		1
V. Sehwag c Duminy b Parnell	109	– c Smith b Steyn		16
M. Vijay b Steyn	4	– c Morkel b Harris		32
S. R. Tendulkar c Boucher b Steyn	7	– b Harris		100
S. Badrinath c Prince b Steyn	56	– c Boucher b Parnell		6
*†M. S. Dhoni c Kallis b Harris	6	– c de Villiers b Harris		25
W. P. Saha b Steyn	0	– lbw b Steyn		36
Harbhajan Singh lbw b Steyn	8	– lbw b Parnell		39
Zaheer Khan b Steyn	2	– c Harris b Kallis		33
A. Mishra b Steyn	0	– b Steyn		0
I. Sharma not out	0	– not out		0
B 14, l-b 6, w 5, n-b 4	29	B 15, l-b 8, w 6, n-b 2		31
(64.4 overs)	233	(107.1 overs)		319

1/31 (1) 2/40 (3) 3/56 (4) 4/192 (2) 5/221 (6) 6/221 (5)
7/222 (7) 8/226 (9) 9/228 (10) 10/233 (8)

1/1 (1) 2/24 (2) 3/96 (3) 4/122 (5) 5/192 (4)
6/209 (6) 7/259 (8) 8/318 (9) 9/318 (7) 10/319 (10)

Steyn 16.4–6–51–7; Morkel 15–4–58–1; Harris 17–2–39–1; Parnell 7–1–31–1; Kallis 6–0–14–0; Duminy 3–0–20–0. *Second Innings*—Steyn 18.1–1–57–3; Morkel 21–6–65–1; Parnell 13–2–58–2; Harris 38–17–76–3; Kallis 12–3–19–1; Duminy 5–0–21–0.

Umpires: S. J. Davis *(Australia)* (22) and I. J. Gould *(England)* (10).
Third umpire: A. M. Saheba *(India)*. Referee: A. J. Pycroft *(Zimbabwe)* (9).

Close of play: First day, South Africa 291–2 (Amla 115, Kallis 159); Second day, India 25–0 (Gambhir 12, Sehwag 9); Third day, India 66–2 (Vijay 27, Tendulkar 15).

INDIA v SOUTH AFRICA 2009–10 (2nd Test)

At Eden Gardens, Kolkata, on 14, 15, 16, 17, 18 February, 2010.
Toss: South Africa.   Result: INDIA WON BY AN INNINGS AND 57 RUNS.
Debuts: South Africa – A. N. Petersen.
Man of the Match: H. M. Amla. Man of the Series: H. M. Amla.

Revenge was swift for India, but South Africa made it easier for them to square the series with a first-day collapse. They reached 218 for one, with Amla racing to another sublime century and Alviro Petersen (replacing Boucher, whose run of 54 consecutive Tests was ended by back trouble; de Villiers kept wicket) making a quality hundred on debut – only the third for his country after Andrew Hudson (1991–92) and Jacques Rudolph (2002–03). But Zaheer Khan removed both, and South Africa ultimately failed to reach 300. Sehwag blasted 39 from his first 20 balls, and later he and Tendulkar cruised along at five an over without difficulty, both completing centuries. After a wobble, Laxman (back after a finger injury) and Dhoni steered India to their highest total against South Africa during an unbeaten stand of 259, a national seventh-wicket record, beating 235 by Ravi Shastri and Syed Kirmani against England at Bombay in 1984–85. Bad weather shortened the fourth day, and South Africa's hopes of a series-clinching draw grew as Amla held the fort on the fifth: Parnell survived 101 minutes, and last man Morkel for over an hour. Sehwag incurred five penalty runs after kicking the ball over the rope in an unsuccessful attempt to deny Amla the strike. There were only 16 minutes left when Harbhajan Singh trapped Morkel in front. Only five players had made more runs in a two-Test series than Amla's 490, the most being Sanath Jayasuriya's 571 for Sri Lanka against India in 1997–98.

South Africa

*G. C. Smith b Zaheer Khan	4	– lbw b Mishra	20
A. N. Petersen c Dhoni b Zaheer Khan	100	– c Badrinath b Harbhajan Singh	21
H. M. Amla c Dhoni b Zaheer Khan	114	– not out	123
J. H. Kallis c Laxman b Harbhajan Singh	10	– c Dhoni b Mishra	20
†A. B. de Villiers run out	12	– (6) lbw b Mishra	3
A. G. Prince lbw b Harbhajan Singh	1	– (5) c Sharma b Harbhajan Singh	23
J-P. Duminy lbw b Harbhajan Singh	0	– lbw b Harbhajan Singh	6
D. W. Steyn lbw b Mishra	5	– lbw b Harbhajan Singh	1
P. L. Harris c Dhoni b Sharma	1	– (10) c sub (K. D. Karthik) b Sharma	4
W. D. Parnell lbw b Zaheer Khan	12	– (9) c Harbhajan Singh b Sharma	22
M. Morkel not out	11	– lbw b Harbhajan Singh	12
B 1, l-b 4, w 10, n-b 11	26	B 6, l-b 5, w 1, n-b 18, p 5	35
(85 overs)	296	(131.3 overs)	290

1/9 (1) 2/218 (2) 3/229 (3) 4/251 (4) 5/253 (6)
6/253 (7) 7/254 (5) 8/255 (9) 9/261 (8) 10/296 (10)

1/36 (1) 2/54 (2) 3/111 (4) 4/158 (5) 5/164 (6)
6/172 (7) 7/180 (8) 8/250 (9) 9/264 (10) 10/290 (11)

Zaheer Khan 22–5–90–4; Sharma 18–3–67–1; Mishra 21–3–70–1; Harbhajan Singh 24–2–64–3. *Second Innings*—Zaheer Khan 6–0–32–0; Harbhajan Singh 48.3–23–59–5; Sharma 25–5–84–2; Mishra 40–12–78–3; Sehwag 10–2–20–0; Tendulkar 2–1–1–0.

India

G. Gambhir run out	25
V. Sehwag c Prince b Duminy	165
M. Vijay c de Villiers b Morkel	7
S. R. Tendulkar c Kallis b Harris	106
V. V. S. Laxman not out	143
S. Badrinath b Steyn	1
A. Mishra c Kallis b Morkel	28
*†M. S. Dhoni not out	132
B 6, l-b 9, w 13, n-b 8	36
(6 wkts dec, 153 overs)	643

1/73 (1) 2/82 (3) 3/331 (2) 4/335 (4) 5/336 (6) 6/384 (7)

Harbhajan Singh, Zaheer Khan and I. Sharma did not bat.

Steyn 30–5–115–1; Morkel 26–3–115–2; Parnell 20–1–103–0; Kallis 12–1–40–0; Harris 50–5–182–1; Duminy 15–0–73–1.

Umpires: S. J. Davis *(Australia)* (23) and I. J. Gould *(England)* (11).
Third umpire: S. K. Tarapore *(India)*. Referee: A. J. Pycroft *(Zimbabwe)* (10).

Close of play: First day, South Africa 266–9 (Parnell 2, Morkel 3); Second day, India 342–5 (Laxman 9, Mishra 1); Third day, South Africa 6–0 (Smith 5, Petersen 1); Fourth day, South Africa 115–3 (Amla 49, Prince 0).

NEW ZEALAND v BANGLADESH 2009–10 (Only Test)

At Seddon Park, Hamilton, on 15, 16, 17, 18, 19 February, 2009.
Toss: Bangladesh.   Result: NEW ZEALAND WON BY 121 RUNS.
Debuts: New Zealand – P. J. Ingram.
Man of the Match: M. J. Guptill.

Put in, New Zealand declined to 158 for five, three falling to the lively Rubel Hossain, who later completed his maiden five-for. But then Guptill and McCullum piled on 339 – a New Zealand sixth-wicket record (beating 246 by Jeff Crowe and Richard Hadlee in Colombo in 1986–87), their third-best for any wicket, and only 12 short of the sixth-wicket record in all Tests. McCullum, in his 50th Test, showed a tenacity and willpower not always apparent, and reached the highest score by a New Zealand wicketkeeper. Guptill allied sound defence to some classical front-foot driving in his maiden Test hundred, batting nearly seven and a half hours. New Zealand probably expected to roll Bangladesh over after declaring at 553 – but Tamim Iqbal charged to 50 in 39 balls on the second evening and, though five wickets fell before lunch next day, Shakib Al Hasan and Mahmudullah put on 145, a national seventh-wicket record, before Shakib was given out caught behind. Mahmudullah remained, to avert the follow-on, complete his first century, and raise the 400. Shakib soon threw out Watling with a direct hit, the first of three run-outs involving McIntosh, but Vettori's second declaration left Bangladesh nearly four sessions to make 404. Vettori bowled the sixth over, and his fourth delivery removed Tamim. Shakib fought back valiantly, but without real hope. He reached the third maiden century of this Test, and seemed to wobble at the knees with excitement: Southee bowled him two balls later, and victory arrived soon afterwards.

New Zealand

T. G. McIntosh c Imrul Kayes b Shafiul Islam	7	– (2) run out		89
B-J. Watling c Junaid Siddique b Rubel Hossain	13	– (1) run out		1
P. J. Ingram c Shahadat Hossain b Rubel Hossain	42	– run out		13
L. R. P. L. Taylor c Mushfiqur Rahim b Rubel Hossain	40	– c Imrul Kayes b Mahmudullah		51
M. J. Guptill c Mushfiqur Rahim b Rubel Hossain	189	– not out		56
*D. L. Vettori b Shakib Al Hasan	10	– c Mohammad Ashraful b Mahmudullah		13
†B. B. McCullum b Rubel Hossain	185	– not out		19
D. R. Tuffey not out	31			
J. S. Patel not out	12			
B 1, l-b 10, w 5, n-b 8	24	B 5, l-b 2, w 6, n-b 3		16
(7 wkts dec, 135 overs)	553	(5 wkts dec, 71 overs)		258

1/17 (1) 2/57 (2) 3/66 (3) 4/126 (4) 5/158 (6)
6/497 (7) 7/525 (5)   1/2 (1) 2/52 (3) 3/124 (4) 4/196 (2) 5/227 (6)

T. G. Southee and C. S. Martin did not bat.

Shahadat Hossain 24–1–136–0; Shafiul Islam 31–2–111–1; Rubel Hossain 29–1–166–5; Shakib Al Hasan 37–6–89–1; Aftab Ahmed 4–0–10–0; Mahmudullah 7–0–21–0; Mohammad Ashraful 3–0–9–0. *Second Innings—* Shahadat Hossain 11–2–32–0; Shafiul Islam 14–3–47–0; Shakib Al Hasan 15–1–44–0; Rubel Hossain 12–0–44–0; Mahmudullah 19–1–84–2.

Bangladesh

Tamim Iqbal c McCullum b Southee	68	– c Tuffey b Vettori		30
Imrul Kayes c Taylor b Vettori	28	– b Patel		29
Junaid Siddique c Taylor b Martin	21	– b Martin		8
Aftab Ahmed c Taylor b Tuffey	33	– run out		8
Mohammad Ashraful c Watling b Tuffey	12	– lbw b Vettori		2
*Shakib Al Hasan c McCullum b Martin	87	– b Southee		100
†Mushfiqur Rahim c Guptill b Vettori	7	– c McIntosh b Tuffey		22
Mahmudullah lbw b Vettori	115	– c Tuffey b Patel		42
Shahadat Hossain c McCullum b Martin	13	– not out		17
Shafiul Islam not out	12	– c McCullum b Southee		13
Rubel Hossain run out	0	– c McIntosh b Southee		0
B 4, l-b 1, w 7	12	B 4, l-b 1, w 6		11
(97.3 overs)	408	(76 overs)		282

1/79 (2) 2/118 (1) 3/132 (3) 4/162 (5) 5/179 (4)   1/35 (1) 2/51 (3) 3/72 (4) 4/78 (5) 5/78 (2)
6/196 (7) 7/341 (6) 8/362 (9) 9/402 (8) 10/408 (11)   6/157 (7) 7/225 (8) 8/252 (6) 9/282 (10) 10/282 (11)

Martin 25–2–116–3; Southee 16–2–62–1; Patel 10–3–53–0; Tuffey 18–2–84–2; Vettori 28.3–7–88–3. *Second Innings—* Martin 12–1–48–1; Southee 11–4–41–3; Vettori 24–6–80–2; Tuffey 12–5–33–1; Patel 17–2–75–2.

Umpires: R. E. Koertzen (*South Africa*) (106) and R. J. Tucker (*Australia*) (1).
Third umpire: S. J. A. Taufel (*Australia*). Referee: A. G. Hurst (*Australia*) (37).

Close of play: First day, New Zealand 258–5 (Guptill 80, McCullum 58); Second day, Bangladesh 87–1 (Tamim Iqbal 56, Junaid Siddique 3); Third day, New Zealand 9–1 (McIntosh 5, Ingram 2); Fourth day, Bangladesh 88–5 (Shakib Al Hasan 0, Mushfiqur Rahim 10).

BANGLADESH v ENGLAND 2009–10 (1st Test)

At Zohur Ahmed Chowdhury Stadium, Chittagong, on 12, 13, 14, 15, 16 March, 2010.
Toss: Bangladesh.   Result: ENGLAND WON BY 181 RUNS.
Debuts: England – M. A. Carberry, S. T. Finn.
Man of the Match: G. P. Swann.

Cook celebrated his first Test as captain (Andrew Strauss gave this tour a miss) with a century, reached with a rare six, and Swann became the first specialist England off-spinner to take ten wickets in a Test since Jim Laker in 1956. Bangladesh were outplayed for two days – hoping for early life they inserted England and had to watch them make almost 600 – but then fought hard, assisted by a soporific pitch. Tamim Iqbal made a bright 86, but had little support until Mushfiqur Rahim and Naeem Islam produced a Bangladesh record eighth-wicket stand of 113, ended by the debutant Michael Carberry's brilliant chase and return. Swann cleaned up the tail in the next three balls – one of them a blinding one-handed catch at midwicket by James Tredwell, substituting for that one delivery after Cook went off. The follow-on was waived to rest the bowlers, and the target swelled: Bell took his freakish Test average against Bangladesh to 350. When Shakib Al Hasan was adjudged lbw sweeping Swann, Bangladesh were 110 for five: with tea still 20 minutes away, England sensed a quick kill... but made no more progress until after lunch next day, as Junaid and Mushfiqur ground out 167 in 70 overs. Swann finally dismissed both, and fittingly added the final wicket, Carberry taking a slick catch at midwicket. Swann's efforts were tarnished by his send-off of Junaid Siddique, whose stubborn forward-defensive had become etched on the mind during a 385-minute innings of 106, his first Test century.

England

*A. N. Cook c and b Mahmudullah	173	– c Aftab Ahmed b Mahmudullah		39
M. A. Carberry lbw b Mahmudullah	30	– lbw b Abdur Razzak		34
I. J. L. Trott c Mushfiqur Rahim b Rubel Hossain	39	– c Junaid Siddique b Shakib Al Hasan		14
K. P. Pietersen b Abdur Razzak	99	– lbw b Shakib Al Hasan		32
P. D. Collingwood c Tamim Iqbal b Abdur Razzak	145	– c Mahmudullah b Abdur Razzak		3
I. R. Bell c Rubel Hossain b Shakib Al Hasan	84	– not out		39
†M. J. Prior not out	0	– c Shahadat Hossain b Shakib Al Hasan		7
G. P. Swann (did not bat)		– c Junaid Siddique b Shakib Al Hasan		32
B 6, l-b 9, w 3, n-b 11	29	B 5, l-b 2, n-b 2		9
(6 wkts dec, 138.3 overs)	599	(7 wkts dec, 49.3 overs)		209

1/72 (2) 2/149 (3) 3/319 (4) 4/412 (1) 5/596 (5) 6/599 (6)

1/65 (1) 2/87 (3) 3/126 (4) 4/130 (2) 5/131 (5)
6/144 (7) 7/209 (8)

S. C. J. Broad, T. T. Bresnan and S. T. Finn did not bat.

Shahadat Hossain 17–2–73–0; Rubel Hossain 19–0–97–1; Shakib Al Hasan 34.3–4–133–1; Naeem Islam 12–1–42–0; Mahmudullah 23–1–78–2; Abdur Razzak 31–1–157–2; Aftab Ahmed 1–0–2–0; Tamim Iqbal 1–0–2–0. *Second Innings*—Shahadat Hossain 6–0–19–0; Rubel Hossain 6–1–28–0; Mahmudullah 8–0–26–1; Naeem Islam 3–0–14–0; Shakib Al Hasan 16.3–1–62–4; Abdur Razzak 10–2–53–2.

Bangladesh

Tamim Iqbal b Bresnan	86	– b Swann		14
Imrul Kayes c Prior b Broad	4	– c Prior b Finn		23
Junaid Siddique c and b Broad	7	– c Collingwood b Swann		106
Aftab Ahmed c Bell b Swann	1	– c Prior b Bresnan		26
Mahmudullah c Collingwood b Swann	51	– b Bresnan		5
*Shakib Al Hasan b Swann	1	– lbw b Swann		4
Shahadat Hossain c Collingwood b Finn	14	– (10) c Prior b Bresnan		12
†Mushfiqur Rahim c sub (J. C. Tredwell) b Swann	79	– (7) b Swann		95
Naeem Islam run out	38	– (8) c Carberry b Swann		36
Abdur Razzak not out	0	– (9) lbw b Broad		1
Rubel Hossain b Swann	0	– not out		0
B 1, l-b 12, w 1, n-b 1	15	B 2, l-b 7		9
(90.3 overs)	296	(124 overs)		331

1/13 (2) 2/27 (3) 3/51 (4) 4/145 (5) 5/149 (6)
6/159 (1) 7/183 (7) 8/296 (9) 9/296 (8) 10/296 (11)

1/33 (1) 2/45 (2) 3/99 (4) 4/105 (5) 5/110 (6)
6/277 (3) 7/294 (7) 8/301 (9) 9/327 (10) 10/331 (8)

Broad 21–4–70–2; Bresnan 25–10–72–1; Swann 29.3–8–90–5; Finn 14–5–48–1; Pietersen 1–0–3–0. *Second Innings*—Broad 24–7–65–1; Bresnan 24–7–63–3; Finn 18–7–47–1; Swann 49–11–127–5; Pietersen 7–1–15–0; Trott 2–0–5–0.

Umpires: A. L. Hill *(New Zealand)* (16) and R. J. Tucker *(Australia)* (2).
Third umpire: Enamul Haque, sen. *(Bangladesh)*. Referee: J. J. Crowe *(New Zealand)* (39).

Close of play: First day, England 374–3 (Cook 158, Collingwood 32); Second day, Bangladesh 154–5 (Tamim Iqbal 81, Shahadat Hossain 0); Third day, England 131–5 (Bell 0, Prior 0); Fourth day, Bangladesh 191–5 (Junaid Siddique 68, Mushfiqur Rahim 47).

BANGLADESH v ENGLAND 2009–10 (2nd Test)

At Shere Bangla National Stadium, Mirpur, Dhaka, on 20, 21, 22, 23, 24 March, 2010.
Toss: Bangladesh.   Result: ENGLAND WON BY NINE WICKETS.
Debuts: Bangladesh – Jahurul Islam. England – J. C. Tredwell.
Man of the Match: Shakib Al Hasan. Man of the Series: G. P. Swann.

England needed another fifth-day finish, but still won an attritional Test comfortably. Cook rounded things off with his 12th Test hundred, his second in two matches as captain, as England made light of chasing 209 in 54 overs. The game started on Tamim Iqbal's 21st birthday, and he hurtled to 85 before falling 30 minutes before lunch: England had five boundary fielders by the end of the first hour. Finally an attempted sweep bobbled round to Prior, a fortuitous maiden Test wicket for Kent off-spinner James Tredwell. Bangladesh eventually reached their third-highest total, and England – with only five specialist batsmen – were under pressure. Trott took 33 balls to open his account (one fewer than Tamim needed to reach 50), and laboured for 64 overs for 64 by the close. He departed quickly next day, but Bell helped stretch the lead to 77, his tenth Test hundred being his first in an innings in which no one else scored one – although Bresnan nearly did after a responsible knock. Shakib Al Hasan delivered 66 overs for four top-six wickets, and later top-scored with 96. Tredwell's presence alongside Swann proved essential as England slowly dismantled Bangladesh's second innings: they bowled 64 of the 102 overs, and each finished with six wickets in the match. Tamim was less impressive this time, dropped three times in making 52. The other debutant Jahurul Islam, after a first-innings duck, emulated team-mate Shafiul Islam (against India in January) when his first two scoring shots in Test cricket were sixes.

Bangladesh

Tamim Iqbal c Prior b Tredwell	85	– c Broad b Swann		52
Imrul Kayes c Finn b Broad	12	– b Broad		4
Junaid Siddique lbw b Swann	39	– c and b Tredwell		34
Jahurul Islam lbw b Swann	0	– b Swann		43
Mahmudullah c Collingwood b Finn	59	– c Prior b Bresnan		6
*Shakib Al Hasan lbw b Tredwell	49	– st Prior b Tredwell		96
†Mushfiqur Rahim c Prior b Bresnan	30	– b Broad		3
Naeem Islam not out	59	– (9) c Pietersen b Tredwell		3
Abdur Razzak lbw b Swann	3	– (10) lbw b Finn		8
Shafiul Islam c Prior b Bresnan	53	– (8) c Trott b Tredwell		28
Rubel Hossain c Prior b Swann	17	– not out		0
B 1, l-b 10, n-b 2	13	L-b 3, w 5		8
(117.1 overs)	419	(102 overs)		285

1/53 (2) 2/119 (1) 3/122 (4) 4/167 (3) 5/226 (5)   1/23 (2) 2/86 (1) 3/110 (3) 4/130 (5) 5/156 (4)
6/254 (6) 7/301 (7) 8/314 (9) 9/388 (10) 10/419 (11)   6/169 (7) 7/232 (8) 8/258 (9) 9/275 (10) 10/285 (6)

Broad 18–5–69–1; Bresnan 21–7–57–2; Swann 36.1–5–114–4; Finn 10–2–61–1; Tredwell 31–5–99–2; Collingwood 1–0–8–0. *Second Innings*—Broad 16–2–72–2; Bresnan 13–2–34–1; Tredwell 34–8–82–4; Finn 9–3–21–1; Swann 30–7–73–2.

England

*A. N. Cook c Imrul Kayes b Abdur Razzak	21	– not out		109
I. J. L. Trott b Shakib Al Hasan	64	– run out		19
K. P. Pietersen c Imrul Kayes b Shakib Al Hasan	45	– not out		74
P. D. Collingwood lbw b Rubel Hossain	0			
I. R. Bell c Jahurul Islam b Shakib Al Hasan	138			
†M. J. Prior b Shakib Al Hasan	62			
T. T. Bresnan st Mushfiqur Rahim b Abdur Razzak	91			
G. P. Swann run out	6			
S. C. J. Broad lbw b Mahmudullah	3			
J. C. Tredwell st Mushfiqur Rahim b Abdur Razzak	37			
S. T. Finn not out	0			
B 9, l-b 12, w 1, n-b 7	29	B 2, l-b 4, n-b 1		7
(173.3 overs)	496	(1 wkt, 44 overs)		209

1/29 (1) 2/105 (3) 3/107 (4) 4/174 (2) 5/272 (6)
6/415 (5) 7/426 (8) 8/434 (9) 9/481 (7) 10/496 (10)   1/42 (2)

Shafiul Islam 14–3–45–0; Abdur Razzak 39.3–8–132–3; Shakib Al Hasan 66–27–124–4; Mahmudullah 20–4–53–1; Rubel Hossain 26–4–88–1; Naeem Islam 7–0–29–0; Tamim Iqbal 1–0–4–0. *Second Innings*—Shafiul Islam 6–0–22–0; Abdur Razzak 15–0–67–0; Shakib Al Hasan 8–0–31–0; Mahmudullah 7–1–38–0; Rubel Hossain 4–0–26–0; Naeem Islam 4–0–19–0.

Umpires: A. L. Hill *(New Zealand)* (17) and R. J. Tucker *(Australia)* (3).
Third umpire: Nadir Shah *(Bangladesh)*. Referee: J. J. Crowe *(New Zealand)* (40).

Close of play: First day, Bangladesh 330–8 (Naeem Islam 33, Shafiul Islam 8); Second day, England 171–3 (Trott 64, Bell 25); Third day, England 440–8 (Bresnan 74, Tredwell 0); Fourth day, Bangladesh 172–6 (Shakib Al Hasan 25, Shafiul Islam 0).

NEW ZEALAND v AUSTRALIA 2009–10 (1st Test)

At Basin Reserve, Wellington, on 19, 20, 21, 22, 23 March, 2010.
Toss: Australia.   Result: AUSTRALIA WON BY TEN WICKETS.
Debuts: New Zealand – B. J. Arnel. Australia – R. J. Harris.
Man of the Match: M. J. Clarke.

Australia ran out emphatic winners in the end, and owed their success to players who had been under pressure. North, out of form for much of the season, produced a flawless century, while Hughes – included only when Shane Watson was ruled out with a hip strain – sealed victory with an attacking innings on the final day. Meanwhile Clarke, recovering from a very public break-up with his model fiancée, repaid his captain Ponting – who gave him a pep talk when he belatedly arrived in New Zealand – with his highest Test score: he and North put on 253 for the fifth wicket. After Ponting's declaration, Bollinger skittled New Zealand out for 157: celebrating his fifth wicket, he meant to kiss the Australian crest on his shirt but chose the wrong side, planting his lips on the sponsor's beercan logo instead. New Zealand did better in the follow-on, amid weather so windy that it prevented the use of the replay equipment. When McCullum had 52, the Australians tried to refer an lbw appeal, but the tracking cameras were shaking too much to work properly. Hauritz bowled 49 overs into the wind for three wickets, while the debutant fast bowler Ryan Harris claimed three of his four victims pushing into the gale. McCullum's fifth Test century lifted New Zealand to respectability, but still left Australia needing only 106. Hughes threw himself out of his shoes with every attacking shot: his 86 came from just 75 balls. Katich, with 18 from 65, played second fiddle to perfection.

Australia

P. J. Hughes c Taylor b Arnel	20	– not out	86
S. M. Katich lbw b Arnel	79	– not out	18
*R. T. Ponting run out	41		
M. E. K. Hussey c Watling b Martin	4		
M. J. Clarke st McCullum b Vettori	168		
M. J. North not out	112		
†B. J. Haddin not out	11		
B 2, l-b 15, w 2, n-b 5	24	N-b 2	2
(5 wkts dec, 131 overs)	459	(no wkt, 23 overs)	106

1/25 (1) 2/104 (3) 3/115 (4) 4/176 (2) 5/429 (5)

M. G. Johnson, N. M. Hauritz, R. J. Harris and D. E. Bollinger did not bat.

Martin 30–3–115–1; Southee 19–4–68–0; Arnel 26–4–89–2; Tuffey 22–7–49–0; Vettori 33–5–111–1; Guptill 1–0–10–0. *Second Innings*—Martin 6–0–43–0; Arnel 10–2–31–0; Vettori 7–1–32–0.

New Zealand

T. G. McIntosh c Hussey b Harris	9	– (2) c Katich b Hauritz	83
B-J. Watling lbw b Bollinger	0	– (1) lbw b Bollinger	33
P. J. Ingram run out	5	– c Haddin b Bollinger	1
L. R. P. L. Taylor c North b Bollinger	21	– lbw b Hauritz	25
M. J. Guptill c Haddin b Bollinger	30	– c North b Harris	6
*D. L. Vettori c Ponting b Harris	46	– b Hauritz	77
†B. B. McCullum c Harris b Bollinger	24	– c Clarke b Harris	104
D. R. Tuffey run out	0	– not out	47
T. G. Southee c Haddin b Johnson	5	– c Clarke b Harris	0
B. J. Arnel c Ponting b Bollinger	0	– lbw b Harris	3
C. S. Martin not out	0	– b Johnson	1
L-b 4, w 2, n-b 11	17	B 1, l-b 14, w 1, n-b 11	27
(59.1 overs)	157	(134.5 overs)	407

1/3 (2) 2/14 (3) 3/31 (1) 4/43 (4) 5/112 (6)   1/70 (1) 2/78 (3) 3/115 (4) 4/136 (5) 5/183 (2)
6/148 (7) 7/148 (5) 8/154 (8) 9/156 (10) 10/157 (9)   6/309 (6) 7/388 (7) 8/392 (9) 9/396 (10) 10/407 (11)

Bollinger 13–4–28–5; Harris 17–4–42–2; Johnson 11.1–5–38–1; Hauritz 14–4–39–0; North 4–1–6–0. *Second Innings*—Bollinger 27–3–80–2; Harris 24–3–77–4; Johnson 29.5–7–107–1; Hauritz 49–16–119–3; North 5–2–9–0.

Umpires: Asad Rauf *(Pakistan)* (29) and I. J. Gould *(England)* (12).
Third umpire: Aleem Dar *(Pakistan)*. Referee: J. Srinath *(India)* (14).

Close of play: First day, Australia 316–4 (Clarke 100, North 52); Second day, New Zealand 108–4 (Guptill 19, Vettori 42); Third day, New Zealand 187–5 (Vettori 18, McCullum 4); Fourth day, New Zealand 369–6 (McCullum 94, Tuffey 23).

NEW ZEALAND v AUSTRALIA 2009–10 (2nd Test)

At Seddon Park, Hamilton, on 27, 28, 29, 30, 31 March, 2010.
Toss: Australia.   Result: AUSTRALIA WON BY 176 RUNS.
Debuts: none.
Man of the Match: M. G. Johnson.

Vettori made an excellent start to his 100th Test, on his home ground, when he took four wickets and ran out Ponting, and later Taylor's whirlwind hundred gave New Zealand a first-innings lead. But the game slipped away: the ultimate outcome mimicked the First Test – a crushing home defeat before lunch on the last day. Ponting claimed first use of a firm, batsman-friendly pitch. Not long afterwards Vettori's superb throw from mid-off beat him home, a record 13th run-out in Tests for Ponting, one ahead of Allan Border, Matthew Hayden and Rahul Dravid. Australia were further set back by Southee, and their eventual 231 looked inadequate. However, New Zealand struggled themselves, and had the catching been half as good as the bowling, the fightback would have been even more effective. Taylor was dropped three times, and cantered to New Zealand's fastest Test century from 81 balls, beating Vettori's 82 at Harare in 2005–06. He then lifted Hauritz for three successive sixes in an over costing 25, and finally fell having hit exactly 100 in boundaries from just 104 balls. It left New Zealand 33 in front, but Katich and Hussey slowly reversed the momentum, adding 155, before Clarke and North put on 142. New Zealand had five sessions to pursue an unlikely 479, but lost half their side by the fourth-day close. Johnson took the first three, including the prize wicket of Taylor, and next day claimed the last three in successive overs to finish with ten in the match.

Australia

S. R. Watson c Arnel b Southee	12	– c Watling b Southee		65
S. M. Katich c Watling b Vettori	88	– c McCullum b Arnel		106
*R. T. Ponting run out	22	– c Watling b Southee		6
M. E. K. Hussey c McCullum b Southee	22	– c McCullum b Arnel		67
M. J. Clarke c Southee b Patel	28	– lbw b Arnel		63
M. J. North lbw b Southee	9	– c McCullum b Vettori		90
†B. J. Haddin c and b Southee	12	– b Patel		48
M. G. Johnson c McIntosh b Vettori	0	– c Patel b Vettori		0
N. M. Hauritz not out	12	– not out		41
R. J. Harris lbw b Vettori	10	– not out		18
D. E. Bollinger b Vettori	4			
B 4, l-b 6, n-b 2	12	B 2, l-b 1, n-b 4		7
(74.3 overs)	231	(8 wkts dec, 153 overs)		511

1/25 (1) 2/63 (3) 3/129 (4) 4/172 (5) 5/180 (2)
6/199 (7) 7/200 (8) 8/200 (6) 9/217 (10) 10/231 (11)

1/85 (1) 2/91 (3) 3/246 (4) 4/247 (2) 5/389 (5)
6/443 (6) 7/443 (8) 8/453 (7)

Martin 12–3–42–0; Southee 19–3–61–4; Arnel 12–2–53–0; Vettori 19.3–5–36–4; Patel 12–2–29–1. *Second Innings*—Martin 14–1–60–0; Southee 23–4–89–2; Arnel 26–6–77–3; Vettori 48–10–140–2; Patel 39–8–141–1; Sinclair 3–2–1–0.

New Zealand

T. G. McIntosh b Bollinger	4	– (2) b Johnson		19
B-J. Watling b Bollinger	46	– (1) c Haddin b Johnson		24
M. S. Sinclair b Johnson	11	– lbw b Clarke		29
L. R. P. L. Taylor c Haddin b Bollinger	138	– c Haddin b Johnson		22
M. J. Guptill c Ponting b Harris	4	– c Ponting b Johnson		58
*D. L. Vettori c Haddin b Harris	15	– lbw b Hauritz		22
†B. B. McCullum c Ponting b Johnson	5	– c Hussey b Bollinger		51
J. S. Patel c Ponting b Johnson	7	– c North b Bollinger		3
T. G. Southee not out	22	– c Clarke b Johnson		45
B. J. Arnel c Haddin b Johnson	7	– c Haddin b Johnson		0
C. S. Martin b Harris	0	– not out		5
W 1, n-b 4	5	B 12, l-b 10, n-b 2		24
(63.3 overs)	264	(91.1 overs)		302

1/4 (1) 2/30 (3) 3/114 (2) 4/143 (5) 5/167 (6)
6/193 (7) 7/234 (8) 8/236 (4) 9/263 (10) 10/264 (11)

1/40 (2) 2/53 (1) 3/107 (4) 4/119 (3) 5/152 (6)
6/239 (7) 7/249 (8) 8/273 (5) 9/295 (10) 10/302 (9)

Bollinger 14–3–57–3; Harris 15.3–3–50–3; Johnson 16–2–59–4; Hauritz 13–1–68–0; Watson 5–1–30–0. *Second Innings*—Bollinger 16–2–87–2; Harris 14–3–38–0; Watson 6–2–18–0; Johnson 20.1–6–73–6; Clarke 16–4–27–1; Hauritz 17–5–37–1; North 2–2–0–0.

Umpires: Aleem Dar *(Pakistan)* (60) and Asad Rauf *(Pakistan)* (30).
Third umpire: I. J. Gould *(England)*. Referee: J. Srinath *(India)* (15).

Close of play: First day, New Zealand 19–1 (Watling 6, Sinclair 8); Second day, Australia 35–0 (Watson 28, Katich 6); Third day, Australia 333–4 (Clarke 42, North 42); Fourth day, New Zealand 185–5 (Guptill 29, McCullum 19).

ENGLAND v BANGLADESH 2010 (1st Test)

At Lord's, London, on 27, 28, 29, 30, 31 May, 2010.
Toss: Bangladesh.   Result: ENGLAND WON BY EIGHT WICKETS.
Debuts: England – E. J. G. Morgan. Bangladesh – Robiul Islam.
Man of the Match: S. T. Finn.

England, fresh from winning the World Twenty20 in the Caribbean – their first global competition victory – completed their seventh win in seven Tests against Bangladesh, but it took them until tea on the fifth day (Bangladesh's previous Test at Lord's, in 2005, was over on the third morning). In Tamim Iqbal's coruscating second-innings hundred Bangladesh provided the most entertaining moments of a genuine scrap, a Test in reality, not just name. But England were always likely winners after racking up 505 on the back of Trott's patient 226, made in 490 minutes before becoming one of Shahadat Hossain's five wickets. On television Geoffrey Boycott called Bangladesh's attack unfit for Test cricket: next day in the follow-on Tamim (who thought the slight was levelled at the whole team) set about putting the record straight. He slog-swept Swann for two sixes, and later disdainfully despatched a length delivery over mid-on to reach Bangladesh's fastest Test hundred, from 94 balls. In celebration, Tamim ebulliently gestured for the signwriter to start work on the honours board. However, although Imrul Kayes finally passed 50 at his 24th attempt (no Test opener had waited longer), the middle order crumbled again, failing to knuckle down when they might have denied England the time to push for victory. As it was, they were left to get 160 in two full sessions, and cantered home. With the scores level, Pietersen dead-batted the last scheduled over before tea. But the umpires sensibly kept the players on – and, next ball, Trott finished the job.

England

*A. J. Strauss b Mahmudullah	83	– c Mushfiqur Rahim b Shakib Al Hasan	82
A. N. Cook lbw b Shahadat Hossain	7	– lbw b Mahmudullah	23
I. J. L. Trott c Imrul Kayes b Shahadat Hossain	226	– not out	36
K. P. Pietersen b Shakib Al Hasan	18	– not out	10
I. R. Bell b Rubel Hossain	17		
E. J. G. Morgan c Mushfiqur Rahim b Shahadat Hossain	44		
†M. J. Prior run out	16		
T. T. Bresnan c Junaid Siddique b Shahadat Hossain	25		
G. P. Swann c Rubel Hossain b Shakib Al Hasan	22		
J. M. Anderson b Shahadat Hossain	13		
S. T. Finn not out	3		
L-b 10, w 8, n-b 13	31	L-b 5, w 1, n-b 6	12
(125 overs)	505	(2 wkts, 35.1 overs)	163

1/7 (2) 2/188 (1) 3/227 (4) 4/258 (5) 5/370 (6)
6/400 (7) 7/463 (8) 8/478 (3) 9/498 (9) 10/505 (10)   1/67 (2) 2/147 (1)

Shahadat Hossain 28–3–98–5; Robiul Islam 22–2–107–0; Shakib Al Hasan 27–3–109–2; Rubel Hossain 23–0–109–1; Mahmudullah 23–3–59–1; Mohammad Ashraful 2–0–13–0. *Second Innings*—Shahadat Hossain 2–0–19–0; Robiul Islam 1–0–12–0; Shakib Al Hasan 16–1–48–1; Rubel Hossain 1–0–8–0; Mahmudullah 15.1–1–71–1.

Bangladesh

Tamim Iqbal run out	55	– c Trott b Finn	103
Imrul Kayes c Strauss b Finn	43	– c Bell b Finn	75
Junaid Siddique c Prior b Finn	58	– c Bresnan b Finn	74
Jahurul Islam c Prior b Anderson	20	– c and b Trott	46
Mohammad Ashraful lbw b Finn	4	– c Prior b Anderson	21
*Shakib Al Hasan c Strauss b Anderson	25	– (7) c Morgan b Finn	16
†Mushfiqur Rahim b Finn	16	– (8) c Prior b Finn	0
Mahmudullah b Anderson	17	– (9) c Prior b Bresnan	19
Shahadat Hossain b Anderson	20	– b Bresnan	0
Rubel Hossain c Cook b Bresnan	9	– c Strauss b Bresnan	4
Robiul Islam not out	9	– not out	0
L-b 2, w 3, n-b 1	6	B 7, l-b 14, w 2, n-b 1	24
(93 overs)	282	(110.2 overs)	382

1/88 (1) 2/134 (2) 3/179 (3) 4/185 (5) 5/191 (4)
6/221 (6) 7/234 (7) 8/255 (9) 9/266 (8) 10/282 (10)

1/185 (1) 2/189 (2) 3/289 (4) 4/321 (5) 5/322 (6)
6/347 (7) 7/354 (3) 8/361 (8) 9/381 (10) 10/382 (9)

Anderson 31–6–78–4; Bresnan 24–5–76–1; Finn 25–5–100–4; Swann 11–6–19–0; Trott 2–0–7–0. *Second Innings*—Anderson 29–8–84–1; Bresnan 26.2–9–93–3; Finn 24–6–87–5; Swann 27–5–81–0; Trott 4–0–16–1.

Umpires: B. F. Bowden *(New Zealand)* (60) and E. A. R. de Silva *(Sri Lanka)* (44).
Third umpire: R. K. Illingworth *(England)*. Referee: A. G. Hurst *(Australia)* (38).

Close of play: First day, England 362–4 (Trott 175, Morgan 40); Second day, Bangladesh 172–2 (Junaid Siddique 53, Jahurul Islam 16); Third day, Bangladesh 237–7 (Mahmudullah 7, Shahadat Hossain 3); Fourth day, Bangladesh 328–5 (Junaid Siddique 66, Shakib Al Hasan 2).

ENGLAND v BANGLADESH 2010 (2nd Test)

At Old Trafford, Manchester, on 4, 5, 6 June, 2010.
Toss: England.   Result: ENGLAND WON BY AN INNINGS AND 80 RUNS.
Debuts: England – A. Shahzad.
Man of the Match: I. R. Bell. Men of the Series: S. T. Finn and Tamim Iqbal.

At 4.24pm on the second day, Bangladesh's players could look back proudly on five sessions of hard-fought cricket in which they had shared the spoils. After England were restricted to 419 – Bell and Prior put on 153 before both fell to Shakib Al Hasan – Tamim Iqbal and Imrul Kayes opened up with 126 in 23.5 overs of uninhibited strokeplay. Taking the game into a fifth day seemed eminently feasible; embarrassing England was not impossible. Yet less than 24 hours later, England's players were spraying the champagne – Bangladesh lost all 20 wickets in scoring 213 further runs in 64.3 overs. Ten fell in Saturday's prolonged evening session, chiefly to Swann and the impressive debutant Ajmal Shahzad; then, on a cloudy Sunday afternoon, all ten were swept aside, again in a single extended session, in 34.1 overs of carnage. Once they lost Tamim – who had flayed 108 the previous afternoon, becoming the first Bangladeshi to score successive Test centuries – the other batsmen's techniques were mercilessly exposed, in conditions beloved of English seamers but rarely seen in Chittagong. The lofty Finn, who took 15 wickets in the two Tests, dismissed Kayes (hooking to deep backward square) with a short ball for the fourth time out of four. At 39 for six in the 14th over, Bangladesh were threatening their lowest Test total (62 against Sri Lanka in 2007), but Mahmudullah averted that indignity. Tamim's heroics led to him becoming the first Bangladeshi to be named one of *Wisden's* Five Cricketers of the Year.

England

*A. J. Strauss c Imrul Kayes b Shafiul Islam		21
A. N. Cook c Junaid Siddique b Abdur Razzak		29
I. J. L. Trott b Shafiul Islam		3
K. P. Pietersen st Mushfiqur Rahim b Shakib Al Hasan		64
I. R. Bell b Shakib Al Hasan		128
E. J. G. Morgan c Jahurul Islam b Shahadat Hossain		37
†M. J. Prior c Jahurul Islam b Shakib Al Hasan		93
G. P. Swann lbw b Abdur Razzak		20
A. Shahzad c Abdur Razzak b Shakib Al Hasan		5
J. M. Anderson not out		2
S. T. Finn lbw b Shakib Al Hasan		0
B 6, l-b 5, w 4, n-b 2		17
(121.3 overs)		419

1/44 (1) 2/48 (3) 3/83 (2) 4/153 (4) 5/223 (6) 6/376 (5)
7/399 (8) 8/414 (9) 9/419 (7) 10/419 (11)

Shahadat Hossain 21–3–84–1; Shafiul Islam 21–2–63–2; Mahmudullah 12–1–31–0; Shakib Al Hasan 37.3–4–121–5; Abdur Razzak 30–3–109–2.

Bangladesh

Tamim Iqbal c Prior b Anderson	108	– c Prior b Anderson	2
Imrul Kayes c Shahzad b Finn	36	– c Shahzad b Finn	9
Junaid Siddique c Prior b Swann	1	– c Pietersen b Anderson	6
Jahurul Islam b Swann	5	– (5) c Prior b Finn	0
Mohammad Ashraful c Morgan b Shahzad	11	– (4) c Trott b Anderson	14
*Shakib Al Hasan c Anderson b Swann	10	– b Shahzad	1
†Mushfiqur Rahim c Anderson b Swann	11	– c sub (K. R. Brown) b Finn	13
Mahmudullah b Shahzad	8	– c Prior b Finn	38
Shafiul Islam b Shahzad	4	– (10) c Strauss b Finn	4
Abdur Razzak not out	0	– (9) c Morgan b Swann	19
Shahadat Hossain lbw b Swann	0	– not out	4
B 4, l-b 7, w 8, n-b 3	22	B 13	13
(54.1 overs)	216	(34.1 overs)	123

1/126 (2) 2/153 (3) 3/169 (1) 4/169 (4) 5/185 (6) 1/2 (1) 2/14 (2) 3/18 (3) 4/21 (5) 5/37 (4)
6/200 (5) 7/210 (8) 8/214 (9) 9/216 (7) 10/216 (11) 6/39 (6) 7/76 (7) 8/97 (8) 9/119 (10) 10/123 (9)

Anderson 14–4–45–1; Finn 8–1–39–1; Swann 22.1–4–76–5; Shahzad 10–2–45–3. *Second Innings*—Anderson 10–3–16–3; Finn 10–2–42–5; Shahzad 7–2–18–1; Swann 7.1–0–34–1.

Umpires: B. F. Bowden *(New Zealand)* (61) and E. A. R. de Silva *(Sri Lanka)* (45).
Third umpire: R. A. Kettleborough *(England)*. Referee: A. G. Hurst *(Australia)* (39).

Close of play: First day, England 275–5 (Bell 87, Prior 21); Second day, Bangladesh 216.

WEST INDIES v SOUTH AFRICA 2010 (1st Test)

At Queen's Park Oval, Port-of-Spain, Trinidad, on 10, 11, 12, 13 June, 2010.
Toss: South Africa.　　　Result: SOUTH AFRICA WON BY 163 RUNS.
Debuts: West Indies – N. T. Pascal, S. Shillingford. South Africa – L. L. Tsotsobe.
Man of the Match: D. W. Steyn.

The pace and hostility of Steyn and Morkel, even on a benign pitch, were too much for a fragile West Indian team (without the injured Adrian Barath and Ramnaresh Sarwan) which had just been beaten in all seven limited-overs matches. Despite persistent rain allowing only 34 overs on the first day, South Africa surged to victory with a day to spare. Benn and Shillingford – the rarity of two front-line spinners in a West Indian team – used early turn to good effect as South Africa slipped to 107 for five, but de Villiers and Prince, eventually taken at leg slip in Gayle's solitary over, added 122, then Boucher and the markedly improved Steyn put on 86. West Indies' competitiveness evaporated with a spectacular batting collapse. Morkel used his height well to prise out the top three, and later the last seven tumbled for 31 once Chanderpaul gloved a nasty lifter. Steyn took five for two in 16 balls, including his 200th wicket (Benn) in his 39th Test; only Clarrie Grimmett (36), Dennis Lillee and Waqar Younis (both 38) got there in fewer matches. It was West Indies' lowest total against South Africa. Smith waived the follow-on and cashed in against a lethargic attack: the declaration, an hour into the fourth day, set an improbable 457. Gayle's 73 led a steelier display, but Morkel and Steyn were again superb. A late flourish threatened to take play into the final day but, after Smith claimed the extra half-hour, Steyn fittingly ended the contest.

South Africa

*G. C. Smith c Bravo b Shillingford	23 – b Benn	90
A. N. Petersen lbw b Shillingford	31 – lbw b Benn	22
H. M. Amla c Bravo b Benn	2 – c Deonarine b Shillingford	5
J. H. Kallis lbw b Shillingford	28 – lbw b Benn	40
P. L. Harris c Shillingford b Benn	10	
A. B. de Villiers c Ramdin b Benn	68 – (5) not out	19
A. G. Prince c Dowlin b Gayle	57 – (6) not out	16
†M. V. Boucher c Pascal b Bravo	69	
D. W. Steyn st Ramdin b Benn	39	
M. Morkel b Benn	2	
L. L. Tsotsobe not out	3	
B 9, l-b 4, w 1, n-b 6	20	B 6, l-b 3, n-b 5 ... 14
(129.4 overs)	352	(4 wkts dec, 62 overs) ... 206

1/55 (1) 2/60 (3) 3/68 (2) 4/91 (5) 5/107 (4)
6/229 (7) 7/238 (6) 8/324 (9) 9/330 (10) 10/352 (8)　　1/56 (2) 2/79 (3) 3/157 (4) 4/178 (1)

Rampaul 19–3–56–0; Pascal 11–1–32–0; Bravo 16.4–6–33–1; Benn 47–9–120–5; Shillingford 35–4–96–3; Gayle 1–0–2–1. *Second Innings*—Rampaul 6–2–21–0; Pascal 6–1–27–0; Benn 25–3–74–3; Shillingford 21–2–66–1; Bravo 4–1–9–0.

West Indies

*C. H. Gayle b Morkel	6 – lbw b Morkel	73
T. M. Dowlin c Smith b Morkel	4 – lbw b Morkel	1
B. P. Nash c Boucher b Morkel	1 – c Boucher b Steyn	13
S. Chanderpaul c Boucher b Steyn	26 – c de Villiers b Kallis	15
N. Deonarine b Steyn	29 – lbw b Steyn	23
D. J. Bravo c Boucher b Morkel	1 – c Prince b Harris	49
†D. Ramdin not out	25 – c de Villiers b Tsotsobe	9
S. Shillingford lbw b Steyn	0 – c Petersen b Harris	27
S. J. Benn b Steyn	0 – lbw b Petersen	42
R. Rampaul b Steyn	0 – not out	18
N. T. Pascal c Petersen b Kallis	2 – b Steyn	10
B 2, l-b 3, w 2, n-b 1	8	B 11, l-b 2 ... 13
(47.1 overs)	102	(80.3 overs) ... 293

1/7 (2) 2/9 (3) 3/12 (1) 4/71 (4) 5/72 (6) 6/72 (5)　　1/2 (2) 2/39 (3) 3/94 (4) 4/114 (1) 5/152 (5)
7/72 (8) 8/75 (9) 9/75 (10) 10/102 (11)　　6/192 (6) 7/194 (7) 8/260 (9) 9/264 (8) 10/293 (11)

Steyn 14–5–29–5; Morkel 13–7–19–4; Tsotsobe 8–0–18–0; Harris 6–1–25–0; Kallis 6.1–2–6–1. *Second Innings*—Steyn 15.3–1–65–3; Morkel 12–3–49–2; Tsotsobe 13–5–20–1; Harris 26.3–3–91–2; Kallis 11–3–49–1; Smith 0.3–0–4–0; Petersen 2–1–2–1.

Umpires: Asad Rauf *(Pakistan)* (31) and S. J. Davis *(Australia)* (24).
Third umpire: S. J. A. Taufel *(Australia)*. Referee: R. S. Mahanama *(Sri Lanka)* (29).

Close of play: First day, South Africa 70–3 (Kallis 6, Harris 0); Second day, South Africa 352; Third day, South Africa 155–2 (Smith 79, Kallis 40).

WEST INDIES v SOUTH AFRICA 2010 (2nd Test)

At Warner Park, Basseterre, St Kitts, on 18, 19, 20, 21, 22 June, 2010.
Toss: South Africa.   Result: MATCH DRAWN.
Debuts: none.
Man of the Match: S. Chanderpaul.

At the toss for only the second Test played at Warner Park, Gayle called the grassless, straw-coloured pitch "a road". And after five days of dour batsman-dominated cricket that drew just a few hundred spectators and did Test cricket no favours, no one could argue. Smith, dropped at 79 and 112, made the first of the match's five centuries, and passed 7,000 Test runs too. Kallis leapfrogged Steve Waugh (10,927) on the Test-runs list, and later joined Tendulkar, Lara, Ponting, Dravid and Border in passing 11,000 – but again he could not convert a century (his 35th in Tests) into that elusive double, top-edging a sweep. The carefree de Villiers hit 135, including six of the innings's 15 sixes on probably Test cricket's smallest outfield. One of them, off Benn, took him to three figures. West Indies were 151 for three before a counter-attacking stand of 220 in 200 minutes. Chanderpaul was felled by Steyn's bouncer when five, but rose to register his 22nd Test century; Nash, watched by his parents, wife and infant son, over from their home in Australia, made his second. But West Indies reverted to defence on the fourth day despite being in a decent position: Chanderpaul used up another 93 balls for 15 more runs. West Indies eventually led by three; more significant was Boucher becoming the first wicketkeeper to make 500 Test dismissals, when he caught Rampaul. South Africa enjoyed a glorified net on the last day, ensuring they retained the Sir Vivian Richards Trophy.

South Africa

*G. C. Smith b Roach	132	– c Ramdin b Shillingford	46
A. N. Petersen c Roach b Shillingford	52	– b Bravo	39
H. M. Amla c Bravo b Shillingford	44	– c sub (D. J. G. Sammy) b Shillingford	41
J. H. Kallis c Rampaul b Shillingford	110	– not out	62
A. B. de Villiers not out	135	– not out	31
A. G. Prince c Gayle b Benn	9		
†M. V. Boucher run out	17		
D. W. Steyn not out	20		
L-b 5, w 2, n-b 17	24	B 1, l-b 1, w 13, n-b 1	16
(6 wkts dec, 147 overs)	543	(3 wkts dec, 94 overs)	235

1/99 (2) 2/211 (3) 3/283 (1) 4/421 (4) 5/442 (6) 6/490 (7)   1/74 (1) 2/131 (3) 3/131 (2)

P. L. Harris, M. Morkel and L. L. Tsotsobe did not bat.

Roach 22–4–72–1; Rampaul 18–4–65–0; Benn 30–3–124–1; Bravo 18–2–58–0; Shillingford 52–4–193–3; Deonarine 3–0–20–0; Nash 4–0–6–0. *Second Innings*—Roach 13–3–33–0; Rampaul 2–0–7–0; Benn 28–4–61–0; Shillingford 30–5–80–2; Bravo 11–4–37–1; Nash 9–4–12–0; Dowlin 1–0–3–0.

West Indies

*C. H. Gayle b Morkel	50
T. M. Dowlin c de Villiers b Morkel	10
N. Deonarine b Steyn	65
S. Chanderpaul c and b Harris	166
B. P. Nash run out	114
D. J. Bravo c Boucher b Harris	53
†D. Ramdin c Petersen b Tsotsobe	1
S. Shillingford c de Villiers b Kallis	7
S. J. Benn c Kallis b Morkel	26
R. Rampaul c Boucher b Morkel	31
K. A. J. Roach not out	1
B 1, l-b 7, w 7, n-b 7	22
(181.1 overs)	546

1/13 (2) 2/106 (1) 3/151 (3) 4/371 (5) 5/471 (4)
6/476 (7) 7/486 (6) 8/486 (8) 9/545 (10) 10/546 (9)

Steyn 29–4–105–1; Morkel 34.1–9–116–4; Tsotsobe 28–10–68–1; Harris 62–9–165–2; Kallis 23–7–65–1; Petersen 5–0–19–0.

Umpires: Asad Rauf *(Pakistan)* (32) and S. J. A. Taufel *(Australia)* (62).
Third umpire: S. J. Davis *(Australia)*. Referee: J. J. Crowe *(New Zealand)* (41).

Close of play: First day, South Africa 296–3 (Kallis 45, de Villiers 7); Second day, West Indies 86–1 (Gayle 42, Deonarine 33); Third day, West Indies 424–4 (Chanderpaul 151, Bravo 21); Fourth day, South Africa 23–0 (Smith 13, Petersen 8).

WEST INDIES v SOUTH AFRICA 2010 (3rd Test)

At Kensington Oval, Bridgetown, Barbados, on 26, 27, 28, 29 June, 2010.
Toss: West Indies.   Result: SOUTH AFRICA WON BY SEVEN WICKETS.
Debuts: West Indies – B. J. Bess.
Man of the Match: J. Botha. Man of the Series: D. W. Steyn.

Brittle West Indian batting contributed to another hefty defeat, this one completed half an hour before lunch on the fourth day. South Africa thus took the series 2–0, and made the overall score 9–0 in ten international games on their tour. The match was sullied by unpleasant clashes which resulted in heavy fines for Steyn and Roach, and Benn's second suspension in six months. West Indies were forced to call up Brandon Bess – a Guyanese fast bowler at the new High Performance Center in Barbados – after Pascal suffered a neck injury. Bess arrived for his debut shortly after the match began. South Africa balanced their attack by including off-spinner Botha for his first Test since 2008: it was the first time they had gone into a Test with two specialist spinners since October 2003 in Pakistan. His clever variations brought him seven wickets and the match award. Richards fell in the fourth over before scoring; next over Gayle played on for the third time in the series. Bravo and Ramdin added 76 to make up for a middle-order meltdown, but 231 never looked enough. South Africa dipped to 145 for five before de Villiers gradually took control, putting on 134 with Prince, who stretched the lead to 115. Steyn scotched any notions of a fightback with three quick wickets before Botha struck again, and only Chanderpaul – who played his usual role on a sinking ship with a four-hour 71 – and Shillingford prolonged the contest into the fourth day.

West Indies

*C. H. Gayle b Steyn	20	– c Boucher b Steyn	10
D. M. Richards lbw b Morkel	0	– c Petersen b Steyn	17
N. Deonarine b Botha	46	– c Prince b Steyn	0
S. Chanderpaul c Kallis b Botha	22	– not out	71
B. P. Nash lbw b Botha	2	– c Kallis b Botha	12
D. J. Bravo c Smith b Steyn	61	– b Harris	2
†D. Ramdin c Steyn b Kallis	27	– c Boucher b Botha	1
S. Shillingford c Botha b Kallis	0	– lbw b Botha	25
S. J. Benn c Amla b Botha	24	– b Morkel	9
K. A. J. Roach c Boucher b Steyn	2	– c Boucher b Morkel	8
B. J. Bess not out	11	– c Kallis b Morkel	0
B 4, l-b 7, w 5	16	B 1, l-b 1, w 1, n-b 3	6
(73.5 overs)	231	(65.1 overs)	161

1/12 (2) 2/21 (1) 3/76 (4) 4/90 (5) 5/105 (3)
6/181 (7) 7/187 (8) 8/204 (6) 9/207 (10) 10/231 (9)

1/27 (2) 2/27 (3) 3/36 (1) 4/70 (5) 5/74 (6)
6/75 (7) 7/128 (8) 8/151 (9) 9/161 (10) 10/161 (11)

Steyn 13–3–37–3; Morkel 10–2–48–1; Kallis 12–1–36–2; Botha 19.5–2–56–4; Harris 19–3–43–0. *Second Innings*—Steyn 11–4–36–3; Morkel 14.1–5–33–3; Harris 16–3–34–1; Botha 20–5–46–3; Kallis 4–0–10–0.

South Africa

*G. C. Smith c Richards b Benn	70	– c Chanderpaul b Roach	10
A. N. Petersen c Chanderpaul b Roach	1	– b Roach	6
H. M. Amla c Nash b Benn	5	– c Benn b Roach	25
P. L. Harris c Gayle b Bess	11		
J. H. Kallis b Benn	43	– (4) not out	0
A. B. de Villiers c Ramdin b Benn	73	– (5) not out	4
A. G. Prince not out	78		
†M. V. Boucher run out	17		
J. Botha lbw b Benn	9		
D. W. Steyn b Roach	4		
M. Morkel c Bravo b Benn	9		
B 5, l-b 6, w 7, n-b 8	26	W 2, n-b 2	4
(134.4 overs)	346	(3 wkts, 8.4 overs)	49

1/17 (2) 2/41 (3) 3/60 (4) 4/122 (1) 5/145 (5)
6/279 (6) 7/312 (8) 8/326 (9) 9/333 (10) 10/346 (11)

1/14 (1) 2/29 (2) 3/45 (3)

Roach 25–6–59–2; Bess 9–0–65–1; Shillingford 25–2–85–0; Benn 46.4–13–81–6; Bravo 27–12–43–0; Gayle 2–1–2–0. *Second Innings*—Roach 4.4–1–22–3; Bess 4–0–27–0.

Umpires: S. J. Davis *(Australia)* (25) and S. J. A. Taufel *(Australia)* (63).
Third umpire: Asad Rauf *(Pakistan)*. Referee: J. J. Crowe *(New Zealand)* (42).

Close of play: First day, South Africa 46–2 (Smith 35, Harris 2); Second day, South Africa 285–6 (Prince 55, Boucher 4); Third day, West Indies 134–7 (Chanderpaul 57, Benn 4).

PAKISTAN v AUSTRALIA 2010 (1st Test)

At Lord's, London, on 13, 14, 15, 16 July, 2010.
Toss: Pakistan.   Result: AUSTRALIA WON BY 150 RUNS.
Debuts: Pakistan – Azhar Ali, Umar Amin. Australia – T. D. Paine, S. P. D. Smith.
Men of the Match: S. M. Katich and Salman Butt.

Sixteen months after the attack on the Sri Lankans in Lahore, Lord's staged the first of two Pakistan "home" matches in a series sponsored by MCC, the first neutral Tests in England since the 1912 Triangular Tournament. Since their 3–0 defeat in Australia six months previously, Pakistan had appointed their ninth Test captain in ten years: Shahid Afridi, surely the wildest spirit ever to lead his country, found himself recalled after four years playing only limited-overs internationals. He didn't last long: after hitting out manically in both innings, Afridi resigned immediately after Pakistan lost their 13th successive Test against Australia, a record for one nation against another. Even so, the feeling that the Aussies were not the force of old was reinforced when they were limited to 229 for nine in the 70 overs possible on a cloudy first day, despite Katich's vigilant 80. Next day, Salman Butt defended with sound judgment as wickets fell swiftly around him, until he was ninth out. Watson pitched the ball up and swung it to take a maiden five-for (another followed the next week), but Australia were soon in trouble again: when North was seventh out at 188 the game was still in the balance. But typical Australian resolution left Pakistan chasing a distant 440. Just as they were beginning to dream, at 186 for two, off-spinner North dismissed Butt with his first ball, with the debutant wicketkeeper Tim Paine making an accomplished stumping, and went on to a career-best six for 55.

Australia

S. R. Watson b Mohammad Aamer	4	– c Imran Farhat b Mohammad Asif	31
S. M. Katich c Kamran Akmal b Mohammad Asif	80	– c Kamran Akmal b Umar Gul	83
*R. T. Ponting c Umar Amin b Mohammad Aamer	26	– lbw b Mohammad Asif	0
M. J. Clarke lbw b Mohammad Asif	47	– b Umar Gul	12
M. E. K. Hussey not out	56	– c Imran Farhat b Umar Gul	0
M. J. North b Mohammad Asif	0	– (7) c Kamran Akmal b Mohammad Asif	20
†T. D. Paine c Kamran Akmal b Umar Gul	7	– (8) b Shahid Afridi	47
S. P. D. Smith lbw b Danish Kaneria	1	– (9) lbw b Danish Kaneria	12
M. G. Johnson b Danish Kaneria	3	– (6) b Umar Gul	30
B. W. Hilfenhaus b Mohammad Aamer	1	– not out	56
D. E. Bollinger b Mohammad Aamer	4	– b Danish Kaneria	21
B 10, l-b 2, w 2, n-b 10	24	B 6, l-b 5, w 2, n-b 9	22
(76.5 overs)	253	(91 overs)	334

1/8 (1) 2/51 (3) 3/171 (4) 4/174 (2) 5/174 (6)
6/206 (7) 7/208 (8) 8/213 (9) 9/222 (10) 10/253 (11)

1/61 (1) 2/73 (3) 3/97 (4) 4/97 (5) 5/149 (6)
6/188 (2) 7/188 (7) 8/208 (9) 9/282 (8) 10/334 (11)

Mohammad Aamer 19.5–2–72–4; Mohammad Asif 19–5–63–3; Umar Gul 17–3–32–1; Shahid Afridi 3–0–25–0; Danish Kaneria 18–7–49–2. *Second Innings*—Mohammad Aamer 18–3–67–0; Mohammad Asif 21–3–77–3; Umar Gul 21–5–61–4; Danish Kaneria 17–2–74–2; Shahid Afridi 14–0–44–1.

Pakistan

Imran Farhat c Paine b Hilfenhaus	4	– c Watson b Smith	24
Salman Butt b Watson	63	– st Paine b North	92
Azhar Ali c Paine b Hilfenhaus	16	– c Paine b Hilfenhaus	42
Umar Amin c Paine b Johnson	1	– c Katich b North	33
Umar Akmal lbw b Watson	5	– c Clarke b North	22
†Kamran Akmal lbw b Watson	0	– b Smith	46
*Shahid Afridi c Johnson b Watson	31	– c Hussey b North	2
Mohammad Aamer c Paine b Bollinger	0	– c Hussey b North	19
Umar Gul c Watson b Bollinger	7	– c Ponting b Smith	1
Danish Kaneria c Smith b Watson	14	– c Ponting b North	2
Mohammad Asif not out	4	– not out	1
L-b 2, n-b 1	3	B 2, l-b 1, n-b 2	5
(40.5 overs)	148	(91.1 overs)	289

1/11 (1) 2/45 (3) 3/54 (4) 4/75 (5) 5/83 (6) 6/117 (7)
7/117 (8) 8/129 (9) 9/133 (2) 10/148 (10)

1/50 (1) 2/152 (3) 3/186 (2) 4/216 (5) 5/227 (4)
6/229 (7) 7/283 (6) 8/285 (8) 9/287 (9) 10/289 (10)

Bollinger 11–3–38–2; Hilfenhaus 12–2–37–2; Johnson 10–2–31–1; Watson 7.5–1–40–5. *Second Innings*—Bollinger 12–4–43–0; Hilfenhaus 16–8–37–1; Johnson 18–5–74–0; Smith 21–5–51–3; Watson 6–0–26–0; North 18.1–1–55–6.

Umpires: I. J. Gould *(England)* (13) and R. E. Koertzen *(South Africa)* (107).
Third umpire: Ahsan Raza *(Pakistan)*. Referee: B. C. Broad *(England)* (39).

Close of play: First day, Australia 229–9 (Hussey 39, Bollinger 0); Second day, Australia 100–4 (Katich 49, Johnson 2); Third day, Pakistan 114–1 (Salman Butt 58, Azhar Ali 28).

PAKISTAN v AUSTRALIA 2010 (2nd Test)

At Headingley, Leeds, on 21, 22, 23, 24 July, 2010.
Toss: Australia.   Result: PAKISTAN WON BY THREE WICKETS.
Debuts: none.
Men of the Match: Mohammad Aamer and S. R. Watson.

Pakistan had lost every competitive match on their recent tour of Australia. They had lost their 13 previous Tests against them, and had not won one for 15 years. But despite a second-innings collapse which betrayed their lack of a senior batsman, and all those memories, they edged home. Australia never recovered from being bowled out for 88 – their lowest total for 25 years, and their worst against Pakistan since they first met on the Karachi mat in 1956–57. Ponting chose to bat, against local opinion: he had not bowled first since losing to England at Edgbaston in 2005. Mohammad Asif swung the ball both ways in a superlative opening spell: he kept drawing Ponting across his crease with outswingers, until pinning him in front so decisively that he walked. Pakistan were in the lead soon after tea, with Salman Butt digging in on his captaincy debut, but Watson improved his career-best figures for the second week running. Still, a lead of 170 looked decisive. Ponting became the second man after Tendulkar to reach 12,000 Test runs, and later Steve Smith, in his second Test, hit 77 from 100 balls. The target was 180: Azhar Ali and Imran Farhat, dropped by Watson at slip off Bollinger when four, calmly added 110, but then the nerves set in, and six wickets tumbled for 42. Kamran Akmal fell with the scores level, and Umar Gul was almost caught next ball but ran the winning single. This was umpire Rudi Koertzen's 108th and final Test.

Australia

S. R. Watson lbw b Mohammad Asif	5 – b Umar Amin	24
S. M. Katich lbw b Mohammad Aamer	13 – b Mohammad Aamer	11
*R. T. Ponting lbw b Mohammad Asif	6 – c Kamran Akmal b Mohammad Aamer	66
M. J. Clarke b Umar Gul	3 – c Kamran Akmal b Mohammad Asif	77
M. E. K. Hussey lbw b Umar Gul	5 – c Umar Akmal b Mohammad Aamer	8
M. J. North c Kamran Akmal b Umar Amin	16 – b Mohammad Aamer	0
†T. D. Paine c Kamran Akmal b Mohammad Asif	17 – c Azhar Ali b Danish Kaneria	33
S. P. D. Smith b Mohammad Aamer	10 – b Umar Gul	77
M. G. Johnson b Mohammad Aamer	0 – lbw b Mohammad Asif	12
B. W. Hilfenhaus run out	3 – c Umar Akmal b Danish Kaneria	17
D. E. Bollinger not out	2 – not out	0
L-b 6, n-b 2	8	B 4, l-b 10, w 2, n-b 8	24
(33.1 overs)	88	(95.3 overs)	349

1/20 (2) 2/20 (1) 3/27 (4) 4/29 (3) 5/41 (5)
6/60 (6) 7/73 (8) 8/73 (9) 9/86 (10) 10/88 (7)

1/15 (2) 2/55 (1) 3/144 (3) 4/158 (5) 5/164 (6)
6/217 (4) 7/246 (7) 8/283 (9) 9/320 (10) 10/349 (8)

Mohammad Aamer 11–4–20–3; Mohammad Asif 10.1–1–30–3; Umar Gul 9–3–16–2; Umar Amin 2–0–7–1; Danish Kaneria 1–0–9–0. *Second Innings*—Mohammad Aamer 27–6–86–4; Mohammad Asif 26–4–83–2; Umar Gul 15.3–1–80–1; Umar Amin 6–1–12–1; Danish Kaneria 21–2–74–2.

Pakistan

Imran Farhat lbw b Watson	43 – b Bollinger	67
*Salman Butt b Hilfenhaus	45 – c Clarke b Hilfenhaus	13
Azhar Ali c Paine b Watson	30 – c Paine b Bollinger	51
Umar Amin c North b Hilfenhaus	25 – c Paine b Bollinger	0
Umar Akmal c Paine b Johnson	21 – c Paine b Hilfenhaus	8
Shoaib Malik c Paine b Watson	26 – c North b Hilfenhaus	10
†Kamran Akmal c North b Watson	15 – c Hussey b Johnson	13
Mohammad Aamer lbw b Watson	0 – not out	5
Umar Gul b Watson	0 – not out	1
Danish Kaneria run out	15		
Mohammad Asif not out	9		
B 11, l-b 9, n-b 9	29	L-b 7, n-b 5	12
(64.5 overs)	258	(7 wkts, 50.4 overs)	180

1/80 (2) 2/133 (1) 3/140 (3) 4/171 (5) 5/195 (4)
6/222 (7) 7/222 (8) 8/224 (9) 9/234 (6) 10/258 (10)

1/27 (2) 2/137 (1) 3/137 (4) 4/146 (3)
5/150 (5) 6/161 (6) 7/179 (7)

Bollinger 17–4–50–0; Hilfenhaus 20.5–3–77–2; Watson 11–3–33–6; Johnson 15–0–71–1; Smith 1–0–7–0. *Second Innings*—Bollinger 13–2–51–3; Hilfenhaus 13–2–39–3; Johnson 10.4–1–41–1; Watson 5–1–18–0; Smith 9–2–24–0.

Umpires: I. J. Gould *(England)* (14) and R. E. Koertzen *(South Africa)* (108).
Third umpire: Nadeem Ghauri *(Pakistan)*. Referee: B. C. Broad *(England)* (40).

Close of play: First day, Pakistan 148–3 (Umar Amin 1, Umar Akmal 8); Second day, Australia 136–2 (Ponting 61, Clarke 32); Third day, Pakistan 140–3 (Azhar Ali 47, Umar Akmal 2).

SRI LANKA v INDIA 2010 (1st Test)

At Galle International Stadium on 18, 19 (*no play*), 20, 21, 22 July, 2010.
Toss: Sri Lanka.   Result: SRI LANKA WON BY TEN WICKETS.
Debuts: India – A. Mithun.
Man of the Match: S. L. Malinga.

Muttiah Muralitharan had previously intimated that he would bow out from Test cricket at the end of 2010. But after the Sri Lankan board arranged a mid-year series against India, he decided that this Test would be his last, although he remained available for one-day cricket until the 2011 World Cup. He went into the match with 792 Test wickets, and the whole of Sri Lanka praying he would claim the eight he needed for 800. It was a close-run thing, but in the end Murali's Test career had the fairytale ending the nation craved: the landmark wicket ended India's resistance and set up a ten-wicket victory, completed shortly after tea on the final day. The loss of the second day to rain meant that for Sri Lanka to win – and probably for Murali to make it to 800 – they had to bowl India out twice after running up 520. Murali stretched his record number of Test five-fors to 67 as India struggled despite a brilliant century from Sehwag, and made it to 799 as they lurched to 197 for seven in the follow-on. But he had to toil through 23.4 further overs – during which he twice narrowly failed to run out one of the last pair – before Ojha edged low to slip, where Mahela Jayawardene grasped his 77th catch off Murali's bowling, a Test record for a bowler and non-wicketkeeper. The entire stadium erupted. Muralitharan was given a 21-gun salute, an honour normally reserved for visiting heads of state.

Sri Lanka

N. T. Paranavitana c Dhoni b Sharma	111	– not out		23
T. M. Dilshan c Dhoni b Mithun	25	– not out		68
*K. C. Sangakkara c Tendulkar b Sehwag	103			
D. P. M. D. Jayawardene lbw b Sharma	48			
T. T. Samaraweera lbw b Mithun	0			
A. D. Mathews c Laxman b Sharma	41			
†H. A. P. W. Jayawardene lbw b Mithun	27			
H. M. R. K. B. Herath not out	80			
S. L. Malinga c Harbhajan Singh b Mithun	64			
M. Muralitharan not out	5			
B 2, l-b 9, n-b 5	16	W 1, n-b 4		5
(8 wkts dec, 124 overs)	520	(no wkt, 14.1 overs)		96

1/55 (2) 2/236 (3) 3/259 (1) 4/260 (5) 5/322 (4)
6/344 (6) 7/393 (7) 8/508 (9)

U. W. M. B. C. A. Welagedara did not bat.

Sharma 28–5–145–3; Mithun 28–3–105–4; Harbhajan Singh 30–4–98–0; Ojha 28–1–115–0; Sehwag 10–0–46–1. *Second Innings*—Mithun 5–0–33–0; Sharma 4–0–28–0; Ojha 3–0–11–0; Harbhajan Singh 2.1–0–24–0.

India

G. Gambhir lbw b Malinga	2	– c H. A. P. W. Jayawardene b Malinga	0
V. Sehwag c Paranavitana b Welagedara	109	– c D. P. M. D. Jayawardene b Welagedara	31
R. Dravid run out	18	– c Sangakkara b Malinga	44
S. R. Tendulkar lbw b Muralitharan	8	– lbw b Malinga	84
V. V. S. Laxman c Dilshan b Malinga	22	– run out	69
Yuvraj Singh c D. P. M. D. Jayawardene b Muralitharan	52	– c D. P. M. D. Jayawardene b Muralitharan	5
*†M. S. Dhoni b Muralitharan	33	– b Malinga	4
Harbhajan Singh st H. A. P. W. Jayawardene b Herath	2	– lbw b Muralitharan	8
I. Sharma not out	5	– (10) not out	31
P. P. Ojha c D. P. M. D. Jayawardene b Muralitharan	3	– (11) c D. P. M. D. Jayawardene b Muralitharan	13
A. Mithun b Muralitharan	8	– (9) lbw b Malinga	25
B 1, l-b 1, w 2, n-b 10	14	B 5, l-b 9, w 2, n-b 8	24
(65 overs)	276	(115.4 overs)	338

1/2 (1) 2/68 (3) 3/101 (4) 4/169 (2) 5/178 (5) 6/252 (7)
7/259 (6) 8/259 (8) 9/266 (10) 10/276 (11)

1/0 (1) 2/42 (2) 3/161 (3) 4/172 (4) 5/181 (6)
6/186 (7) 7/197 (8) 8/246 (9) 9/314 (5) 10/338 (11)

Malinga 13–0–55–2; Welagedara 11–1–69–1; Herath 18–1–62–1; Mathews 5–0–19–0; Muralitharan 17–1–63–5; Dilshan 1–0–6–0. *Second Innings*—Malinga 17–2–50–5; Welagedara 10–2–43–1; Herath 27–3–60–0; Mathews 7–3–13–0; Muralitharan 44.4–7–128–3; Dilshan 10–1–30–0.

Umpires: D. J. Harper (*Australia*) (89) and R. J. Tucker (*Australia*) (4).
Third umpire: T. H. Wijewardene (*Sri Lanka*). Referee: A. J. Pycroft (*Zimbabwe*) (11).

Close of play: First day, Sri Lanka 256–2 (Paranavitana 110, D. P. M. D. Jayawardene 8); Second day, No play; Third day, India 140–3 (Sehwag 85, Laxman 18); Fourth day, India 181–5 (Laxman 9).

SRI LANKA v INDIA 2010 (2nd Test)

At Sinhalese Sports Club, Colombo, on 26, 27, 28, 29, 30 July, 2010.
Toss: Sri Lanka.   Result: MATCH DRAWN.
Debuts: Sri Lanka – S. Randiv *(full name H. K. S. R. Kaluhalamulla)*. India – S. K. Raina.
Man of the Match: K. C. Sangakkara.

After the Lord Mayor's Show of the First Test, this was a bore-draw. A pitch with less life than a dodo produced two double-centuries, three single hundreds and a 99, but overall this was a poor advertisement for Test cricket. Unusually for a winning team, Sri Lanka changed all four specialist bowlers: Muralitharan must have been delighted he had retired before encountering this pitch. The man given the thankless task of replacing him was Suraj Randiv, a 25-year-old off-spinner. Injuries meant Suresh Raina played his first Test after a record 98 one-day internationals, and he knuckled down for nearly five hours, becoming the 12th Indian to score a debut century (the first since Sehwag in 2001–02). He put on 256 with Tendulkar, who batted for 8½ hours and collected his 48th century (and fifth double). India finished up with 707, their second-biggest Test total after 726 against Sri Lanka at Mumbai in 2009–10, and the highest by a visiting team in Sri Lanka. Sehwag had earlier become only the third man to be stumped for 99 in a Test, following Maqsood Ahmed of Pakistan (1954–55) and New Zealand's John Wright (1991–92). This was after Sri Lanka's own massive total, in which Sangakkara extended his third successive century into his seventh double, while Jayawardene completed his tenth Test hundred at the SSC to surpass Don Bradman's record of nine at a single ground (Melbourne). It was only the fourth time in Tests that both sides reached 600 in their first innings.

Sri Lanka

N. T. Paranavitana b Sharma	100	– c Laxman b Harbhajan Singh	34
T. M. Dilshan c Laxman b Ojha	54	– c Sharma b Mithun	14
*K. C. Sangakkara c Dravid b Sehwag	219	– not out	42
D. P. M. D. Jayawardene c Raina b Harbhajan Singh	174	– lbw b Sehwag	5
T. T. Samaraweera not out	76	– not out	10
B 4, l-b 8, w 2, n-b 5	19	B 8, l-b 8, n-b 8	24
(4 wkts dec, 159.4 overs)	642	(3 wkts dec, 45 overs)	129

1/99 (2) 2/273 (1) 3/466 (3) 4/642 (4)   1/50 (2) 2/73 (1) 3/97 (4)

A. D. Mathews, †H. A. P. W. Jayawardene, K. T. G. D. Prasad, S. Randiv, B. A. W. Mendis and C. R. D. Fernando did not bat.

Mithun 23–5–117–0; Sharma 23–5–102–1; Ojha 46–9–172–1; Harbhajan Singh 42.4–4–147–1; Sehwag 20–0–71–1; Raina 5–0–21–0. *Second Innings*—Mithun 6–1–17–1; Sharma 4–0–31–0; Sehwag 9–1–17–1; Harbhajan Singh 13–0–35–1; Ojha 13–6–13–0.

India

M. Vijay lbw b Mendis	58
V. Sehwag st H. A. P. W. Jayawardene b Randiv	99
R. Dravid lbw b Randiv	3
S. R. Tendulkar c H. A. P. W. Jayawardene b Dilshan	203
V. V. S. Laxman lbw b Mendis	29
S. K. Raina c Sangakkara b Mendis	120
*†M. S. Dhoni c and b Dilshan	76
Harbhajan Singh c Sangakkara b Dilshan	0
A. Mithun b Mendis	41
I. Sharma c Sangakkara b Fernando	27
P. P. Ojha not out	18
B 9, l-b 7, w 4, n-b 13	33
(225.2 overs)	707

1/165 (2) 2/169 (1) 3/173 (3) 4/241 (5) 5/497 (6)
6/592 (4) 7/592 (8) 8/643 (7) 9/668 (9) 10/707 (10)

Prasad 22–2–101–0; Fernando 31.2–1–116–1; Mathews 9–1–24–0; Randiv 73–16–222–2; Mendis 63–10–172–4; Dilshan 27–6–56–3.

Umpires: D. J. Harper *(Australia)* (90) and R. J. Tucker *(Australia)* (5).
Third umpire: R. E. J. Martinesz *(Sri Lanka)*. Referee: A. J. Pycroft *(Zimbabwe)* (12).

Close of play: First day, Sri Lanka 312–2 (Sangakkara 130, D. P. M. D. Jayawardene 13); Second day, India 95–0 (Vijay 22, Sehwag 64); Third day, India 382–4 (Tendulkar 108, Raina 66); Fourth day, India 669–9 (Sharma 10, Ojha 0).

SRI LANKA v INDIA 2010 (3rd Test)

At P. Sara Oval, Colombo, on 3, 4, 5, 6, 7 August, 2010.
Toss: Sri Lanka.   Result: INDIA WON BY FIVE WICKETS.
Debuts: none.
Man of the Match: V. V. S. Laxman. Man of the Series: V. Sehwag.

The pitch for the final Test contained a lot more life than the previous one. Samaraweera batted six hours for an unbeaten 137, but the last six wickets managed only 95. Sehwag led the reply with his 21st Test hundred, passing 7,000 runs in the process: only Wally Hammond got there quicker (131 innings to Sehwag's 134; Don Bradman was famously stranded four short of 7,000 after 80 innings). Malinga became the third Sri Lankan to take 100 Test wickets when he had Tendulkar caught behind, but the last three wickets added 86, to manufacture a slender lead. Then Sri Lanka lost both openers cheaply to Sehwag's seemingly innocuous off-breaks, and next morning their strong batting line-up buckled. Six wickets went down for 62 in a dramatic session, with the spinners in charge, before Samaraweera and Mendis added 118, a national ninth-wicket record. India needed a tantalising 257, and after three quick wickets Tendulkar, then 18, was put down by Dilshan at forward short leg off Randiv, in the eighth over of the final day. That would have been 67 for five. Instead, Tendulkar – in his 169th match, passing Steve Waugh as the most-capped Test player – went on to 54 before gloving a sweep. With half the side out (all to Randiv), India still needed 86 to square the series, but Laxman completed his 16th Test century, despite a lot of discomfort from his back later in his innings, and Raina ended proceedings by smashing Welagedara over long-on for six.

Sri Lanka

N. T. Paranavitana c Dhoni b Sharma	8	– c Dhoni b Sehwag		16
T. M. Dilshan run out	41	– c Vijay b Sehwag		13
*K. C. Sangakkara c Sehwag b Ojha	75	– c Raina b Ojha		28
D. P. M. D. Jayawardene lbw b Ojha	56	– (5) c Dravid b Ojha		5
T. T. Samaraweera not out	137	– (6) c Dhoni b Mithun		83
A. D. Mathews lbw b Ojha	45	– (7) c Tendulkar b Mishra		5
†H. A. P. W. Jayawardene lbw b Ojha	9	– (8) lbw b Mishra		0
S. Randiv c Dravid b Sehwag	8	– (4) lbw b Ojha		6
S. L. Malinga c and b Mishra	4	– lbw b Sehwag		15
B. A. W. Mendis c Raina b Sharma	3	– c Raina b Mishra		78
U. W. M. B. C. A. Welagedara c Dhoni b Sharma	4	– not out		4
B 8, l-b 4, w 7, n-b 16	35		L-b 4, w 4, n-b 6	14
(138 overs)	425		(85.2 overs)	267

1/15 (1) 2/102 (2) 3/157 (3) 4/241 (4) 5/330 (6)   1/32 (1) 2/39 (2) 3/63 (4) 4/77 (5) 5/78 (3)
6/359 (7) 7/381 (8) 8/386 (9) 9/421 (10) 10/425 (11)   6/87 (7) 7/87 (8) 8/125 (9) 9/243 (6) 10/267 (10)

Mithun 22–2–78–0; Sharma 23–6–72–3; Mishra 42–3–140–1; Ojha 46–10–115–4; Sehwag 5–0–8–1. *Second Innings*—Mithun 8–1–22–1; Sharma 17–3–54–0; Ojha 28–5–89–3; Sehwag 15–0–51–3; Mishra 17.2–1–47–3.

India

M. Vijay c Mendis b Malinga	14	– c D. P. M. D. Jayawardene b Randiv		27
V. Sehwag c Welagedara b Randiv	109	– c D. P. M. D. Jayawardene b Randiv		0
R. Dravid lbw b Mathews	23	– b Randiv		7
S. R. Tendulkar c H. A. P. W. Jayawardene b Malinga	41	– c H. A. P. W. Jayawardene b Randiv		54
V. V. S. Laxman c D. P. M. D. Jayawardene b Mendis	56	– (6) not out		103
S. K. Raina c Sangakkara b Mendis	62	– (7) not out		41
*†M. S. Dhoni c H. A. P. W. Jayawardene b Malinga	15			
A. Mithun c D. P. M. D. Jayawardene b Randiv	46			
A. Mishra c Dilshan b Randiv	40			
I. Sharma c Paranavitana b Randiv	8	– (5) c Sangakkara b Randiv		4
P. P. Ojha not out	1			
B 6, l-b 6, w 1, n-b 8	21		B 5, l-b 6, w 2, n-b 9	22
(106.1 overs)	436		(5 wkts, 68.3 overs)	258

1/49 (1) 2/92 (3) 3/183 (4) 4/199 (2) 5/304 (5)
6/321 (6) 7/350 (7) 8/414 (8) 9/433 (9) 10/436 (10)   1/10 (2) 2/27 (3) 3/49 (1) 4/62 (5) 5/171 (4)

Malinga 30–3–119–3; Welagedara 15–0–88–0; Mendis 30–4–109–2; Mathews 4–0–13–1; Randiv 25.1–6–80–4; Dilshan 2–0–15–0. *Second Innings*—Malinga 12–1–49–0; Randiv 29–3–82–5; Mathews 2–0–5–0; Welagedara 8.3–2–34–0; Mendis 14–0–65–0; Dilshan 3–0–12–0.

Umpires: S. J. A. Taufel *(Australia)* (64) and R. J. Tucker *(Australia)* (6).
Third umpire: H. D. P. K. Dharmasena *(Sri Lanka)*. Referee: A. J. Pycroft *(Zimbabwe)* (13).

Close of play: First day, Sri Lanka 293–4 (Samaraweera 65, Mathews 26); Second day, India 180–2 (Sehwag 97, Tendulkar 40); Third day, Sri Lanka 45–2 (Sangakkara 12, Randiv 0); Fourth day, India 53–3 (Tendulkar 11, Sharma 2).

ENGLAND v PAKISTAN 2010 (1st Test)

At Trent Bridge, Nottingham, on 29, 30, 31 July, 1 August, 2010.
Toss: England.   Result: ENGLAND WON BY 354 RUNS.
Debuts: none.
Man of the Match: J. M. Anderson.

Pakistan had just defeated Australia at Headingley, but found England a different proposition, crashing to their heaviest Test defeat by runs. Under the leaden skies which prevailed almost throughout, Kamran Akmal helped Strauss settle by dropping a dolly early on. Strauss recovered, but Akmal regressed, grappling with the ball like a baby with his first toy. Nevertheless, Mohammad Aamer and Mohammad Asif reduced England to 118 for four, despite Trott becoming the first batsman in a Test in England successfully to challenge his "dismissal": the Hot-Spot infra-red cameras showed he had edged the ball to which he was originally adjudged lbw. But when the skies cleared, Collingwood and Morgan – who reached his maiden Test century with a straight six off Shoaib Malik – added 219, an England fifth-wicket record against Pakistan beating 192 by Denis Compton and Trevor Bailey on the same ground in 1954. Asif derailed England on the second morning, reaching 100 wickets in 20 Tests, level with Waqar Younis as the fastest for Pakistan. The last six wickets went for 17, but then Anderson, on his 28th birthday, showed he could swing it too: Pakistan slumped to 47 for six. Umar Gul biffed a bright maiden half-century to avert the follow-on, and then England made an uncertain start. But Prior's third Test century helped them regroup from 98 for six, and the eventual target was a distant 435. Pakistan never got close, subsiding for just 80, their lowest total against England at the time, again obliterated by Anderson's swing.

England

*A. J. Strauss c Kamran Akmal b Mohammad Aamer	45	– c Kamran Akmal b Mohammad Aamer		0
A. N. Cook c Imran Farhat b Mohammad Aamer	8	– c Kamran Akmal b Mohammad Asif		12
I. J. L. Trott lbw b Mohammad Aamer	38	– b Umar Gul		26
K. P. Pietersen b Mohammad Asif	9	– c Kamran Akmal b Umar Gul		22
P. D. Collingwood lbw b Mohammad Asif	82	– lbw b Umar Gul		1
E. J. G. Morgan lbw b Mohammad Asif	130	– run out		17
†M. J. Prior run out	6	– not out		102
G. P. Swann lbw b Mohammad Asif	2	– lbw b Danish Kaneria		28
S. C. J. Broad b Umar Gul	3	– c Imran Farhat b Shoaib Malik		24
J. M. Anderson lbw b Mohammad Asif	0	– c Kamran Akmal b Shoaib Malik		2
S. T. Finn not out	0	– not out		9
B 5, l-b 14, w 5, n-b 7	31	B 4, l-b 11, w 1, n-b 3		19
(104.1 overs)	354	(9 wkts dec, 75.3 overs)		262

1/42 (2) 2/93 (1) 3/116 (4) 4/118 (3) 5/337 (5)
6/344 (6) 7/351 (7) 8/354 (8) 9/354 (10) 10/354 (9)

1/2 (1) 2/18 (2) 3/65 (4) 4/66 (3) 5/72 (5)
6/98 (6) 7/147 (8) 8/203 (9) 9/213 (10)

Mohammad Aamer 24–7–41–3; Mohammad Asif 27–9–77–5; Umar Gul 18.1–5–61–1; Danish Kaneria 21–0–100–0; Shoaib Malik 11–2–39–0; Azhar Ali 1–0–9–0; Umar Amin 1–0–3–0; Imran Farhat 1–0–5–0. *Second Innings—* Mohammad Aamer 16–3–35–1; Mohammad Asif 17–1–56–1; Umar Gul 15–2–41–3; Umar Amin 5–1–13–0; Danish Kaneria 12–0–71–1; Shoaib Malik 10.3–0–31–2.

Pakistan

Imran Farhat b Anderson	19	– c Strauss b Anderson		15
*Salman Butt c Prior b Anderson	1	– c Collingwood b Broad		8
Azhar Ali c Prior b Anderson	14	– lbw b Broad		0
Umar Amin c Swann b Finn	2	– lbw b Anderson		1
Umar Akmal c Swann b Finn	4	– (6) lbw b Anderson		4
Shoaib Malik c Strauss b Anderson	38	– (7) c Collingwood b Anderson		9
†Kamran Akmal c Collingwood b Finn	0	– (8) lbw b Finn		0
Mohammad Aamer c Swann b Anderson	25	– (5) c Pietersen b Finn		4
Umar Gul not out	65	– c Collingwood b Anderson		9
Danish Kaneria b Broad	7	– not out		16
Mohammad Asif run out	0	– c Swann b Anderson		0
B 5, l-b 2	7	B 4, l-b 8, w 1, n-b 1		14
(54 overs)	182	(29 overs)		80

1/5 (2) 2/32 (1) 3/35 (4) 4/41 (3) 5/45 (5) 6/47 (7)
7/105 (6) 8/108 (8) 9/147 (10) 10/182 (11)

1/10 (2) 2/10 (3) 3/11 (4) 4/31 (1) 5/37 (6)
6/41 (5) 7/41 (8) 8/50 (9) 9/65 (7) 10/80 (11)

Anderson 22–7–54–5; Broad 17–4–59–1; Finn 13–5–50–3; Swann 2–1–12–0. *Second Innings—*Anderson 15–8–17–6; Broad 8–2–23–2; Finn 6–3–28–2.

Umpires: E. A. R. de Silva *(Sri Lanka)* (46) and A. L. Hill *(New Zealand)* (18).
Third umpire: M. Erasmus *(South Africa)*. Referee: R. S. Madugalle *(Sri Lanka)* (116).

Close of play: First day, England 331–4 (Collingwood 81, Morgan 125); Second day, Pakistan 147–9 (Umar Gul 30, Mohammad Asif 0); Third day, Pakistan 15–3 (Imran Farhat 6, Mohammad Aamer 0).

ENGLAND v PAKISTAN 2010 (2nd Test)

At Edgbaston, Birmingham, on 6, 7, 8, 9 August, 2010.
Toss: Pakistan.   Result: ENGLAND WON BY NINE WICKETS.
Debuts: Pakistan – Zulqarnain Haider.
Man of the Match: G. P. Swann.

Another crushing England victory was all but guaranteed not long after lunch on the first day, as Pakistan were bowled out for under 100 for the second time in six days. Their problems were exacerbated by dropping ten catches, at least two almost comically easy. Anderson and Broad took advantage of helpful conditions, and some supine batting: Imran Farhat (24 balls) and Azhar Ali (33) each made long-winded ducks. England also struggled, but Trott and Pietersen added 133: both were put down in single figures. Pietersen was dropped at least twice more, and also escaped when, distracted, he pulled away just as Mohammad Asif bowled. He absent-mindedly swiped the ball to mid-off where, amazingly, it was caught. Umpire Erasmus said he had called dead ball as it left Asif's hand. Saeed Ajmal took his maiden five-for as the last seven wickets added only 46, but then Swann mesmerised the batsmen, at one stage delivering 67 dot-balls in a row. At 101 for six, still 78 behind, Pakistan looked likely to lose before tea on the third day – but the last four wickets added 195, led by the debutant wicketkeeper Zulqarnain Haider, who spanked 88 after being given out lbw to Swann for a king pair but reprieved on review. He was also struck on the hand (probably not helping a finger cracked before the match) when Broad threw the ball towards him; whether it was intended to strike Zulqarnain was unclear, but Broad was fined 50% of his match fee.

Pakistan

Imran Farhat c Prior b Broad	0	– b Swann		29
*Salman Butt c Swann b Finn	7	– c Strauss b Anderson		0
Azhar Ali lbw b Broad	0	– b Swann		19
Shoaib Malik c Prior b Anderson	3	– c Prior b Finn		3
Umar Akmal lbw b Finn	17	– lbw b Swann		20
Umar Amin c Collingwood b Broad	23	– st Prior b Swann		14
†Zulqarnain Haider c Prior b Broad	0	– c Strauss b Swann		88
Mohammad Aamer c Cook b Anderson	12	– c Strauss b Broad		16
Umar Gul c Pietersen b Anderson	0	– (10) not out		13
Saeed Ajmal not out	5	– (9) c Collingwood b Swann		50
Mohammad Asif c Pietersen b Anderson	0	– c Pietersen b Broad		14
L-b 4, n-b 1	5	B 16, l-b 14		30
(39.3 overs)	72	(117.5 overs)		296

1/8 (1) 2/9 (2) 3/12 (4) 4/29 (3) 5/33 (5) 6/36 (7)
7/63 (6) 8/64 (9) 9/67 (8) 10/72 (11)

1/1 (2) 2/53 (1) 3/54 (3) 4/76 (4) 5/82 (5)
6/101 (6) 7/153 (8) 8/268 (9) 9/269 (7) 10/296 (11)

Anderson 14.3–6–20–4; Broad 17–7–38–4; Finn 8–3–10–2. *Second Innings*—Anderson 28–13–62–1; Broad 28.5–8–66–2; Finn 16–5–57–1; Swann 37–20–65–6; Collingwood 7–2–14–0; Pietersen 1–0–2–0.

England

*A. J. Strauss c Zulqarnain Haider b Mohammad Aamer	25	– not out	53
A. N. Cook c Umar Akmal b Mohammad Asif	17	– b Mohammad Aamer	4
I. J. L. Trott c sub (Yasir Hameed) b Umar Amin	55	– not out	53
K. P. Pietersen c and b Saeed Ajmal	80		
P. D. Collingwood c Imran Farhat b Saeed Ajmal	28		
E. J. G. Morgan c Zulqarnain Haider b Mohammad Asif	6		
†M. J. Prior lbw b Saeed Ajmal	15		
G. P. Swann c and b Saeed Ajmal	4		
S. C. J. Broad c sub (Yasir Hameed) b Saeed Ajmal	0		
J. M. Anderson lbw b Mohammad Aamer	0		
S. T. Finn not out	0		
B 10, l-b 9, w 1, n-b 1	21	B 5, n-b 3	8
(83.1 overs)	251	(1 wkt, 36.3 overs)	118

1/44 (2) 2/44 (1) 3/177 (3) 4/205 (4) 5/220 (6)
6/243 (7) 7/248 (5) 8/248 (9) 9/251 (10) 10/251 (8)   1/7 (2)

Mohammad Aamer 20–4–57–2; Mohammad Asif 20–5–41–2; Umar Gul 9–1–24–0; Saeed Ajmal 26.1–5–82–5; Umar Amin 8–2–28–1. *Second Innings*—Mohammad Aamer 11–1–31–1; Mohammad Asif 6–0–20–0; Saeed Ajmal 14.3–1–42–0; Shoaib Malik 5–0–20–0.

Umpires: S. J. Davis *(Australia)* (26) and M. Erasmus *(South Africa)* (3).
Third umpire: A. L. Hill *(New Zealand)*. Referee: R. S. Madugalle *(Sri Lanka)* (117).

Close of play: First day, England 112–2 (Trott 31, Pietersen 36); Second day, Pakistan 19–1 (Imran Farhat 10, Azhar Ali 5); Third day, Pakistan 291–9 (Umar Gul 9, Mohammad Asif 13).

ENGLAND v PAKISTAN 2010 (3rd Test)

At Kennington Oval, London, 18, 29, 20, 21 August, 2010.
Toss: England.   Result: PAKISTAN WON BY FOUR WICKETS.
Debuts: Pakistan – Wahab Riaz.
Man of the Match: Mohammad Aamer.

After winning six straight Tests, England were ignominiously undone. They batted first, but slumped to 94 for seven after 31 overs: Wahab Riaz, a rangy 25-year-old left-armer, had four wickets, three of them caught by the unpredictable keeper Kamran Akmal, restored because Zulqarnain Haider had broken a finger. Prior and Broad put on 119, at better than four an over, but 233 still looked insipid. Mohammad Yousuf, summoned late to England after a ban for supposed indiscretions in Australia, survived a jittery start before becoming Swann's 100th wicket in his 23rd Test (the same rate as Shane Warne), but Azhar Ali stretched the lead to 75. Strauss edged the fourth ball of the second innings to second slip, but Cook – his place in jeopardy after only 106 runs in his previous eight innings – decided to counter-attack. He unveiled some uncharacteristic cover-drives: his century effectively saved his place for the upcoming Ashes tour. By tea on the third day England had 194 for three and the match seemed well balanced: by 5.15pm, though, it was all over, bar another Pakistan batting catastrophe. Seven wickets tumbled for 28 in 16 overs, with Mohammad Aamer becoming the youngest to take a Test five-for in England. Pakistan needed only 148, but predictably made a meal of it: at 131 Yousuf was stunningly yorked by Anderson, and when the sixth wicket fell one run later, 16 more were required. Umar Akmal and Aamer, Pakistan's two youngest players, spent 33 agonising minutes compiling the winning runs.

England

*A. J. Strauss c Kamran Akmal b Wahab Riaz	15	– c Yasir Hameed b Mohammad Aamer		4
A. N. Cook c Kamran Akmal b Mohammad Asif	6	– c Kamran Akmal b Wahab Riaz		110
I. J. L. Trott c Yasir Hameed b Wahab Riaz	12	– (4) c Azhar Ali b Mohammad Aamer		36
K. P. Pietersen c Kamran Akmal b Wahab Riaz	6	– (5) b Saeed Ajmal		23
P. D. Collingwood b Mohammad Aamer	5	– (6) c Kamran Akmal b Mohammad Aamer		3
E. J. G. Morgan c Kamran Akmal b Wahab Riaz	17	– (7) b Saeed Ajmal		5
†M. J. Prior not out	84	– (8) c Kamran Akmal b Mohammad Aamer		5
G. P. Swann c Umar Akmal b Mohammad Asif	8	– (9) b Saeed Ajmal		6
S. C. J. Broad lbw b Wahab Riaz	48	– (10) c Mohammad Asif b Mohammad Aamer		6
J. M. Anderson lbw b Mohammad Asif	0	– (3) c Kamran Akmal b Saeed Ajmal		11
S. T. Finn lbw b Saeed Ajmal	0	– not out		1
B 10, l-b 11, w 6, n-b 5	32	L-b 5, w 2, n-b 5		12
(62.3 overs)	233	(77 overs)		222

1/9 (2) 2/35 (1) 3/40 (3) 4/47 (5) 5/67 (4) 6/74 (6)   1/4 (1) 2/40 (3) 3/156 (2) 4/194 (5) 5/195 (4)
7/94 (8) 8/213 (9) 9/214 (10) 10/233 (11)   6/202 (6) 7/206 (7) 8/210 (8) 9/220 (9) 10/222 (10)

Mohammad Aamer 15–4–49–1; Mohammad Asif 20–5–68–3; Wahab Riaz 18–6–63–5; Saeed Ajmal 9.3–1–32–1. *Second Innings*—Mohammad Aamer 19–5–52–5; Mohammad Asif 16–7–45–0; Wahab Riaz 8–1–40–1; Saeed Ajmal 31–7–71–4; Imran Farhat 3–0–9–0.

Pakistan

Imran Farhat b Anderson	11	– lbw b Swann		33
Yasir Hameed c Prior b Finn	36	– c Swann b Anderson		0
Wahab Riaz lbw b Swann	27			
*Salman Butt c Prior b Swann	17	– (3) c Collingwood b Swann		48
Mohammad Yousuf c and b Swann	56	– (4) b Anderson		33
Azhar Ali not out	92	– (5) run out		5
Umar Akmal run out	38	– (6) not out		16
†Kamran Akmal c Morgan b Broad	10	– (7) lbw b Swann		0
Mohammad Aamer c Prior b Broad	6	– (8) not out		4
Saeed Ajmal b Anderson	0			
Mohammad Asif c Anderson b Swann	8			
L-b 4, w 1, n-b 2	7	B 4, l-b 2, w 2, n-b 1		9
(100.2 overs)	308	(6 wkts, 41.4 overs)		148

1/48 (1) 2/48 (2) 3/76 (4) 4/110 (3) 5/179 (5)   1/5 (2) 2/57 (1) 3/103 (3) 4/124 (5) 5/131 (4)
6/236 (7) 7/251 (8) 8/269 (9) 9/270 (10) 10/308 (11)   6/132 (7)

Anderson 24–6–79–2; Broad 25–4–72–2; Finn 20–4–74–1; Swann 27.2–9–68–4; Collingwood 4–0–11–0. *Second Innings*—Anderson 14–5–39–2; Broad 6–0–35–0; Swann 18.4–4–50–3; Finn 3–0–18–0.

Umpires: S. J. Davis *(Australia)* (27) and A. L. Hill *(New Zealand)* (19).
Third umpire: B. F. Bowden *(New Zealand)*. Referee: R. S. Madugalle *(Sri Lanka)* (118).

Close of play: First day, Pakistan 48–1 (Yasir Hameed 36, Wahab Riaz 0); Second day, England 6–1 (Cook 0, Anderson 2); Third day, England 221–9 (Broad 6, Finn 0).

ENGLAND v PAKISTAN 2010 (4th Test)

At Lord's, London, on 26, 27, 28, 29 August, 2010.
Toss: Pakistan.   Result: ENGLAND WON BY AN INNINGS AND 225 RUNS.
Debuts: none.
Man of the Match: S. C. J. Broad. Men of the Series: I. J. L. Trott and Mohammad Aamer.

The last Test of Pakistan's previous visit in 2006 had ended in Test cricket's first forfeiture. The last Test this time was even more controversial. On the third evening, news broke of a conspiracy involving some of Pakistan's leading players. The *News of the World* had paid an agent, Mazhar Majeed, £150,000 to arrange "spot-fixing" – specifically for Pakistan's opening bowlers to deliver three no-balls at pre-arranged moments. Mohammad Aamer, Mohammad Asif and Pakistan's captain Salman Butt, were banned by ICC: all three (and the agent) subsequently served jail terms. The controversy overshadowed England's fine performance: they recovered from 102 for seven – four falling to Aamer for ducks – through Trott and Broad's eighth-wicket partnership of 332, a Test record, beating 313 by Pakistan's Wasim Akram and Saqlain Mushtaq against Zimbabwe at Sheikhupura in 1996–97. Broad extended his maiden first-class century to 169, the second-highest Test score by a No. 9 after Ian Smith's 173 for New Zealand against India at Auckland in 1990–91; only Gubby Allen and John Murray had previously made hundreds from there for England. Stuart and Chris Broad were the first father and son to score centuries for England. Seventeen wickets fell on the third day, 14 of them Pakistan's: they heard about the newspaper story towards the end of the day, and were understandably detached next morning, slumping to their heaviest Test defeat. The presentations were moved indoors, where the ECB chairman Giles Clarke refused to shake the hand of Aamer, Pakistan's Man of the Series.

England

*A. J. Strauss b Mohammad Asif	13
A. N. Cook c Kamran Akmal b Mohammad Aamer....	10
I. J. L. Trott c Kamran Akmal b Wahab Riaz	184
K. P. Pietersen c Kamran Akmal b Mohammad Aamer...	0
P. D. Collingwood lbw b Mohammad Aamer	0
E. J. G. Morgan c Yasir Hameed b Mohammad Aamer	0
†M. J. Prior c Kamran Akmal b Mohammad Aamer ...	22
G. P. Swann c Azhar Ali b Mohammad Aamer	0
S. C. J. Broad lbw b Saeed Ajmal	169
J. M. Anderson c Yasir Hameed b Saeed Ajmal	6
S. T. Finn not out	0
B 4, l-b 17, w 7, n-b 14	42
(139.2 overs)	446

1/31 (1) 2/39 (2) 3/39 (4) 4/39 (5) 5/47 (6)
6/102 (7) 7/102 (8) 8/434 (9) 9/446 (10) 10/446 (3)

Mohammad Aamer 28–6–84–6; Mohammad Asif 29–6–97–1; Wahab Riaz 27.2–4–92–1; Saeed Ajmal 44–5–126–2; Yasir Hameed 1–1–0–0; Imran Farhat 10–1–26–0.

Pakistan

Imran Farhat c Prior b Anderson	6	– c Cook b Broad	5
Yasir Hameed c Swann b Broad	2	– lbw b Anderson	3
*Salman Butt b Swann	26	– lbw b Swann	21
Mohammad Yousuf b Broad	0	– c Trott b Finn	10
Azhar Ali c Cook b Swann	10	– b Swann	12
Umar Akmal b Finn	6	– not out	79
†Kamran Akmal c Prior b Finn	13	– c Prior b Anderson	1
Mohammad Aamer lbw b Finn	0	– b Swann	0
Wahab Riaz lbw b Swann	2	– c Pietersen b Swann	0
Saeed Ajmal not out	4	– run out	8
Mohammad Asif c and b Swann	0	– c Collingwood b Swann	1
L-b 4, n-b 1	5	B 1, l-b 2, w 3, n-b 1	7
(33 overs)	74	(36.5 overs)	147

1/9 (2) 2/9 (1) 3/10 (4) 4/46 (3) 5/53 (5) 6/57 (6)
7/57 (8) 8/70 (7) 9/74 (9) 10/74 (11)

1/7 (1) 2/9 (2) 3/41 (3) 4/41 (4) 5/63 (5)
6/64 (7) 7/65 (8) 8/73 (9) 9/97 (10) 10/147 (11)

Anderson 10–6–10–1; Broad 6–4–10–2; Finn 9–4–38–3; Swann 8–3–12–4. *Second Innings*—Anderson 13–4–35–2; Broad 6–1–24–1; Finn 4–0–23–1; Swann 13.5–1–62–5.

Umpires: B. F. Bowden *(New Zealand)* (62) and A. L. Hill *(New Zealand)* (20).
Third umpire: S. J. Davis *(Australia)*. Referee: R. S. Madugalle *(Sri Lanka)* (119).

Close of play: First day, England 39–1 (Cook 10, Trott 8); Second day, England 346–7 (Trott 149, Broad 125); Third day, Pakistan 41–4 (Azhar Ali 0, Umar Akmal 0).

INDIA v AUSTRALIA 2010–11 (1st Test)

At Punjab C. A. Stadium, Mohali, Chandigarh, on 1, 2, 3, 4, 5 October, 2010.
Toss: Australia.   Result: INDIA WON BY ONE WICKET.
Debuts: none.
Man of the Match: Zaheer Khan.

India scrambled to the narrowest of their 106 victories – only the 12th Test to end in a one-wicket victory – despite requiring 92 when the eighth wicket fell. India won thanks to Laxman – always at his best against Australia – despite back spasms which forced him to bat at No. 10 in the first innings. Even he couldn't have done it without Ishant Sharma, who survived 106 minutes and 92 balls. Only 11 were needed when Hilfenhaus finally dismissed Sharma. With six required, Johnson pinned Ojha in front. The Australians' shock at umpire Bowden's refusal (he perceived an inside edge) turned to grief when substitute Steve Smith at point threw at the stumps but conceded four overthrows. Two leg-byes a couple of balls later ended proceedings. Earlier, Watson had been dropped from the match's second ball, and went on to a fine century. Paine swelled the total, but Sehwag responded with a rapid-fire fifty before Tendulkar settled in. He surprisingly fell for 98, playing across North's off-spin, precipitating a collapse of five for 23. Australia's openers then put on 87 before all ten wickets tumbled for 105. Needing 216, India lost four quick wickets. On the final morning Tendulkar and Laxman (more supple now) added 43. Thus Bollinger dismissed Tendulkar, Dhoni was run out in a muddle with Laxman's runner (Raina), and Harbhajan fended lamely to slip and the Australians mistakenly felt that the day was theirs. At the start of the match Katich and Hussey had identical figures of 3,981 runs from 52 Tests.

Australia

S. R. Watson c Gambhir b Harbhajan Singh	126	– b Sharma	56
S. M. Katich lbw b Zaheer Khan	6	– c Dhoni b Ojha	37
*R. T. Ponting run out	71	– c Raina b Sharma	4
M. J. Clarke c Dravid b Harbhajan Singh	14	– c Dhoni b Sharma	4
M. E. K. Hussey lbw b Zaheer Khan	17	– lbw b Harbhajan Singh	28
M. J. North b Zaheer Khan	0	– c sub (C. A. Pujara) b Harbhajan Singh	10
†T. D. Paine c Laxman b Zaheer Khan	92	– c sub (C. A. Pujara) b Ojha	9
M. G. Johnson c Dhoni b Zaheer Khan	47	– c Dhoni b Zaheer Khan	3
N. M. Hauritz c Gambhir b Harbhajan Singh	9	– b Zaheer Khan	9
B. W. Hilfenhaus not out	20	– b Zaheer Khan	6
D. E. Bollinger c Sharma b Ojha	0	– not out	5
B 4, l-b 9, n-b 13	26	B 12, l-b 4, n-b 5	21
(151.4 overs)	428	(60.5 overs)	192

1/13 (2) 2/154 (3) 3/172 (4) 4/218 (5) 5/222 (6)
6/275 (1) 7/357 (8) 8/373 (9) 9/427 (7) 10/428 (11)

1/87 (1) 2/91 (3) 3/96 (4) 4/138 (2) 5/154 (5)
6/165 (6) 7/165 (7) 8/170 (8) 9/183 (9) 10/192 (10)

Zaheer Khan 30–7–94–5; Sharma 11.4–1–71–0; Ojha 51.4–16–113–1; Harbhajan Singh 49–12–114–3; Sehwag 9.2–1–23–0. *Second Innings*—Zaheer Khan 11.5–1–43–3; Sharma 9–2–34–3; Harbhajan Singh 23–7–40–2; Ojha 17–1–59–2.

India

G. Gambhir lbw b Johnson	25	– lbw b Hilfenhaus	0
V. Sehwag c Clarke b Johnson	59	– c Hussey b Hilfenhaus	17
R. Dravid c Paine b Bollinger	77	– c Paine b Bollinger	13
I. Sharma b Bollinger	18	– (10) lbw b Hilfenhaus	31
S. R. Tendulkar lbw b North	98	– (4) c Hussey b Bollinger	38
S. K. Raina lbw b Johnson	86	– (5) c North b Hilfenhaus	0
*†M. S. Dhoni c Watson b Johnson	14	– (8) run out	2
Harbhajan Singh c Paine b Johnson	0	– (9) c Ponting b Bollinger	2
Zaheer Khan b Hauritz	6	– (6) c Clarke b Hauritz	10
V. V. S. Laxman c Clarke b Hauritz	2	(7) not out	73
P. P. Ojha not out	0	– not out	5
B 5, l-b 13, w 1, n-b 1	20	B 10, l-b 8, w 6, n-b 1	25
(108.1 overs)	405	(9 wkts, 58.4 overs)	216

1/81 (1) 2/106 (2) 3/151 (4) 4/230 (3) 5/354 (5)
6/382 (7) 7/382 (8) 8/399 (9) 9/401 (6) 10/405 (10)

1/0 (1) 2/31 (3) 3/48 (2) 4/48 (5) 5/76 (6)
6/119 (4) 7/122 (8) 8/124 (9) 9/205 (10)

Hilfenhaus 25–2–100–0; Bollinger 16–2–49–2; Johnson 20–5–64–5; Hauritz 29.1–4–116–2; Watson 6–0–19–0; North 12–3–39–1. *Second Innings*—Hilfenhaus 19–3–57–4; Bollinger 8–0–32–3; Johnson 16.4–2–50–0; Hauritz 9–1–45–1; North 4–0–8–0; Watson 2–0–6–0.

Umpires: B. F. Bowden *(New Zealand)* (63) and I. J. Gould *(England)* (15).
Third umpire: S. S. Hazare *(India)*. Referee: B. C. Broad *(England)* (41).

Close of play: First day, Australia 224–5 (Watson 101, Paine 1); Second day, India 110–2 (Dravid 21, Sharma 0); Third day, India 405; Fourth day, India 55–4 (Tendulkar 10, Zaheer Khan 5).

INDIA v AUSTRALIA 2010–11 (2nd Test)

At M. Chinnaswamy Stadium, Bangalore, on 9, 10, 11, 12, 13 October, 2010.
Toss: Australia.   Result: INDIA WON BY SEVEN WICKETS.
Debuts: India – C. A. Pujara. Australia – P. R. George.
Man of the Match: S. R. Tendulkar. Man of the Series: S. R. Tendulkar.

Another fluctuating match was effectively clinched by Cheteshwar Pujara, in concert with another relative newcomer Murali Vijay, with a partnership of 72 that was brief but ferocious. Pujara had replaced the injured Laxman after a mountain of domestic runs: he averaged 60 before this match and had a first-class triple-century to his name. Australia again batted first, and again might have scored even more: Ponting scored 77 before gifting Raina a distinguished maiden Test wicket, then North made a fluent century and added 149 with Paine, reprieved after being caught behind when TV showed Sreesanth had overstepped. India started slowly, but then Vijay, with his maiden Test century, and Tendulkar, with his sixth double, added 308. Johnson finally separated them, and in the same over conjured up a shooter for the unfortunate Pujara, who had sat padded up through 90.3 overs, the longest wait for any debutant. Eventually Peter George found some old-ball swing to become the 19th debutant to dismiss Tendulkar: for all his dominance, India led by only 17. Australia again started well then surrendered quick wickets, as Zaheer Khan and Sreesanth summoned treacherous amounts of reverse swing on the fourth evening. Needing quick strikes, Australia soon dismissed Sehwag – but were surprised when Pujara was promoted to No. 3 ahead of Dravid. He soon showed why, making a forthright 72, and fittingly Tendulkar completed the 2–0 series victory. All this was watched and cheered by one of the largest and most buoyant Test crowds in India this century.

Australia

S. R. Watson c Dhoni b Ojha	57	– lbw b Ojha	32
S. M. Katich c Dravid b Harbhajan Singh	43	– c Dhoni b Harbhajan Singh	24
*R. T. Ponting lbw b Raina	77	– lbw b Zaheer Khan	72
M. J. Clarke c Raina b Harbhajan Singh	14	– st Dhoni b Ojha	3
M. E. K. Hussey c Sehwag b Zaheer Khan	34	– lbw b Ojha	20
M. J. North c Sreesanth b Harbhajan Singh	128	– b Harbhajan Singh	3
†T. D. Paine st Dhoni b Ojha	59	– c Dhoni b Sreesanth	23
M. G. Johnson lbw b Ojha	0	– b Zaheer Khan	11
N. M. Hauritz run out	17	– not out	21
B. W. Hilfenhaus not out	16	– b Sreesanth	0
P. R. George st Dhoni b Harbhajan Singh	2	– c Dhoni b Zaheer Khan	0
B 9, l-b 12, w 1, n-b 9	31	B 1, l-b 5, w 3, n-b 5	14
(141 overs)	478	(75.2 overs)	223

1/99 (2) 2/113 (1) 3/132 (4) 4/198 (5) 5/256 (3)   1/58 (1) 2/58 (2) 3/65 (4) 4/126 (5) 5/131 (6)
6/405 (7) 7/415 (8) 8/458 (6) 9/459 (9) 10/478 (11)   6/181 (3) 7/185 (7) 8/217 (8) 9/218 (10) 10/223 (11)

Zaheer Khan 23–5–84–1; Sreesanth 21–1–79–0; Ojha 42–7–120–3; Harbhajan Singh 43–3–148–4; Sehwag 4–1–7–0; Raina 8–1–19–1. *Second Innings*—Zaheer Khan 11.2–1–41–3; Sreesanth 14–2–48–2; Ojha 25–5–57–3; Harbhajan Singh 21–2–63–2; Sehwag 4–0–8–0.

India

M. Vijay c Paine b Johnson	139	– lbw b Watson	37
V. Sehwag c Johnson b Hilfenhaus	30	– c Paine b Hilfenhaus	7
R. Dravid c North b Johnson	1	– (5) not out	21
S. R. Tendulkar b George	214	– not out	53
C. A. Pujara lbw b Johnson	4	– (3) b Hauritz	72
S. K. Raina c Hilfenhaus b Clarke	32		
*†M. S. Dhoni c Clarke b Hauritz	30		
Harbhajan Singh c Ponting b Watson	4		
Zaheer Khan c Clarke b George	1		
P. P. Ojha not out	0		
S. Sreesanth lbw b Hauritz	0		
B 6, l-b 26, w 8	40	B 8, l-b 5, w 4	17
(144.5 overs)	495	(3 wkts, 45 overs)	207

1/37 (2) 2/38 (3) 3/346 (1) 4/350 (5) 5/411 (6)
6/486 (4) 7/491 (8) 8/494 (9) 9/495 (7) 10/495 (11)   1/17 (2) 2/89 (1) 3/146 (3)

Hilfenhaus 31–6–77–1; Johnson 28–2–105–3; George 21–3–48–2; Hauritz 39.5–4–153–2; Clarke 8–0–27–1; Watson 12–2–35–1; Katich 5–0–18–0. *Second Innings*—Hilfenhaus 7–0–27–1; Johnson 14–4–42–0; Hauritz 12–0–76–1; George 7–0–29–0; Watson 5–0–20–1.

Umpires: B. F. Bowden *(New Zealand)* (64) and I. J. Gould *(England)* (16).
Third umpire: A. M. Saheba *(India)*. Referee: B. C. Broad *(England)* (42).

Close of play: First day, Australia 285–5 (North 43, Paine 8); Second day, India 128–2 (Vijay 42, Tendulkar 44); Third day, India 435–5 (Tendulkar 191, Dhoni 11); Fourth day, Australia 202–7 (Johnson 7, Hauritz 8).

INDIA v NEW ZEALAND 2010–11 (1st Test)

At Sardar Patel Stadium, Motera, Ahmedabad, on 4, 5, 6, 7, 8 November, 2010.
Toss: India.   Result: MATCH DRAWN.
Debuts: New Zealand – H. K. Bennett, K. S. Williamson.
Man of the Match: Harbhajan Singh.

Chris Martin breathed some life into a comatose Test with an intoxicating spell of inswing. India were tottering at 15 for five on the fourth evening, but their crisis man, Laxman, added 163 with Harbhajan Singh, who hit his maiden hundred, to force a draw. Before this, bat had dominated ball for almost four days: the game looked dead and buried before Martin produced an inspired opening salvo of 9–6–15–4. However, India escaped: Harbhajan was only the second No. 8 to score a half-century and a hundred in the same Test, after Eric Dalton of South Africa at The Oval in 1935. On the first day, Sehwag collected 173 from 199 balls, and Dravid slowly dragged himself back into form with a sedate 30th Test century as India meandered to a large total. On the third day New Zealand's batsmen regrouped after a nightmarish Bangladesh tour, where their side had suffered an embarrassing 4–0 one-day whitewash. McCullum, who had decided to stop keeping wicket in Tests, made 65, but it was Ryder and the 20-year-old Kane Williamson who really sparkled. Ryder's foot movement was minimal but precise, the backlift short, and he showed good solidity in defence and conviction in attack. Williamson, who batted for 6½ hours, became the eighth and youngest New Zealander to make a century in his first Test. New Zealand's other debutant, fast bowler Hamish Bennett, was not so lucky: he suffered a groin strain on the first day and went home.

India

G. Gambhir b Ryder	21	– c Hopkins b Martin		0
V. Sehwag b Vettori	173	– run out		1
R. Dravid b Martin	104	– c Hopkins b Martin		1
S. R. Tendulkar c and b Patel	40	– b Martin		12
V. V. S. Laxman lbw b Patel	40	– lbw b Vettori		91
S. K. Raina c McCullum b Williamson	3	– c Taylor b Martin		0
*†M. S. Dhoni c Watling b Vettori	10	– b Martin		22
Harbhajan Singh c Hopkins b Vettori	69	– c Watling b Taylor		115
Zaheer Khan b Vettori	1	– lbw b Vettori		0
P. P. Ojha lbw b Patel	11	– not out		9
S. Sreesanth not out	2	– c Hopkins b Taylor		4
B 5, l-b 2, w 1, n-b 5	13	B 10, n-b 1		11
(151.5 overs)	487	(102.4 overs)		266

1/60 (1) 2/297 (2) 3/317 (3) 4/383 (4) 5/392 (6)   1/0 (1) 2/1 (2) 3/2 (3) 4/15 (4) 5/15 (6)
6/392 (5) 7/410 (7) 8/412 (9) 9/478 (10) 10/487 (8)   6/65 (7) 7/228 (5) 8/228 (9) 9/260 (8) 10/266 (11)

Martin 24–5–75–1; Bennett 15–2–47–0; Vettori 54.5–12–118–4; Ryder 17–4–56–1; Patel 29–6–135–3; Williamson 12–0–49–1. *Second Innings*—Martin 27–8–63–5; Vettori 38–8–81–2; Patel 23–1–72–0; Williamson 4–0–18–0; Taylor 4.4–2–4–2; McCullum 6–1–18–0.

New Zealand

T. G. McIntosh c Dhoni b Zaheer Khan	0	– lbw b Zaheer Khan		0
B. B. McCullum st Dhoni b Ojha	65	– not out		11
B-J. Watling b Ojha	6	– not out		2
L. R. P. L. Taylor c Laxman b Harbhajan Singh	56			
J. D. Ryder lbw b Sreesanth	103			
K. S. Williamson c Laxman b Ojha	131			
*D. L. Vettori c Dhoni b Raina	41			
†G. J. Hopkins lbw b Ojha	14			
J. S. Patel b Sreesanth	14			
H. K. Bennett b Zaheer Khan	4			
C. S. Martin not out	3			
B 5, l-b 12, n-b 5	22	B 4, w 5		9
(165.4 overs)	459	(1 wkt, 10 overs)		22

1/8 (1) 2/27 (3) 3/131 (4) 4/137 (2) 5/331 (5)   1/4 (1)
6/417 (6) 7/417 (7) 8/445 (8) 9/445 (9) 10/459 (10)

Zaheer Khan 28.4–6–70–2; Sreesanth 26–2–88–2; Ojha 53–14–107–4; Harbhajan Singh 43–7–112–1; Sehwag 1–0–7–0; Raina 12–1–42–1; Tendulkar 2–0–16–0. *Second Innings*—Zaheer Khan 4–2–7–1; Sreesanth 1–0–4–0; Ojha 3–2–1–0; Raina 1–0–1–0; Dhoni 1–0–5–0.

Umpires: S. J. Davis *(Australia)* (28) and H. D. P. K. Dharmasena *(Sri Lanka)* (1).
Third umpire: S. K. Tarapore *(India)*. Referee: R. S. Madugalle *(Sri Lanka)* (120).

Close of play: First day, India 329–3 (Tendulkar 13, Laxman 7); Second day, New Zealand 69–2 (McCullum 38, Taylor 18); Third day, New Zealand 331–5 (Williamson 87); Fourth day, India 82–6 (Laxman 34, Harbhajan Singh 12).

INDIA v NEW ZEALAND 2010–11 (2nd Test)

At Rajiv Gandhi International Stadium, Uppal, Hyderabad, on 12, 13, 14, 15, 16 November, 2010.
Toss: New Zealand.   Result: MATCH DRAWN.
Debuts: none.
Man of the Match: B. B. McCullum.

This Test, like the First, came alive on the fourth day. New Zealand started it by wiping out a lead of 122, the first century stand by their openers since 2004. Shortly before tea, an umpiring error denied McIntosh a fifty to go with his first-innings century, but he had already become the 17th player to follow a pair with a Test century. India bounced back with three further wickets, but McCullum battled hard for his third century in five Tests in 2010. On the final day he dashed any hopes of a home win, beginning quietly before racing to his maiden double-century. Dhoni packed the leg side, so McCullum unleashed a reverse scoop. India paid dearly for dropping him on 148 – the lead was 185 at the time – when substitute Cheteshwar Pujara at short leg failed to hold on to a sharp chance off Harbhajan Singh. McCullum batted for 543 minutes, hit 22 fours and four sixes from 308 balls. Harbhajan had earlier played a big part in extending India's lead to 122 after Sehwag's 96, becoming the first No. 8 to score back-to-back Test centuries. But if his batting stats were superb, his bowling ones were atrocious: only six for 305 in the series. The absence of Zaheer, who pulled an abdominal muscle, was crucial. The draw had become a stronger possibility with every passing day at the 101st ground to stage Test cricket – the 21st in India and the second in Hyderabad, after the Lal Bahadur Shastri Stadium, which last hosted one in December 1988.

New Zealand

T. G. McIntosh b Zaheer Khan	102	– c sub (C. A. Pujara) b Ojha			49
B. B. McCullum c Dhoni b Sreesanth	4	– c Raina b Sreesanth			225
M. J. Guptill lbw b Ojha	85	– c Dhoni b Ojha			18
L. R. P. L. Taylor c Dhoni b Zaheer Khan	24	– b Sreesanth			7
J. D. Ryder c Laxman b Harbhajan Singh	70	– c Dhoni b Raina			20
†G. J. Hopkins lbw b Zaheer Khan	4	– (8) not out			11
K. S. Williamson lbw b Zaheer Khan	4	– (6) lbw b Harbhajan Singh			69
*D. L. Vettori lbw b Harbhajan Singh	11	– (7) c Dravid b Raina			23
T. G. Southee st Dhoni b Harbhajan Singh	10	– b Harbhajan Singh			11
B. J. Arnel not out	6	– not out			1
C. S. Martin c Sehwag b Harbhajan Singh	3				
B 2, l-b 20, w 1, n-b 4	27	B 4, l-b 3, w 2, n-b 5			14
(117.3 overs)	350	(8 wkts dec, 135 overs)			448

1/4 (2) 2/151 (3) 3/206 (4) 4/253 (1) 5/269 (6)   1/125 (1) 2/174 (3) 3/187 (4) 4/221 (5)
6/287 (7) 7/312 (8) 8/331 (5) 9/338 (9) 10/350 (11)   5/345 (6) 6/396 (7) 7/431 (2) 8/447 (9)

Zaheer Khan 27–8–69–4; Sreesanth 21–1–88–1; Harbhajan Singh 35.3–10–76–4; Ojha 27–4–80–1; Raina 7–2–15–0. *Second Innings*—Zaheer Khan 7.3–1–21–0; Sreesanth 27–5–121–3; Ojha 47.3–14–137–2; Harbhajan Singh 38–3–117–1; Tendulkar 2–0–7–0; Raina 13–2–38–2.

India

G. Gambhir c Hopkins b Southee	54	– not out	14
V. Sehwag b Vettori	96	– not out	54
R. Dravid lbw b Southee	45		
S. R. Tendulkar c Taylor b Vettori	13		
V. V. S. Laxman lbw b Martin	74		
S. K. Raina c Guptill b Vettori	20		
*†M. S. Dhoni c McCullum b Vettori	14		
Harbhajan Singh not out	111		
Zaheer Khan c Arnel b Southee	7		
P. P. Ojha run out	0		
S. Sreesanth lbw b Vettori	24		
B 4, l-b 8, w 1, n-b 1	14		
(143.4 overs)	472	(no wkt, 17 overs)	68

1/160 (2) 2/160 (1) 3/184 (4) 4/259 (3) 5/311 (6)
6/326 (5) 7/336 (7) 8/355 (9) 9/367 (10) 10/472 (11)

Martin 29–6–87–1; Southee 33–6–119–3; Arnel 24–5–79–0; Vettori 49.4–7–135–5; Williamson 7–0–31–0; Taylor 1–0–9–0. *Second Innings*—Southee 4–0–11–0; Arnel 5–1–11–0; Guptill 5–0–33–0; Taylor 3–0–13–0.

Umpires: H. D. P. K. Dharmasena *(Sri Lanka)* (2) and S. J. A. Taufel *(Australia)* (65).
Third umpire: A. M. Saheba *(India)*. Referee: R. S. Madugalle *(Sri Lanka)* (121).

Close of play: First day, New Zealand 258–4 (Ryder 22, Hopkins 0); Second day, India 178–2 (Dravid 7, Tendulkar 11); Third day, India 436–9 (Harbhajan Singh 85, Sreesanth 14); Fourth day, New Zealand 237–4 (McCullum 124, Williamson 12).

INDIA v NEW ZEALAND 2010–11 (3rd Test)

At Vidarbha C. A. Stadium, Jamtha, Nagpur, on 20, 21, 22, 23 November, 2010.
Toss: New Zealand.   Result: INDIA WON BY AN INNINGS AND 198 RUNS.
Debuts: New Zealand – A. J. McKay.
Man of the Match: R. Dravid. Man of the Series: Harbhajan Singh.

New Zealand were upbeat after two refreshing performances, but now their batting misfired on the first day, and they couldn't recover. India, protecting their No. 1 Test ranking, seized a 373-run lead, and went on to a simple victory. New Zealand's problems began even before the start: McCullum tweaked his back during catching practice, and couldn't open the innings. Sreesanth started the slide, producing a cracking leg-cutter to Guptill, then gated McIntosh. Ishant Sharma – replacing the injured Zaheer Khan – extracted some extra bounce and occasional movement, and the middle order surrendered. There was a brief revival from the under-the-weather pair of Ryder (who had injured his calf in the First Test) and McCullum, who made 40 from No. 8. Ryder made 59, but a smart slip catch left New Zealand 124 for seven. Southee contributed a breezy 38, but 193 was never enough. Dravid piled on the agony on a flat pitch by making 191 in 9½ hours after the openers' fiery start. Dravid kept working the angles, while Dhoni clattered a rapid 98 to ensure a big lead. New Zealand's batsmen under-performed again, and slid to defeat with a day to spare. The ball turned and bounced on the fourth day, and India were all over New Zealand like a rash: two debatable umpiring decisions – Guptill and Taylor were the unlucky victims – didn't help. The ball kicked and spat: only Southee, who biffed three more sixes, passed 30 as the spinners shared seven wickets to clinch India's series win.

New Zealand

T. G. McIntosh b Sreesanth	....	4 – lbw b Harbhajan Singh	8
M. J. Guptill c Dhoni b Sreesanth	....	6 – (4) lbw b Ojha	0
L. R. P. L. Taylor lbw b Sharma	....	20 – (5) c sub (C. A. Pujara) b Harbhajan Singh	29
J. D. Ryder c Raina b Harbhajan Singh	....	59 – (6) c Sharma b Raina	22
K. S. Williamson c Sehwag b Ojha	....	0 – (7) b Sharma	8
*D. L. Vettori b Sharma	....	3 – (8) lbw b Raina	13
†G. J. Hopkins c Raina b Ojha	....	7 – (3) c Gambhir b Harbhajan Singh	8
B. B. McCullum c Dhoni b Sharma	....	40 – (2) lbw b Ojha	25
T. G. Southee c Sehwag b Ojha	....	38 – b Sharma	31
A. J. McKay b Sharma	....	5 – not out	20
C. S. Martin not out	....	2 – b Sharma	0
B 1, l-b 5, n-b 3	 9	B 10, l-b 1	11
(66.3 overs)	 193	(51.2 overs)	175

1/11 (2) 2/16 (1) 3/42 (3) 4/43 (5) 5/51 (6) 6/82 (7)
7/124 (4) 8/159 (8) 9/165 (10) 10/193 (9)

1/18 (1) 2/38 (2) 3/38 (4) 4/62 (3) 5/93 (5)
6/110 (7) 7/123 (6) 8/124 (8) 9/175 (9) 10/175 (11)

Sreesanth 12–4–28–2; Sharma 18–4–43–4; Ojha 19.3–2–57–3; Harbhajan Singh 17–2–59–1. *Second Innings*—Sreesanth 7–3–25–0; Sharma 6.2–2–15–3; Ojha 17–2–67–2; Harbhajan Singh 19–4–56–3; Raina 2–1–1–2.

India

G. Gambhir c Taylor b Southee	78
V. Sehwag c and b Vettori	74
R. Dravid c Guptill b Williamson	191
S. R. Tendulkar c Hopkins b McKay	61
V. V. S. Laxman b Martin	12
S. K. Raina c sub (B-J. Watling) b Vettori	3
*†M. S. Dhoni c and b Vettori	98
Harbhajan Singh c McCullum b Martin	20
I. Sharma not out	7
S. Sreesanth not out	0
B 12, l-b 5, w 4, n-b 1	22
(8 wkts dec, 165 overs)	566

1/113 (2) 2/192 (1) 3/296 (4) 4/309 (5) 5/328 (6)
6/521 (7) 7/549 (3) 8/562 (8)

P. P. Ojha did not bat.

Martin 28–4–82–2; Southee 29–5–94–1; McKay 31–5–120–1; Vettori 58–7–178–3; Williamson 11–0–45–1; Guptill 7–0–27–0; Taylor 1–0–3–0.

Umpires: N. J. Llong *(England)* (9) and S. J. A. Taufel *(Australia)* (66).
Third umpire: S. S. Hazare *(India)*. Referee: R. S. Madugalle *(Sri Lanka)* (122).

Close of play: First day, New Zealand 148–7 (McCullum 34, Southee 7); Second day, India 292–2 (Dravid 69, Tendulkar 57); Third day, New Zealand 24–1 (McCullum 15, Hopkins 1).

PAKISTAN v SOUTH AFRICA 2010–11 (1st Test)

At Dubai International Cricket Stadium on 12, 13, 14, 15, 16 November, 2010.
Toss: South Africa.   Result: MATCH DRAWN.
Debuts: Pakistan – Adnan Akmal.
Man of the Match: Younis Khan.

With Pakistan forced to play "home" matches in the Gulf, the inaugural Test in Dubai moved along briskly at first, both teams making good starts before suffering near-identical collapses. This was puzzling, because the pitch played well throughout at the 102nd Test venue (the match started a few hours after Uppal in Hyderabad became the 101st). After a watchful opening stand of 153, Smith completed his 22nd Test century, a record 20th as captain. Adnan, the third Akmal brother to keep wicket for Pakistan in internationals, later caught Amla and Kallis after they added 117. Early humidity encouraged lively first sessions each day, and South Africa were dismissed for 380 shortly after lunch on the second. Pakistan, showing seven changes from their controversial previous Test against England, also started well: Mohammad Hafeez and Taufeeq Umar – in his first Test for more than four years – collected 60 from the first nine overs, but next morning Botha and Morkel skittled Pakistan for 248. Amla, with his 11th Test century, and Kallis (36th) then shared a record partnership for South Africa's third wicket against Pakistan. It was their eighth century stand in Tests, including two of more than 300. Starting 450 behind, Pakistan lost the openers quickly, but on the final day Younis Khan, recalled after 15 months, made his 17th Test century. Misbah-ul-Haq, Pakistan's new captain, delightedly declared the draw a "gift for the nation" after helping his side to its highest fourth-innings total. Only three wickets fell on the last two days.

South Africa

*G. C. Smith c Taufeeq Umar b Wahab Riaz	100	– (2) lbw b Saeed Ajmal	34
A. N. Petersen c Younis Khan b Abdur Rehman	67	– (1) lbw b Abdur Rehman	26
H. M. Amla c Adnan Akmal b Wahab Riaz	80	– not out	118
J. H. Kallis c Adnan Akmal b Saeed Ajmal	73	– not out	135
P. L. Harris c Younis Khan b Umar Gul	0		
A. B. de Villiers b Umar Gul	5		
A. G. Prince lbw b Umar Gul	1		
†M. V. Boucher lbw b Abdur Rehman	9		
J. Botha b Abdur Rehman	10		
D. W. Steyn not out	10		
M. Morkel lbw b Saeed Ajmal	10		
B 9, l-b 2, w 1, n-b 3	15	B 1, l-b 2, w 1, n-b 1	5
(123 overs)	380	(2 wkts dec, 95 overs)	318

1/153 (2) 2/190 (1) 3/307 (3) 4/318 (5) 5/327 (6)
6/329 (7) 7/345 (8) 8/347 (4) 9/363 (9) 10/380 (11)   1/47 (1) 2/76 (2)

Umar Gul 30–4–100–3; Wahab Riaz 18–3–61–2; Abdur Rehman 32–2–101–3; Saeed Ajmal 35–6–95–2; Mohammad Hafeez 1–0–1–0; Younis Khan 7–2–11–0. *Second Innings*—Umar Gul 18–0–73–0; Younis Khan 3–0–15–0; Abdur Rehman 36–5–105–1; Mohammad Hafeez 11–3–20–0; Saeed Ajmal 27–2–102–1.

Pakistan

Mohammad Hafeez c Smith b Harris	60	– c Botha b Steyn	34
Taufeeq Umar lbw b Morkel	42	– c Kallis b Botha	22
Azhar Ali c Amla b Morkel	56	– b Harris	63
Younis Khan c de Villiers b Botha	35	– not out	131
*Misbah-ul-Haq c Amla b Botha	9	– not out	76
Umar Akmal c Steyn b Botha	4		
†Adnan Akmal c Boucher b Steyn	10		
Abdur Rehman c de Villiers b Morkel	1		
Umar Gul not out	12		
Wahab Riaz c Boucher b Morkel	5		
Saeed Ajmal c Boucher b Morkel	2		
L-b 12	12	B 6, l-b 4, w 5, n-b 2	17
(95 overs)	248	(3 wkts, 117 overs)	343

1/105 (1) 2/111 (2) 3/176 (4) 4/196 (5) 5/202 (6)
6/220 (7) 7/225 (8) 8/228 (3) 9/246 (10) 10/248 (11)   1/41 (1) 2/75 (2) 3/157 (3)

Steyn 18–3–58–1; Morkel 21–7–54–5; Harris 25–7–47–1; Kallis 8–3–16–0; Botha 23–6–61–3. *Second Innings*—Steyn 22–6–82–1; Morkel 22–4–46–0; Harris 31–10–57–1; Botha 38–7–138–1; Kallis 4–2–10–0.

Umpires: E. A. R. de Silva *(Sri Lanka)* (47) and D. J. Harper *(Australia)* (91).
Third umpire: Ahsan Raza *(Pakistan)*. Referee: A. J. Pycroft *(Zimbabwe)* (14).

Close of play: First day, South Africa 311–3 (Kallis 53, Harris 0); Second day, Pakistan 144–2 (Azhar Ali 12, Younis Khan 21); Third day, South Africa 139–2 (Amla 44, Kallis 32); Fourth day, Pakistan 109–2 (Azhar Ali 37, Younis Khan 11).

PAKISTAN v SOUTH AFRICA 2010–11 (2nd Test)

At Sheikh Zayed Stadium, Abu Dhabi, on 20, 21, 22, 23, 24 November, 2010.
Toss: Pakistan.   Result: MATCH DRAWN.
Debuts: Pakistan – Asad Shafiq, Tanvir Ahmed.
Man of the Match: A. B. de Villiers. Man of the Series: J. H. Kallis.

Pakistan made a fine start on a green-tinged pitch at Test cricket's 103rd ground. Their chief weapon was almost a local: Tanvir Ahmed, the 31-year-old seamer making his debut after an injury to Wahab Riaz, was born in Kuwait. He removed Petersen with his third ball and Amla with the eighth, and added Smith in his sixth over. But by the end of a rollicking opening session the score had shot to 114 from only 25 overs, with Kallis leading the charge: his 37th century came from just 135 balls. Then de Villiers, after his tenth hundred partnership with Kallis, batted for a minute over ten hours in all for South Africa's highest Test score, beating Smith's 277 at Edgbaston in 2003. Tanvir persevered for six for 120, but the last pair's unbeaten stand eclipsed South Africa's last-wicket record, the 103 of Tuppy Owen-Smith and Sandy Bell at Headingley in 1929. Pakistan faced a grim battle for the draw, but avoided the follow-on with some ease on a now-bland pitch. Azhar Ali made his third consecutive fifty, Asad Shafiq an assured 61 on debut, and Misbah-ul-Haq was rock-solid again. South Africa built quickly on their lead of 150. Amla, opening instead of Smith (injured thumb), struck a scintillating 62 from 64 balls, but Smith was not going to give Pakistan a sniff, and his declaration set 354 from 82 overs. Harris and Botha teased out three wickets in eight balls, but South Africa never looked likely to take all ten.

South Africa

*G. C. Smith c Adnan Akmal b Tanvir Ahmed	10		
A. N. Petersen c Misbah-ul-Haq b Tanvir Ahmed	2	– (1) c Younis Khan b Abdur Rehman	35
H. M. Amla c Adnan Akmal b Tanvir Ahmed	4	– (2) b Abdur Rehman	62
J. H. Kallis b Tanvir Ahmed	105	– c Taufeeq Umar b Mohammad Hafeez	10
A. B. de Villiers not out	278	– (3) lbw b Abdur Rehman	25
A. G. Prince c Asad Shafiq b Mohammad Hafeez	32	– (5) not out	47
†M. V. Boucher b Tanvir Ahmed	45	– (6) b Umar Gul	15
J. Botha b Abdur Rehman	12	– (7) not out	7
D. W. Steyn c Mohammad Hafeez b Abdur Rehman	27		
P. L. Harris c Adnan Akmal b Tanvir Ahmed	19		
M. Morkel not out	35		
B 6, l-b 1, w 2, n-b 6	15	L-b 1, n-b 1	2
(9 wkts dec, 153 overs)	584	(5 wkts dec, 55 overs)	203

1/2 (2) 2/6 (3) 3/33 (1) 4/212 (4) 5/268 (6)
6/341 (7) 7/383 (8) 8/442 (9) 9/477 (10)   1/81 (1) 2/113 (2) 3/130 (3) 4/148 (4) 5/182 (6)

Umar Gul 36–6–137–0; Tanvir Ahmed 28–6–120–6; Mohammad Sami 24–1–101–0; Younis Khan 3–1–11–0; Abdur Rehman 50–9–150–2; Mohammad Hafeez 12–0–58–1. *Second Innings*—Umar Gul 7–0–32–1; Tanvir Ahmed 5–1–29–0; Abdur Rehman 22–1–81–3; Mohammad Sami 5–0–28–0; Mohammad Hafeez 16–4–32–1.

Pakistan

Mohammad Hafeez lbw b Steyn	2	– lbw b Harris	34
Taufeeq Umar c Amla b Kallis	43	– lbw b Botha	30
Azhar Ali c Smith b Steyn	90	– not out	28
Younis Khan c Amla b Steyn	14	– lbw b Harris	0
*Misbah-ul-Haq lbw b Steyn	77	– not out	58
Asad Shafiq c Kallis b Harris	61		
†Adnan Akmal c Amla b Harris	17		
Abdur Rehman lbw b Botha	60		
Umar Gul lbw b Harris	21		
Tanvir Ahmed c Prince b Morkel	30		
Mohammad Sami not out	2		
B 5, l-b 8, w 2, n-b 2	17	L-b 2, w 1	3
(144.1 overs)	434	(3 wkts, 67 overs)	153

1/2 (1) 2/119 (2) 3/153 (4) 4/156 (3) 5/263 (6)
6/309 (7) 7/317 (5) 8/353 (9) 9/412 (10) 10/434 (8)   1/66 (2) 2/66 (1) 3/66 (4)

Steyn 30–8–98–4; Morkel 33–13–94–1; Kallis 21–6–77–1; Botha 14.1–3–54–1; Harris 46–17–98–3. *Second Innings*—Steyn 13–2–40–0; Morkel 11–3–29–0; Harris 23–14–28–2; Kallis 2–0–13–0; Botha 17–4–40–1; Petersen 1–0–1–0.

Umpires: E. A. R. de Silva *(Sri Lanka)* (48) and D. J. Harper *(Australia)* (92).
Third umpire: Nadeem Ghauri *(Pakistan)*. Referee: A. J. Pycroft *(Zimbabwe)* (15).

Close of play: First day, South Africa 311–5 (de Villiers 120, Boucher 26); Second day, Pakistan 59–1 (Taufeeq Umar 16, Azhar Ali 34); Third day, Pakistan 317–6 (Misbah-ul-Haq 77, Abdur Rehman 0); Fourth day, South Africa 173–4 (Prince 27, Boucher 13).

SRI LANKA v WEST INDIES 2010–11 (1st Test)

At Galle International Stadium on 15, 16, 17, 18, 19 November, 2010.
Toss: West Indies.　　Result: MATCH DRAWN.
Debuts: West Indies – D. M. Bravo, A. D. Russell.
Man of the Match: C. H. Gayle.

In his first Test since being relieved of the West Indian captaincy after rejecting a central contract, Chris Gayle joined Don Bradman, Brian Lara and Virender Sehwag in scoring two Test triple-centuries in Tests, his 333 – the highest for West Indies outside the Caribbean – adding to 317 against South Africa in Antigua in 2005. Gayle spent 19 balls over his first run, but then plundered 34 fours and nine sixes, a West Indian record. He was less commanding on the second day, escaping twice thanks to reviewed decisions. At 559 for three, it looked as if West Indies could amass 700 if they chose: but suddenly, after his first 54 overs had yielded just one wicket, Mendis recaptured his magic with mesmerising effect, taking five for 12 in 23 balls. That included Gayle, defeated by his 437th delivery after 649 minutes, and the new captain, Darren Sammy, clueless about a first-ball googly. Sri Lanka immediately lost Dilshan, to Andre Russell's second ball in Test cricket, but 67 overs were lost to rain on the third day. Roach and Shillingford (later reported for a suspect action) chipped away, and despite Prasad's breezy late 47, West Indies made the opposition follow on for the first time since 2005. An opening stand of 102 then reassured Sri Lanka, and although Dilshan and Sangakkara fell early on the final day the only other casualties were Paranavitana, caught at slip for 95, and Mahela Jayawardene, just before the weather closed in for the final time.

West Indies

C. H. Gayle b Mendis		333
A. B. Barath c D. P. M. D. Jayawardene b Randiv		50
D. M. Bravo c Samaraweera b Mendis		58
S. Chanderpaul c D. P. M. D. Jayawardene b Randiv		32
B. P. Nash lbw b Mendis		64
D. J. Bravo lbw b Mendis		5
†C. S. Baugh not out		8
*D. J. G. Sammy b Mendis		0
A. D. Russell b Mendis		2
S. Shillingford st H. A. P. W. Jayawardene b Randiv		1
B 2, l-b 6, w 7, n-b 12		27
(9 wkts dec, 163.2 overs)		580

1/110 (2) 2/306 (3) 3/392 (4) 4/559 (5) 5/565 (6)
6/566 (1) 7/566 (8) 8/579 (9) 9/580 (10)

K. A. J. Roach did not bat.

Mirando 21–4–79–0; Prasad 30–3–116–0; Mendis 59–6–169–6; Randiv 48.2–3–183–3; Dilshan 3–0–15–0; Mathews 2–0–10–0.

Sri Lanka

N. T. Paranavitana b Roach	10	– c Sammy b Shillingford	95
T. M. Dilshan c Shillingford b Russell	0	– b Roach	54
*K. C. Sangakkara b D. J. Bravo	73	– c Sammy b Roach	4
D. P. M. D. Jayawardene c Baugh b Roach	59	– c and b Nash	58
T. T. Samaraweera run out	52	– not out	19
A. D. Mathews c Sammy b Shillingford	27	– not out	5
†H. A. P. W. Jayawardene c Roach b Shillingford	58		
S. Randiv b Shillingford	12		
K. T. G. D. Prasad c Russell b Shillingford	47		
B. A. W. Mendis c D. M. Bravo b Roach	4		
M. T. T. Mirando not out	4		
B 8, l-b 8, w 3, n-b 13	32	L-b 1, w 4, n-b 1	6
(95.2 overs)	378	(4 wkts, 81.2 overs)	241

1/6 (2) 2/61 (1) 3/132 (3) 4/193 (4) 5/227 (5)
6/264 (6) 7/295 (8) 8/367 (9) 9/374 (10) 10/378 (7)　　　　1/102 (2) 2/110 (3) 3/197 (1) 4/233 (4)

Roach 19–2–75–3; Russell 15–1–73–1; Shillingford 33.2–3–123–4; Sammy 11–2–41–0; D. J. Bravo 16–4–47–1; Gayle 1–0–3–0. *Second Innings*—Roach 17–3–55–2; Russell 8–1–31–0; D. J. Bravo 12.2–1–40–0; Shillingford 30–4–79–1; Sammy 9–2–14–0; Nash 5–0–21–1.

Umpires: S. J. Davis *(Australia)* (29) and R. A. Kettleborough *(England)* (1).
Third umpire: Asad Rauf *(Pakistan)*. Referee: A. G. Hurst *(Australia)* (40).

Close of play: First day, West Indies 362–2 (Gayle 219, Chanderpaul 20); Second day, Sri Lanka 54–1 (Paranavitana 10, Sangakkara 33); Third day, Sri Lanka 165–3 (D. P. M. D. Jayawardene 51, Samaraweera 11); Fourth day, Sri Lanka 89–0 (Paranavitana 44, Dilshan 44).

SRI LANKA v WEST INDIES 2010–11 (2nd Test)

At R. Premadasa Stadium, Colombo, on 23, 24, 25, 26 (*no play*), 27 November, 2010.
Toss: Sri Lanka.   Result: MATCH DRAWN.
Debuts: Sri Lanka – R. A. S. Lakmal.
Man of the Match: K. C. Sangakkara.

After winning the toss, Sangakkara pondered his options like a schoolboy faced with a tricky exam question, his uncertainty prompted by a brand-new pitch and weeks of rain. He eventually decided to bat, only for his side to stumble to 34 for three on a surface more Chester-le-Street than Colombo. Sangakkara spent 6¾ hours putting matters right. He offered a tough slip catch to Sammy off Roach when two, and a difficult leg-side chance to wicketkeeper Baugh off Dwayne Bravo when 118, before he was finally taken by the diving Gayle at first slip. Sangakkara's stand of 170 with Samaraweera shifted the pressure on to West Indies, who had preferred left-arm spinner Benn to paceman Russell. It meant Sammy took the new ball for the first time, sending down 17 consecutive overs of tame medium-pace on the reduced opening day. Lacking incisive support, Roach deserved even better than his five for 100. Darren Bravo's exquisite strokeplay, strikingly similar to his cousin Brian Lara's, brought him four sixes, and helped rescue West Indies from 77 for three. Eventually Dilshan was tried: he dismissed Nash, after a stand of 83, with his tenth ball and Bravo with his 12th, to Herath's leaping catch at cover from an unbecoming slog. At 165 for five, two testing days lay ahead for West Indies, but the weather eased their worries; the fourth day was completely lost, and no play was possible until after lunch on the fifth. Once Baugh saved the follow-on, they were safe.

Sri Lanka

N. T. Paranavitana c D. J. Bravo b Roach	16	– not out		20
T. M. Dilshan b Roach	4	– c Baugh b D. J. Bravo		26
*K. C. Sangakkara c Gayle b Sammy	150	– not out		1
D. P. M. D. Jayawardene b Sammy	2			
T. T. Samaraweera c Shillingford b D. J. Bravo	80			
A. D. Mathews c Baugh b Roach	25			
†H. A. P. W. Jayawardene b Benn	34			
K. M. D. N. Kulasekara c D. J. Bravo b Roach	17			
H. M. R. K. B. Herath not out	24			
B. A. W. Mendis b Roach	2			
B 4, l-b 12, w 14, n-b 3	33	B 5, l-b 4, w 1		10
(9 wkts dec, 115.2 overs)	387	(1 wkt dec, 15 overs)		57

1/10 (2) 2/31 (1) 3/34 (4) 4/204 (5) 5/273 (6)
6/325 (3) 7/349 (7) 8/383 (8) 9/387 (10)   1/55 (2)

R. A. S. Lakmal did not bat.

Roach 28.2–5–100–5; Sammy 35–8–80–2; D. J. Bravo 18–5–61–1; Benn 19–4–57–1; Shillingford 15–0–73–0. *Second Innings*—Roach 5–0–15–0; Sammy 4–1–16–0; D. J. Bravo 4–1–8–1; Benn 2–0–9–0.

West Indies

C. H. Gayle c Mathews b Lakmal	30	– c D. P. M. D. Jayawardene b Dilshan		3
A. B. Barath lbw b Kulasekara	3	– lbw b Mendis		8
D. M. Bravo c Herath b Dilshan	80	– not out		0
S. Chanderpaul lbw b Mendis	8	– not out		0
B. P. Nash lbw b Dilshan	29			
D. J. Bravo st H. A. P. W. Jayawardene b Herath	20			
†C. S. Baugh b Herath	50			
*D. J. G. Sammy c Mathews b Lakmal	2			
S. J. Benn c Paranavitana b Herath	0			
S. Shillingford not out	5			
K. A. J. Roach b Mendis	3			
L-b 5, n-b 8	13	N-b 1		1
(71.3 overs)	243	(2 wkts, 11 overs)		12

1/7 (2) 2/51 (1) 3/77 (4) 4/160 (5) 5/161 (3)
6/205 (6) 7/208 (8) 8/209 (9) 9/240 (7) 10/243 (11)   1/9 (2) 2/11 (1)

Mendis 16.3–1–56–2; Lakmal 16–1–84–2; Kulasekara 11–5–17–1; Herath 23–3–76–3; Mathews 3–2–1–0; Dilshan 2–0–4–2. *Second Innings*—Lakmal 2–0–7–0; Dilshan 5–2–4–1; Mendis 3–2–1–1; Herath 1–1–0–0.

Umpires: Asad Rauf *(Pakistan)* (33) and R. A. Kettleborough *(England)* (2).
Third umpire: S. J. Davis *(Australia)*. Referee: A. G. Hurst *(Australia)* (41).

Close of play: First day, Sri Lanka 84–3 (Sangakkara 25, Samaraweera 26); Second day, Sri Lanka 294–5 (Sangakkara 135, H. A. P. W. Jayawardene 12); Third day, West Indies 165–5 (D. J. Bravo 1, Baugh 4); Fourth day, No play.

SRI LANKA v WEST INDIES 2010–11 (3rd Test)

At Muttiah Muralitharan Stadium, Pallekele, on 1, 2, 3 (*no play*), 4, 5 (*no play*) December, 2010.
Toss: Sri Lanka.   Result: MATCH DRAWN.
Debuts: none.
Man of the Match: no award. Man of the Series: K. A. J. Roach.

Pallekele, a half-hour drive from Kandy, had a sensational initiation as Test cricket's 104th venue when Gayle was trapped lbw by the first delivery. It was only the third ground to witness a wicket to its first ball in a Test, following Jullundur (Mohsin Khan dismissed by Kapil Dev in 1983–84) and Jaipur (Sunil Gavaskar by Imran Khan in 1986–87). The start was delayed by 70 minutes, and rain was never far away. There was no play on the third and fifth days, and each of the others was appreciably shortened, allowing only 103.3 overs in all. Another sparkling innings by Darren Bravo – who batted as if playing for his club in Port-of-Spain – and Herath's probing left-arm spin were the highlights of what play there was. Bravo's confidence, in the third half-century of his debut series, helped settle Devon Smith, drafted in for his first Test for 18 months after Barath's late withdrawal with flu. Chanderpaul's dismissal set off a familiar clatter of wickets. Five fell for 33, four in succession to Herath, before Benn and Roach held firm as the series splashed to its inevitable soggy end at ten to one on the fourth afternoon. During the tour, Sri Lanka's heaviest and most widespread rainfall in 18 years had caused flash floods and landslides. Fewer than half the allocated overs (656.2 of 1,350) could be bowled in the three Tests, none of which came close to a positive result. The limited-overs matches that were supposed to follow were cancelled.

West Indies

C. H. Gayle lbw b Lakmal	0
D. S. Smith lbw b Mendis	55
D. M. Bravo lbw b Fernando	68
S. Chanderpaul c D. P. M. D. Jayawardene b Mendis ..	54
B. P. Nash c H. A. P. W. Jayawardene b Herath	67
D. J. Bravo st H. A. P. W. Jayawardene b Herath	0
†C. S. Baugh lbw b Herath	2
*D. J. G. Sammy lbw b Herath	8
S. J. Benn not out	29
K. A. J. Roach not out	12
L-b 4, w 1, n-b 3	8
(8 wkts, 103.3 overs)	303

1/0 (1) 2/115 (2) 3/142 (3) 4/241 (4) 5/242 (6)
6/252 (5) 7/253 (7) 8/274 (8)

N. T. Pascal did not bat.

Lakmal 17.3–5–41–1; Mathews 10–4–34–0; Dilshan 10–1–20–0; Fernando 15–2–72–1; Mendis 28–6–78–2; Herath 23–5–54–4.

Sri Lanka

N. T. Paranavitana, T. M. Dilshan, *K. C. Sangakkara, D. P. M. D. Jayawardene, T. T. Samaraweera, A. D. Mathews, †H. A. P. W. Jayawardene, H. M. R. K. B. Herath, B. A. W. Mendis, C. R. D. Fernando and R. A. S. Lakmal.

Umpires: Asad Rauf *(Pakistan)* (34) and B. N. J. Oxenford *(Australia)* (1).
Third umpire: R. J. Tucker *(Australia)*. Referee: A. G. Hurst *(Australia)* (42).

Close of play: First day, West Indies 134–2 (D. M. Bravo 63, Chanderpaul 11); Second day, West Indies 244–5 (Nash 62, Baugh 0); Third day, No play; Fourth day, West Indies 303–8 (Benn 29, Roach 12).

AUSTRALIA v ENGLAND 2010–11 (1st Test)

At Woolloongabba, Brisbane, on 25, 26, 27, 28, 29 November, 2010.
Toss: England.   Result: MATCH DRAWN.
Debuts: Australia – X. J. Doherty.
Man of the Match: A. N. Cook.

Australia's proud record of not losing at Brisbane since 1988–89 remained intact, but a draw felt like a defeat considering their position of superiority after a first-innings lead of 221. That owed much to a sixth-wicket stand of 307 between Hussey, whose 195 probably saved his place after an indifferent run, and Haddin, who reached three figures with a straight six off Swann. They had come together at 143 for five. What came next, though, flattened Australia and set the tone for the series: England amassed 517 for one to mock the ground's reputation as a fast bowler's haven – the pacemen bowled 98 wicketless overs between them. It was only the sixth time any side had passed 500 for the loss of just one wicket in a Test. All three batsmen scored centuries, with Cook going to an epic 235 not out, second only to Wally Hammond (251 at Sydney in 1928–29) for England in Australia, and the highest by anyone at the Gabba, beating Don Bradman's 226 against South Africa in 1931–32. Cook put on 188 with Strauss, during which they eclipsed Jack Hobbs and Herbert Sutcliffe (3,249 runs together) as England's most productive opening pair, then an unbroken 329 – England's highest for any wicket in Australia – with Trott. It had all looked very different on the opening day, when Straus fell to the third ball of the match, then Siddle pouched Australia's 11th Test hat-trick – on his 26th birthday – with the wickets of Cook, Prior and Broad.

England

*A. J. Strauss c Hussey b Hilfenhaus	0	– st Haddin b North	110
A. N. Cook c Watson b Siddle	67	– not out	235
I. J. L. Trott b Watson	29	– not out	135
K. P. Pietersen c Ponting b Siddle	43		
P. D. Collingwood c North b Siddle	4		
I. R. Bell c Watson b Doherty	76		
†M. J. Prior b Siddle	0		
S. C. J. Broad lbw b Siddle	0		
G. P. Swann lbw b Siddle	10		
J. M. Anderson b Doherty	11		
S. T. Finn not out	0		
L-b 8, w 7, n-b 5	20	B 17, l-b 4, w 10, n-b 6	37
(76.5 overs)	260	(1 wkt dec, 152 overs)	517

1/0 (1) 2/41 (3) 3/117 (4) 4/125 (5) 5/197 (2)
6/197 (7) 7/197 (8) 8/228 (9) 9/254 (6) 10/260 (10)   1/188 (1)

Hilfenhaus 19–4–60–1; Siddle 16–3–54–6; Johnson 15–2–66–0; Watson 12–2–30–1; Doherty 13.5–3–41–2; North 1–0–1–0. *Second Innings*—Hilfenhaus 32–8–82–0; Siddle 24–4–90–0; North 19–3–47–1; Johnson 27–5–104–0; Doherty 35–5–107–0; Watson 15–2–66–0.

Australia

S. R. Watson c Strauss b Anderson	36	– not out	41
S. M. Katich c and b Finn	50	– c Strauss b Broad	4
*R. T. Ponting c Prior b Anderson	10	– not out	51
M. J. Clarke c Prior b Finn	9		
M. E. K. Hussey c Cook b Finn	195		
M. J. North c Collingwood b Swann	1		
†B. J. Haddin c Collingwood b Swann	136		
M. G. Johnson b Finn	0		
X. J. Doherty c Cook b Finn	16		
P. M. Siddle c Swann b Finn	6		
B. W. Hilfenhaus not out	1		
B 4, l-b 12, w 4, n-b 1	21	B 4, l-b 1, w 1, p 5	11
(158.4 overs)	481	(1 wkt, 26 overs)	107

1/78 (1) 2/96 (3) 3/100 (2) 4/140 (4) 5/143 (6)
6/450 (7) 7/458 (5) 8/462 (8) 9/472 (10) 10/481 (9)   1/5 (2)

Anderson 37–13–99–2; Broad 33–7–72–0; Swann 43–5–128–2; Finn 33.4–1–125–6; Collingwood 12–1–41–0. *Second Innings*—Anderson 5–2–15–0; Broad 7–1–18–1; Swann 8–0–33–0; Finn 4–0–25–0; Pietersen 2–0–6–0.

Umpires: Aleem Dar *(Pakistan)* (61) and B. R. Doctrove *(West Indies)* (30).
Third umpire: A. L. Hill *(New Zealand)*. Referee: J. J. Crowe *(New Zealand)* (43).

Close of play: First day, Australia 25–0 (Watson 9, Katich 15); Second day, Australia 220–5 (Hussey 81, Haddin 22); Third day, England 19–0 (Strauss 11, Cook 6); Fourth day, England 309–1 (Cook 132, Trott 54).

AUSTRALIA v ENGLAND 2010–11 (2nd Test)

At Adelaide Oval on 3, 4, 5, 6, 7 December, 2010.
Toss: Australia.   Result: ENGLAND WON BY AN INNINGS AND 71 RUNS.
Debuts: none.
Man of the Match: K. P. Pietersen.

England seized control in the first over and never relinquished it – Australia were nought for two after five balls, two for three after 13, and never discovered any equilibrium. Afterwards, Ponting was forced to admit: "They outbowled us, they outbatted us, they outfielded us the entire game." The upshot was England's first innings win over Australia since the Ashes clincher at Melbourne in December 1986; their first win in any Test in Australia since then with the Ashes still at stake; and Australia's first innings defeat in 101 home Tests against anyone since February 1993. Hussey, again helped by Haddin, repaired some of the damage caused by the poor start, but England put Australia's total into perspective by motoring to 620 at more than four an over. Cook made another hundred, putting on 173 with Trott and 175 with Pietersen, who went on to England's seventh Test double-century in Australia, a week after the sixth. Almost 400 behind, Australia started defiantly, with Watson and Katich (battling an Achilles injury in what turned out to be his 56th and last Test) putting on 84, then Clarke batted with more of his usual élan before popping a catch to short leg off Pietersen's occasional off-spin. Only the inevitable Hussey could make much of Swann, who completed the first five-for by an England spinner at Adelaide since Derek Underwood in 1974–75. Just to compound Australia's misery, the heavens opened two hours after the match ended, and produced Adelaide's wettest recorded December day.

Australia

S. R. Watson c Pietersen b Anderson	51	– c Strauss b Finn	57
S. M. Katich run out	0	– c Prior b Swann	43
*R. T. Ponting c Swann b Anderson	0	– c Collingwood b Swann	9
M. J. Clarke c Swann b Anderson	2	– c Cook b Pietersen	80
M. E. K. Hussey c Collingwood b Swann	93	– c Anderson b Finn	52
M. J. North c Prior b Finn	26	– lbw b Swann	22
†B. J. Haddin c Finn b Broad	56	– c Prior b Anderson	12
R. J. Harris lbw b Swann	0	– lbw b Anderson	0
X. J. Doherty run out	6	– b Swann	5
P. M. Siddle c Cook b Anderson	3	– b Swann	6
D. E. Bollinger not out	0	– not out	7
L-b 6, w 1, n-b 1	8	B 5, l-b 1, w 5	11
(85.5 overs)	245	(99.1 overs)	304

1/0 (2) 2/0 (3) 3/2 (4) 4/96 (1) 5/156 (6) 6/207 (5)
7/207 (8) 8/226 (9) 9/243 (10) 10/245 (7)

1/84 (2) 2/98 (3) 3/134 (1) 4/238 (4) 5/261 (5)
6/286 (7) 7/286 (8) 8/286 (6) 9/295 (9) 10/304 (10)

Anderson 19–4–51–4; Broad 18.5–6–39–1; Finn 16–1–71–1; Swann 29–2–70–2; Collingwood 3–0–8–0. *Second Innings*—Anderson 22–4–92–2; Broad 11–3–32–0; Swann 41.1–12–91–5; Finn 18–2–60–2; Collingwood 4–0–13–0; Pietersen 3–0–10–1.

England

*A. J. Strauss b Bollinger	1
A. N. Cook c Haddin b Harris	148
I. J. L. Trott c Clarke b Harris	78
K. P. Pietersen c Katich b Doherty	227
P. D. Collingwood lbw b Watson	42
I. R. Bell not out	68
†M. J. Prior not out	27
B 8, l-b 13, w 8	29
(5 wkts dec, 152 overs)	620

1/3 (1) 2/176 (3) 3/351 (2) 4/452 (5) 5/568 (4)

S. C. J. Broad, G. P. Swann, J. M. Anderson and S. T. Finn did not bat.

Harris 29–5–84–2; Bollinger 29–1–130–1; Siddle 30–3–121–0; Watson 19–7–44–1; Doherty 27–3–158–1; North 18–0–62–0.

Umpires: M. Erasmus *(South Africa)* (4) and A. L. Hill *(New Zealand)* (21).
Third umpire: B. R. Doctrove *(West Indies)*. Referee: J. J. Crowe *(New Zealand)* (44).

Close of play: First day, England 1–0 (Strauss 0, Cook 0); Second day, England 317–2 (Cook 136, Pietersen 85); Third day, England 551–4 (Pietersen 213, Bell 41); Fourth day, Australia 238–4 (Hussey 44).

AUSTRALIA v ENGLAND 2010–11 (3rd Test)

At W. A. C. A. Ground, Perth, on 16, 17, 18, 19 December, 2010.
Toss: England.   Result: AUSTRALIA WON BY 267 RUNS.
Debuts: none.
Man of the Match: M. G. Johnson.

England departed from the game-plan that otherwise served them well in this series. Attempting to wrap up the Ashes before Christmas, as never before, they gave up their strategy of patience and plenty of spin, and tried short balls and verbals. It was an outright failure. Australia went for all-out attack with a barrage of words and four fast bowlers, levelled the series, and maintained the WACA as England's least successful ground (they had won only one of 12 previous Tests there, against a weakened Australian side in 1978–79). England also ran into Johnson at his best, as Australia's fast left-armer briefly rediscovered his swing. At 69 for five on the first day Australia were rocking, but Hussey and Haddin saved them yet again, before Johnson clubbed 62 from 93 balls. Then, after the openers had put on 78, Johnson the bowler claimed four for seven. He was helped by a hot wind that blew from the east – and Johnson bowled not only with the wind but like it. Building on a lead of 81, Watson and Hussey showed England how to bat at Perth, using vertical or horizontal bats, nothing in between. Chasing an unlikely 391, England slumped to 81 for five on the third evening, and were ripped apart within an hour next morning. Harris improved his Test-best; like Johnson, he took nine wickets in the match. Ponting was unable to field on the fourth day, his 36th birthday, as he had broken his little finger palming a catch from Trott to Haddin.

Australia

S. R. Watson lbw b Finn	13	– lbw b Tremlett			95
P. J. Hughes b Tremlett	2	– c Collingwood b Finn			12
*R. T. Ponting c Collingwood b Anderson	12	– c Prior b Finn			1
M. J. Clarke c Prior b Tremlett	4	– b Tremlett			20
M. E. K. Hussey c Prior b Swann	61	– c Swann b Tremlett			116
S. P. D. Smith c Strauss b Tremlett	7	– c Prior b Tremlett			36
†B. J. Haddin c Swann b Anderson	53	– b Tremlett			7
M. G. Johnson c Anderson b Finn	62	– c Bell b Collingwood			1
R. J. Harris b Anderson	3	– c Bell b Finn			1
P. M. Siddle not out	35	– c Collingwood b Anderson			8
B. W. Hilfenhaus c Cook b Swann	13	– not out			0
L-b 3	3	L-b 6, w 4, n-b 2			12
(76 overs)	268	(86 overs)			309

1/2 (2) 2/17 (3) 3/28 (4) 4/36 (1) 5/69 (6) 6/137 (5)   1/31 (2) 2/34 (3) 3/64 (4) 4/177 (1) 5/252 (6)
7/189 (7) 8/201 (9) 9/233 (8) 10/268 (11)   6/271 (7) 7/276 (8) 8/284 (9) 9/308 (10) 10/309 (5)

Anderson 20–3–61–3; Tremlett 23–3–63–3; Finn 15–1–86–2; Collingwood 2–0–3–0; Swann 16–0–52–2. *Second Innings*—Anderson 26–7–65–1; Tremlett 24–4–87–5; Finn 21–4–97–3; Swann 9–0–51–0; Collingwood 6–3–3–1.

England

*A. J. Strauss c Haddin b Harris	52	– c Ponting b Johnson			15
A. N. Cook c Hussey b Johnson	32	– lbw b Harris			13
I. J. L. Trott lbw b Johnson	4	– c Haddin b Johnson			31
K. P. Pietersen lbw b Johnson	0	– c Watson b Hilfenhaus			3
P. D. Collingwood lbw b Johnson	5	– c Smith b Harris			11
I. R. Bell c Ponting b Harris	53	– (7) lbw b Harris			16
†M. J. Prior b Siddle	12	– (8) c Hussey b Harris			10
G. P. Swann c Haddin b Harris	11	– (9) b Johnson			9
C. T. Tremlett b Johnson	2	– (10) not out			1
J. M. Anderson c Watson b Johnson	0	– (6) b Harris			3
S. T. Finn not out	1	– c Smith b Harris			2
B 8, l-b 4, w 1, n-b 2	15	L-b 8, n-b 1			9
(62.3 overs)	187	(37 overs)			123

1/78 (2) 2/82 (3) 3/82 (4) 4/94 (1) 5/98 (5) 6/145 (7)   1/23 (2) 2/37 (1) 3/55 (4) 4/81 (3) 5/81 (5)
7/181 (8) 8/186 (6) 9/186 (9) 10/187 (10)   6/94 (6) 7/111 (7) 8/114 (8) 9/120 (9) 10/123 (11)

Hilfenhaus 21–6–53–0; Harris 15–4–59–3; Siddle 9–2–25–1; Johnson 17.3–5–38–6. *Second Innings*—Hilfenhaus 10–4–16–1; Harris 11–1–47–6; Johnson 12–3–44–3; Siddle 4–1–8–0.

Umpires: B. R. Doctrove *(West Indies)* (31) and M. Erasmus *(South Africa)* (5).
Third umpire: Aleem Dar *(Pakistan)*. Referee: J. J. Crowe *(New Zealand)* (45).

Close of play: First day, England 29–0 (Strauss 12, Cook 17); Second day, Australia 119–3 (Watson 61, Hussey 24); Third day, England 81–5 (Anderson 0).

AUSTRALIA v ENGLAND 2010–11 (4th Test)

At Melbourne Cricket Ground on 26, 27, 28, 29 December, 2010.
Toss: England.   Result: ENGLAND WON BY AN INNINGS AND 157 RUNS.
Debuts: none.
Man of the Match: I. J. L. Trott.

After playing what their coach called a "perfect" game at Adelaide, England went close to improving on perfection in the Boxing Day Test, rebounding from their Perth setback to lead throughout, ensuring the retention of the Ashes just before noon on the fourth day. England savoured first use of a pitch with an unusual carpet of grass: Australia were demolished for 98, only their tenth sub-100 total against England since 1896, and the first since the 1968 Lord's Test. England were well in front by the end of the first day, and although Cook fell early next morning Trott dropped anchor, putting on 173 with Prior – who had taken six catches in the first innings – and remaining undefeated with 168 (his third century in five Tests against Australia) as England ended up 415 ahead. Australia were still just alive at 95 for one at tea on the third day, but three quick wickets, including Hussey for a duck, prised their fingers from the window ledge. Haddin made another combative fifty, and put on 86 with Siddle, but it was only a matter of time. Bresnan finally had Hilfenhaus caught behind, leaving Swann to organise the team's new signature "Sprinkler" dance in front of the Barmy Army. Ponting aggravated his injured finger during the match, and was forced to miss the final Test. England got their selection just right: Tremlett, tall and fast, took four wickets in the first innings, and Bresnan – preferred to the tiring Finn – six in the match.

Australia

S. R. Watson c Pietersen b Tremlett	5	– lbw b Bresnan	54
P. J. Hughes c Pietersen b Bresnan	16	– run out	23
*R. T. Ponting c Swann b Tremlett	10	– b Bresnan	20
M. J. Clarke c Prior b Anderson	20	– c Strauss b Swann	13
M. E. K. Hussey c Prior b Anderson	8	– c Bell b Bresnan	0
S. P. D. Smith c Prior b Anderson	6	– b Anderson	38
†B. J. Haddin c Strauss b Bresnan	5	– not out	55
M. G. Johnson c Prior b Anderson	0	– b Tremlett	6
R. J. Harris not out	10	– absent hurt	
P. M. Siddle c Prior b Tremlett	11	– (9) c Pietersen b Swann	40
B. W. Hilfenhaus c Prior b Tremlett	0	– (10) c Prior b Bresnan	0
L-b 2, n-b 5	7	B 1, l-b 6, w 2	9
(42.5 overs)	98	(85.4 overs)	258

1/15 (1) 2/37 (2) 3/37 (3) 4/58 (5) 5/66 (6) 6/77 (4) 7/77 (7) 8/77 (8) 9/92 (10) 10/98 (11)

1/53 (2) 2/99 (1) 3/102 (3) 4/104 (5) 5/134 (4) 6/158 (6) 7/172 (8) 8/258 (9) 9/258 (10)

Anderson 16–4–44–4; Tremlett 11.5–5–26–4; Bresnan 13–6–25–2; Swann 2–1–1–0. *Second Innings*—Anderson 20–1–71–1; Tremlett 17–3–71–1; Swann 27–11–59–2; Bresnan 21.4–8–50–4.

England

*A. J. Strauss c Hussey b Siddle	69
A. N. Cook c Watson b Siddle	82
I. J. L. Trott not out	168
K. P. Pietersen lbw b Siddle	51
P. D. Collingwood c Siddle b Johnson	8
I. R. Bell c Siddle b Johnson	1
†M. J. Prior c Ponting b Siddle	85
T. T. Bresnan c Haddin b Siddle	4
G. P. Swann c Haddin b Hilfenhaus	22
C. T. Tremlett b Hilfenhaus	4
J. M. Anderson b Siddle	1
B 10, l-b 2, w 3, n-b 3	18
(159.1 overs)	513

1/159 (2) 2/170 (1) 3/262 (4) 4/281 (5) 5/286 (6) 6/459 (7) 7/465 (8) 8/508 (9) 9/512 (10) 10/513 (11)

Hilfenhaus 37–13–83–2; Harris 28.4–9–91–0; Johnson 29–2–134–2; Siddle 33.1–10–75–6; Watson 10–1–34–0; Smith 18–3–71–0; Clarke 3.2–0–13–0.

Umpires: Aleem Dar *(Pakistan)* (62) and A. L. Hill *(New Zealand)* (22).
Third umpire: M. Erasmus *(South Africa)*. Referee: R. S. Madugalle *(Sri Lanka)* (123).

Close of play: First day, England 157–0 (Strauss 64, Cook 80); Second day, England 444–5 (Trott 141, Prior 75); Third day, Australia 169–6 (Haddin 11, Johnson 6).

AUSTRALIA v ENGLAND 2010–11 (5th Test)

At Sydney Cricket Ground on 3, 4, 5, 6, 7 January, 2011.
Toss: Australia.   Result: ENGLAND WON BY AN INNINGS AND 83 RUNS.
Debuts: Australia – M. A. Beer, U. T. Khawaja.
Man of the Match: A. N. Cook. Man of the Series: A. N. Cook.

England completed an unprecedented third innings victory of an Ashes series, the 3–1 triumph set up by another huge total: 644 was their third-highest against Australia, the other two both coming in 1938. Clarke, Australia's 43rd Test captain, did England a favour by batting first on a damp, patchy pitch under overcast skies. This may have been the residue of paranoia about Ponting's 2005 Edgbaston blunder – there had not been one single insertion by Australia since. But although six batsmen reached 30, the highest was Johnson's 53 in the face of another fine performance from Anderson, who finished the rubber with 24 wickets. England's policy of "bowling dry" – keeping the runs down – meant Australia's middling 280 took 106.1 overs to arrive. And when England batted, that total was again dwarfed, mainly by Cook, whose 189 gave him 766 runs at 127.66 in the five Tests. Prior (who finished the series with 23 catches, equalling Alec Stewart's England Ashes record) added England's fastest Ashes century since Ian Botham's at Old Trafford in 1981: never previously had the sixth, seventh and eighth wickets all managed century partnerships in the same Test innings, and England had never before reached 500 four times in any series. Australia again kept losing batsmen when set, and only a perky eighth-wicket stand of 86 between Smith and Siddle prolonged the match into the final day. Strauss became only the third England captain, after Len Hutton and Mike Brearley, to win Ashes series both home and away.

Australia

S. R. Watson c Strauss b Bresnan	45	– run out 38
P. J. Hughes c Collingwood b Tremlett	31	– c Prior b Bresnan 13
U. T. Khawaja c Trott b Swann	37	– c Prior b Anderson 21
*M. J. Clarke c Anderson b Bresnan	4	– c Prior b Anderson 41
M. E. K. Hussey b Collingwood	33	– c Pietersen b Bresnan 12
†B. J. Haddin c Prior b Anderson	6	– c Prior b Tremlett 30
S. P. D. Smith c Collingwood b Anderson	18	– not out 54
M. G. Johnson b Bresnan	53	– b Tremlett 0
P. M. Siddle c Strauss b Anderson	2	– c Anderson b Swann 43
B. W. Hilfenhaus c Prior b Anderson	34	– c Prior b Anderson 7
M. A. Beer not out	2	– b Tremlett 2
B 5, l-b 7, w 1, n-b 2	15	B 11, l-b 4, w 3, n-b 2 20
(106.1 overs)	280	(84.4 overs) 281

1/55 (2) 2/105 (1) 3/113 (4) 4/134 (3) 5/143 (6)
6/171 (5) 7/187 (7) 8/189 (9) 9/265 (8) 10/280 (10)

1/46 (1) 2/52 (2) 3/117 (3) 4/124 (4) 5/161 (5)
6/171 (6) 7/171 (8) 8/257 (9) 9/267 (10) 10/281 (11)

Anderson 30.1–7–66–4; Tremlett 26–9–71–1; Bresnan 30–5–89–3; Swann 16–4–37–1; Collingwood 4–2–5–1.
Second Innings—Anderson 18–5–61–3; Tremlett 20.4–4–79–3; Swann 28–8–75–1; Bresnan 18–6–51–2.

England

*A. J. Strauss b Hilfenhaus	60
A. N. Cook c Hussey b Watson	189
I. J. L. Trott b Johnson	0
K. P. Pietersen c Beer b Johnson	36
J. M. Anderson b Siddle	7
P. D. Collingwood c Hilfenhaus b Beer	13
I. R. Bell c Clarke b Johnson	115
†M. J. Prior c Haddin b Hilfenhaus	118
T. T. Bresnan c Clarke b Johnson	35
G. P. Swann not out	36
C. T. Tremlett c Haddin b Hilfenhaus	12
B 3, l-b 11, w 5, n-b 4	23
(177.5 overs)	644

1/98 (1) 2/99 (3) 3/165 (4) 4/181 (5) 5/226 (6)
6/380 (2) 7/487 (7) 8/589 (9) 9/609 (8) 10/644 (11)

Hilfenhaus 38.5–7–121–3; Johnson 36–5–168–4; Siddle 31–5–111–1; Watson 20–7–49–1; Beer 38–3–112–1; Smith 13–0–67–0; Hussey 1–0–2–0.

Umpires: Aleem Dar *(Pakistan)* (63) and B. F. Bowden *(New Zealand)* (65).
Third umpire: A. L. Hill *(New Zealand)*. Referee: R. S. Madugalle *(Sri Lanka)* (124).

Close of play: First day, Australia 134–4 (Hussey 12); Second day, England 167–3 (Cook 61, Anderson 1); Third day, England 488–7 (Prior 54, Bresnan 0); Fourth day, Australia 213–7 (Smith 24, Siddle 17).

SOUTH AFRICA v INDIA 2010–11 (1st Test)

At Centurion Park, Pretoria, on 16, 17, 18, 19, 20 December, 2010.
Toss: South Africa.   Result: SOUTH AFRICA WON BY AN INNINGS AND 25 RUNS.
Debuts: India – J. D. Unadkat.
Man of the Match: J. H. Kallis.

Sachin Tendulkar scored his 50th Test century – but that was the end of the good news for India, who were otherwise as meek and submissive as on previous tours to South Africa, which they had sworn would not be the case this time now they were ranked No. 1 in the world. When play started four hours late after rain, the rot started immediately: Sehwag sliced to third man before he had scored, and wickets tumbled regularly thereafter. Tendulkar counter-attacked briefly, before a Steyn delivery swung too fast and too late for him, while Morkel's five for 20 did not flatter him. South Africa soon overhauled India's puny total, and eventually left it nearly 500 behind. Kallis was a man on a mission, finally adding a Test double-century to his CV. His hundred was, at 130 deliveries, the quickest of his 38 in Tests, although that was put in the shade by de Villiers, whose own 75-ball century was fully 20 quicker than South Africa's previous-fastest, by Denis Lindsay against Australia in 1966–67. Kallis put on 230 with Amla, and 224 with the rampaging de Villiers. India's second innings was much better than their first. Gambhir and Sehwag put on 137, then Dhoni added 172 with the imperious Tendulkar, who was in such command that even Steyn admitted he had "given up trying to get him out once he'd reached about 40 – I was just attacking the other guy". Still, it wasn't quite enough to make South Africa bat again.

India

G. Gambhir c Harris b Morkel	5	– lbw b Steyn		80
V. Sehwag c Amla b Steyn	0	– c Smith b Harris		63
R. Dravid lbw b Morkel	14	– c Boucher b Morkel		43
S. R. Tendulkar lbw b Steyn	36	– (5) not out		111
V. V. S. Laxman b Steyn	7	– (6) c de Villiers b Tsotsobe		8
S. K. Raina c Prince b Kallis	1	– (7) c Harris b Kallis		5
*†M. S. Dhoni lbw b Morkel	33	– (8) c Boucher b Steyn		90
Harbhajan Singh run out	27	– (9) c Kallis b Harris		1
I. Sharma c Kallis b Morkel	0	– (4) c Amla b Steyn		23
S. Sreesanth c Steyn b Morkel	0	– c de Villiers b Morkel		3
J. D. Unadkat not out	1	– c Prince b Steyn		1
L-b 6, w 3, n-b 3	12	B 13, l-b 5, w 8, n-b 5		31
(38.4 overs)	136	(128.1 overs)		459

1/1 (2) 2/24 (1) 3/27 (3) 4/66 (5) 5/67 (6) 6/71 (4)   1/137 (2) 2/170 (1) 3/214 (4) 4/242 (3) 5/256 (6)
7/110 (8) 8/110 (9) 9/116 (10) 10/136 (7)   6/277 (7) 7/449 (8) 8/450 (9) 9/456 (10) 10/459 (11)

Steyn 10–1–34–3; Morkel 12.4–5–20–5; Tsotsobe 9–2–50–0; Kallis 6–1–20–1; Harris 1–0–6–0. *Second Innings*—Steyn 30.1–6–105–4; Morkel 31–6–94–2; Tsotsobe 24–3–98–1; Harris 30–5–88–2; Kallis 13–3–56–1.

South Africa

*G. C. Smith c Dhoni b Harbhajan Singh	62
A. N. Petersen c Gambhir b Harbhajan Singh	77
H. M. Amla c Dhoni b Sharma	140
J. H. Kallis not out	201
A. B. de Villiers c Dhoni b Sharma	129
B 2, l-b 3, w 2, n-b 4	11
(4 wkts dec, 130.1 overs)	620

1/111 (1) 2/166 (2) 3/396 (3) 4/620 (5)

A. G. Prince, †M. V. Boucher, D. W. Steyn, P. L. Harris, M. Morkel and L. L. Tsotsobe did not bat.

Sreesanth 24–1–97–0; Sharma 27.1–2–120–2; Unadkat 26–4–101–0; Harbhajan Singh 36–2–169–2; Raina 7–0–77–0; Tendulkar 10–1–51–0.

Umpires: S. J. Davis *(Australia)* (30) and I. J. Gould *(England)* (17).
Third umpire: S. George *(South Africa)*. Referee: A. J. Pycroft *(Zimbabwe)* (16).

Close of play: First day, India 136–9 (Dhoni 33, Unadkat 1); Second day, South Africa 366–2 (Amla 116, Kallis 102); Third day, India 190–2 (Dravid 28, Sharma 7); Fourth day, India 454–8 (Tendulkar 107, Sreesanth 3).

SOUTH AFRICA v INDIA 2010–11 (2nd Test)

At Kingsmead, Durban, on 26, 27, 28, 29 December, 2010.
Toss: South Africa.   Result: INDIA WON BY 87 RUNS.
Debuts: none.
Man of the Match: V. V. S. Laxman.

After their implosion at Centurion, and faced with a green pitch and the loss of Gambhir with a hand injury, India seemed ripe for the slaughter. What happened next stunned the sceptics, and left even the optimists confused. After Dhoni lost his 12th toss out of 13 in 2010, several of his batsmen got starts, but none could push on: top-scorer Laxman (38) was sensationally caught by Tsotsobe one-handed at midwicket, one of six scalps for Steyn. South Africa looked handily placed at 67 for two – but then Kallis was run out when Amla's straight-drive hit the stumps via Sharma's hand, and Harbhajan took four quick wickets as the innings was wrapped up for 131. Wickets continued to tumble – 18 on the second day, during which all 22 players batted at some point – and India looked to be squandering their hard-earned advantage until the determined Laxman was joined by Zaheer Khan at 148 for seven – the same score at which they had come together at Johannesburg in 2006–07, when India won their first Test in South Africa. In an exact repeat, they again added 70. Laxman was last out, trying for his century. South Africa needed 303, but after an opening stand of 63 Sreesanth disposed of the danger men – Amla caught behind, and Kallis caught off the glove at gully after receiving a jaffa that climbed on him and jagged back off a good length. India's second win in South Africa was only a matter of time after that.

India

V. Sehwag c Kallis b Steyn	25	– c Boucher b Tsotsobe	32		
M. Vijay c Boucher b Steyn	19	– c Amla b Morkel	9		
R. Dravid c Boucher b Steyn	25	– c Boucher b Tsotsobe	2		
S. R. Tendulkar c Kallis b Tsotsobe	13	– c de Villiers b Steyn	6		
V. V. S. Laxman c Tsotsobe b Steyn	38	– c Boucher b Steyn	96		
C. A. Pujara c Boucher b Tsotsobe	19	– b Morkel	10		
*†M. S. Dhoni c Petersen b Steyn	35	– c Boucher b Tsotsobe	21		
Harbhajan Singh c de Villiers b Steyn	21	– c Kallis b Morkel	4		
Zaheer Khan c Boucher b Morkel	0	– c de Villiers b Harris	27		
I. Sharma not out	1	– c Amla b Kallis	0		
S. Sreesanth c Boucher b Morkel	0	– not out	0		
B 1, l-b 2, w 4, n-b 2	9	B 8, l-b 4, w 9	21		
(65.1 overs)	205	(70.5 overs)	228		

1/43 (1) 2/48 (2) 3/79 (4) 4/117 (3) 5/130 (5)   1/42 (1) 2/44 (2) 3/48 (3) 4/56 (4) 5/93 (6)
6/156 (6) 7/190 (8) 8/193 (9) 9/205 (7) 10/205 (11)   6/141 (7) 7/148 (8) 8/218 (9) 9/223 (10) 10/228 (5)

Steyn 19–6–50–6; Morkel 19.1–3–68–2; Tsotsobe 11–3–40–2; Kallis 8–2–18–0; Harris 8–1–26–0. *Second Innings*—Steyn 15.5–1–60–2; Morkel 15–1–47–3; Tsotsobe 13–3–43–3; Kallis 13–2–30–1; Harris 14–2–36–1.

South Africa

A. N. Petersen b Zaheer Khan	24	– (2) c Pujara b Harbhajan Singh	26		
*G. C. Smith c Dhoni b Zaheer Khan	9	– (1) c Dhoni b Sreesanth	37		
H. M. Amla lbw b Harbhajan Singh	33	– c Dhoni b Sreesanth	16		
J. H. Kallis run out	10	– c Sehwag b Sreesanth	17		
A. B. de Villiers c Dhoni b Sreesanth	0	– lbw b Harbhajan Singh	33		
A. G. Prince b Zaheer Khan	13	– not out	39		
†M. V. Boucher not out	16	– lbw b Zaheer Khan	1		
D. W. Steyn c Dravid b Harbhajan Singh	1	– c Pujara b Zaheer Khan	10		
P. L. Harris c Pujara b Harbhajan Singh	0	– b Zaheer Khan	7		
M. Morkel c Harbhajan Singh b Sharma	10	– c Dhoni b Sharma	20		
L. L. Tsotsobe c Vijay b Harbhajan Singh	0	– run out	0		
L-b 2, w 1, n-b 12	15	L-b 1, n-b 8	9		
(37.2 overs)	131	(72.3 overs)	215		

1/23 (2) 2/46 (1) 3/67 (4) 4/74 (5) 5/96 (3) 6/100 (6)   1/63 (1) 2/82 (2) 3/82 (3) 4/123 (4) 5/136 (5)
7/103 (8) 8/103 (9) 9/127 (10) 10/131 (11)   6/143 (7) 7/155 (8) 8/182 (9) 9/215 (10) 10/215 (11)

Zaheer Khan 13–2–36–3; Sreesanth 8–0–41–1; Sharma 9–2–42–1; Harbhajan Singh 7.2–2–10–4. *Second Innings*—Zaheer Khan 17–3–57–3; Sharma 11.3–0–36–1; Sreesanth 14–2–45–3; Harbhajan Singh 29–5–70–2; Tendulkar 1–0–6–0.

Umpires: Asad Rauf *(Pakistan)* (35) and S. J. Davis *(Australia)* (31).
Third umpire: J. D. Cloete *(South Africa)*. Referee: A. J. Pycroft *(Zimbabwe)* (17).

Close of play: First day, India 183–6 (Dhoni 20, Harbhajan Singh 15); Second day, India 92–4 (Laxman 23, Pujara 10); Third day, South Africa 111–3 (Kallis 12, de Villiers 17).

SOUTH AFRICA v INDIA 2010–11 (3rd Test)

At Newlands, Cape Town, 2, 3, 4, 5, 6 January, 2011.
Toss: India.   Result: MATCH DRAWN.
Debuts: none.
Man of the Match: J. H. Kallis. Man of the Series: J. H. Kallis.

A draw meant the fifth series between these sides in South Africa ended level at 1–1 – the first time that India had not lost there. But Dhoni conceded that his side had missed the chance of a famous victory: they were denied largely by Kallis, whose twin centuries (his 39th and 40th in Tests) took him to 498 runs in the series at an average of 166. Amla made 59 in the first innings and Boucher a vital 55 in the second, joining the immovable Kallis at 130 for six – an overall lead of 128 – with India clear favourites. They put on 103, then the remaining wickets somehow eked out a further 108. Harbhajan bore the brunt of the bowling, sending down 38 overs for seven for 120, figures only he himself had bettered for India against South Africa. Kallis's batting heroics were matched by Tendulkar, who refused to be perturbed by several close shaves, including being dropped early on by de Villiers at second slip off Tsotsobe. He marched to 146, his 51st (and, as it turned out, last) Test century, and shepherded his side to a narrow lead, helped by 93 from Gambhir. After Kallis's second tour de force, India needed 340 to win – although more realistically their target was to survive 90 overs for the draw. Despite another failure from Sehwag, they managed it easily: Gambhir hung on for more than 4½ hours for 64, while Tendulkar was uncharacteristically restrained in making 14 from 91 balls.

South Africa

A. N. Petersen c Dhoni b Sharma	21	– (2) lbw b Harbhajan Singh	22
*G. C. Smith lbw b Zaheer Khan	6	– (1) lbw b Harbhajan Singh	29
H. M. Amla c Pujara b Sreesanth	59	– (4) b Harbhajan Singh	2
J. H. Kallis c Dhoni b Zaheer Khan	161	– (5) not out	109
A. B. de Villiers c Dhoni b Sreesanth	26	– (6) b Zaheer Khan	13
A. G. Prince b Sreesanth	47	– (7) c Sreesanth b Sharma	22
†M. V. Boucher c Dhoni b Sreesanth	0	– (8) lbw b Tendulkar	55
D. W. Steyn c Pujara b Zaheer Khan	0	– (9) c sub (M. Vijay) b Harbhajan Singh	32
M. Morkel c Dhoni b Sreesanth	8	– (10) c Sreesanth b Harbhajan Singh	28
P. L. Harris c Pujara b Sharma	7	– (3) lbw b Harbhajan Singh	0
L. L. Tsotsobe not out	8	– c Sehwag b Harbhajan Singh	8
B 1, l-b 6, w 1, n-b 11	19	L-b 7, w 2, n-b 12	21
(112.5 overs)	362	(102 overs)	341

1/17 (2) 2/34 (1) 3/106 (3) 4/164 (5) 5/262 (6)
6/262 (7) 7/272 (8) 8/283 (9) 9/310 (10) 10/362 (4)

1/50 (1) 2/52 (3) 3/53 (2) 4/64 (5) 5/98 (6)
6/130 (7) 7/233 (8) 8/287 (9) 9/333 (10) 10/341 (11)

Zaheer Khan 29.5–6–89–3; Sreesanth 29–0–114–5; Sharma 27–6–77–2; Harbhajan Singh 27–3–75–0. *Second Innings*—Zaheer Khan 20–2–64–1; Sreesanth 24–3–79–0; Sharma 18–1–62–1; Harbhajan Singh 38–1–120–7; Tendulkar 2–0–9–1.

India

G. Gambhir c Boucher b Harris	93	– c Boucher b Steyn	64
V. Sehwag c Smith b Steyn	13	– c Smith b Morkel	11
R. Dravid run out	5	– c Prince b Tsotsobe	31
S. R. Tendulkar b Morkel	146	– not out	14
V. V. S. Laxman run out	15	– not out	32
C. A. Pujara lbw b Steyn	2		
*†M. S. Dhoni c Prince b Steyn	0		
Harbhajan Singh c sub (J-P. Duminy) b Steyn	40		
Zaheer Khan c Prince b Morkel	23		
I. Sharma c Boucher b Steyn	1		
S. Sreesanth not out	4		
L-b 20, w 1, n-b 1	22	B 7, w 5, n-b 2	14
(117.1 overs)	364	(3 wkts, 82 overs)	166

1/19 (2) 2/28 (3) 3/204 (1) 4/235 (5) 5/237 (6)
6/247 (7) 7/323 (8) 8/341 (4) 9/350 (10) 10/364 (9)

1/27 (2) 2/106 (3) 3/120 (1)

Steyn 31–11–75–5; Morkel 29.1–7–106–2; Tsotsobe 26–5–82–0; Harris 29–8–72–1; Petersen 2–0–9–0. *Second Innings*—Steyn 18–6–43–1; Morkel 15–6–26–1; Tsotsobe 13–4–29–1; Harris 30–19–29–0; Smith 4–0–27–0; Petersen 2–0–5–0.

Umpires: I. J. Gould *(England)* (18) and S. J. A. Taufel *(Australia)* (67).
Third umpire: B. G. Jerling *(South Africa)*. Referee: A. J. Pycroft *(Zimbabwe)* (18).

Close of play: First day, South Africa 232–4 (Kallis 81, Prince 28); Second day, India 142–2 (Gambhir 65, Tendulkar 49); Third day, South Africa 52–2 (Petersen 22, Amla 0); Fourth day, South Africa 341.

NEW ZEALAND v PAKISTAN 2010–11 (1st Test)

At Seddon Park, Hamilton, on 7, 8, 9 January, 2011.
Toss: Pakistan.　　Result: PAKISTAN WON BY TEN WICKETS.
Debuts: New Zealand – R. A. Young.
Man of the Match: Abdur Rehman.

No sooner had this game threatened to come to the boil than it was over. New Zealand had reached 36 without loss shortly after tea on the third day, just 56 behind, when they suffered a crippling collapse. All ten wickets fell for 74 inside a session, leaving a derisory target. Vettori lamented the "sour taste" left by a "familiar batting performance in the third innings". The damage was done in four helter-skelter overs – 60 for two became 61 for six on a good pitch. Only Martin's gallows-humour milestone of 100 Test runs – achieved in his 87th innings, 47 more than the next-worst, India's Bhagwat Chandrasekhar – cheered up the locals. New Zealand had started brightly enough, but the middle order succumbed to Abdur Rehman before a stand of 84 between Williamson and Southee propelled them to 275. Taufeeq Umar's first Test fifty since October 2003 was a curious affair – his first 35 runs came off 33 balls, his next 19 off 71 – but Pakistan were tottering at 107 for four before Asad Shafiq, in only his second Test, kept Misbah-ul-Haq company in a match-turning stand of 149 that occupied nearly 60 overs. New Zealand still harboured hopes of a come-from-behind victory. But Rehman – brought on as early as the tenth over – extracted more turn than Vettori, who had looked out of sorts. McCullum was unlucky to be given out caught behind down the leg side off his thigh pad, but the procession that followed had nothing to do with misfortune.

New Zealand

T. G. McIntosh c Younis Khan b Tanvir Ahmed	5	– st Adnan Akmal b Abdur Rehman	3
B. B. McCullum c Azhar Ali b Umar Gul	56	– c Adnan Akmal b Wahab Riaz	35
M. J. Guptill c Misbah-ul-Haq b Abdur Rehman	50	– c Taufeeq Umar b Abdur Rehman	11
L. R. P. L. Taylor c Adnan Akmal b Abdur Rehman	6	– run out	8
J. D. Ryder run out	22	– lbw b Wahab Riaz	0
K. S. Williamson c Adnan Akmal b Tanvir Ahmed	50	– c Azhar Ali b Wahab Riaz	1
†R. A. Young lbw b Abdur Rehman	14	– c Azhar Ali b Umar Gul	12
*D. L. Vettori lbw b Tanvir Ahmed	0	– lbw b Abdur Rehman	3
T. G. Southee c Younis Khan b Umar Gul	56	– c sub (Umar Akmal) b Umar Gul	17
B. J. Arnel c Wahab Riaz b Tanvir Ahmed	8	– not out	8
C. S. Martin not out	0	– c Younis Khan b Umar Gul	7
L-b 6, w 1, n-b 1	8	N-b 5	5
(97.5 overs)	275	(38.3 overs)	110

1/9 (1) 2/92 (2) 3/99 (4) 4/135 (5) 5/158 (3)
6/176 (7) 7/177 (8) 8/261 (9) 9/274 (6) 10/275 (10)

1/36 (1) 2/44 (2) 3/60 (3) 4/60 (5) 5/61 (4)
6/61 (6) 7/71 (8) 8/90 (9) 9/96 (7) 10/110 (11)

Umar Gul 24–3–84–2; Tanvir Ahmed 18.5–2–63–4; Wahab Riaz 17–4–47–0; Younis Khan 6–1–20–0; Abdur Rehman 30–13–51–3; Mohammad Hafeez 2–1–4–0. *Second Innings*—Umar Gul 8.3–3–28–3; Tanvir Ahmed 4–1–20–0; Abdur Rehman 15–6–24–3; Wahab Riaz 11–1–38–3.

Pakistan

Mohammad Hafeez c McIntosh b Martin	0	– (2) not out	9
Taufeeq Umar c Williamson b Arnel	54	– (1) not out	12
Azhar Ali c Young b Martin	24		
Younis Khan c and b Arnel	23		
*Misbah-ul-Haq lbw b Arnel	62		
Asad Shafiq lbw b Southee	83		
†Adnan Akmal c Ryder b Southee	44		
Abdur Rehman b Arnel	28		
Umar Gul lbw b Vettori	17		
Tanvir Ahmed c Southee b Martin	18		
Wahab Riaz not out	0		
B 4, l-b 6, w 1, n-b 3	14		
(122.1 overs)	367	(no wkt, 3.4 overs)	21

1/0 (1) 2/72 (3) 3/104 (2) 4/107 (4) 5/256 (6)
6/256 (5) 7/332 (7) 8/332 (8) 9/365 (9) 10/367 (10)

Martin 25.1–7–86–3; Southee 32–10–82–2; Arnel 28–6–95–4; Vettori 29–12–48–1; Williamson 6–0–33–0; Guptill 2–0–13–0. *Second Innings*—Martin 2–0–11–0; Southee 1.4–0–10–0.

Umpires: D. J. Harper *(Australia)* (93) and R. J. Tucker *(Australia)* (7).
Third umpire: G. A. V. Baxter *(New Zealand)*. Referee: R. S. Mahanama *(Sri Lanka)* (30).

Close of play: First day, New Zealand 260–7 (Williamson 44, Southee 56); Second day, Pakistan 235–4 (Misbah-ul-Haq 50, Asad Shafiq 74).

NEW ZEALAND v PAKISTAN 2010–11 (2nd Test)

At Basin Reserve, Wellington, on 15, 16, 17, 18, 19 January, 2011.
Toss: New Zealand.   Result: MATCH DRAWN.
Debuts: none.
Man of the Match: Misbah-ul-Haq.

Misbah-ul-Haq secured Pakistan's first Test series win since December 2006, their first outside the subcontinent since beating New Zealand in 2003–04. Misbah batted for 622 minutes in all, and kept New Zealand at bay on what had shaped up to be a captivating final day. Seven years earlier, Pakistan had successfully chased 274 here: now, faced with an identical target, they opted for safety after losing three wickets in the first 13 overs, including Taufeeq Umar, their only survivor from 2003–04. Misbah added an unbeaten 70 to his first-innings 99, and although Martin moved to 199 Test wickets, Vettori – who stepped down as Test captain afterwards – made little impression. And yet without Vettori's heroics with the bat, New Zealand would not have been in any sort of position to push for what would have been only his seventh victory in 32 Tests in charge. At 180 for six Vettori joined Young, who eventually became Adnan Akmal's sixth victim, in a gritty stand of 138; he completed his sixth Test century (third against Pakistan) with last man Martin for company. Two big stands lifted Pakistan to 286 for three, but Younis Khan was wrongly given out caught at short leg – one of several poor decisions in a series played, for financial reasons, without DRS – while Misbah walked across his stumps one short of his hundred. Guptill and McCullum responded with an opening stand of 120. Umar Gul bowled well, but Taylor's second fifty left Pakistan with just too much to do.

New Zealand

M. J. Guptill c Adnan Akmal b Tanvir Ahmed	29	– lbw b Abdur Rehman		73
B. B. McCullum lbw b Umar Gul	2	– c Tanvir Ahmed b Abdur Rehman		64
K. S. Williamson c Adnan Akmal b Umar Gul	21	– c Adnan Akmal b Tanvir Ahmed		15
L. R. P. L. Taylor c Adnan Akmal b Wahab Riaz	78	– lbw b Umar Gul		52
J. D. Ryder c Adnan Akmal b Tanvir Ahmed	0	– b Mohammad Hafeez		17
J. E. C. Franklin c Adnan Akmal b Abdur Rehman	33	– c Younis Khan b Mohammad Hafeez		6
†R. A. Young c Adnan Akmal b Tanvir Ahmed	57	– c Azhar Ali b Abdur Rehman		20
*D. L. Vettori c Misbah-ul-Haq b Abdur Rehman	110	– b Umar Gul		1
T. G. Southee c Misbah-ul-Haq b Umar Gul	1	– not out		22
B. J. Arnel lbw b Umar Gul	1	– lbw b Umar Gul		0
C. S. Martin not out	4	– c Adnan Akmal b Umar Gul		1
B 7, l-b 1, w 10, n-b 2	20	B 2, l-b 6, w 1, n-b 13		22
(127.1 overs)	356	(90.5 overs)		293

1/3 (2) 2/46 (3) 3/98 (1) 4/98 (5) 5/166 (6) 6/180 (4)   1/120 (2) 2/166 (3) 3/166 (1) 4/192 (5) 5/208 (6)
7/318 (7) 8/322 (9) 9/338 (10) 10/356 (8)   6/268 (7) 7/268 (4) 8/275 (8) 9/275 (10) 10/293 (11)

Umar Gul 32–3–87–4; Tanvir Ahmed 25–5–93–3; Younis Khan 1–0–9–0; Wahab Riaz 16–3–46–1; Abdur Rehman 45.1–11–96–2; Mohammad Hafeez 8–0–17–0. *Second Innings*—Umar Gul 20.5–4–61–4; Tanvir Ahmed 10–0–36–1; Abdur Rehman 39–6–119–3; Wahab Riaz 8–1–38–0; Mohammad Hafeez 13–3–31–2.

Pakistan

Taufeeq Umar c Guptill b Vettori	70	– (2) lbw b Southee		0
Mohammad Hafeez c Young b Southee	1	– (1) c Taylor b Martin		32
Azhar Ali c Taylor b Martin	67	– lbw b Martin		10
Younis Khan c Ryder b Vettori	73	– c Young b Southee		81
*Misbah-ul-Haq lbw b Martin	99	– not out		70
Asad Shafiq c Taylor b Vettori	0	– lbw b Vettori		24
†Adnan Akmal c Martin b Vettori	22	– not out		2
Abdur Rehman c McCullum b Martin	5			
Umar Gul c McCullum b Martin	19			
Tanvir Ahmed c Taylor b Southee	7			
Wahab Riaz not out	7			
B 1, l b 2, w 2, n b 1	6	L-b 6, n-b 1		7
(133 overs)	376	(5 wkts, 92 overs)		226

1/2 (2) 2/134 (1) 3/144 (3) 4/286 (4) 5/294 (6)
6/324 (7) 7/333 (8) 8/360 (5) 9/363 (9) 10/376 (10)   1/4 (2) 2/35 (3) 3/42 (1) 4/160 (4) 5/215 (6)

Martin 32–7–91–4; Southee 28–7–102–2; Arnel 16–4–50–0; Franklin 9–1–30–0; Vettori 47–11–100–4; Guptill 1–1–0–0. *Second Innings*—Martin 24–6–63–2; Southee 15–2–49–2; Vettori 34–13–57–1; Arnel 9–5–17–0; Franklin 5–1–6–0; Guptill 3–0–16–0; Ryder 2–0–12–0.

Umpires: D. J. Harper *(Australia)* (94) and R. J. Tucker *(Australia)* (8).
Third umpire: C. B. Gaffaney *(New Zealand)*. Referee: R. S. Mahanama *(Sri Lanka)* (31).

Close of play: First day, New Zealand 246–6 (Young 28, Vettori 38); Second day, Pakistan 134–2 (Azhar Ali 62); Third day, New Zealand 9–0 (Guptill 1, McCullum 6); Fourth day, New Zealand 293.

WEST INDIES v PAKISTAN 2010–11 (1st Test)

At National Stadium, Providence, Guyana, on 12, 13, 14, 15 May, 2011.
Toss: West Indies.   Result: WEST INDIES WON BY 40 RUNS.
Debuts: West Indies – D. Bishoo. Pakistan – Mohammad Salman.
Man of the Match: D. J. G. Sammy.

West Indies' first Test win since February 2009 was especially satisfying. Gayle had been dropped after an outspoken radio interview, so victory was important for Sammy, whose place had come under scrutiny: his accurate medium-pace produced match figures of 29–13–45–7. The pitch was hard and dry, which led to 20 lbws (three more than the previous Test record), and kept the run-rate to 2.4 an over, with just one individual fifty. Pakistan's spinners claimed 17 wickets, 11 to Saeed Ajmal. Only Simmons, in his first Test since 2009, played with much fluency at first, although he was briefly forced to retire hurt with a knee injury. The tail inched the total to 226. Batting was no easier for Pakistan: only a steady knock from No. 8 Abdur Rehman reduced the deficit to 66. Smith then fell quickly again to Mohammad Hafeez's off-spin, and the lead was only 170 when Rampaul was ninth out. But three sharp close catches were missed, Chanderpaul was lucky to survive a run-out appeal, and the last pair added 48. Pakistan began their quest for 219 on the third afternoon. Rampaul and Roach – both exceeding 90mph – caused early mayhem, but Asad Shafiq and Misbah-ul-Haq set up a tense finale. Rampaul's sharp in-cutter bowled Shafiq in the third over next morning, but Misbah and Umar Akmal kept Pakistan in touch. However, an unplayable delivery was never far away – and Sammy suddenly conjured them almost at will to take five for 11 in 52 balls.

West Indies

D. S. Smith b Mohammad Hafeez	13	– lbw b Mohammad Hafeez	1
L. M. P. Simmons lbw b Saeed Ajmal	49	– c Azhar Ali b Wahab Riaz	21
D. M. Bravo lbw b Wahab Riaz	25	– lbw b Saeed Ajmal	8
R. R. Sarwan c Mohammad Salman b Abdur Rehman	23	– (5) c Asad Shafiq b Saeed Ajmal	11
S. Chanderpaul b Saeed Ajmal	27	– (6) not out	36
B. P. Nash lbw b Saeed Ajmal	5	– (7) run out	3
†C. S. Baugh lbw b Saeed Ajmal	4	– (8) c Umar Akmal b Saeed Ajmal	7
*D. J. G. Sammy c Umar Akmal b Abdur Rehman	12	– (9) lbw b Abdur Rehman	9
K. A. J. Roach c Azhar Ali b Saeed Ajmal	24	– (4) lbw b Saeed Ajmal	3
R. Rampaul lbw b Mohammad Hafeez	14	– c Azhar Ali b Saeed Ajmal	2
D. Bishoo not out	15	– c Umar Akmal b Saeed Ajmal	24
B 5, l-b 7, w 1, n-b 2	15	B 7, l-b 17, w 2, n-b 1	27
(98 overs)	226	(61.5 overs)	152

1/15 (1) 2/71 (3) 3/127 (4) 4/136 (6) 5/142 (7)   1/3 (1) 2/23 (3) 3/35 (4) 4/47 (2) 5/59 (5)
6/159 (8) 7/162 (5) 8/175 (2) 9/198 (10) 10/226 (9)   6/74 (7) 7/86 (8) 8/99 (9) 9/104 (10) 10/152 (11)

In the first innings Simmons, when 41, retired hurt at 81 and resumed at 159.

Umar Gul 13–0–40–0; Mohammad Hafeez 13–5–22–2; Abdur Rehman 29–11–51–2; Saeed Ajmal 33–14–69–5; Wahab Riaz 10–1–32–1. *Second Innings*—Umar Gul 8–2–21–0; Mohammad Hafeez 9–1–15–1; Abdur Rehman 11–1–25–1; Saeed Ajmal 23.5–6–42–6; Wahab Riaz 10–1–25–1.

Pakistan

Mohammad Hafeez b Rampaul	4	– lbw b Roach	2
Taufeeq Umar lbw b Sammy	19	– lbw b Rampaul	0
Azhar Ali b Sammy	34	– c Baugh b Rampaul	0
*Misbah-ul-Haq lbw b Bishoo	2	– (5) lbw b Sammy	52
Asad Shafiq lbw b Bishoo	2	– (4) b Rampaul	42
Umar Akmal c Baugh b Bishoo	33	– lbw b Sammy	47
†Mohammad Salman lbw b Bishoo	4	– lbw b Sammy	0
Abdur Rehman not out	40	– c Smith b Rampaul	6
Umar Gul c Baugh b Rampaul	5	– lbw b Sammy	1
Saeed Ajmal lbw b Rampaul	1	– (11) b Sammy	3
Wahab Riaz c Baugh b Roach	5	– (10) not out	11
B 6, l-b 3, n-b 2	11	B 2, l-b 11, n-b 1	14
(64.4 overs)	160	(73 overs)	178

1/5 (1) 2/57 (2) 3/60 (4) 4/62 (3) 5/66 (5) 6/80 (7)   1/2 (2) 2/2 (3) 3/2 (1) 4/83 (4) 5/135 (5) 6/135 (7)
7/130 (6) 8/135 (9) 9/141 (10) 10/160 (11)   7/160 (8) 8/163 (9) 9/166 (6) 10/178 (11)

Roach 10.4–2–40–1; Rampaul 17–5–27–3; Sammy 12–6–16–2; Bishoo 25–6–68–4. *Second Innings*—Roach 13–1–30–1; Rampaul 21–6–48–4; Bishoo 21–5–56–0; Sammy 17–7–29–5; Nash 1–0–2–0.

Umpires: B. F. Bowden *(New Zealand)* (66) and A. L. Hill *(New Zealand)* (23).
Third umpire: E. A. R. de Silva *(Sri Lanka)*. Referee: A. G. Hurst *(Australia)* (43).

Close of play: First day, West Indies 209–9 (Roach 16, Bishoo 10); Second day, West Indies 34–2 (Simmons 18, Roach 3); Third day, Pakistan 80–3 (Asad Shafiq 40, Misbah-ul-Haq 34).

WEST INDIES v PAKISTAN 2010–11 (2nd Test)

At Warner Park, Basseterre, St Kitts, on 20, 21, 22, 23, 24 May, 2011.
Toss: Pakistan.   Result: PAKISTAN WON BY 196 RUNS.
Debuts: West Indies – K. C. Brathwaite.
Man of the Match: Taufeeq Umar. Man of the Series: Saeed Ajmal.

After their hard-fought win in Guyana, West Indies not unreasonably expected St Kitts to serve up the featherbed of the previous year's Test against South Africa, on which despairing bowlers conceded five individual centuries, and 1,324 runs in all for 19 wickets. Instead, the pitch – hard and dry, encouraging turn and bounce – was tailor-made for Pakistan's spinners, who shared 15 wickets, while second-innings hundreds from Taufeeq Umar and Misbah-ul-Haq put the match beyond West Indies' grasp: Pakistan levelled the series midway through the final day. Tanvir Ahmed's robust 57, and his last-wicket partnership of 78 with Saeed Ajmal on the second morning, took advantage of some tame tactics to raise a challenging total. But after Roach and Rampaul helped limit the deficit to 49 by adding 60 for West Indies' ninth wicket, Roach's no-ball reprieved Mohammad Hafeez after he edged to the keeper, while Taufeeq was twice missed in the slips early on, again off the unfortunate Roach. He proceeded to his first Test hundred since October 2003, carefully accumulated off 314 balls. The Barbadian opener Kraigg Brathwaite was, at 18 years 170 days, West Indies' youngest player since Robin Bynoe in 1958–59, while Chanderpaul's late withdrawal with a shoulder niggle allowed Samuels to return for his first Test since his suspension for contact with an alleged Indian bookmaker. He top-scored with a cautious 57. Ajmal's six wickets brought his total in the short series to 17: the batsmen found his doosra as impossible to read as an Urdu text.

Pakistan

Mohammad Hafeez c Simmons b Rampaul	8	– b Sammy	32	
Taufeeq Umar c Baugh b Rampaul	11	– run out	135	
Azhar Ali run out	67	– c Sammy b Bishoo	53	
Asad Shafiq c Bishoo b Rampaul	0	– c Baugh b Roach	4	
*Misbah-ul-Haq c Samuels b Bishoo	25	– not out	102	
Umar Akmal c Rampaul b Sammy	56	– b Bishoo	30	
†Mohammad Salman c Samuels b Bishoo	13	– c Roach b Rampaul	8	
Abdur Rehman c Baugh b Sammy	3			
Tanvir Ahmed lbw b Bishoo	57	– (8) not out	4	
Wahab Riaz c Baugh b Roach	0			
Saeed Ajmal not out	23			
L-b 3, w 4, n-b 2	9	W 7, n-b 2	9	
(109.5 overs)	272	(6 wkts dec, 112.2 overs)	377	

1/17 (2) 2/22 (1) 3/24 (4) 4/74 (5) 5/167 (6)   1/82 (1) 2/158 (3) 3/167 (4) 4/296 (2) 5/358 (6)
6/176 (3) 7/187 (8) 8/187 (7) 9/194 (10) 10/272 (9)   6/367 (7)

Roach 23–9–51–1; Rampaul 26–4–68–3; Sammy 28–6–70–2; Bishoo 32.5–11–80–3. *Second Innings*—Roach 21–6–58–1; Rampaul 24.2–6–87–1; Sammy 23–3–64–1; Bishoo 38–5–149–2; Nash 6–0–19–0.

West Indies

L. M. P. Simmons c Taufeeq Umar b Tanvir Ahmed	0	– c Mohammad Hafeez b Abdur Rehman	24	
K. C. Brathwaite c Taufeeq Umar b Wahab Riaz	15	– b Tanvir Ahmed	0	
D. M. Bravo c Asad Shafiq b Mohammad Hafeez	24	– lbw b Wahab Riaz	50	
R. R. Sarwan st Mohammad Salman b Saeed Ajmal	20	– lbw b Abdur Rehman	0	
M. N. Samuels c Taufeeq Umar b Saeed Ajmal	57	– c Mohammad Salman b Abdur Rehman	6	
B. P. Nash c Misbah-ul-Haq b Mohammad Hafeez	6	– c Taufeeq Umar b Saeed Ajmal	30	
†C. S. Baugh lbw b Abdur Rehman	6	– lbw b Abdur Rehman	18	
*D. J. G. Sammy c Umar Akmal b Abdur Rehman	16	– c Misbah-ul-Haq b Saeed Ajmal	41	
K. A. J. Roach lbw b Mohammad Hafeez	29	– run out	12	
R. Rampaul not out	32	– c Umar Akmal b Saeed Ajmal	20	
D. Bishoo c Taufeeq Umar b Saeed Ajmal	1	– not out	3	
B 4, l-b 4, n-b 9	17	B 8, l-b 6, w 6, n-b 6	26	
(83.5 overs)	223	(80.3 overs)	230	

1/0 (1) 2/22 (2) 3/54 (4) 4/94 (3) 5/100 (6) 6/107 (7)   1/5 (2) 2/59 (1) 3/63 (4) 4/77 (5) 5/115 (3)
7/144 (8) 8/158 (5) 9/218 (9) 10/223 (11)   6/135 (6) 7/171 (7) 8/193 (8) 9/227 (10) 10/230 (9)

Tanvir Ahmed 7–1–22–1; Wahab Riaz 11–1–59–1; Abdur Rehman 29–10–55–2; Saeed Ajmal 28.5–10–56–3; Mohammad Hafeez 8–0–23–3. *Second Innings*—Tanvir Ahmed 5–0–10–1; Wahab Riaz 10–1–39–1; Abdur Rehman 24.3–10–65–4; Saeed Ajmal 31–7–79–3; Mohammad Hafeez 10–1–23–0.

Umpires: B. F. Bowden *(New Zealand)* (67) and E. A. R. de Silva *(Sri Lanka)* (49).
Third umpire: A. L. Hill *(New Zealand)*. Referee: A. G. Hurst *(Australia)* (44).

Close of play: First day, Pakistan 180–6 (Mohammad Salman 8, Abdur Rehman 1); Second day, West Indies 184–8 (Roach 10, Rampaul 15); Third day, Pakistan 202–3 (Taufeeq Umar 97, Misbah-ul-Haq 13); Fourth day, West Indies 130–5 (Nash 30, Baugh 7).

ENGLAND v SRI LANKA 2011 (1st Test)

At Sophia Gardens, Cardiff, on 26, 27, 28, 29, 30 May, 2011.
Toss: Sri Lanka.   Result: ENGLAND WON BY AN INNINGS AND 14 RUNS.
Debuts: Sri Lanka – N. L. T. C. Perera.
Man of the Match: I. J. L. Trott.

Cardiff's second Test seemed destined for a soggy draw when the heaviest rain finally relented on the last afternoon: play had started on time only on the second day, and a day and a half lost overall. When play restarted, 55 overs remained, and England were only 91 ahead in their first innings. Two overs were used up to allow Bell to reach his 13th Test century, and two more shaved off by the change of innings. With Anderson unable to bowl (side strain), it was, admitted Strauss, "a long shot". But, in an astonishing afternoon, Sri Lanka were demolished in 24.4 overs, by one delivery their shortest-ever Test innings. It was England's third successive innings victory, and fourth in five matches. In their first Test outside Asia for three years, Sri Lanka had no answer to the hostility of Tremlett and the fizzing menace of Swann. They had not hinted at such ineptitude in the first innings, reaching 400 in conditions less benign than they looked thanks to 112 from Prasanna Jayawardene. Broad took his 100th Test wicket (Perera), at 24 the youngest to get there for England apart from Ian Botham. Only seven times previously had a total of 400-plus not been enough to avoid an innings defeat – all, save one Bradman-inspired instance in 1930, since 2000. When England batted, Trott put on 251 with Cook, and 160 with Bell: only Pietersen failed, dismissed by a slow left-armer for the 20th time in his last 62 Test innings.

Sri Lanka

N. T. Paranavitana b Tremlett	66	– c Strauss b Tremlett	0
*T. M. Dilshan b Swann	50	– c and b Tremlett	10
K. C. Sangakkara c Prior b Anderson	11	– c Strauss b Swann	14
D. P. M. D. Jayawardene c Strauss b Anderson	4	– c Strauss b Tremlett	15
T. T. Samaraweera c Swann b Anderson	58	– b Swann	0
†H. A. P. W. Jayawardene c Prior b Broad	112	– c Prior b Tremlett	3
M. F. Maharoof run out	16	– c Prior b Swann	0
N. L. T. C. Perera c Tremlett b Broad	25	– c Bell b Broad	20
H. M. R. K. B. Herath c Trott b Swann	25	– lbw b Swann	3
B. A. W. Mendis not out	1	– not out	12
R. A. S. Lakmal c Broad b Swann	2	– c Cook b Broad	0
B 9, l-b 21	30	B 5	5
(118.4 overs)	400	(24.4 overs)	82

1/93 (2) 2/114 (3) 3/133 (4) 4/159 (1) 5/243 (5)
6/278 (7) 7/346 (8) 8/397 (9) 9/397 (6) 10/400 (11)

1/1 (1) 2/10 (2) 3/33 (4) 4/36 (5) 5/43 (3)
6/43 (7) 7/43 (6) 8/52 (9) 9/82 (8) 10/82 (11)

Anderson 28–8–66–3; Broad 33–4–113–2; Tremlett 26–9–81–1; Swann 24.4–2–78–3; Trott 6–0–29–0; Pietersen 1–0–3–0. *Second Innings*—Broad 7.4–1–21–2; Tremlett 10–2–40–4; Swann 7–1–16–4.

England

*A. J. Strauss c D. P. M. D. Jayawardene b Lakmal	20
A. N. Cook c H. A. P. W. Jayawardene b Maharoof	133
J. M. Anderson c D. P. M. D. Jayawardene b Mendis	1
I. J. L. Trott b Dilshan	203
K. P. Pietersen lbw b Herath	3
I. R. Bell not out	103
E. J. G. Morgan not out	14
B 10, l-b 4, n-b 5	19
(5 wkts dec, 155 overs)	496

1/46 (1) 2/47 (3) 3/298 (2) 4/305 (5) 5/465 (4)

†M. J. Prior, S. C. J. Broad, G. P. Swann and C. T. Tremlett did not bat.

Lakmal 22–4–68–1; Perera 24–5–81–0; Dilshan 16–1–60–1; Maharoof 28–3–92–1; Mendis 21–4–66–1; Herath 44–7–115–1.

Umpires: Aleem Dar *(Pakistan)* (64) and B. R. Doctrove *(West Indies)* (32).
Third umpire: R. J. Tucker *(Australia)*. Referee: J. Srinath *(India)* (16).

Close of play: First day, Sri Lanka 133–2 (Paranavitana 58, D. P. M. D. Jayawardene 4); Second day, England 47–1 (Cook 24, Anderson 1); Third day, England 287–2 (Cook 129, Trott 125); Fourth day, England 491–5 (Bell 98, Morgan 14).

ENGLAND v SRI LANKA 2011 (2nd Test)

At Lord's, London, on 3, 4, 5, 6, 7 June, 2011.
Toss: Sri Lanka.   Result: MATCH DRAWN.
Debuts: none.
Man of the Match: T. M. Dilshan.

It looked like business as usual for England as, after an initial stumble to 22 for three, they ran up 486, Prior making a forthright fifth Test century after Cook just missed his 18th (he atoned in the second innings). But, missing the injured Anderson, England's bowlers frequently strayed down leg; Dilshan dominated an opening stand of 207 and, driving well, completed Sri Lanka's highest score at Lord's, beating Sidath Wettimuny's 190 in 1984. One run before he was out for 193, Dilshan was hit on the right thumb for the second time by Tremlett, suffering a fracture which kept him out of the Third Test. England's bowling perked up, and the last seven wickets fell for 85: Sri Lanka were only seven behind, helped by 52 extras. England pushed on initially – they were 231 ahead an hour into the final day – but then slowed down, Cook and Pietersen managing only 20 in ten overs; Cook's second fifty occupied 137 balls, before he was stumped for the first time in 269 first-class innings. Strauss gave his bowlers 58 overs to bowl Sri Lanka out, but there was no repeat of the First Test. It was the first draw in the last six Tests at Lord's. After Prior was run out he accidentally smashed a dressing-room window: among those beneath who were showered with glass was 22-year-old Emma Baker, whose brother Daniel had had a similar experience at Wellington in March 2005 when Adam Gilchrist smashed a window with a six.

England

*A. J. Strauss lbw b Welagedara	4	– lbw b Welagedara	0
A. N. Cook c Maharoof b Fernando	96	– st H. A. P. W. Jayawardene b Herath	106
I. J. L. Trott lbw b Lakmal	2	– b Herath	58
K. P. Pietersen c Dilshan b Lakmal	2	– b Herath	72
I. R. Bell c Paranavitana b Welagedara	52	– not out	57
E. J. G. Morgan lbw b Lakmal	79	– c Lakmal b Fernando	4
†M. J. Prior b Herath	126	– run out	4
S. C. J. Broad lbw b Welagedara	54	– c H. A. P. W. Jayawardene b Fernando	3
G. P. Swann c Paranavitana b Welagedara	4		
C. T. Tremlett not out	24		
S. T. Finn b Herath	19		
B 3, l-b 7, w 4, n-b 10	24	L-b 12, w 1, n-b 18	31
(112.5 overs)	486	(7 wkts dec, 78.1 overs)	335

1/5 (1) 2/18 (3) 3/22 (4) 4/130 (5) 5/201 (2)   1/0 (1) 2/117 (3) 3/244 (4) 4/305 (2)
6/302 (6) 7/410 (8) 8/414 (9) 9/452 (7) 10/486 (11)   5/312 (6) 6/319 (7) 7/335 (8)

Welagedara 28–4–122–4; Lakmal 25–2–126–3; Maharoof 17–5–57–0; Fernando 17–2–77–1; Herath 18.5–1–64–2; Dilshan 7–1–30–0. *Second Innings*—Welagedara 10–1–50–1; Lakmal 17–0–70–0; Maharoof 7–0–24–0; Fernando 20.1–2–92–2; Herath 24–2–87–3.

Sri Lanka

N. T. Paranavitana c Strauss b Finn	65	– lbw b Trott	44
*T. M. Dilshan b Finn	193		
K. C. Sangakkara c Prior b Tremlett	26	– (2) c Morgan b Tremlett	12
D. P. M. D. Jayawardene c Cook b Finn	49	– (3) c Pietersen b Broad	25
T. T. Samaraweera c Prior b Tremlett	9	– (4) not out	17
†H. A. P. W. Jayawardene c Swann b Finn	40	– (5) not out	12
M. F. Maharoof lbw b Broad	2		
H. M. R. K. B. Herath st Prior b Swann	26		
C. R. D. Fernando c Strauss b Swann	5		
R. A. S. Lakmal not out	0		
U. W. M. B. C. A. Welagedara c Broad b Swann	6		
B 25, l-b 23, w 8, n-b 2	58	B 7, l b 3, w 6, n-b 1	17
(131.4 overs)	479	(3 wkts, 43 overs)	127

1/207 (1) 2/288 (3) 3/370 (2) 4/394 (4) 5/394 (5)   1/13 (2) 2/66 (3) 3/96 (1)
6/409 (7) 7/466 (8) 8/472 (6) 9/472 (9) 10/479 (11)

Broad 32–5–125–1; Tremlett 30–8–85–2; Finn 33–8–108–4; Swann 32.4–5–101–3; Pietersen 4–0–12–0. *Second Innings*—Tremlett 9–1–31–1; Broad 9–2–29–1; Finn 8–2–31–0; Trott 4–1–5–1; Pietersen 1–0–2–0.

Umpires: B. R. Doctrove *(West Indies)* (33) and R. J. Tucker *(Australia)* (9).
Third umpire: Aleem Dar *(Pakistan)*. Referee: J. Srinath *(India)* (17).

Close of play: First day, England 342–6 (Prior 73, Broad 17); Second day, Sri Lanka 231–1 (Dilshan 127, Sangakkara 13); Third day, Sri Lanka 372–3 (D. P. M. D. Jayawardene 40, Samaraweera 1); Fourth day, England 149–2 (Cook 61, Pietersen 15).

ENGLAND v SRI LANKA 2011 (3rd Test)

At The Rose Bowl, Southampton, on 16, 17, 18, 19, 20 June, 2011.
Toss: England.   Result: MATCH DRAWN.
Debuts: Sri Lanka – H. D. R. L. Thirimanne.
Man of the Match: C. T. Tremlett. Men of the Series: C. T. Tremlett and H. A. P. W. Jayawardene.

Heavy showers strafed the first-ever Test on the South Coast (the Rose Bowl became the 105th ground to stage one), delaying the start and hastening the end. In between, a greenish pitch combined the true bounce of Perth with the lateral movement of Nottingham, a mixture that proved perfect for Tremlett, born and bred in Hampshire. He took a Test-best six for 48 as Sri Lanka were hustled out for 184, then sat back as England eased to a lead of nearly 200. Cook, in his 66th successive Test (beating the national record previously shared by Alan Knott and Ian Botham), became only the fourth to reach 50 in six successive innings for England, then Bell extended his fifth fifty in a row into his 14th Test century. It gave him 1,066 runs in his last 12 Tests, at an average of 106.60, the longest period over which any England batsman had averaged more than 100. Strauss, by contrast, managed only 27 runs in the series at 6.75. His declaration came just before tea on the fourth day, but hopes of a 2–0 series victory were dashed by more rain – and by Sangakkara, reluctantly restored to the captaincy by Dilshan's injury. His 17 previous Test innings in England had not produced a century, but he put that right with an attractive 119: his stand of 141 with Samaraweera had saved the game even before the final showers swept in at tea. In all, 184 overs were lost to the weather.

Sri Lanka

N. T. Paranavitana lbw b Tremlett	11	– c Swann b Anderson	10
H. D. R. L. Thirimanne c Strauss b Anderson	10	– c Strauss b Tremlett	38
*K. C. Sangakkara c Prior b Anderson	2	– c sub (A. P. Rouse) b Anderson	119
D. P. M. D. Jayawardene c Prior b Tremlett	4	– c Prior b Broad	6
T. T. Samaraweera c Pietersen b Tremlett	31	– (6) not out	87
†H. A. P. W. Jayawardene c Morgan b Swann	43	– (7) not out	6
N. L. T. C. Perera c Prior b Tremlett	2		
H. M. R. K. B. Herath c Anderson b Tremlett	12	– (5) lbw b Swann	36
C. R. D. Fernando not out	39		
R. A. S. Lakmal c Prior b Tremlett	0		
U. W. M. B. C. A. Welagedara c Morgan b Broad	7		
B 2, l-b 15, w 4, n-b 2	23	B 16, l-b 9, w 1, n-b 6	32
(64.2 overs)	184	(5 wkts, 104 overs)	334

1/23 (2) 2/23 (1) 3/29 (3) 4/39 (4) 5/89 (5) 6/91 (7)
7/117 (8) 8/158 (6) 9/166 (10) 10/184 (11)

1/25 (1) 2/86 (2) 3/110 (4) 4/185 (5)
5/326 (3)

Anderson 23–7–56–2; Broad 19.2–3–51–1; Tremlett 20–5–48–6; Swann 2–0–12–1. *Second Innings*—Anderson 30–9–81–2; Tremlett 21–5–66–1; Broad 18–4–51–1; Swann 25–6–57–1; Pietersen 7–1–30–0; Trott 3–0–24–0.

England

*A. J. Strauss c Paranavitana b Welagedara	3
A. N. Cook c Samaraweera b Fernando	55
I. J. L. Trott c H. A. P. W. Jayawardene b Lakmal	4
K. P. Pietersen c H. A. P. W. Jayawardene b Perera	85
I. R. Bell not out	119
J. M. Anderson c H. A. P. W. Jayawardene b Welagedara	27
E. J. G. Morgan c H. A. P. W. Jayawardene b Lakmal	71
†M. J. Prior c D. P. M. D. Jayawardene b Perera	0
S. C. J. Broad c sub (S. Randiv) b Lakmal	0
L-b 2, w 3, n-b 8	13
(8 wkts dec, 92.4 overs)	377

1/4 (1) 2/14 (3) 3/120 (2) 4/191 (4) 5/236 (6)
6/373 (7) 7/374 (8) 8/377 (9)

G. P. Swann and C. T. Tremlett did not bat.

Welagedara 24–3–90–2; Lakmal 24.2–2–99–3; Fernando 10.2–0–47–1; Perera 24–3–101–2; Herath 9–0–33–0; D. P. M. D. Jayawardene 1–0–5–0.

Umpires: Aleem Dar *(Pakistan)* (65) and R. J. Tucker *(Australia)* (10).
Third umpire: B. R. Doctrove *(West Indies)*. Referee: A. G. Hurst *(Australia)* (45).

Close of play: First day, Sri Lanka 81–4 (Samaraweera 24, H. A. P. W. Jayawardene 10); Second day, Sri Lanka 177–9 (Fernando 33, Welagedara 7); Third day, England 195–4 (Bell 39, Anderson 0); Fourth day, Sri Lanka 112–3 (Sangakkara 44, Herath 2).

WEST INDIES v INDIA 2011 (1st Test)

At Sabina Park, Kingston, Jamaica, on 20, 21, 22, 23 June, 2011.
Toss: India.   Result: INDIA WON BY 63 RUNS.
Debuts: India – V. Kohli, P. Kumar, A. Mukund.
Man of the Match: R. Dravid.

India's response to potential trouble in each innings proved the difference in a low-scoring match on a pitch offering pace and bounce. Shortly after lunch on the first day they were 85 for six, but Raina and Harbhajan counter-attacked to add 146 in 28 overs. They mauled Bishoo, whose leg-spin had accounted for Laxman (with his first delivery), Dravid and Dhoni in his first 20 balls: he finished with three for 75 from 11 overs. Second time round, India were guided by Dravid, whose 32nd Test century was the basis of only their fifth win in 43 matches in the West Indies. He was, however, badly missed at second slip by Sammy off Rampaul when only six. He glided calmly on, and eclipsed Sunil Gavaskar (1,404) as the leading visiting run-scorer in the Caribbean. West Indies' batsmen under-performed, only Barath making a half-century: but for the last two wickets adding 74 when all was virtually lost, the margin would have been much wider. India were without Tendulkar (allowed to rest before the forthcoming England tour), and regular openers Gambhir and Sehwag (both with shoulder injuries). Instead they picked three debutants for the first time since 2001–02 (Sanjay Bangar, Iqbal Siddiqui and Tinu Yohannan, against England at Mohali). One of them, Praveen Kumar, was banned from bowling in the first innings by umpire Harper for running down the pitch: after the match Dhoni was critical of this decision, and several others, causing Harper to withdraw from the Second Test and retire.

India

A. Mukund b Rampaul	11	– c Baugh b Bishoo	25
M. Vijay c Bishoo b Rampaul	8	– lbw b Rampaul	0
R. Dravid c Sammy b Bishoo	40	– c Sarwan b Bishoo	112
V. V. S. Laxman c Sammy b Bishoo	12	– c and b Sammy	0
V. Kohli c Baugh b Edwards	4	– c Baugh b Edwards	15
S. K. Raina c Bishoo b Rampaul	82	– c Sammy b Bishoo	27
*†M. S. Dhoni c Simmons b Bishoo	0	– c Edwards b Bishoo	16
Harbhajan Singh c Bishoo b Edwards	70	– lbw b Sammy	5
P. Kumar lbw b Edwards	4	– b Sammy	0
A. Mishra c Sarwan b Edwards	6	– c Bravo b Sammy	28
I. Sharma not out	0	– not out	5
B 1, l-b 2, n-b 6	9	B 8, l-b 2, n-b 9	19
(61.2 overs)	246	(94.5 overs)	252

1/15 (2) 2/30 (1) 3/64 (4) 4/69 (5) 5/83 (3) 6/85 (7)
7/231 (8) 8/236 (9) 9/246 (10) 10/246 (6)

1/0 (2) 2/56 (1) 3/57 (4) 4/100 (5) 5/148 (6)
6/166 (7) 7/183 (8) 8/183 (9) 9/239 (10) 10/252 (3)

Edwards 16–1–56–4; Rampaul 18.2–2–59–3; Sammy 13–3–42–0; Bishoo 11–2–75–3; Simmons 2–0–8–0; Nash 1–0–3–0. *Second Innings*—Edwards 20–1–70–1; Rampaul 22–3–49–1; Sammy 27–11–52–4; Bishoo 24.5–2–65–4; Nash 1–0–6–0.

West Indies

A. B. Barath c Dhoni b Kumar	64	– c Raina b Kumar	38
L. M. P. Simmons c Vijay b Sharma	3	– b Sharma	27
R. R. Sarwan lbw b Sharma	3	– c Kohli b Sharma	0
D. M. Bravo c Dhoni b Kumar	18	– b Kumar	41
S. Chanderpaul c Mukund b Harbhajan Singh	23	– c Raina b Kumar	30
B. P. Nash c Raina b Kumar	1	– lbw b Mishra	9
†C. S. Baugh c Vijay b Harbhajan Singh	27	– c Kohli b Harbhajan Singh	0
*D. J. G. Sammy b Sharma	1	– c Laxman b Mishra	25
R. Rampaul not out	14	– c Dhoni b Sharma	34
F. H. Edwards c Dhoni b Mishra	7	– not out	15
D. Bishoo c Raina b Mishra	4	– b Raina	26
B 1, l-b 3, n-b 4	8	B 1, l-b 13, w 2, n-b 1	17
(67.5 overs)	173	(68.2 overs)	262

1/18 (2) 2/35 (3) 3/91 (1) 4/95 (4) 5/102 (6)
6/147 (7) 7/148 (8) 8/152 (5) 9/169 (10) 10/173 (11)

1/62 (1) 2/63 (3) 3/80 (2) 4/148 (4) 5/149 (5)
6/150 (7) 7/181 (8) 8/188 (6) 9/223 (9) 10/262 (11)

Kumar 18–5–38–3; Sharma 17–6–29–3; Mishra 13.5–1–51–2; Harbhajan Singh 19–5–53–2. *Second Innings*—Kumar 16–3–42–3; Sharma 17–3–81–3; Mishra 13–1–62–2; Harbhajan Singh 16–3–54–1; Raina 6.2–1–9–1.

Umpires: I. J. Gould *(England)* (19) and D. J. Harper *(Australia)* (95).
Third umpire: N. A. Malcolm *(West Indies)*. Referee: J. J. Crowe *(New Zealand)* (46).

Close of play: First day, West Indies 34–1 (Barath 26, Sarwan 2); Second day, India 91–3 (Dravid 45, Kohli 14); Third day, West Indies 131–3 (Bravo 30, Chanderpaul 24).

WEST INDIES v INDIA 2011 (2nd Test)

At Kensington Oval, Bridgetown, Barbados, on 28, 39, 30 June, 1, 2 July, 2011.
Toss: West Indies.   Result: MATCH DRAWN.
Debuts: none.
Man of the Match: I. Sharma.

Unseasonal rain robbed the game of the equivalent of more than four sessions and denied India a likely victory following Dhoni's challenging last-day declaration. Set 280 in 77 overs, West Indies had reached 202 for seven in 71.3 before, amid increasing tension and with the light fading, India settled for the draw that preserved their series lead. Seamers claimed 28 of the 33 wickets to fall on a lively pitch – 20 of them to catches in the cordon. India, sent in, were quickly reduced to 38 for four as Rampaul reached lunch with figures of 8–5–4–3, before a restorative stand of 117. But Raina fell to a disputed bat-pad catch (he was later fined for dissent), then Laxman slapped a leg-break to point the over after becoming the fourth Indian to reach 8,000 Test runs. India's 201 was below par, but their seamers redressed the balance: Sharma took six for 55, and went on to complete India's first ten-for in the West Indies. On a rain-hit second day limited to 25.3 overs, Chanderpaul (who hit only one of his 117 balls for four) and Samuels checked the decline in their contrasting styles. But India then took control, despite Edwards swinging the ball at pace for five wickets. Laxman again dropped anchor for more than four hours, eventually becoming the tenth batsman to be dismissed twice in the eighties in the same Test (and only the second Indian, after Rusi Modi against West Indies at Calcutta in 1948–49).

India

A. Mukund c Samuels b Rampaul	1	– c Baugh b Edwards	48
M. Vijay c Baugh b Rampaul	11	– c Baugh b Rampaul	3
R. Dravid c Baugh b Sammy	5	– c Sarwan b Edwards	55
V. V. S. Laxman c Barath b Bishoo	85	– c Sammy b Edwards	87
V. Kohli c Sammy b Rampaul	0	– c Sammy b Edwards	27
S. K. Raina c Barath b Bishoo	53	– not out	12
*†M. S. Dhoni c Chanderpaul b Edwards	2	– c Chanderpaul b Edwards	5
Harbhajan Singh c Barath b Edwards	5	– not out	6
P. Kumar st Baugh b Bishoo	12		
A. Mithun b Edwards	0		
I. Sharma not out	1		
B 5, l-b 4, w 11, n-b 6	26	B 4, l-b 9, w 5, n-b 8	26
(68 overs)	201	(6 wkts dec, 102 overs)	269

1/1 (1) 2/8 (3) 3/38 (2) 4/38 (5) 5/155 (6) 6/167 (7) 1/26 (2) 2/89 (1) 3/154 (3) 4/232 (5) 5/247 (4)
7/183 (8) 8/187 (4) 9/189 (10) 10/201 (9) 6/253 (7)

Edwards 19–2–56–3; Rampaul 16–6–38–3; Sammy 19–4–52–1; Bishoo 14–1–46–3. *Second Innings*—Edwards 23–4–76–5; Rampaul 28–6–72–1; Sammy 24–8–45–0; Bishoo 27–4–63–0.

West Indies

A. B. Barath c Kohli b Sharma	3	– c Raina b Sharma	27
L. M. P. Simmons c Dhoni b Kumar	2	– c Dravid b Sharma	14
R. R. Sarwan lbw b Sharma	18	– c Raina b Kumar	8
D. M. Bravo c Dhoni b Mithun	9	– c Dhoni b Mithun	73
D. Bishoo c Kohli b Sharma	13		
S. Chanderpaul b Mithun	37	– (5) lbw b Harbhajan Singh	12
M. N. Samuels not out	78	– (6) lbw b Sharma	9
†C. S. Baugh c Dravid b Harbhajan Singh	2	– (7) not out	46
*D. J. G. Sammy lbw b Sharma	15	– (8) lbw b Sharma	0
R. Rampaul c Vijay b Sharma	0	– (9) not out	0
F. H. Edwards c Dhoni b Sharma	0		
L-b 3, w 5, n-b 5	13	B 5, l-b 6, n-b 2	13
(73.5 overs)	190	(7 wkts, 71.3 overs)	202

1/3 (1) 2/5 (2) 3/30 (4) 4/53 (5) 5/57 (3) 6/134 (6) 1/18 (2) 2/27 (3) 3/55 (1) 4/109 (5) 5/132 (6)
7/143 (8) 8/186 (9) 9/190 (10) 10/190 (11) 6/201 (4) 7/202 (8)

Kumar 23–3–67–1; Sharma 21.5–7–55–6; Mithun 15–6–34–2; Harbhajan Singh 14–3–31–1. *Second Innings*— Kumar 16–6–41–1; Sharma 19.3–4–53–4; Mithun 13–3–50–1; Harbhajan Singh 19–2–42–1; Raina 4–1–5–0.

Umpires: Asad Rauf *(Pakistan)* (36) and I. J. Gould *(England)* (20).
Third umpire: G. O. Brathwaite *(West Indies)*. Referee: B. C. Broad *(England)* (43).

Close of play: First day, West Indies 30–3 (Sarwan 10, Bishoo 0); Second day, West Indies 98–5 (Chanderpaul 20, Samuels 21); Third day, India 23–0 (Mukund 8, Vijay 3); Fourth day, India 229–3 (Laxman 72, Kohli 26).

WEST INDIES v INDIA 2011 (3rd Test)

At Windsor Park, Roseau, Dominica, on 6, 7, 8, 9, 10 July, 2011.
Toss: India.   Result: MATCH DRAWN.
Debuts: West Indies – K. A. Edwards, K. O. A. Powell.
Man of the Match: S. Chanderpaul. Man of the Series: I. Sharma

Dhoni called off India's run-chase when, with only 86 needed from 15 overs and seven wickets left, he settled for the series win which maintained his side's position atop the rankings ahead of their tour of England. Hearteningly, the last day was watched by a crowd of around 11,000 in the tiny Dominican capital, at the 106th ground to host a Test. After rain limited the first day to 31.1 overs, Sharma added five wickets to his ten at Bridgetown, and West Indies only scraped past 200 thanks to Bravo's careful 50 and a gutsy 60 from Baugh, who then provided Harbhajan with his 400th Test wicket: he was the third Indian – and the 11th overall – to get there. India started slowly against some tight bowling, but eventually Raina and Dhoni broke free. Laxman had fallen after 3½ hours, slickly stumped by Baugh as he momentarily lifted his heel: it was Chanderpaul's first wicket for almost nine years, in his West Indian-record 133rd Test. West Indies' batting stuttered again, before a rearguard from Kirk Edwards, who became the 13th West Indian to score a debut century, and Chanderpaul – dropped by Dravid when 25 – who survived 343 minutes over 501 minutes for his 23rd. Still, the lead was only 113 when No. 10 Fidel Edwards joined Chanderpaul on the final morning. But they lasted more than 2½ hours, and 222 balls. Even so, India's eventual target of 180 from 47 overs did not seem beyond a team stuffed with IPL players.

West Indies

A. B. Barath b Sharma	12	– c Kohli b Kumar		6
K. O. A. Powell c Laxman b Kumar	3	– c Raina b Sharma		4
K. A. Edwards c Dhoni b Sharma	6	– c Dhoni b Harbhajan Singh		110
D. M. Bravo c Dhoni b Sharma	50	– c Kumar b Harbhajan Singh		14
S. Chanderpaul c Dhoni b Patel	23	– not out		116
M. N. Samuels b Kumar	9	– lbw b Harbhajan Singh		0
†C. S. Baugh b Harbhajan Singh	60	– c Mukund b Kumar		10
*D. J. G. Sammy c Mukund b Harbhajan Singh	20	– c Mukund b Harbhajan Singh		17
F. H. Edwards b Sharma	3	– (10) c Kumar b Raina		30
R. Rampaul not out	0	– (9) run out		1
D. Bishoo b Sharma	0	– c Dravid b Raina		1
B 8, l-b 10	18	B 8, l-b 2, w 1, n-b 2		13
(76.3 overs)	204	(131.3 overs)		322

1/17 (2) 2/24 (1) 3/35 (3) 4/84 (5) 5/99 (6) 6/158 (4)
7/199 (8) 8/200 (7) 9/204 (9) 10/204 (11)

1/8 (2) 2/10 (1) 3/40 (4) 4/201 (3) 5/201 (6) 6/223 (7)
7/255 (8) 8/256 (9) 9/321 (10) 10/322 (11)

Kumar 16–7–22–2; Sharma 21.3–4–77–5; Patel 20–7–48–1; Harbhajan Singh 15–7–26–2; Raina 4–1–13–0. *Second Innings*—Kumar 21–6–44–2; Sharma 27–5–76–1; Patel 24–5–71–0; Harbhajan Singh 42–14–75–4; Raina 15.3–2–32–2; Mukund 2–0–14–0.

India

A. Mukund c Barath b Bishoo	62	– lbw b F. H. Edwards		0
M. Vijay c Baugh b F. H. Edwards	5	– c Bishoo b Rampaul		45
R. Dravid b Sammy	5	– not out		34
V. V. S. Laxman st Baugh b Chanderpaul	56	– (5) not out		3
V. Kohli c Baugh b Sammy	30			
S. K. Raina lbw b F. H. Edwards	50	– (4) c and b Rampaul		8
*†M. S. Dhoni c Bishoo b F. H. Edwards	74			
Harbhajan Singh c Baugh b F. H. Edwards	12			
P. Kumar c Samuels b Bishoo	23			
I. Sharma c Barath b F. H. Edwards	2			
M. M. Patel not out	4			
B 8, l-b 3, w 3, n-b 10	24	L-b 1, n b 3		4
(108.2 overs)	347	(3 wkts, 32 overs)		94

1/13 (2) 2/18 (3) 3/116 (1) 4/168 (5) 5/172 (4) 6/275 (6)
7/308 (8) 8/339 (7) 9/343 (9) 10/347 (10)

1/0 (1) 2/73 (2) 3/86 (4)

F. H. Edwards 28.2–3–103–5; Sammy 28–7–51–2; Bishoo 38–2–125–2; K. A. Edwards 4–0–19–0; Chanderpaul 10–0–38–1. *Second Innings*—F. H. Edwards 8–1–19–1; Rampaul 11–2–31–2; Sammy 5–0–26–0; Bishoo 8–1–17–0.

Umpires: Asad Rauf *(Pakistan)* (37) and R. A. Kettleborough *(England)* (3).
Third umpire: J. S. Wilson *(West Indies)*. Referee: B. C. Broad *(England)* (44).

Close of play: First day, West Indies 75–3 (Bravo 22, Chanderpaul 17); Second day, India 8–0 (Mukund 6, Vijay 1); Third day, India 308–6 (Dhoni 65, Harbhajan Singh 12); Fourth day, West Indies 224–6 (Chanderpaul 73, Sammy 1).

ENGLAND v INDIA 2011 (1st Test)

At Lord's, London, 21, 22, 23, 24, 25 July, 2011.
Toss: India.   Result: ENGLAND WON BY 196 RUNS.
Debuts: none.
Man of the Match: K. P. Pietersen.

This was the 2,000th Test match, and England's 100th against India. But an even more magical number never happened: Tendulkar went into the game with 99 international centuries, and left with his highest score from five Lord's Tests still only 37. England dominated after a hesitant start, and closed in on another important figure: India's No. 1 Test ranking. And they did so in front of a last-day crowd of 27,728 – perhaps the most vivid number of the lot. On an overcast first morning, Zaheer Khan started with 7–3–9–1, then reeled off four maidens after lunch. Soon, though, he tweaked his right hamstring, and limped off – and out of the series. The release of tension was palpable: Pietersen rolled on to a double-century after being reprieved when given out caught behind during a rare spell from Dhoni, the first designated wicketkeeper to bowl in a Test at Lord's. Dravid stood almost alone for India, batting beautifully for his 33rd Test century. England collapsed to 62 for five on the fourth morning, as Sharma refound his fire, but a superb century from Prior, who added 162 with Broad, took them to an unassailable lead. India, with Gambhir hit while fielding and Tendulkar suffering from a virus, were always up against it. Laxman made a classy half-century, then Raina survived past tea on the final day – but fell to the new ball as the last four wickets tumbled in 29 balls. England won with nearly 30 overs to spare.

England

*A. J. Strauss c Sharma b Zaheer Khan	22	– lbw b Harbhajan Singh	32
A. N. Cook lbw b Zaheer Khan	12	– c Dhoni b Kumar	1
I. J. L. Trott lbw b Kumar	70	– b Sharma	22
K. P. Pietersen not out	202	– c Dhoni b Sharma	1
I. R. Bell c Dhoni b Kumar	45	– c Dhoni b Sharma	0
E. J. G. Morgan c Dhoni b Kumar	0	– c Gambhir b Sharma	19
†M. J. Prior c Dhoni b Kumar	71	– not out	103
S. C. J. Broad lbw b Kumar	0	– not out	74
G. P. Swann b Raina	24		
C. T. Tremlett not out	4		
B 14, l-b 8, w 1, n-b 1	24	B 7, l-b 8, w 2	17
(8 wkts dec, 131.4 overs)	474	(6 wkts dec, 71 overs)	269

1/19 (2) 2/62 (1) 3/160 (3) 4/270 (5) 5/270 (6)
6/390 (7) 7/390 (8) 8/451 (9)

1/23 (2) 2/54 (1) 3/55 (4) 4/55 (5)
5/62 (3) 6/107 (6)

J. M. Anderson did not bat.

Zaheer Khan 13.3–8–18–2; Kumar 40.3–10–106–5; Sharma 32–5–128–0; Harbhajan Singh 35–3–152–0; Dhoni 8–1–23–0; Raina 2.4–1–25–1. *Second Innings*—Kumar 20–2–70–1; Sharma 22–6–59–4; Harbhajan Singh 21–1–66–1; Raina 6–1–43–0; Dhoni 2–0–16–0.

India

A. Mukund b Broad	49	– b Broad	12
G. Gambhir b Broad	15	– (4) lbw b Swann	22
R. Dravid not out	103	– (2) c Prior b Anderson	36
S. R. Tendulkar c Swann b Broad	34	– (5) lbw b Anderson	12
V. V. S. Laxman c Trott b Tremlett	10	– (3) c Bell b Anderson	56
S. K. Raina lbw b Swann	0	– c Prior b Anderson	78
*†M. S. Dhoni c Swann b Tremlett	28	– c Prior b Tremlett	16
Harbhajan Singh c Prior b Tremlett	0	– c Tremlett b Anderson	12
P. Kumar c Strauss b Broad	17	– b Broad	2
Zaheer Khan b Anderson	0	– not out	0
I. Sharma c Prior b Anderson	0	– lbw b Broad	1
B 5, l-b 12, w 1, n-b 12	30	B 2, l-b 6, n-b 6	14
(95.5 overs)	286	(96.3 overs)	261

1/63 (2) 2/77 (1) 3/158 (4) 4/182 (5) 5/183 (6)
6/240 (7) 7/241 (8) 8/276 (9) 9/284 (10) 10/286 (11)

1/19 (1) 2/94 (2) 3/131 (3) 4/135 (4) 5/165 (5)
6/225 (7) 7/243 (8) 8/256 (9) 9/260 (6) 10/261 (11)

Anderson 23.5–6–87–2; Tremlett 24–5–80–3; Broad 22–8–37–4; Trott 6–1–12–0; Swann 19–3–50–1; Pietersen 1–0–3–0. *Second Innings*—Anderson 28–7–65–5; Tremlett 21–4–44–1; Broad 20.3–4–57–3; Swann 22–3–64–1; Trott 2–0–11–0; Pietersen 3–0–12–0.

Umpires: Asad Rauf *(Pakistan)* (38) and B. F. Bowden *(New Zealand)* (68).
Third umpire: M. Erasmus *(South Africa)*. Referee: R. S. Madugalle *(Sri Lanka)* (125).

Close of play: First day, England 127–2 (Trott 58, Pietersen 22); Second day, India 17–0 (Mukund 8, Gambhir 7); Third day, England 5–0 (Strauss 3, Cook 0); Fourth day, India 80–1 (Dravid 34, Laxman 32).

ENGLAND v INDIA 2011 (2nd Test)

At Trent Bridge, Nottingham, on 29, 20, 31 July, 1 August, 2011.
Toss: India.   Result: ENGLAND WON BY 319 RUNS.
Debuts: none.
Man of the Match: S. C. J. Broad.

England came out on top in a topsy-turvy match, by virtue of a massive third innings after conceding a deficit of 67. Victory had looked unlikely at first as they slipped to 124 for eight against some fine seam bowling, but Broad conjured 97 from the last two wickets. Dravid, pressed into service as an opener, made another studious century, and was ninth out. He had passed Ricky Ponting's run aggregate at Lord's, and when he was briefly joined by Tendulkar it was the first time Test cricket's two leading scorers had batted together since 1911–12 (Clem Hill and Victor Trumper of Australia). India looked set for a big lead at 267 for four, but Broad, who had been part of Peter Siddle's hat-trick at Brisbane the previous November, now took one himself to limit the advantage. Pushed up to No. 3 as Trott had hurt his shoulder, Bell continued the fightback during successive hundred partnerships. However, he was run out from the last ball before tea on the third day, after walking off with 137, believing the ball was dead. Dhoni sportingly revoked the appeal, and Bell resumed after the break, to widespread applause all round. Prior and Bresnan (with his highest Test score) swelled the total to 544. India were quickly up against it; Yuvraj had his finger broken just before he was out, and Dhoni shouldered arms to his first ball. Soon it was 55 for six, and only Tendulkar's tenacious 56 held England up for long.

England

*A. J. Strauss c Raina b Kumar	32	– c Dhoni b Sreesanth	16
A. N. Cook lbw b Sharma	2	– c Yuvraj Singh b Sharma	5
I. J. L. Trott c Laxman b Sreesanth	4	– (7) c Dravid b Kumar	2
K. P. Pietersen c Raina b Sreesanth	29	– c Dhoni b Sreesanth	63
I. R. Bell c Dhoni b Sharma	31	– (3) c Laxman b Yuvraj Singh	159
E. J. G. Morgan lbw b Kumar	0	– (5) c Dhoni b Kumar	70
†M. J. Prior c Dravid b Sreesanth	1	– (6) c Dhoni b Kumar	73
T. T. Bresnan c Dravid b Sharma	11	– c Dravid b Kumar	90
S. C. J. Broad c Tendulkar b Harbhajan Singh	64	– run out	44
G. P. Swann c Mukund b Kumar	28	– c sub (W. P. Saha) b Sharma	3
J. M. Anderson not out	6	– not out	1
B 2, l-b 8, w 3	13	B 9, l-b 5, w 2, n-b 2	18
(68.4 overs)	221	(120.2 overs)	544

1/7 (2) 2/23 (3) 3/73 (4) 4/85 (1) 5/85 (6) 6/88 (7)   1/6 (2) 2/57 (1) 3/219 (4) 4/323 (3) 5/329 (5)
7/117 (8) 8/124 (5) 9/197 (10) 10/221 (9)   6/339 (7) 7/458 (6) 8/540 (9) 9/540 (8) 10/544 (10)

Kumar 22–8–45–3; Sharma 22–4–66–3; Sreesanth 19–1–77–3; Harbhajan Singh 4.4–0–22–1; Yuvraj Singh 1–0–1–0. *Second Innings*—Kumar 36–5–124–4; Sharma 29.2–4–131–2; Sreesanth 27–5–135–2; Yuvraj Singh 11–0–51–1; Harbhajan Singh 9–1–47–0; Raina 8–0–42–0.

India

A. Mukund c Pietersen b Anderson	0	– c Strauss b Bresnan	3
R. Dravid c Cook b Bresnan	117	– c Prior b Broad	6
V. V. S. Laxman c Prior b Bresnan	54	– b Anderson	4
S. R. Tendulkar c Strauss b Broad	16	– lbw b Anderson	56
S. K. Raina c Morgan b Anderson	12	– c sub (S. L. Elstone) b Bresnan	1
Yuvraj Singh c Prior b Broad	62	– c Cook b Bresnan	8
*†M. S. Dhoni c Anderson b Broad	5	– lbw b Bresnan	0
Harbhajan Singh lbw b Broad	0	– c sub (S. L. Elstone) b Bresnan	46
P. Kumar b Broad	0	– b Anderson	25
I. Sharma c Bell b Broad	3	– not out	8
S. Sreesanth not out	7	– b Broad	0
B 4, l b 3, w 4, n b 1	12	B 1	1
(91.1 overs)	288	(47.4 overs)	158

1/0 (1) 2/93 (3) 3/119 (4) 4/139 (5) 5/267 (6) 6/273 (7)   1/6 (2) 2/13 (3) 3/31 (1) 4/37 (5) 5/55 (6) 6/55 (7)
7/273 (8) 8/273 (9) 9/273 (2) 10/288 (10)   7/107 (4) 8/129 (8) 9/153 (9) 10/158 (11)

Anderson 26–8–80–2; Broad 24.1–8–46–6; Bresnan 21–6–48–2; Trott 4–1–18–0; Swann 12–0–76–0; Pietersen 4–0–13–0. *Second Innings*—Anderson 17–3–51–3; Broad 14.4–5–30–2; Bresnan 12–2–48–5; Swann 3–0–21–0; Pietersen 1–0–7–0.

Umpires: Asad Rauf *(Pakistan)* (39) and M. Erasmus *(South Africa)* (6).
Third umpire: B. F. Bowden *(New Zealand)*. Referee: R. S. Madugalle *(Sri Lanka)* (126).

Close of play: First day, India 24–1 (Dravid 7, Laxman 13); Second day, England 24–1 (Strauss 6, Bell 9); Third day, England 441–6 (Prior 64, Bresnan 47).

ENGLAND v INDIA 2011 (3rd Test)

At Edgbaston, Birmingham, on 10, 11, 12, 13 August, 2011.
Toss: England.   Result: ENGLAND WON BY AN INNINGS AND 242 RUNS.
Debuts: none.
Man of the Match: A. N. Cook.

England displaced India at the top of the Test rankings after overwhelming them in Birmingham, where recent unrest made for a tense start to the match. India were soon in trouble again, with Sehwag – rushed back into the side after shoulder surgery despite looking unfit – completing the first half of a king pair. England's seamers made the most of the pitch, the overcast sky, and the doubts in the minds of India's despairing batsmen. Broad and Bresnan made the initial inroads, and finished with four wickets apiece. Dhoni organised a something of a recovery from 111 for seven, but India's total was dwarfed by England's marathon effort. Cook, who had scored only 20 runs in four previous knocks in this series, settled in for 773 minutes and 545 balls, hitting 33 fours in England's sixth-highest individual innings. It was his 19th Test hundred, and his second double. Several substantial partnerships included one of 222 with Morgan, who was dropped twice en route to his second Test century. When Cook finally fell, Strauss declared with England's third-highest total, and their third-largest lead. It was clearly going to be enough after Sehwag fell first ball again, Dravid was given out caught after the ball flicked the metal aglet on his bootlace, and Tendulkar was stranded when bowler Swann finger-tipped Dhoni's straight-drive into the stumps. Dhoni made partial amends with another fighting seventy, but India were sunk before tea on the fourth day. England had enjoyed only four larger innings victories in Tests.

India

G. Gambhir b Bresnan	38 – c Swann b Anderson	14
V. Sehwag c Prior b Broad	0 – c Strauss b Anderson	0
R. Dravid b Bresnan	22 – c Prior b Anderson	18
S. R. Tendulkar c Anderson b Broad	1 – run out	40
V. V. S. Laxman c Broad b Bresnan	30 – c Prior b Anderson	2
S. K. Raina b Anderson	4 – lbw b Swann	10
*†M. S. Dhoni c Strauss b Broad	77 – not out	74
A. Mishra c Prior b Broad	4 – c Broad b Swann	22
P. Kumar c Prior b Bresnan	26 – c Bopara b Broad	40
I. Sharma c Cook b Anderson	4 – lbw b Broad	0
S. Sreesanth not out	0 – c Pietersen b Bresnan	5
B 4, l-b 14	18	B 6, l-b 6, w 7	19
(62.2 overs)	224	(55.3 overs)	244

1/8 (2) 2/59 (1) 3/60 (4) 4/75 (3) 5/92 (6) 6/100 (5)
7/111 (8) 8/195 (9) 9/224 (7) 10/224 (10)

1/3 (2) 2/35 (1) 3/40 (3) 4/56 (5) 5/87 (6) 6/89 (4)
7/130 (8) 8/205 (9) 9/221 (10) 10/244 (11)

Anderson 21.2–3–69–2; Broad 17–6–53–4; Bresnan 20–4–62–4; Swann 4–0–22–0. *Second Innings*—Anderson 18–3–85–4; Broad 12–4–28–2; Bresnan 10.3–3–19–1; Swann 13–1–88–2; Pietersen 2–0–12–0.

England

*A. J. Strauss b Mishra	87
A. N. Cook c Raina b Sharma	294
I. R. Bell b Kumar	34
K. P. Pietersen lbw b Kumar	63
E. J. G. Morgan c Sehwag b Raina	104
R. S. Bopara lbw b Mishra	7
†M. J. Prior c Tendulkar b Mishra	5
T. T. Bresnan not out	53
B 11, l-b 34, w 3, n-b 15	63
(7 wkts dec, 188.1 overs)	710

1/186 (1) 2/252 (3) 3/374 (4) 4/596 (5) 5/605 (6)
6/613 (7) 7/710 (2)

S. C. J. Broad, G. P. Swann and J. M. Anderson did not bat.

Kumar 40–13–98–2; Sreesanth 36–4–158–0; Sharma 37.1–7–159–1; Mishra 43–2–150–3; Raina 28–1–83–1; Tendulkar 4–0–17–0.

Umpires: S. J. Davis *(Australia)* (32) and S. J. A. Taufel *(Australia)* (68).
Third umpire: R. J. Tucker *(Australia)*. Referee: R. S. Madugalle *(Sri Lanka)* (127).

Close of play: First day, England 84–0 (Strauss 52, Cook 27); Second day, England 456–3 (Cook 182, Morgan 44); Third day, India 35–1 (Gambhir 14, Dravid 18).

ENGLAND v INDIA 2011 (4th Test)

At Kennington Oval, London, on 18, 19, 20, 21, 22 August, 2011.
Toss: England.   Result: ENGLAND WON BY AN INNINGS AND EIGHT RUNS.
Debuts: none.
Man of the Match: I. R. Bell. Men of the Series: S. C. J. Broad and R. Dravid.

England completed a clean sweep against demoralised opposition; their only previous whitewashes had been against West Indies in 2004 (4–0) and India in 1959 (5–0), both much weaker teams. England again made the game safe with an imposing total. Bell piled on 350 with Pietersen, a third-wicket record for either side in these Tests. They were an intriguing study in contrasts, Bell full of back-foot elegance, Pietersen a front-foot force of nature. Bell's maiden double-century gave him 835 Test runs in the summer, exceeded for England at home only by Graham Gooch (1,058 in 1990) and Michael Vaughan (900 in 2002). Sehwag again fell in the first over, and wickets continued to tumble, Swann chipping in with three late on the third day. Dravid rolled on, completing his 35th Test century and carrying his bat, only the third instance for India after Sunil Gavaskar (v Pakistan at Faisalabad in 1982–83) and Sehwag (against Sri Lanka at Galle in July 2008). Cruelly, though, Dravid was soon batting again – and managed only 13 in the follow-on. Nightwatchman Mishra held England up on the final day, reaching a Test-best 84 and putting on 144 with Tendulkar, who threatened that elusive 100th international century before swishing across the line at 91. Raina completed a gruesome 42-ball pair, and England were almost home. It was Strauss's 44th Test win as a player, beating Colin Cowdrey's England record. For the 16th match running England did not include a debutant, another national record. The overall mark is South Africa's 21 in 2007–08.

England

*A. J. Strauss c Dhoni b Sreesanth	40
A. N. Cook c Sehwag b Sharma	34
I. R. Bell lbw b Raina	235
K. P. Pietersen c and b Raina	175
J. M. Anderson c Laxman b Sreesanth	13
E. J. G. Morgan c Dhoni b Sreesanth	1
R. S. Bopara not out	44
†M. J. Prior not out	18
B 6, l-b 8, w 7, n-b 10	31
(6 wkts dec, 153 overs)	591

1/75 (2) 2/97 (1) 3/447 (4) 4/480 (5) 5/487 (6) 6/548 (3)

T. T. Bresnan, S. C. J. Broad and G. P. Swann did not bat.

Singh 34–7–118–0; Sharma 31–7–97–1; Sreesanth 29–2–123–3; Raina 19–2–58–2; Mishra 38–3–170–0; Tendulkar 2–0–11–0.

India

V. Sehwag lbw b Anderson	8	– b Swann	33
R. Dravid not out	146	– c Cook b Swann	13
V. V. S. Laxman c Prior b Broad	2	– b Anderson	24
S. R. Tendulkar c Anderson b Swann	23	– lbw b Bresnan	91
S. K. Raina st Prior b Swann	0	– (6) lbw b Swann	0
I. Sharma c Cook b Swann	1	– (10) not out	7
*†M. S. Dhoni c Prior b Anderson	17	– c Swann b Broad	3
A. Mishra c Bell b Bresnan	43	– (5) b Swann	84
G. Gambhir c Pietersen b Broad	10	– (8) c Morgan b Swann	3
R. P. Singh c Anderson b Bresnan	25	– (9) c Prior b Broad	0
S. Sreesanth c Morgan b Bresnan	0	– b Swann	6
B 8, l-b 9, w 7, n-b 1	25	B 12, l-b 7	19
(94 overs)	300	(91 overs)	283

1/8 (1) 2/13 (3) 3/68 (4) 4/93 (5) 5/95 (6) 6/137 (7) 7/224 (8) 8/264 (9) 9/300 (10) 10/300 (11)

1/49 (2) 2/64 (1) 3/118 (3) 4/262 (5) 5/262 (4) 6/266 (6) 7/269 (7) 8/269 (9) 9/275 (8) 10/283 (11)

Anderson 16–7–49–2; Broad 21–3–51–2; Bresnan 17–3–54–3; Swann 31–5–102–3; Pietersen 7–1–27–0; Bopara 2–2–0–0. *Second Innings*—Anderson 17–4–54–1; Broad 20–6–44–2; Swann 38–6–106–6; Bresnan 11–2–30–1; Bopara 3–0–13–0; Pietersen 2–0–17–0.

Umpires: S. J. A. Taufel *(Australia)* (69) and R. J. Tucker *(Australia)* (11).
Third umpire: S. J. Davis *(Australia)*. Referee: R. S. Madugalle *(Sri Lanka)* (128).

Close of play: First day, England 75–0 (Strauss 38, Cook 34); Second day, England 457–3 (Bell 181, Anderson 3); Third day, India 103–5 (Dravid 57, Dhoni 5); Fourth day, India 129–3 (Tendulkar 35, Mishra 8).

ZIMBABWE v BANGLADESH 2011 (Only Test)

At Harare Sports Club on 4, 5, 6, 7, 8 August, 2011.
Toss: Bangladesh.   Result: ZIMBABWE WON BY 130 RUNS.
Debuts: Zimbabwe – C. R. Ervine, K. M. Jarvis, T. M. K. Mawoyo, B. V. Vitori.
Man of the Match: B. R. M. Taylor.

It was quite a comeback: nearly six years after withdrawing from Test cricket, after a series of thumping defeats, Zimbabwe returned with their ninth victory, the fifth in nine games against Bangladesh. Hardened into a team by 108 one-day internationals during the non-Test years, they showed discipline and patience with the bat (one careless collapse aside) and refreshing energy with the ball. Taylor became the seventh player – and the second Zimbabwean, after Dave Houghton – to register his maiden century in his first Test as captain, while Masakadza added a second ten years after his first. Put in on a seamer-friendly pitch, Sibanda and Mawoyo eased to a century opening stand before lunch, and Zimbabwe reached 304 for two on the second morning before imploding: Masakadza undid five hours' vigilance with a loose drive to give Robiul Islam his first Test wicket, triggering a collapse of eight wickets for 66. Yet anything Zimbabwe could do, Bangladesh could do worse: the young new-ball pairing of Brian Vitori and Kyle Jarvis was particularly impressive, and the last five wickets went down for 41. Taylor's undefeated hundred – and his partnerships with Taibu and Ervine – lifted the lead to 374, and his enterprising declaration gave his bowlers four sessions to complete victory. They needed barely two, as Bangladesh's batsmen again failed to screw their courage to the sticking place. Tamim Iqbal, after a lively start, was the first of five to be bowled, and the partying started in earnest when Jarvis trapped Robiul in front.

Zimbabwe

T. M. K. Mawoyo c Mahmudullah b Rubel Hossain....	43	– b Robiul Islam..	35
V. Sibanda c Mushfiqur Rahim b Rubel Hossain.........	78	– c sub (Nasir Hossain) b Rubel Hossain..............	38
H. Masakadza c Imrul Kayes b Robiul Islam	104	– c and b Shakib Al Hasan	5
*B. R. M. Taylor c Mushfiqur Rahim b Robiul Islam....	71	– not out	105
C. R. Ervine lbw b Mahmudullah.................................	6	– (7) not out..	35
†T. Taibu c Shahriar Nafees b Shakib Al Hasan	23	– c Robiul Islam b Shafiul Islam	59
E. Chigumbura c Shafiul Islam b Shakib Al Hasan.....	5		
R. W. Price lbw b Rubel Hossain	4	– (5) lbw b Abdur Razzak	4
K. M. Jarvis not out	4		
B. V. Vitori c Robiul Islam b Shakib Al Hasan	12		
C. B. Mpofu st Mushfiqur Rahim b Abdur Razzak	2		
B 4, l-b 11, w 1, n-b 2	18	L-b 2, w 4, n-b 4..............................	10
(131 overs)	370	(5 wkts dec, 92 overs)	291

1/102 (1) 2/162 (2) 3/304 (3) 4/317 (5) 5/317 (4)
6/326 (7) 7/344 (8) 8/352 (6) 9/368 (10) 10/370 (11)   1/69 (2) 2/79 (1) 3/83 (3) 4/92 (5) 5/205 (6)

Shafiul Islam 22–8–38–0; Robiul Islam 30–4–106–2; Rubel Hossain 29–3–84–3; Shakib Al Hasan 26–5–62–3; Abdur Razzak 22–2–57–1; Mahmudullah 2–0–8–1. *Second Innings*—Shafiul Islam 11–3–29–1; Robiul Islam 13–1–48–1; Abdur Razzak 20–5–49–1; Rubel Hossain 17–2–75–1; Mahmudullah 12–3–27–0; Shakib Al Hasan 18–4–60–1; Imrul Kayes 1–0–1–0.

Bangladesh

Tamim Iqbal c Taylor b Vitori	15	– b Mpofu...	43
Imrul Kayes c Price b Vitori.......................................	4	– c Taibu b Jarvis...	31
Shahriar Nafees b Price..	50	– b Jarvis	9
Mohammad Ashraful c Taibu b Chigumbura..............	73	– b Vitori	39
Mahmudullah c Mawoyo b Vitori	13	– (6) c Taibu b Mpofu	11
*Shakib Al Hasan c Taibu b Mpofu	68	– (7) c Taylor b Chigumbura	6
†Mushfiqur Rahim c Mawoyo b Vitori	27	– (5) c Ervine b Mpofu	28
Abdur Razzak lbw b Mpofu..	11	– b Chigumbura..	43
Shafiul Islam b Jarvis...	5	– b Jarvis	7
Rubel Hossain not out..	16	– not out	8
Robiul Islam lbw b Price..	0	– lbw b Jarvis	12
B 1, n-b 4...	5	B 4, l-b 2, n-b 1	7
(96.2 overs)	287	(57.3 overs)	244

1/13 (2) 2/36 (1) 3/102 (3) 4/136 (5) 5/190 (4)   1/65 (1) 2/87 (2) 3/102 (3) 4/140 (4) 5/167 (6)
6/246 (6) 7/258 (8) 8/266 (7) 9/275 (9) 10/287 (11)   6/174 (7) 7/174 (5) 8/224 (8) 9/228 (9) 10/244 (11)

Vitori 24–5–66–4; Jarvis 16–1–67–1; Mpofu 23–5–72–2; Chigumbura 19–4–47–1; Price 14.2–4–34–2. *Second Innings*—Vitori 14–1–56–1; Jarvis 16.3–4–61–4; Chigumbura 15–3–50–2; Mpofu 10–0–51–3; Price 2–0–20–0.

Umpires: H. D. P. K. Dharmasena *(Sri Lanka)* (3) and B. N. J. Oxenford *(Australia)* (2).
Third umpire: T. J. Matibiri *(Zimbabwe)*. Referee: R. S. Mahanama *(Sri Lanka)* (32).

Close of play: First day, Zimbabwe 264–2 (Masakadza 88, Taylor 40); Second day, Bangladesh 107–3 (Mohammad Ashraful 34, Mahmudullah 4); Third day, Zimbabwe 92–4 (Taylor 5, Taibu 0); Fourth day, Bangladesh 112–3 (Mohammad Ashraful 19, Mushfiqur Rahim 4).

SRI LANKA v AUSTRALIA 2011–12 (1st Test)

At Galle International Stadium on 31 August, 1, 2, 3 September, 2011.
Toss: Australia.   Result: AUSTRALIA WON BY 125 RUNS.
Debuts: Australia – T. A. Copeland, N. M. Lyon.
Man of the Match: M. E. K. Hussey.

It quickly became apparent that the pitch had been designed as a secondary defence against invaders in case the Galle Fort failed to do the job. The problem for Sri Lanka, though, was that the invaders won the toss, thus robbing Dilshan of the chance to let his spinners loose on a crumbling fourth-innings surface. Excessive early turn and uneven bounce on a track later rated "poor" by ICC meant Australia's 273 – in which Hussey survived four hours for a superb 95 – felt more than respectable. Copeland then took a wicket with his second ball in Tests, Ponting clinging on cat-like at short cover, before Lyon went one better, luring Sangakkara into a fatal push at his first delivery. His off-breaks brought him five wickets as Sri Lanka toppled for just 105. Clarke's aggressive 60 held Australia together, and the last three wickets added 80: a target of 379 looked mountainous. Sri Lanka lost Paranavitana first ball, and predictably fell short, despite a brilliant 29th Test century from Jayawardene. He batted for 311 minutes, and put on 142 – a record for Sri Lanka's sixth wicket against Australia – with Mathews. But he finally fell to the second new ball, to snuff out any hope of a famous win. Galle was the scene of Ponting's first win as Test captain, back in March 2004, and now Clarke's too. It was also an unprecedented 100th Test win for Ponting as a player, before he headed home for the birth of his second child.

Australia

S. R. Watson c H. A. P. W. Jayawardene b Herath	22	– c Samaraweera b Welagedara	0
P. J. Hughes c Paranavitana b Lakmal	12	– lbw b Dilshan	28
R. T. Ponting c Mathews b Herath	44	– c Herath b Lakmal	4
*M. J. Clarke lbw b Herath	23	– c H. A. P. W. Jayawardene b Herath	60
M. E. K. Hussey lbw b Dilshan	95	– c Paranavitana b Herath	15
U. T. Khawaja b Welagedara	21	– lbw b Welagedara	26
†B. J. Haddin c Mathews b Randiv	24	– c D. P. M. D. Jayawardene b Herath	0
M. G. Johnson c H. A. P. W. Jayawardene b Lakmal	14	– c H. A. P. W. Jayawardene b Herath	8
R. J. Harris lbw b Lakmal	1	– c and b Herath	23
T. A. Copeland c Paranavitana b Randiv	12	– not out	23
N. M. Lyon not out	0	– c Samaraweera b Dilshan	13
B 3, l-b 2	5	B 4, l-b 4, n-b 2	10
(86.4 overs)	273	(59.2 overs)	210

1/28 (1) 2/36 (2) 3/91 (4) 4/112 (3) 5/157 (6)   1/0 (1) 2/5 (3) 3/61 (2) 4/110 (4) 5/110 (5)
6/205 (7) 7/234 (8) 8/236 (9) 9/251 (10) 10/273 (5)   6/112 (7) 7/130 (8) 8/170 (6) 9/178 (9) 10/210 (11)

Welagedara 15–5–61–1; Lakmal 17–2–55–3; Herath 24–3–54–3; Randiv 21–2–76–2; Dilshan 9.4–1–22–1. *Second Innings*—Welagedara 6–3–13–2; Lakmal 8–3–23–1; Herath 23–3–79–5; Randiv 14–3–61–0; Dilshan 8.2–1–26–2.

Sri Lanka

N. T. Paranavitana lbw b Watson	29	– lbw b Harris	0
*T. M. Dilshan c Ponting b Copeland	4	– b Harris	12
K. C. Sangakkara c Clarke b Lyon	10	– c Hussey b Watson	17
D. P. M. D. Jayawardene run out	11	– b Harris	105
T. T. Samaraweera lbw b Watson	26	– c Haddin b Johnson	0
†H. A. P. W. Jayawardene lbw b Watson	0	– b Harris	0
A. D. Mathews b Lyon	5	– b Watson	95
S. Randiv c Ponting b Lyon	9	– c Clarke b Johnson	0
H. M. R. K. B. Herath c Johnson b Lyon	0	– c Copeland b Harris	12
R. A. S. Lakmal not out	2	– c Johnson b Lyon	5
U. W. M. B. C. A. Welagedara c and b Lyon	1	– not out	4
L-b 4, w 1, n-b 3	8	B 1, l-b 1, w 1	3
(50 overs)	105	(95.5 overs)	253

1/4 (2) 2/24 (3) 3/44 (4) 4/87 (5) 5/87 (6) 6/88 (1)   1/0 (1) 2/15 (2) 3/52 (3) 4/63 (5) 5/68 (6)
7/100 (7) 8/100 (9) 9/103 (8) 10/105 (11)   6/210 (4) 7/221 (8) 8/242 (9) 9/249 (7) 10/253 (10)

Harris 8–5–6–0; Copeland 12–3–24–1; Johnson 9–1–26–0; Lyon 15–3–34–5; Watson 6–1–11–3. *Second Innings*—Harris 20–5–62–5; Copeland 16–6–20–0; Johnson 19–6–56–2; Lyon 19.5–2–73–1; Clarke 6–0–16–0; Watson 13–6–19–2; Ponting 2–0–5–0.

Umpires: Aleem Dar *(Pakistan)* (66) and R. A. Kettleborough *(England)* (4).
Third umpire: A. L. Hill *(New Zealand)*. Referee: B. C. Broad *(England)* (45).

Close of play: First day, Australia 273; Second day, Australia 115–6 (Khawaja 2, Johnson 3); Third day, Sri Lanka 120–5 (D. P. M. D. Jayawardene 57, Mathews 32).

SRI LANKA v AUSTRALIA 2011–12 (2nd Test)

At Muttiah Muralitharan Stadium, Pallekele, on 8, 9, 10, 11, 12 September, 2011.
Toss: Sri Lanka.   Result: MATCH DRAWN.
Debuts: Sri Lanka – S. Prasanna. Australia – S. E. Marsh.
Man of the Match: M. E. K. Hussey.

This was a good match for the Marsh family. Left-hander Shaun, called up as Ponting's replacement, received his baggy green cap from his father Geoff, who played 50 Tests for Australia. Shaun, 28, responded by becoming the 19th Australian to score a century on debut. Meanwhile Geoff, who had flown over just to watch his son, found himself courted by Sri Lanka and was later unveiled as their new coach. This was only the second Test at Pallekele: bad weather ruined the first (against West Indies the previous December), and rain and bad light robbed this one of more than a day, again preventing a result. Sri Lanka's 174 owed much to Sangakkara, who battled more than three hours, and Mathews, whose 58 from No. 7 included three sixes. Sangakkara's dismissal was cunningly contrived by Clarke, who thought Hussey's rarely seen wobblers might induce a catch forward of the wicket. He was successful after only three balls, and taken off after six. Two days later, he was raising his bat to celebrate his 14th Test century. Most of the attention, however, was grabbed by Marsh, who proved he was not just a one-day dasher, batting for exactly seven hours; his stand of 258 with Hussey allowed Clarke to declare at 411. Sri Lanka made a better fist of their second innings, but Hussey intervened again, this time removing Paranavitana for a watchful 55. Sangakkara and Jayawardene then shared their 13th century partnership in Tests, and Sri Lanka comfortably avoided defeat.

Sri Lanka

N. T. Paranavitana c Haddin b Harris	0	– c Haddin b Hussey	55
*T. M. Dilshan b Copeland	4	– c Watson b Harris	36
K. C. Sangakkara c Hughes b Hussey	48	– c Clarke b Harris	69
D. P. M. D. Jayawardene c Hussey b Copeland	4	– c Clarke b Copeland	51
T. T. Samaraweera c Haddin b Harris	17	– c Haddin b Watson	43
†H. A. P. W. Jayawardene c Harris b Lyon	18	– c Haddin b Harris	21
A. D. Mathews c Haddin b Johnson	58	– not out	11
S. Randiv c and b Lyon	4	– not out	4
S. Prasanna b Harris	5		
R. A. S. Lakmal not out	7		
U. W. M. B. C. A. Welagedara c Copeland b Johnson	2		
B 2, l-b 4, n-b 1	7	B 6, l-b 20, n-b 1	27
(64.1 overs)	174	(6 wkts, 114.3 overs)	317

1/2 (1) 2/10 (2) 3/14 (4) 4/57 (5) 5/76 (6) 6/128 (3)   1/81 (2) 2/128 (1) 3/229 (3) 4/270 (4)
7/133 (8) 8/150 (9) 9/166 (7) 10/174 (11)   5/301 (6) 6/307 (5)

Harris 16–7–38–3; Copeland 12–5–24–2; Watson 10–5–17–0; Johnson 15.1–1–48–2; Lyon 10–2–41–2; Hussey 1–1–0–1. *Second Innings*—Harris 22–8–54–3; Copeland 27–10–63–1; Johnson 23.3–4–61–0; Watson 20–9–43–1; Lyon 15–1–52–0; Hussey 4–2–2–1; Clarke 3–0–16–0.

Australia

S. R. Watson b Lakmal	36
P. J. Hughes c Paranavitana b Randiv	36
S. E. Marsh c Sangakkara b Lakmal	141
*M. J. Clarke c D. P. M. D. Jayawardene b Welagedara	13
M. E. K. Hussey c Sangakkara b Samaraweera	142
U. T. Khawaja not out	13
†B. J. Haddin c Sangakkara b Randiv	1
M. G. Johnson b Randiv	0
R. J. Harris not out	9
L-b 9, w 1, n-b 10	20
(7 wkts dec, 132 overs)	411

1/60 (1) 2/95 (2) 3/116 (4) 4/374 (5) 5/391 (3)
6/392 (7) 7/392 (8)

T. A. Copeland and N. M. Lyon did not bat.

Welagedara 23–3–74–1; Lakmal 23–2–102–2; Prasanna 23–3–80–0; Dilshan 14–4–32–0; Randiv 43–7–103–3; Sangakkara 2–0–4–0; Samaraweera 4–0–7–1.

Umpires: A. L. Hill *(New Zealand)* (24) and R. A. Kettleborough *(England)* (5).
Third umpire: S. K. Tarapore *(India)*. Referee: B. C. Broad *(England)* (46).

Close of play: First day, Australia 60–0 (Watson 36, Hughes 23); Second day, Australia 264–3 (Marsh 87, Hussey 76); Third day, Australia 411–7 (Khawaja 13, Harris 9); Fourth day, Sri Lanka 223–2 (Sangakkara 69, D. P. M. D. Jayawardene 38).

SRI LANKA v AUSTRALIA 2011–12 (3rd Test)

At Sinhalese Sports Club, Colombo, on 16, 17, 18, 19, 20 September, 2011.
Toss: Sri Lanka.   Result: MATCH DRAWN.
Debuts: Sri Lanka – R. M. S. Eranga.
Man of the Match: M. E. K. Hussey. Man of the Series: M. E. K. Hussey.

A high-scoring draw enabled Clarke to complete a series victory in his first proper outing as Test captain. His side started poorly, losing Hughes in the second over and Watson in the ninth, to seamer Shaminda Eranga's first ball in Test cricket (only Chamila Gamage Lakshitha, against Bangladesh on this ground in July 2002, had previously managed this for Sri Lanka). Marsh and the returning Ponting steadied the ship, then Hussey shored things up with another century. Sri Lanka gained a big lead, but much of the advantage was squandered by a painfully slow maiden century from Mathews, who batted for 404 minutes in all. Australia needed to avoid an early collapse, and duly did so, thanks to two previously out-of-form batsmen: Hughes reined in his attacking instincts to bat for 314 minutes and compile his first Test hundred since making two in only his second match, against South Africa at Durban in March 2009, while Clarke glided to his first century in 23 innings. The Sinhalese Sports Club pitch might just be the best road in the country, and its benign nature soon made it apparent there would be no result. Herath persevered well, and was rewarded with the wickets of the top five, finishing the series with 16 wickets from two matches. Hussey fell seven short of a third successive hundred, but did manage a third successive match award, a unique feat: only Ian Botham, in the six-match 1981 Ashes series, had won three in one rubber before.

Australia

S. R. Watson c Dilshan b Eranga		8	– lbw b Herath		21
P. J. Hughes b Lakmal		0	– c Thirimanne b Herath		126
S. E. Marsh b Herath		81	– c Thirimanne b Herath		18
R. T. Ponting c H. A. P. W. Jayawardene b Lakmal		48	– c D. P. M. D. Jayawardene b Herath		28
*M. J. Clarke c H. A. P. W. Jayawardene b Eranga		6	– c Paranavitana b Herath		112
M. E. K. Hussey b Eranga		118	– c Welagedara b Dilshan		93
†B. J. Haddin c H. A. P. W. Jayawardene b Eranga		35	– c Lakmal b Herath		30
M. G. Johnson c Herath b Welagedara		8	– c Eranga b Welagedara		4
P. M. Siddle c Paranavitana b Welagedara		0	– lbw b Herath		26
T. A. Copeland c D. P. M. D. Jayawardene b Welagedara		1	– c Paranavitana b Eranga		3
N. M. Lyon not out		3	– not out		1
L-b 4, w 1, n-b 3		8	B 5, l-b 11, w 6, n-b 4		26
(104.3 overs)		316	(138.5 overs)		488

1/0 (2) 2/22 (1) 3/101 (4) 4/120 (5) 5/190 (3) 6/265 (7)
7/293 (8) 8/293 (9) 9/295 (10) 10/316 (6)

1/62 (1) 2/122 (3) 3/188 (4) 4/220 (2) 5/396 (5)
6/448 (6) 7/452 (8) 8/471 (7) 9/486 (9) 10/488 (10)

Welagedara 21–6–75–3; Lakmal 21–3–60–2; Eranga 23.3–6–65–4; Herath 27–5–78–1; Dilshan 12–0–34–0.
Second Innings—Eranga 18.5–2–62–1; Lakmal 22–2–86–0; Welagedara 24–3–88–1; Herath 52–11–157–7; Dilshan 19–0–62–1; Thirimanne 1–0–7–0; Paranavitana 2–0–10–0.

Sri Lanka

N. T. Paranavitana c Ponting b Johnson		46	– not out		2
H. D. R. L. Thirimanne b Siddle		28	– not out		4
K. C. Sangakkara c Haddin b Siddle		79			
D. P. M. D. Jayawardene c Haddin b Watson		51			
*T. M. Dilshan c Haddin b Copeland		83			
A. D. Mathews not out		105			
†H. A. P. W. Jayawardene c Clarke b Copeland		47			
R. M. S. Eranga b Siddle		12			
H. M. R. K. B. Herath lbw b Siddle		3			
U. W. M. B. C. A. Welagedara run out		1			
R. A. S. Lakmal b Johnson		13			
B 1, l-b 2, n-b 2		5	W 1		1
(174 overs)		473	(no wkt, 2 overs)		7

1/56 (2) 2/97 (1) 3/198 (4) 4/210 (3) 5/331 (5) 6/412 (7)
7/436 (8) 8/444 (9) 9/450 (10) 10/473 (11)

Copeland 40–10–93–2; Siddle 35–8–91–4; Johnson 35–6–122–2; Watson 26–8–54–1; Lyon 34–5–91–0; Hussey 2–1–5–0; Ponting 2–0–14–0. *Second Innings*—Copeland 1–0–3–0; Lyon 1–0–4–0.

Umpires: Aleem Dar *(Pakistan)* (67) and A. L. Hill *(New Zealand)* (25).
Third umpire: R. A. Kettleborough *(England)*. Referee: B. C. Broad *(England)* (47).

Close of play: First day, Australia 235–5 (Hussey 63, Haddin 21); Second day, Sri Lanka 166–2 (Sangakkara 61, D. P. M. D. Jayawardene 31); Third day, Sri Lanka 428–6 (Mathews 85, Eranga 5); Fourth day, Australia 209–3 (Hughes 122, Clarke 8).

ZIMBABWE v PAKISTAN 2011–12 (Only Test)

At Queens Sports Club, Bulawayo, on 1, 2, 3, 4, 5 September, 2011.
Toss: Pakistan.   Result: PAKISTAN WON BY SEVEN WICKETS.
Debuts: Zimbabwe – G. A. Lamb. Pakistan – Aizaz Cheema, Junaid Khan.
Man of the Match: Mohammad Hafeez.

Zimbabwe's encouraging return was rudely interrupted by Pakistan, who inflicted a hard-fought defeat four weeks after Taylor's team had triumphantly seen off Bangladesh. Saeed Ajmal was the main difference, while seamer Aizaz Cheema claimed eight for 103: only Mohammad Zahid (11 for 130 against New Zealand at Rawalpindi in 1996–97) had recorded better debut figures for Pakistan. The result was harsh on Tino Mawoyo, who lasted 645 minutes to become only the third player to carry his bat for Zimbabwe; Mark Dekker and Grant Flower also did it against Pakistan. In only his second Test, Mawoyo made good use of a flat, dry pitch – Misbah-ul-Haq's insertion was a surprise, despite a substantial covering of grass – and hit 20 fours from 453 balls. Mawoyo struggled against Ajmal's doosra, but did not succumb to it, although he was fortunate on 98 when Adnan Akmal made a hash of a stumping. But from 365 for five halfway through the second day Zimbabwe lost five for 47, including four to Cheema's slower balls and yorkers. Mohammad Hafeez kick-started Pakistan's reply: badly dropped twice, he pulled and drove powerfully to his third Test hundred, the first since November 2006. Six catches went down as Pakistan, bowled out shortly after lunch on the fourth day, compiled a handy lead of 54. Zimbabwe then collapsed fatally, and led by only 15 at the fall of the eighth wicket. Taibu and Jarvis forced the match into the last day, but Cheema celebrated his 32nd birthday with the last two wickets.

Zimbabwe

T. M. K. Mawoyo not out	163	– b Saeed Ajmal	12
V. Sibanda st Adnan Akmal b Saeed Ajmal	45	– c Saeed Ajmal b Aizaz Cheema	5
H. Masakadza b Saeed Ajmal	11	– b Aizaz Cheema	8
*B. R. M. Taylor lbw b Saeed Ajmal	10	– lbw b Saeed Ajmal	5
†T. Taibu c Adnan Akmal b Sohail Khan	44	– c Adnan Akmal b Aizaz Cheema	58
C. R. Ervine c and b Junaid Khan	49	– lbw b Mohammad Hafeez	6
G. A. Lamb lbw b Saeed Ajmal	39	– lbw b Mohammad Hafeez	7
R. W. Price c Azhar Ali b Aizaz Cheema	6	– b Mohammad Hafeez	0
B. V. Vitori c Younis Khan b Aizaz Cheema	14	– c Taufeeq Umar b Mohammad Hafeez	7
K. M. Jarvis b Aizaz Cheema	0	– not out	25
C. B. Mpofu b Aizaz Cheema	8	– c Adnan Akmal b Aizaz Cheema	0
B 7, l-b 13, w 1, n-b 2	23	B 4, l-b 1, w 2, n-b 1	8
(150.4 overs)	412	(56.3 overs)	141

1/71 (2) 2/91 (3) 3/111 (4) 4/176 (5) 5/270 (6)
6/365 (7) 7/374 (8) 8/394 (9) 9/394 (10) 10/412 (11)

1/9 (2) 2/19 (1) 3/31 (4) 4/31 (3) 5/45 (6) 6/61 (7)
7/61 (8) 8/69 (9) 9/135 (5) 10/141 (11)

Sohail Khan 24–8–62–1; Aizaz Cheema 28.4–11–79–4; Junaid Khan 29–14–55–1; Saeed Ajmal 54–13–143–4; Mohammad Hafeez 9–1–30–0; Azhar Ali 6–1–23–0. *Second Innings*—Sohail Khan 6–1–19–0; Aizaz Cheema 11.3–5–24–4; Saeed Ajmal 22–4–53–2; Mohammad Hafeez 15–4–31–4; Junaid Khan 2–0–9–0.

Pakistan

Mohammad Hafeez c Lamb b Masakadza	119	– b Price	38
Taufeeq Umar lbw b Jarvis	4	– c Taibu b Jarvis	8
Azhar Ali c Taibu b Lamb	75	– c Lamb b Price	22
Younis Khan c Taylor b Price	88	– not out	14
*Misbah-ul-Haq c Vitori b Lamb	66	– not out	6
Umar Akmal c Taylor b Lamb	15		
†Adnan Akmal run out	36		
Saeed Ajmal b Price	28		
Sohail Khan c Ervine b Mpofu	11		
Junaid Khan c Ervine b Mpofu	6		
Aizaz Cheema not out	0		
B 4, l-b 14	18		
(156.1 overs)	466	(3 wkts, 21.4 overs)	88

1/8 (2) 2/196 (1) 3/218 (3) 4/318 (5) 5/357 (6) 6/415 (7)
7/424 (4) 8/455 (9) 9/466 (10) 10/466 (8)

1/19 (2) 2/49 (1) 3/80 (3)

Vitori 25–3–103–0; Jarvis 24–4–79–1; Mpofu 22–5–64–2; Price 50.1–24–69–2; Lamb 28–2–120–3; Masakadza 7–2–13–1. *Second Innings*—Jarvis 5–0–17–1; Price 10.4–2–35–2; Vitori 2–0–15–0; Lamb 4–0–21–0.

Umpires: I. J. Gould *(England)* (21) and R. J. Tucker *(Australia)* (12).
Third umpire: T. J. Matibiri *(Zimbabwe)*. Referee: D. C. Boon *(Australia)* (1).

Close of play: First day, Zimbabwe 245–4 (Mawoyo 82, Ervine 38); Second day, Pakistan 116–1 (Mohammad Hafeez 79, Azhar Ali 27); Third day, Pakistan 357–5 (Younis Khan 61); Fourth day, Zimbabwe 135–8 (Taibu 58, Jarvis 20).

PAKISTAN v SRI LANKA 2011–12 (1st Test)

At Sheikh Zayed Stadium, Abu Dhabi, on 18, 29, 20, 21, 22 October, 2011.
Toss: Pakistan.   Result: MATCH DRAWN.
Debuts: Sri Lanka – A. N. P. R. Fernando *(usually known as Nuwan Pradeep)*.
Man of the Match: K. C. Sangakkara.

Catches win matches, goes the saying: Pakistan dropped several after working themselves into a strong position, and Sri Lanka escaped with a draw. They had begun their second innings 314 behind, and lost Paravitana first ball. Defeat loomed. But on the fourth morning the usually reliable Mohammad Hafeez dropped Thirimanne three times – twice in successive balls at first slip off Junaid Khan, then, as lunch approached, at gully off Saeed Ajmal. Three overs later, Hafeez the bowler saw Younis Khan miss a difficult slip chance off Sangakkara. Much later in the day the substitute Wahab Riaz spilled the easiest one of all at short midwicket, with Sri Lanka five down and still nearly 60 behind. Prasanna Jayawardene, then 11, went on to 120: his eventual partnership of 201 with Sangakkara stretched deep into the fifth day. Sangakkara completed his eighth Test double-century, one more than Wally Hammond; only Don Bradman (12) and Brian Lara (nine) lay ahead. This was an immense effort, nearly 11 hours long, most of which were spent in concentrated defence. Still, his double-hundred was still easier on the eye than Taufeeq Umar's, the first by a Pakistan opener since Aamir Sohail's 205 at Old Trafford in 1992. For vast, boundary-free portions, it was scratchy and ponderous, never imposing. He faced 496 balls in 712 minutes, the fourth-longest innings for Pakistan. Taufeeq's marathon built on a riveting first day, when Pakistan bowled with great gusto. Junaid – young, left-armed, yorker-happy – announced himself with three wickets in five balls.

Sri Lanka

N. T. Paranavitana c Adnan Akmal b Umar Gul	37	– lbw b Umar Gul		0
H. D. R. L. Thirimanne c Younis Khan b Saeed Ajmal	20	– run out		68
K. C. Sangakkara c Adnan Akmal b Aizaz Cheema	2	– lbw b Azhar Ali		211
D. P. M. D. Jayawardene c Mohammad Hafeez b Junaid Khan...	28	– b Saeed Ajmal		4
*T. M. Dilshan c Adnan Akmal b Saeed Ajmal	19	– b Junaid Khan		9
A. D. Mathews not out	52	– lbw b Umar Gul		22
†H. A. P. W. Jayawardene b Junaid Khan	0	– c Adnan Akmal b Aizaz Cheema		120
H. M. R. K. B. Herath lbw b Junaid Khan	0	– not out		23
R. A. S. Lakmal c Mohammad Hafeez b Umar Gul	18	– (10) b Umar Gul		0
U. W. M. B. C. A. Welagedara c Taufeeq Umar b Junaid Khan...	11	– (9) c Adnan Akmal b Umar Gul		8
A. N. P. R. Fernando c Adnan Akmal b Junaid Khan	1	– run out		0
L-b 3, w 1, n-b 5	9	B 4, l-b 11, n-b 3		18
(74.1 overs)	197	(168 overs)		483

1/48 (2) 2/51 (3) 3/79 (1) 4/112 (5) 5/112 (4) 6/112 (7)
7/114 (8) 8/168 (9) 9/193 (10) 10/197 (11)

1/0 (1) 2/153 (2) 3/160 (4) 4/191 (5)
5/233 (6) 6/434 (3) 7/466 (7) 8/477 (9)
9/481 (10) 10/483 (11)

Umar Gul 11–1–37–2; Aizaz Cheema 15–5–51–1; Mohammad Hafeez 9–3–12–0; Junaid Khan 14.1–3–38–5; Saeed Ajmal 25–5–56–2. *Second Innings*—Umar Gul 25–3–64–4; Aizaz Cheema 32–1–108–1; Saeed Ajmal 55–8–167–1; Junaid Khan 31–6–83–1; Mohammad Hafeez 22–4–42–0; Azhar Ali 3–1–4–1.

Pakistan

Mohammad Hafeez lbw b Herath	75	– not out		12
Taufeeq Umar run out	236	– lbw b Welagedara		2
Azhar Ali b Welagedara	70	– not out		4
Younis Khan lbw b Welagedara	33			
*Misbah-ul-Haq c H. A. P. W. Jayawardene b Herath	46			
Asad Shafiq not out	26			
Umar Gul c Mathews b Herath	0			
B 3, l-b 3, w 3, n-b 16	25	N-b 3		3
(6 wkts dec, 174.4 overs)	511	(1 wkt, 10 overs)		21

1/118 (1) 2/278 (3) 3/360 (4) 4/436 (5) 5/511 (2) 6/511 (7)   1/7 (2)

†Adnan Akmal, Aizaz Cheema, Saeed Ajmal and Junaid Khan did not bat.

Welagedara 30–5–80–2; Lakmal 24–3–108–0; Herath 61.4–16–126–3; Fernando 27–1–107–0; Dilshan 32–6–84–0. *Second Innings*—Welagedara 5–2–9–1; Lakmal 2–1–1–0; Herath 2–0–8–0; Fernando 1–0–3–0.

Umpires: A. L. Hill *(New Zealand)* (26) and R. J. Tucker *(Australia)* (13).
Third umpire: Ahsan Raza *(Pakistan)*. Referee: D. C. Boon *(Australia)* (2).

Close of play: First day, Pakistan 27–0 (Mohammad Hafeez 17, Taufeeq Umar 8); Second day, Pakistan 259–1 (Taufeeq Umar 109, Azhar Ali 60); Third day, Sri Lanka 47–1 (Thirimanne 20, Sangakkara 27); Fourth day, Sri Lanka 298–5 (Sangakkara 161, H. A. P. W. Jayawardene 25).

PAKISTAN v SRI LANKA 2011–12 (2nd Test)

At Dubai International Cricket Stadium on 26, 27, 28, 29 October, 2011.
Toss: Sri Lanka.   Result: PAKISTAN WON BY NINE WICKETS.
Debuts: Sri Lanka – J. K. Silva.
Man of the Match: Saeed Ajmal.

The pitch for Dubai's second Test was a humdinger. At first, it deceived both captains. Dilshan thought it flat enough to bat first; Misbah-ul-Haq thought it dry enough to drop a paceman for a second spinner. Misbah was ultimately proved right, but had it not been for outstanding long opening spells from Umar Gul and Junaid Khan, he might have looked foolish. The first session was the decisive one. Gul struck three times in his first five overs, and Sri Lanka lunched in disarray at 78 for five. The pitch then began to ease, and Sangakkara – not for the first time seemingly batting on a different pitch from his team-mates – and the tail dragged their side to a reasonable total. Welagedara, whose previous-highest score was 11, survived two hours for 48: spinners Saeed Ajmal and Abdur Rehman took the last five wickets. Pakistan ground out a big lead, the highlight Azhar Ali's breakthrough maiden hundred after ten unconverted half-centuries. He spent a nervous 30 balls in the nineties, but finally a paddle sweep got him to 100. Just as well: they could easily have been given as byes, and he was leg-before off an inside edge – there was no DRS for this series – without addition soon after. By the time Sri Lanka addressed their 164-run deficit, the pitch was offering big turn and inconsistent bounce. Ajmal and Rehman worked through nearly 64 tight, unflashy overs to seal Pakistan's first Test win over Sri Lanka for five and a half years.

Sri Lanka

N. T. Paranavitana c Misbah-ul-Haq b Umar Gul	6	– c Younis Khan b Saeed Ajmal		72
H. D. R. L. Thirimanne lbw b Umar Gul	1	– b Mohammad Hafeez		8
K. C. Sangakkara c Asad Shafiq b Abdur Rehman	78	– lbw b Abdur Rehman		30
D. P. M. D. Jayawardene c Misbah-ul-Haq b Umar Gul	6	– b Saeed Ajmal		5
*T. M. Dilshan c Misbah-ul-Haq b Junaid Khan	7	– lbw b Junaid Khan		3
A. D. Mathews c Adnan Akmal b Junaid Khan	19	– not out		52
†J. K. Silva lbw b Abdur Rehman	20	– c Saeed Ajmal b Junaid Khan		8
K. T. G. D. Prasad c Adnan Akmal b Saeed Ajmal	7	– b Abdur Rehman		33
H. M. R. K. B. Herath c Younis Khan b Saeed Ajmal	29	– c Misbah-ul-Haq b Saeed Ajmal		15
U. W. M. B. C. A. Welagedara st Adnan Akmal b Saeed Ajmal	48	– lbw b Saeed Ajmal		4
R. A. S. Lakmal not out	0	– b Saeed Ajmal		8
B 5, l-b 7, n-b 6	18	B 14, l-b 3, n-b 2		19
(79 overs)	239	(109.5 overs)		257

1/3 (2) 2/24 (1) 3/30 (4) 4/45 (5) 5/73 (6) 6/127 (7)
7/154 (8) 8/154 (3) 9/229 (9) 10/239 (10)

1/22 (2) 2/95 (3) 3/113 (4) 4/116 (5) 5/141 (1)
6/166 (7) 7/222 (8) 8/243 (9) 9/247 (10) 10/257 (11)

Umar Gul 19–2–78–3; Junaid Khan 15–2–57–2; Saeed Ajmal 26–9–45–3; Abdur Rehman 17–5–40–2; Mohammad Hafeez 2–0–7–0. *Second Innings*—Umar Gul 15–3–39–0; Junaid Khan 17–4–38–2; Mohammad Hafeez 14–2–30–1; Abdur Rehman 33–7–65–2; Saeed Ajmal 30.5–9–68–5.

Pakistan

Mohammad Hafeez lbw b Prasad	33	– not out		59
Taufeeq Umar c Silva b Prasad	27	– b Herath		1
Azhar Ali lbw b Dilshan	100	– not out		29
Younis Khan b Dilshan	55			
*Misbah-ul-Haq c Jayawardene b Welagedara	41			
Saeed Ajmal c Mathews b Welagedara	20			
Asad Shafiq c Jayawardene b Prasad	59			
†Adnan Akmal c Silva b Dilshan	41			
Abdur Rehman b Herath	0			
Umar Gul lbw b Herath	2			
Junaid Khan not out	0			
B 10, l-b 10, w 2, n-b 3	25	B 4, l-b 1		5
(141.1 overs)	403	(1 wkt, 24.1 overs)		94

1/63 (2) 2/64 (1) 3/181 (4) 4/275 (3) 5/283 (5)
6/324 (6) 7/394 (7) 8/397 (9) 9/399 (10) 10/403 (8)

1/17 (2)

Welagedara 29–7–79–2; Prasad 32–2–104–3; Herath 37–5–89–2; Lakmal 24–8–54–0; Dilshan 19.1–1–57–3. *Second Innings*—Prasad 3–0–23–0; Welagedara 2–1–1–0; Herath 10.1–2–29–1; Dilshan 9–0–36–0.

Umpires: A. L. Hill *(New Zealand)* (27) and S. K. Tarapore *(India)* (1).
Third umpire: Zameer Haider *(Pakistan)*. Referee: D. C. Boon *(Australia)* (3).

Close of play: First day, Pakistan 42–0 (Mohammad Hafeez 18, Taufeeq Umar 20); Second day, Pakistan 281–4 (Misbah-ul-Haq 40, Saeed Ajmal 5); Third day, Sri Lanka 88–1 (Paranavitana 42, Sangakkara 29).

PAKISTAN v SRI LANKA 2011–12 (3rd Test)

At Sharjah C. A. Stadium on 3, 4, 5, 6, 7 November, 2011.
Toss: Sri Lanka.　　　Result: MATCH DRAWN.
Debuts: Sri Lanka – C. K. B. Kulasekara.
Man of the Match: K. C. Sangakkara. Men of the Series: Saeed Ajmal and K. C. Sangakkara.

Sharjah's first Test for nine years started against the backdrop of the spot-fixing trial in London – the jail sentences for Salman Butt, Mohammad Asif and Mohammad Aamer were handed down on the first day – and ended up showing how far Pakistan had already dragged themselves from those bleak times. A draw sealed their series victory, although Misbah-ul-Haq still faced criticism for ignoring a final-day target. Once rain – rain in Sharjah! – had wiped out the morning session, Pakistan were left 61 overs to chase 255. They teased for about five overs until Mohammad Hafeez was run out, and then didn't so much shut up shop as deny it ever existed. When the captains shook hands, Pakistan had crept to 87 for four from 57 overs; Misbah was still there, after dead-batting for nine off 86 balls. Before all this, Sri Lanka's strong position had been set up by Dilshan's return to form and another hundred from Sangakkara – the second Sri Lankan to 9,000 Test runs, following Mahela Jayawardene, but the fastest from anywhere in terms of innings (172; Rahul Dravid was next with 176). Younis Khan's third-day hundred already felt like an innings played to save a Test, more so for the dawdling support from Misbah (333 minutes for 89) and Azhar Ali. By the time Pakistan's first innings was done, the match was well into the fourth day. Sri Lanka did at least try to push on, led yet again by Sangakkara, but the next morning's rain dampened the equation.

Sri Lanka

N. T. Paranavitana c Younis Khan b Umar Gul	4	– not out	76
*T. M. Dilshan c Younis Khan b Saeed Ajmal	92	– c Mohammad Hafeez b Umar Gul	4
K. C. Sangakkara c Younis Khan b Saeed Ajmal	144	– c Asad Shafiq b Mohammad Hafeez	51
D. P. M. D. Jayawardene lbw b Junaid Khan	39	– lbw b Umar Gul	20
A. D. Mathews c Adnan Akmal b Abdur Rehman	17	– lbw b Saeed Ajmal	13
†J. K. Silva c Azhar Ali b Saeed Ajmal	39	– lbw b Saeed Ajmal	0
C. K. B. Kulasekara lbw b Saeed Ajmal	15	– b Saeed Ajmal	7
S. Randiv lbw b Umar Gul	1		
K. T. G. D. Prasad c Adnan Akmal b Junaid Khan	17		
H. M. R. K. B. Herath not out	34	– (8) not out	1
U. W. M. B. C. A. Welagedara b Umar Gul	0		
L-b 5, n-b 6	11	L-b 6, w 1, n-b 2	9
(153.3 overs)	413	(6 wkts dec, 58 overs)	181

1/4 (1) 2/177 (2) 3/261 (4) 4/300 (5) 5/304 (3)　　　1/5 (2) 2/80 (3) 3/127 (4) 4/155 (5) 5/155 (6)
6/330 (7) 7/331 (8) 8/359 (9) 9/413 (6) 10/413 (11)　6/178 (7)

Umar Gul 29.3–10–76–3; Junaid Khan 27–4–94–2; Saeed Ajmal 51–4–132–4; Abdur Rehman 45–14–103–1; Mohammad Hafeez 1–0–3–0. *Second Innings*—Umar Gul 15–1–44–2; Junaid Khan 5–3–9–0; Abdur Rehman 12–1–38–0; Mohammad Hafeez 10–1–34–1; Saeed Ajmal 16–2–50–3.

Pakistan

Mohammad Hafeez c Jayawardene b Welagedara	6	– run out	13
Taufeeq Umar st Silva b Herath	19	– c Sangakkara b Randiv	39
Azhar Ali b Kulasekara	53	– lbw b Herath	7
Younis Khan b Welagedara	122	– c sub (H. D. R. L. Thirimanne) b Welagedara	11
*Misbah-ul-Haq c Dilshan b Randiv	89	– not out	9
Asad Shafiq c Silva b Welagedara	16	– not out	7
†Adnan Akmal lbw b Herath	7		
Abdur Rehman c Paranavitana b Welagedara	3		
Umar Gul c Mathews b Herath	5		
Saeed Ajmal not out	12		
Junaid Khan b Welagedara	0		
L-b 2, w 3, n-b 3	8	L-b 1	1
(138.2 overs)	340	(4 wkts, 57 overs)	87

1/8 (1) 2/35 (2) 3/133 (3) 4/233 (4) 5/258 (6)
6/277 (7) 7/282 (8) 8/289 (9) 9/336 (5) 10/340 (11)　　1/20 (1) 2/30 (3) 3/57 (4) 4/77 (2)

Welagedara 35.2–10–87–5; Prasad 4–0–9–0; Kulasekara 25–7–65–1; Herath 42–14–85–3; Randiv 25–5–74–1; Dilshan 7–1–18–0. *Second Innings*—Welagedara 9–3–19–1; Kulasekara 3–0–15–0; Herath 22–14–19–1; Randiv 19–9–21–1; Dilshan 4–0–12–0.

Umpires: S. K. Tarapore *(India)* (2) and S. J. A. Taufel *(Australia)* (70).
Third umpire: Shozab Raza *(Pakistan)*. Referee: D. C. Boon *(Australia)* (4).

Close of play: First day, Sri Lanka 245–2 (Sangakkara 112, Jayawardene 32); Second day, Pakistan 35–2 (Azhar Ali 10, Younis Khan 0); Third day, Pakistan 282–6 (Misbah-ul-Haq 50, Abdur Rehman 3); Fourth day, Sri Lanka 164–5 (Paranavitana 66, Kulasekara 4).

79

BANGLADESH v WEST INDIES 2011–12 (1st Test)

At Zohur Ahmed Chowdhury Stadium, Chittagong, on 21, 22 (*no play*), 23 (*no play*), 24, 25 October, 2011.
Toss: Bangladesh.   Result: MATCH DRAWN.
Debuts: Bangladesh – Elias Sunny, Nasir Hossain.
Man of the Match: Elias Sunny.

The shortcomings of the drainage system proved a major embarrassment to the locals – and possibly cost their team a rare Test victory too. On a spin-friendly pitch, Bangladesh might have expected to press home the advantage of a first-innings lead of 106. But they didn't get the chance: after overnight rain washed out the second day, the third dawned bright and sunny – but the ground resembled a bog, and it was announced as early as 10.30 that there could be no play. Bangladesh had reached 255 for four before the rain, one of their better Test displays as the batsmen for once exhibited discipline and patience, running 106 singles against puzzlingly defensive field-settings. Top-scorer Mushfiqur Rahim was able to declare – only Bangladesh's fourth in 70 Tests – and did so again on the final day in a brave bid to enliven a dead match, becoming only the fourth man to declare twice in his first as captain, after Waqar Younis, Andrew Strauss and Alastair Cook. West Indies ignored the target of 226 in 37 overs, although they did bat with more composure than in the first innings, when their total would have been even lower but for a spirited maiden Test half-century from Sammy, and five penalty runs after Bangladesh's batsmen twice ran down the pitch during their first innings. Brathwaite survived having two stumps uprooted during the second over, after Rubel Hossain overstepped. Slow left-armer Elias Sunny flighted the ball craftily for seven wickets, despite having two early chances dropped.

Bangladesh

Tamim Iqbal c Brathwaite b Samuels	52	– c Baugh b Sammy		37
Imrul Kayes c Baugh b Rampaul	10	– c Baugh b Rampaul		13
Shahriar Nafees c Baugh b F. H. Edwards	32	– b Samuels		50
Raqibul Hasan lbw b Sammy	41	– not out		10
*†Mushfiqur Rahim c Bishoo b F. H. Edwards	68	– not out		2
Shakib Al Hasan c Baugh b Samuels	40			
Naeem Islam not out	36			
Nasir Hossain c Baugh b Bishoo	34			
Elias Sunny c Sammy b Bishoo	0			
Shahadat Hossain st Baugh b Bishoo	9			
Rubel Hossain not out	5			
B 8, l-b 5, w 5, n-b 5	23	B 4, l-b 2, n-b 1		7
(9 wkts dec, 122.4 overs)	350	(3 wkts dec, 42 overs)		119

1/26 (2) 2/110 (1) 3/159 (4) 4/238 (6) 5/255 (5)
6/274 (3) 7/317 (8) 8/317 (9) 9/345 (10)   1/32 (2) 2/72 (1) 3/116 (3)

In the first innings Shahriar Nafees, when 21, retired hurt at 58 for one and resumed at 255 for five.

F. H. Edwards 18.4–1–88–2; Rampaul 23–8–42–1; Sammy 26–8–53–1; Samuels 25–4–73–2; Bishoo 30–6–81–3. *Second Innings*—F. H. Edwards 9–0–37–0; Rampaul 11–1–26–1; Samuels 16–3–41–1; Sammy 6–1–9–1.

West Indies

L. M. P. Simmons c Raqibul Hasan b Shahadat Hossain	7	– c Rubel Hossain b Shakib Al Hasan		44
K. C. Brathwaite c Imrul Kayes b Elias Sunny	33	– lbw b Elias Sunny		0
K. A. Edwards lbw b Elias Sunny	17	– not out		28
D. M. Bravo c Shahriar Nafees b Elias Sunny	2	– not out		24
S. Chanderpaul c Shahriar Nafees b Elias Sunny	49			
M. N. Samuels c Raqibul Hasan b Elias Sunny	24			
†C. S. Baugh b Elias Sunny	30			
*D. J. G. Sammy b Shakib Al Hasan	58			
R. Rampaul c Mushfiqur Rahim b Shakib Al Hasan	8			
F. H. Edwards not out	0			
D. Bishoo b Shakib Al Hasan	0			
B 2, l-b 2, n-b 7, p 5	16	L-b 2, n-b 2		4
(68 overs)	244	(2 wkts, 22 overs)		100

1/19 (1) 2/44 (3) 3/52 (4) 4/114 (2) 5/137 (5) 6/152 (6)
7/212 (7) 8/229 (9) 9/244 (8) 10/244 (11)   1/5 (2) 2/58 (1)

Shahadat Hossain 5–1–19–1; Rubel Hossain 15–2–52–0; Shakib Al Hasan 18–2–53–3; Elias Sunny 23–0–94–6; Nasir Hossain 7–1–17–0. *Second Innings*—Elias Sunny 6–0–34–1; Shahadat Hossain 4–0–21–0; Shakib Al Hasan 6–1–34–1; Rubel Hossain 2–0–3–0; Nasir Hossain 2–0–4–0.

Umpires: H. D. P. K. Dharmasena *(Sri Lanka)* (4) and N. J. Llong *(England)* (10).
Third umpire: Enamul Haque, sen. *(Bangladesh)*. Referee: A. J. Pycroft *(Zimbabwe)* (19).

Close of play: First day, Bangladesh 255–4 (Mushfiqur Rahim 68, Naeem Islam 8); Second day, No play; Third day, No play; Fourth day, West Indies 144–5 (Samuels 17, Baugh 6).

BANGLADESH v WEST INDIES 2011–12 (2nd Test)

At Shere Bangla National Stadium, Mirpur, Dhaka, on 29, 30, 31 October, 1, 2 November, 2011.
Toss: West Indies.   Result: WEST INDIES WON BY 229 RUNS.
Debuts: Bangladesh – Suhrawadi Shuvo.
Man of the Match: K. A. Edwards. Man of the Series: Shakib Al Hasan.

Sammy was upbeat after a victory that atoned for Bangladesh's 2009 triumph over a weakened team in the Caribbean. It was West Indies' first away win since beating South Africa in December 2007, and first series triumph overseas since Zimbabwe in November 2003. The end came quickly. Five overs before lunch on the final day, Bangladesh – chasing a notional 508 – looked reasonably comfortable at 256 for five. But Shakib Al Hasan carelessly spiralled a leading edge to backward point, and the last five wickets tumbled for 22. Leg-spinner Bishoo claimed his first Test five-for: his match figures were the best by any West Indian spinner away from home since Lance Gibbs's nine for 143 at Bombay in 1974–75. West Indies batted for 126.4 overs in their first innings, and 111.3 in the second; Bangladesh lasted less than 150 overs in total. In the first innings, their fifth wicket went down in only the ninth over, although the score was already 59; Fidel Edwards took all five in 29 balls. Despite a partial recovery, the deficit was still 124. Brathwaite and Powell made maiden fifties in West Indies' first innings, while Kirk Edwards survived more than six hours for his second century in only his third Test. In the second innings Darren Bravo, in his tenth Test, reached his maiden hundred from the last ball of the third day, and went on to 195 before attempting a second consecutive six off slow left-armer Suhrawadi Shuvo, a late replacement for Elias Sunny (stomach upset).

West Indies

K. C. Brathwaite c Imrul Kayes b Rubel Hossain	50	– run out	0
K. O. A. Powell b Suhrawadi Shuvo	72	– c Nasir Hossain b Shakib Al Hasan	12
K. A. Edwards lbw b Shakib Al Hasan	121	– b Suhrawadi Shuvo	86
D. M. Bravo lbw b Nasir Hossain	12	– c Mushfiqur Rahim b Suhrawadi Shuvo	195
S. Chanderpaul c Mushfiqur Rahim b Nasir Hossain..	18	– (6) not out	59
K. A. J. Roach b Shakib Al Hasan	6	– (5) c Naeem Islam b Suhrawadi Shuvo	12
M. N. Samuels c and b Nasir Hossain	48		
†C. S. Baugh c Imrul Kayes b Shakib Al Hasan	6		
*D. J. G. Sammy hit wkt b Shakib Al Hasan	1		
F. H. Edwards lbw b Shakib Al Hasan	9		
D. Bishoo not out	2		
B 2, l-b 4, w 3, n-b 1	10	B 6, l-b 4, w 5, n-b 4	19
(126.4 overs)	355	(5 wkts dec, 111.3 overs)	383

1/100 (1) 2/155 (2) 3/180 (4) 4/226 (5) 5/232 (6)
6/319 (7) 7/337 (8) 8/339 (9) 9/348 (3) 10/355 (10)   1/0 (1) 2/33 (2) 3/184 (3) 4/240 (5) 5/383 (4)

Shahadat Hossain 16–1–76–0; Rubel Hossain 24–3–71–1; Shakib Al Hasan 34.4–12–63–5; Nasir Hossain 25–6–52–3; Suhrawadi Shuvo 23–3–73–1; Naeem Islam 4–0–14–0. *Second Innings*—Rubel Hossain 12–2–36–0; Nasir Hossain 25–5–78–0; Shakib Al Hasan 21–1–79–1; Naeem Islam 12–2–38–0; Suhrawadi Shuvo 26.3–3–73–3; Shahadat Hossain 11–0–57–0; Raqibul Hasan 4–0–12–0.

Bangladesh

Tamim Iqbal c Bravo b F. H. Edwards	14	– c Sammy b Bishoo	83
Imrul Kayes c Brathwaite b F. H. Edwards	29	– c K. A. Edwards b F. H. Edwards	9
Shahriar Nafees c Bravo b F. H. Edwards	7	– c and b Sammy	18
Raqibul Hasan lbw b F. H. Edwards	0	– c Sammy b Samuels	17
*†Mushfiqur Rahim c Chanderpaul b F. H. Edwards	0	– b Bishoo	69
Shakib Al Hasan b Bishoo	73	– c Chanderpaul b Sammy	55
Naeem Islam run out	45	– lbw b Bishoo	3
Nasir Hossain c K. A. Edwards b Samuels	42	– lbw b Bishoo	3
Suhrawadi Shuvo c Brathwaite b Bishoo	15	– c Sammy b Bishoo	0
Shahadat Hossain b Bishoo	4	– not out	1
Rubel Hossain not out	2	– b Roach	7
		B 6, l-b 1, n-b 6	13
(68 overs)	231	(80.2 overs)	278

1/14 (1) 2/36 (3) 3/46 (4) 4/46 (5) 5/59 (2) 6/143 (6)   1/26 (2) 2/73 (3) 3/124 (4) 4/168 (1) 5/256 (6)
7/195 (7) 8/225 (9) 9/225 (8) 10/231 (10)   6/260 (5) 7/264 (8) 8/264 (9) 9/271 (7) 10/278 (11)

F. H. Edwards 13–0–63–5; Roach 9–0–52–0; Sammy 10–3–32–0; Bishoo 23–4–62–3; Samuels 13–2–22–1. *Second Innings*—F. H. Edwards 14–0–56–1; Roach 13.2–2–49–1; Sammy 13–4–19–2; Bishoo 25–6–90–5; Samuels 15–2–57–1.

Umpires: H. D. P. K. Dharmasena *(Sri Lanka)* (5) and N. J. Llong *(England)* (11).
Third umpire: Nadir Shah *(Bangladesh)*. Referee: A. J. Pycroft *(Zimbabwe)* (20).

Close of play: First day, West Indies 253–5 (K. A. Edwards 71, Samuels 16); Second day, Bangladesh 204–7 (Nasir Hossain 34, Suhrawadi Shuvo 2); Third day, West Indies 207–3 (Bravo 100, Roach 4); Fourth day, Bangladesh 164–3 (Tamim Iqbal 82, Mushfiqur Rahim 33).

ZIMBABWE v NEW ZEALAND 2011–12 (Only Test)

At Queens Sports Club, Bulawayo, on 1, 2, 3, 4, 5 November, 2011.
Toss: New Zealand.   Result: NEW ZEALAND WON BY 34 RUNS.
Debuts: Zimbabwe – R. W. Chakabva, N. Ncube, M. N. Waller. New Zealand – D. A. J. Bracewell,
    D. G. Brownlie.
Man of the Match: D. L. Vettori.

Few gave Zimbabwe a chance when they were set 366. But, with Brendan Taylor making a superb century, they came close to one of Test cricket's most unlikely victories: that they didn't even draw felt cruel. Taylor mixed attack and defence, whacking four leg-side sixes – three of them in ten balls off Patel – in his second Test hundred, Zimbabwe's first in the fourth innings since Kevin Arnott's against New Zealand at Bulawayo in 1992–93. At tea, with seven wickets left, they needed 101. Moments before, Watling had claimed a catch at deep point from Taylor's sliced drive off Martin (who earlier in the match had become the fourth New Zealander to take 200 Test wickets, when he dismissed Jarvis), but it was ruled not out by the TV-watching umpire. Two balls after the break, Taylor carved a long-hop to the same place; this time it was clearly held. Vettori, who had taken his 350th Test wicket in the first innings, then removed Taibu, and debutant seamer Bracewell struck three times in four overs. Finally Vettori trapped Mpofu to clinch a nailbiting victory with 35 balls to spare. Earlier, Guptill had grafted to his second Test century, while Ross Taylor, in his first Test in charge, made 76 in both innings. Sibanda played beautifully for his 93, while Malcolm Waller passed fifty on Test debut, as his father Andy had done, also at Bulawayo, against England in 1996–97. This was the first Test in which both captains shared the same surname.

New Zealand

M. J. Guptill c Taibu b Masakadza	109 – (2) b Jarvis	0
B. B. McCullum b Jarvis	14 – (1) lbw b Price	11
K. S. Williamson run out	49 – lbw b Jarvis	68
*L. R. P. L. Taylor c Chakabva b Ncube	76 – (5) lbw b Jarvis	76
B-J. Watling c Chakabva b Mpofu	39 – (6) c Taylor b Price	3
D. G. Brownlie c Taylor b Price	63 – (8) b Jarvis	9
D. L. Vettori c Taylor b Mpofu	40 – c Ncube b Mpofu	31
†R. A. Young not out	9 – (9) not out	35
D. A. J. Bracewell b Mpofu	0 – (10) not out	1
J. S. Patel c Mawoyo b Mpofu	12 – (4) b Jarvis	9
C. S. Martin b Price	0	
B 7, l-b 3, w 2, n-b 3	15	B 3, l-b 3, n-b 3	9
(143.3 overs)	426	(8 wkts dec, 71 overs)	252

1/40 (2) 2/115 (3) 3/247 (1) 4/275 (4) 5/320 (5) 6/401 (6)
7/407 (7) 8/407 (9) 9/425 (10) 10/426 (11)

1/5 (2) 2/23 (1) 3/36 (4) 4/155 (3) 5/167 (6)
6/179 (5) 7/199 (8) 8/236 (7)

Jarvis 28–6–98–1; Ncube 25–4–80–1; Mpofu 34–10–92–4; Price 42.3–7–118–2; Masakadza 11–4–20–1; Waller 3–0–8–0. *Second Innings*—Jarvis 18–1–64–5; Ncube 10–0–41–0; Price 29–5–87–2; Mpofu 14–1–54–1.

Zimbabwe

T. M. K. Mawoyo c Watling b Vettori	5 – b Guptill	52
V. Sibanda c Taylor b Brownlie	93 – lbw b Bracewell	13
H. Masakadza b Bracewell	22 – c Brownlie b Bracewell	19
*B. R. M. Taylor lbw b Vettori	50 – c Watling b Martin	117
T. Taibu c Patel b Vettori	20 – c Guptill b Vettori	63
M. N. Waller not out	72 – lbw b Vettori	29
†R. W. Chakabva run out	37 – c Young b Bracewell	5
R. W. Price lbw b Vettori	0 – (9) c Young b Bracewell	4
K. M. Jarvis c Taylor b Martin	6 – (10) not out	2
C. B. Mpofu c Williamson b Vettori	0 – (11) lbw b Vettori	0
N. Ncube b Martin	3 – (8) b Bracewell	14
L-b 3, w 1, n-b 1	5	B 5, l-b 4, n-b 4	13
(121.5 overs)	313	(108.1 overs)	331

1/24 (1) 2/83 (3) 3/159 (2) 4/193 (4) 5/198 (5) 6/284 (7)
7/286 (8) 8/299 (9) 9/300 (10) 10/313 (11)

1/25 (2) 2/61 (3) 3/157 (1) 4/265 (4) 5/287 (5)
6/303 (7) 7/321 (8) 8/329 (9) 9/329 (6) 10/331 (11)

Martin 25.5–6–74–2; Bracewell 23–12–51–1; Vettori 43–13–70–5; Patel 23–1–91–0; Brownlie 4–0–13–1; Williamson 2–0–9–0; Guptill 1–0–2–0. *Second Innings*—Martin 22–3–85–1; Bracewell 25–2–85–5; Vettori 38.1–14–71–3; Patel 13–1–51–0; Guptill 9–0–28–1; Brownlie 1–0–2–0.

Umpires: M. Erasmus *(South Africa)* (7) and B. N. J. Oxenford *(Australia)* (3).
Third umpire: T. J. Matibiri *(Zimbabwe)*. Referee: B. C. Broad *(England)* (48).

Close of play: First day, New Zealand 275–3 (Taylor 76, Watling 16); Second day, Zimbabwe 82–1 (Sibanda 53, Masakadza 22); Third day, New Zealand 28–2 (Williamson 13, Patel 4); Fourth day, Zimbabwe 61–2 (Mawoyo 27).

INDIA v WEST INDIES 2011–12 (1st Test)

At Feroz Shah Kotla, Delhi, on 6, 7, 8, 9 November, 2011.
Toss: West Indies.　　Result: INDIA WON BY FIVE WICKETS.
Debuts: India – R. Ashwin, U. T. Yadav.
Man of the Match: R. Ashwin.

Back in November 1987, in their last Test in Delhi, West Indies had hunted down 276 – still the highest successful run-chase by a visiting team in India. But now it was India who finished up with 276 for a victory that relieved some of the pressure after a disastrous England tour. It was their first win in seven matches, but the 11th in 20 home Tests since the start of 2008. Chanderpaul's 24th Test century underpinned a solid first innings: Ojha finished with his first Test five-for, while Dhoni passed Syed Kirmani's Indian-record 198 dismissals with his smart stumping of the adhesive Brathwaite, and later claimed his 200th (Samuels) as 269 for five turned into 304 all out. India's openers clattered 89 in 12.3 overs before Sammy finger-tipped a Sehwag drive into the stumps with Gambhir stranded; Dravid apart, the batting subsided. West Indies lost two quick wickets, making 17 in all on the second day. That soon became 63 for six, and India's eventual target was less than it might have been. Tendulkar ended the third day with 33, which took him past 15,000 Test runs. Next day Fidel Edwards uprooted Dravid's off and middle stumps – but Tendulkar was largely untroubled before missing a straight one from Bishoo. The sepulchral silence that followed was eventually broken only by the applause that accompanied the winning runs. Ravichandran Ashwin took nine for 128, debut figures bettered for India only by Narendra Hirwani's 16 for 136 against West Indies at Madras in 1987–88.

West Indies

K. C. Brathwaite st Dhoni b Ojha	63	– lbw b Ojha	2
K. O. A. Powell lbw b Ojha	14	– c Gambhir b Ashwin	0
K. A. Edwards c and b Ojha	15	– b Yadav	33
D. M. Bravo b Ashwin	12	– (5) lbw b Ashwin	12
S. Chanderpaul lbw b Sharma	118	– (6) lbw b Ashwin	47
M. N. Samuels c Dhoni b Ashwin	15	– (7) b Yadav	0
†C. S. Baugh lbw b Ojha	27	– (8) c Dhoni b Yadav	7
*D. J. G. Sammy lbw b Ojha	5	– (9) b Ashwin	42
R. Rampaul lbw b Ashwin	12	– (10) c Ojha b Ashwin	18
F. H. Edwards c Sehwag b Ojha	10	– (4) c Dhoni b Sharma	1
D. Bishoo not out	0	– not out	9
B 4, l-b 8, n-b 1	13	B 1, l-b 8	9
(108.2 overs)	304	(57.3 overs)	180

1/25 (2) 2/45 (3) 3/72 (4) 4/180 (1) 5/200 (6) 6/269 (7)　　1/0 (2) 2/17 (1) 3/26 (4) 4/53 (3) 5/63 (5) 6/63 (7)
7/281 (8) 8/281 (5) 9/304 (9) 10/304 (10)　　7/84 (8) 8/124 (6) 9/157 (9) 10/180 (10)

Sharma 25–5–80–1; Yadav 19–5–52–0; Ojha 34.2–9–72–6; Ashwin 27–4–81–3; Sehwag 2–0–5–0; Yuvraj Singh 1–0–2–0. *Second Innings*—Ojha 14–4–37–1; Ashwin 21.3–5–47–6; Yuvraj Singh 1–0–2–0; Sharma 14–2–49–1; Yadav 7–0–36–2.

India

G. Gambhir run out	41	– lbw b Samuels	22
V. Sehwag st Baugh b Bishoo	55	– b Sammy	55
R. Dravid c Sammy b Rampaul	54	– b F. H. Edwards	31
S. R. Tendulkar lbw b F. H. Edwards	7	– lbw b Bishoo	76
V. V. S. Laxman c Baugh b Bishoo	1	– not out	58
Yuvraj Singh c K. A. Edwards b Sammy	23	– b Sammy	18
*†M. S. Dhoni b Sammy	0	– not out	0
R. Ashwin c Baugh b Sammy	0		
I. Sharma c Baugh b Samuels	17		
P. P. Ojha not out	3		
U. T. Yadav b Rampaul	0		
B 5, w 1, n-b 2	8	B 1, l-b 14, n-b 1	16
(52.5 overs)	209	(5 wkts, 80.4 overs)	276

1/89 (1) 2/100 (2) 3/113 (4) 4/120 (5) 5/152 (6) 6/152 (7)
7/154 (8) 8/203 (9) 9/209 (3) 10/209 (11)　　1/51 (1) 2/95 (2) 3/162 (3) 4/233 (4) 5/275 (6)

F. H. Edwards 11–1–57–1; Rampaul 14.5–2–44–2; Sammy 8–1–35–3; Bishoo 14–0–55–2; Samuels 5–0–13–1. *Second Innings*—F. H. Edwards 15–3–51–1; Rampaul 10–0–34–0; Sammy 16–0–56–2; Samuels 16–0–57–1; Bishoo 22–2–56–1; Brathwaite 1.4–0–7–0.

Umpires: H. D. P. K. Dharmasena *(Sri Lanka)* (6) and R. J. Tucker *(Australia)* (14).
Third umpire: S. Asnani *(India)*. Referee: J. J. Crowe *(New Zealand)* (47).

Close of play: First day, West Indies 256–5 (Chanderpaul 111, Baugh 19); Second day, West Indies 21–2 (K. A. Edwards 15, F. H. Edwards 0); Third day, India 152–2 (Dravid 30, Tendulkar 33).

INDIA v WEST INDIES 2011–12 (2nd Test)

At Eden Gardens, Kolkata, on 14, 15, 16, 17 November, 2011.
Toss: India.   Result: INDIA WON BY AN INNINGS AND 15 RUNS.
Debuts: none.
Man of the Match: V. V. S. Laxman.

This was an old-style Indian thrashing. Dravid produced another masterclass for his 36th Test century, his fifth of 2011, then the screw was turned in a seventh-wicket partnership of 224 – Laxman all eased drives, tucks and nudges in his 17th Test century (fifth at Kolkata), Dhoni relying on immense power to propel the ball to (and five times over) the ropes. His declaration at 631 meant West Indies would have to bat long to save the game: their first effort didn't even make it past lunch on the third day. The game-changer was Yadav, who found rhythm rarely in evidence during his nervy Delhi debut. The innings lasted just 48 overs and, with a lead of 478, Dhoni bucked the modern-day trend by imposing the follow-on. West Indies had only once conceded a bigger first-innings lead – 563 to England at Kingston in 1929–30. Finally they knuckled down: Barath made a cultured half-century, and Kirk Edwards a solid 60. But the star was Darren Bravo, a cousin of Brian Lara and reminiscent of him in batting style. After this match, his 12th, Bravo had 941 runs at 47.05, identical figures to Lara's after a dozen Tests. At 401 for four it looked certain India would have to bat again. But the bowlers kept at it, and claimed their rewards late on the fourth afternoon, when Bravo's eventual dismissal – edging to slip after 321 minutes – triggered a collapse. India's innings victory was only their second over West Indies, following Mumbai in 2002–03.

India

G. Gambhir c Barath b F. H. Edwards	65
V. Sehwag c Barath b Sammy	38
R. Dravid b Brathwaite	119
S. R. Tendulkar c Samuels b Bishoo	38
V. V. S. Laxman not out	176
I. Sharma c Baugh b Roach	0
Yuvraj Singh lbw b Sammy	25
*†M. S. Dhoni c Baugh b Roach	144
R. Ashwin not out	4
B 6, l-b 5, w 2, n-b 9	22
(7 wkts dec, 151.2 overs)	631

1/66 (2) 2/149 (1) 3/205 (4) 4/345 (3) 5/346 (6)
6/396 (7) 7/620 (8)

P. P. Ojha and U. T. Yadav did not bat.

F. H. Edwards 22.2–1–81–1; Sammy 25–0–132–2; Roach 26–1–106–2; Samuels 27–0–104–0; Bishoo 45–2–154–1; Brathwaite 6–0–43–1.

West Indies

A. B. Barath c Sehwag b Yadav	1	– c Laxman b Sharma	62
K. C. Brathwaite c Gambhir b Ashwin	17	– c Dhoni b Yadav	9
K. A. Edwards lbw b Ojha	16	– lbw b Sharma	60
D. M. Bravo b Yadav	30	– c Dravid b Ojha	136
S. Chanderpaul lbw b Ashwin	4	– b Yadav	47
M. N. Samuels b Yadav	25	– lbw b Ashwin	84
†C. S. Baugh lbw b Ojha	13	– c Dravid b Ojha	3
*D. J. G. Sammy c Dhoni b Ojha	18	– b Yadav	32
K. A. J. Roach run out	2	– b Ashwin	1
F. H. Edwards lbw b Ojha	16	– not out	15
D. Bishoo not out	8	– b Yadav	0
L-b 3	3	B 9, l-b 4, w 1	14
(48 overs)	153	(126.3 overs)	463

1/3 (1) 2/30 (2) 3/42 (3) 4/46 (5) 5/92 (4) 6/99 (6)   1/23 (2) 2/116 (1) 3/161 (3) 4/269 (5) 5/401 (4)
7/120 (8) 8/129 (9) 9/129 (7) 10/153 (10)   6/411 (7) 7/417 (6) 8/421 (9) 9/463 (8) 10/463 (11)

Ojha 22–5–64–4; Yadav 7–1–23–3; Ashwin 14–3–49–2; Sharma 5–2–14–0. *Second Innings*—Yadav 17.3–1–80–4; Sharma 25–4–95–2; Ojha 32–5–104–2; Ashwin 40–4–137–2; Yuvraj Singh 3–0–14–0; Sehwag 9–2–20–0.

Umpires: B. N. J. Oxenford *(Australia)* (4) and R. J. Tucker *(Australia)* (15).
Third umpire: S. Ravi *(India)*. Referee: J. J. Crowe *(New Zealand)* (48).

Close of play: First day, India 346–5 (Laxman 73); Second day, West Indies 34–2 (K. A. Edwards 12, Bravo 4); Third day, West Indies 195–3 (Bravo 38, Chanderpaul 21).

INDIA v WEST INDIES 2011–12 (3rd Test)

At Wankhede Stadium, Mumbai, on 22, 23, 24, 25, 26 November, 2011.
Toss: West Indies.   Result: MATCH DRAWN.
Debuts: India – V. R. Aaron.
Man of the Match: R. Ashwin. Man of the Series: R. Ashwin.

Only once before had a Test ended as a draw with the scores level after the fourth innings, when England failed to beat Zimbabwe at Bulawayo in 1996–97, also with a last-ball run-out. Ashwin, who had made a hundred from No. 8 in the first innings, was left to score two off the final two balls: the first went straight to a fielder then, after thumping the last to long-on, he was slow setting off and was run out going for the vital second. West Indies celebrated as if they had won. The match had looked like a cast-iron draw – only 22 wickets fell on the first four days – but with the spinners extracting more bounce, West Indies were shot out for 134 before lunch on the final day. Ojha and Ashwin shared all ten wickets, finishing the series with 42 between them. Needing 243 in 64 overs, India were cruising at first – 101 for one at above five an over. But once Sehwag miscued a daft reverse paddle-sweep, India collapsed too, with Dravid following Tendulkar not just past 13,000 Test runs but back to the pavilion. Kohli was left to pilot the chase. His 63 got India so close, but in truth West Indies deserved a share of the spoils. Bravo followed his Kolkata century with a dazzling 166 as his side batted into the third day: had Ashwin completed that second run, their 590 would have been the highest first-innings total in Tests to have led to defeat.

West Indies

A. B. Barath c Dhoni b Ashwin	62	– c Laxman b Ojha	3
K. C. Brathwaite c Kohli b Ashwin	68	– c Tendulkar b Ojha	35
K. A. Edwards c Dhoni b Sharma	86	– st Dhoni b Ojha	17
D. M. Bravo c Dhoni b Aaron	166	– c and b Ojha	48
K. O. A. Powell c Dhoni b Ojha	81	– lbw b Ashwin	11
M. N. Samuels c Dravid b Ashwin	61	– st Dhoni b Ojha	0
†C. S. Baugh b Aaron	4	– b Ashwin	1
*D. J. G. Sammy c Dhoni b Aaron	3	– c Dhoni b Ashwin	10
R. Rampaul c Kohli b Ashwin	10	– c Tendulkar b Ojha	0
F. H. Edwards not out	11	– not out	2
D. Bishoo b Ashwin	12	– lbw b Ashwin	0
B 8, l-b 16, n-b 2	26	B 3, l-b 4	7
(184.1 overs)	590	(57.2 overs)	134

1/137 (1) 2/150 (2) 3/314 (3) 4/474 (5) 5/518 (4)
6/524 (7) 7/540 (8) 8/563 (9) 9/566 (6) 10/590 (11)

1/6 (1) 2/30 (3) 3/91 (2) 4/112 (4) 5/112 (6)
6/117 (7) 7/120 (5) 8/129 (9) 9/134 (8) 10/134 (11)

Sharma 32–9–84–1; Aaron 28–4–106–3; Ojha 48–10–126–1; Ashwin 52.1–6–156–5; Sehwag 16–1–61–0; Kohli 2–0–9–0; Tendulkar 6–0–24–0. *Second Innings*—Ojha 27–5–47–6; Sharma 8–2–15–0; Aaron 4–0–23–0; Ashwin 15.2–0–34–4; Sehwag 2–0–3–0; Tendulkar 1–0–5–0.

India

G. Gambhir c Baugh b Rampaul	55	– c Sammy b F. H. Edwards	12
V. Sehwag b Sammy	37	– c Sammy b Bishoo	60
R. Dravid b Samuels	82	– c sub (D. Ramdin) b Samuels	33
S. R. Tendulkar c Sammy b Rampaul	94	– c K. A. Edwards b Samuels	3
V. V. S. Laxman c Samuels b F. H. Edwards	32	– c Barath b Rampaul	31
V. Kohli c F. H. Edwards b Bishoo	52	– c Sammy b Bishoo	63
*†M. S. Dhoni b Sammy	8	– c K. A. Edwards b Rampaul	13
R. Ashwin c Barath b Rampaul	103	– run out	14
I. Sharma c Bravo b Samuels	5	– b Rampaul	10
V. R. Aaron b Samuels	4	– not out	2
P. P. Ojha not out	0		
B 1, w 4, n-b 5	10	N-b 1	1
(135.4 overs)	482	(9 wkts, 64 overs)	242

1/67 (2) 2/138 (1) 3/224 (3) 4/287 (5) 5/322 (4)
6/331 (7) 7/428 (6) 8/455 (9) 9/463 (10) 10/482 (8)

1/19 (1) 2/101 (2) 3/106 (4) 4/113 (3) 5/165 (5)
6/189 (7) 7/224 (6) 8/239 (9) 9/242 (8)

F. H. Edwards 28–4–116–1; Rampaul 24.4–3–95–3; Sammy 26–3–90–2; Samuels 17–0–74–3; Bishoo 40–6–106–1. *Second Innings*—F. H. Edwards 7–0–28–1; Rampaul 16–1–56–3; Samuels 25–0–93–2; Bishoo 16–0–65–2.

Umpires: A. L. Hill *(New Zealand)* (28) and B. N. J. Oxenford *(Australia)* (5).
Third umpire: S. K. Tarapore *(India)*. Referee: D. C. Boon *(Australia)* (5).

Close of play: First day, West Indies 267–2 (K. A. Edwards 65, Bravo 57); Second day, West Indies 575–9 (F. H. Edwards 7, Bishoo 2); Third day, India 281–3 (Tendulkar 67, Laxman 32); Fourth day, West Indies 81–2 (Brathwaite 34, Bravo 27).

SOUTH AFRICA v AUSTRALIA 2011–12 (1st Test)

At Newlands, Cape Town, on 9, 10, 11 November, 2011.
Toss: South Africa.   Result: SOUTH AFRICA WON BY EIGHT WICKETS.
Debuts: South Africa – Imran Tahir, V. D. Philander.
Man of the Match: V. D. Philander.

An astonishing match was over before lunch on the third day after Australia were bundled out for 47, their lowest total since 1902. It might have been worse: no Test side had ever been 21 for nine before, as Australia flirted with New Zealand's Test-record-low of 26. But the last pair doubled the total, Lyon becoming the eighth No. 11 to top-score in a Test innings. The pitch served up for only the third Test held in Cape Town in November (the other two, against Australia in 1902–03 and 1921–22, also ended inside three days) was tricky but far from unplayable, as Clarke showed with a superb 151 in Australia's first innings, in the face of some lively seam bowling. Boucher was the first wicketkeeper to make 500 Test dismissals when he caught Hughes. But 23 wickets – the most in any Test for 110 years – cascaded on the second day, which featured part of all four innings (only the third such instance, after Lord's 2000 and Hamilton 2002–03). Both Clarke and Rudolph – in his first Test for five years – were dismissed twice in the day. South Africa, 49 for one at lunch, were shot out for 96, Watson's five including Kallis for his first Test duck since December 2007. Then South Africa's seamers ripped Australia apart, Vernon Philander marking his debut with five for 15. A target of 236 looked mountainous in the circumstances – but suddenly things returned to normal, Smith and Amla completing unruffled centuries on the third morning.

Australia

S. R. Watson c Kallis b Steyn	3	– lbw b Steyn		4
P. J. Hughes c Boucher b Philander	9	– c Rudolph b Morkel		9
S. E. Marsh lbw b Steyn	44	– (10) lbw b Philander		0
R. T. Ponting lbw b Steyn	8	– (3) lbw b Philander		0
*M. J. Clarke b Morkel	151	– (4) lbw b Philander		2
M. E. K. Hussey c Boucher b Morkel	1	– (5) c Prince b Morkel		0
†B. J. Haddin c Prince b Steyn	5	– (6) c Boucher b Philander		0
M. G. Johnson c Morkel b Philander	20	– (7) c Amla b Philander		3
R. J. Harris c Morkel b Philander	5	– (8) c Smith b Morkel		3
P. M. Siddle c de Villiers b Morkel	20	– (9) not out		12
N. M. Lyon not out	1	– c de Villiers b Steyn		14
B 5, l-b 7, w 1, n-b 4	17			
(75 overs)	284	(18 overs)		47

1/9 (1) 2/13 (2) 3/40 (4) 4/143 (3) 5/158 (6) 6/163 (7)   1/4 (1) 2/11 (3) 3/13 (2) 4/13 (5) 5/15 (4)
7/202 (8) 8/214 (9) 9/273 (10) 10/284 (5)   6/18 (6) 7/21 (8) 8/21 (7) 9/21 (10) 10/47 (11)

Steyn 20–4–55–4; Philander 21–3–63–3; Morkel 18–2–82–3; Imran Tahir 10–1–35–0; Kallis 6–0–37–0. *Second Innings*—Steyn 5–1–23–2; Philander 7–3–15–5; Morkel 6–1–9–3.

South Africa

J. A. Rudolph b Harris	18	– (2) c Haddin b Siddle		14
*G. C. Smith b Watson	37	– (1) not out		101
H. M. Amla lbw b Watson	3	– c Clarke b Johnson		112
J. H. Kallis c Ponting b Watson	0	– not out		2
A. B. de Villiers lbw b Harris	8			
A. G. Prince lbw b Watson	0			
†M. V. Boucher lbw b Watson	4			
V. D. Philander c Ponting b Harris	4			
D. W. Steyn not out	9			
M. Morkel run out	1			
Imran Tahir b Harris	5			
L-b 4, w 1, n-b 2	7	L-b 4, w 1, n-b 2		7
(24.3 overs)	96	(2 wkts, 50.2 overs)		236

1/24 (1) 2/49 (3) 3/49 (4) 4/73 (2) 5/73 (6) 6/77 (5)   1/27 (2) 2/222 (3)
7/77 (7) 8/81 (8) 9/83 (10) 10/96 (11)

Harris 10.3–3–33–4; Johnson 5–0–26–0; Siddle 4–1–16–0; Watson 5–2–17–5. *Second Innings*—Harris 14–2–67–0; Siddle 12.2–0–49–1; Watson 10–0–44–0; Johnson 11–1–61–1; Lyon 3–1–11–0.

Umpires: B. R. Doctrove *(West Indies)* (34) and I. J. Gould *(England)* (22).
Third umpire: B. F. Bowden *(New Zealand)*. Referee: R. S. Mahanama *(Sri Lanka)* (33).

Close of play: First day, Australia 214–8 (Clarke 107, Siddle 0); Second day, South Africa 81–1 (Smith 36, Amla 29).

SOUTH AFRICA v AUSTRALIA 2011–12 (2nd Test)

At The Wanderers, Johannesburg, on 17, 18, 19, 20, 21 November, 2011.
Toss: South Africa.   Result: AUSTRALIA WON BY TWO WICKETS.
Debuts: Australia – P. J. Cummins.
Man of the Match: P. J. Cummins. Man of the Series: V. D. Philander.

Australia held their nerve in conditions as orthodox as Cape Town's were outlandish. The pitch demanded old-fashioned application, but only Kallis (the fourth to reach 12,000 Test runs), de Villiers and Prince provided that on the first day. Australia grabbed a lead of 30, thanks almost exclusively to Watson and Hughes, who both scored 88; from 174 without loss, Australia lost all ten wickets for 122. Amla, with his 14th Test century, then put on 147 with de Villiers, helped by the absence of Watson (hamstring strain), which put the spotlight on Pat Cummins, in only his fourth first-class match and, at 18, the youngest-ever Australian Test cricketer apart from Ian Craig (17 in 1952–53). He finished with six for 79, the first Australian paceman to take a debut five-for since Stuart Clark at Cape Town in 2005–06. He roughed up Kallis in classic style, eventually despatching him via a snorter nicked to slip. The fall of seven wickets for 102 meant Australia – at one stage apparently out of it – now had a sniff, even if they needed 310, the biggest total to win at the Wanderers. After two quick wickets, Ponting and Khawaja steadied the ship, then the middle order nursed, nurdled and nuked Australia towards their target. But Philander's smoking aggression kept South Africa in it and, when Steyn despatched Siddle with 18 needed, all four results were possible until Cummins smeared Tahir for the runs that squared an enthralling series. Never had two Tests seemed so insufficient.

South Africa

J. A. Rudolph c Haddin b Watson	30	– (2) c Haddin b Cummins	24
*G. C. Smith c Clarke b Johnson	11	– (1) c Hughes b Lyon	36
H. M. Amla c Ponting b Cummins	19	– c Haddin b Johnson	105
J. H. Kallis c Khawaja b Siddle	54	– c Clarke b Cummins	2
A. B. de Villiers c Cummins b Siddle	64	– c Clarke b Cummins	73
A. G. Prince c Johnson b Lyon	50	– run out	2
†M. V. Boucher c Lyon b Siddle	3	– c Watson b Lyon	13
V. D. Philander lbw b Lyon	0	– c Haddin b Cummins	23
D. W. Steyn not out	15	– c Haddin b Cummins	41
M. Morkel c Watson b Clarke	6	– b Cummins	0
Imran Tahir c Hughes b Clarke	0	– not out	4
B 9, l-b 2, w 2, n-b 1	14	B 5, l-b 2, w 7, n-b 2	16
(71 overs)	266	(110 overs)	339

1/24 (2) 2/43 (1) 3/123 (4) 4/129 (3) 5/241 (6)   1/40 (2) 2/75 (1) 3/90 (4) 4/237 (5) 5/249 (6)
6/243 (5) 7/243 (8) 8/245 (7) 9/258 (10) 10/266 (11)   6/260 (3) 7/266 (7) 8/314 (8) 9/314 (10) 10/339 (9)

Johnson 16.1–4–67–1; Cummins 15–3–38–1; Siddle 15–4–69–3; Watson 3.5–1–13–1; Lyon 13–2–52–2; Hussey 4–0–10–0; Clarke 4–1–6–2. *Second Innings*—Johnson 30–4–101–1; Cummins 29–5–79–6; Siddle 27–10–71–0; Lyon 16–4–57–2; Hussey 5–0–14–0; Clarke 2–1–2–0; Ponting 1–0–8–0.

Australia

S. R. Watson c Imran Tahir b Kallis	88	– b Philander	0
P. J. Hughes c de Villiers b Philander	88	– c Kallis b Philander	11
U. T. Khawaja lbw b Steyn	12	– c Kallis b Imran Tahir	65
R. T. Ponting lbw b Steyn	0	– c Rudolph b Morkel	62
*M. J. Clarke c de Villiers b Morkel	11	– b Philander	2
M. E. K. Hussey b Steyn	20	– lbw b Philander	39
†B. J. Haddin lbw b Imran Tahir	16	– c Boucher b Philander	55
M. G. Johnson not out	38	– not out	40
P. M. Siddle b Imran Tahir	0	– c Imran Tahir b Steyn	4
P. J. Cummins c Boucher b Steyn	2	– not out	13
N. M. Lyon lbw b Imran Tahir	2		
B 4, l-b 8, w 3, n-b 4	19	B 1, l-b 7, w 4, n b 7	19
(76.4 overs)	296	(8 wkts, 86.5 overs)	310

1/174 (2) 2/192 (1) 3/193 (4) 4/212 (5) 5/228 (3)   1/0 (1) 2/19 (2) 3/141 (3) 4/145 (5) 5/165 (4)
6/233 (6) 7/255 (7) 8/255 (9) 9/285 (10) 10/296 (11)   6/215 (6) 7/287 (7) 8/292 (9)

Steyn 18–3–64–4; Philander 15–4–47–1; Morkel 17–4–62–1; Kallis 13–2–56–1; Imran Tahir 13.4–2–55–3. *Second Innings*—Philander 20–3–70–5; Steyn 23–1–98–1; Morkel 19–6–43–1; Imran Tahir 15.5–0–63–1; Kallis 9–1–28–0.

Umpires: B. F. Bowden *(New Zealand)* (69) and I. J. Gould *(England)* (23).
Third umpire: B. R. Doctrove *(West Indies)*. Referee: R. S. Mahanama *(Sri Lanka)* (34).

Close of play: First day, South Africa 266; Second day, South Africa 0–0 (Smith 0, Rudolph 0); Third day, South Africa 229–3 (Amla 89, de Villiers 70); Fourth day, Australia 142–3 (Ponting 54, Clarke 1).

AUSTRALIA v NEW ZEALAND 2011–12 (1st Test)

At Woolloongabba, Brisbane, on 1, 2, 3, 4 December, 2011.
Toss: New Zealand.   Result: AUSTRALIA WON BY NINE WICKETS.
Debuts: Australia – J. L. Pattinson, M. A. Starc, D. A. Warner.
Man of the Match: J. L. Pattinson.

New Zealand started well but, hampered by sloppy fielding, surrendered the advantage. By the 11th over, they had reached 44 – but then threw away five for 52. Brownlie, Perth-born, shared a national sixth-wicket record of 148 against Australia with Vettori, who looked set for his first century against Australia, but at 96 took on Hussey's arm from mid-off, and lost. Australia's reply swung on a vital let-off when Clarke, on 23, was bowled by Bracewell – but replays revealed a no-ball. Clarke thundered on, although he was dropped twice. Young, one of the culprits, was later struck in the face by a Vettori delivery; while he had 12 stitches in his top lip, McCullum kept wicket without pads. Clarke and Haddin put on 108, then Starc was dropped second ball and survived an hour as the lead stretched to 132. It proved crucial. Third-innings collapses had become a New Zealand trademark and, in the best batting conditions of the match, they did it again here. On a remarkable fourth morning, Pattinson took three wickets in four balls, including Taylor for his first duck in 59 Test innings; only A. B. de Villiers (78) and Aravinda de Silva (75) had more before falling for nought. Bracewell soon followed, giving Pattinson dream debut figures of 7–5–7–5, and New Zealand folded in less than 50 overs. Pattinson's brother, Darren, won one cap for England in 2008. They were the third siblings to play Tests for different sides, the other two both in the 1890s.

New Zealand

B. B. McCullum c Warner b Starc	34	– (2) c Ponting b Pattinson	1
M. J. Guptill c Haddin b Siddle	13	– (1) c Khawaja b Pattinson	12
K. S. Williamson c Khawaja b Lyon	19	– (4) c Ponting b Pattinson	0
*L. R. P. L. Taylor b Pattinson	14	– (5) c Haddin b Pattinson	0
J. D. Ryder c Warner b Starc	6	– (6) c Hussey b Lyon	36
D. G. Brownlie not out	77	– (7) c Warner b Siddle	42
D. L. Vettori run out	96	– (8) c Clarke b Hussey	17
†R. A. Young c Clarke b Siddle	2	– (9) not out	11
D. A. J. Bracewell c Clarke b Lyon	0	– (3) c Haddin b Pattinson	2
T. G. Southee c Hussey b Lyon	17	– c Warner b Lyon	8
C. S. Martin b Lyon	1	– c Starc b Lyon	0
B 9, l-b 1, w 3, n-b 3	16	L-b 15, w 2, n-b 4	21
(82.5 overs)	295	(49.4 overs)	150

1/44 (2) 2/56 (1) 3/78 (3) 4/93 (4) 5/96 (5) 6/254 (7)
7/256 (8) 8/259 (9) 9/290 (10) 10/295 (11)

1/10 (2) 2/17 (1) 3/17 (4) 4/17 (5) 5/28 (3) 6/69 (6)
7/121 (8) 8/123 (7) 9/141 (10) 10/150 (11)

Pattinson 15–1–64–1; Siddle 24–8–57–2; Starc 20–1–90–2; Lyon 21.5–1–69–4; Hussey 2–0–5–0. *Second Innings*— Pattinson 11–5–27–5; Siddle 16–3–44–1; Starc 6–0–33–0; Lyon 11.4–2–19–3; Hussey 4–1–7–1; Warner 1–0–5–0.

Australia

D. A. Warner c Young b Southee	3	– (2) not out	12
P. J. Hughes c Guptill b Martin	10	– (1) c Guptill b Martin	7
U. T. Khawaja run out	38	– not out	0
R. T. Ponting lbw b Martin	78		
*M. J. Clarke c Southee b Martin	139		
M. E. K. Hussey c Ryder b Vettori	15		
†B. J. Haddin c Martin b Guptill	80		
P. M. Siddle c Taylor b Vettori	0		
J. L. Pattinson c Taylor b Bracewell	12		
M. A. Starc not out	32		
N. M. Lyon c Brownlie b Southee	5		
L-b 6, w 3, n-b 6	15		
(129.2 overs)	427	(1 wkt, 2.2 overs)	19

1/3 (1) 2/25 (2) 3/91 (3) 4/177 (4) 5/237 (6) 6/345 (5)
7/345 (8) 8/374 (9) 9/418 (7) 10/427 (11)   1/11 (1)

Vettori 37–13–88–2; Southee 28.2–5–103–2; Martin 28–5–89–3; Bracewell 26–3–104–1; Guptill 3–0–18–1; Brownlie 3–0–11–0; Williamson 4–0–8–0. *Second Innings*—Southee 1–0–11–0; Martin 1–1–0–1; Bracewell 0.2–0–8–0.

Umpires: Aleem Dar *(Pakistan)* (68) and Asad Rauf *(Pakistan)* (40).
Third umpire: N. J. Llong *(England)*. Referee: A. J. Pycroft *(Zimbabwe)* (21).

Close of play: First day, New Zealand 176–5 (Brownlie 32, Vettori 45); Second day, Australia 154–3 (Ponting 67, Clarke 28); Third day, New Zealand 10–1 (Guptill 7, Bracewell 0).

AUSTRALIA v NEW ZEALAND 2011–12 (2nd Test)

At Bellerive Oval, Hobart, on 9, 10, 11, 12 December, 2011.
Toss: Australia.　　Result: NEW ZEALAND WON BY SEVEN RUNS.
Debuts: New Zealand – T. A. Boult.
Man of the Match: D. A. Warner. Man of the Series: J. L. Pattinson.

New Zealand squared the series with their first win over Australia since 1992–93, their first *in* Australia since 1985–86. It was desperately close. Left seven sessions to score 241, Australia flowed to 72 without loss at the third-day close then – with Hughes uniquely being caught by Guptill off Martin for the fourth innings running – ebbed to 199 for nine next day. It looked all over, but Warner and Lyon conjured 34 to reduce the target to single figures. New Zealand thought they had won when umpire Llong pronounced Lyon lbw to Southee, but the review showed otherwise... but finally Bracewell, in his 16th over of the day, seamed one back through the gate to knock back Lyon's middle stump after 43 minutes and 27 balls. Warner, in only his second Test and previously branded a Twenty20 specialist, carried his bat after 317 minutes. Australia had topped 500 in the previous two Tests at Hobart, but now, on a grassy pitch, the two first innings were done and dusted inside 100 overs. New Zealand's second successive total of 150 – which included a patient 56 from Brownlie, and Martin's 32nd duck in his 64th Test – improbably proved enough for a lead, as Australia were seamed out for 136. Left-armer Boult, making his debut after Vettori tweaked a hamstring, took three wickets. By stumps on the second day, New Zealand looked in control at 139 for three – but Williamson fell without addition next morning, and the last six wickets cobbled together only 55.

New Zealand

B. B. McCullum c Haddin b Pattinson	16	– (2) c Hughes b Pattinson	12
M. J. Guptill c Haddin b Siddle	3	– (1) c Haddin b Siddle	16
J. D. Ryder lbw b Pattinson	0	– st Haddin b Hussey	16
*L. R. P. L. Taylor lbw b Siddle	6	– c Clarke b Pattinson	56
K. S. Williamson c Haddin b Starc	19	– c Ponting b Siddle	34
D. G. Brownlie b Pattinson	56	– c Haddin b Pattinson	21
†R. A. Young b Pattinson	0	– lbw b Siddle	9
D. A. J. Bracewell c Clarke b Siddle	12	– b Lyon	4
T. G. Southee b Starc	18	– c Hussey b Lyon	13
T. A. Boult not out	0	– c Hussey b Lyon	21
C. S. Martin b Pattinson	0	– not out	2
B 2, l-b 12, w 1, n-b 5	20	B 4, l-b 11, w 5, n-b 2	22
(45.5 overs)	150	(78.3 overs)	226

1/10 (2) 2/11 (3) 3/25 (4) 4/56 (5) 5/60 (1) 6/60 (7)　　1/36 (2) 2/36 (1) 3/73 (3) 4/139 (5) 5/171 (4)
7/105 (8) 8/146 (9) 9/150 (6) 10/150 (11)　　6/178 (6) 7/190 (7) 8/203 (9) 9/203 (8) 10/226 (10)

Pattinson 13.5–3–51–5; Siddle 13–3–42–3; Starc 11–4–30–2; Lyon 8–4–13–0. *Second Innings*—Pattinson 21–7–54–3; Siddle 25–11–66–3; Starc 19–6–47–0; Hussey 5–0–15–1; Lyon 7.3–1–25–3; Ponting 1–0–4–0.

Australia

D. A. Warner c Taylor b Martin	15	– (2) not out	123
P. J. Hughes c Guptill b Martin	4	– (1) c Guptill b Martin	20
U. T. Khawaja c Young b Martin	7	– c Taylor b Boult	23
R. T. Ponting lbw b Southee	5	– c Southee b Bracewell	16
*M. J. Clarke b Bracewell	22	– c Taylor b Bracewell	0
M. E. K. Hussey c Young b Boult	8	– lbw b Bracewell	0
†B. J. Haddin c McCullum b Bracewell	5	– c Taylor b Southee	15
P. M. Siddle c Guptill b Bracewell	36	– c Ryder b Southee	2
J. L. Pattinson c Williamson b Boult	17	– c Guptill b Bracewell	4
M. A. Starc lbw b Boult	4	– b Bracewell	0
N. M. Lyon not out	1	– b Bracewell	9
B 1, l-b 8, n-b 3	12	B 3, l-b 18	21
(51 overs)	136	(63.4 overs)	233

1/7 (2) 2/24 (1) 3/31 (4) 4/35 (3) 5/58 (6) 6/69 (7)　　1/72 (1) 2/122 (3) 3/159 (4) 4/159 (5) 5/159 (6)
7/75 (5) 8/131 (8) 9/131 (9) 10/136 (10)　　6/192 (7) 7/194 (8) 8/199 (9) 9/199 (10) 10/233 (11)

Martin 16–1–46–3; Boult 13–4–29–3; Southee 12–2–32–1; Bracewell 10–3–20–3. *Second Innings*—Martin 16–4–44–1; Boult 12–1–51–1; Southee 19–3–77–2; Bracewell 16.4–4–40–6.

Umpires: Asad Rauf *(Pakistan)* (41) and N. J. Llong *(England)* (12).
Third umpire: Aleem Dar *(Pakistan)*. Referee: A. J. Pycroft *(Zimbabwe)* (22).

Close of play: First day, Australia 12–1 (Warner 7, Khawaja 1); Second day, New Zealand 139–3 (Taylor 42, Williamson 34); Third day, Australia 72–0 (Hughes 20, Warner 47).

BANGLADESH v PAKISTAN 2011–12 (1st Test)

At Zohur Ahmed Chowdhury Stadium, Chittagong, on 9, 10, 11, 12 December, 2011.
Toss: Pakistan.   Result: PAKISTAN WON BY AN INNINGS AND 184 RUNS.
Debuts: Bangladesh — Nazimuddin.
Man of the Match: Younis Khan.

Pakistan's batsmen gave a masterclass in old-fashioned Test-match batting, which proved far too much for their hosts. Victory came midway through the fourth day; it was Bangladesh's 35th innings reverse in 72 Tests, and their 62nd defeat in all. It was inevitable once they folded for 135 after Misbah-ul-Haq bowled first in what seemed like perfect batting conditions – but the batsmen played too many shots and kept the slip cordon interested. The debutant opener Nazimuddin was the exception, grafting 132 minutes for 31 – but otherwise only No. 8 Nasir Hossain lasted longer than three-quarters of an hour. Pakistan's openers were not parted until Bangladesh's puny total had been passed, with Mohammad Hafeez batting for seven minutes short of six hours for his fourth Test century. He was out only because umpire Doctrove missed a thick inside-edge (DRS was not used in this series for cost reasons). But the agony was not over for Bangladesh: Younis Khan extended his 19th Test century into his third double, galloping through the 190s – where he had twice previously been dismissed – in the space of eight balls. One of Younis's three sixes took him past 6,000 Test runs, and he put on 259 with Asad Shafiq, who made his maiden Test hundred. Bangladesh fared better second time round, but as they were trailing by 459 they already needed a near-miracle just to make Pakistan bat again. Mohammad Ashraful, controversially recalled after missing the West Indies series, made one and nought – and was promptly dumped again.

Bangladesh

Tamim Iqbal c Adnan Akmal b Aizaz Cheema	9	– b Mohammad Hafeez		15
Nazimuddin c Mohammad Hafeez b Umar Gul	31	– c Saeed Ajmal b Abdur Rehman		78
Shahriar Nafees c Younis Khan b Aizaz Cheema	0	– lbw b Saeed Ajmal		28
Mohammad Ashraful c Adnan Akmal b Umar Gul	1	– c Mohammad Hafeez b Abdur Rehman		0
*†Mushfiqur Rahim lbw b Saeed Ajmal	4	– (7) lbw b Abdur Rehman		49
Shakib Al Hasan c Mohammad Hafeez b Abdur Rehman	8	– lbw b Abdur Rehman		51
Mahmudullah lbw b Saeed Ajmal	18	– (8) b Saeed Ajmal		0
Nasir Hossain c Azhar Ali b Abdur Rehman	41	– (5) c Mohammad Hafeez b Aizaz Cheema		3
Elias Sunny c Younis Khan b Saeed Ajmal	2	– not out		20
Shahadat Hossain b Abdur Rehman	8	– c Umar Gul b Aizaz Cheema		21
Rubel Hossain not out	3	– absent hurt		
L-b 9, n-b 1	10	B 2, l-b 5, n-b 3		10
(51.2 overs)	135	(82.3 overs)		275

1/17 (1) 2/19 (3) 3/20 (4) 4/28 (5) 5/47 (6) 6/71 (2) 7/81 (7) 8/97 (9) 9/118 (10) 10/135 (8)

1/24 (1) 2/74 (3) 3/75 (4) 4/80 (5) 5/158 (6) 6/205 (2) 7/210 (8) 8/252 (7) 9/275 (10)

Mohammad Hafeez 3–1–9–0; Umar Gul 13–5–33–2; Aizaz Cheema 11–4–35–2; Saeed Ajmal 18–5–40–3; Abdur Rehman 6.2–2–9–3. *Second Innings*—Umar Gul 13–2–45–0; Aizaz Cheema 7.3–1–40–2; Mohammad Hafeez 7–2–21–1; Saeed Ajmal 25–7–74–2; Abdur Rehman 30–7–88–4.

Pakistan

Mohammad Hafeez lbw b Elias Sunny	143
Taufeeq Umar lbw b Mahmudullah	61
Azhar Ali c Mushfiqur Rahim b Shahadat Hossain	26
Younis Khan not out	200
*Misbah-ul-Haq lbw b Elias Sunny	20
Asad Shafiq c Shahriar Nafees b Elias Sunny	104
†Adnan Akmal not out	6
L-b 21, w 1, n-b 12	34
(5 wkts dec, 176.5 overs)	594

1/164 (2) 2/220 (3) 3/265 (1) 4/311 (5) 5/570 (6)

Abdur Rehman, Umar Gul, Saeed Ajmal and Aizaz Cheema did not bat.

Shahadat Hossain 27–3–113–1; Rubel Hossain 25–1–97–0; Mahmudullah 30–7–94–1; Shakib Al Hasan 41.5–7–121–0; Elias Sunny 47–7–123–3; Nasir Hossain 2–0–5–0; Mohammad Ashraful 4–0–20–0.

Umpires: B. R. Doctrove *(West Indies)* (35) and S. K. Tarapore *(India)* (3).
Third umpire: Enamul Haque, sen. *(Bangladesh)*. Referee: J. Srinath *(India)* (18).

Close of play: First day, Pakistan 132–0 (Mohammad Hafeez 74, Taufeeq Umar 53); Second day, Pakistan 415–4 (Younis Khan 96, Asad Shafiq 40); Third day, Bangladesh 134–4 (Nazimuddin 41, Shakib Al Hasan 41).

BANGLADESH v PAKISTAN 2011–12 (2nd Test)

At Shere Bangla National Stadium, Mirpur, Dhaka, on 17, 18, 19, 20, 21 December, 2011.
Toss: Pakistan.   Result: PAKISTAN WON BY SEVEN WICKETS.
Debuts: none.
Man of the Match: Shakib Al Hasan. Man of the Series: Younis Khan.

As Pakistan chased down a modest target of 103 from 40 overs, their main opponent was the light-meter: not long before Misbah-ul-Haq's six clinched Pakistan's sixth victory in ten Tests, the umpires had consulted. Morning fog and fading light later were a feature throughout: even the floodlights could not ensure 90 overs on the first four days. When play began, 75 minutes late, it was no surprise that Misbah again bowled first: Aizaz Cheema struck three times in his opening spell. But Shakib Al Hasan made a superb century, putting on 180 – Bangladesh's fifth-wicket record – with Shahriar Nafees. Eventually Mushfiqur Rahim ran out Shakib, then was dismissed himself next ball, and the tail was swept away. Pakistan ground out a lead of 132 in reply. Nazmul Hossain had Mohammad Hafeez caught behind from his opening delivery; in fact, it was two in two, as Nazmul had dismissed Harbhajan Singh with his final ball of his debut in December 2004. Taufeeq Umar dropped anchor for his seventh Test century, but was missed three times; four other chances were spurned as the lead swelled. Shakib was the 21st man – the first from Bangladesh – to score a century and take a five-for in the same Test; only South Africa's Jimmy Sinclair (1898–99), and Vinoo Mankad of India (1952) had previously ended up losing. Nasir Hossain and Mushfiqur put on 117 to raise hopes of a draw, but Pakistan's spinners winkled out the last five wickets for 22, leaving their batsmen just enough time.

Bangladesh

Tamim Iqbal c Aizaz Cheema b Umar Gul	14 – c Misbah-ul-Haq b Umar Gul	21
Nazimuddin lbw b Aizaz Cheema	0 – b Abdur Rehman	12
Shahriar Nafees c Adnan Akmal b Umar Gul	97 – lbw b Umar Gul	0
Mahmudullah b Aizaz Cheema	0 – c Abdur Rehman b Aizaz Cheema	32
Nasir Hossain c Adnan Akmal b Aizaz Cheema	7 – b Umar Gul	79
Shakib Al Hasan run out	144 – c Azhar Ali b Aizaz Cheema	6
*†Mushfiqur Rahim c Adnan Akmal b Umar Gul	40 – c Saeed Ajmal b Abdur Rehman	53
Elias Sunny lbw b Saeed Ajmal	12 – b Saeed Ajmal	4
Shahadat Hossain not out	21 – c Younis Khan b Abdur Rehman	1
Nazmul Hossain run out	0 – not out	8
Robiul Islam lbw b Saeed Ajmal	0 – st Adnan Akmal b Saeed Ajmal	0
L-b 3	3	B 9, l-b 8, w 1	18
(107.2 overs)	338	(82.1 overs)	234

1/0 (2) 2/16 (1) 3/21 (4) 4/43 (5) 5/223 (3) 6/305 (6) 7/305 (7)
8/331 (8) 9/332 (10) 10/338 (11)

1/24 (1) 2/24 (3) 3/54 (2) 4/76 (4) 5/95 (6) 6/212 (5)
7/221 (7) 8/226 (9) 9/228 (8) 10/234 (11)

Umar Gul 28–1–102–3; Aizaz Cheema 26–4–73–3; Mohammad Hafeez 9–3–27–0; Saeed Ajmal 24.2–3–64–2; Abdur Rehman 19–0–66–0; Younis Khan 1–0–3–0. *Second Innings*—Umar Gul 13–4–34–2; Aizaz Cheema 15–2–61–2; Abdur Rehman 27–12–51–4; Saeed Ajmal 23.1–6–55–2; Mohammad Hafeez 3–0–8–0; Azhar Ali 1–0–8–0.

Pakistan

Mohammad Hafeez c Mushfiqur Rahim b Nazmul Hossain	14 – c Shahadat Hossain b Shakib Al Hasan	47
Taufeeq Umar c Shahriar Nafees b Nazmul Hossain	130 – c Nazimuddin b Nazmul Hossain	3
Azhar Ali c Mushfiqur Rahim b Shakib Al Hasan	57 – b Elias Sunny	34
Younis Khan c Mushfiqur Rahim b Elias Sunny	49 – not out	16
*Misbah-ul-Haq c Mahmudullah b Shakib Al Hasan	70 – not out	6
Asad Shafiq lbw b Robiul Islam	42		
†Adnan Akmal st Mushfiqur Rahim b Shakib Al Hasan	53		
Abdur Rehman c Mahmudullah b Shakib Al Hasan	24		
Umar Gul c Elias Sunny b Shakib Al Hasan	11		
Saeed Ajmal b Shakib Al Hasan	0		
Aizaz Cheema not out	1		
L-b 3, n-b 16	19	N-b 1	1
(154.5 overs)	470	(3 wkts, 20.5 overs)	107

1/23 (1) 2/150 (3) 3/245 (2) 4/293 (4) 5/359 (5) 6/389 (6)
7/430 (8) 8/464 (9) 9/465 (10) 10/470 (7)

1/7 (2) 2/70 (1) 3/101 (3)

Shahadat Hossain 16–1–82–0; Robiul Islam 23–3–78–1; Nazmul Hossain 24–5–61–2; Mahmudullah 15–2–45–0; Shakib Al Hasan 40.5–7–82–6; Elias Sunny 27–4–95–1; Nasir Hossain 9–0–24–0. *Second Innings*—Nazmul Hossain 5–1–19–1; Shakib Al Hasan 10–1–47–1; Shahadat Hossain 4–0–26–0; Robiul Islam 1–0–8–0; Elias Sunny 0.5–0–7–1.

Umpires: B. R. Doctrove *(West Indies)* (36) and S. K. Tarapore *(India)* (4).
Third umpire: Enamul Haque, sen. *(Bangladesh)*. Referee: D. C. Boon *(Australia)* (6).

Close of play: First day, Bangladesh 234–5 (Shakib Al Hasan 108, Mushfiqur Rahim 5); Second day, Pakistan 87–1 (Taufeeq Umar 44, Azhar Ali 26); Third day, Pakistan 292–3 (Younis Khan 48, Misbah-ul-Haq 26); Fourth day, Bangladesh 114–5 (Nasir Hossain 30, Mushfiqur Rahim 7).

SOUTH AFRICA v SRI LANKA 2011–12 (1st Test)

At Centurion Park, Pretoria, on 15, 16, 17 December, 2011.
Toss: South Africa.   Result: SOUTH AFRICA WON BY AN INNINGS AND 81 RUNS.
Debuts: none.
Man of the Match: V. D. Philander.

South Africa continued their love affair with Centurion, winning the 13th of 17 Tests there. Sri Lanka, in their first Test in South Africa for nine years, struggled from the start on a greentop, and reached 180 only thanks to a cautious stand of 65 between Samaraweera and Mathews, before the last six wickets tumbled for 24. Philander dismissed Samaraweera and Silva with successive balls, both after reviews. Rudolph, who made only seven from his first 53 deliveries, added 88 with Smith, but after a fiery spell from Fernando South Africa were five down and still behind. De Villiers and Prince dragged their side in front, and although de Villiers fell for 99 to a low gully catch, the lead was swelled by Boucher – with only his second fifty of a lean patch stretching back to mid-2010 – and Tahir to 231. It proved enough. Steyn had taken the last two first-innings wickets in consecutive balls, and only his booming inswing denied him a hat-trick when Paranavitana was struck on the pad by one doing too much. Nonetheless Sri Lanka were soon 19 for three, and there was never any doubt from 70 for six. Boucher collected six catches, while Philander finished with his second five-for in the match, giving him four in his first three Tests, a feat previously achieved only by Charlie Turner, Tom Richardson and Rodney Hogg. Sri Lanka's plight was summed up when Jayawardene was run out trying for what would have been his 10,000th run in Tests.

Sri Lanka

N. T. Paranavitana b Philander	32	– c Boucher b Steyn	4
*T. M. Dilshan c Philander b Steyn	6	– c Boucher b Philander	6
K. C. Sangakkara c Kallis b Philander	1	– c Boucher b Philander	2
D. P. M. D. Jayawardene c Smith b Steyn	30	– run out	15
T. T. Samaraweera c Boucher b Philander	36	– c Boucher b Morkel	32
A. D. Mathews c Kallis b Philander	38	– c Boucher b Philander	5
†J. K. Silva c Boucher b Philander	0	– c Kallis b Imran Tahir	17
N. L. T. C. Perera c Kallis b Imran Tahir	1	– c Smith b Steyn	21
H. M. R. K. B. Herath not out	14	– c Boucher b Philander	23
U. W. M. B. C. A. Welagedara b Steyn	4	– c and b Philander	10
C. R. D. Fernando b Steyn	0	– not out	4
B 1, l-b 7, w 4, n-b 6	18	L-b 1, n-b 10	11
(47.4 overs)	180	(39.1 overs)	150

1/11 (2) 2/12 (3) 3/66 (1) 4/91 (4) 5/156 (5) 6/156 (7)
7/157 (8) 8/175 (6) 9/180 (10) 10/180 (11)

1/11 (2) 2/11 (1) 3/19 (3) 4/37 (4) 5/66 (6)
6/70 (5) 7/104 (8) 8/133 (7) 9/145 (10) 10/150 (9)

Steyn 10.4–3–18–4; Philander 13–2–53–5; Morkel 10–1–48–0; Kallis 8–2–31–0; Imran Tahir 6–0–22–1. *Second Innings*—Steyn 10–2–36–2; Philander 11.1–1–49–5; Kallis 5–3–13–0; Morkel 9–0–36–1; Imran Tahir 4–1–15–1.

South Africa

J. A. Rudolph c Paranavitana b Perera	44
*G. C. Smith lbw b Fernando	61
D. W. Steyn run out	0
H. M. Amla c Mathews b Perera	18
J. H. Kallis c Mathews b Welagedara	31
A. B. de Villiers c sub (F. D. M. Karunaratne) b Perera	99
A. G. Prince c Silva b Mathews	39
†M. V. Boucher c Silva b Welagedara	65
V. D. Philander c Jayawardene b Dilshan	4
M. Morkel c Samaraweera b Welagedara	4
Imran Tahir not out	29
B 1, l-b 1, w 3, n-b 12	17
(122 overs)	411

1/88 (2) 2/90 (3) 3/125 (4) 4/136 (1) 5/173 (5) 6/270 (7)
7/303 (6) 8/344 (9) 9/350 (10) 10/411 (8)

Welagedara 31–4–96–3; Perera 24–1–114–3; Mathews 9–4–13–1; Fernando 28–2–128–1; Dilshan 7–1–17–1; Herath 23–4–41–0.

Umpires: S. J. Davis *(Australia)* (33) and R. J. Tucker *(Australia)* (16).
Third umpire: R. A. Kettleborough *(England)*. Referee: B. C. Broad *(England)* (49).

Close of play: First day, South Africa 90–1 (Rudolph 27, Steyn 0); Second day, South Africa 389–9 (Boucher 49, Imran Tahir 24).

SOUTH AFRICA v SRI LANKA 2011–12 (2nd Test)

At Kingsmead, Durban, on 26, 27, 28, 29 December, 2011.
Toss: Sri Lanka.   Result: SRI LANKA WON BY 208 RUNS.
Debuts: South Africa – M. de Lange. Sri Lanka – L. D. Chandimal.
Man of the Match: H. M. R. K. B. Herath.

Sri Lanka turned the tables in stunning style for their first Test win in South Africa: it was their 62nd victory overall, but only the sixth outside Asia or Zimbabwe. It helped that South Africa had not won any of their last three Tests at Durban, and that Philander was ruled out with knee trouble. His replacement, Marchant de Lange, responded with seven for 81, debut figures bettered at the time for South Africa only by Lance Klusener (1996–97) and Alf Hall (1922–23). But, with Tahir proving innocuous, Samaraweera settled in for only Sri Lanka's second Test century in South Africa, after Hashan Tillekeratne's at Centurion in 2002–03. It was Samaraweera's 13th in Tests, and only his second outside the subcontinent; to celebrate he pointed his bat like a machine-gun, perhaps surprising for a man once shot by terrorists in Lahore. He put on 111 with Chandimal; earlier Jayawardene's first run was his 10,000th in Tests, a first for his country. South Africa were rolled for 168, their lowest total against Sri Lanka; Kallis was one of five victims for left-arm seamer Welagedara for the first half of his first pair in 149 Tests. Sangakkara made the most of being dropped at slip when three to make his 28th Test hundred. Chandimal became only the second wicketkeeper to score two half-centuries on Test debut, after Dilawar Hussain of India in 1933–34. Chasing 450, South Africa were soon 133 for six: de Villiers and Steyn added 99 to reduce the margin.

Sri Lanka

N. T. Paranavitana c Boucher b de Lange	12	– c Prince b Morkel			9
*T. M. Dilshan c Morkel b Imran Tahir	47	– c Smith b Steyn			4
K. C. Sangakkara c Boucher b de Lange	0	– c Smith b Imran Tahir			108
D. P. M. D. Jayawardene b Morkel	31	– lbw b de Lange			14
T. T. Samaraweera c Prince b de Lange	102	– b Imran Tahir			43
A. D. Mathews c and b de Lange	30	– c Boucher b Steyn			3
†L. D. Chandimal c Boucher b Morkel	58	– c Boucher b Steyn			54
N. L. T. C. Perera c Amla b de Lange	12	– c Kallis b Steyn			12
H. M. R. K. B. Herath c Boucher b de Lange	30	– not out			8
U. W. M. B. C. A. Welagedara c Amla b de Lange	2	– c Amla b Steyn			10
C. R. D. Fernando not out	0	– c Prince b Morkel			3
L-b 8, n-b 6	14	B 5, l-b 3, w 1, n-b 2			11
(108.2 overs)	338	(78.2 overs)			279

1/35 (1) 2/47 (3) 3/84 (2) 4/117 (4) 5/162 (6)   1/4 (2) 2/20 (1) 3/44 (4) 4/138 (5) 5/141 (6)
6/273 (7) 7/289 (8) 8/335 (9) 9/337 (10) 10/338 (5)   6/245 (7) 7/245 (3) 8/262 (8) 9/276 (10) 10/279 (11)

Steyn 23–5–63–0; Morkel 21–3–61–2; de Lange 23.2–3–81–7; Imran Tahir 32–3–101–1; Kallis 9–1–24–0. *Second Innings*—Morkel 18.2–4–46–2; Steyn 20–3–73–5; de Lange 13–2–45–1; Kallis 11–1–43–0; Imran Tahir 16–1–64–2.

South Africa

*G. C. Smith c Chandimal b Welagedara	15	– (2) c Jayawardene b Fernando			26
J. A. Rudolph c Welagedara b Perera	7	– (1) c Jayawardene b Perera			22
H. M. Amla c Chandimal b Welagedara	54	– run out			51
J. H. Kallis c Jayawardene b Welagedara	0	– c Paranavitana b Herath			0
A. B. de Villiers c Jayawardene b Welagedara	25	– (6) lbw b Herath			69
A. G. Prince c Jayawardene b Herath	11	– (5) c Paranavitana b Fernando			7
†M. V. Boucher c Dilshan b Herath	3	– lbw b Herath			7
D. W. Steyn not out	29	– lbw b Herath			43
M. Morkel b Herath	0	– lbw b Dilshan			5
Imran Tahir st Chandimal b Herath	11	– not out			0
M. de Lange c Chandimal b Welagedara	9	– b Herath			0
W 1, n-b 3	4	B 6, l-b 1, w 3, n-b 1			11
(54.4 overs)	168	(87.3 overs)			241

1/22 (2) 2/27 (1) 3/27 (4) 4/103 (5) 5/106 (3)   1/37 (2) 2/88 (1) 3/97 (4) 4/106 (3) 5/116 (5)
6/118 (7) 7/119 (6) 8/119 (9) 9/145 (10) 10/168 (11)   6/133 (7) 7/232 (6) 8/241 (9) 9/241 (8) 10/241 (11)

Welagedara 16.4–3–52–5; Perera 9–3–27–1; Dilshan 1–1–0–0; Herath 20–7–49–4; Mathews 2–0–11–0; Fernando 6–0–29–0. *Second Innings*—Welagedara 16–5–33–0; Perera 13–0–48–1; Fernando 13–3–29–2; Dilshan 11–2–35–1; Herath 30.3–7–79–5; Mathews 3–0–9–0; Samaraweera 1–0–1–0.

Umpires: S. J. Davis *(Australia)* (34) and R. A. Kettleborough *(England)* (6).
Third umpire: R. J. Tucker *(Australia)*. Referee: B. C. Broad *(England)* (50).

Close of play: First day, Sri Lanka 289–7 (Samaraweera 86); Second day, Sri Lanka 7–1 (Paranavitana 0, Sangakkara 3); Third day, Sri Lanka 256–7 (Perera 6, Herath 5).

SOUTH AFRICA v SRI LANKA 2011–12 (3rd Test)

At Newlands, Cape Town, on 3, 4, 5, 6 January, 2012.
Toss: Sri Lanka.   Result: SOUTH AFRICA WON BY TEN WICKETS.
Debuts: none.
Man of the Match: J. H, Kallis. Man of the Series: A. B. de Villiers.

Now it was South Africa's turn to bounce back, winning a home Test series for the first time since 2008–09. Kallis, in his 150th match, bounced back too, after his pair at Durban; surviving an early scare when Welagedara at fine leg failed to spot an airy pull, he cruised to a career-best 224. He added 205 with Petersen, restored to open, and 192 with de Villiers, who then pasted another 127 with Rudolph before the declaration near tea on the second day. Dilshan started briskly, and Sri Lanka surged past 50 in the 13th over. It couldn't last, though: he fell to a superb catch in the deep late in the day. Sangakkara fell first thing next morning, and the pacemen got to work. Leading by 341, Smith enforced the follow-on – and an early finish looked likely when Sri Lanka dipped to 98 for four, their big guns gone. But Samaraweera reprised his Durban defiance, adding 142 with Mathews in a stand that stretched beyond lunch on the fourth day. However, the irrepressible Philander broke through afterwards, and soon added Chandimal, one of six catches in the match for Kallis, who completed a memorable game by wrapping up the innings. South Africa needed just two to win, and got there without facing a legal delivery – the first such instance in Test history – when Prasad overstepped and Petersen pushed a single. This was Smith's 41st win as captain, putting him level with Steve Waugh and behind only Ricky Ponting (48).

South Africa

*G. C. Smith b Prasad	16	– (2) not out	0
A. N. Petersen c Dilshan b Welagedara	109	– (1) not out	1
H. M. Amla lbw b Prasad	16		
J. H. Kallis c Mathews b Herath	224		
A. B. de Villiers not out	160		
J. A. Rudolph not out	51		
L-b 1, w 1, n-b 2	4	N-b 1	1
(4 wkts dec, 139 overs)	580	(no wkt, 0 overs)	2

1/25 (1) 2/56 (3) 3/261 (2) 4/453 (4)

†M. V. Boucher, V. D. Philander, D. W. Steyn, M. Morkel and Imran Tahir did not bat.

Welagedara 29–7–107–1; Perera 22–1–131–0; Prasad 30–2–154–2; Mathews 12–0–47–0; Herath 42–4–108–1; Dilshan 4–0–32–0. *Second Innings*—Prasad 0–0–2–0.

Sri Lanka

H. D. R. L. Thirimanne b Morkel	23	– c Amla b Kallis	30
*T. M. Dilshan c Smith b Imran Tahir	78	– c Boucher b Philander	5
K. C. Sangakkara c Amla b Steyn	35	– c Kallis b Imran Tahir	34
D. P. M. D. Jayawardene c Kallis b Steyn	30	– c Kallis b Morkel	12
T. T. Samaraweera c Kallis b Philander	11	– not out	115
A. D. Mathews c Boucher b Steyn	1	– lbw b Philander	63
†L. D. Chandimal c Boucher b Morkel	35	– c Kallis b Philander	1
N. L. T. C. Perera b Imran Tahir	5	– c Morkel b Imran Tahir	30
H. M. R. K. B. Herath lbw b Philander	1	– c and b Kallis	0
K. T. G. D. Prasad c Petersen b Philander	9	– st Boucher b Imran Tahir	16
U. W. M. B. C. A. Welagedara not out	0	– b Kallis	14
B 6, l-b 3, n-b 2	11	B 1, l-b 15, w 6	22
(73.5 overs)	239	(107.5 overs)	342

1/70 (1) 2/126 (2) 3/149 (3) 4/184 (5) 5/189 (4)   1/12 (2) 2/79 (1) 3/83 (3) 4/98 (4) 5/240 (6)
6/194 (6) 7/219 (8) 8/220 (9) 9/236 (10) 10/239 (7)   6/248 (7) 7/304 (8) 8/306 (9) 9/327 (10) 10/342 (11)

Steyn 20–5–56–3; Philander 19–7–46–3; Morkel 13.5–2–74–2; Imran Tahir 21–1–54–2. *Second Innings*—Steyn 20–3–56–0; Philander 20–4–54–3; Morkel 19–4–68–1; Imran Tahir 32–7–106–3; Kallis 14.5–2–35–3; Smith 2–0–7–0.

Umpires: R. A. Kettleborough *(England)* (7) and R. J. Tucker *(Australia)* (17).
Third umpire: S. J. Davis *(Australia)*. Referee: B. C. Broad *(England)* (51).

Close of play: First day, South Africa 347–3 (Kallis 159, de Villiers 45); Second day, Sri Lanka 149–2 (Sangakkara 35, Jayawardene 7); Third day, Sri Lanka 138–4 (Samaraweera 19, Mathews 28).

AUSTRALIA v INDIA 2011–12 (1st Test)

At Melbourne Cricket Ground on 26, 27, 28, 29 December, 2011.
Toss: Australia. Result: AUSTRALIA WON BY 122 RUNS.
Debuts: Australia – E. J. M. Cowan.
Man of the Match: J. L. Pattinson.

India's travelling woes continued with a disappointing attempt at a gettable fourth-day target of 292: Tendulkar top-scored, as so often, but 32 wasn't enough as the seamers shared nine wickets. Australia had started sedately on Boxing Day, debutant opener Ed Cowan inching to 68 in 68 overs. "That first hour," he declared, "I was just trying to leave well." Hussey was given out first ball, caught off his sleeve in a series played without DRS because of India's opposition; Ponting's 62, and Haddin's stand of 72 with Siddle, pushed Australia to 333. With Sehwag biffing 67 of the first 97, India reached 214 for two in reply, before a passage that shaped the match, and arguably the series. Siddle had just castled Dravid with a no-ball, but sheared through Tendulkar in the second day's last over; Dravid followed second ball next morning, part of Hilfenhaus's first five-for in his 18th Test, and one of seven wickets in the session as India's potential lead crumbled into a deficit of 51. Still, Australia lost four batsmen before clearing that off, being rescued by old hands Ponting and Hussey in a watchful stand of 115. With Zaheer and Yadav sharing seven wickets, it looked rocky at 166 for eight, but Hussey and the tail eked out another 74 vital runs. Hilfenhaus prevented any Sehwag heroics, the "unbowlable" Dravid was bowled for the third time in the match (including Siddle's no-ball), and India's hopes were extinguished when Tendulkar's departure made it 81 for six.

Australia

E. J. M. Cowan c Dhoni b Ashwin	68	– (2) lbw b Yadav	8
D. A. Warner c Dhoni b Yadav	37	– (1) b Yadav	5
S. E. Marsh c Kohli b Yadav	0	– b Yadav	3
R. T. Ponting c Laxman b Yadav	62	– c Sehwag b Zaheer Khan	60
*M. J. Clarke b Zaheer Khan	31	– b Sharma	1
M. E. K. Hussey c Dhoni b Zaheer Khan	0	– c Dhoni b Zaheer Khan	89
†B. J. Haddin c Sehwag b Zaheer Khan	27	– c Laxman b Zaheer Khan	6
P. M. Siddle c Dhoni b Zaheer Khan	41	– c Dhoni b Yadav	4
J. L. Pattinson not out	18	– (10) not out	37
B. W. Hilfenhaus c Kohli b Ashwin	19	– (11) c Laxman b Sharma	14
N. M. Lyon b Ashwin	6	– (9) lbw b Ashwin	0
L-b 21, w 2, n-b 1	24	B 5, l-b 2, w 1, n-b 5	13
(110 overs)	333	(76.3 overs)	240

1/46 (2) 2/46 (3) 3/159 (4) 4/205 (5) 5/205 (6)
6/214 (1) 7/286 (7) 8/291 (8) 9/318 (10) 10/333 (11)

1/13 (1) 2/16 (2) 3/24 (3) 4/27 (5) 5/142 (4)
6/148 (7) 7/163 (8) 8/166 (9) 9/197 (6) 10/240 (11)

Zaheer Khan 31–6–77–4; Sharma 24–7–48–0; Yadav 26–5–106–3; Ashwin 29–3–81–3. *Second Innings*—Zaheer Khan 20–4–53–3; Yadav 20–4–70–4; Sharma 12.3–0–43–2; Ashwin 22–4–60–1; Sehwag 2–0–7–0.

India

G. Gambhir c Haddin b Hilfenhaus	3	– c Ponting b Siddle	13
V. Sehwag b Pattinson	67	– c Hussey b Hilfenhaus	7
R. Dravid b Hilfenhaus	68	– b Pattinson	10
S. R. Tendulkar b Siddle	73	– c Hussey b Siddle	32
I. Sharma c Haddin b Hilfenhaus	11	– (10) not out	6
V. V. S. Laxman c Haddin b Siddle	2	– (5) c Cowan b Pattinson	1
V. Kohli c Haddin b Hilfenhaus	11	– (6) lbw b Hilfenhaus	0
*†M. S. Dhoni c Hussey b Hilfenhaus	6	– (7) b Pattinson	23
R. Ashwin c Haddin b Siddle	31	– (8) c Cowan b Siddle	30
Zaheer Khan b Pattinson	4	– (9) c Cowan b Pattinson	13
U. T. Yadav not out	2	– c Warner b Lyon	21
W 1, n-b 3	4	L-b 10, w 2, n-b 1	13
(94.1 overs)	282	(47.5 overs)	169

1/22 (1) 2/97 (2) 3/214 (4) 4/214 (3) 5/221 (6) 6/238 (7)
7/245 (8) 8/254 (5) 9/259 (10) 10/282 (9)

1/17 (2) 2/39 (1) 3/58 (3) 4/68 (5) 5/69 (6) 6/81 (4)
7/117 (8) 8/141 (9) 9/142 (7) 10/169 (11)

Pattinson 23–6–55–2; Hilfenhaus 26–5–75–5; Siddle 21.1–2–63–3; Lyon 17–2–66–0; Hussey 5–0–15–0; Warner 2–0–8–0. *Second Innings*—Pattinson 15–2–53–4; Hilfenhaus 18–4–39–2; Siddle 9–1–42–3; Lyon 5.5–0–25–1.

Umpires: M. Erasmus *(South Africa)* (8) and I. J. Gould *(England)* (24).
Third umpire: P. R. Reiffel *(Australia)*. Referee: R S. Madugalle *(Sri Lanka)* (129).

Close of play: First day, Australia 277–6 (Haddin 21, Siddle 34); Second day, India 214–3 (Dravid 68, Sharma 0); Third day, Australia 179–8 (Hussey 79, Pattinson 3).

AUSTRALIA v INDIA 2011–12 (2nd Test)

At Sydney Cricket Ground on 3, 4, 5, 6 January, 2012.
Toss: India.　　　Result: AUSTRALIA WON BY AN INNINGS AND 68 RUNS.
Debuts: none.
Man of the Match: M. J. Clarke.

Sydney's 100th Test duly became a carnival of centuries: after Australia slipped to 37 for three, Ponting extended his 100th score of 50 or more to his 40th Test century, while Hussey made a largely untroubled undefeated 150, strafing the off field. Dwarfing both of them, though, was Clarke, who extended his own 18th hundred to 329 not out, only the third Test triple-century in Australia after Matthew Hayden's 380 in 2003–04, and Bob Cowper's 307 in 1965–66. It was the highest Test score at the SCG, beating Tip Foster's 287 for England in 1903–04; only Don Bradman (twice) had made a higher first-class score there. Some were surprised that Clarke declared halfway through the third day – but Australia did lead by 468, after India had succumbed on a pitch at its spiciest on the first day. All ten wickets fell to the seamers: Tendulkar dragged Pattinson on, but the others all fell to pokes and prods, as the facility of modern Twenty20-inflected batsmanship against the moving ball came into question again. India were able to make 400 in their second innings without seriously threatening to subvert Australia's eventual triumph. There were four half-centuries, but Clarke proved it was unquestionably his match – during a spell mainly designed to expedite the new ball – by making one pop at Tendulkar, whose snick brushed Haddin's gloves and was caught at slip. Victory was completed late on the fourth day: Clarke had been on the field the entire game, bar the first 50 minutes of Australia's innings.

India

G. Gambhir c Clarke b Pattinson	0	– c Warner b Siddle	83
V. Sehwag c Haddin b Pattinson	30	– c Warner b Hilfenhaus	4
R. Dravid c Cowan b Siddle	5	– b Hilfenhaus	29
S. R. Tendulkar b Pattinson	41	– c Hussey b Clarke	80
V. V. S. Laxman c Marsh b Pattinson	2	– b Hilfenhaus	66
V. Kohli c Haddin b Siddle	23	– lbw b Pattinson	9
*†M. S. Dhoni not out	57	– c and b Hilfenhaus	2
R. Ashwin c Clarke b Hilfenhaus	20	– c Lyon b Hilfenhaus	62
Zaheer Khan c Cowan b Hilfenhaus	0	– c Marsh b Siddle	35
I. Sharma c Cowan b Hilfenhaus	0	– lbw b Lyon	11
U. T. Yadav c Haddin b Siddle	0	– not out	0
B 3, l-b 6, w 2, n-b 2	13	B 6, l-b 3, w 2, n-b 8	19
(59.3 overs)	191	(110.5 overs)	400

1/0 (1) 2/30 (3) 3/55 (2) 4/59 (5) 5/96 (6) 6/124 (4)　　1/18 (2) 2/100 (3) 3/168 (1) 4/271 (4) 5/276 (5)
7/178 (8) 8/178 (9) 9/186 (10) 10/191 (11)　　6/286 (7) 7/286 (6) 8/342 (9) 9/384 (10) 10/400 (8)

Pattinson 14–3–43–4; Hilfenhaus 22–9–51–3; Siddle 13.3–3–55–3; Hussey 2–0–8–0; Lyon 8–0–25–0. *Second Innings*—Pattinson 23–4–106–1; Hilfenhaus 32.5–8–106–5; Siddle 24–8–88–2; Lyon 20–2–64–1; Clarke 9–0–22–1; Hussey 2–0–5–0.

Australia

D. A. Warner c Tendulkar b Zaheer Khan	8
E. J. M. Cowan lbw b Zaheer Khan	16
S. E. Marsh c Laxman b Zaheer Khan	0
R. T. Ponting c Tendulkar b Sharma	134
*M. J. Clarke not out	329
M. E. K. Hussey not out	150
B 2, l-b 13, w 4, n-b 3	22
(4 wkts dec, 163 overs)	659

1/8 (1) 2/8 (3) 3/37 (2) 4/325 (4)

†B. J. Haddin, P. M. Siddle, J. L. Pattinson, B. W. Hilfenhaus and N. M. Lyon did not bat.

Zaheer Khan 31–4–122–3; Yadav 24–2–123–0; Sharma 33–2–144–1; Ashwin 44–5–157–0; Sehwag 23–1–75–0; Kohli 8–0–23–0.

Umpires: M. Erasmus *(South Africa)* (9) and I. J. Gould *(England)* (25).
Third umpire: B. N. J. Oxenford *(Australia)*. Referee: R S. Madugalle *(Sri Lanka)* (130).

Close of play: First day, Australia 116–3 (Ponting 44, Clarke 47); Second day, Australia 482–4 (Clarke 251, Hussey 55); Third day, India 114–2 (Gambhir 68, Tendulkar 8).

AUSTRALIA v INDIA 2011–12 (3rd Test)

At W. A. C. A. Ground, Perth, on 13, 14, 15 January, 2012.
Toss: Australia.   Result: AUSTRALIA WON BY AN INNINGS AND 37 RUNS.
Debuts: India – R. Vinay Kumar.
Man of the Match: D. A. Warner.

Perth welcomed the teams with bright sunshine, hot summer days and a bouncy pitch. India wouldn't have minded the first two, but the third threatened to lay low a side already reeling on the ropes. Put in against a high-octane four-pronged pace attack – Harris and Starc returned for off-spinner Lyon and the injured Pattinson – India floundered to 161 after brief resistance from Laxman and Kohli, and never recovered. All four fast bowlers operated in excess of 87mph, and also found excellent lengths. In reply Warner played his own game – Test20 if you like – flaying 180 from 159 balls and 258 minutes of mayhem, which included 20 fours and five sixes. The pick of them, a lofted cover-drive off Zaheer Khan, flew into the stand named after John Inverarity, the WA stalwart who had become Australian cricket's chief selector. Warner reached three figures in only 69 balls – the joint-fourth-fastest hundred in Tests where balls faced are known – and dominated an opening stand of 214 with fellow left-hander Cowan, whose three-hour 74 was no dirge. All ten wickets fell for 155 after that, the pacy Yadav enjoying the conditions for his first Test five-for, but Australia still led by 208. It was more than enough: India struggled again, although Dravid rolled back the years with a cultured 47, and Kohli gave a glimpse of the future with 75. But India's last six tumbled for 36 – they had managed only 30 in the first innings – and the last four for none at all.

India

G. Gambhir c Haddin b Hilfenhaus	31	– c Hussey b Starc		14
V. Sehwag c Ponting b Hilfenhaus	0	– c Haddin b Siddle		10
R. Dravid b Siddle	9	– b Harris		47
S. R. Tendulkar lbw b Harris	15	– lbw b Starc		8
V. V. S. Laxman c Clarke b Siddle	31	– c Marsh b Hilfenhaus		0
V. Kohli c Warner b Siddle	44	– c Haddin b Siddle		75
*†M. S. Dhoni c Ponting b Hilfenhaus	12	– c Ponting b Siddle		2
R. Vinay Kumar lbw b Starc	5	– c Clarke b Hilfenhaus		6
Zaheer Khan c Clarke b Hilfenhaus	2	– c Clarke b Hilfenhaus		0
I. Sharma c Haddin b Starc	3	– c Cowan b Hilfenhaus		0
U. T. Yadav not out	4	– not out		0
B 2, l-b 2, w 1	5	B 1, l-b 5, w 3		9
(60.2 overs)	161	(63.2 overs)		171

1/4 (2) 2/32 (3) 3/59 (4) 4/63 (1) 5/131 (6) 6/138 (5)
7/152 (8) 8/152 (7) 9/157 (9) 10/161 (10)

1/24 (1) 2/25 (2) 3/42 (4) 4/51 (5) 5/135 (3)
6/148 (7) 7/171 (8) 8/171 (9) 9/171 (10) 10/171 (6)

Harris 18–6–33–1; Hilfenhaus 18–5–43–4; Starc 12.2–3–39–2; Siddle 12–3–42–3. *Second Innings*—Harris 16–3–34–1; Hilfenhaus 18–6–54–4; Starc 12–4–31–2; Siddle 15.2–5–43–3; Hussey 2–0–3–0.

Australia

E. J. M. Cowan b Yadav	74
D. A. Warner c Yadav b Sharma	180
S. E. Marsh c Laxman b Yadav	11
R. T. Ponting b Yadav	7
*M. J. Clarke c Dhoni b Zaheer Khan	18
M. E. K. Hussey c Sehwag b Vinay Kumar	14
†B. J. Haddin c Dhoni b Zaheer Khan	0
P. M. Siddle b Yadav	30
R. J. Harris c Gambhir b Yadav	9
M. A. Starc not out	15
B. W. Hilfenhaus c Kohli b Sehwag	6
L-b 3, w 2	5
(76.2 overs)	369

1/214 (1) 2/230 (3) 3/242 (4) 4/290 (2) 5/301 (5)
6/303 (7) 7/339 (6) 8/343 (8) 9/357 (9) 10/369 (11)

Zaheer Khan 21–3–91–2; Yadav 17–2–93–5; Vinay Kumar 13–0–73–1; Sharma 18–0–89–1; Sehwag 7.2–0–20–1.

Umpires: Aleem Dar *(Pakistan)* (69) and H. D. P. K. Dharmasena *(Sri Lanka)* (7).
Third umpire: P. R. Reiffel *(Australia)*. Referee: R S. Madugalle *(Sri Lanka)* (131).

Close of play: First day, Australia 149–0 (Cowan 40, Warner 104); Second day, India 88–4 (Dravid 32, Kohli 21).

AUSTRALIA v INDIA 2011–12 (4th Test)

At Adelaide Oval on 24, 25, 26, 27, 28 January, 2012.
Toss: Australia.   Result: AUSTRALIA WON BY 298 RUNS.
Debuts: none.
Man of the Match: P. M. Siddle. Man of the Series: M. J. Clarke.

Australia duly completed a 4–0 whitewash, India's second such reverse in a row away from home after a similar scoreline in England. It was a tour too far for 39-year-old Dravid, who later announced his retirement with 13,288 runs at 52.31 from 164 Tests. To emphasise the changing of the guard, Kohli made his first Test century, India's only one of the series, although he was nearly run out for 99, attempting a crazy single. But – in the story of India's tour – Kohli's defiance came in an otherwise inadequate reply, this time to Australia's imposing 604. That included a stand of 386 between Ponting – whose 221 was his 41st (and, as it turned out, last) Test century – and Clarke, who joined Don Bradman (against England in 1930) and Wally Hammond (in New Zealand in 1932–33) as the only men to make triple- and double-centuries in the same series. India were skittled by Siddle and Hilfenhaus, both of whom had been slated for a rest under Australia's sometimes controversial rotation policy. Clarke gave them a breather, anyway, eventually setting India 500 – but they didn't get halfway, undone first by seam then by the under-rated off-spin of Lyon. Sehwag, captaining as Dhoni had been suspended for India's slow over-rate at Perth, signed off with 62 before trying to slog Lyon into the Torrens River; no one else made more than 35. Australia won the series despite their No. 3, Marsh, enduring a horror stretch – only 17 runs at 2.83, with three ducks.

Australia

E. J. M. Cowan c Laxman b Ashwin	30	– (2) lbw b Ashwin	10
D. A. Warner lbw b Zaheer Khan	8	– (1) c and b Ashwin	28
S. E. Marsh b Ashwin	3	– lbw b Zaheer Khan	0
R. T. Ponting c Tendulkar b Zaheer Khan	221	– not out	60
*M. J. Clarke b Yadav	210	– c Saha b Yadav	37
M. E. K. Hussey run out	25	– lbw b Sharma	15
†B. J. Haddin not out	42	– not out	11
P. M. Siddle c Saha b Ashwin	2		
R. J. Harris not out	35		
B 3, l-b 17, w 8	28	L-b 6	6
(7 wkts dec, 157 overs)	604	(5 wkts dec, 46 overs)	167

1/26 (2) 2/31 (3) 3/84 (1) 4/470 (5) 5/520 (6)
6/530 (4) 7/533 (8)

1/39 (1) 2/40 (3) 3/40 (2) 4/111 (5) 5/147 (6)

B. W. Hilfenhaus and N. M. Lyon did not bat.

Zaheer Khan 31–4–96–2; Yadav 26–1–136–1; Ashwin 53–6–194–3; Sharma 30–6–100–0; Sehwag 16–0–55–0; Kohli 1–0–3–0. *Second Innings*—Zaheer Khan 13–1–38–1; Ashwin 20–2–73–2; Sharma 8–0–27–1; Yadav 5–0–23–1.

India

G. Gambhir c Hussey b Siddle	34	– c Haddin b Harris	3
*V. Sehwag c and b Siddle	18	– c Ponting b Lyon	62
R. Dravid b Hilfenhaus	1	– c Hussey b Harris	25
S. R. Tendulkar c Ponting b Siddle	25	– c Cowan b Lyon	13
V. V. S. Laxman c Haddin b Lyon	18	– c Marsh b Lyon	35
V. Kohli lbw b Hilfenhaus	116	– run out	22
†W. P. Saha b Harris	35	– (8) c Haddin b Siddle	3
R. Ashwin lbw b Siddle	5	– (9) not out	15
Zaheer Khan c Haddin b Siddle	0	– (10) c Warner b Hilfenhaus	15
I. Sharma b Hilfenhaus	16	– (7) c Haddin b Harris	2
U. T. Yadav not out	0	– c Haddin b Lyon	1
B 1, w 1, n-b 2	4	L-b 3, w 2	5
(95.1 overs)	272	(69.4 overs)	201

1/26 (2) 2/31 (3) 3/78 (4) 4/87 (1) 5/111 (5) 6/225 (7)
7/230 (8) 8/230 (9) 9/263 (10) 10/272 (6)

1/14 (1) 2/80 (2) 3/100 (3) 4/110 (4) 5/162 (5)
6/166 (6) 7/166 (7) 8/170 (8) 9/193 (10) 10/201 (11)

Harris 25–7–71–1; Hilfenhaus 22.1–5–62–3; Siddle 15–2–49–5; Lyon 21–5–48–1; Clarke 6–1–23–0; Hussey 6–0–18–0. *Second Innings*—Harris 19–5–41–3; Hilfenhaus 11–2–35–1; Siddle 14–5–47–1; Lyon 21.4–4–63–4; Hussey 2–0–3–0; Clarke 2–0–9–0.

Umpires: Aleem Dar *(Pakistan)* (70) and H. D. P. K. Dharmasena *(Sri Lanka)* (8).
Third umpire: S. D. Fry *(Australia)*. Referee: R S. Madugalle *(Sri Lanka)* (132).

Close of play: First day, Australia 335–3 (Ponting 137, Clarke 140); Second day, India 61–2 (Gambhir 30, Tendulkar 12); Third day, Australia 50–3 (Ponting 1, Clarke 9); Fourth day, India 166–6 (Sharma 2, Saha 0).

PAKISTAN v ENGLAND 2011–12 (1st Test)

At Dubai International Cricket Stadium on 17, 18, 19 January, 2012.
Toss: England.　　Result: PAKISTAN WON BY TEN WICKETS.
Debuts: none.
Man of the Match: Saeed Ajmal.

A little over two months after three Pakistani players were jailed for spot-fixing during their previous Test against England, at Lord's in August 2010, the sides met at the neutral venue of Dubai. But the ground did not preside over neutral cricket – at least not from Pakistan, who immediately located top gear to despatch England inside three days. The main destroyer was Saeed Ajmal, whose mixture of off-breaks and doosras brought him ten for 97 in the match: only Abdul Qadir (four times), Fazal Mahmood and Imran Khan had previously taken ten in a match for Pakistan against England. Seven of his victims were lbw, one short of the Test record shared by Mohammad Zahid (on debut in 1996–97) and Chaminda Vaas (2001–02). England looked anything but a side recently elevated to No. 1 in the world rankings, failing to reach 200 in either innings. Only Prior in the first innings, and Swann in both, batted with much confidence against Ajmal, although Trott grafted to 49 in the second before becoming one of four wickets for the impressive Umar Gul. The DRS seemed to make England's batsmen doubly jittery. Before the series, Pietersen had referred to it as "that bloody machine", and now displayed all the existential angst of Edvard Munch's *The Scream* before Ajmal put him out of his misery for two from 29 balls. England's bowlers did reasonably well to restrict Pakistan to 338 after a century opening stand, but their batsmen's failings meant it counted for nothing.

England

*A. J. Strauss b Saeed Ajmal	19	– c Adnan Akmal b Umar Gul		6
A. N. Cook c Adnan Akmal b Mohammad Hafeez	3	– c Adnan Akmal b Umar Gul		5
I. J. L. Trott c Adnan Akmal b Aizaz Cheema	17	– c Adnan Akmal b Umar Gul		49
K. P. Pietersen lbw b Saeed Ajmal	2	– c Abdur Rehman b Umar Gul		0
I. R. Bell c Adnan Akmal b Saeed Ajmal	0	– lbw b Saeed Ajmal		4
E. J. G. Morgan lbw b Saeed Ajmal	24	– c Adnan Akmal b Abdur Rehman		14
†M. J. Prior not out	70	– lbw b Saeed Ajmal		4
S. C. J. Broad lbw b Saeed Ajmal	8	– c Asad Shafiq b Abdur Rehman		17
G. P. Swann b Abdur Rehman	34	– c Asad Shafiq b Saeed Ajmal		39
C. T. Tremlett lbw b Saeed Ajmal	1	– c Mohammad Hafeez b Abdur Rehman		0
J. M. Anderson lbw b Saeed Ajmal	12	– not out		15
L-b 2	2	B 4, l-b 1, n-b 2		7
(72.3 overs)	192	(57.5 overs)		160

1/10 (2) 2/31 (3) 3/42 (1) 4/42 (5) 5/43 (4) 6/82 (6)　　1/6 (1) 2/25 (2) 3/25 (4) 4/35 (5) 5/74 (6)
7/94 (8) 8/151 (9) 9/168 (10) 10/192 (11)　　6/87 (3) 7/87 (7) 8/135 (8) 9/135 (10) 10/160 (9)

Umar Gul 12–4–35–0; Aizaz Cheema 12–0–43–1; Mohammad Hafeez 6–3–5–1; Abdur Rehman 18–5–52–1; Saeed Ajmal 24.3–7–55–7. *Second Innings*—Umar Gul 19–5–63–4; Aizaz Cheema 7.2–1–9–0; Mohammad Hafeez 2–0–4–0; Saeed Ajmal 17.3–4–42–3; Abdur Rehman 12–2–37–3.

Pakistan

Mohammad Hafeez lbw b Swann	88	– not out		15
Taufeeq Umar b Broad	58	– not out		0
Azhar Ali c Prior b Broad	1			
Younis Khan lbw b Trott	37			
*Misbah-ul-Haq lbw b Swann	52			
Asad Shafiq c Prior b Anderson	16			
†Adnan Akmal st Prior b Swann	61			
Abdur Rehman b Anderson	4			
Umar Gul c Morgan b Broad	0			
Saeed Ajmal c Cook b Swann	12			
Aizaz Cheema not out	0			
B 2, l-b 5, n-b 2	9			
(119.5 overs)	338	(no wkt, 3.4 overs)		15

1/114 (2) 2/128 (3) 3/176 (1) 4/202 (4) 5/231 (6)
6/283 (5) 7/288 (8) 8/289 (9) 9/319 (10) 10/338 (7)

Anderson 30–7–71–2; Tremlett 21–6–53–0; Broad 31–8–84–3; Swann 29.5–3–107–4; Trott 8–2–16–1. *Second Innings*—Anderson 2–1–7–0; Broad 1.4–1–8–0.

Umpires: B. F. Bowden *(New Zealand)* (70) and B. N. J. Oxenford *(Australia)* (6).
Third umpire: S. J. Davis *(Australia)*. Referee: J. Srinath *(India)* (19).

Close of play: First day, Pakistan 42–0 (Mohammad Hafeez 22, Taufeeq Umar 18); Second day, Pakistan 288–7 (Adnan Akmal 24).

PAKISTAN v ENGLAND 2011–12 (2nd Test)

At Sheikh Zayed Stadium, Abu Dhabi, on 25, 26, 27, 28 January, 2012.
Toss: Pakistan.   Result: PAKISTAN WON BY 72 RUNS.
Debuts: none.
Man of the Match: Abdur Rehman.

After this match, few recalled England's excellent bowling, the dogged stand between Cook and Trott that seemed to have put them in charge, Broad's counter-attacking half-century, or Panesar's six second-innings wickets in his first Test since July 2009. Instead, the stark memories were of England's second innings. Set just 145 to win, they did not even get halfway, capitulating for 72 to lose the series. It was comfortably their lowest total against Pakistan, outdoing 130, at The Oval in 1954 and Lahore in 1987–88. And it was only the second time in more than a century that England had lost chasing a target under 150; the previous occasion was at Wellington in 1977–78 (out for 64 chasing 137), which followed similar collapses against Australia in 1882 (in the match that spawned the Ashes), 1888 and 1902. It all started so well: Pakistan were bowled out for 257 despite a century partnership between Misbah-ul-Haq and Asad Shafiq, then England countered the spinners well enough to take a lead of 70. Cook fell just short of a hundred, defeated by Saeed Ajmal's doosra, but added 139 with Trott, and later Broad cracked 58 from 62 balls. Pakistan were still behind at 58 for four, but Azhar Ali's 68 in 4¼ hours helped them to a lead of 144, which looked barely sufficient – until Ajmal and Abdur Rehman got to work against batsmen seemingly paralysed with fear and uncertainty. Strauss survived for 29 overs, but when he was fifth out the end was nigh.

Pakistan

Mohammad Hafeez b Panesar	31	–	lbw b Panesar		22
Taufeeq Umar b Swann	16	–	b Swann		7
Azhar Ali b Broad	24	–	c Prior b Anderson		68
Younis Khan b Broad	24	–	b Panesar		1
*Misbah-ul-Haq lbw b Broad	84	–	lbw b Panesar		12
Asad Shafiq lbw b Swann	58	–	c Anderson b Panesar		43
†Adnan Akmal lbw b Broad	9	–	c Strauss b Broad		13
Abdur Rehman b Swann	0	–	lbw b Swann		10
Saeed Ajmal lbw b Anderson	0	–	c Anderson b Panesar		17
Umar Gul not out	0	–	not out		10
Junaid Khan c Swann b Anderson	0	–	b Panesar		0
B 8, l-b 1, n-b 2	11		B 5, l-b 6		11
(96.4 overs)	257		(99.2 overs)		214

1/51 (2) 2/61 (1) 3/98 (4) 4/103 (3) 5/203 (6)
6/216 (7) 7/243 (8) 8/257 (5) 9/257 (9) 10/257 (11)

1/29 (1) 2/29 (2) 3/36 (4) 4/54 (5) 5/142 (6)
6/170 (3) 7/172 (7) 8/198 (8) 9/208 (9) 10/214 (11)

Anderson 19.4–5–46–2; Broad 24–4–47–4; Panesar 33–9–91–1; Swann 18–2–52–3; Trott 2–0–12–0. *Second Innings*—Anderson 14–3–39–1; Broad 20–9–36–1; Panesar 38.2–18–62–6; Swann 27–5–66–2.

England

*A. J. Strauss c Asad Shafiq b Mohammad Hafeez	11	–	lbw b Abdur Rehman		32
A. N. Cook lbw b Saeed Ajmal	94	–	c and b Mohammad Hafeez		7
I. J. L. Trott b Abdur Rehman	74	–	(7) lbw b Abdur Rehman		1
K. P. Pietersen c Mohammad Hafeez b Saeed Ajmal	14	–	lbw b Abdur Rehman		1
I. R. Bell lbw b Umar Gul	29	–	(3) b Saeed Ajmal		3
E. J. G. Morgan c Mohammad Hafeez b Saeed Ajmal	3	–	(5) b Abdur Rehman		0
†M. J. Prior lbw b Saeed Ajmal	3	–	(6) c Asad Shafiq b Saeed Ajmal		18
S. C. J. Broad not out	58	–	b Abdur Rehman		0
G. P. Swann lbw b Abdur Rehman	15	–	lbw b Saeed Ajmal		0
J. M. Anderson b Mohammad Hafeez	13	–	c Umar Gul b Abdur Rehman		1
M. S. Panesar lbw b Mohammad Hafeez	0	–	not out		0
B 5, l-b 7, n-b 1	13		L-b 9		9
(112 overs)	327		(36.1 overs)		72

1/27 (1) 2/166 (3) 3/198 (2) 4/203 (4) 5/207 (6)
6/227 (7) 7/268 (5) 8/291 (9) 9/327 (10) 10/327 (11)

1/21 (2) 2/26 (3) 3/33 (4) 4/37 (5) 5/56 (1)
6/68 (7) 7/68 (8) 8/71 (9) 9/72 (6) 10/72 (10)

Umar Gul 13–1–53–1; Junaid Khan 8–0–33–0; Mohammad Hafeez 22–4–54–3; Saeed Ajmal 40–6–108–4; Abdur Rehman 29–9–67–2. *Second Innings*—Mohammad Hafeez 8–3–11–1; Umar Gul 3–0–5–0; Saeed Ajmal 15–7–22–3; Abdur Rehman 10.1–4–25–6.

Umpires: S. J. Davis *(Australia)* (35) and B. N. J. Oxenford *(Australia)* (7).
Third umpire: B. F. Bowden *(New Zealand)*. Referee: J. Srinath *(India)* (20).

Close of play: First day, Pakistan 256–7 (Misbah-ul-Haq 83, Saeed Ajmal 0); Second day, England 207–5 (Bell 4); Third day, Pakistan 125–4 (Azhar Ali 46, Asad Shafiq 35).

PAKISTAN v ENGLAND 2011–12 (3rd Test)

At Dubai International Cricket Stadium on 3, 4, 5, 6 February, 2012.
Toss: Pakistan.   Result: PAKISTAN WON BY 71 RUNS.
Debuts: none.
Man of the Match: Azhar Ali. Man of the Series: Saeed Ajmal.

It seemed appropriate that this match, which produced Pakistan's first clean sweep over England, should end on a referred lbw decision. The DRS, and the way it was implemented by the officials, had been a leitmotif of the Tests – so much so that the final demise of Panesar was the 43rd lbw in all, an unprecedented number for a three-Test series. England were left to wonder how they could dismiss Pakistan for 99 – they were 44 for seven before lunch on the first day – and still lose. Only twice before – in the Ashes match at The Oval in 1882, and South Africa's first win, in Johannesburg in 1905–06 – had England lost after bowling the opposition out for under 100 in the first innings. The problem was that England, their brains well and truly scrambled by Pakistani spin, mustered only 141 in reply, when batting conditions were at their best; then they were unable to separate Azhar Ali and Younis Khan during a stand of 216 that seemed to mock the loss of 22 wickets for 268 (16 on the first day) which preceded it. Azhar batted for seven minutes short of nine hours, and faced 442 balls. England needed 324, and started well enough: Cook, 27, became the second-youngest (after Sachin Tendulkar) to make 6,000 Test runs. But the spinners chipped away, then Umar Gul took four wickets in 30 balls. Fittingly, Saeed Ajmal and Abdur Rehman finished things off, ending up with 43 wickets between them in the whitewash.

Pakistan

Mohammad Hafeez lbw b Broad	13	– lbw b Panesar	21
Taufeeq Umar lbw b Anderson	0	– c Strauss b Anderson	6
Azhar Ali c Prior b Broad	1	– c Cook b Swann	157
Younis Khan c Prior b Broad	4	– lbw b Broad	127
*Misbah-ul-Haq lbw b Anderson	1	– lbw b Panesar	31
Asad Shafiq lbw b Panesar	45	– lbw b Panesar	5
†Adnan Akmal lbw b Broad	6	– b Panesar	0
Abdur Rehman c Pietersen b Swann	1	– c Anderson b Swann	1
Saeed Ajmal lbw b Panesar	12	– c Anderson b Swann	1
Umar Gul b Anderson	13	– lbw b Panesar	4
Aizaz Cheema not out	0	– not out	0
L-b 3	3	B 10, l-b 1, n-b 1	12
(44.1 overs)	99	(152.4 overs)	365

1/1 (2) 2/8 (3) 3/18 (4) 4/21 (1) 5/21 (5) 6/39 (7)
7/44 (8) 8/78 (9) 9/85 (6) 10/99 (10)

1/16 (2) 2/28 (1) 3/244 (4) 4/331 (5) 5/339 (6)
6/345 (7) 7/346 (8) 8/350 (9) 9/363 (3) 10/365 (10)

Anderson 14.1–3–35–3; Broad 16–5–36–4; Panesar 13–4–25–2; Swann 1–1–0–1. *Second Innings*—Anderson 28–7–51–1; Broad 24–7–55–1; Panesar 56.4–13–124–5; Swann 39–6–101–3; Trott 2–0–14–0; Pietersen 3–0–9–0.

England

*A. J. Strauss st Adnan Akmal b Abdur Rehman	56	– lbw b Abdur Rehman	26
A. N. Cook c Adnan Akmal b Umar Gul	1	– c Younis Khan b Saeed Ajmal	49
I. J. L. Trott lbw b Umar Gul	2	– c Abdur Rehman b Saeed Ajmal	18
K. P. Pietersen lbw b Abdur Rehman	32	– b Saeed Ajmal	18
I. R. Bell st Adnan Akmal b Saeed Ajmal	5	– c Asad Shafiq b Umar Gul	10
E. J. G. Morgan lbw b Abdur Rehman	10	– c Adnan Akmal b Umar Gul	31
†M. J. Prior b Abdur Rehman	6	– not out	49
J. M. Anderson b Abdur Rehman	4	– (10) c Younis Khan b Saeed Ajmal	9
S. C. J. Broad lbw b Saeed Ajmal	4	– (8) c Taufeeq Umar b Umar Gul	18
G. P. Swann c Abdur Rehman b Saeed Ajmal	16	– (9) c Asad Shafiq b Umar Gul	1
M. S. Panesar not out	0	– lbw b Abdur Rehman	8
B 1, l-b 4	5	B 4, l-b 8, n-b 3	15
(55 overs)	141	(97.3 overs)	252

1/5 (2) 2/7 (3) 3/64 (4) 4/75 (5) 5/88 (6) 6/98 (7)
7/106 (8) 8/121 (9) 9/133 (1) 10/141 (10)

1/48 (1) 2/85 (3) 3/116 (4) 4/119 (2) 5/156 (5)
6/159 (6) 7/196 (8) 8/203 (9) 9/237 (10) 10/252 (11)

Umar Gul 7–1–28–2; Aizaz Cheema 4–0–9–0; Saeed Ajmal 23–6–59–3; Abdur Rehman 21–4–40–5. *Second Innings*—Umar Gul 20–5–61–4; Aizaz Cheema 4–0–9–0; Mohammad Hafeez 5–2–6–0; Abdur Rehman 41.3–10–97–2; Saeed Ajmal 27–9–67–4.

Umpires: S. J. Davis *(Australia)* (36) and S. J. A. Taufel *(Australia)* (71).
Third umpire: S. K. Tarapore *(India)*. Referee: J. J. Crowe *(New Zealand)* (49).

Close of play: First day, England 104–6 (Strauss 41, Anderson 3); Second day, Pakistan 222–2 (Azhar Ali 75, Younis Khan 115); Third day, England 36–0 (Strauss 19, Cook 15).

NEW ZEALAND v ZIMBABWE 2011–12 (Only Test)

At McLean Park, Napier, on 26, 27, 28 January, 2012.
Toss: Zimbabwe.   Result: NEW ZEALAND WON BY AN INNINGS AND 301 RUNS.
Debuts: Zimbabwe – S. W. Masakadza, F. Mutizwa.
Man of the Match: C. S. Martin.

Zimbabwe had performed well enough in three home matches since resuming Test cricket in 2011, including a close-run game against New Zealand at Bulawayo a few months previously. But now, in unfamiliar conditions away from home, they crumbled embarrassingly to their heaviest Test defeat. They were bowled out twice on the third day, only the third such occurrence overall, following India against England at Old Trafford in 1952 and Zimbabwe themselves against New Zealand at Harare in August 2005, one of the results that persuaded them to take a break from the five-day game in the first place. Here they were skittled for 51 in the first innings, their lowest in Tests and also the lowest against New Zealand. Record-books were being thumbed when Zimbabwe plummeted to 12 for five in the follow-on, but Chakabva, in only his second Test, saved a few blushes with a tidy half-century. Martin wrapped things up with two wickets in two balls to complete his best first-class figures, and eight for 31 in the match. Thirteen catches were taken in the cordon, five by Brownlie at third sip. New Zealand's imposing total, most of it made on the first day (rain allowed only 15.2 overs on the second), included a century opening stand after being put in, a hundred from Taylor before he pulled a calf muscle, and a maiden one from Watling in his first Test as the designated wicketkeeper. Remarkably, it was New Zealand's first win in all ten Tests at Napier.

New Zealand

B. B. McCullum	lbw b Jarvis	83
M. J. Guptill	c Taibu b S. W. Masakadza	51
K. S. Williamson	run out	4
*L. R. P. L. Taylor	retired hurt	122
D. G. Brownlie	c Taibu b H. Masakadza	0
D. L. Vettori	st Taibu b Cremer	38
†B-J. Watling	not out	102
D. A. J. Bracewell	b Vitori	11
T. G. Southee	c Waller b Cremer	44
T. A. Boult	not out	5
	B 1, l-b 21, w 2, n-b 11	35
	(7 wkts dec, 123.4 overs)	495

1/124 (2) 2/131 (3) 3/195 (1) 4/196 (5) 5/278 (6)
6/392 (8) 7/466 (9)

C. S. Martin did not bat. *Taylor retired hurt at 365–5.*

Jarvis 32.4–7–120–1; Vitori 25–3–94–1; S. W. Masakadza 23–2–102–1; H. Masakadza 21–6–45–1; Cremer 22–2–112–2.

Zimbabwe

T. M. K. Mawoyo	b Martin	2	– c Guptill b Martin		2
H. Masakadza	c Brownlie b Boult	0	– c McCullum b Martin		0
F. Mutizwa	b Martin	6	– c Watling b Bracewell		18
*B. R. M. Taylor	c Guptill b Bracewell	9	– c Watling b Martin		2
†T. Taibu	c Brownlie b Boult	2	– c Williamson b Bracewell		4
M. N. Waller	c Brownlie b Southee	23	– lbw b Bracewell		0
R. W. Chakabva	lbw b Bracewell	3	– c Brownlie b Martin		63
A. G. Cremer	lbw b Vettori	3	– c Bracewell b Williamson		26
S. W. Masakadza	not out	3	– c Watling b Martin		21
K. M. Jarvis	run out	0	– not out		0
B. V. Vitori	c Brownlie b Southee	0	– c Watling b Martin		0
			B 4, l-b 3		7
	(28.5 overs)	51	(48.3 overs)		143

1/2 (1) 2/8 (3) 3/8 (2) 4/19 (4) 5/19 (5) 6/24 (7) 7/46 (8)
8/50 (6) 9/50 (10) 10/51 (11)

1/2 (1) 2/3 (2) 3/5 (4) 4/12 (5) 5/12 (6) 6/37 (3)
7/100 (8) 8/134 (9) 9/143 (7) 10/143 (11)

Martin 6–2–5–2; Boult 9–3–24–2; Bracewell 6–2–12–2; Vettori 4–3–2–1; Southee 3.5–0–8–2. *Second Innings*—Martin 8.3–3–26–6; Southee 8–2–20–0; Bracewell 10–4–26–3; Vettori 10–1–25–0; Boult 9–4–15–0; Guptill 1–0–12–0; Williamson 2–0–12–1.

Umpires: Enamul Haque, sen. *(Bangladesh)* (1) and R. J. Tucker *(Australia)* (18).
Third umpire: N. J. Llong *(England)*. Referee: D. C. Boon *(Australia)* (7).

Close of play: First day, New Zealand 331–5 (Taylor 111, Watling 15); Second day, New Zealand 392–5 (Watling 52, Bracewell 11).

NEW ZEALAND v SOUTH AFRICA 2011–12 (1st Test)

At University Oval, Dunedin, on 7, 8, 9, 10, 11 (*no play*) March, 2012.
Toss: New Zealand.   Result: MATCH DRAWN.
Debuts: New Zealand – R. J. Nicol, C. F. K. van Wyk.
Man of the Match: G. C. Smith.

Set 401 in over four sessions after Smith's enterprising declaration, New Zealand ended the fourth day on 137 for two with McCullum and Taylor well set, raising hopes of an upset. The forecast warned of the strong possibility of showers in the morning; in fact, it started raining on the fourth evening – and didn't stop. On the first day, Martin had knocked over Smith, Kallis and de Villiers in the space of four deliveries, Smith starting the stumble with a loose drive to cover just after tea. Rudolph collected a calm half-century as South Africa scraped together 238. New Zealand reached 106 for two in reply, but McCullum nudged a full-toss back to Tahir, and Taylor slashed outside off. Vettori, up at No. 6, made a gutsy 46 before Kallis clasped a good return catch, and the eventual lead was only 35. Smith and Kallis batted for most of the third day, adding 200 to nullify that, then Rudolph made his sixth Test century, more than six years after the fifth. He had 12 when Aleem Dar's lbw decision in favour of Bracewell was overturned, after replays showed the ball pitched fractionally outside leg. Rudolph was so convinced he was out that he started walking, but was persuaded by Kallis to review. South African-born Kruger van Wyk, called up to keep wicket after Watling injured his hip, was the first to make his Test debut against his native country since the Hollioake brothers against Australia at Trent Bridge in 1997.

South Africa

*G. C. Smith c Nicol b Martin	53	– (2) b Bracewell	115
A. N. Petersen lbw b Boult	11	– (1) c Southee b Bracewell	25
H. M. Amla c Taylor b Vettori	62	– c Guptill b Bracewell	2
J. H. Kallis c Taylor b Martin	0	– c Nicol b Boult	113
A. B. de Villiers lbw b Martin	0	– (6) c McCullum b Williamson	29
J. A. Rudolph c Boult b Bracewell	52	– (5) not out	105
†M. V. Boucher run out	4	– not out	34
D. W. Steyn c Taylor b Bracewell	9		
V. D. Philander c Williamson b Martin	22		
M. Morkel not out	13		
Imran Tahir run out	10		
L-b 1, n-b 1	2	B 2, l-b 6, w 1, n-b 3	12
(68.2 overs)	238	(5 wkts dec, 140 overs)	435

1/34 (2) 2/86 (1) 3/90 (4) 4/90 (5) 5/156 (3) 6/161 (7)
7/179 (8) 8/214 (9) 9/222 (6) 10/238 (11)   1/45 (1) 2/47 (3) 3/247 (2) 4/283 (4) 5/353 (6)

Martin 18–2–56–4; Southee 10–1–40–0; Boult 8–0–58–1; Bracewell 16.2–2–52–2; Vettori 15–4–31–1; Nicol 1–1–0–0. *Second Innings*—Martin 23–4–74–0; Boult 26–4–93–1; Bracewell 25–3–70–3; Southee 26–4–100–0; Vettori 32–5–65–0; Nicol 1–0–9–0; Williamson 7–4–16–1.

New Zealand

R. J. Nicol c Smith b Philander	6	– c Smith b Imran Tahir	19
M. J. Guptill b Morkel	16	– c de Villiers b Philander	6
B. B. McCullum c and b Imran Tahir	48	– not out	58
*L. R. P. L. Taylor c Boucher b Morkel	44	– not out	48
K. S. Williamson c Boucher b Philander	11		
D. L. Vettori c and b Kallis	46		
†C. F. K. van Wyk c Smith b Philander	36		
D. A. J. Bracewell b Steyn	25		
T. G. Southee c Smith b Philander	0		
T. A. Boult not out	33		
C. S. Martin c Amla b Steyn	5		
L-b 3	3	L-b 2, w 2, n-b 2	6
(88.2 overs)	273	(2 wkts, 41 overs)	137

1/7 (1) 2/41 (2) 3/106 (3) 4/116 (4) 5/135 (5)
6/188 (6) 7/229 (7) 8/229 (9) 9/239 (8) 10/273 (11)   1/16 (2) 2/55 (1)

Steyn 20.2–4–79–2; Philander 18–1–72–4; Morkel 18–5–52–2; Imran Tahir 24–6–55–1; Kallis 8–2–12–1. *Second Innings*—Steyn 8–2–25–0; Philander 12–2–29–1; Morkel 9–2–33–0; Imran Tahir 8–2–33–1; Kallis 4–1–15–0.

Umpires: Aleem Dar *(Pakistan)* (71) and B. R. Doctrove *(West Indies)* (37).
Third umpire: R. A. Kettleborough *(England)*. Referee: R. S. Mahanama *(Sri Lanka)* (35).

Close of play: First day, South Africa 191–7 (Rudolph 46, Philander 4); Second day, New Zealand 243–9 (Boult 8, Martin 0); Third day, South Africa 268–3 (Kallis 107, Rudolph 13); Fourth day, New Zealand 137–2 (McCullum 58, Taylor 48).

NEW ZEALAND v SOUTH AFRICA 2011–12 (2nd Test)

At Seddon Park, Hamilton, on 15, 16, 17 March, 2012.
Toss: South Africa.   Result: SOUTH AFRICA WON BY NINE WICKETS.
Debuts: none.
Man of the Match: V. D. Philander.

Only twice before had five wickets fallen on the same score during a Test innings, in 1945–46 and 1964–65, both times by New Zealand. The latest episode, on the first evening here, rewarded classic fast bowling. South Africa went on to win in 2½ days, but it was a peculiar contest: they never really landed another memorable punch after that five-for-nothing flurry. McCullum and Taylor had displayed resilience in nursing their side to 133 for two on a nippy pitch and under overcast skies. There was always the feeling that a wicket could fall… but not five at once. Suddenly, within the space of 20 balls after tea, Steyn and the unstoppable Philander derailed New Zealand completely as the total turned into 133 for seven. South Africa's dominance was shaken on the second day, when a magnificent morning spell from Gillespie reduced them to 88 for six, but the New Zealand bowlers ran out of steam against de Villiers and the tail, conceding a lead of 68. Then their batsmen slid to seven for three after 25 balls, and a two-day finish seemed possible – but Williamson's 77 scotched that, and at 141 for five next day, a lead of 73, local hopes were rising again. But van Wyk fell an over before lunch, and the remaining four wickets lasted just 29 balls after it, Philander finishing with six for 44. South Africa needed only 101, and were anchored to victory by the imperturbable Smith, the master of the run-chase.

New Zealand

R. J. Nicol c Boucher b Philander	2	– b Philander		1
M. J. Guptill b Steyn	22	– c Amla b Steyn		1
B. B. McCullum c Rudolph b Steyn	61	– lbw b Philander		5
*L. R. P. L. Taylor c Smith b Philander	44	– lbw b Steyn		17
K. S. Williamson c Smith b Steyn	0	– c Boucher b Philander		77
D. L. Vettori b Philander	0	– c Boucher b Kallis		21
†C. F. K. van Wyk lbw b Morkel	21	– b Philander		20
D. A. J. Bracewell c Boucher b Philander	0	– b Morkel		0
M. R. Gillespie c Petersen b Imran Tahir	27	– c Boucher b Philander		14
B. J. Arnel lbw b Imran Tahir	3	– not out		8
C. S. Martin not out	0	– b Philander		0
L-b 3, n-b 2	5	L-b 4		4
(61.2 overs)	185	(67.5 overs)		168

1/11 (1) 2/44 (2) 3/133 (3) 4/133 (4) 5/133 (5)   1/1 (1) 2/7 (3) 3/7 (2) 4/64 (4) 5/99 (6)
6/133 (6) 7/133 (8) 8/176 (7) 9/184 (9) 10/185 (10)   6/141 (7) 7/142 (5) 8/142 (8) 9/160 (9) 10/168 (11)

Steyn 18–5–49–3; Philander 15–3–70–4; Kallis 9–4–9–0; Morkel 14–2–42–1; Imran Tahir 5.2–1–12–2. *Second Innings*—Steyn 16–5–31–2; Philander 15.5–3–44–6; Morkel 13–5–26–1; Imran Tahir 17–2–52–0; Kallis 6–3–11–1.

South Africa

*G. C. Smith c van Wyk b Martin	13	– (2) not out		55
A. N. Petersen lbw b Gillespie	29	– (1) c van Wyk b Bracewell		1
D. W. Steyn c van Wyk b Martin	4			
H. M. Amla c Williamson b Gillespie	16	– (3) not out		46
J. H. Kallis c van Wyk b Gillespie	6			
A. B. de Villiers b Vettori	83			
J. A. Rudolph c van Wyk b Gillespie	1			
†M. V. Boucher b Gillespie	24			
V. D. Philander b Bracewell	14			
M. Morkel not out	35			
Imran Tahir c Gillespie b Williamson	16			
B 1, l-b 9, w 1, n-b 1	12	N-b 1		1
(77.3 overs)	253	(1 wkt, 19.5 overs)		103

1/14 (1) 2/18 (3) 3/63 (4) 4/69 (5) 5/84 (2) 6/88 (7)
7/151 (8) 8/185 (9) 9/219 (6) 10/253 (11)   1/5 (1)

Martin 16–6–38–2; Bracewell 18–7–50–1; Gillespie 15–2–59–5; Vettori 19–3–49–1; Arnel 9–2–46–0; Williamson 0.3–0–1–1. *Second Innings*—Martin 3–1–18–0; Bracewell 5–0–14–1; Vettori 2–0–2–0; Gillespie 4–0–24–0; Arnel 3–0–18–0; Williamson 2–0–3–0; Nicol 0.5–0–4–0.

Umpires: B. R. Doctrove *(West Indies)* (38) and R. A. Kettleborough *(England)* (8).
Third umpire: Aleem Dar *(Pakistan)*. Referee: R. S. Madugalle *(Sri Lanka)* (133).

Close of play: First day, South Africa 27–2 (Petersen 8, Amla 2); Second day, New Zealand 65–4 (Williamson 41, Vettori 0).

NEW ZEALAND v SOUTH AFRICA 2011–12 (3rd Test)

At Basin Reserve, Wellington, on 23, 24, 25, 26, 27 March, 2012.
Toss: New Zealand.   Result: MATCH DRAWN.
Debuts: none.
Man of the Match: M. Morkel.

Frequent rain-breaks – around a day's play was lost overall – helped New Zealand draw, chiefly thanks to a calm century by Williamson, who entered at one for two. The weather meant South Africa's first innings lasted beyond tea on the third day, with Petersen returning to form with a restrained 156 and Duminy – a late replacement for Kallis (stiff neck) making 103. Amla edged Martin into his groin when 33; he hobbled off 30 runs later and went straight to hospital for emergency surgery. A draw seemed certain, even with around 200 overs still available. Flynn and Guptill opened with 86, and at 263 for five – effectively six, as Morkel had broken Taylor's left arm – only 12 were needed to avoid the follow-on. But three wickets went down at the same score, and it was left to Gillespie to conjure up the necessary dozen, courtesy of successive edged fours. South Africa scooted to a lead of 388, with 81 overs remaining. New Zealand survived, despite Morkel, who took all six wickets to fall. Boucher's catch of Flynn was his 999th dismissal in international cricket (998 as wicketkeeper); but a freak eye injury in July, on the first day of the tour of England, forced his retirement one short of 1,000. Philander had earlier taken his 50th wicket in his seventh Test; only the 19th-century Australian Charles Turner had ever got there in fewer matches (six). Rodney Hogg (116 days) was the only man to reach 50 faster than Philander's 139 days.

South Africa

*G. C. Smith c van Wyk b Bracewell	5	– (2) c Bracewell b Vettori	41
A. N. Petersen lbw b Martin	156	– (1) run out	39
H. M. Amla c van Wyk b Gillespie	63		
J-P. Duminy c Taylor b Gillespie	103	– not out	33
A. B. de Villiers b Martin	38	– (3) c Williamson b Bracewell	68
J. A. Rudolph c van Wyk b Gillespie	11		
†M. V. Boucher c Williamson b Gillespie	46		
D. W. Steyn c Guptill b Gillespie	0		
V. D. Philander c Flynn b Gillespie	29		
M. Morkel not out	10		
B 6, l-b 1, w 3, n-b 3	13	L-b 3, w 3, n-b 2	8
(9 wkts dec, 148.4 overs)	474	(3 wkts dec, 29.4 overs)	189

1/13 (1) 2/106 (3) 3/306 (4) 4/362 (2) 5/381 (5)
6/388 (6) 7/404 (8) 8/459 (7) 9/474 (9)   1/77 (1) 2/106 (2) 3/189 (3)

M. de Lange did not bat.

Martin 28–5–95–2; Bracewell 30–3–106–1; Gillespie 33.4–7–113–6; Vettori 42–11–98–0; Brownlie 2–0–20–0; Williamson 13–1–35–0. *Second Innings*—Martin 10–0–44–0; Bracewell 6.4–0–47–1; Gillespie 6–0–55–0; Vettori 7–1–40–1.

New Zealand

D. R. Flynn c Boucher b Philander	45	– (2) c Boucher b Morkel	0
M. J. Guptill lbw b Philander	59	– (1) c Rudolph b Morkel	18
B. B. McCullum c Boucher b Steyn	31	– lbw b Morkel	0
*L. R. P. L. Taylor retired hurt	18		
K. S. Williamson c Boucher b Steyn	39	– (4) not out	102
D. G. Brownlie c Steyn b Philander	29	– (5) b Morkel	15
D. L. Vettori c Rudolph b Philander	30	– (6) b Morkel	0
†C. F. K. van Wyk c sub (Imran Tahir) b de Lange	7	– (7) c and b Morkel	39
D. A. J. Bracewell b Philander	0	– (8) not out	20
M. R. Gillespie c de Villiers b Philander	10		
C. S. Martin not out	2		
L-b 2, w 2, n-b 1	5	L-b 6	6
(96 overs)	275	(6 wkts, 80.4 overs)	200

1/86 (1) 2/136 (3) 3/145 (2) 4/219 (6) 5/242 (5)   1/1 (2) 2/1 (3) 3/32 (1) 4/83 (5) 5/83 (6)
6/263 (7) 7/263 (9) 8/263 (8) 9/275 (10)   6/163 (7)

In the first innings Taylor retired hurt at 160–3.

Steyn 23–8–41–2; Philander 22–4–81–6; Morkel 20–6–54–0; de Lange 21–1–74–1; Duminy 10–0–23–0. *Second Innings*—Morkel 16.4–7–23–6; Philander 18.4–6–29–0; de Lange 17.2–4–77–0; Steyn 15–9–14–0; Duminy 13–2–51–0.

Umpires: Aleem Dar *(Pakistan)* (72) and R. A. Kettleborough *(England)* (9).
Third umpire: B. R. Doctrove *(West Indies)*. Referee: R. S. Madugalle *(Sri Lanka)* (134).

Close of play: First day, South Africa 136–2 (Petersen 44, Duminy 23); Second day, South Africa 246–2 (Petersen 96, Duminy 76); Third day, New Zealand 65–0 (Flynn 35, Guptill 28); Fourth day, South Africa 75–0 (Petersen 38, Smith 34).

SRI LANKA v ENGLAND 2011–12 (1st Test)

At Galle International Stadium on 26, 27, 28, 29 March, 2012.
Toss: Sri Lanka.   Result: SRI LANKA WON BY 75 RUNS.
Debuts: England – S. R. Patel.
Man of the Match: H. M. R. K. B. Herath.

England slipped to their fourth successive defeat since attaining top spot in the ICC's Test rankings, after an inconsistent batting effort at Galle. Several of their batsmen perished on the sweep: four of them were lbw, while Prior thumped one into Thirimanne's midriff at short leg, signalling the end of any hopes England might have had of reaching a testing target of 340. Trott's seventh Test century – the first one to come in a defeat – had given them a sniff, but Prior's rather unlucky demise came with 107 still needed, and shortly afterwards the last five wickets tumbled for 12. Herath finished with six wickets in both innings, his match figures the best by any slow left-armer against England apart from Vinoo Mankad's 12 for 108 for India at Madras in 1951–52. Sri Lanka's batting star was Mahela Jayawardene, who extended his 30th Test century – his seventh both at Galle and against England – to 180 out of 318, or 56% of the total. He was missed four times, twice late on by Panesar as the last two wickets added 65 important runs. Jayawardene faced 315 balls, his ten team-mates 268 between them; his runs included 51 singles, 23 more than England would manage in the first innings. England, in turn, were helped by tail-end runs; they recovered from 122 for seven, but still trailed by 125. Sri Lanka then dipped to 115 for seven, before the other Jayawardene – Prasanna – coaxed 99 more runs to put the target beyond England's grasp.

Sri Lanka

H. D. R. L. Thirimanne c Swann b Anderson	3	– b Swann		6
T. M. Dilshan c Strauss b Broad	11	– b Broad		0
K. C. Sangakkara c Prior b Anderson	0	– c Bell b Swann		14
*D. P. M. D. Jayawardene c Prior b Anderson	180	– c Anderson b Swann		5
T. T. Samaraweera run out	20	– st Prior b Swann		36
L. D. Chandimal c Bell b Patel	27	– c Pietersen b Panesar		31
†H. A. P. W. Jayawardene lbw b Anderson	23	– (8) not out		61
S. Randiv run out	12	– (7) lbw b Swann		18
H. M. R. K. B. Herath lbw b Patel	5	– b Swann		7
U. W. M. B. C. A. Welagedara b Anderson	19	– c Strauss b Panesar		13
R. A. S. Lakmal not out	0	– run out		13
L-b 14, n-b 4	18	B 1, l-b 4, w 1, n-b 4		10
(96.3 overs)	318	(84.3 overs)		214

1/11 (1) 2/11 (3) 3/15 (2) 4/67 (5) 5/128 (6) 6/170 (7)
7/191 (8) 8/253 (9) 9/307 (10) 10/318 (4)

1/4 (2) 2/8 (1) 3/14 (4) 4/41 (3) 5/72 (5) 6/114 (6)
7/115 (7) 8/127 (9) 9/167 (10) 10/214 (11)

Anderson 20.3–5–72–5; Broad 21–3–71–1; Panesar 23–11–42–0; Swann 23–3–92–0; Patel 9–1–27–2. *Second Innings*—Anderson 10.3–2–26–0; Broad 11–2–33–1; Swann 30–5–82–6; Panesar 24–6–59–2; Patel 9–4–9–0.

England

*A. J. Strauss lbw b Herath	26	– c Dilshan b Herath		27
A. N. Cook lbw b Lakmal	0	– c H. A. P. W. Jayawardene b Herath		14
I. J. L. Trott st H. A. P. W. Jayawardene b Herath	12	– c Dilshan b Randiv		112
K. P. Pietersen b Welagedara	3	– c D. P. M. D. Jayawardene b Randiv		30
I. R. Bell b Herath	52	– lbw b Herath		13
†M. J. Prior lbw b Herath	7	– c Thirimanne b Herath		41
S. R. Patel lbw b Herath	2	– c Dilshan b Herath		9
S. C. J. Broad lbw b Herath	28	– not out		5
G. P. Swann c Dilshan b Randiv	24	– lbw b Herath		1
J. M. Anderson not out	23	– c H. A. P. W. Jayawardene b Randiv		5
M. S. Panesar lbw b Randiv	13	– c Dilshan b Randiv		0
L-b 2, w 1	3	L-b 6, w 1		7
(46.4 overs)	193	(99 overs)		264

1/0 (2) 2/40 (3) 3/43 (1) 4/65 (4) 5/72 (6) 6/92 (7)
7/122 (8) 8/157 (9) 9/157 (5) 10/193 (11)

1/31 (2) 2/48 (1) 3/118 (4) 4/152 (5) 5/233 (6)
6/252 (7) 7/256 (3) 8/259 (9) 9/264 (10) 10/264 (11)

Welagedara 11–2–46–1; Lakmal 9–2–45–1; Herath 19–5–74–6; Randiv 7.4–0–26–2. *Second Innings*—Welagedara 13–2–40–0; Lakmal 10–5–22–0; Herath 38–9–97–6; Dilshan 12–1–25–0; Randiv 26–2–74–4.

Umpires: Asad Rauf *(Pakistan)* (42) and R. J. Tucker *(Australia)* (19).
Third umpire: B. N. J. Oxenford *(Australia)*. Referee: J. Srinath *(India)* (21).

Close of play: First day, Sri Lanka 289–8 (D. P. M. D. Jayawardene 168, Welagedara 10); Second day, Sri Lanka 84–5 (Chandimal 17, Randiv 2); Third day, England 111–2 (Trott 40, Pietersen 29).

SRI LANKA v ENGLAND 2011–12 (2nd Test)

At P. Sara Oval, Colombo, on 3, 4, 5, 6, 7 April, 2012.
Toss: Sri Lanka.   Result: ENGLAND WON BY EIGHT WICKETS.
Debuts: none.
Man of the Match: K. P. Pietersen. Man of the Series: D. P. M. D. Jayawardene.

In their last game of a chastening winter, England finally showed they were capable of winning a Test in Asia, the batsmen finally giving proper support to the valiant bowlers. England replicated their victory from their previous visit to the cosy Sara stadium, for Sri Lanka's inaugural Test 30 years before. Anderson quickly reduced Sri Lanka to 30 for three, but Mahela Jayawardene responded with another century, which included the two-millionth run in Test history. Strauss and Cook responded by putting on 122, Trott added 64, then Pietersen belied his problems against left-arm spin with a superb 151, his 20th Test century, including six sixes as well as 16 fours. His trademark switch-hit led to an unusual warning; three times in one over Dilshan refused to release the ball as Pietersen – who started the over on 86 and finished it with 104 – was busy changing into a left-hander. Umpire Rauf, reasoning that Pietersen was causing the impasse that prevented the ball from being delivered, warned that a repeat would incur a five-run penalty. Swann conjured two important wickets in the fourth day's penultimate over to set Sri Lanka back, and next morning disposed of Jayawardene too on the way to six wickets in the innings and ten in the match. England needed 94 and – despite two early wickets – did not hang around. Pietersen ended things with his eighth six of the match as England squared the series and clung on to their No. 1 ranking, just ahead of South Africa.

Sri Lanka

H. D. R. L. Thirimanne lbw b Anderson	8	– (2) c Strauss b Anderson	11
T. M. Dilshan c Prior b Anderson	14	– (3) c Anderson b Swann	35
K. C. Sangakkara c Strauss b Anderson	0	– (4) c Prior b Swann	21
*D. P. M. D. Jayawardene lbw b Swann	105	– (5) c Cook b Swann	64
T. T. Samaraweera lbw b Bresnan	54	– (6) b Swann	47
A. D. Mathews c Strauss b Swann	57	– (8) c Strauss b Finn	46
†H. A. P. W. Jayawardene c Prior b Finn	7	– (9) b Swann	2
S. Randiv c Pietersen b Swann	12	– (7) b Swann	0
K. T. G. D. Prasad not out	12	– (1) c Bresnan b Finn	34
H. M. R. K. B. Herath c Prior b Bresnan	2	– c Anderson b Patel	2
R. A. S. Lakmal b Swann	0	– not out	4
B 4	4	B 4, l-b 6, w 2	12
(111.1 overs)	275	(118.5 overs)	278

1/21 (2) 2/21 (3) 3/30 (1) 4/154 (5) 5/216 (4)   1/23 (2) 2/64 (1) 3/104 (3) 4/125 (4) 5/215 (6)
6/227 (7) 7/258 (8) 8/261 (6) 9/270 (10) 10/275 (11)   6/215 (7) 7/238 (5) 8/242 (9) 9/251 (10) 10/278 (8)

Anderson 22–5–62–3; Finn 22–4–51–1; Bresnan 21–3–47–2; Patel 16–3–32–0; Swann 28.1–4–75–4; Pietersen 2–0–4–0. *Second Innings*—Anderson 20–6–36–1; Finn 15.5–1–30–2; Swann 40–1–106–6; Bresnan 14–5–24–0; Patel 25–7–54–1; Pietersen 4–0–18–0.

England

*A. J. Strauss c H. A. P. W. Jayawardene b Dilshan	61	– b Dilshan	0
A. N. Cook c D. P. M. D. Jayawardene b Dilshan	94	– not out	49
I. J. L. Trott c D. P. M. D. Jayawardene b Herath	64	– lbw b Herath	5
K. P. Pietersen lbw b Herath	151	– not out	42
I. R. Bell c Randiv b Prasad	18		
†M. J. Prior c Prasad b Herath	11		
S. R. Patel c Prasad b Randiv	29		
T. T. Bresnan b Herath	5		
G. P. Swann c Dilshan b Herath	17		
J. M. Anderson lbw b Herath	2		
S. T. Finn not out	2		
B 1, l-b 2, w 1, n-b 2	6	L-b 1	1
(152.3 overs)	460	(2 wkts, 19.4 overs)	97

1/122 (1) 2/213 (2) 3/253 (3) 4/347 (5) 5/380 (6)
6/411 (4) 7/419 (8) 8/454 (9) 9/458 (10) 10/460 (7)   1/0 (1) 2/31 (3)

Lakmal 22–4–81–0; Prasad 23–8–63–1; Herath 53–9–133–6; Dilshan 20–4–73–2; Randiv 34.3–4–107–1. *Second Innings*—Dilshan 7.4–1–43–1; Herath 9–0–37–1; Randiv 3–0–16–0.

Umpires: Asad Rauf *(Pakistan)* (43) and B. N. J. Oxenford *(Australia)* (8).
Third umpire: R. J. Tucker *(Australia)*. Referee: J. Srinath *(India)* (22).

Close of play: First day, Sri Lanka 238–6 (Mathews 41, Randiv 5); Second day, England 154–1 (Cook 77, Trott 15); Third day, Sri Lanka 4–0 (Prasad 0, Thirimanne 0); Fourth day, Sri Lanka 218–6 (D. P. M. D. Jayawardene 55, Mathews 3).

WEST INDIES v AUSTRALIA 2011–12 (1st Test)

At Kensington Oval, Bridgetown, Barbados, on 7, 8, 9, 10, 11 April, 2012.
Toss: West Indies.　　Result: AUSTRALIA WON BY THREE WICKETS.
Debuts: Australia – M. S. Wade.
Man of the Match: R. J. Harris.

West Indies made 449 in their first innings, with Chanderpaul scoring a leisurely 25th Test century… but still ended up losing, allowing Australia, behind for vast tracts of the match, to burst past them at the death. The teenaged Brathwaite, opening because Gayle was still in dispute with the West Indian board, survived more than 4½ hours, while Kirk Edwards and Darren Bravo contributed more attacking fifties. All 11 batsmen reached double figures, only the 12th such instance in Tests, and the first by West Indies. With his pacemen off-colour, Clarke tried eight bowlers in 153 overs, before Sammy allowed himself the luxury of West Indies' first declaration against Australia in 21 years. A big lead looked likely as Australia dipped to 250 for seven, but Test-bests for Harris and Lyon spirited them past 400 too. West Indies needed a good start – but were soon four for three, all to Hilfenhaus. Harris and Siddle joined in, and West Indies were rolled for 148, leaving a teasing target of 192 in 62 overs, with the light – which faded early each day – also a factor. With Cowan dropping anchor, to the irritation of some spectators, Australia reached 61 for one from 22 overs by tea, and came out swinging afterwards. Watson made 52 before becoming the first of four victims for Deonarine's gentle off-spin. Roach removed Wade with 15 needed, and Hussey with only three to go, but the winning runs came as the sun hid behind the Hall and Griffith Stand.

West Indies

A. B. Barath c Siddle b Harris	22 – b Hilfenhaus	2
K. C. Brathwaite c Wade b Siddle	57 – c Wade b Hilfenhaus	0
K. A. Edwards c and b Warner	61 – lbw b Hilfenhaus	1
D. M. Bravo c Hussey b Watson	51 – c Wade b Siddle	32
S. Chanderpaul not out	103 – c Wade b Harris	12
N. Deonarine c Wade b Harris	21 – lbw b Harris	21
†C. S. Baugh run out	22 – c Harris b Hilfenhaus	23
*D. J. G. Sammy c Cowan b Hilfenhaus	41 – b Watson	14
K. A. J. Roach c Clarke b Lyon	16 – b Harris	25
F. H. Edwards c Hussey b Warner	10 – c Watson b Siddle	3
D. Bishoo not out	18 – not out	7
B 12, l-b 9, w 4, n-b 2	27　　B 4, l-b 3, n-b 1	8
(9 wkts dec, 153 overs)	449　　(66.4 overs)	148

1/38 (1) 2/142 (3) 3/167 (2) 4/240 (4) 5/285 (6)　　1/2 (1) 2/3 (2) 3/4 (3) 4/17 (5) 5/67 (4) 6/75 (6)
6/316 (7) 7/369 (8) 8/402 (9) 9/421 (10)　　7/106 (8) 8/116 (7) 9/125 (10) 10/148 (9)

Harris 29–8–83–2; Hilfenhaus 33–12–67–1; Siddle 31–10–83–1; Lyon 31–11–94–1; Clarke 2–0–4–0; Watson 15–5–46–1; Warner 10–0–45–2; Hussey 2–0–6–0. *Second Innings*—Hilfenhaus 17–7–27–4; Watson 12–1–30–1; Harris 8.4–2–31–3; Siddle 17–2–32–2; Lyon 11–4–19–0; Clarke 1–0–2–0.

Australia

E. J. M. Cowan c Baugh b Sammy	14 – (2) c Chanderpaul b Deonarine	34
D. A. Warner c Bravo b Sammy	42 – (1) c Baugh b Sammy	22
S. R. Watson c Baugh b Roach	39 – c sub (K. O. A. Powell) b Deonarine	52
R. T. Ponting run out	4 – b Deonarine	14
*M. J. Clarke c Deonarine b Bishoo	73 – c and b Deonarine	6
M. E. K. Hussey c Baugh b Roach	48 – b Roach	32
†M. S. Wade c Bravo b F. H. Edwards	28 – c Bishoo b Roach	18
P. M. Siddle c K. A. Edwards b F. H. Edwards	0	
R. J. Harris not out	68 – (8) not out	4
B. W. Hilfenhaus b Roach	24 – (9) not out	2
N. M. Lyon not out	40	
L-b 16, w 5, n-b 5	26　　B 1, l-b 3, w 2, n-b 2	8
(9 wkts dec, 145 overs)	406　　(7 wkts, 47 overs)	192

1/50 (1) 2/65 (2) 3/84 (4) 4/133 (3) 5/215 (5)　　1/31 (1) 2/106 (3) 3/126 (2) 4/131 (4) 5/140 (5)
6/249 (6) 7/250 (8) 8/285 (7) 9/329 (10)　　6/177 (7) 7/189 (6)

F. H. Edwards 31–4–92–2; Roach 29–8–72–3; Bishoo 45–10–125–1; Sammy 21–6–65–2; Deonarine 19–5–36–0. *Second Innings*—Roach 12–0–45–2; F. H. Edwards 6–0–19–0; Sammy 10–2–27–1; Bishoo 8–0–44–0; Deonarine 11–1–53–4.

Umpires: I. J. Gould *(England)* (26) and A. L. Hill *(New Zealand)* (29).
Third umpire: M. Erasmus *(South Africa)*. Referee: J. J. Crowe *(New Zealand)* (50).

Close of play: First day, West Indies 179–3 (Bravo 20, Chanderpaul 8); Second day, Australia 44–0 (Cowan 13, Warner 27); Third day, Australia 248–5 (Hussey 47, Wade 19); Fourth day, West Indies 71–5 (Deonarine 20, Baugh 2).

WEST INDIES v AUSTRALIA 2011–12 (2nd Test)

At Queen's Park Oval, Port-of-Spain, Trinidad, on 15, 16, 17, 18, 19 April, 2012.
Toss: Australia.   Result: MATCH DRAWN.
Debuts: none.
Man of the Match: K. A. J. Roach.

The weather had the final say in an interesting contest, ensuring Australia retained the Frank Worrell Trophy they had held for 17 years. West Indies, set an enticing 215 from 59 overs, had made a brisk start, with Sammy promoting himself to No. 3 – but then the rain closed in for good. On a subcontinental-type pitch, both sides included two spinners, Australia for the first time since Nagpur in 2008–09. Clarke was delighted to win the toss, but his own struggles – 129 minutes for 45 – showed the problems posed by the pitch and some accurate bowling. Hussey spent four hours over 73, and later admitted he had seldom felt so drained. His seventh-wicket partnership of 89 with Pattinson helped the innings stagger past 300. Clarke's knack for the lateral was demonstrated again when he handed the new ball to slow left-armer Michael Beer – recalled for his second Test after 15 months – the first Australian spinner to open the bowling in the opposition's first innings since 1938, when leg-spinner Bill O'Reilly partnered Ernie McCormick at Trent Bridge. Beer did the trick, trapping Barath in his third over, while Hilfenhaus and Pattinson prospered at the other end. West Indies were 230 for four, but Lyon suddenly got the ball to fizz as six wickets tumbled for 27. Australia's efforts to set a target quickly were undone by Roach – who completed West Indies' first ten-for against Australia since Curtly Ambrose in 1992–93 – and the rain, which restricted the fourth day to 30.4 overs.

Australia

D. A. Warner c Sammy b Shillingford	29	– (2) c Bravo b Roach	17
E. J. M. Cowan lbw b Roach	28	– (1) lbw b Roach	20
S. R. Watson c Barath b Shillingford	56	– b Roach	0
R. T. Ponting c Sammy b Roach	7	– c Powell b Edwards	41
*M. J. Clarke c Shillingford b Deonarine	45	– c and b Sammy	15
M. E. K. Hussey c Brathwaite b Deonarine	73	– b Roach	24
†M. S. Wade c Bravo b Roach	11	– not out	31
J. L. Pattinson c Bravo b Shillingford	32		
B. W. Hilfenhaus b Roach	5	– (8) b Roach	0
N. M. Lyon not out	7	– (9) c Sammy b Shillingford	3
M. A. Beer lbw b Roach	2		
B 5, l-b 5, w 1, n-b 5	16	B 4, l-b 1, w 1, n-b 3	9
(135 overs)	311	(8 wkts dec, 61.5 overs)	160

1/53 (1) 2/65 (2) 3/83 (4) 4/167 (5) 5/178 (3)
6/208 (7) 7/297 (6) 8/297 (8) 9/309 (9) 10/311 (11)

1/26 (2) 2/26 (3) 3/57 (1) 4/93 (4) 5/95 (5)
6/145 (6) 7/149 (8) 8/160 (9)

Edwards 23–11–45–0; Roach 27–5–105–5; Sammy 16–6–27–0; Shillingford 49–17–92–3; Deonarine 20–6–32–2. *Second Innings*—Edwards 10–2–28–1; Shillingford 23.5–4–55–1; Roach 18–4–41–5; Sammy 8–0–17–1; Deonarine 2–0–14–0.

West Indies

A. B. Barath lbw b Beer	7	– c Clarke b Hilfenhaus	5
K. C. Brathwaite lbw b Hilfenhaus	0		
K. O. A. Powell lbw b Pattinson	19	– (2) lbw b Hilfenhaus	4
D. M. Bravo lbw b Hussey	38	– not out	8
S. Chanderpaul lbw b Lyon	94		
N. Deonarine st Wade b Lyon	55		
†C. S. Baugh lbw b Beer	21		
*D. J. G. Sammy c Hussey b Lyon	1	– (3) not out	30
S. Shillingford c Cowan b Lyon	4		
K. A. J. Roach c Wade b Lyon	0		
F. H. Edwards not out	0		
B 1, l b 8, w 1, n-b 8	18	B 6	6
(104.4 overs)	257	(2 wkts, 11 overs)	53

1/0 (2) 2/26 (1) 3/38 (3) 4/100 (4) 5/230 (6)
6/231 (5) 7/237 (8) 8/241 (9) 9/249 (10) 10/257 (7)

1/6 (2) 2/13 (1)

Beer 25.4–9–56–2; Hilfenhaus 16–4–39–1; Lyon 29–9–68–5; Pattinson 11–2–40–1; Hussey 6–1–19–1; Watson 12–5–14–0; Warner 3–1–9–0; Clarke 2–0–3–0. *Second Innings*—Beer 4–1–10–0; Hilfenhaus 4–0–22–2; Watson 3–1–15–0.

Umpires: M. Erasmus *(South Africa)* (10) and I. J. Gould *(England)* (27).
Third umpire: A. L. Hill *(New Zealand)*. Referee: J. J. Crowe *(New Zealand)* (51)

Close of play: First day, Australia 208–5 (Hussey 26, Wade 11); Second day, West Indies 49–3 (Bravo 16, Chanderpaul 1); Third day, West Indies 252–9 (Baugh 17, Edwards 0); Fourth day, Australia 73–3 (Ponting 32, Clarke 3).

WEST INDIES v AUSTRALIA 2011–12 (3rd Test)

At Windsor Park, Roseau, Dominica, on 23, 24, 25, 26, 27 April, 2012.
Toss: Australia.   Result: AUSTRALIA WON BY 75 RUNS.
Debuts: none.
Man of the Match: M. S. Wade. Man of the Series: S. Chanderpaul.

A match originally scheduled for Guyana, but moved after a dispute with the local board, proved a mixed blessing for Dominica, where celebrations at local man Shane Shillingford's ten wickets were diminished by a 2–0 series defeat. Australia had looked in trouble at 169 for seven, with Shillingford finding bounce and quick turn to interest a cluster of close fielders, led by skipper Sammy, who grasped five catches in the match. But wicketkeeper Wade played superbly for a century, and the last three wickets almost doubled the score. West Indies struggled in turn, and were in danger of following on at 120 for eight before Chanderpaul added 98 with Rampaul and Roach. Still, the deficit of 110 felt decisive. Cowan and Ponting added blue-collar half-centuries, while Shillingford completed only the second ten-for by a West Indian spinner in the Caribbean, after Wilf Ferguson's against England in 1947–48. But 370 always looked well beyond a West Indies side prone to collapse. Hilfenhaus quickly nabbed Barath, before Clarke had a rare bowl: he whirred down his slow left-armers and confounded Brathwaite, Powell and, pivotally, Chanderpaul, who had earlier become only the tenth batsman – and the second West Indian, after Brian Lara – to pass 10,000 Test runs. The final day ultimately offered up a microcosm of the series. West Indies fought doughtily, without ever suggesting they might win; Sammy's 51-ball 61 at least provided some entertainment, before Clarke – with his second Test five-for, more than seven years after the first – and Lyon mopped up.

Australia

E. J. M. Cowan lbw b Rampaul	1	– (2) c Sammy b Deonarine	55
D. A. Warner c Powell b Shillingford	50	– (1) c Chanderpaul b Roach	11
S. R. Watson c Deonarine b Sammy	41	– c Sammy b Shillingford	5
R. T. Ponting c Sammy b Shillingford	23	– c Chanderpaul b Roach	57
*M. J. Clarke c Barath b Shillingford	24	– c Bravo b Shillingford	25
M. E. K. Hussey c Sammy b Shillingford	10	– c Sammy b Shillingford	32
†M. S. Wade c Bravo b Shillingford	106	– lbw b Deonarine	4
R. J. Harris c Baugh b Roach	4	– c Baugh b Deonarine	9
M. A. Starc run out	35	– b Roach	21
B. W. Hilfenhaus b Shillingford	19	– c Brathwaite b Shillingford	6
N. M. Lyon not out	0	– not out	12
B 4, l-b 6, w 3, n-b 2	15	B 8, l-b 9, w 1, n-b 4	22
(114.5 overs)	328	(85 overs)	259

1/1 (1) 2/84 (3) 3/105 (2) 4/142 (4) 5/157 (5)
6/164 (6) 7/169 (8) 8/226 (9) 9/328 (7) 10/328 (10)

1/17 (1) 2/25 (3) 3/112 (2) 4/168 (4) 5/171 (5)
6/196 (7) 7/220 (6) 8/230 (8) 9/237 (10) 10/259 (9)

Roach 23–5–72–1; Rampaul 24–6–65–1; Sammy 21–7–48–1; Shillingford 42.5–9–119–6; Deonarine 4–0–14–0. *Second Innings*—Rampaul 9–1–37–0; Roach 13–2–40–3; Shillingford 39–7–100–4; Sammy 10–4–20–0; Deonarine 14–1–45–3.

West Indies

A. B. Barath c Cowan b Lyon	29	– c Cowan b Hilfenhaus	0
K. C. Brathwaite c Harris b Hilfenhaus	0	– lbw b Clarke	14
K. O. A. Powell b Lyon	40	– b Clarke	24
D. M. Bravo c Cowan b Warner	10	– c Wade b Watson	45
S. Chanderpaul lbw b Starc	68	– lbw b Clarke	69
N. Deonarine lbw b Harris	7	– c and b Clarke	13
†C. S. Baugh c Cowan b Lyon	5	– c Ponting b Lyon	12
*D. J. G. Sammy run out	10	– c Hilfenhaus b Lyon	61
S. Shillingford b Starc	0	– (11) not out	31
R. Rampaul c Warner b Lyon	31	– c Warner b Clarke	11
K. A. J. Roach not out	9	– (9) c Clarke b Lyon	2
B 1, l-b 2, w 1, n-b 5	9	B 3, l-b 9	12
(87.2 overs)	218	(96.3 overs)	294

1/1 (2) 2/62 (1) 3/73 (4) 4/85 (3) 5/96 (6) 6/103 (7)
7/120 (8) 8/120 (9) 9/186 (10) 10/218 (5)

1/0 (1) 2/28 (2) 3/45 (3) 4/155 (4) 5/173 (5)
6/180 (6) 7/206 (7) 8/234 (9) 9/245 (10) 10/294 (8)

Hilfenhaus 18–6–30–1; Starc 12.2–4–29–2; Harris 13–0–36–1; Watson 4–0–12–0; Lyon 33–7–69–4; Warner 5–0–21–1; Clarke 2–0–18–0. *Second Innings*—Hilfenhaus 13–5–23–1; Starc 9–2–26–0; Lyon 29.3–6–87–3; Harris 12–2–34–0; Clarke 23–1–86–5; Watson 9–2–20–1; Warner 1–0–6–0.

Umpires: M. Erasmus *(South Africa)* (11) and A. L. Hill *(New Zealand)* (30).
Third umpire: I. J. Gould *(England)*. Referee: J. J. Crowe *(New Zealand)* (52).

Close of play: First day, Australia 212–7 (Wade 22, Starc 24); Second day, West Indies 165–8 (Chanderpaul 34, Rampaul 24); Third day, Australia 200–6 (Hussey 17, Harris 4); Fourth day, West Indies 173–5 (Deonarine 11).

ENGLAND v WEST INDIES 2012 (1st Test)

At Lord's, London, 17, 18, 19, 20, 21 May, 2012.
Toss: England.   Result: ENGLAND WON BY FIVE WICKETS.
Debuts: England – J. M. Bairstow. West Indies – S. T. Gabriel.
Man of the Match: S. C. J. Broad.

Lord's is not a happy hunting ground for visiting teams in May. This was the 12th such Test since the extension of the international season in 2000, and England had now won eight of them, with four draws. Thanks to Strauss, who produced a timely return to form with his 20th Test century – his fifth at his home ground – West Indies were never quite close enough to threaten an upset. Nonetheless, with Chanderpaul scoring 178 runs for once out in ten hours 25 minutes, they made England sweat. His 87 not out underpinned West Indies' first innings of 243, although the limelight was stolen by the absent Gayle, 4,000 miles away in the IPL, where he smashed 128 not out from 62 balls. Anderson tormented the top order, but Broad knocked over the rest, finishing with seven for 72 (and 11 in the match). Strauss's century – his first for 18 months and 26 innings – and an unruffled 61 from Bell massaged England's lead past 150, then West Indies lost three wickets for no runs, and were later 65 for four before a stand of 157 between Chanderpaul – eventually out sweeping for 91 – and the rehabilitated Samuels turned an apparently routine defeat into a genuine bid for the spoils. Ramdin and Sammy swelled the target to 191, and England lost Strauss and nightwatchman Anderson on the fourth evening. Two more wickets next morning had West Indies briefly dreaming, but Cook's resolve and Bell's elegance soon woke them up.

West Indies

A. B. Barath c Anderson b Broad	42	– c Prior b Bresnan	24
K. O. A. Powell b Anderson	5	– c Bell b Broad	8
K. A. Edwards lbw b Anderson	1	– run out	0
D. M. Bravo run out	29	– b Swann	21
S. Chanderpaul not out	87	– lbw b Swann	91
M. N. Samuels c Bairstow b Broad	31	– c Swann b Broad	86
†D. Ramdin c Strauss b Broad	6	– b Anderson	43
*D. J. G. Sammy c Bresnan b Broad	17	– c Prior b Broad	37
K. A. J. Roach c and b Broad	6	– c Bell b Broad	4
F. H. Edwards c Prior b Broad	2	– not out	10
S. T. Gabriel c Swann b Broad	0	– b Swann	13
B 6, l-b 8, n-b 3	17	L-b 7, n-b 1	8
(89.5 overs)	243	(130.5 overs)	345

1/13 (2) 2/32 (3) 3/86 (1) 4/100 (4) 5/181 (6)
6/187 (7) 7/219 (8) 8/231 (9) 9/243 (10) 10/243 (11)

1/36 (1) 2/36 (2) 3/36 (3) 4/65 (4) 5/222 (6)
6/261 (5) 7/307 (8) 8/313 (9) 9/325 (7) 10/345 (11)

Anderson 25–8–59–2; Broad 24.5–6–72–7; Bresnan 20–7–39–0; Swann 18–6–52–0; Trott 2–0–7–0. *Second Innings*—Anderson 36–11–67–1; Broad 34–6–93–4; Bresnan 36–11–105–1; Swann 18.5–4–59–3; Trott 6–0–14–0.

England

*A. J. Strauss c Ramdin b Roach	122	– c Powell b Roach	1
A. N. Cook b Roach	26	– c K. A. Edwards b Sammy	79
I. J. L. Trott c Ramdin b Sammy	58	– (4) c Sammy b Roach	13
K. P. Pietersen c Ramdin b Samuels	32	– (5) c Ramdin b Gabriel	13
I. R. Bell c Powell b Gabriel	61	– (6) not out	63
J. M. Bairstow lbw b Roach	16	– (7) not out	0
†M. J. Prior b Gabriel	19		
T. T. Bresnan c Ramdin b Sammy	0		
S. C. J. Broad b F. H. Edwards	10		
G. P. Swann b Gabriel	30		
J. M. Anderson not out	0	– (3) c Ramdin b Roach	6
B 9, l-b 3, n-b 12	24	B 4, l-b 3, n-b 11	18
(113.3 overs)	398	(5 wkts, 46.1 overs)	193

1/47 (2) 2/194 (3) 3/244 (4) 4/266 (1) 5/292 (6)
6/320 (7) 7/323 (8) 8/342 (9) 9/397 (10) 10/398 (5)

1/1 (1) 2/10 (3) 3/29 (4) 4/57 (5) 5/189 (2)

F. H. Edwards 25–1–88–1; Roach 25–3–108–3; Gabriel 21.3–2–60–3; Sammy 28–1–92–2; Samuels 14–3–38–1. *Second Innings*—F. H. Edwards 8–0–24–0; Roach 13–2–60–3; Gabriel 5–1–26–1; Sammy 10–1–25–1; Samuels 10.1–0–51–0.

Umpires: Aleem Dar *(Pakistan)* (73) and M. Erasmus *(South Africa)* (12).
Third umpire: Asad Rauf *(Pakistan)*. Referee: R. S. Mahanama *(Sri Lanka)* (36).

Close of play: First day, West Indies 243–9 (Chanderpaul 87); Second day, England 259–3 (Strauss 121, Bell 5); Third day, West Indies 120–4 (Chanderpaul 34, Samuels 26); Fourth day, England 10–2 (Cook 0, Trott 0).

ENGLAND v WEST INDIES 2012 (2nd Test)

At Trent Bridge, Nottingham, on 25, 26, 27, 28 May, 2012.
Toss: West Indies.   Result: ENGLAND WON BY NINE WICKETS.
Debuts: none.
Man of the Match: T. T. Bresnan.

West Indies came to Nottingham, where they had never lost any of their 22 first-class games – and slid to a four-day defeat. Although their side looked more united than for some time, you don't win many Tests from 63 for four in the first innings, or 61 for six in the second. The contest between England's four leading bowlers and West Indies' top four batsmen looked like one of the most uneven in Test history: Kirk Edwards rounded off a disastrous series with seven and (suffering from flu) nought, to follow one and nought at Lord's. A rollicking seventh-wicket stand of 204 between Samuels (who hit 16 fours) and Sammy, who clobbered 17 fours and a six in his maiden Test century, rescued West Indies in the first innings. Cook was twice caught off Roach no-balls before falling for 24, but Strauss reprised his Lord's hundred: it was only the second instance, after Jackie McGlew of South Africa and England's Peter May at Old Trafford in 1955, of both captains reaching centuries on the same day. England were slowed down by three lbws on the third morning, as Strauss laboured to 141. But the eventual lead of 58 proved vital; Anderson soon removed both openers, and only Samuels stood in the way of England's bowling machine. A crude collection of swipes and prods left England with only 108 to chase for a record seventh consecutive series victory at home, a sequence dating back to West Indies' previous visit in 2009.

West Indies

A. B. Barath c Anderson b Broad	0	– lbw b Anderson		7
K. O. A. Powell c Anderson b Broad	33	– b Anderson		1
K. A. Edwards b Anderson	7	– (7) lbw b Bresnan		0
D. M. Bravo c Swann b Anderson	3	– (3) lbw b Bresnan		22
S. Chanderpaul lbw b Swann	46	– (4) c Trott b Broad		11
M. N. Samuels c Anderson b Bresnan	117	– (5) not out		76
†D. Ramdin b Bresnan	1	– (6) lbw b Bresnan		6
*D. J. G. Sammy c Pietersen b Bresnan	106	– lbw b Bresnan		25
K. A. J. Roach c Strauss b Bresnan	7	– lbw b Anderson		14
S. Shillingford st Prior b Swann	16	– c Anderson b Swann		0
R. Rampaul not out	6	– c Bresnan b Anderson		0
B 8, l-b 18, w 1, n-b 1	28	B 1, l-b 2		3
(109.2 overs)	370	(60.1 overs)		165

1/9 (1) 2/26 (3) 3/42 (4) 4/63 (2) 5/125 (5) 6/136 (7)   1/5 (2) 2/14 (1) 3/31 (4) 4/45 (3) 5/61 (6) 6/61 (7)
7/340 (8) 8/341 (6) 9/360 (9) 10/370 (10)   7/110 (8) 8/139 (9) 9/148 (10) 10/165 (11)

Anderson 30–12–73–2; Broad 27–4–81–2; Bresnan 27–4–104–4; Swann 20.2–4–62–2; Trott 5–0–24–0. *Second Innings*—Anderson 20.1–6–43–4; Broad 17–5–58–1; Swann 6–1–24–1; Bresnan 17–5–37–4.

England

*A. J. Strauss c Ramdin b Sammy	141	– c Bravo b Samuels		45
A. N. Cook c Ramdin b Rampaul	24	– not out		43
I. J. L. Trott lbw b Rampaul	35	– not out		17
K. P. Pietersen lbw b Rampaul	80			
I. R. Bell lbw b Roach	22			
J. M. Bairstow c Chanderpaul b Roach	4			
†M. J. Prior b Sammy	16			
T. T. Bresnan not out	39			
S. C. J. Broad c Sammy b Shillingford	25			
G. P. Swann c Sammy b Samuels	1			
J. M. Anderson lbw b Samuels	0			
B 9, l-b 10, w 4, n-b 18	41	B 5, n-b 1		6
(123.4 overs)	428	(1 wkt, 30.4 overs)		111

1/43 (2) 2/123 (3) 3/267 (4) 4/300 (5) 5/308 (6)
6/336 (7) 7/363 (1) 8/416 (9) 9/426 (10) 10/428 (11)   1/89 (1)

Roach 25–1–90–2; Rampaul 32–8–75–3; Sammy 34–3–120–2; Shillingford 26–4–110–1; Samuels 6.4–2–14–2. *Second Innings*—Roach 5–2–16–0; Rampaul 6–2–12–0; Sammy 6–0–32–0; Samuels 5.4–0–18–1; Shillingford 8–1–28–0.

Umpires: Aleem Dar *(Pakistan)* (74) and Asad Rauf *(Pakistan)* (44).
Third umpire: M. Erasmus *(South Africa)*. Referee: R. S. Mahanama *(Sri Lanka)* (37).

Close of play: First day, West Indies 304–6 (Samuels 107, Sammy 88); Second day, England 259–2 (Strauss 102, Pietersen 72); Third day, West Indies 61–6 (Samuels 13, Sammy 0).

ENGLAND v WEST INDIES 2012 (3rd Test)

At Edgbaston, Birmingham, on 7 (*no play*), 8 (*no play*), 9, 10, 11 June (*no play*), 2012.
Toss: England.　　Result: MATCH DRAWN.
Debuts: West Indies – A. B. Fudadin, S. P. Narine.
Man of the Match: T. L. Best. Men of the Series: A. J. Strauss and M. N. Samuels.

Not since 1964, and Australia's visit to Lord's, had the first two days of a Test in England been washed out. But, after Samuels took his series aggregate to 386 runs, a cast-iron draw was rescued from watery obscurity on the fourth day, when Tino Best smashed 95, the highest Test score by a No. 11 (beating Zaheer Khan's 75 for India against Bangladesh at Dhaka in 2004–05). Best, whose previous-highest score was 27, slammed 14 fours and a six, helped by England's decision to rest Anderson and Broad. He was finally caught just short of a fairytale century, but the way Strauss threw the ball away told of his frustration, despite equalling the England record of 120 Test catches, shared by Colin Cowdrey and Ian Botham. Best added 143 with Ramdin, a West Indian last-wicket record and the third-highest in Tests. Ramdin caused controversy – and was fined 20% of his match fee – when, after reaching his second Test hundred (both against England), he unfurled a handwritten sign saying "Yea Viv, talk nah", a jibe at Viv Richards, who had described him as looking "totally lost" during the Second Test. England slipped to 49 for three before Bell and Pietersen added 137, but the final day was rained off. The soggy finale ended Bresnan's England-record run of 13 successive victories since his debut in 2009. Only Adam Gilchrist, who kicked off his Test career with 15 wins, had a better start; Stuart Clark, another recent Australian, also started with 13.

West Indies

A. B. Barath lbw b Onions		41
K. O. A. Powell c Swann b Bresnan		24
A. B. Fudadin c Bell b Bresnan		28
D. M. Bravo c and b Finn		6
M. N. Samuels lbw b Bresnan		76
N. Deonarine c Strauss b Onions		7
†D. Ramdin not out		107
*D. J. G. Sammy c Strauss b Finn		16
S. P. Narine b Onions		11
R. Rampaul c Prior b Finn		2
T. L. Best c Strauss b Onions		95
	B 4, l-b 8, w 1	13
	(129.3 overs)	426

1/49 (2) 2/90 (1) 3/99 (4) 4/128 (3) 5/152 (6) 6/208 (5)
7/241 (8) 8/267 (9) 9/283 (10) 10/426 (11)

Onions 29.3–7–88–4; Bresnan 34–9–111–3; Finn 32–6–109–3; Swann 26–5–85–0; Trott 8–1–21–0.

England

*A. J. Strauss c Bravo b Best		17
A. N. Cook lbw b Rampaul		4
I. J. L. Trott b Sammy		17
K. P. Pietersen c Sammy b Samuels		78
I. R. Bell not out		76
J. M. Bairstow b Best		18
S. T. Finn not out		0
	B 1, l-b 7, n-b 3	11
	(5 wkts, 58 overs)	221

1/13 (2) 2/40 (3) 3/49 (1) 4/186 (4) 5/215 (6)

†M. J. Prior, T. T. Bresnan, G. P. Swann and G. Onions did not bat.

Best 12–2–37–2; Rampaul 14–1–55–1; Sammy 8–1–22–1; Narine 15–1–70–0; Samuels 9–0–29–1.

Umpires: H. D. P. K. Dharmasena (*Sri Lanka*) (9) and A. L. Hill (*New Zealand*) (31).
Third umpire: Aleem Dar (*Pakistan*). Referee: R. S. Mahanama (*Sri Lanka*) (38).

Close of play: First day, no play; Second day, no play; Third day, West Indies 280–8 (Ramdin 60, Rampaul 2); Fourth day, England 221–5 (Bell 76, Finn 0).

SRI LANKA v PAKISTAN 2012 (1st Test)

At Galle International Stadium on 22, 23, 24, 25 June, 2012.
Toss: Sri Lanka.　　Result: SRI LANKA WON BY 209 RUNS.
Debuts: Pakistan – Mohammad Ayub.
Man of the Match: K. C. Sangakkara.

Sri Lanka had won only two of their previous 19 Tests, but controlled this one from the start. The pitch had a helpful covering of grass, but nonetheless Dilshan – with his first Test hundred at home since August 2009 – and Sangakkara rocketed Sri Lanka to 300 for two on the first day. On the second, a scoreboard error probably deprived Sangakkara of his ninth Test double-century. With the board reading 194, he slogged Saeed Ajmal for six and began to celebrate – only to be informed he was still one short. Somewhat frazzled, he failed to score off the last ball of the over, leaving the No. 11 on strike. Pradeep Fernando was castled second ball, to the mortification of Sangakkara, the second man to be stranded on 199 in a Test after Zimbabwe's Andy Flower against South Africa at Harare 11 years earlier. Pakistan lurched to 44 for five, and were routed next day for 100. Jayawardene waived the follow-on, instead building the lead to an impregnable 509. When Pakistan dipped to 38 for four on the fourth morning, complete humiliation was on the cards. But Younis Khan and Asad Shafiq ground it out for nearly two sessions, adding 151. Pakistan were eight down by the scheduled close, but Randiv struck in successive overs in the extra half-hour. Misbah-ul-Haq missed the match, suspended after slow over-rates in the preceding one-day series; his replacement Mohammad Ayub became, at 32 years 283 days, Pakistan's fifth-eldest debutant, and the oldest since the 1950s.

Sri Lanka

N. T. Paranavitana st Adnan Akmal b Saeed Ajmal	24	– lbw b Saeed Ajmal	25
T. M. Dilshan lbw b Saeed Ajmal	101	– lbw b Junaid Khan	56
K. C. Sangakkara not out	199	– c Taufeeq Umar b Saeed Ajmal...........................	1
*D. P. M. D. Jayawardene b Saeed Ajmal....................	62	– c Adnan Akmal b Junaid Khan...................	14
T. T. Samaraweera st Adnan Akmal b Saeed Ajmal	6	– c Younis Khan b Junaid Khan	15
A. D. Mathews c and b Saeed Ajmal............................	0	– not out	7
†H. A. P. W. Jayawardene c Adnan Akmal b Mohammad Hafeez	48	– not out	9
S. Randiv c and b Abdur Rehman	8		
K. M. D. N. Kulasekara c Mohammad Ayub b Mohammad Hafeez	0		
H. M. R. K. B. Herath run out...................................	0		
A. N. P. R. Fernando b Mohammad Hafeez.................	0		
B 10, l-b 7, w 5, n-b 2	24	B 6, l-b 2, n-b 2	10
(153.2 overs)	472	(5 wkts dec, 41 overs)	137

1/63 (1) 2/187 (2) 3/315 (4) 4/335 (5) 5/335 (6)
6/415 (7) 7/438 (8) 8/439 (9) 9/455 (10) 10/472 (11)　　　1/81 (1) 2/85 (2) 3/93 (3) 4/114 (4) 5/119 (5)

Umar Gul 27–8–76–0; Junaid Khan 18–5–52–0; Mohammad Hafeez 19.2–3–55–3; Saeed Ajmal 46–9–146–5; Abdur Rehman 43–7–126–1. *Second Innings*—Umar Gul 4–0–11–0; Junaid Khan 13–2–44–3; Abdur Rehman 5–0–25–0; Saeed Ajmal 17–3–47–2; Younis Khan 2–0–2–0.

Pakistan

*Mohammad Hafeez lbw b Randiv	20	– c D. P. M. D. Jayawardene b Kulasekara	4
Taufeeq Umar lbw b Kulasekara..................................	9	– b Kulasekara...	10
Azhar Ali c H. A. P. W. Jayawardene b Kulasekara......	0	– c Samaraweera b Herath........................	7
Younis Khan lbw b Herath	29	– c H. A. P. W. Jayawardene b Kulasekara ...	87
Saeed Ajmal c Paranavitana b Randiv.........................	0	– run out	12
Asad Shafiq c H. A. P. W. Jayawardene b Herath........	0	– c D. P. M. D. Jayawardene b Herath	80
Mohammad Ayub lbw b Herath..................................	25	– lbw b Fernando......................................	22
†Adnan Akmal run out..	9	– not out	40
Abdur Rehman lbw b Randiv......................................	1	– c Sangakkara b Randiv...........................	14
Umar Gul c H. A. P. W. Jayawardene b Randiv............	2	– c Samaraweera b Randiv	4
Junaid Khan not out	2	– c sub (B. M. A. J. Mendis) b Randiv	8
L-b 2, w 1...	3	B 9, l-b 2, w 1.................................	12
(54.3 overs)	100	(114 overs)	300

1/17 (2) 2/17 (3) 3/43 (1) 4/43 (5) 5/44 (6) 6/65 (4)　　　1/8 (1) 2/21 (3) 3/25 (2) 4/38 (5) 5/189 (6)
7/88 (8) 8/94 (9) 9/98 (7) 10/100 (10)　　　6/212 (4) 7/243 (7) 8/266 (9) 9/280 (10) 10/300 (11)

Kulasekara 13–7–27–2; Fernando 9–2–28–0; Herath 21–6–30–3; Mathews 2–2–0–0; Randiv 9.3–1–13–4. *Second Innings*—Kulasekara 23–8–48–3; Fernando 15–4–56–1; Herath 42–9–91–2; Mathews 4–1–8–0; Randiv 30–4–86–3.

Umpires: S. J. Davis *(Australia)* (37) and I. J. Gould *(England)* (28).
Third umpire: R. E. J. Martinesz *(Sri Lanka)*. Referee: D. C. Boon *(Australia)* (8).

Close of play: First day, Sri Lanka 300–2 (Sangakkara 111, D. P. M. D. Jayawardene 55); Second day, Pakistan 48–5 (Younis Khan 15, Mohammad Ayub 1); Third day, Pakistan 36–3 (Younis Khan 0, Saeed Ajmal 11).

SRI LANKA v PAKISTAN 2012 (2nd Test)

At Sinhalese Sports Club, Colombo, on 30 June, 1, 2, 3, 4 July, 2012.
Toss: Sri Lanka.   Result: MATCH DRAWN.
Debuts: none.
Man of the Match: Junaid Khan.

Sri Lanka nearly paid the price for bowling first on a placid track, the weather helping them escape with a draw. Pakistan ran up 551; the usually sedate Taufeeq Umar plundered 65 of an opening stand of 78, while Mohammad Hafeez returned to form with a career-best 196 in seven hours seven minutes. He added 287 – the highest by any visiting pair in Sri Lanka – with Azhar Ali, who scored 157 for the second time in Tests. Pakistan's charge was halted by rain, which allowed only 44.2 overs on the second day. Younis Khan was struck outside the line, but given out; for the third time in three innings, DRS – not used in this series for cost reasons – would have reprieved him. Misbah-ul-Haq, restored as captain, batted on for an hour on the third morning before declaring. Between rain-breaks, Dilshan (who passed 5,000 Test runs during his century) and Sangakkara then added 225, but four others made ducks. Sangakkara again missed out on a double-century, reaching 192 before he charged Abdur Rehman and slapped to midwicket. Only Mohammad Yousuf of Pakistan had previously made three 190s in Tests. But Sangakkara's 30th Test hundred put him past Don Bradman; no one had scored more than nine against Pakistan, and he also overtook Sunil Gavaskar's 2,089 runs against them. Once the follow-on was avoided, there was little hope of a positive result. No Pakistan bowler had bowled as many as 34 overs in an innings without a maiden before, as Saeed Ajmal did.

Pakistan

Mohammad Hafeez b Herath	196	– c Dilshan b Randiv	21
Taufeeq Umar c H. A. P. W. Jayawardene b Mathews..	65	– not out	42
Azhar Ali c Kulasekara b Randiv	157		
Younis Khan lbw b Herath	32		
*Misbah-ul-Haq not out	66		
Asad Shafiq run out	2		
†Adnan Akmal c Dilshan b Herath	5	– (4) not out	0
Abdur Rehman not out	18	– (3) b Randiv	36
L-b 5, w 1, n-b 4	10	N-b 1	1
(6 wkts dec, 147 overs)	551	(2 wkts dec, 18 overs)	100

1/78 (2) 2/365 (1) 3/435 (4) 4/486 (3) 5/491 (6)
6/519 (7)

1/51 (1) 2/99 (3)

Saeed Ajmal, Aizaz Cheema and Junaid Khan did not bat.

Kulasekara 27–6–84–0; Mathews 15–1–55–1; Fernando 24–3–103–0; Randiv 31–0–131–1; Herath 49–5–164–3; Dilshan 1–0–9–0. *Second Innings*—Kulasekara 5–0–23–0; Fernando 8–0–48–0; Randiv 4–0–28–2; Herath 1–0–1–0.

Sri Lanka

N. T. Paranavitana c Azhar Ali b Junaid Khan	0	– lbw b Saeed Ajmal	32
T. M. Dilshan lbw b Junaid Khan	121	– lbw b Abdur Rehman	28
K. C. Sangakkara c Taufeeq Umar b Abdur Rehman	192	– not out	24
*D. P. M. D. Jayawardene lbw b Junaid Khan	0	– not out	1
T. T. Samaraweera lbw b Saeed Ajmal	0		
S. Randiv lbw b Abdur Rehman	5		
A. D. Mathews c Adnan Akmal b Junaid Khan	47		
†H. A. P. W. Jayawardene c Adnan Akmal b Abdur Rehman	6		
K. M. D. N. Kulasekara b Junaid Khan	0		
H. M. R. K. B. Herath not out	10		
A. N. P. R. Fernando c Saeed Ajmal b Abdur Rehman	1		
B 4, l-b 5	9	L-b 1	1
(124.4 overs)	391	(2 wkts, 22 overs)	86

1/11 (1) 2/236 (2) 3/250 (4) 4/259 (5) 5/278 (6)
6/370 (7) 7/378 (3) 8/379 (9) 9/385 (8) 10/391 (11)

1/48 (2) 2/78 (1)

Aizaz Cheema 24–5–86–0; Junaid Khan 28–6–73–5; Saeed Ajmal 34–0–106–1; Abdur Rehman 26.4–5–78–4; Mohammad Hafeez 8–0–29–0; Azhar Ali 4–0–10–0. *Second Innings*—Junaid Khan 4–0–21–0; Aizaz Cheema 2–0–11–0; Abdur Rehman 9–2–19–1; Saeed Ajmal 7–0–34–1.

Umpires: I. J. Gould *(England)* (29) and S. J. A. Taufel *(Australia)* (72).
Third umpire: R. S. A. Palliyaguruge *(Sri Lanka)*. Referee: D. C. Boon *(Australia)* (9).

Close of play: First day, Pakistan 334–1 (Mohammad Hafeez 172, Azhar Ali 92); Second day, Pakistan 488–4 (Misbah-ul-Haq 29, Asad Shafiq 1); Third day, Sri Lanka 70–1 (Dilshan 46, Sangakkara 22); Fourth day, Sri Lanka 278–5 (Sangakkara 144).

SRI LANKA v PAKISTAN 2012 (3rd Test)

At Muttiah Muralitharan Stadium, Pallekele, on 8, 9 (*no play*), 10, 11, 12 July, 2012.
Toss: Sri Lanka.   Result: MATCH DRAWN.
Debuts: none.
Man of the Match: Asad Shafiq. Man of the Series: K. C. Sangakkara.

Hill-country Sri Lanka was lush from months of rain, and offered the bowlers a juicy pitch. Jayawardene put Pakistan in again, and got it right this time: with Perera swinging the ball appreciably, they subsided for 226. Dilhara Fernando – on his 17th comeback to the Test side – bowled too short, but did fracture Adnan Akmal's left ring finger; Taufeeq Umar had to keep wicket instead. Sri Lanka slipped to 44 for three by stumps. Sangakkara, whose 190s in the first two Tests had shut Pakistan out, was this time tormented by Junaid Khan's inward movement; almost lbw to the first two balls, he had his stumps rearranged by the third. After a blank second day, Sri Lanka were rescued by Paranavitana and Samaraweera, who ground out 143 in 47 overs before Perera and Kulasekara boosted the lead towards 111. Pakistan wiped out the deficit with only two wickets down, and built a lead on Azhar Ali's third century against Sri Lanka, and Asad Shafiq's second in Tests. Herath became the third Sri Lankan, after Muttiah Muralitharan and Chaminda Vaas, to take 100 Test wickets at home. Adnan appeared at No. 10 following painkilling injections, and defended stoutly to see Shafiq to his hundred. Sri Lanka were left 270 in 71 overs; they set off positively, but the quality of the Pakistani attack – and Sri Lanka's 1–0 series lead – meant the shutters soon came down. It was Misbah's first series defeat as captain, although he had missed the match that mattered.

Pakistan

Mohammad Hafeez b Perera	22	– c Paranavitana b Fernando	52
Taufeeq Umar lbw b Perera	29	– lbw b Kulasekara	4
Azhar Ali c Samaraweera b Perera	0	– c H. A. P. W. Jayawardene b Fernando	136
Younis Khan c H. A. P. W. Jayawardene b Kulasekara ...	0	– c Paranavitana b Herath	19
*Misbah-ul-Haq c H. A. P. W. Jayawardene b Perera...	40	– c D. P. M. D. Jayawardene b Herath	5
Asad Shafiq c H. A. P. W. Jayawardene b Herath........	75	– not out	100
†Adnan Akmal b Herath	24	– (10) not out	35
Mohammad Sami c Perera b Mathews	9	– (7) lbw b Fernando	3
Umar Gul b Kulasekara	7	– (8) lbw b Herath	0
Saeed Ajmal lbw b Herath	6	– (9) lbw b Herath	5
Junaid Khan not out	3		
L-b 11	11	B 6, l-b 8, w 7	21
(72.5 overs)	226	(8 wkts dec, 128.4 overs)	380

1/35 (1) 2/41 (3) 3/50 (4) 4/56 (2) 5/141 (5) 6/175 (8)
7/198 (7) 8/217 (9) 9/217 (6) 10/226 (10)

1/16 (2) 2/110 (1) 3/158 (4) 4/176 (5) 5/276 (3)
6/280 (7) 7/281 (8) 8/299 (9)

In the first innings Adnan Akmal, when 10, retired hurt at 162–5 and resumed at 175–6.

Kulasekara 16–4–44–2; Perera 18–5–63–4; Mathews 8–3–20–1; Herath 18.5–6–40–3; Fernando 12–1–48–0. *Second Innings*—Kulasekara 28–9–65–1; Perera 25–2–88–0; Herath 39.4–4–99–4; Fernando 23–1–74–3; Mathews 12–0–38–0; Samaraweera 1–0–2–0.

Sri Lanka

N. T. Paranavitana b Saeed Ajmal	75	– c Younis Khan b Junaid Khan	22
L. D. Chandimal lbw b Junaid Khan	8	– c Asad Shafiq b Saeed Ajmal	65
K. C. Sangakkara b Junaid Khan	0	– not out	74
*D. P. M. D. Jayawardene lbw b Mohammad Sami	12	– c Mohammad Hafeez b Saeed Ajmal	11
T. T. Samaraweera lbw b Saeed Ajmal	73	– b Saeed Ajmal	10
A. D. Mathews c Asad Shafiq b Junaid Khan	9	– not out	1
†H. A. P. W. Jayawardene lbw b Umar Gul	20		
N. L. T. C. Perera b Junaid Khan	75		
K. M. D. N. Kulasekara c Taufeeq Umar b Junaid Khan..	33		
H. M. R. K. B. Herath lbw b Saeed Ajmal	2		
C. R. D. Fernando not out	0		
B 16, l-b 7, w 6, n-b 1	30	B 2, l-b 10	12
(100.2 overs)	337	(4 wkts, 62 overs)	195

1/14 (2) 2/14 (3) 3/44 (4) 4/187 (5) 5/200 (6) 6/204 (1)
7/236 (7) 8/320 (9) 9/337 (10) 10/337 (8)

1/44 (1) 2/132 (2) 3/150 (4) 4/178 (5)

Umar Gul 22–3–90–1; Junaid Khan 28.2–3–70–5; Mohammad Sami 17–1–69–1; Saeed Ajmal 25–5–66–3; Younis Khan 3–0–9–0; Mohammad Hafeez 5–0–10–0. *Second Innings*—Umar Gul 9–2–43–0; Junaid Khan 10–0–45–1; Mohammad Hafeez 9–1–22–0; Saeed Ajmal 26–8–50–3; Mohammad Sami 8–0–23–0.

Umpires: S. J. Davis *(Australia)* (38) and S. J. A. Taufel *(Australia)* (73).
Third umpire: R. E. J. Martinesz *(Sri Lanka)*. Referee: D. C. Boon *(Australia)* (10).

Close of play: First day, Sri Lanka 44–3 (Paranavitana 13); Second day, no play; Third day, Pakistan 27–1 (Mohammad Hafeez 8, Azhar Ali 6); Fourth day, Pakistan 299–8 (Asad Shafiq 55, Adnan Akmal 0).

ENGLAND v SOUTH AFRICA 2012 (1st Test)

At Kennington Oval, London, on 19, 20, 21, 22, 23 July, 2012.
Toss: England.   Result: SOUTH AFRICA WON BY AN INNINGS AND 12 RUNS.
Debuts: none.
Man of the Match: H. M. Amla.

South Africa had never won in 13 previous Tests at The Oval, but put that right in emphatic fashion. England did not make the most of a placid pitch, despite Cook's 20th Test century, but South Africa certainly did. Smith was the seventh to score a hundred in his 100th Test (including Ricky Ponting, who made two), and added 259 with Amla – who, it turned out, was just getting started. He and Kallis piled on 377 without being separated. It was Kallis's 20th double-century stand in Tests, two more than Sachin Tendulkar. Amla, meanwhile, flowed past de Villiers's national record of 277, and completed South Africa's first Test triple-century; in all he batted for 790 minutes and 529 balls, hitting 35 fours. It was the first Test triple in England since Graham Gooch's 333 in 1990, and the first by a visiting batsman since 1964, when Australia's Bob Simpson also made 311. England were done for, although Bell's 189-ball fifty – his slowest in Tests, as Smith's had been – delayed the inevitable. De Villiers was playing his 75th successive Tests, equalling the South African record of Mark Boucher, whose place he had taken behind the stumps after Boucher's career-ending eye injury in the first match of the tour. It was only the fifth Test victory by a team losing only two wickets; South Africa (against Bangladesh at Chittagong in 2003) had also been the last. No one was sure when England had been so utterly outflanked, although Hastings 1066 was a possibility.

England

*A. J. Strauss lbw b Morkel	0	– c Philander b Imran Tahir	27
A. N. Cook b Steyn	115	– c de Villiers b Philander	0
I. J. L. Trott c de Villiers b Morkel	71	– c de Villiers b Steyn	10
K. P. Pietersen c de Villiers b Kallis	42	– b Morkel	16
I. R. Bell b Kallis	13	– c Kallis b Steyn	55
R. S. Bopara c de Villiers b Steyn	0	– b Steyn	22
†M. J. Prior c de Villiers b Morkel	60	– c Kallis b Imran Tahir	40
T. T. Bresnan b Imran Tahir	8	– not out	20
S. C. J. Broad b Philander	16	– c de Villiers b Steyn	0
G. P. Swann not out	15	– c Petersen b Steyn	7
J. M. Anderson c de Villiers b Morkel	2	– lbw b Imran Tahir	4
B 2, l-b 24, w 3, n-b 14	43	B 11, l-b 15, w 1, n-b 12	39
(125.5 overs)	385	(97 overs)	240

1/0 (1) 2/170 (3) 3/251 (4) 4/271 (2) 5/272 (6)
6/284 (5) 7/313 (8) 8/358 (9) 9/383 (7) 10/385 (11)

1/2 (2) 2/32 (3) 3/57 (4) 4/67 (1) 5/117 (6)
6/203 (7) 7/210 (5) 8/210 (9) 9/218 (10) 10/240 (11)

Morkel 24.5–2–72–4; Philander 27–4–79–1; Steyn 30–7–99–2; Kallis 19–7–38–2; Imran Tahir 19–0–61–1; Duminy 6–1–10–0. *Second Innings*—Morkel 16–0–41–1; Philander 19–6–29–1; Steyn 21–6–56–5; Imran Tahir 32–7–63–3; Kallis 7–1–22–0; Duminy 2–1–3–0.

South Africa

*G. C. Smith b Bresnan	131
A. N. Petersen lbw b Anderson	0
H. M. Amla not out	311
J. H. Kallis not out	182
B 5, l-b 4, w 2, n-b 2	13
(2 wkts dec, 189 overs)	637

1/1 (2) 2/260 (1)

†A. B. de Villiers, J. A. Rudolph, J-P. Duminy, V. D. Philander, D. W. Steyn, M. Morkel and Imran Tahir did not bat.

Anderson 41–7–116–1; Broad 34–6–118–0; Swann 52–10–151–0; Bresnan 37–2–140–1; Bopara 18–1–78–0; Pietersen 3–0–13–0; Trott 4–0–12–0.

Umpires: Asad Rauf *(Pakistan)* (45) and S. J. Davis *(Australia)* (39).
Third umpire: H. D. P. K. Dharmasena *(Sri Lanka)*. Referee: J. J. Crowe *(New Zealand)* (53).

Close of play: First day, England 267–3 (Cook 114, Bell 10); Second day, South Africa 86–1 (Smith 37, Amla 47); Third day, South Africa 403–2 (Amla 183, Kallis 82); Fourth day, England 102–4 (Bell 14, Bopara 15).

ENGLAND v SOUTH AFRICA 2012 (2nd Test)

At Headingley, Leeds, on 2, 3, 4, 5, 6 August, 2012.
Toss: England.   Result: MATCH DRAWN.
Debuts: England – J. W. A. Taylor.
Man of the Match: K. P. Pietersen.

An absorbing Test was played out against the weird backdrop of the Kevin Pietersen saga. After a dazzling 149, KP hinted at a press conference that the next Test might be his last – but later, when it emerged he had sent South African players apparently derogatory text messages about Strauss, he was dropped anyway. England omitted Swann, wicketless at The Oval, in favour of a fourth pace bowler – but Cook, at second slip instead of Swann, dropped Petersen when he had 29. Next over, Smith was reprieved after being bowled, as Finn had broken the stumps with his knee in delivery (the law was later changed to make this a no-ball rather than a dead ball, as was called here). South Africa's openers survived to add 120, Petersen went on to 182, and the total passed 400. Thanks mainly to Pietersen, who made exactly 100 in an elongated final session on the third day, England went past that. But thunderstorms allowed only 38.4 overs on the fourth day, then on the fifth day Smith made an enterprising declaration not long after Broad had taken five wickets in 37 balls. England needed 253 in 39 overs; unlikely, but not impossible. Pietersen, promoted to open, and Strauss both passed 7,000 Test runs, and England contemplated the chase until Prior was run out. Had the weather allowed just one more session, it might have been a thriller: as it was, with Pietersen about to face the press, the fun and games had barely begun.

South Africa

A. N. Petersen c Prior b Broad	182	– (8) not out		16
*G. C. Smith c Bell b Bresnan	52	– c Taylor b Pietersen		52
H. M. Amla run out	9	– c Cook b Pietersen		28
J. H. Kallis c Cook b Anderson	19	– (5) c Prior b Broad		27
†A. B. de Villiers b Broad	47	– (4) lbw b Broad		44
D. W. Steyn b Finn	0	– (9) c and b Anderson		3
J. A. Rudolph st Prior b Pietersen	19	– (1) lbw b Pietersen		69
J-P. Duminy not out	48	– (6) lbw b Broad		0
V. D. Philander c Bresnan b Finn	13	– (7) lbw b Broad		6
M. Morkel c Cook b Broad	19	– c Cook b Broad		10
Imran Tahir c Cook b Anderson	0			
B 5, l-b 6	11	L-b 2, w 1		3
(139.2 overs)	419	(9 wkts dec, 67.4 overs)		258

1/120 (2) 2/132 (3) 3/157 (4) 4/254 (5) 5/259 (6)   1/120 (1) 2/129 (2) 3/182 (3) 4/209 (4)
6/318 (7) 7/353 (1) 8/375 (9) 9/414 (10) 10/419 (11)   5/209 (6) 6/223 (7) 7/230 (5) 8/247 (9) 9/258 (10)

Anderson 33.2–10–61–2; Broad 35–10–96–3; Finn 32–3–118–2; Bresnan 27–4–98–1; Trott 5–1–9–0; Pietersen 7–0–26–1. *Second Innings*—Anderson 19–7–40–1; Broad 16.4–2–69–5; Finn 14–2–55–0; Bresnan 9–2–40–0; Pietersen 9–1–52–3.

England

*A. J. Strauss c de Villiers b Steyn	37	– (3) c and b Duminy		22
A. N. Cook lbw b Philander	24	– c Rudolph b Steyn		46
I. J. L. Trott c Smith b Steyn	35	– (4) not out		30
K. P. Pietersen lbw b Morkel	149	– (1) c Imran Tahir b Philander		12
I. R. Bell c Smith b Kallis	11	– (6) not out		3
J. W. A. Taylor b Morkel	34			
†M. J. Prior c Steyn b Imran Tahir	68	– (5) run out		7
T. T. Bresnan c Smith b Philander	9			
S. C. J. Broad c sub (F. du Plessis) b Imran Tahir	1			
J. M. Anderson b Imran Tahir	8			
S. T. Finn not out	0			
B 7, l-b 17, w 14, n-b 11	49	L-b 8, w 1, n-b 1		10
(126.4 overs)	425	(4 wkts, 33 overs)		130

1/65 (2) 2/85 (1) 3/142 (3) 4/173 (5) 5/320 (6)
6/351 (4) 7/396 (8) 8/407 (9) 9/420 (7) 10/425 (10)   1/21 (1) 2/75 (3) 3/90 (2) 4/106 (5)

Morkel 32–9–96–2; Philander 30–10–72–2; Steyn 28–8–102–2; Kallis 12–3–34–1; Imran Tahir 23.4–0–92–3; Duminy 1–0–5–0. *Second Innings*—Morkel 10–4–33–0; Philander 6–1–26–1; Steyn 7–1–26–1; Imran Tahir 4–0–20–0; Duminy 2–0–10–1; Kallis 4–2–7–0.

Umpires: S. J. Davis *(Australia)* (40) and R. J. Tucker *(Australia)* (20).
Third umpire: Asad Rauf *(Pakistan)*. Referee: J. J. Crowe *(New Zealand)* (54).

Close of play: First day, South Africa 262–5 (Petersen 124, Rudolph 1); Second day, England 48–0 (Strauss 19, Cook 20); Third day, England 351–5 (Pietersen 149, Prior 20); Fourth day, South Africa 39–0 (Rudolph 21, Smith 17).

ENGLAND v SOUTH AFRICA 2012 (3rd Test)

At Lord's, London, on 16, 17, 18, 19, 20 August, 2012.
Toss: South Africa.   Result: SOUTH AFRICA WON BY 51 RUNS.
Debuts: none.
Man of the Match: V. D. Philander. Men of the Series: H. M. Amla and M. J. Prior.

When a brainless run-out reduced England to 45 for four on the final morning, still 300 adrift, embarrassment loomed – and with it the tame surrender of that hard-earned No. 1 Test ranking. England did lose in the end, but only after a thrilling fightback which briefly persuaded an enthralled crowd that a miracle was possible. The touch-paper was lit by a 41-ball fifty from the coathanger-shouldered Bairstow, playing only because Pietersen had been dropped for textual impropriety. Prior and Broad carried on the fight, and Swann swung lustily. But just as Smith, captaining for a record 94th time, was beginning to look nervous, Swann was run out, and the bouncy Philander wrapped things up with a five-for to set alongside two vital batting contributions. England had been on top initially, reducing South Africa to 163 for six before Duminy and Philander got them past 300. England struggled too, before Bairstow's first fine innings. But he was marooned on 95 for 14 balls before trying one on-drive too many, and it was left to the last pair to pinch a lead of six, as at Headingley. Amla's luscious 121 underpinned his side's total, which again included a healthy contribution from the tail. England needed 346 – a few too many, as it turned out. This was Strauss's 100th Test, the 50th as captain: he announced his retirement shortly afterwards. The match was played later than usual at Lord's as the ground had staged the archery events at the London Olympics three weeks previously.

South Africa

*G. C. Smith c Prior b Anderson	14	– (2) lbw b Swann	23
A. N. Petersen c Prior b Finn	22	– (1) lbw b Broad	24
H. M. Amla b Finn	13	– b Finn	121
J. H. Kallis c Prior b Finn	3	– lbw b Finn	31
†A. B. de Villiers c Cook b Anderson	27	– (6) c Strauss b Finn	43
J. A. Rudolph b Swann	42	– (7) c Prior b Finn	11
J-P. Duminy c Prior b Anderson	61	– (8) not out	26
V. D. Philander st Prior b Swann	61	– (9) c Bairstow b Anderson	35
D. W. Steyn c Swann b Broad	26	– (5) c Taylor b Broad	9
M. Morkel c Prior b Finn	25	– st Prior b Swann	9
Imran Tahir not out	2	– b Anderson	1
B 7, l-b 5, w 1	13	B 6, l-b 8, w 2, n-b 2	18
(101.2 overs)	309	(124.2 overs)	351

1/22 (1) 2/49 (2) 3/50 (3) 4/54 (4) 5/105 (5)   1/46 (2) 2/50 (1) 3/131 (4) 4/164 (5) 5/259 (3)
6/163 (6) 7/235 (7) 8/270 (9) 9/307 (10) 10/309 (8)   6/268 (6) 7/282 (7) 8/336 (9) 9/348 (10) 10/351 (11)

Anderson 29–5–76–3; Broad 24–4–69–1; Finn 18–2–75–4; Swann 24.2–6–63–2; Trott 6–1–14–0. *Second Innings*— Anderson 25.2–4–73–2; Broad 21–2–85–2; Swann 47–14–94–2; Finn 27–5–74–4; Trott 4–0–11–0.

England

*A. J. Strauss b Morkel	20	– lbw b Philander	1
A. N. Cook c Kallis b Steyn	7	– lbw b Philander	3
I. J. L. Trott lbw b Steyn	8	– c Kallis b Steyn	63
I. R. Bell c Petersen b Philander	58	– c Smith b Philander	4
J. W. A. Taylor c Smith b Morkel	10	– run out	4
J. M. Bairstow b Morkel	95	– b Imran Tahir	54
†M. J. Prior c Kallis b Philander	27	– c Smith b Philander	73
S. C. J. Broad c Amla b Steyn	16	– c Amla b Kallis	37
G. P. Swann not out	37	– run out	41
J. M. Anderson c Rudolph b Steyn	12	– not out	4
S. T. Finn c Duminy b Morkel	10	– c Kallis b Philander	0
L-b 10, w 1, n-b 4	15	B 7, w 2, n-b 1	10
(107.3 overs)	315	(82.5 overs)	294

1/29 (1) 2/38 (3) 3/39 (2) 4/54 (5) 5/178 (4)   1/5 (2) 2/6 (1) 3/34 (4) 4/45 (5) 5/134 (6)
6/221 (7) 7/252 (8) 8/264 (6) 9/283 (10) 10/315 (11)   6/146 (3) 7/208 (8) 8/282 (9) 9/294 (7) 10/294 (11)

Morkel 28.3–6–80–4; Philander 24–9–48–2; Steyn 29–4–94–4; Kallis 12–3–29–0; Imran Tahir 14–3–54–0. *Second Innings*—Morkel 17–3–58–0; Philander 14.5–4–30–5; Steyn 16–4–61–1; Kallis 11–2–50–1; Imran Tahir 24–3–88–1.

Umpires: H. D. P. K. Dharmasena *(Sri Lanka)* (10) and S. J. A. Taufel *(Australia)* (74).
Third umpire: R. J. Tucker *(Australia)*. Referee: J. J. Crowe *(New Zealand)* (55).

Close of play: First day, South Africa 262–7 (Philander 46, Steyn 21); Second day, England 208–5 (Bairstow 72, Prior 22); Third day, South Africa 145–3 (Amla 57, Steyn 0); Fourth day, England 16–2 (Trott 6, Bell 4).

WEST INDIES v NEW ZEALAND 2012 (1st Test)

At Sir Vivian Richards Stadium, North Sound, Antigua, on 25, 26, 27, 28, 29 July, 2012.
Toss: New Zealand.   Result: WEST INDIES WON BY NINE WICKETS.
Debuts: New Zealand – N. Wagner.
Man of the Match: S. P. Narine.

West Indies' first Test victory over New Zealand since April 1996 was built upon Gayle's resounding return 16 months after his contentious exclusion, his crushing opening stand with Powell, and the way Narine and Roach overcame a sluggish pitch. New Zealand had started well, reaching 223 for two before Taylor and Guptill – who spent 11 overs moving from 90 to 97 – fell just before stumps. Next day, it took Bracewell's robust 39 to carry them past 350. Gayle despatched the last four balls of Martin's opening over for four, but should have gone at 36, when Flynn misjudged a head-high catch at point off Bracewell. Aside from a first-ball dismissal for Chanderpaul – only his sixth in 244 Test innings – there was little subsequent encouragement for New Zealand's bowlers. The longer Gayle batted, the more subdued he became, taking 39 balls for his first fifty, 90 for his second, and eventually spending 206 deliveries in making 150, his 14th Test century. The tall, relaxed Powell completed his first during a stand of 254. Sammy's forthright fifty, with three sixes, sent the total past 500. Guptill and McCullum carried New Zealand within one run of parity before they both fell late on the fourth day. Next morning 26 overs before lunch yielded 26 runs; Wagner – nightwatchman for the second time on debut – occupied 83 balls for nine, but no one had an answer to Roach, who had four for 16 on the day. Requiring 102 off 46 overs, Gayle did not hang around.

New Zealand

D. R. Flynn c Powell b Narine	45	– (2) lbw b Narine	20
M. J. Guptill c Deonarine b Narine	97	– (1) c Fudadin b Narine	67
B. B. McCullum c Deonarine b Roach	25	– b Roach	84
*L. R. P. L. Taylor b Narine	45	– lbw b Roach	21
N. Wagner c Sammy b Narine	4	– c Ramdin b Roach	13
K. S. Williamson b Roach	19	– b Roach	0
D. G. Brownlie c Ramdin b Rampaul	23	– c Gayle b Rampaul	5
†C. F. K. van Wyk c Fudadin b Narine	11	– b Roach	30
D. L. Vettori c Deonarine b Sammy	17	– c Ramdin b Rampaul	13
D. A. J. Bracewell c Chanderpaul b Rampaul	39	– lbw b Narine	0
C. S. Martin not out	4	– not out	0
B 14, l-b 1, w 1, n-b 6	22	B 7, l-b 8, n-b 4	19
(129.1 overs)	351	(105.2 overs)	272

1/97 (1) 2/133 (3) 3/223 (4) 4/228 (2) 5/233 (5)
6/273 (6) 7/281 (7) 8/308 (9) 9/309 (8) 10/351 (10)

1/47 (2) 2/170 (1) 3/194 (3) 4/217 (4) 5/217 (6)
6/225 (5) 7/225 (7) 8/251 (9) 9/258 (10) 10/272 (8)

Rampaul 23.1–9–44–2; Roach 23–8–55–2; Sammy 26–7–76–1; Narine 43–9–132–5; Samuels 6–2–14–0; Fudadin 5–1–11–0; Deonarine 3–1–4–0. *Second Innings*—Rampaul 17–3–52–2; Roach 23.2–4–60–5; Narine 42–13–91–3; Sammy 16–6–25–0; Samuels 3–1–22–0; Deonarine 4–2–7–0.

West Indies

C. H. Gayle c McCullum b Williamson	150	– not out	64
K. O. A. Powell c van Wyk b Wagner	134	– c Brownlie b Bracewell	30
A. B. Fudadin c McCullum b Williamson	55	– not out	7
M. N. Samuels b Martin	28		
S. Chanderpaul c van Wyk b Martin	0		
N. Deonarine b Martin	79		
†D. Ramdin b Bracewell	3		
*D. J. G. Sammy c and b Vettori	50		
S. P. Narine run out	4		
K. A. J. Roach not out	6		
R. Rampaul lbw b Bracewell	1		
L-b 9, n-b 3	12	W 1	1
(163.3 overs)	522	(1 wkt, 19.3 overs)	102

1/254 (1) 2/304 (2) 3/355 (4) 4/355 (5) 5/410 (3)
6/428 (7) 7/497 (6) 8/502 (9) 9/516 (8) 10/522 (11)

1/77 (2)

Martin 30–9–134–3; Bracewell 29.3–5–96–2; Wagner 33–8–112–1; Vettori 51–14–124–1; Williamson 20–2–47–2. *Second Innings*—Bracewell 6–0–25–1; Martin 4–0–12–0; Williamson 3–1–30–0; Wagner 5–0–32–0; Vettori 1.3–0–3–0.

Umpires: R. A. Kettleborough *(England)* (10) and P. R. Reiffel *(Australia)* (1).
Third umpire: M. Erasmus *(South Africa)*. Referee: R. S. Madugalle *(Sri Lanka)* (135).

Close of play: First day, New Zealand 232–4 (Wagner 4, Williamson 2); Second day, West Indies 145–0 (Gayle 85, Powell 58); Third day, West Indies 442–6 (Deonarine 54, Sammy 8); Fourth day, New Zealand 199–3 (Taylor 11, Wagner 4).

WEST INDIES v NEW ZEALAND 2012 (2nd Test)

At Sabina Park, Kingston, Jamaica, on 2, 3, 4, 5 August, 2012.
Toss: West Indies.   Result: WEST INDIES WON BY FIVE WICKETS.
Debuts: none.
Man of the Match: M. N. Samuels. Man of the Series: K. A. J. Roach.

A 2–0 series victory was another modest sign of a West Indian revival after several years of struggles at Test level. It was also apt that, on the eve of the 50th anniversary of Jamaica's independence, it was Kingston native Marlon Samuels who led the way. His exceptional 123, out of a first-innings 209, averted the humiliation of a double-digit total, and limited the deficit to 51. Only four West Indian batsmen had been responsible for a greater share of a completed innings than Samuels's 58.85%. New Zealand had again wasted opportunities in their first innings; Taylor slashed unwisely at the recalled Best, then top-scorer Guptill – hampered by a groin twinge – was run out by a direct hit from cover after van Wyk unwisely called for a quick single. Then, after Samuels's masterclass, New Zealand's second effort was a disaster. Both openers fell within sight of the second-day close, lbw to Deonarine's undemanding off-spin, then next day the last eight wickets tumbled for 74, only Brownlie surviving as long as an hour and a half. West Indies needed 206, no formality given their recent travails, but after Samuels passed 50 for the sixth time in seven innings, a forthright career-best from nightwatchman Roach all but settled matters. The match timings had been adjusted to allow spectators to watch the 100 metres final from the London Olympics, but West Indies completed victory a full 4½ hours before the planned break to watch the first of local boy Usain Bolt's three golds.

New Zealand

B-J. Watling c Gayle b Roach	2	– (2) lbw b Deonarine	11
M. J. Guptill run out	71	– (1) lbw b Deonarine	42
B. B. McCullum c Ramdin b Best	0	– (4) c Fudadin b Deonarine	19
*L. R. P. L. Taylor c Ramdin b Best	60	– (5) c Ramdin b Best	0
K. S. Williamson c Sammy b Deonarine	22	– (6) c Sammy b Deonarine	8
D. G. Brownlie c Ramdin b Roach	0	– (7) c Deonarine b Narine	35
†C. F. K. van Wyk b Deonarine	16	– (8) c Chanderpaul b Narine	5
D. A. J. Bracewell b Narine	14	– (9) c Fudadin b Narine	14
N. Wagner c Best b Roach	23	– (3) c Ramdin b Best	6
T. G. Southee c Sammy b Roach	18	– c Narine b Roach	7
T. A. Boult not out	14	– not out	0
B 6, l-b 2, w 1, n-b 11	20	L-b 1, w 1, n-b 5	7
(82.5 overs)	260	(65.2 overs)	154

1/10 (1) 2/11 (3) 3/114 (4) 4/161 (5) 5/162 (6)
6/170 (2) 7/202 (8) 8/202 (7) 9/225 (10) 10/260 (9)

1/55 (2) 2/56 (1) 3/80 (3) 4/80 (5) 5/85 (4)
6/98 (6) 7/105 (8) 8/142 (9) 9/151 (7) 10/154 (10)

Roach 17.5–2–70–4; Best 16–1–40–2; Sammy 10–1–31–0; Narine 26–7–66–1; Samuels 1–0–2–0; Deonarine 12–3–43–2. *Second Innings*—Roach 12.2–3–34–1; Best 13–2–44–2; Sammy 6–2–19–0; Narine 12–1–19–3; Deonarine 22–7–37–4.

West Indies

C. H. Gayle c Watling b Wagner	8	– lbw b Boult	8
K. O. A. Powell c Brownlie b Boult	10	– lbw b Southee	6
A. B. Fudadin lbw b Boult	5	– b Wagner	27
M. N. Samuels c Wagner b Bracewell	123	– c Taylor b Bracewell	52
S. Chanderpaul c Taylor b Southee	9	– not out	43
N. Deonarine c van Wyk b Boult	0	– (7) not out	15
†D. Ramdin c Williamson b Wagner	15		
*D. J. G. Sammy lbw b Southee	32		
S. P. Narine c Guptill b Bracewell	1		
K. A. J. Roach c Guptill b Bracewell	0	– (6) c Southee b Williamson	41
T. L. Best not out	0		
L-b 4, w 2	6	B 4, l-b 2, w 8	14
(64.3 overs)	209	(5 wkts, 63.2 overs)	206

1/11 (2) 2/17 (3) 3/53 (1) 4/82 (5) 5/83 (6) 6/113 (7)
7/162 (8) 8/177 (9) 9/183 (10) 10/209 (4)

1/20 (1) 2/20 (2) 3/94 (3) 4/113 (4) 5/183 (6)

Boult 17–2–58–3; Bracewell 15.3–3–46–3; Southee 19–5–70–2; Wagner 10–3–24–2; Williamson 3–0–7–0. *Second Innings*—Boult 12–1–46–1; Bracewell 13–0–38–1; Southee 14–4–30–1; Wagner 12–3–41–1; Williamson 7.2–1–18–1; Guptill 4–0–21–0; Brownlie 1–0–6–0.

Umpires: M. Erasmus *(South Africa)* (13) and P. R. Reiffel *(Australia)* (2).
Third umpire: R. A. Kettleborough *(England)*. Referee: R. S. Madugalle *(Sri Lanka)* (136).

Close of play: First day, West Indies 11–0 (Gayle 1, Powell 10); Second day, New Zealand 59–2 (Wagner 2, McCullum 1); Third day, West Indies 135–4 (Chanderpaul 20, Roach 10).

INDIA v NEW ZEALAND 2012–13 (1st Test)

At Rajiv Gandhi International Stadium, Uppal, Hyderabad, on 23, 24, 25, 26 August, 2012.
Toss: India.   Result: INDIA WON BY AN INNINGS AND 115 RUNS.
Debuts: none.
Man of the Match: R. Ashwin.

In their first Test since the retirements of Rahul Dravid and V. V. S. Laxman, India were always heavy favourites – but even they must have been pleasantly surprised at the ease and swiftness of victory. New Zealand came unstuck against probing spin. Ojha took six wickets, while Ashwin finished with 12 for 85, match figures bettered against New Zealand only by Courtney Walsh, with 13 for 55 for West Indies at Wellington in 1994–95. All eyes were on India's relatively inexperienced middle order. Pujara, in his first Test for more than 18 months, compiled a masterful 159. He and Kohli doubled the score from an uncertain 125 for three then, after another mini-stutter, India were baled out by Pujara and Dhoni in a stand of 127. New Zealand's batting woes began almost immediately: McCullum skimmed a low catch into the covers in Ojha's first over. New Zealand then seemingly left footwork and soft hands behind in the dressing-room; they were shot out in a shade over four hours and, with the weather closing in, Dhoni had no hesitation in enforcing the follow-on. New Zealand showed greater character but – after McCullum and Williamson had inched to 98 for one in 45 overs – the floodgates opened once Yadav won a fortuitous leg-before shout against McCullum, despite a big edge (with no DRS to save him, as this was India). The last nine wickets clattered for just 66; Taylor's dismissal – offering no stroke to Ashwin as the ball hit the top of off – epitomised the tourists' uncertainty.

India

G. Gambhir c van Wyk b Boult 22
V. Sehwag c Guptill b Bracewell 47
C. A. Pujara c Franklin b Patel 159
S. R. Tendulkar b Boult 19
V. Kohli c Guptill b Martin 58
S. K. Raina c van Wyk b Patel 3
*†M. S. Dhoni c Bracewell b Patel 73
R. Ashwin st van Wyk b Patel 37
Zaheer Khan c van Wyk b Boult 0
P. P. Ojha not out 4
U. T. Yadav run out 4
     B 6, l-b 4, w 2 12
     (134.3 overs) 438

1/49 (1) 2/77 (2) 3/125 (4) 4/250 (5) 5/260 (6)
6/387 (3) 7/411 (7) 8/414 (9) 9/430 (8) 10/438 (11)

Martin 27–4–76–1; Boult 27–4–93–3; Bracewell 19.1–1–88–1; Franklin 13.2–0–40–0; Patel 41–9–100–4; Williamson 7–0–31–0.

New Zealand

B. B. McCullum c Kohli b Ojha	22	– (2) lbw b Yadav	42
M. J. Guptill c Kohli b Ashwin	2	– (1) lbw b Ojha	16
K. S. Williamson c Sehwag b Ojha	32	– c Sehwag b Ojha	52
*L. R. P. L. Taylor c Kohli b Ashwin	2	– b Ashwin	7
D. R. Flynn lbw b Ashwin	16	– lbw b Ashwin	11
J. E. C. Franklin not out	43	– c Sehwag b Ashwin	5
†C. F. K. van Wyk lbw b Yadav	0	– lbw b Ashwin	13
D. A. J. Bracewell st Dhoni b Ojha	17	– c Kohli b Ojha	1
J. S. Patel c and b Ashwin	10	– not out	6
T. A. Boult c Gambhir b Ashwin	4	– c Sehwag b Ashwin	0
C. S. Martin b Ashwin	0	– lbw b Ashwin	0
B 4, l-b 7	11	B 1, l-b 10	11
(61.3 overs)	159	(79.5 overs)	164

1/25 (1) 2/29 (2) 3/35 (4) 4/55 (5) 5/99 (3) 6/111 (7)   1/26 (1) 2/98 (2) 3/105 (4) 4/138 (3) 5/142 (5)
7/141 (8) 8/153 (9) 9/159 (10) 10/159 (11)   6/145 (6) 7/148 (8) 8/160 (7) 9/164 (10) 10/164 (11)

Zaheer Khan 11–4–33–0; Yadav 8–0–24–1; Ojha 21–6–44–3; Ashwin 16.3–5–31–6; Sehwag 2–0–4–0; Raina 2–0–6–0; Tendulkar 1–0–6–0. *Second Innings*—Ojha 28–9–48–3; Zaheer Khan 13–5–17–0; Yadav 10–1–32–1; Ashwin 26.5–9–54–6; Raina 2–1–2–0.

Umpires: S. J. Davis *(Australia)* (41) and I. J. Gould *(England)* (30).
Third umpire: V. A. Kulkarni *(India)*. Referee: B. C. Broad *(England)* (52).

Close of play: First day, India 307–5 (Pujara 119, Dhoni 29); Second day, New Zealand 106–5 (Franklin 31, van Wyk 0); Third day, New Zealand 41–1 (McCullum 16, Williamson 3).

INDIA v NEW ZEALAND 2012–13 (2nd Test)

At M. Chinnaswamy Stadium, Bangalore, on 31 August, 1, 2, 3 September, 2012.
Toss: New Zealand.   Result: INDIA WON BY FIVE WICKETS.
Debuts: none.
Man of the Match: V. Kohli. Man of the Series: R. Ashwin.

After the First Test, when New Zealand struggled to match Pujara's 159 in either innings, this was expected to be another procession. That it wasn't owed much to a tremendous counter-attacking hundred from Taylor, and a superb display of swing and seam from Southee, whose figures were New Zealand's best in India, beating Dion Nash's six for 27 at Mohali in 1999–2000. The end result was no different, though: India completed a 2–0 victory, but had to work for their fifth-highest successful run-chase after a stumble to 166 for five. In the first innings, Kohli's second Test century had rescued his side after the early loss of Gambhir (in his 50th Test) and Pujara; he shared handy stands with Raina and Dhoni to limit the deficit to 12. New Zealand tried to build on that: eight batsmen reached double figures, but the highest score was 41. Yadav hit van Wyk on the helmet and, next ball, broke his forearm, but he battled on for another six overs (McCullum kept wicket later). But Ashwin dismantled the middle order, and India were eventually set 261. The openers gave them a solid base, before both fell in quick succession. Pujara and Tendulkar rebuilt, but three quick wickets gave New Zealand a sniff: Tendulkar was bowled for the third time running, his frustration apparent as he briefly threatened to smash the stumps. With 95 still needed, coolness was required – and it was provided by Kohli and Dhoni, who finished things off with his second six.

New Zealand

M. J. Guptill c Gambhir b Ojha	53	– (2) b Yadav		7
B. B. McCullum lbw b Zaheer Khan	0	– (1) c Dhoni b Yadav		23
K. S. Williamson lbw b Ojha	17	– c Sehwag b Ashwin		13
*L. R. P. L. Taylor lbw b Ojha	113	– lbw b Ojha		35
D. R. Flynn lbw b Ashwin	33	– c Sehwag b Ashwin		31
J. E. C. Franklin c Raina b Ojha	8	– st Dhoni b Ashwin		41
†C. F. K. van Wyk c Raina b Zaheer Khan	71	– lbw b Ashwin		31
D. A. J. Bracewell run out	43	– lbw b Ojha		22
T. G. Southee lbw b Ojha	14	– b Ashwin		2
J. S. Patel c Gambhir b Yadav	0	– c Dhoni b Zaheer Khan		22
T. A. Boult not out	2	– not out		4
B 2, l-b 9	11	B 4, l-b 12, w 1		17
(90.1 overs)	365	(73.2 overs)		248

1/0 (2) 2/63 (3) 3/89 (1) 4/196 (5) 5/215 (6) 6/246 (4) 7/345 (7) 8/353 (8) 9/353 (10) 10/365 (9)

1/30 (2) 2/31 (1) 3/69 (3) 4/111 (4) 5/140 (5) 6/195 (7) 7/216 (6) 8/222 (9) 9/222 (8) 10/248 (10)

Ojha 28.1–10–99–5; Zaheer Khan 22–2–83–2; Yadav 16–1–90–1; Ashwin 24–5–82–1. *Second Innings*—Zaheer Khan 14.2–2–46–1; Yadav 15–0–68–2; Ojha 21–6–49–2; Ashwin 22–1–69–5; Raina 1–1–0–0.

India

G. Gambhir b Southee	2	– c Taylor b Boult		34
V. Sehwag c Flynn b Bracewell	43	– b Patel		38
C. A. Pujara c Boult b Southee	9	– c Flynn b Patel		48
S. R. Tendulkar b Bracewell	17	– b Southee		27
V. Kohli lbw b Southee	103	– not out		51
S. K. Raina c van Wyk b Southee	55	– b Patel		0
*†M. S. Dhoni lbw b Southee	62	– not out		48
R. Ashwin not out	32			
Zaheer Khan c van Wyk b Southee	7			
P. P. Ojha c van Wyk b Southee	0			
U. T. Yadav b Boult	4			
B 11, l-b 2, w 1, n-b 5	19	B 4, l-b 6, w 5, n-b 1		16
(96.5 overs)	353	(5 wkts, 63.2 overs)		262

1/5 (1) 2/27 (3) 3/67 (2) 4/80 (4) 5/179 (6) 6/301 (5) 7/312 (7) 8/320 (9) 9/320 (10) 10/353 (11)

1/77 (2) 2/83 (1) 3/152 (4) 4/158 (3) 5/166 (6)

Boult 23.5–2–90–1; Southee 24–6–64–7; Bracewell 20–4–91–2; Franklin 10–4–17–0; Patel 19–5–78–0. *Second Innings*—Boult 16–4–64–1; Southee 18–3–68–1; Bracewell 14–3–52–0; Patel 15.2–3–68–3.

Umpires: S. J. Davis *(Australia)* (42) and I. J. Gould *(England)* (31).
Third umpire: S. Asnani *(India)*. Referee: B. C. Broad *(England)* (53).

Close of play: First day, New Zealand 328–6 (van Wyk 63, Bracewell 30); Second day, India 283–5 (Kohli 93, Dhoni 46); Third day, New Zealand 232–9 (Patel 10, Boult 0).

AUSTRALIA v SOUTH AFRICA 2012–13 (1st Test)

At Wolloongabba, Brisbane, on 9, 10 (*no play*), 11, 12, 13 November, 2012.
Toss: South Africa.   Result: MATCH DRAWN.
Debuts: Australia – R. J. Quiney. South Africa – R. K. Kleinveldt.
Man of the Match: M. J. Clarke.

Rain that fell for one day, and a pitch that stayed slow for five, condemned this to a draw – although a late thrust by Australia pushed the game into the last hour. Batsmen enjoyed themselves, particularly Clarke, who stayed the longest and made the most; his chanceless unbeaten 259 was the highest score at the Gabba, beating Alastair Cook's 235 not out in 2010–11, and Australia's first double-century there since Greg Chappell's 201 against Pakistan in 1981–82. Clarke shared successive stands of 259 with Cowan, whose maiden Test hundred was ended only by a deflection by the bowler (Steyn), and 228 with Hussey, who fell shortly after completing his 18th century to a fine catch by Faf du Plessis at short cover, the first wicket to fall to a bowler for 120 overs. Clarke declared on the fifth day 115 ahead, but South Africa kept their noses to the grindstone, proceeding at around two an over, apart from two before tea in which Lyon was clubbed for 26 – although Australia were briefly interested after Amla and Kallis, who had shared a stand of 165 in the first innings, departed with the lead barely scrubbed off. Amla, who had passed 5,000 runs earlier in the game, was bowled by Pattinson but became the third man reprieved after TV replays showed up a no-ball (Cowan and Clarke both survived slip catches). Duminy strained an Achilles tendon exercising on the outfield after the first day's play, and played no part in the match.

South Africa

*G. C. Smith lbw b Pattinson	10	– (2) c Quiney b Pattinson	23
A. N. Petersen c Hussey b Lyon	64	– (1) c Wade b Pattinson	5
H. M. Amla lbw b Siddle	104	– c Hussey b Siddle	38
J. H. Kallis c Quiney b Pattinson	147	– c Clarke b Lyon	49
†A. B. de Villiers c Warner b Pattinson	40	– not out	29
J. A. Rudolph c Quiney b Lyon	31	– lbw b Lyon	11
V. D. Philander c Clarke b Siddle	11	– not out	1
D. W. Steyn c Wade b Hilfenhaus	15		
R. K. Kleinveldt not out	17		
M. Morkel c Siddle b Hilfenhaus	0		
J-P. Duminy absent hurt			
B 1, l-b 1, w 3, n-b 6	11	B 2, w 4, n-b 4	10
(151.4 overs)	450	(5 wkts, 68 overs)	166

1/29 (1) 2/119 (2) 3/284 (3) 4/374 (4) 5/377 (5)
6/403 (7) 7/426 (6) 8/446 (8) 9/450 (10)   1/6 (1) 2/55 (2) 3/102 (3) 4/129 (4) 5/165 (6)

Hilfenhaus 32.4–9–73–2; Pattinson 34–6–93–3; Siddle 36–6–111–2; Lyon 37–4–136–2; Hussey 4–0–21–0; Quiney 7–3–10–0; Clarke 1–0–4–0. *Second Innings*—Hilfenhaus 15–3–26–0; Pattinson 19–3–58–2; Siddle 17–4–36–1; Lyon 13–5–41–2; Quiney 4–3–3–0.

Australia

E. J. M. Cowan run out	136
D. A. Warner c Kallis b Steyn	4
R. J. Quiney c Steyn b Morkel	9
R. T. Ponting c Kallis b Morkel	0
*M. J. Clarke not out	259
M. E. K. Hussey c sub (F. du Plessis) b Morkel	100
†M. S. Wade not out	19
L-b 14, w 1, n-b 23	38
(5 wkts dec, 138 overs)	565

1/13 (2) 2/30 (3) 3/40 (4) 4/299 (1) 5/527 (6)

P. M. Siddle, J. L. Pattinson, B. W. Hilfenhaus and N. M. Lyon did not bat.

Steyn 30–3–129–1; Philander 30–3–103–0; Morkel 31–6–127–3; Kleinveldt 21–1–97–0; Kallis 12–3–30–0; Smith 9–0–36–0; Amla 2–0–9–0; Petersen 3–0–20–0.

Umpires: Asad Rauf *(Pakistan)* (46) and B. F. Bowden *(New Zealand)* (71).
Third umpire: R. A. Kettleborough *(England)*. Referee: R. S. Madugalle *(Sri Lanka)* (137).

Close of play: First day, South Africa 255–2 (Amla 90, Kallis 84); Second day, no play; Third day, Australia 111–3 (Cowan 49, Clarke 34); Fourth day, Australia 487–4 (Clarke 218, Hussey 86).

AUSTRALIA v SOUTH AFRICA 2012–13 (2nd Test)

At Adelaide Oval on 22, 23, 24, 25, 26 November, 2012.
Toss: Australia.   Result: MATCH DRAWN.
Debuts: South Africa – F. du Plessis.
Man of the Match: F. du Plessis.

South Africa staged a four-day rearguard after a disastrous start, and had just enough in reserve to keep the series all square. In effect, it was Duminy's Brisbane injury which saved them, as it led to a first cap for 28-year-old Faf du Plessis. Calm, collected and compact, he batted for 11 hours 11 minutes in the game, including the whole of the final day, unconquerable as South Africa stumbled towards sanctuary. Australia had sprinted to 482 from 86.5 overs on the first, the most on the opening day of any Test apart from Australia's 494 for six against South Africa at Sydney in 1910–11. Warner biffed a 93-ball hundred, then Clarke – the first to score four Test double-centuries in the same year – and Hussey piled on 282 in less than 50 overs. They were particularly severe on Tahir's leg-spin; South Africa's attack, already lacking Philander (sore neck), also lost Kallis, who pulled up with hamstring trouble in his fourth over. Smith and Petersen opened with 138, but wickets fell regularly after that until the hobbling Kallis emerged at No. 9 and gritted out 58, adding 93 with du Plessis, who finally fell for 78 with last man Tahir at the other end. Ponting failed again, and Quiney completed a pair, but Hussey helped set up a distant target of 430 in 148 overs. At 45 for four, survival looked inconceivable – but de Villiers made 33 in four hours, then Kallis hung on for 39 overs with the determined du Plessis.

Australia

D. A. Warner c Smith b Morkel	119	– (2) c du Plessis b Kleinveldt	41
E. J. M. Cowan c and b Kallis	10	– (1) b Kleinveldt	29
R. J. Quiney c Smith b Morkel	0	– c de Villiers b Kleinveldt	0
R. T. Ponting b Kallis	4	– b Steyn	16
*M. J. Clarke b Morkel	230	– lbw b Steyn	38
M. E. K. Hussey b Steyn	103	– (7) c Steyn b Morkel	54
†M. S. Wade c de Villiers b Morkel	6	– (8) c de Villiers b Morkel	18
P. M. Siddle c Smith b Kleinveldt	6	– (6) c de Villiers b Morkel	1
J. L. Pattinson c Smith b Steyn	42	– not out	29
B. W. Hilfenhaus c Kleinveldt b Morkel	0	– not out	18
N. M. Lyon not out	7		
L-b 11, w 1, n-b 11	23	B 4, l-b 10, n-b 9	23
(107.2 overs)	550	(8 wkts dec, 70 overs)	267

1/43 (2) 2/44 (3) 3/55 (4) 4/210 (1) 5/482 (6)   1/77 (2) 2/77 (3) 3/91 (1) 4/98 (4) 5/103 (6)
6/494 (5) 7/501 (7) 8/503 (8) 9/504 (10) 10/550 (9)   6/173 (5) 7/206 (7) 8/220 (8)

Steyn 23.4–4–79–2; Morkel 30–5–146–5; Kallis 3.3–1–19–2; Kleinveldt 20.1–4–81–1; Imran Tahir 23–0–180–0; du Plessis 7–0–34–0. *Second Innings*—Steyn 17–5–50–2; Morkel 19–4–50–3; Imran Tahir 14–1–80–0; Kleinveldt 19–2–65–3; du Plessis 1–0–8–0.

South Africa

*G. C. Smith c Wade b Siddle	122	– (2) c Ponting b Hilfenhaus	0
A. N. Petersen run out	54	– (1) b Siddle	24
H. M. Amla st Wade b Warner	11	– c Clarke b Lyon	17
J. A. Rudolph c Quiney b Lyon	29	– c Cowan b Lyon	3
†A. B. de Villiers lbw b Siddle	1	– b Siddle	33
F. du Plessis c Clarke b Hilfenhaus	78	– not out	110
D. W. Steyn c Ponting b Hilfenhaus	1	– (8) c Quiney b Siddle	0
R. K. Kleinveldt b Hilfenhaus	0	– (9) b Siddle	3
J. H. Kallis c Wade b Clarke	58	– (7) c Cowan b Lyon	46
M. Morkel b Lyon	6	– not out	8
Imran Tahir not out	10		
B 7, l-b 2, w 3, n-b 6	18	B 1, l-b 1, w 1, n-b 1	4
(124.3 overs)	388	(8 wkts, 148 overs)	248

1/138 (2) 2/169 (3) 3/233 (4) 4/233 (1) 5/240 (5)   1/3 (2) 2/36 (3) 3/45 (4) 4/45 (1) 5/134 (5)
6/246 (7) 7/250 (8) 8/343 (9) 9/352 (10) 10/388 (6)   6/233 (7) 7/234 (8) 8/240 (9)

Hilfenhaus 19.3–6–49–3; Pattinson 9.1–0–41–0; Lyon 44–7–91–2; Siddle 30.5–6–130–2; Clarke 7–1–22–1; Hussey 1–0–7–0; Warner 5–0–27–1; Quiney 8–3–12–0. *Second Innings*—Hilfenhaus 34–16–65–1; Siddle 33–15–65–4; Clarke 18–5–34–0; Lyon 50–31–49–3; Warner 6–0–29–0; Quiney 6–3–4–0; Ponting 1–1–0–0.

Umpires: B. F. Bowden *(New Zealand)* (72) and R. A. Kettleborough *(England)* (11).
Third umpire: Asad Rauf *(Pakistan)*. Referee: R. S. Madugalle *(Sri Lanka)* (138).

Close of play: First day, Australia 482–5 (Clarke 224); Second day, South Africa 217–2 (Smith 111, Rudolph 25); Third day, Australia 111–5 (Clarke 9, Hussey 5); Fourth day, South Africa 77–4 (de Villiers 12, du Plessis 19).

AUSTRALIA v SOUTH AFRICA 2012–13 (3rd Test)

At W. A. C. A. Ground, Perth, on 30 November, 1, 2, 3 December, 2012.
Toss: South Africa.   Result: SOUTH AFRICA WON BY 309 RUNS.
Debuts: Australia – J. W. Hastings. South Africa – D. Elgar.
Man of the Match: H. M. Amla. Man of the Series: M. J. Clarke.

South Africa capitalised on their Adelaide escape with an overwhelming victory to take the series. It meant a subdued farewell for the retiring Ricky Ponting: given a guard of honour by the opposition, he was out cheaply twice, finishing with 13,378 runs (in 168 Tests, equalling Steve Waugh's national record). Australia, with a remodelled pace attack, had South Africa 75 for six on the first day, before du Plessis raised his Test average to 265, and supervised the acquisition of 150 more runs. On the second day, Australia were outclassed and overwhelmed on all fronts. Their batsmen were cowed by Steyn and Philander – soon it was 45 for six – and their tail was bemused by slow left-armer Peterson, then their bowlers were towelled by Smith and Amla, who added 178 in 153 balls. Amla continued serenely on the third day, reaching 196 before Johnson's fine return catch, but the star turn was de Villiers, who reached his 14th Test century (his first as the designated keeper) with three consecutive reverse-sweeps off Lyon. De Villiers eventually scored 169 from 184 balls, 36 fewer than in making 33 at Adelaide a week earlier. The Mitchells – Starc and Johnson – shared all ten wickets, Johnson inflicting a debut pair on Elgar, but the lead was a colossal 621. Peterson chipped in with three more wickets, and Australia made it past halfway only because the last pair added 87. It was the first time since 2001–02 that Australia had not won a Test in a home series.

South Africa

*G. C. Smith c Clarke b Watson	16	– (2) c Lyon b Starc	84
A. N. Petersen b Starc	30	– (1) c and b Johnson	23
H. M. Amla run out	11	– c and b Johnson	196
J. H. Kallis b Starc	2	– c Johnson b Starc	37
†A. B. de Villiers c Clarke b Hastings	4	– c Wade b Starc	169
D. Elgar c Wade b Johnson	0	– lbw b Johnson	0
F. du Plessis not out	78	– c Clarke b Johnson	27
R. J. Peterson c Wade b Lyon	31	– c Johnson b Starc	0
V. D. Philander c Hussey b Lyon	30	– not out	14
D. W. Steyn b Johnson	2	– c Wade b Starc	8
M. Morkel c Hastings b Lyon	17	– b Starc	0
L-b 2, w 2	4	B 4, l-b 4, w 3	11
(74 overs)	225	(111.5 overs)	569

1/38 (1) 2/61 (2) 3/63 (4) 4/67 (3) 5/67 (5) 6/75 (6)
7/132 (8) 8/196 (9) 9/206 (10) 10/225 (11)

1/28 (1) 2/206 (2) 3/287 (4) 4/436 (3) 5/436 (6)
6/538 (7) 7/539 (8) 8/557 (5) 9/569 (10) 10/569 (11)

Starc 16–3–55–2; Hastings 20–2–51–1; Watson 9–2–22–1; Johnson 17–3–54–2; Lyon 12–1–41–3. *Second Innings*—Starc 28.5–3–154–6; Watson 9–3–24–0; Johnson 25–1–110–4; Hastings 19–1–102–0; Lyon 22–2–128–0; Hussey 4–0–26–0; Warner 3–0–14–0; Ponting 1–0–3–0.

Australia

D. A. Warner c de Villiers b Steyn	13	– (2) c Smith b Philander	29
E. J. M. Cowan c Kallis b Steyn	0	– (1) c Elgar b Steyn	53
S. R. Watson lbw b Philander	10	– c Smith b Morkel	25
N. M. Lyon c du Plessis b Steyn	7	– (11) c Smith b Steyn	31
R. T. Ponting lbw b Philander	4	– (4) c Kallis b Peterson	8
*M. J. Clarke c de Villiers b Steyn	5	– (5) st de Villiers b Peterson	44
M. E. K. Hussey c Smith b Morkel	12	– (6) c de Villiers b Steyn	26
†M. S. Wade b Peterson	68	– (7) c Smith b Peterson	10
J. W. Hastings c Petersen b Peterson	32	– (8) c Smith b Morkel	20
M. G. Johnson b Peterson	7	– (9) c de Villiers b Philander	3
M. A. Starc not out	0	– (10) not out	68
L-b 5	5	L-b 3, w 2	5
(53.1 overs)	163	(82.5 overs)	322

1/3 (2) 2/18 (3) 3/34 (1) 4/35 (4) 5/43 (5) 6/45 (6)
7/100 (7) 8/140 (8) 9/162 (10) 10/163 (9)

1/40 (2) 2/81 (3) 3/102 (4) 4/130 (1) 5/188 (5)
6/198 (6) 7/198 (7) 8/204 (9) 9/235 (8) 10/322 (11)

Steyn 16–4–40–4; Philander 16–0–55–2; Morkel 13–6–19–1; Peterson 8.1–1–44–3. *Second Innings*—Steyn 22.5–6–72–3; Philander 21–8–41–2; Morkel 16–2–57–2; Peterson 20–2–127–3; Elgar 1–0–4–0; du Plessis 2–0–18–0.

Umpires: Asad Rauf *(Pakistan)* (47) and R. A. Kettleborough *(England)* (12).
Third umpire: B. F. Bowden *(New Zealand)*. Referee: R. S. Madugalle *(Sri Lanka)* (139).

Close of play: First day, Australia 33–2 (Warner 12, Lyon 7); Second day, South Africa 230–2 (Amla 99, Kallis 17); Third day, Australia 40–0 (Cowan 9, Warner 29).

BANGLADESH v WEST INDIES 2012–13 (1st Test)

At Shere Bangla National Stadium, Mirpur, Dhaka, on 13, 14, 15, 16, 17 November, 2012.
Toss: West Indies.   Result: WEST INDIES WON BY 77 RUNS.
Debuts: Bangladesh – Sohag Gazi. West Indies – V. Permaul.
Man of the Match: K. O. A. Powell.

The match had a unique start: the first ball was hit over long-on for six by Gayle. The bowler, Sohag Gazi, was the first debutant spinner to take the new ball in the first innings of a Test since the England leg-tweaker Douglas Carr against Australia at The Oval in 1909. Off-spinner Gazi soon had his revenge, as Gayle holed out at long-off in his third over. And a Test which started so dramatically had an equally exciting finish: after both teams passed 500 – Bangladesh's 556 was a new national record – a draw seemed likely until West Indies slid from 209 for one to 273 all out. Gazi took the last four wickets on the final morning (including Chanderpaul, down at No. 11 after illness) to finish with Bangladesh's best debut figures. That left a tempting target of 245 for a rare Test victory – only for the batsmen to crumble in depressingly familiar fashion. West Indies' first innings included Powell's second Test hundred (the third followed in the second innings), then Chanderpaul extended his 26th Test century to his second score of 203 not out, putting on 296 with Ramdin. In reply, Naeem Islam made his maiden hundred, and Nasir Hossain just missed his. But Bangladesh's second effort was less inspired. Best took his first five-for in Tests, finally castling Mahmudullah an hour into the final session. Bangladesh had taken a first-innings lead for only the ninth time in their 74 Tests – but still slid to their 64th defeat.

West Indies

C. H. Gayle c Mahmudullah b Sohag Gazi	24	– c Mushfiqur Rahim b Rubel Hossain	19
K. O. A. Powell b Sohag Gazi	117	– c Mushfiqur Rahim b Shakib Al Hasan	110
D. M. Bravo c Rubel Hossain b Sohag Gazi	14	– c Mushfiqur Rahim b Rubel Hossain	76
M. N. Samuels c Sohag Gazi b Shahadat Hossain	16	– c Shahriar Nafees b Sohag Gazi	1
S. Chanderpaul not out	203	– (11) lbw b Sohag Gazi	1
†D. Ramdin not out	126	– (5) lbw b Shakib Al Hasan	5
*D. J. G. Sammy (did not bat)		– (6) lbw b Sohag Gazi	16
V. Permaul (did not bat)		– (7) b Sohag Gazi	10
S. P. Narine (did not bat)		– (8) not out	22
R. Rampaul (did not bat)		– (9) b Sohag Gazi	5
T. L. Best (did not bat)		– b Sohag Gazi	0
B 4, l-b 13, w 2, n-b 8	27	B 1, l-b 3, n-b 4	8
(4 wkts dec, 144 overs)	527	(74.2 overs)	273

1/32 (1) 2/74 (3) 3/106 (4) 4/231 (2)

1/20 (1) 2/209 (3) 3/212 (4) 4/218 (2) 5/225 (5)
6/244 (7) 7/249 (6) 8/265 (9) 9/265 (10) 10/273 (11)

Sohag Gazi 47–7–145–3; Shahadat Hossain 21–3–85–1; Rubel Hossain 18–0–89–0; Mahmudullah 14–0–45–0; Shakib Al Hasan 34–4–104–0; Naeem Islam 8–1–24–0; Nasir Hossain 1–0–8–0; Tamim Iqbal 1–0–10–0. *Second Innings*—Sohag Gazi 23.2–2–74–6; Rubel Hossain 19–4–53–2; Mahmudullah 3–0–12–0; Shahadat Hossain 7–1–34–0; Shakib Al Hasan 11–2–56–2; Naeem Islam 8–0–22–0; Nasir Hossain 3–0–18–0.

Bangladesh

Tamim Iqbal c Narine b Sammy	72	– c Ramdin b Rampaul	5
Junaid Siddique c Bravo b Rampaul	7	– c Ramdin b Best	20
Shahriar Nafees c Ramdin b Rampaul	31	– c and b Best	23
Naeem Islam c Ramdin b Sammy	108	– lbw b Permaul	26
Shakib Al Hasan c sub (A. B. Fudadin) b Rampaul	89	– c Ramdin b Best	2
*†Mushfiqur Rahim c and b Permaul	43	– lbw b Best	16
Nasir Hossain c Gayle b Best	96	– b Permaul	21
Mahmudullah c Powell b Narine	62	– b Best	29
Sohag Gazi b Narine	4	– c sub (N. Deonarine) b Permaul	19
Shahadat Hossain b Narine	13	– c Powell b Rampaul	4
Rubel Hossain not out	0	– not out	0
B 8, l-b 12, w 3, n-b 8	31	B 1, n-b 1	2
(148.3 overs)	556	(54.3 overs)	167

1/25 (2) 2/88 (3) 3/119 (1) 4/286 (5) 5/362 (4)
6/368 (6) 7/489 (8) 8/493 (9) 9/554 (7) 10/556 (10)

1/10 (1) 2/44 (2) 3/51 (3) 4/55 (5) 5/85 (6)
6/106 (4) 7/119 (7) 8/155 (9) 9/159 (10) 10/167 (8)

Rampaul 32–2–118–3; Best 23–3–77–1; Sammy 23–3–83–2; Narine 32.3–5–148–3; Permaul 29–7–75–1; Gayle 3–0–14–0; Samuels 6–0–21–0. *Second Innings*—Rampaul 11–1–32–2; Narine 18–1–56–0; Best 12.3–2–24–5; Permaul 8–0–32–3; Sammy 3–0–9–0; Samuels 2–0–9–0.

Umpires: R. K. Illingworth *(England)* (1) and B. N. J. Oxenford *(Australia)* (9).
Third umpire: Enamul Haque, sen. *(Bangladesh)*. Referee: D. C. Boon *(Australia)* (11).

Close of play: First day, West Indies 361–4 (Chanderpaul 123, Ramdin 52); Second day, Bangladesh 164–3 (Naeem Islam 27, Shakib Al Hasan 16); Third day, Bangladesh 455–6 (Nasir Hossain 33, Mahmudullah 42); Fourth day, West Indies 244–6 (Sammy 15).

BANGLADESH v WEST INDIES 2012–13 (2nd Test)

At Shaikh Abu Naser Stadium, Khulna, on 21, 22, 23, 24, 25 November, 2012.
Toss: Bangladesh.　　　Result: WEST INDIES WON BY TEN WICKETS.
Debuts: Bangladesh – Abul Hasan.
Man of the Match: M. N. Samuels. Man of the Series: S. Chanderpaul.

West Indies won their fourth match running, a sequence unmatched since 1992–93, the dying days of their glory years. Khulna's ground was the 107th to stage a Test, a matter of great pride to the locals. Bangladesh misfired at first, and it was 193 for eight when Abul Hasan, a 20-year-old debutant fast bowler, strolled in… and smashed a hundred from 106 balls. He was only the fourth No. 10 to score a Test century (the second on debut after Australia's Reggie Duff in 1901–02), and dominated a stand of 184 with the more experienced Mahmudullah. However, after scoring 113, Abul conceded 113 with the ball – and failed to take a wicket as West Indies marched to a huge lead. Samuels shared stands of 326 with Bravo, and 177 with the inevitable Chanderpaul, who finished with a series average of 354. Samuels batted for 618 minutes, often exploiting the slowness of the pitch by standing almost square-on and working the spinners to leg during his first double-century. At one point Shakib Al Hasan had none for 134 from 48 overs, but then claimed four quick wickets, including his 100th in Tests (Sammy, caught at slip); he was the second Bangladeshi to get there after Mohammad Rafique, another slow left-armer. Bangladesh dipped to 82 for five, but although Best improved his Test-best for the second match running, despite a hamstring niggle, nineties from Shakib and Nasir Hossain (his second of the series) at least ensured West Indies had to bat again.

Bangladesh

Tamim Iqbal b Sammy	32	– b Best	28
Nazimuddin c Powell b Edwards	4	– lbw b Edwards	0
Shahriar Nafees c Ramdin b Sammy	26	– c Sammy b Best	21
Naeem Islam b Edwards	16	– b Best	2
Shakib Al Hasan c Ramdin b Edwards	17	– c Best b Permaul	97
*†Mushfiqur Rahim c Ramdin b Edwards	38	– b Permaul	10
Nasir Hossain c Edwards b Permaul	52	– b Best	94
Mahmudullah c and b Sammy	76	– c Ramdin b Permaul	2
Sohag Gazi lbw b Edwards	0	– b Best	7
Abul Hasan c Sammy b Edwards	113	– not out	7
Rubel Hossain not out	5	– c Bravo b Best	14
B 4, l-b 3, n-b 1	8	L-b 3, w 1, n-b 1	5
(91.1 overs)	387	(70.1 overs)	287

1/5 (2) 2/64 (3) 3/77 (1) 4/93 (4) 5/98 (5) 6/185 (7)
7/193 (6) 8/193 (9) 9/377 (8) 10/387 (10)

1/1 (2) 2/49 (1) 3/51 (4) 4/62 (3) 5/82 (6) 6/226 (5)
7/228 (8) 8/254 (9) 9/269 (7) 10/287 (11)

Edwards 18.1–2–90–6; Best 10–3–31–0; Sammy 23–4–74–3; Narine 19–0–91–0; Permaul 19–2–79–1; Samuels 2–0–15–0. *Second Innings*—Edwards 17–0–95–1; Narine 9–0–48–0; Permaul 20–2–67–3; Best 12.1–1–40–6; Gayle 4–0–15–0; Sammy 8–3–19–0.

West Indies

C. H. Gayle c Mushfiqur Rahim b Sohag Gazi	25	– not out	20
K. O. A. Powell c Shakib Al Hasan b Rubel Hossain	13	– not out	9
D. M. Bravo lbw b Sohag Gazi	127		
M. N. Samuels c sub (Elias Sunny) b Rubel Hossain	260		
S. Chanderpaul not out	150		
†D. Ramdin c Mushfiqur Rahim b Shakib Al Hasan	31		
*D. J. G. Sammy c Mahmudullah b Shakib Al Hasan	0		
V. Permaul c Sohag Gazi b Shakib Al Hasan	13		
S. P. Narine c Shahriar Nafees b Shakib Al Hasan	0		
F. H. Edwards c Shakib Al Hasan b Sohag Gazi	2		
B 10, l-b 7, w 2, n-b 8	27	W 1	1
(9 wkts dec, 200.3 overs)	648	(no wkt, 4.4 overs)	30

1/37 (2) 2/43 (1) 3/369 (3) 4/546 (4) 5/621 (6) 6/621 (7)
7/639 (8) 8/639 (9) 9/648 (10)

T. L. Best did not bat.

Sohag Gazi 57.3–4–167–3; Abul Hasan 24–0–113–0; Rubel Hossain 31–8–86–2; Naeem Islam 14–1–43–0; Shakib Al Hasan 52–11–151–4; Mahmudullah 10–0–42–0; Nasir Hossain 12–1–29–0. *Second Innings*—Sohag Gazi 1–0–8–0; Rubel Hossain 2–0–14–0; Naeem Islam 1.4–1–8–0.

Umpires: R. K. Illingworth *(England)* (2) and B. N. J. Oxenford *(Australia)* (10).
Third umpire: Enamul Haque, sen. *(Bangladesh)*. Referee: D. C. Boon *(Australia)* (12).

Close of play: First day, Bangladesh 365–8 (Mahmudullah 72, Abul Hasan 100); Second day, West Indies 241–2 (Bravo 85, Samuels 109); Third day, West Indies 564–4 (Chanderpaul 109, Ramdin 4); Fourth day, Bangladesh 226–6 (Nasir Hossain 64).

INDIA v ENGLAND 2012–13 (1st Test)

At Sardar Patel Stadium, Motera, Ahmedabad, on 15, 16, 17, 18, 19 November, 2012.
Toss: India.   Result: INDIA WON BY NINE WICKETS.
Debuts: England – N. R. D. Compton.
Man of the Match: C. A. Pujara.

England continued their worrying penchant for starting series slowly, as India ran up a huge score then made them follow on. Cook, in his first match as permanent captain after Strauss's retirement, then dropped anchor for 556 minutes, but India still completed victory on the fifth afternoon. Prior batted for more than 60 overs, putting on 157 with Cook; his 91 was the highest by an England wicketkeeper in India apart from Dick Spooner's 92 in 1951–52. But Cook soon followed, another of Ojha's nine wickets in the match, and the end came quickly after that. India's big total was set up by Sehwag, with his 23rd (and, barring a surprise comeback, last) Test century, and a superb unbeaten 203 from Pujara. He put on 130 with Yuvraj Singh, in his first Test for a year after cancer treatment. England subsided to 191, a deficit of 330, with Prior top-scoring from No. 8. Pietersen, having been "reintegrated" following the text-messaging saga, got into a tangle against Ojha, and Bell chipped the next ball to deepish mid-off. Experienced observers wondered whether it was the worst stroke they had seen from an established Test batsman. England did much better second time round – but it was too late. Nick Compton followed his grandfather Denis as a Test player; the only other such combination for England was Maurice and Chris Tremlett. After scoring nine from 53 balls Compton provided Ashwin with his 50th wicket in only his ninth Test, beating Anil Kumble's Indian record of ten.

India

G. Gambhir b Swann	45			
V. Sehwag b Swann	117	– (1) c Pietersen b Swann		25
C. A. Pujara not out	206	– (2) not out		41
S. R. Tendulkar c Patel b Swann	13			
V. Kohli b Swann	19	– (3) not out		14
Yuvraj Singh c Swann b Patel	74			
*†M. S. Dhoni b Swann	5			
R. Ashwin c Prior b Pietersen	23			
Zaheer Khan c Trott b Anderson	7			
P. P. Ojha not out	0			
B 1, l-b 10, n-b 1	12			
(8 wkts dec, 160 overs)	521	(1 wkt, 15.3 overs)		80

1/134 (1) 2/224 (2) 3/250 (4) 4/283 (5) 5/413 (6)
6/444 (7) 7/510 (8) 8/519 (9)   1/57 (1)

U. T. Yadav did not bat.

Anderson 27–7–75–1; Broad 24–1–97–0; Bresnan 19–2–73–0; Swann 51–8–144–5; Patel 31–3–96–1; Pietersen 8–1–25–1. *Second Innings*—Anderson 2–0–10–0; Swann 7.3–1–46–1; Patel 6–0–24–0.

England

*A. N. Cook c Sehwag b Ashwin	41	– b Ojha		176
N. R. D. Compton b Ashwin	9	– lbw b Zaheer Khan		37
J. M. Anderson c Gambhir b Ojha	2	– (11) not out		0
I. J. L. Trott c Pujara b Ashwin	0	– (3) c Dhoni b Ojha		17
K. P. Pietersen b Ojha	17	– (4) b Ojha		2
I. R. Bell c Tendulkar b Ojha	0	– (5) lbw b Yadav		22
S. R. Patel lbw b Yadav	10	– (6) lbw b Yadav		0
†M. J. Prior b Ojha	48	– (7) c and b Ojha		91
T. T. Bresnan c Kohli b Ojha	19	– (8) c sub (A. M. Rahane) b Zaheer Khan		20
S. C. J. Broad lbw b Zaheer Khan	25	– (9) c and b Yadav		3
G. P. Swann not out	3	– (10) b Ashwin		17
B 5, l-b 12	17	B 14, l-b 6, w 1		21
(74.2 overs)	191	(154.3 overs)		406

1/26 (2) 2/29 (3) 3/30 (4) 4/69 (5) 5/69 (6) 6/80 (1)   1/123 (2) 2/156 (3) 3/160 (4) 4/199 (5) 5/199 (6)
7/97 (7) 8/144 (9) 9/187 (10) 10/191 (8)   6/356 (7) 7/365 (1) 8/378 (9) 9/406 (10) 10/406 (8)

Ashwin 27–9–80–3; Zaheer Khan 15–7–23–1; Ojha 22.2–8–45–5; Yuvraj Singh 3–0–12–0; Yadav 7–2–14–1. *Second Innings*—Yadav 23–2–70–3; Ojha 55–16–120–4; Ashwin 43–9–111–1; Sehwag 1–0–1–0; Zaheer Khan 27.3–5–59–2; Tendulkar 1–0–8–0; Yuvraj Singh 4–0–17–0.

Umpires: Aleem Dar *(Pakistan)* (75) and A. L. Hill *(New Zealand)* (32).
Third umpire: S. Asnani *(India)*. Referee: R. S. Mahanama *(Sri Lanka)* (39).

Close of play: First day, India 323–4 (Pujara 98, Yuvraj Singh 24); Second day, England 41–3 (Cook 22, Pietersen 6); Third day, England 111–0 (Cook 74, Compton 34); Fourth day, England 340–5 (Cook 168, Prior 84).

INDIA v ENGLAND 2012–13 (2nd Test)

At Wankhede Stadium, Mumbai, on 23, 24, 25, 26 November, 2012.
Toss: India.   Result: ENGLAND WON BY TEN WICKETS.
Debuts: none.
Man of the Match: K. P. Pietersen.

After India's emphatic victory at Ahmedabad, Dhoni called for a spinning pitch at Mumbai. He got one, then won the toss – and saw England romp to victory in under ten sessions. India's vaunted spinners were outbowled by Swann, who took four wickets in each innings, and the returning Panesar, who claimed 11 in the match, his extra pace through the air leaving the batsmen reluctant to commit to the front foot on the bouncy surface. After Anderson removed Gambhir in the first over of the match, the remaining 29 wickets all fell to spin. Thanks to another patient century from Pujara and a late flourish from Ashwin, India reached 327. Running out of partners, Pujara was eventually stumped after batting for 1,015 minutes in the series; the bowler, Swann, had just taken his 200th Test wicket (Harbhajan Singh). England briefly feared the worst – but then Cook and Pietersen added 206, both making their 22nd Test centuries to equal the England record shared by Wally Hammond, Colin Cowdrey and Geoff Boycott. Pietersen was particularly majestic: he called it his best innings, and was probably right, even if he was helped by the spinners' tendency to drop short. England led by 86, but no one was prepared for what happened next – in the 33 overs remaining on the third evening, India lost seven for 117, five to Panesar. Gambhir was last out next morning, and to square the series England needed only 57, which they joyously knocked off in less than ten overs.

India

G. Gambhir lbw b Anderson	4	– lbw b Swann	65
V. Sehwag b Panesar	30	– c Swann b Panesar	9
C. A. Pujara st Prior b Swann	135	– c Bairstow b Swann	6
S. R. Tendulkar b Panesar	8	– lbw b Panesar	8
V. Kohli c Compton b Panesar	19	– c sub (J. E. Root) b Swann	7
Yuvraj Singh b Swann	0	– c Bairstow b Panesar	8
*†M. S. Dhoni c Swann b Panesar	29	– c Trott b Panesar	6
R. Ashwin lbw b Panesar	68	– c Patel b Panesar	11
Harbhajan Singh lbw b Swann	21	– c Trott b Swann	6
Zaheer Khan c Bairstow b Swann	11	– c Prior b Panesar	1
P. P. Ojha not out	0	– not out	6
L-b 1, n-b 1	2	B 6, l-b 3	9
(115.1 overs)	327	(44.1 overs)	142

1/4 (1) 2/52 (2) 3/60 (4) 4/118 (5) 5/119 (6) 6/169 (7)   1/30 (2) 2/37 (3) 3/52 (4) 4/65 (5) 5/78 (6)
7/280 (8) 8/315 (9) 9/316 (3) 10/327 (10)   6/92 (7) 7/110 (8) 8/128 (9) 9/131 (10) 10/142 (1)

Anderson 18–3–61–1; Broad 12–1–60–0; Panesar 47–12–129–5; Swann 34.1–7–70–4; Patel 4–1–6–0. *Second Innings*—Anderson 4–1–9–0; Panesar 22–3–81–6; Swann 18.1–6–43–4.

England

*A. N. Cook c Dhoni b Ashwin	122	– not out	18
N. R. D. Compton c Sehwag b Ojha	29	– not out	30
I. J. L. Trott lbw b Ojha	0		
K. P. Pietersen c Dhoni b Ojha	186		
J. M. Bairstow c Gambhir b Ojha	9		
S. R. Patel c Kohli b Ojha	26		
†M. J. Prior run out	21		
S. C. J. Broad c Pujara b Harbhajan Singh	6		
G. P. Swann not out	1		
J. M. Anderson lbw b Harbhajan Singh	2		
M. S. Panesar c Zaheer Khan b Ashwin	4		
B 4, l-b 2, w 1	7	B 8, l-b 2	10
(121.3 overs)	413	(no wkt, 9.4 overs)	58

1/66 (2) 2/68 (3) 3/274 (1) 4/298 (5) 5/357 (6)
6/382 (4) 7/406 (7) 8/406 (8) 9/408 (10) 10/413 (11)

Ashwin 42.3–6–145–2; Ojha 40–6–143–5; Zaheer Khan 15–4–37–0; Harbhajan Singh 21–1–74–2; Yuvraj Singh 3–0–8–0. *Second Innings*—Ashwin 3.4–0–22–0; Ojha 4–0–16–0; Harbhajan Singh 2–0–10–0.

Umpires: Aleem Dar *(Pakistan)* (76) and A. L. Hill *(New Zealand)* (33).
Third umpire: S. Ravi *(India)*. Referee: R. S. Mahanama *(Sri Lanka)* (40).

Close of play: First day, India 266–6 (Pujara 114, Ashwin 60); Second day, England 178–2 (Cook 87, Pietersen 62); Third day, India 117–7 (Gambhir 53, Harbhajan Singh 1).

INDIA v ENGLAND 2012–13 (3rd Test)

At Eden Gardens, Kolkata, on 5, 6, 7, 8, 9 December, 2012.
Toss: India.   Result: ENGLAND WON BY SEVEN WICKETS.
Debuts: none.
Man of the Match: A. N. Cook.

England proved their success in Mumbai was no fluke, their bowlers again outperforming India's to set up a seven-wicket victory. India had passed 600 in the last three Tests at Kolkata, so 316 this time was a disappointment, as was Tendulkar's dismissal in sight of yet another century – one of three wickets for the exemplary Anderson, who reversed the ball well. Tendulkar's 76 did take him past Sunil Gavaskar's Indian-record 2,483 runs against England. Cook, batting with authority and purpose, then put on 165 with the adhesive Compton and 173 with Trott. His 23rd century – the England record – was, uniquely, his fifth in his first five Tests as captain, while only four other visiting batsmen (Everton Weekes, Garry Sobers, Ken Barrington and Andy Flower) had previously scored hundreds in three successive Tests in India. After 492 minutes and 377 balls, Cook was run out – his first such dismissal in 312 first-class innings. Only Sobers, Arthur Morris and Younis Khan had previously been run out in the 190s in Tests. England led by 207, but India lunched more comfortably on the fourth day at 86 for none, with Sehwag in battling form. But Swann sneaked the first ball after the break between his bat and pad, and soon India were reeling at 122 for six; only Ashwin's combative 91 made England bat again, enabling Cook to become only the second man – after England's Archie MacLaren at Sydney in 1894–95 – to be stumped in the first over of a Test innings.

India

G. Gambhir c Trott b Panesar	60	– c Prior b Finn	40
V. Sehwag run out	23	– b Swann	49
C. A. Pujara b Panesar	16	– run out	8
S. R. Tendulkar c Prior b Anderson	76	– c Trott b Swann	5
V. Kohli c Swann b Anderson	6	– c Prior b Finn	20
Yuvraj Singh c Cook b Swann	32	– b Anderson	11
*†M. S. Dhoni c Swann b Finn	52	– c Cook b Anderson	0
R. Ashwin b Anderson	21	– not out	91
Zaheer Khan lbw b Panesar	6	– lbw b Finn	0
I. Sharma b Panesar	0	– b Panesar	10
P. P. Ojha not out	0	– b Anderson	3
B 5, l-b 13, w 5, n-b 1	24	B 8, l-b 2	10
(105 overs)	316	(84.4 overs)	247

1/47 (2) 2/88 (3) 3/117 (1) 4/136 (5) 5/215 (6)   1/86 (2) 2/98 (3) 3/103 (1) 4/107 (4) 5/122 (6)
6/230 (4) 7/268 (8) 8/292 (9) 9/296 (10) 10/316 (7)   6/122 (7) 7/155 (5) 8/159 (9) 9/197 (10) 10/247 (11)

Anderson 28–7–89–3; Finn 21–2–73–1; Panesar 40–13–90–4; Swann 16–3–46–1. *Second Innings*—Anderson 15.4–4–38–3; Finn 18–6–45–3; Panesar 22–1–75–1; Swann 28–9–70–2; Patel 1–0–9–0.

England

*A. N. Cook run out	190	– st Dhoni b Ashwin	1
N. R. D. Compton lbw b Ojha	57	– not out	9
I. J. L. Trott c Dhoni b Ojha	87	– lbw b Ojha	3
K. P. Pietersen lbw b Ashwin	54	– c Dhoni b Ashwin	0
I. R. Bell c Dhoni b Sharma	5	– not out	28
S. R. Patel c Sehwag b Ojha	33		
†M. J. Prior c Dhoni b Zaheer Khan	41		
G. P. Swann c Sehwag b Ojha	21		
S. T. Finn not out	4		
J. M. Anderson c Sehwag b Ashwin	9		
M. S. Panesar lbw b Ashwin	0		
B 13, l-b 4, n-b 5	22		
(167.3 overs)	523	(3 wkts, 12.1 overs)	41

1/165 (2) 2/338 (3) 3/359 (1) 4/395 (5) 5/420 (4)
6/453 (6) 7/510 (8) 8/510 (7) 9/523 (10) 10/523 (11)   1/4 (1) 2/7 (3) 3/8 (4)

Zaheer Khan 31–6–94–1; Sharma 29–8–78–1; Ashwin 52.3–9–183–3; Ojha 52–10–142–4; Yuvraj Singh 3–1–9–0. *Second Innings*—Ashwin 6.1–1–31–2; Ojha 6–3–10–1.

Umpires: H. D. P. K. Dharmasena *(Sri Lanka)* (11) and R. J. Tucker *(Australia)* (21).
Third umpire: V. A. Kulkarni *(India)*. Referee: J. J. Crowe *(New Zealand)* (56).

Close of play: First day, India 273–7 (Dhoni 22, Zaheer Khan 0); Second day, England 216–1 (Cook 136, Trott 21); Third day, England 509–6 (Prior 40, Swann 21); Fourth day, India 239–9 (Ashwin 83, Ojha 3).

INDIA v ENGLAND 2012–13 (4th Test)

At Vidarbha C. A. Stadium, Jamtha, Nagpur, on 13, 14, 15, 16, 17 December, 2012.
Toss: England.   Result: MATCH DRAWN.
Debuts: India – R. A. Jadeja. England – J. E. Root.
Man of the Match: J. M. Anderson. Man of the Series: A. N. Cook.

A quiet draw – a rarity in modern Test cricket – enabled England to take the series 2–1, their first win in India since 1984–85 when they also came from behind. A recently relaid pitch played placidly throughout: Dhoni remarked phlegmatically that the game could have continued for another three days and still ended in a draw. England managed only 199 runs in 97 overs on the first day – Pietersen's 73 took 202 minutes, and next day the debutant Joe Root went to 73 in 289 minutes. India were equally circumspect, especially after slipping to 71 for four: they were rescued by a stand of 198 between Kohli, who scored his third Test hundred, and Dhoni, who – after over an hour in the nineties – was run out for 99 by Cook's direct hit from mid-off. It was his first risk of an innings that lasted 398 minutes. India added only 29 in the first hour of the fourth morning before Dhoni declared. England had merely to avoid mishaps, and did: Cook scored one from 46 balls before lunch, while Compton managed a solitary four in 134 deliveries before getting a dubious lbw decision. The draw had been a formality for several hours as Trott and Bell stretched their abstemious partnership to 208, although Trott upset the Indians by claiming the ball after it slipped from bowler Jadeja's hand, and swiping it to the boundary for one of his 18 fours. Anderson's final wicket (Jadeja) was his 528th in international cricket (288 in Tests), equalling Ian Botham's England record.

England

*A. N. Cook lbw b Sharma	1	– c Dhoni b Ashwin	13
N. R. D. Compton c Dhoni b Sharma	3	– lbw b Ojha	34
I. J. L. Trott b Jadeja	44	– c Kohli b Ashwin	143
K. P. Pietersen c Ojha b Jadeja	73	– b Jadeja	6
I. R. Bell c Kohli b Chawla	1	– not out	116
J. E. Root c and b Chawla	73	– not out	20
†M. J. Prior b Ashwin	57		
T. T. Bresnan lbw b Sharma	0		
G. P. Swann lbw b Chawla	56		
J. M. Anderson c Pujara b Chawla	4		
M. S. Panesar not out	1		
B 5, l-b 12	17	B 8, l-b 6, n-b 6	20
(145.5 overs)	330	(4 wkts dec, 154 overs)	352

1/3 (2) 2/16 (1) 3/102 (3) 4/119 (5) 5/139 (4) 6/242 (7)   1/48 (1) 2/81 (2) 3/94 (4) 4/302 (3)
7/242 (8) 8/302 (6) 9/325 (9) 10/330 (10)

Sharma 28–9–49–3; Ojha 35–12–71–0; Jadeja 37–17–58–2; Chawla 21.5–1–69–4; Ashwin 24–3–66–1. *Second Innings*—Sharma 15–3–42–0; Ojha 40–14–70–1; Ashwin 38–11–99–2; Chawla 26–6–64–0; Jadeja 33–17–59–1; Gambhir 2–0–4–0.

India

G. Gambhir c Prior b Anderson	37
V. Sehwag b Anderson	0
C. A. Pujara c Bell b Swann	26
S. R. Tendulkar b Anderson	2
V. Kohli lbw b Swann	103
*†M. S. Dhoni run out	99
R. A. Jadeja lbw b Anderson	12
R. Ashwin not out	29
P. P. Chawla b Swann	1
P. P. Ojha b Panesar	3
I. Sharma not out	2
B 5, l-b 7	12
(9 wkts dec, 143 overs)	326

1/1 (2) 2/59 (3) 3/64 (4) 4/71 (1) 5/269 (5) 6/288 (7)
7/295 (6) 8/297 (9) 9/317 (10)

Anderson 32–5–81–4; Bresnan 26–5–69–0; Panesar 52–15–81–1; Swann 31–10–76–3; Trott 1–0–2–0; Root 1–0–5–0.

Umpires: H. D. P. K. Dharmasena *(Sri Lanka)* (12) and R. J. Tucker *(Australia)* (22).
Third umpire: S. Ravi *(India)*. Referee: J. J. Crowe *(New Zealand)* (57).

Close of play: First day, England 199–5 (Root 31, Prior 34); Second day, India 87–4 (Kohli 11, Dhoni 8); Third day, India 297–8 (Ashwin 7); Fourth day, England 161–3 (Trott 66, Bell 24).

SRI LANKA v NEW ZEALAND 2012–13 (1st Test)

At Galle International Stadium on 17, 18, 19 November, 2012.
Toss: New Zealand.   Result: SRI LANKA WON BY TEN WICKETS.
Debuts: Sri Lanka – F. D. M. Karunaratne.
Man of the Match: H. M. R. K. B. Herath.

Sri Lanka continued to enjoy Galle, pulling off their sixth win in the last eight Tests there, the 12th in 21 overall. Herath also maintained his success rate: his 11 wickets took his tally to 46 at just over 20 apiece, and his match figures were Sri Lanka's best against this opposition. Still, New Zealand's fifth consecutive Test defeat since July – their worst run since losing six in a row in the mid-1950s – owed more to a lack of confidence on a pitch conducive to spin than it did to Herath's bowling. New Zealand struggled from the start, managing just 221 after winning the toss. McCullum and Flynn provided the only partnership of substance, putting on 90 for the fourth wicket. New Zealand did, though, claim a wicket before the close, when Southee's inswinger trapped the debutant opener Dimuth Karunaratne (replacing the injured Tillekeratne Dilshan) for a third-ball duck. Next morning, Paranavitana made a duck too, edging into his leg stump, and by the end of the 16th over they were 50 for five before a face-saving stand of 156 between Mahela Jayawardene – who gave himself out caught off the glove – and his deputy Mathews. But once Franklin broke through with his first Test wicket since April 2009 the floodgates were open again, and the innings was quickly polished off. New Zealand, 26 behind, lost McCullum on the second evening, caught in the deep, then collapsed next morning: all was lost at 96 for eight at lunch.

New Zealand

M. J. Guptill c Mathews b Eranga		11 – b Kulasekara	13
B. B. McCullum b Herath	68	– c Kulasekara b Herath	13
K. S. Williamson c Paranavitana b Eranga	0	– c H. A. P. W. Jayawardene b Kulasekara	10
*L. R. P. L. Taylor b Kulasekara	9	– lbw b Herath	18
D. R. Flynn c H. A. P. W. Jayawardene b Herath	53	– b Herath	20
J. E. C. Franklin lbw b Herath	3	– st H. A. P. W. Jayawardene b Herath	2
†C. F. K. van Wyk b Herath	28	– not out	13
D. A. J. Bracewell c D. P. M. D. Jayawardene b Herath	12	– lbw b Herath	0
T. G. Southee c Mathews b Eranga	16	– st H. A. P. W. Jayawardene b Randiv	16
J. S. Patel not out	12	– c Karunaratne b Herath	0
T. A. Boult b Kulasekara	7	– c D. P. M. D. Jayawardene b Randiv	13
L-b 1, n-b 1	2		
(82.5 overs)	221	(44.1 overs)	118

1/29 (1) 2/29 (3) 3/40 (4) 4/130 (2) 5/142 (6)
6/155 (5) 7/181 (8) 8/196 (7) 9/207 (9) 10/221 (11)

1/18 (2) 2/35 (1) 3/46 (3) 4/60 (4) 5/70 (6)
6/79 (5) 7/79 (8) 8/96 (9) 9/97 (10) 10/118 (11)

Kulasekara 12.5–5–31–2; Eranga 16–5–51–3; Mathews 3–0–11–0; Herath 30–5–65–5; Randiv 21–1–62–0. *Second Innings*—Kulasekara 12–4–28–2; Eranga 4–2–10–0; Herath 18–3–43–6; Randiv 10.1–0–37–2.

Sri Lanka

N. T. Paranavitana b Southee	0	– not out	31
F. D. M. Karunaratne lbw b Southee	0	– not out	60
S. Randiv c Guptill b Southee	9		
K. C. Sangakkara c McCullum b Boult	5		
*D. P. M. D. Jayawardene c van Wyk b Patel	91		
T. T. Samaraweera lbw b Southee	17		
A. D. Mathews c van Wyk b Franklin	79		
†H. A. P. W. Jayawardene c Bracewell b Patel	4		
K. M. D. N. Kulasekara c and b Patel	8		
H. M. R. K. B. Herath not out	11		
R. M. S. Eranga c Bracewell b Boult	4		
B 9, l-b 8, n-b 2	19	W 2	2
(80.2 overs)	247	(no wkt, 18.3 overs)	93

1/2 (2) 2/9 (1) 3/18 (3) 4/20 (4) 5/50 (6) 6/206 (7)
7/215 (8) 8/229 (5) 9/242 (9) 10/247 (11)

Boult 16.2–3–46–2; Southee 18–4–46–4; Bracewell 16–1–67–0; Franklin 7–2–16–1; Patel 23–7–55–3. *Second Innings*—Boult 4–1–15–0; Bracewell 5.3–0–35–0; Patel 5–1–22–0; Franklin 3–0–15–0; Williamson 1–0–6–0.

Umpires: M. Erasmus *(South Africa)* (14) and N. J. Llong *(England)* (13).
Third umpire: R. E. J. Martinesz *(Sri Lanka)*. Referee: J. Srinath *(India)* (23).

Close of play: First day, Sri Lanka 9–1 (Paranavitana 0, Randiv 3); Second day, New Zealand 35–1 (Guptill 13, Williamson 9).

SRI LANKA v NEW ZEALAND 2012–13 (2nd Test)

At P. Sara Oval, Colombo, on 25, 26, 27, 28, 29 November, 2012.
Toss: New Zealand.   Result: NEW ZEALAND WON BY 167 RUNS.
Debuts: New Zealand – T. D. Astle.
Man of the Match: L. R. P. L. Taylor. Man of the Series: H. M. R. K. B. Herath.

New Zealand displayed great resolve to square this short series; their first victory in Sri Lanka since winning by exactly the same margin in May 1998 ended a run of five successive defeats. Taylor reserved his best for what he knew was his last match as captain, as the new coach Mike Hesson planned to replace him. He and Williamson blunted the attack in a stand of 262, a record for any New Zealand wicket in Sri Lanka, beating the 246 of Jeff Crowe and Richard Hadlee at Colombo CC in 1986–87. Taylor, whose century was his first against Sri Lanka, hit only 11 fours from 306 balls; Williamson was equally restrained, with 12 from 305. At 300 for six, Sri Lanka had a chance to limit the damage, but the tail helped Flynn add a further 112. Three important wickets went down before stumps, the impressive Southee removing Dilshan and Sangakkara in three balls. The follow-on looked possible at 128 for six, and although Samaraweera defied a hand injury to avert that, New Zealand claimed a lead of 168 – which they increased to 362, Taylor again leading the way. His declaration left Sri Lanka 16 overs to survive on the fourth evening, and the match was all but decided when four big wickets tumbled. Samaraweera ran himself out early next morning, and although Mathews grafted for five hours, the match ended when he edged Boult to second slip soon after tea. New Zealand's seamers took 17 wickets between them.

New Zealand

M. J. Guptill c Mathews b Kulasekara	4	– c Dilshan b Eranga	11
B. B. McCullum lbw b Eranga	4	– st H. A. P. W. Jayawardene b Herath	35
K. S. Williamson lbw b Herath	135	– c Paranavitana b Kulasekara	18
*L. R. P. L. Taylor lbw b Herath	142	– run out	74
D. R. Flynn lbw b Herath	53	– lbw b Kulasekara	0
†C. F. K. van Wyk b Dilshan	0	– c Paranavitana b Herath	0
T. D. Astle lbw b Herath	3	– c Dilshan b Randiv	35
D. A. J. Bracewell c Herath b Randiv	24	– c Kulasekara b Herath	1
T. G. Southee b Herath	15	– not out	8
J. S. Patel not out	25	– st H. A. P. W. Jayawardene b Randiv	0
T. A. Boult b Herath	1	– not out	6
B 2, l-b 2, n-b 2	6	L-b 4, n-b 2	6
(153 overs)	412	(9 wkts dec, 54 overs)	194

1/4 (1) 2/14 (2) 3/276 (4) 4/290 (3) 5/291 (6)
6/300 (7) 7/346 (8) 8/374 (9) 9/410 (5) 10/412 (11)

1/32 (1) 2/56 (2) 3/74 (3) 4/74 (5) 5/75 (6)
6/172 (7) 7/177 (8) 8/180 (4) 9/182 (10)

Kulasekara 24–2–76–1; Eranga 22–0–91–1; Mathews 10–1–25–0; Herath 49–10–103–6; Randiv 39–3–94–1; Dilshan 9–2–19–1. *Second Innings*—Kulasekara 12–2–47–2; Eranga 10–1–39–1; Herath 21–3–67–3; Randiv 11–1–37–2.

Sri Lanka

N. T. Paranavitana c van Wyk b Southee	40	– lbw b Southee	0
T. M. Dilshan b Southee	5	– c van Wyk b Southee	14
K. C. Sangakkara c Boult b Southee	0	– b Bracewell	16
*D. P. M. D. Jayawardene c Williamson b Boult	4	– c van Wyk b Bracewell	5
A. D. Mathews c Guptill b Southee	47	– (6) c Guptill b Boult	84
T. T. Samaraweera c Guptill b Boult	76	– (5) run out	7
†H. A. P. W. Jayawardene c Williamson b Patel	12	– c van Wyk b Astle	29
S. Randiv lbw b Boult	39	– c Guptill b Boult	0
K. M. D. N. Kulasekara c Taylor b Southee	6	– c Williamson b Boult	18
H. M. R. K. B. Herath c Williamson b Boult	5	– (11) not out	6
R. M. S. Eranga not out	3	– (10) c Williamson b Southee	0
L-b 3, w 1, n-b 3	7	B 4, l-b 11, w 1	16
(94 overs)	244	(85.5 overs)	195

1/7 (2) 2/7 (3) 3/12 (4) 4/102 (1) 5/103 (5) 6/128 (7)
7/225 (6) 8/232 (8) 9/240 (9) 10/244 (10)

1/0 (1) 2/35 (2) 3/41 (3) 4/46 (4) 5/63 (5) 6/119 (7)
7/122 (8) 8/168 (9) 9/169 (10) 10/195 (6)

Southee 22–4–62–5; Boult 21–7–42–4; Patel 22–3–47–1; Astle 13–2–41–0; Bracewell 13–1–44–0; Williamson 3–1–5–0. *Second Innings*—Southee 20–5–58–3; Boult 17.5–6–33–3; Bracewell 13–6–13–2; Patel 16–7–20–0; Astle 18–4–56–1; Flynn 1–1–0–0.

Umpires: M. Erasmus *(South Africa)* (15) and N. J. Llong *(England)* (14).
Third umpire: R. S. A. Palliyaguruge *(Sri Lanka)*. Referee: J. Srinath *(India)* (24).

Close of play: First day, New Zealand 223–2 (Williamson 95, Taylor 119); Second day, Sri Lanka 43–3 (Paranavitana 9, Mathews 20); Third day, Sri Lanka 225–6 (Samaraweera 76, Randiv 34); Fourth day, Sri Lanka 47–4 (Samaraweera 1, Mathews 1).

AUSTRALIA v SRI LANKA 2012–13 (1st Test)

At Bellerive Oval, Hobart, on 14, 15, 16, 17, 18 December, 2012.
Toss: Australia.   Result: AUSTRALIA WON BY 137 RUNS.
Debuts: none.
Man of the Match: P. M. Siddle.

Sri Lanka had lost eight of their ten previous Tests in Australia, without winning any, and the trend continued. They almost escaped defeat here, though: with six wickets in hand at tea on the final day, they collapsed against Starc and Siddle, and lost with only 10.4 overs remaining. The basis for success had been set on the first two days. Australia's batting flourished against some insipid bowling on a sluggish pitch: Hughes's fifty was his first in a home Test, while Hussey's third hundred in four matches arrived when, on 96, he miscued a pull off Eranga to deep midwicket, where Mathews dropped the chance and it bobbled over the rope. Mathews atoned with 75 in a stand of 161 with Dilshan, a Sri Lankan fifth-wicket record against Australia. Still, with the early batting misfiring, Australia led by 114. The openers increased that by 132, although Cowan was lucky an early lbw appeal was not reviewed. Clarke charged to 57 off 46 balls before straining a hamstring, and declared not long afterwards. Sri Lanka never attempted 393 in 130 overs on what their coach Graham Ford called a "minefield" (Jayawardene preferred "challenging"). Jayawardene survived 77 balls for 19, Sangakkara 226 for 63, and Samaraweera 140 for 49 – but all three eventually fell to Siddle, whose match figures of nine for 104 had been bettered for Australia against Sri Lanka only by Shane Warne (twice). Wade became the first Australian wicketkeeper to bowl in a Test since Rod Marsh in 1983–84.

Australia

D. A. Warner run out	57	– (2) c H. A. P. W. Jayawardene b Herath		68
E. J. M. Cowan c Eranga b Welagedara	4	– (1) b Welagedara		56
P. J. Hughes b Welagedara	86	– b Eranga		16
S. R. Watson c D. P. M. D. Jayawardene b Welagedara	30	– st H. A. P. W. Jayawardene b Herath		5
*M. J. Clarke c Sangakkara b Eranga	74	– (6) retired hurt		57
M. E. K. Hussey not out	115	– (7) not out		31
†M. S. Wade not out	68	– (5) c Kulasekara b Herath		11
P. M. Siddle (did not bat)		– c H. A. P. W. Jayawardene b Welagedara		4
M. A. Starc (did not bat)		– lbw b Welagedara		5
N. M. Lyon (did not bat)		– b Herath		11
B. W. Hilfenhaus (did not bat)		– lbw b Herath		0
B 1, l-b 3, w 1, n-b 11	16	L-b 10, n-b 4		14
(5 wkts dec, 131 overs)	450	(73.5 overs)		278

1/18 (2) 2/97 (1) 3/183 (4) 4/198 (3) 5/304 (5)

1/132 (2) 2/140 (1) 3/153 (4) 4/165 (3)
5/181 (5) 6/250 (8) 7/256 (9) 8/271 (10) 9/278 (11)

In the second innings Clarke retired hurt at 238–5.

Kulasekara 32–2–80–0; Welagedara 26–1–130–3; Eranga 25–5–90–1; Mathews 15–3–41–0; Dilshan 7–0–30–0; Herath 26–4–75–0. *Second Innings*—Kulasekara 12–3–24–0; Welagedara 22–3–89–3; Dilshan 2–0–2–0; Eranga 11–0–53–1; Mathews 5–2–5–0; Herath 21.5–2–95–5.

Sri Lanka

F. D. M. Karunaratne c Wade b Hilfenhaus	14	– b Starc		30
T. M. Dilshan b Starc	147	– c Wade b Watson		11
K. C. Sangakkara c Hussey b Siddle	4	– lbw b Siddle		63
*D. P. M. D. Jayawardene lbw b Watson	12	– c Clarke b Siddle		19
T. T. Samaraweera c Wade b Lyon	7	– lbw b Siddle		49
A. D. Mathews lbw b Siddle	75	– c Wade b Siddle		19
†H. A. P. W. Jayawardene lbw b Siddle	40	– c Hussey b Starc		21
K. M. D. N. Kulasekara c sub (J. C. Silk) b Lyon	23	– c Wade b Starc		9
H. M. R. K. B. Herath lbw b Siddle	0	– b Starc		8
R. M. S. Eranga not out	5	– c Wade b Starc		6
U. W. M. B. C. A. Welagedara c Hussey b Siddle	0	– not out		0
B 2, l-b 6, n-b 1	9	B 10, l-b 8, w 1, n-b 1		20
(109.3 overs)	336	(119.2 overs)		255

1/25 (1) 2/42 (3) 3/70 (4) 4/87 (5) 5/248 (6) 6/289 (2)
7/316 (7) 8/320 (9) 9/336 (8) 10/336 (11)

1/26 (2) 2/47 (1) 3/112 (4) 4/151 (3) 5/201 (6)
6/218 (5) 7/235 (7) 8/247 (8) 9/250 (9) 10/255 (10)

Starc 24–3–104–1; Hilfenhaus 12.2–3–30–1; Lyon 25–8–76–2; Siddle 25.3–11–54–5; Watson 20.4–5–55–1; Clarke 2–0–9–0. *Second Innings*—Starc 28.2–7–63–5; Siddle 26–11–50–4; Watson 27–6–54–1; Lyon 32–12–57–0; Hussey 1–0–5–0; Warner 4–0–8–0; Wade 1–1–0–0.

Umpires: A. L. Hill *(New Zealand)* (34) and N. J. Llong *(England)* (15).
Third umpire: Aleem Dar *(Pakistan)*. Referee: B. C. Broad *(England)* (54).

Close of play: First day, Australia 299–4 (Clarke 70, Hussey 37); Second day, Sri Lanka 87–4 (Dilshan 50); Third day, Australia 27–0 (Cowan 16, Warner 8); Fourth day, Sri Lanka 65–2 (Sangakkara 18, D. P. M. D. Jayawardene 5).

AUSTRALIA v SRI LANKA 2012–13 (2nd Test)

At Melbourne Cricket Ground on 26, 27, 28 December, 2012.
Toss: Sri Lanka.   Result: AUSTRALIA WON BY AN INNINGS AND 201 RUNS.
Debuts: Australia – J. M. Bird.
Man of the Match: M. G. Johnson.

Sri Lanka's first-day performance was so abject it set them on the path to their third-heaviest Test defeat. Australia's dramatically recast attack could scarcely believe their good fortune at a string of wrong-headed strokes on a pitch offering bounce but no great lateral movement. The result was further soured for Sri Lanka by injuries, particularly to Sangakkara, the only batsman to make a fight of it on Boxing Day. He punched some admirable drives down the ground, and became the 11th man (the second Sri Lankan, after Mahela Jayawardene) to pass 10,000 Test runs; like Brian Lara and Sachin Tendulkar, he got there in his 195th innings. But he could only watch as Johnson broke Prasanna Jayawardene's thumb with a snorter that was pouched in the slips, then bounced out Prasad next ball. By tea, Australia were batting. Warner hurried them into a dominant position, then Watson added 194 with Clarke, who made his fifth Test century of 2012. Batting again on the third morning 304 behind, Sri Lanka lost Karunaratne (run out) and Dilshan (caught at short leg) in the first over. Jayawardene and Samaraweera were undone by Bird, and shortly afterwards Johnson fractured Sangakkara's left hand so badly it needed surgery. A casualty ward of three meant the match concluded when the seventh wicket fell. Only once before, when five Indians were absent hurt in Jamaica in 1975–76, had a Test innings ended with fewer wickets down. This one was Sri Lanka's shortest in Tests (previously 24.4 overs, at Cardiff in 2011).

Sri Lanka

F. D. M. Karunaratne c Wade b Bird	5	– run out	1
T. M. Dilshan b Johnson	11	– c Cowan b Johnson	0
K. C. Sangakkara c Wade b Johnson	58	– retired hurt	27
*D. P. M. D. Jayawardene c Wade b Siddle	3	– b Bird	0
T. T. Samaraweera c Warner b Bird	10	– lbw b Bird	1
A. D. Mathews c Hussey b Siddle	15	– b Johnson	35
†H. A. P. W. Jayawardene c Hughes b Johnson	24	– absent hurt	
K. T. G. D. Prasad c Wade b Johnson	0	– (7) c Hughes b Lyon	17
H. M. R. K. B. Herath c Cowan b Lyon	14	– (8) not out	11
R. M. S. Eranga not out	4	– (9) c Cowan b Siddle	0
U. W. M. B. C. A. Welagedara c Hussey b Lyon	0	– absent hurt	
L-b 5, n-b 7	12	L-b 10, n-b 1	11
(43.4 overs)	156	(24.2 overs)	103

1/13 (1) 2/19 (2) 3/37 (4) 4/79 (5) 5/99 (6)
6/134 (7) 7/134 (8) 8/147 (3) 9/156 (9) 10/156 (11)

1/1 (1) 2/1 (2) 3/3 (4) 4/13 (5) 5/74 (6)
6/102 (7) 7/103 (9)

In the second innings Sangakkara retired hurt at 62–4.

Johnson 14–2–63–4; Bird 13–5–32–2; Siddle 8–1–30–2; Watson 3–2–3–0; Lyon 5.4–0–23–2. *Second Innings—* Johnson 8–0–16–2; Bird 9–1–29–2; Siddle 5.2–0–32–1; Lyon 2–0–16–1.

Australia

E. J. M. Cowan c D. P. M. D. Jayawardene b Prasad	36
D. A. Warner c Prasad b Mathews	62
P. J. Hughes run out	10
S. R. Watson c Samaraweera b Prasad	83
*M. J. Clarke c D. P. M. D. Jayawardene b Eranga	106
M. E. K. Hussey c Herath b Dilshan	34
†M. S. Wade c Eranga b Prasad	1
M. G. Johnson not out	92
P. M. Siddle c D. P. M. D. Jayawardene b Eranga	13
N. M. Lyon c sub (L. D. Chandimal) b Mathews	1
J. M. Bird b Eranga	0
B 9, l-b 5, w 6, n-b 2	22
(134.4 overs)	460

1/95 (2) 2/117 (3) 3/117 (1) 4/311 (5) 5/313 (4)
6/315 (7) 7/376 (6) 8/434 (9) 9/451 (10) 10/460 (11)

Welagedara 14.4–6–38–0; Eranga 27–2–109–3; Prasad 26–2–106–3; Mathews 16–3–60–2; Herath 39–7–95–0; Dilshan 12–1–38–1.

Umpires: Aleem Dar *(Pakistan)* (77) and N. J. Llong *(England)* (16).
Third umpire: A. L. Hill *(New Zealand)*. Referee: B. C. Broad *(England)* (55).

Close of play: First day, Australia 150–3 (Watson 13, Clarke 20); Second day, Australia 440–8 (Johnson 73, Lyon 0).

AUSTRALIA v SRI LANKA 2012–13 (3rd Test)

At Sydney Cricket Ground on 3, 4, 5, 6 January, 2013.
Toss: Australia.   Result: AUISTRALIA WON BY FIVE WICKETS.
Debuts: none.
Man of the Match: J. M. Bird. Man of the Series: M. J. Clarke.

Australia completed a 3–0 sweep in Mike Hussey's 79th and last Test: he ended it averaging 61.19 in Australia, bettered only by Don Bradman (98.22), Bob Cowper (75.78) and Clarke's 64.93 at the time. Hussey, 37, had stunned his team-mates by announcing his decision during the previous Test. The atmosphere was also subdued following the death of Tony Greig, the former England captain turned Australian TV commentator, the day after the Melbourne Test; his family and colleagues from Channel Nine joined the teams for a minute's silence before the start. Clarke, armed with four fast bowlers, bowled first on winning the toss, but was held up by 72 from Jayawardene and a classy 91 from Thirimanne, Sangakkara's replacement. Hughes and Warner led Australia's reply with panache, but Hussey was disappointingly run out. A second century from Wade, promoted to No. 6, swelled the lead to 138, but he had to work for it: 70 when joined by last man Bird, he farmed the strike so effectively that the No. 11 faced only 11 balls during their stand of 39. A century stand between Karunaratne and Jayawardene narrowed the deficit and, at 155 for two, Sri Lanka were almost on level terms. But a patch of brainless batting gifted four wickets, and despite Chandimal's laudable 62 Australia needed only 141. Warner fell first ball, but Hussey was still there at the end, although the crowd would have preferred it if he, rather than Johnson, had hit the winning run.

Sri Lanka

F. D. M. Karunaratne c Hussey b Bird	5	– c Wade b Bird	85
T. M. Dilshan c Wade b Bird	34	– c Hughes b Johnson	5
*D. P. M. D. Jayawardene c Clarke b Starc	72	– c Clarke b Siddle	60
H. D. R. L. Thirimanne c Warner b Lyon	91	– c Bird b Johnson	7
T. T. Samaraweera lbw b Siddle	12	– c Hussey b Lyon	0
A. D. Mathews c Hussey b Starc	15	– run out	16
†L. D. Chandimal b Starc	24	– not out	62
K. T. G. D. Prasad c Starc b Siddle	2	– c Wade b Starc	15
H. M. R. K. B. Herath c Siddle b Bird	5	– b Bird	10
R. A. S. Lakmal c Hussey b Bird	5	– b Johnson	0
A. N. P. R. Fernando not out	17	– c Wade b Bird	9
L-b 8, w 3, n-b 1	12	B 1, l-b 4, w 1, n-b 3	9
(87.4 overs)	294	(81.2 overs)	278

1/26 (1) 2/72 (2) 3/134 (3) 4/167 (5) 5/222 (6)
6/250 (4) 7/256 (8) 8/271 (7) 9/273 (9) 10/294 (10)

1/24 (2) 2/132 (1) 3/155 (4) 4/158 (5) 5/178 (6)
6/178 (3) 7/202 (8) 8/235 (9) 9/237 (10) 10/278 (11)

Starc 19–0–71–3; Bird 19.4–10–41–4; Siddle 15–3–46–2; Johnson 13–1–58–0; Lyon 19–2–69–1; Hussey 2–1–1–0. *Second Innings*—Starc 12–1–49–1; Bird 21.2–5–76–3; Johnson 15–3–34–3; Siddle 17–4–42–1; Lyon 15–1–66–1; Hussey 1–0–6–0.

Australia

D. A. Warner c Prasad b Dilshan	85	– (2) c Jayawardene b Lakmal	0
E. J. M. Cowan run out	4	– (1) lbw b Herath	36
P. J. Hughes c Chandimal b Herath	87	– lbw b Herath	34
*M. J. Clarke c Karunaratne b Herath	50	– c Thirimanne b Dilshan	29
M. E. K. Hussey run out	25	– not out	27
†M. S. Wade not out	102	– b Herath	9
M. G. Johnson c Chandimal b Fernando	13	– not out	1
P. M. Siddle c Chandimal b Fernando	38		
M. A. Starc lbw b Herath	2		
N. M. Lyon b Herath	4		
J. M. Bird not out	6		
L-b 6, w 7, n-b 3	16	L-b 5	5
(9 wkts dec, 107 overs)	432	(5 wkts, 42.5 overs)	141

1/36 (2) 2/166 (1) 3/195 (3) 4/251 (5) 5/271 (4)
6/307 (7) 7/384 (8) 8/387 (9) 9/393 (10)

1/0 (2) 2/45 (3) 3/104 (4) 4/108 (1) 5/132 (6)

Lakmal 24–4–95–0; Fernando 20–1–114–2; Prasad 11–0–53–0; Mathews 2–0–11–0; Dilshan 19–2–58–1; Herath 31–3–95–4. *Second Innings*—Dilshan 18–2–57–1; Lakmal 6–1–18–1; Herath 16.5–0–47–3; Fernando 2–0–14–0.

Umpires: Aleem Dar *(Pakistan)* (78) and A. L. Hill *(New Zealand)* (35).
Third umpire: N. J. Llong *(England)*. Referee: B. C. Broad *(England)* (56).

Close of play: First day, Sri Lanka 294; Second day, Australia 342–6 (Wade 47, Siddle 16); Third day, Sri Lanka 225–7 (Chandimal 22, Herath 9).

SOUTH AFRICA v NEW ZEALAND 2012–13 (1st Test)

At Newlands, Cape Town, on 2, 3, 4 January, 2013.
Toss: New Zealand.   Result: SOUTH AFRICA WON BY AN INNINGS AND 27 RUNS.
Debuts: none.
Man of the Match: V. D. Philander.

Fully exploiting generous, but not extravagant, seam movement, Philander single-handedly reduced New Zealand to 27 for five in his first 25 balls – the fastest five-for in history from the start of a Test – and that, in effect, was that. Morkel and Steyn, who claimed his 300th Test wicket with a peach of an outswinger to bowl Bracewell, mopped up the tail so quickly there was even time for Smith to be dismissed before lunch. All this after poor McCullum had chosen to bat in his first Test since replacing Ross Taylor (who sat out this series) as captain. South Africa applied themselves diligently on a surface which seemed to improve as the ball got older, Petersen leading the way with his fifth Test century, while Kallis passed 13,000 runs during his 67. Brownlie's maiden Test hundred and a resolutely dull 42 from Watling helped the follow-on span 102 overs, but did little to diminish New Zealand's humiliation. At 116 balls, their first innings was easily their shortest in Tests – even the record-low 26 against England at Auckland in 1954–55 used up 162 deliveries. Williamson was the only one to reach double figures, while the five extras that came in the second over as a leg-bye was swelled by four overthrows accounted for 11% of the total. New Zealand's abject 45 was the lowest Test total by any side in almost 40 years, since Geoff Arnold and Chris Old demolished India for 42 at Lord's in 1974 – and the joint 12th-lowest in all.

New Zealand

M. J. Guptill c de Villiers b Philander	1	– c Amla b Steyn		0
*B. B. McCullum b Philander	7	– lbw b Peterson		51
K. S. Williamson lbw b Philander	13	– c Petersen b Kallis		15
D. G. Brownlie c Smith b Philander	0	– c Peterson b Morkel		109
D. R. Flynn c and b Steyn	8	– c de Villiers b Kallis		14
†B-J. Watling c de Villiers b Philander	0	– c Smith b Philander		42
J. E. C. Franklin c Smith b Morkel	1	– b Steyn		22
D. A. J. Bracewell b Steyn	2	– c Petersen b Philander		0
J. S. Patel c Amla b Morkel	5	– b Steyn		8
T. A. Boult c de Villiers b Morkel	1	– not out		2
C. S. Martin not out	0	– run out		0
L-b 6, n-b 1	7	B 1, l-b 8, w 3		12
(19.2 overs)	45	(102.1 overs)		275

1/7 (1) 2/14 (2) 3/14 (4) 4/27 (3) 5/27 (6) 6/28 (7)
7/31 (8) 8/38 (9) 9/45 (10) 10/45 (5)

1/0 (1) 2/29 (3) 3/118 (2) 4/155 (5) 5/229 (4)
6/252 (6) 7/252 (8) 8/265 (9) 9/274 (7) 10/275 (11)

Steyn 7.2–2–18–2; Philander 6–3–7–5; Morkel 6–2–14–3. *Second Innings*—Steyn 30–6–67–3; Philander 24–8–76–2; Morkel 21–6–50–1; Kallis 11.1–3–31–2; Peterson 16–6–42–1.

South Africa

*G. C. Smith lbw b Bracewell	1
A. N. Petersen b Boult	106
H. M. Amla lbw b Franklin	66
J. H. Kallis c Watling b Boult	60
†A. B. de Villiers b Martin	67
F. du Plessis c Williamson b Martin	15
D. Elgar c Watling b Boult	21
R. J. Peterson b Martin	5
V. D. Philander not out	0
B 1, l-b 2, w 2, n-b 1	6
(8 wkts dec, 95.2 overs)	347

1/1 (1) 2/108 (3) 3/212 (4) 4/255 (2) 5/281 (6)
6/335 (7) 7/342 (5) 8/347 (8)

D. W. Steyn and M. Morkel did not bat.

Boult 21–2–78–3; Bracewell 24–4–93–1; Martin 19.2–4–63–3; Franklin 14–1–50–1; Patel 17–4–60–0.

Umpires: I. J. Gould *(England)* (32) and R. J. Tucker *(Australia)* (23).
Third umpire: H. D. P. K. Dharmasena *(Sri Lanka)*. Referee: D. C. Boon *(Australia)* (13).

Close of play: First day, South Africa 252–3 (Petersen 103, de Villiers 19); Second day, New Zealand 169–4 (Brownlie 69, Watling 10).

SOUTH AFRICA v NEW ZEALAND 2012–13 (2nd Test)

At St George's Park, Port Elizabeth, on 11, 12, 13, 14 January, 2013.
Toss: South Africa.   Result: SOUTH AFRICA WON BY AN INNINGS AND 193 RUNS.
Debuts: New Zealand – C. Munro.
Man of the Match: D. W. Steyn.

South Africa batted superbly on a lively pitch to set up their biggest win against New Zealand, surpassing an innings and 180 runs at Wellington in 1952–53. Amla's clinical century – his 19th in Tests – underpinned a first-day score of 325 for four, which provoked a universal sense of foreboding about New Zealand's fragile batting. Next day a sixth-wicket stand of 131 between du Plessis, with his second Test century, and Elgar, with his first – in his third Test, after a pair on debut – turned the screw. Du Plessis reached 50 and 100 with sixes. Smith declared shortly after tea on the second day, after which New Zealand descended towards defeat with the inevitability of a sunset. Philander's dicky hamstring had ruled him out, but Steyn was so overdue a bagful of wickets he would have been induced had he been pregnant. He ripped out the first two via the slip cordon (after Kallis, unusually, had dropped one in the first over), and returned to leave New Zealand 62 for nine, seemingly set for another embarrassing total. But Watling found a decent hitter in Boult, and they almost doubled the score. In the follow-on, Guptill was reprieved by DRS from a third-ball duck that would have given him just two runs in four innings in the series; instead he managed 48. Brownlie made a tidy half-century, and Watling his second 63 of the match – but it was pillows against machine guns, and South Africa strolled to victory on the fourth morning.

South Africa

A. N. Petersen c Patel b Bracewell		21
*G. C. Smith c Watling b Wagner		54
H. M. Amla c Watling b Boult		110
J. H. Kallis c Watling b Bracewell		8
†A. B. de Villiers c Williamson b Patel		51
F. du Plessis c McCullum b Munro		137
D. Elgar not out		103
R. J. Peterson c Patel b Munro		8
D. W. Steyn c Patel b Bracewell		5
R. K. Kleinveldt not out		7
B 6, l-b 8, w 4, n-b 3		21
(8 wkts dec, 153.5 overs)		525

1/29 (1) 2/121 (2) 3/137 (4) 4/223 (5) 5/336 (3)
6/467 (6) 7/481 (8) 8/508 (9)

M. Morkel did not bat.

Boult 32–5–108–1; Bracewell 34–6–94–3; Wagner 33–4–135–1; Patel 36.5–2–134–1; Munro 18–4–40–2.

New Zealand

M. J. Guptill c Petersen b Steyn		1 – b Kleinveldt		48
*B. B. McCullum c Kallis b Peterson	13	– lbw b Peterson		11
K. S. Williamson c Smith b Steyn		4 – b Peterson		11
D. G. Brownlie c de Villiers b Kleinveldt		10 – c de Villiers b Kallis		53
D. R. Flynn lbw b Kleinveldt		0 – c de Villiers b Kleinveldt		0
†B-J. Watling c Smith b Morkel	63	– b Steyn		63
C. Munro c Elgar b Peterson		0 – c Petersen b Morkel		15
D. A. J. Bracewell c de Villiers b Steyn		7 – c Petersen b Steyn		0
N. Wagner lbw b Steyn		0 – c de Villiers b Steyn		4
J. S. Patel b Steyn		0 – (11) not out		0
T. A. Boult not out	17	– (10) c Peterson b Morkel		3
L-b 5, w 1	6	L-b 2, w 1		3
(44.4 overs)	121	(86.4 overs)		211

1/2 (1) 2/8 (3) 3/27 (4) 4/27 (5) 5/39 (2) 6/39 (7)   1/40 (2) 2/64 (3) 3/84 (1) 4/84 (5) 5/182 (4)
7/61 (8) 8/62 (9) 9/62 (10) 10/121 (6)   6/203 (7) 7/203 (6) 8/204 (8) 9/207 (10) 10/211 (9)

Steyn 13–5–17–5; Morkel 12.4–6–26–1; Kleinveldt 11–3–53–2; Peterson 7–2–20–2; Kallis 1–1–0–0. *Second Innings*—Steyn 15.4–2–48–3; Morkel 16–6–36–2; Kleinveldt 15–8–44–2; Peterson 26–13–47–2; Kallis 9–3–18–1; Smith 1–0–10–0; Petersen 4–0–6–0.

Umpires: H. D. P. K. Dharmasena *(Sri Lanka)* (13) and I. J. Gould *(England)* (33).
Third umpire: R. J. Tucker *(Australia)*. Referee: D. C. Boon *(Australia)* (14).

Close of play: First day, South Africa 325–4 (Amla 106, du Plessis 69); Second day, New Zealand 47–6 (Watling 15, Bracewell 3); Third day, New Zealand 157–4 (Brownlie 44, Watling 41).

SOUTH AFRICA v PAKISTAN 2012–13 (1st Test)

At The Wanderers, Johannesburg, on 1, 2, 3, 4 February, 2013.
Toss: South Africa.   Result: SOUTH AFRICA WON BY 211 RUNS.
Debuts: Pakistan – Nasir Jamshed, Rahat Ali.
Man of the Match: D. W. Steyn.

For the third time in 15 months South Africa shot out the opposition for less than 50, following similar demolitions of Australia (47) and New Zealand (45), both at Cape Town. Pakistan fought hard, but were confronted by fast bowling so intense and unrelenting that it was hard to imagine it had ever been surpassed. Steyn claimed the first three with his trademark late awayswing at extreme pace; Kallis accounted for Azhar Ali with a snorting bouncer worthy of a man 20 years younger, then had Misbah-ul-Haq caught behind in his next over. The cull was completed shortly after lunch by Steyn, who ended with a Victorian-era analysis of six for eight. South Africa had earlier grafted to 253 on a difficult track; Kallis's 78-ball 50 stood out for its passive aggression, although the openers' twenties were no less valuable – they were not separated until the 19th over. Smith waived the follow-on and, against a callow attack, his side were 411 ahead by the second-day close. Next morning de Villiers exploded with a flurry of mouth-watering boundaries to reach his 15th Test century. South Africa looked on course for a three-day win when Pakistan slipped to 82 for four before tea, but a stubborn stand between Misbah and Asad Shafiq, which spanned 53 overs, pushed the match into the fourth day. Steyn completed a national-record fifth ten-for, while de Villiers's five catches gave him a share of the Test record of 11, set by England's Jack Russell here in 1985–86.

South Africa

*G. C. Smith c Sarfraz Ahmed b Umar Gul	24	– (2) c Sarfraz Ahmed b Umar Gul	52
A. N. Petersen c Mohammad Hafeez b Junaid Khan	20	– (1) c Mohammad Hafeez b Umar Gul	27
H. M. Amla c Azhar Ali b Younis Khan	37	– not out	74
J. H. Kallis c Asad Shafiq b Umar Gul	50	– c Asad Shafiq b Saeed Ajmal	7
†A. B. de Villiers c Sarfraz Ahmed b Mohammad Hafeez	31	– not out	103
F. du Plessis b Junaid Khan	41		
D. Elgar c Sarfraz Ahmed b Mohammad Hafeez	27		
R. J. Peterson b Mohammad Hafeez	0		
V. D. Philander run out	1		
D. W. Steyn not out	12		
M. Morkel b Mohammad Hafeez	0		
B 4, l-b 4, w 1, n-b 1	10	L-b 4, w 3, n-b 5	12
(85.2 overs)	253	(3 wkts dec, 62 overs)	275

1/46 (2) 2/46 (1) 3/125 (4) 4/135 (3) 5/199 (5) 6/232 (6)
7/239 (8) 8/240 (7) 9/243 (9) 10/253 (11)   1/82 (1) 2/87 (2) 3/99 (4)

Umar Gul 19–2–56–2; Junaid Khan 18–8–33–2; Rahat Ali 14–0–56–0; Saeed Ajmal 23–4–68–0; Younis Khan 4–0–16–1; Mohammad Hafeez 7.2–1–16–4. *Second Innings*—Umar Gul 14–2–58–2; Junaid Khan 13–1–63–0; Rahat Ali 11–1–44–0; Mohammad Hafeez 5–0–32–0; Saeed Ajmal 18–1–74–1; Younis Khan 1–1–0–0.

Pakistan

Mohammad Hafeez c de Villiers b Steyn	6	– c de Villiers b Philander	2
Nasir Jamshed lbw b Steyn	2	– c Peterson b Steyn	46
Azhar Ali c de Villiers b Kallis	13	– lbw b Kallis	18
Younis Khan c Smith b Steyn	0	– c de Villiers b Morkel	15
*Misbah-ul-Haq c de Villiers b Kallis	12	– c de Villiers b Steyn	64
Asad Shafiq c de Villiers b Philander	1	– c Kallis b Steyn	56
†Sarfraz Ahmed c de Villiers b Steyn	2	– b Philander	6
Umar Gul c Smith b Philander	0	– c de Villiers b Steyn	23
Saeed Ajmal c de Villiers b Steyn	1	– c de Villiers b Morkel	11
Junaid Khan not out	8	– lbw b Steyn	9
Rahat Ali c du Plessis b Steyn	0	– not out	3
L-b 3, w 1	4	B 4, l-b 4, w 3, n-b 4	15
(29.1 overs)	49	(100.4 overs)	268

1/9 (1) 2/12 (2) 3/12 (4) 4/36 (3) 5/37 (5) 6/39 (6)   1/7 (1) 2/64 (2) 3/70 (3) 4/82 (4) 5/209 (6)
7/39 (8) 8/40 (9) 9/41 (7) 10/49 (11)   6/210 (5) 7/218 (7) 8/240 (9) 9/261 (8) 10/268 (10)

Philander 9–5–16–2; Steyn 8.1–6–8–6; Morkel 6–3–11–0; Kallis 6–2–11–2. *Second Innings*—Steyn 28.4–10–52–5; Philander 22–3–60–2; Morkel 25–7–89–2; Kallis 15–5–35–1; Peterson 10–3–24–0.

Umpires: B. F. Bowden *(New Zealand)* (73) and B. N. J. Oxenford *(Australia)* (11).
Third umpire: S. J. Davis *(Australia)*. Referee: J. J. Crowe *(New Zealand)* (58).

Close of play: First day, Pakistan 6–0 (Mohammad Hafeez 6, Nasir Jamshed 0); Second day, South Africa 207–3 (Amla 50, de Villiers 63); Third day, Pakistan 183–4 (Misbah-ul-Haq 44, Asad Shafiq 53).

SOUTH AFRICA v PAKISTAN 2012–13 (2nd Test)

At Newlands, Cape Town, on 14, 15, 16, 17 February, 2013.
Toss: South Africa.   Result: SOUTH AFRICA WON BY FOUR WICKETS.
Debuts: Pakistan – Mohammad Irfan.
Man of the Match: R. J. Peterson.

After the financial disasters of two three-day Tests at Newlands in the previous 15 months, the pitch for Cape Town's 50th Test was dry and bare enough for Smith to worry about Pakistan's spinners. But, although Saeed Ajmal did indeed claim ten wickets, South Africa had enough in reserve to wrap up the series. They were indebted to Amla, who anchored the chase with a responsible 58, falling only with victory in sight. Earlier on that fourth day Pakistan had looked in charge, reaching 114 for three – a lead of 126 – before the last seven wickets clattered for 55, which kept South Africa's target within bounds. Philander bounced in for nine for 99 in the match, while slow left-armer Peterson proved an excellent foil for the seamers. First-innings honours had been roughly even. Pakistan dipped to 33 for four, but were hauled out of a hole by Younis Khan and Asad Shafiq, who both made 111 in a stand of 219. Later a good old-fashioned tailender's crash-bang from Tanvir Ahmed pushed them up to 338. South Africa in turn dipped to 109 for five, Ajmal taking the first three wickets, but recovered thanks to de Villiers and the underrated Peterson, whose 84 was only his second score above 34 in 11 Tests spread over ten years: the last five wickets added 217. The debutant left-arm seamer Mohammad Irfan took three wickets with pace and bounce, unsurprising from the tallest man ever to play Test cricket at a reputed 7ft 1in.

Pakistan

Mohammad Hafeez c Smith b Steyn	17	– lbw b Steyn	0
Nasir Jamshed c de Villiers b Philander	3	– lbw b Philander	0
Azhar Ali c de Villiers b Morkel	4	– c de Villiers b Philander	65
Younis Khan c de Villiers b Philander	111	– b Steyn	14
*Misbah-ul-Haq c Elgar b Morkel	0	– c Smith b Peterson	44
Asad Shafiq c Smith b Philander	111	– b Philander	19
†Sarfraz Ahmed c Petersen b Philander	13	– b Peterson	5
Tanvir Ahmed c Philander b Peterson	44	– not out	10
Umar Gul lbw b Philander	0	– c Petersen b Philander	0
Saeed Ajmal not out	21	– b Peterson	4
Mohammad Irfan b Peterson	6	– c Petersen b Steyn	2
L-b 5, n-b 3	8	L-b 2, w 4	6
(116.2 overs)	338	(75.3 overs)	169

1/10 (2) 2/21 (1) 3/33 (3) 4/33 (5) 5/252 (4) 6/259 (6)
7/266 (7) 8/268 (9) 9/332 (8) 10/338 (11)

1/0 (1) 2/7 (2) 3/45 (4) 4/114 (5) 5/147 (6)
6/152 (7) 7/152 (8) 8/152 (9) 9/158 (10) 10/169 (11)

Steyn 25–7–55–1; Philander 26–10–59–5; Morkel 20.3–6–59–2; Kallis 19.3–2–52–0; Peterson 23.2–0–94–2; Elgar 2–0–14–0. *Second Innings*—Steyn 18.3–5–38–3; Philander 19–6–40–4; Morkel 3.1–0–8–0; Peterson 29–8–73–3; Kallis 5.5–2–8–0.

South Africa

*G. C. Smith lbw b Saeed Ajmal	19	– (2) lbw b Saeed Ajmal	29
A. N. Petersen c Azhar Ali b Saeed Ajmal	17	– (1) lbw b Umar Gul	1
H. M. Amla lbw b Saeed Ajmal	25	– b Saeed Ajmal	58
F. du Plessis c Younis Khan b Saeed Ajmal	28	– (6) lbw b Saeed Ajmal	15
J. H. Kallis lbw b Saeed Ajmal	2	– (4) lbw b Saeed Ajmal	21
†A. B. de Villiers c Umar Gul b Mohammad Irfan	61	– (5) c Sarfraz Ahmed b Tanvir Ahmed	36
D. Elgar c Younis Khan b Saeed Ajmal	23	– not out	11
R. J. Peterson c Umar Gul b Mohammad Hafeez	84	– not out	1
V. D. Philander c Nasir Jamshed b Mohammad Irfan	22		
D. W. Steyn c Sarfraz Ahmed b Mohammad Irfan	10		
M. Morkel not out	8		
B 12, l-b 8, n-b 7	27	B 5, n-b 5	10
(102.1 overs)	326	(6 wkts, 43.1 overs)	182

1/36 (1) 2/50 (2) 3/84 (3) 4/102 (5) 5/109 (4)
6/164 (7) 7/210 (6) 8/277 (9) 9/303 (10) 10/326 (8)

1/10 (1) 2/63 (2) 3/88 (4) 4/150 (3) 5/168 (5)
6/180 (6)

Umar Gul 20–5–74–0; Tanvir Ahmed 10–4–26–0; Mohammad Irfan 21–1–86–3; Saeed Ajmal 42–9–96–6; Mohammad Hafeez 9.1–1–24–1. *Second Innings*—Mohammad Irfan 10–1–35–0; Umar Gul 8–0–46–1; Saeed Ajmal 18.1–2–51–4; Mohammad Hafeez 2–1–11–0; Tanvir Ahmed 5–0–34–1.

Umpires: S. J. Davis *(Australia)* (43) and B. N. J. Oxenford *(Australia)* (12).
Third umpire: B. F. Bowden *(New Zealand)*. Referee: J. J. Crowe *(New Zealand)* (59).

Close of play: First day, Pakistan 253–5 (Asad Shafiq 111, Sarfraz Ahmed 0); Second day, South Africa 139–5 (de Villiers 24, Elgar 11); Third day, Pakistan 100–3 (Azhar Ali 45, Misbah-ul-Haq 36).

SOUTH AFRICA v PAKISTAN 2012–13 (3rd Test)

At Centurion Park, Pretoria, on 22, 23, 24 February, 2013.
Toss: South Africa.   Result: SOUTH AFRICA WON BY AN INNINGS AND 18 RUNS.
Debuts: South Africa – K. J. Abbott. Pakistan – Ehsan Adil.
Man of the Match: K. J. Abbott. Man of the Series: A. B. de Villiers.

After the tension of Cape Town it was business as usual as South Africa completed a 3–0 sweep on the third afternoon. Smith fell to 19-year-old Ehsan Adil's third ball in Tests, but Amla was in glorious touch from the start. He cruised into the nineties before an outside edge gave left-armer Rahat Ali the first of his six wickets. De Villiers was more circumspect, batting for 5½ hours; he was even the junior partner in a seventh-wicket stand of 129 with Philander, whose 74 was a Test-best. When Pakistan batted, Kyle Abbott – a late replacement for Kallis (thigh strain) – had Mohammad Hafeez caught in the gully with his sixth ball, and never looked back on the way to South Africa's best debut figures apart from 8 for 64 by Lance Klusener (now Abbott's coach) at Calcutta in 1996–97. There were five more catches in the cordon, plus an lbw to remove Younis Khan, last out for an obdurate 33. Sensing another quick victory, Smith enforced the follow-on. Steyn bowled a tentative Hafeez off the inside edge first ball, then next morning had Younis Khan caught at first slip, and ran out Azhar Ali with a rocket-like throw from fine leg. Kleinveldt nipped out Misbah-ul-Haq and Asad Shafiq to leave the innings broken-backed at 114 for six shortly after lunch. Sarfraz Ahmed and Saeed Ajmal pushed the match beyond tea with some carefree hitting, before Steyn ended the fun, giving him 33 wickets at 12.36 in five home Tests since January.

South Africa

*G. C. Smith c Younis Khan b Ehsan Adil		5
A. N. Petersen lbw b Rahat Ali		10
H. M. Amla c Sarfraz Ahmed b Rahat Ali		92
F. du Plessis c Sarfraz Ahmed b Ehsan Adil		29
†A. B. de Villiers c Asad Shafiq b Rahat Ali		121
D. Elgar lbw b Rahat Ali		7
R. J. Peterson run out		28
V. D. Philander c Mohammad Hafeez b Younis Khan		74
K. J. Abbott b Rahat Ali		13
R. K. Kleinveldt c Saeed Ajmal b Rahat Ali		0
D. W. Steyn not out		5
B 1, l-b 6, w 6, n-b 12		25
(103.2 overs)		409

1/13 (2) 2/38 (1) 3/107 (4) 4/186 (3) 5/196 (6)
6/248 (7) 7/377 (8) 8/394 (5) 9/402 (10) 10/409 (9)

Mohammad Irfan 21.5–3–80–0; Rahat Ali 27.2–1–127–6; Ehsan Adil 12.1–2–54–2; Saeed Ajmal 29–6–76–0; Younis Khan 6–0–28–1; Mohammad Hafeez 5–0–24–0; Azhar Ali 2–0–13–0.

Pakistan

Mohammad Hafeez c Elgar b Abbott		18	– b Steyn	0
Imran Farhat lbw b Philander		30	– (4) c de Villiers b Abbott	43
Azhar Ali b Philander		6	– (2) run out	27
Younis Khan lbw b Abbott		33	– (3) c Smith b Steyn	11
*Misbah-ul-Haq c Petersen b Abbott		10	– c de Villiers b Kleinveldt	5
Asad Shafiq lbw b Steyn		6	– c Philander b Kleinveldt	6
†Sarfraz Ahmed c Smith b Abbott		17	– c Elgar b Steyn	40
Saeed Ajmal c Smith b Abbott		0	– lbw b Steyn	31
Ehsan Adil c du Plessis b Abbott		9	– c Kleinveldt b Abbott	12
Mohammad Irfan c Elgar b Abbott		0	– (11) not out	6
Rahat Ali not out		0	– (10) lbw b Peterson	22
L-b 17, w 8, n-b 2		27	B 9, l-b 10, w 11, n-b 2	32
(46.4 overs)		156	(78 overs)	235

1/46 (2) 2/56 (1) 3/56 (3) 4/75 (5) 5/95 (6) 6/132 (7)   1/0 (1) 2/39 (3) 3/93 (2) 4/107 (4) 5/107 (5)
7/132 (8) 8/149 (9) 9/149 (10) 10/156 (4)   6/114 (6) 7/183 (8) 8/202 (7) 9/202 (9) 10/235 (10)

Steyn 12–5–25–1; Philander 10–2–30–2; Kleinveldt 12–1–49–0; Abbott 11.4–4–29–7; Peterson 1–0–6–0. *Second Innings*—Steyn 23–5–80–4; Philander 15–4–32–0; Abbott 17–7–39–2; Kleinveldt 13–2–33–2; Peterson 10–2–32–1.

Umpires: B. F. Bowden *(New Zealand)* (74) and S. J. Davis *(Australia)* (44).
Third umpire: B. N. J. Oxenford *(Australia)*. Referee: J. J. Crowe *(New Zealand)* (60).

Close of play: First day, South Africa 334–6 (de Villiers 98, Philander 45); Second day, Pakistan 14–1 (Azhar Ali 5, Younis Khan 8).

INDIA v AUSTRALIA 2012–13 (1st Test)

At M. A. Chidambaram Stadium, Chepauk, Chennai, on 22, 23, 24, 25, 26 February, 2013.
Toss: Australia.　　Result: INDIA WON BY EIGHT WICKETS.
Debuts: India – Bhuvneshwar Kumar. Australia – M. C. Henriques.
Man of the Match: M. S. Dhoni.

A huge crowd thronged the ground on the second day, in anticipation of another hundred from Tendulkar, who had 71 overnight. They missed that – he added only ten – but, after Kohli reached 107, they were treated to a thumping innings from Dhoni, whose 224 was the third-highest in Tests by a wicketkeeper, behind Andy Flower's 232 not out (at Nagpur in 2000–01) and 230 by Kumar Sangakkara the following season at Lahore. Dhoni reached his double-century in 231 balls, in the innings that defined the series: the solid cricket Australia had played on the first two days vanished, never to return. Lyon's 47 overs cost 215, the third-most conceded in any Test innings in India. Australia trailed by nearly 200, despite having reached 380. Clarke, lucky to survive after inside-edging to short leg on 39 (India had declined to use DRS), made 130, adding 151 for the sixth wicket with the impressive Moises Henriques, only the second Test cricketer born in Portugal, after South Africa's Dick Westcott, who had died the previous month. Henriques finally fell sweeping, one of a Test-best seven wickets for Ashwin. It all looked much harder when Australia batted again, with India's three spinners posing different problems. Hughes received a snorter from Jadeja, while Clarke was pinned by a near-shooter from Ashwin. Henriques became the fifth Australian to make twin half-centuries on debut, but Ashwin took his match bag to 12. Tendulkar hurried India towards victory by hitting his first two balls, from Lyon, for six.

Australia

E. J. M. Cowan st Dhoni b Ashwin	29	– lbw b Ashwin	32
D. A. Warner lbw b Ashwin	59	– (3) lbw b Harbhajan Singh	23
P. J. Hughes b Ashwin	6	– (4) c Sehwag b Jadeja	0
S. R. Watson lbw b Ashwin	28	– (2) c Sehwag b Ashwin	17
*M. J. Clarke c Bhuvneshwar Kumar b Jadeja	130	– lbw b Ashwin	31
†M. S. Wade lbw b Ashwin	12	– b Harbhajan Singh	8
M. C. Henriques lbw b Ashwin	68	– not out	81
M. A. Starc b Jadeja	3	– (10) c Tendulkar b Ashwin	8
P. M. Siddle c Sehwag b Harbhajan Singh	19	– (8) b Jadeja	2
J. L. Pattinson not out	15	– (9) c Sehwag b Ashwin	11
N. M. Lyon c Kohli b Ashwin	3	– c Vijay b Jadeja	11
B 1, l-b 7	8	B 15, l-b 2	17
(133 overs)	380	(93 overs)	241

1/64 (1) 2/72 (3) 3/126 (4) 4/131 (2) 5/153 (6)　　1/34 (2) 2/64 (1) 3/65 (4) 4/101 (3) 5/121 (6)
6/304 (7) 7/307 (8) 8/361 (5) 9/364 (9) 10/380 (11)　6/131 (5) 7/137 (8) 8/161 (9) 9/175 (10) 10/241 (11)

Bhuvneshwar Kumar 13–1–52–0; Sharma 17–3–59–0; Harbhajan Singh 25–2–87–1; Ashwin 42–12–103–7; Jadeja 36–10–71–2. *Second Innings*—Ashwin 32–6–95–5; Harbhajan Singh 27–6–55–2; Jadeja 31–8–72–3; Sharma 3–1–2–0.

India

M. Vijay b Pattinson	10	– c Henriques b Pattinson	6
V. Sehwag b Pattinson	2	– c Clarke b Lyon	19
C. A. Pujara b Pattinson	44	– not out	8
S. R. Tendulkar b Lyon	81	– not out	13
V. Kohli c Starc b Lyon	107		
*†M. S. Dhoni c Wade b Pattinson	224		
R. A. Jadeja b Pattinson	16		
R. Ashwin b Lyon	3		
Harbhajan Singh b Henriques	11		
Bhuvneshwar Kumar c Clarke b Siddle	38		
I. Sharma not out	4		
B 14, l-b 14, w 4	32	B 4	4
(154.3 overs)	572	(2 wkts, 11.3 overs)	50

1/11 (1) 2/12 (2) 3/105 (3) 4/196 (4) 5/324 (5)
6/365 (7) 7/372 (8) 8/406 (9) 9/546 (6) 10/572 (10)　　1/16 (1) 2/36 (2)

Starc 25–3–75–0; Pattinson 30–6–96–5; Siddle 24.3–5–66–1; Lyon 47–1–215–3; Henriques 17–4–48–1; Clarke 8–2–25–0; Warner 3–0–19–0. *Second Innings*—Pattinson 3–1–13–1; Lyon 5.3–0–29–1; Siddle 3–2–4–0.

Umpires: H. D. P. K. Dharmasena *(Sri Lanka)* (14) and M. Erasmus *(South Africa)* (16).
Third umpire: V. A. Kulkarni *(India)*. Referee: B. C. Broad *(England)* (57).

Close of play: First day, Australia 316–7 (Clarke 103, Siddle 1); Second day, India 182–3 (Tendulkar 71, Kohli 50); Third day, India 515–8 (Dhoni 206, Bhuvneshwar Kumar 16); Fourth day, Australia 232–9 (Henriques 75, Lyon 8).

INDIA v AUSTRALIA 2012–13 (2nd Test)

At Rajiv Gandhi International Stadium, Uppal, Hyderabad, on 2, 3, 4, 5 March, 2013.
Toss: Australia.   Result: INDIA WON BY AN INNINGS AND 135 RUNS.
Debuts: Australia – G. J. Maxwell.
Man of the Match: C. A. Pujara.

Australia's tenth-heaviest defeat could be summed up by a single statistic: two Indians scored more in one partnership than 11 Australians managed in the entire game. Vijay and Pujara's stand of 370 was a masterclass in batting in Indian conditions. They came together when Sehwag was caught behind, his ninth successive innings without a fifty; he was dropped after this, his 104th Test, seemingly for good. Australia didn't manage another wicket for over seven hours, the batsmen remorselessly increasing the tempo as the bowlers wilted on the second day. Vijay hit 23 fours and two sixes from 361 balls, Pujara 30 fours and a six from 341 in his fourth century – second double – in 11 Tests. Once they were finally parted Australia did well to limit the damage to 503; off-spinner Maxwell took four wickets on debut, and slow left-armer Doherty three, although neither looked particularly menacing. That still meant a deficit of 268 after only Clarke and Wade, who added 145, had lasted for long against the spinners, once the busy Bhuvneshwar Kumar took three early wickets. Cowan and Warner started confidently when Australia batted again – but from 56 for none it all fell apart, only two more batsmen reaching double figures as all ten wickets crashed for 75. Clarke became the first captain to lose by an innings after declaring in the first – admittedly with nine down, in an attempt to nab a wicket before the first-day close. That didn't work – and nor did much else for Australia.

Australia

D. A. Warner b Bhuvneshwar Kumar		6 – (2) b Ashwin		26
E. J. M. Cowan lbw b Bhuvneshwar Kumar		4 – (1) c Sehwag b Jadeja		44
P. J. Hughes c Dhoni b Ashwin	19	– b Ashwin		0
S. R. Watson lbw b Bhuvneshwar Kumar	23	– c Dhoni b Sharma		9
*M. J. Clarke b Jadeja	91	– b Jadeja		16
†M. S. Wade c Bhuvneshwar Kumar b Harbhajan Singh	62	– c Sehwag b Ashwin		10
M. C. Henriques b Jadeja	5	– run out		0
G. J. Maxwell c Dhoni b Jadeja	13	– lbw b Ashwin		8
P. M. Siddle lbw b Harbhajan Singh	0	– c Kohli b Jadeja		4
J. L. Pattinson not out	1	– lbw b Ashwin		0
X. J. Doherty not out	0	– not out		1
B 10, l-b 3	13	B 7, l-b 6		13
(9 wkts dec, 85 overs)	237	(67 overs)		131

1/10 (1) 2/15 (2) 3/57 (4) 4/63 (3) 5/208 (6)   1/56 (2) 2/56 (3) 3/75 (4) 4/108 (5) 5/111 (1)
6/217 (7) 7/233 (8) 8/236 (9) 9/236 (5)   6/111 (7) 7/123 (8) 8/130 (9) 9/130 (6) 10/131 (10)

Bhuvneshwar Kumar 15–2–53–3; Sharma 17–5–45–0; Ashwin 15–6–41–1; Harbhajan Singh 22–2–52–2; Jadeja 16–4–33–3. *Second Innings*—Bhuvneshwar Kumar 6–4–7–0; Ashwin 28–12–63–5; Harbhajan Singh 10–7–10–0; Jadeja 18–8–33–3; Sharma 5–2–5–1.

India

M. Vijay c Cowan b Maxwell	167
V. Sehwag c Wade b Siddle	6
C. A. Pujara c Doherty b Pattinson	204
S. R. Tendulkar c Wade b Pattinson	7
V. Kohli c Cowan b Maxwell	34
*†M. S. Dhoni c Doherty b Maxwell	44
R. A. Jadeja c and b Maxwell	10
R. Ashwin c Hughes b Doherty	1
Harbhajan Singh c Maxwell b Doherty	0
Bhuvneshwar Kumar st Wade b Doherty	10
I. Sharma not out	2
B 1, l-b 13, w 4	18
(154.1 overs)	503

1/17 (2) 2/387 (1) 3/393 (3) 4/404 (4) 5/460 (6) 6/484 (7)
7/485 (8) 8/489 (9) 9/491 (5) 10/503 (10)

Pattinson 29–11–80–2; Siddle 31–6–92–1; Henriques 21–7–45–0; Doherty 46.1–15–131–3; Maxwell 26–2–127–4; Warner 1–0–14–0.

Umpires: H. D. P. K. Dharmasena *(Sri Lanka)* (15) and M. Erasmus *(South Africa)* (17).
Third umpire: S. Ravi *(India)*. Referee: B. C. Broad *(England)* (58).

Close of play: First day, India 5–0 (Vijay 0, Sehwag 4); Second day, India 311–1 (Vijay 129, Pujara 162); Third day, Australia 74–2 (Cowan 26, Watson 9).

INDIA v AUSTRALIA 2012–13 (3rd Test)

At Punjab C. A. Stadium, Mohali, Chandigarh, on 14 (*no play*), 15, 16, 17, 18 March, 2013.
Toss: Australia. Result: INDIA WON BY SIX WICKETS.
Debuts: India – S. Dhawan.
Man of the Match: S. Dhawan.

India regained the Border–Gavaskar Trophy with another emphatic win, set up by a whirlwind innings from Sehwag's replacement, left-hander Shikhar Dhawan, who blitzed the fastest Test-debut century in 85 balls. He and Vijay, who made his third Test hundred – all against Australia – added 289, all bar six of them in 58 overs on the third day. These fireworks came after Australia had seemingly done well to reach 408. Cowan, who batted for almost five hours, added 139 with Warner, but Clarke became only the second Australian (after Ricky Ponting at Chennai in 2000–01) to be stumped first ball in a Test. Smith moved his feet well for 92, and finally Starc hit out before becoming the 21st Australian to be out for 99 in a Test (only Shane Warne of the others never made a hundred). Siddle limited India's advantage to 91, but it felt like more after Dhawan's onslaught – and even more at 143 for eight on the final day. Australia's tail stretched that by 80, and India needed 133 in little over a session. Clarke, reasoning that only a win would keep the series alive, rushed through 21 overs in the penultimate hour, but with 17 needed off four overs, Dhoni biffed three successive fours off Starc. The match was overshadowed by "homeworkgate": four Australians, including vice-captain Watson, were suspended after failing to complete a task set by the management. Haddin was flown in to replace Wade, who sprained his ankle playing basketball on a day off.

Australia

E. J. M. Cowan c Kohli b Ashwin	86	– (2) lbw b Bhuvneshwar Kumar		8
D. A. Warner c Dhoni b Jadeja	71	– (1) c Dhoni b Bhuvneshwar Kumar		2
*M. J. Clarke st Dhoni b Jadeja	0	– (6) c Pujara b Jadeja		18
P. J. Hughes c Dhoni b Ojha	2	– (3) lbw b Ashwin		69
S. P. D. Smith st Dhoni b Ojha	92	– (4) b Bhuvneshwar Kumar		5
†B. J. Haddin b Sharma	21	– (7) lbw b Ashwin		30
M. C. Henriques b Sharma	0	– (8) c and b Jadeja		2
P. M. Siddle lbw b Jadeja	0	– (9) b Ojha		13
M. A. Starc c Dhoni b Sharma	99	– (10) c Ashwin b Jadeja		35
N. M. Lyon not out	9	– (5) c Dhoni b Ojha		18
X. J. Doherty lbw b Ashwin	5	– not out		18
B 8, l-b 12, n-b 3	23	L-b 3, w 1, n-b 1		5
(141.5 overs)	408	(89.2 overs)		223

1/139 (2) 2/139 (3) 3/151 (4) 4/198 (1) 5/244 (6) 1/2 (1) 2/35 (2) 3/55 (4) 4/89 (5) 5/119 (6)
6/244 (7) 7/251 (8) 8/348 (5) 9/399 (9) 10/408 (11) 6/123 (3) 7/126 (8) 8/143 (9) 9/179 (7) 10/223 (10)

Bhuvneshwar Kumar 9–0–44–0; Sharma 30–8–72–3; Ashwin 43.5–9–97–2; Ojha 28–5–98–2; Jadeja 31–7–77–3. *Second Innings*—Bhuvneshwar Kumar 10–1–31–3; Sharma 9–1–34–0; Ashwin 31–9–72–2; Jadeja 16.2–6–35–3; Ojha 21–6–46–2; Tendulkar 2–0–2–0.

India

M. Vijay lbw b Starc	153	– st Haddin b Doherty		26
S. Dhawan c Cowan b Lyon	187			
C. A. Pujara lbw b Siddle	1	– (2) lbw b Lyon		28
S. R. Tendulkar c Cowan b Smith	37	– run out		21
V. Kohli not out	67	– (3) c Hughes b Siddle		34
*†M. S. Dhoni lbw b Starc	4	– (5) not out		18
R. A. Jadeja c Haddin b Siddle	8	– (6) not out		8
R. Ashwin c Haddin b Siddle	4			
Bhuvneshwar Kumar c Haddin b Henriques	18			
I. Sharma c Haddin b Siddle	0			
P. P. Ojha b Siddle	1			
B 5, l-b 13, n-b 1	19	W 1		1
(132.1 overs)	499	(4 wkts, 33.3 overs)		136

1/289 (2) 2/292 (3) 3/384 (4) 4/412 (1) 5/416 (6)
6/427 (7) 7/431 (8) 8/492 (9) 9/493 (10) 10/499 (11) 1/42 (1) 2/70 (2) 3/103 (3) 4/116 (4)

Starc 23–5–74–2; Siddle 29.1–9–71–5; Henriques 15–1–62–1; Lyon 31–4–124–1; Doherty 24–8–87–0; Smith 10–0–63–1. *Second Innings*—Starc 10.3–1–51–0; Siddle 11–2–34–1; Lyon 5–0–27–1; Doherty 7–2–24–1.

Umpires: Aleem Dar *(Pakistan)* (79) and R. A. Kettleborough *(England)* (13).
Third umpire: S. Asnani *(India)*. Referee: R. S. Madugalle *(Sri Lanka)* (140).

Close of play: First day, no play; Second day, Australia 273–7 (Smith 58, Starc 20); Third day, India 283–0 (Vijay 83, Dhawan 185); Fourth day, Australia 75–3 (Hughes 53, Lyon 4).

INDIA v AUSTRALIA 2012–13 (4th Test)

At Feroz Shah Kotla, Delhi, on 22, 23, 24 March, 2013.
Toss: Australia.　　　Result: INDIA WON BY SIX WICKETS.
Debuts: India – A. M. Rahane.
Man of the Match: R. A. Jadeja. Man of the Series: R. Ashwin.

India completed an unprecedented 4–0 clean sweep – reversing the scoreline of their 2011–12 series in Australia – with a three-day victory. Australia's batsmen struggled on a challenging pitch, although this time they were at least in touch on first innings: it was their collapse for 164 in the second that cost them. Spin did most of the damage: Ashwin and Jadeja took seven wickets each, and Lyon nine. Clarke rested a back injury, so Australia were captained for the first time by Watson, who had been suspended for the previous Test. He won the toss, but failed twice with the bat. Australia dipped to 136 for seven before being rescued by Siddle and Pattinson, then India's batting also misfired after an opening stand of 108 between Vijay and Pujara, promoted to open as Dhawan had been injured in the field after his rapid hundred in the previous Test (Ajinkya Rahane made his debut down the order). But then Australia failed again, Jadeja taking his first Test five-for: once again the top-scorer was Siddle, who became the first No. 9 to make two half-centuries in a Test. Needing only 155, India soon lost Vijay, bowled by Maxwell, the first Australian since Percy Hornibrook in 1928–29 to open the batting and bowling in the same Test. Lyon shared the new ball, only the third time Australia had opened the bowling with two spinners. It didn't make much difference: Pujara and Kohli took India close, and Dhoni completed the whitewash with a boundary.

Australia

E. J. M. Cowan b Ashwin	38	– (3) lbw b Jadeja	24
D. A. Warner c Kohli b Sharma	0	– (1) lbw b Jadeja	8
P. J. Hughes b Sharma	45	– (4) lbw b Ashwin	6
*S. R. Watson st Dhoni b Jadeja	17	– (5) b Ojha	5
S. P. D. Smith c Rahane b Ashwin	46	– (6) b Jadeja	18
†M. S. Wade c Vijay b Ashwin	2	– (7) c Dhoni b Ojha	19
G. J. Maxwell c Sharma b Jadeja	10	– (2) b Jadeja	8
M. G. Johnson b Ashwin	3	– b Jadeja	0
P. M. Siddle b Ashwin	51	– st Dhoni b Ashwin	50
J. L. Pattinson c Kohli b Ojha	30	– b Sharma	11
N. M. Lyon not out	8	– not out	5
B 5, l-b 7	12	B 8, l-b 2	10
(112.1 overs)	262	(46.3 overs)	164

1/4 (2) 2/71 (3) 3/106 (1) 4/115 (4) 5/117 (6)　　　1/15 (2) 2/20 (1) 3/41 (4) 4/51 (5) 5/53 (3)
6/129 (7) 7/136 (8) 8/189 (5) 9/243 (9) 10/262 (10)　　6/94 (6) 7/94 (8) 8/122 (7) 9/157 (10) 10/164 (9)

Bhuvneshwar Kumar 9–1–43–0; Sharma 14–3–35–2; Ashwin 34–18–57–5; Ojha 26.1–6–75–1; Jadeja 29–8–40–2. *Second Innings*—Bhuvneshwar Kumar 2–0–9–0; Ashwin 15.3–2–55–2; Jadeja 16–2–58–5; Ojha 11–2–19–2; Sharma 2–0–13–1.

India

M. Vijay c Wade b Siddle	57	– b Maxwell	11
C. A. Pujara b Lyon	52	– not out	82
V. Kohli lbw b Lyon	1	– lbw b Lyon	41
S. R. Tendulkar lbw b Lyon	32	– lbw b Lyon	1
A. M. Rahane c Smith b Lyon	7	– c Lyon b Maxwell	1
*†M. S. Dhoni c Watson b Pattinson	24	– not out	12
R. A. Jadeja lbw b Maxwell	43		
R. Ashwin lbw b Lyon	12		
Bhuvneshwar Kumar not out	14		
I. Sharma b Lyon	0		
P. P. Ojha lbw b Lyon	0		
B 12, l-b 18	30	B 9, l-b 1	10
(70.2 overs)	272	(4 wkts, 31.2 overs)	158

1/108 (2) 2/114 (3) 3/148 (1) 4/165 (5) 5/180 (4)
6/210 (6) 7/254 (7) 8/266 (8) 9/272 (10) 10/272 (11)　　1/19 (1) 2/123 (3) 3/127 (4) 4/128 (5)

Johnson 17–3–44–0; Pattinson 14–1–54–1; Siddle 12–3–38–1; Lyon 23.2–4–94–7; Maxwell 4–0–12–1. *Second Innings*—Lyon 15.2–0–71–2; Maxwell 11–0–54–2; Johnson 2–0–16–0; Pattinson 3–0–7–0.

Umpires: Aleem Dar *(Pakistan)* (80) and R. A. Kettleborough *(England)* (14).
Third umpire: S. Ravi *(India)*. Referee: R. S. Madugalle *(Sri Lanka)* (141).

Close of play: First day, Australia 231–8 (Siddle 47, Pattinson 11); Second day, India 266–8 (Bhuvneshwar Kumar 10).

NEW ZEALAND v ENGLAND 2012–13 (1st Test)

At University Oval, Dunedin, on 6 (*no play*), 7, 8, 9, 10 March, 2013.
Toss: New Zealand.   Result: MATCH DRAWN.
Debuts: New Zealand – B. P. Martin, H. D. Rutherford.
Man of the Match: no award.

New Zealand secured a draw against the side now ranked No. 2 in the world – and could easily have gone one up, as they had on England's previous visit in 2007–08, despite a first-day washout. Put in, England were soon 18 for three, and although Trott lasted nearly three hours for 45 a total of 164 was distinctly underwhelming. Wagner's inswinger to undo Pietersen first ball was the delivery of the match, but his other three wickets were free gifts. The debutant slow left-armer Bruce Martin was another recipient of England's largesse: his four wickets included three heaves across the line and Prior's miscued cut. By the end of the second day New Zealand's openers had made 131, and took their stand to 158 next morning. Left-hander Hamish Rutherford cut and drove powerfully, storming to a debut 171, a rather different start to his father, the former national skipper Ken Rutherford, who collected a first-up pair against West Indies in 1984–85. McCullum cracked three sixes in 59 balls as the lead reached 293, to widespread disbelief. England's resolve stiffened: the openers survived almost to the end of the fourth day, Cook scoring his 24th Test century and Compton his first, "the biggest relief of my life". They were still behind going into the last day, but the pitch was playing few tricks: nightwatchman Finn survived 4¾ hours for his maiden first-class fifty, at one stage facing 49 successive dot-balls. Bell and Prior occupied the last 16 overs to ensure the draw.

England

*A. N. Cook c Rutherford b Wagner	10	– c Watling b Boult	116
N. R. D. Compton b Southee	0	– lbw b Wagner	117
I. J. L. Trott c Boult b Martin	45	– (4) c and b Wagner	52
K. P. Pietersen lbw b Wagner	0	– (5) c Watling b Wagner	12
I. R. Bell c Rutherford b Wagner	24	– (6) not out	26
J. E. Root c Brownlie b Boult	4	– (7) run out	0
†M. J. Prior c Williamson b Martin	23	– (8) not out	23
S. C. J. Broad c Brownlie b Martin	10		
S. T. Finn c Rutherford b Wagner	20	– (3) lbw b Martin	56
J. M. Anderson c Wagner b Martin	23		
M. S. Panesar not out	1		
B 4, l-b 1, w 2	7	B 6, l-b 11, w 1, n-b 1	19
(55 overs)	167	(6 wkts, 170 overs)	421

1/5 (2) 2/18 (1) 3/18 (4) 4/64 (5) 5/71 (6) 6/108 (7)   1/231 (1) 2/265 (2) 3/355 (4) 4/367 (5)
7/109 (3) 8/119 (8) 9/166 (9) 10/167 (10)   5/386 (3) 6/390 (7)

Southee 15–3–45–1; Boult 15–4–32–1; Wagner 11–2–42–4; Martin 14–4–43–4. *Second Innings*—Southee 36–8–94–0; Boult 35–12–49–1; Wagner 43–9–141–3; Martin 44–13–90–1; Williamson 12–3–30–0.

New Zealand

P. G. Fulton c Prior b Anderson	55
H. D. Rutherford c sub (C. R. Woakes) b Anderson	171
K. S. Williamson b Panesar	24
L. R. P. L. Taylor c Trott b Anderson	31
D. G. Brownlie b Anderson	27
*B. B. McCullum c Anderson b Broad	74
†B-J. Watling b Broad	0
T. G. Southee b Broad	25
B. P. Martin c Prior b Finn	41
N. Wagner not out	4
L-b 8	8
(9 wkts dec, 116.4 overs)	460

1/158 (1) 2/249 (3) 3/267 (2) 4/310 (4) 5/321 (5)
6/326 (7) 7/370 (8) 8/447 (6) 9/460 (9)

T. A. Boult did not bat.

Anderson 33–2–137–4; Finn 26.4–3–102–1; Broad 28–3–118–3; Panesar 22–2–83–1; Trott 2–0–4–0; Root 5–1–8–0.

Umpires: Asad Rauf *(Pakistan)* (48) and P. R. Reiffel *(Australia)* (3).
Third umpire: R. J. Tucker *(Australia)*. Referee: R. S. Mahanama *(Sri Lanka)* (41).

Close of play: First day, no play; Second day, New Zealand 131–0 (Fulton 46, Rutherford 77); Third day, New Zealand 402–7 (McCullum 44, Martin 17); Fourth day, England 234–1 (Compton 102, Finn 0).

NEW ZEALAND v ENGLAND 2012–13 (2nd Test)

At Basin Reserve, Wellington, on 14, 15, 16, 17, 18 (*no play*) March, 2013.
Toss: New Zealand.   Result: MATCH DRAWN.
Debuts: none.
Man of the Match: no award.

The weather which blanked the first day of the First Test now returned to wash out the last day of this one. It removed any prospect of an England victory, although New Zealand's batsmen – at 162 for two after following on – had already gone some way towards saving their side before Cyclone Sandra finished the job. McCullum probably erred by sending England in: his bowlers had spent 180 overs in the field the previous weekend, and were now condemned to another 147. Compton – still reassuringly stodgy but playing with more conviction off the front foot – made his second successive hundred to set up England's big total, along with Trott's ninth Test century. Pietersen made a workmanlike 73 despite clearly being restricted by a knee problem (he returned home after this match). Finally Prior, carving through the off side like a chef mutilating the Sunday roast with a chainsaw, smote 82. Broad picked up the gauntlet superbly, steaming in for six wickets. New Zealand were soon 89 for five, and although McCullum and Watling put on exactly 100, England were able to enforce the follow-on for the first time in an overseas Test since Durban in 1999–2000. There was brief hope when Panesar snared Rutherford in the leg trap, but once Williamson and Taylor (who had returned to the side for this series after missing the preceding tour of South Africa following his removal as captain) had seen off 31 overs the weather set in. In all, 145 overs were lost.

England

*A. N. Cook	c Fulton b Wagner	17
N. R. D. Compton	c Taylor b Martin	100
I. J. L. Trott	c Watling b Boult	121
K. P. Pietersen	c Fulton b Martin	73
I. R. Bell	c Fulton b Martin	11
J. E. Root	c Watling b Martin	10
†M. J. Prior	c Wagner b Williamson	82
S. C. J. Broad	c Watling b Boult	6
S. T. Finn	c McCullum b Wagner	24
J. M. Anderson	not out	8
M. S. Panesar	c Taylor b Williamson	0
	L-b 3, w 7, n-b 3	13
	(146.5 overs)	465

1/26 (1) 2/236 (2) 3/267 (3) 4/302 (5) 5/325 (6)
6/366 (4) 7/374 (8) 8/457 (9) 9/465 (7) 10/465 (11)

Southee 32–9–77–0; Boult 30–4–117–2; Wagner 33–5–122–2; Martin 48–11–130–4; Williamson 3.5–0–16–2.

New Zealand

P. G. Fulton	c Cook b Anderson	1	– c Cook b Anderson	45
H. D. Rutherford	c Cook b Broad	23	– c Bell b Panesar	15
K. S. Williamson	c and b Broad	42	– not out	55
L. R. P. L. Taylor	b Broad	0	– not out	41
D. G. Brownlie	lbw b Anderson	18		
*B. B. McCullum	c Trott b Finn	69		
†B-J. Watling	c Prior b Broad	60		
T. G. Southee	c Broad b Finn	3		
B. P. Martin	not out	21		
N. Wagner	c Prior b Broad	0		
T. A. Boult	c Prior b Broad	2		
	L-b 10, w 2, n-b 3	15	L-b 1, w 5	6
	(89.2 overs)	254	(2 wkts, 68 overs)	162

1/6 (1) 2/48 (2) 3/48 (4) 4/85 (3) 5/89 (5) 6/189 (6)
7/197 (8) 8/239 (7) 9/252 (10) 10/254 (11)   1/25 (2) 2/81 (1)

Anderson 25–6–68–2; Finn 20–2–72–2; Broad 17.2–2–51–6; Panesar 26–11–47–0; Root 1–0–6–0. *Second Innings*—Anderson 12–4–27–1; Broad 14–6–32–0; Finn 11–2–36–0; Panesar 26–12–44–1; Trott 3–0–10–0; Root 2–0–12–0.

Umpires: Asad Rauf *(Pakistan)* (49) and R. J. Tucker *(Australia)* (24).
Third umpire: P. R. Reiffel *(Australia)*. Referee: R. S. Mahanama *(Sri Lanka)* (42).

Close of play: First day, England 267–2 (Trott 121, Pietersen 18); Second day, New Zealand 66–3 (Williamson 32, Brownlie 8); Third day, New Zealand 77–1 (Fulton 41, Williamson 16); Fourth day, New Zealand 162–2 (Williamson 55, Taylor 41).

NEW ZEALAND v ENGLAND 2012–13 (3rd Test)

At Eden Park, Auckland, on 22, 23, 24, 25, 26 March, 2013.
Toss: England.　　　Result: MATCH DRAWN.
Debuts: none.
Man of the Match: no award.

In the end, the series boiled down to the last over, to be faced – initially at least – by Panesar, England's often hapless No. 11. It was the 143rd over, but Boult, who had taken six wickets in the first innings, skipped in. Panesar clumped a single third ball, virtually sealing the draw: his partner had been entrenched for more than 4½ hours. Prior did have one slice of outrageous good fortune: at 28, a Wagner bouncer hit bat-handle and helmet before looping back into middle stump, without dislodging the bails. Prior had starred in the first innings, too, with 73 of England's inadequate 204. Earlier, the lanky Fulton had become, at 34, the second-oldest New Zealander to score a maiden hundred, after Zin Harris (35 in 1961–62). Having finally reached three figures, in his 13th Test, Fulton promptly made another, joining Glenn Turner, Geoff Howarth and Andrew Jones as the only Kiwis to make two in the same match. Fulton put on 181 with Williamson in the first innings then, with his side eight for three after waiving the follow-on, 117 with McCullum. England were left around a day and a half to survive. Four wickets fell on the fourth evening, after which it was actually a superb effort to survive. Bell ground out 75 in almost six hours, then Broad did not score a run until a record 102 minutes into his 137-minute stay. Still, Williamson's two late strikes looked to have sunk England, only for Prior and Panesar to hold firm.

New Zealand

P. G. Fulton c Prior b Finn	136	– c Root b Finn	110
H. D. Rutherford c Cook b Finn	37	– c Bell b Broad	0
K. S. Williamson c Prior b Anderson	91	– b Anderson	1
L. R. P. L. Taylor c and b Panesar	19	– lbw b Broad	3
D. G. Brownlie c Compton b Anderson	36	– c Bell b Panesar	28
*B. B. McCullum c Prior b Trott	38	– not out	67
†B-J. Watling c Prior b Finn	21	– c Compton b Panesar	18
T. G. Southee c Prior b Finn	44		
B. P. Martin c Trott b Finn	10		
N. Wagner not out	2		
T. A. Boult c Compton b Finn	0		
B 4, l-b 4, n-b 1	9	B 4, l-b 10	14
(152.3 overs)	443	(6 wkts dec, 57.2 overs)	241

1/79 (2) 2/260 (3) 3/289 (4) 4/297 (1) 5/365 (6)
6/373 (5) 7/424 (8) 8/436 (9) 9/443 (7) 10/443 (11)　　　1/4 (2) 2/5 (3) 3/8 (4) 4/82 (5) 5/199 (1) 6/241 (7)

Anderson 30–8–79–2; Broad 30–6–94–0; Finn 37.3–8–125–6; Panesar 47–17–123–1; Trott 6–3–9–1; Root 2–1–5–0. *Second Innings*—Anderson 17–6–59–1; Broad 17–5–54–2; Finn 13–1–57–1; Panesar 9.2–4–53–2; Trott 1–0–4–0.

England

*A. N. Cook c Watling b Boult	4	– c Brownlie b Williamson	43
N. R. D. Compton lbw b Southee	13	– c Watling b Southee	2
I. J. L. Trott lbw b Boult	27	– c Watling b Wagner	37
I. R. Bell lbw b Southee	17	– c Southee b Wagner	75
J. E. Root b Southee	45	– (6) lbw b Boult	29
J. M. Bairstow lbw b Boult	3	– (7) c Taylor b Southee	6
†M. J. Prior c Rutherford b Wagner	73	– (8) not out	110
S. C. J. Broad c Rutherford b Boult	16	– (9) c Taylor b Williamson	6
S. T. Finn c Taylor b Boult	0	– (5) c Southee b Williamson	0
J. M. Anderson c Watling b Boult	4	– c Taylor b Williamson	0
M. S. Panesar not out	0	– not out	2
W 2	2	L-b 4, n-b 1	5
(89.2 overs)	204	(9 wkts, 143 overs)	315

1/8 (1) 2/44 (3) 3/61 (2) 4/65 (4) 5/72 (6) 6/173 (7)
7/200 (8) 8/200 (9) 9/204 (10) 10/204 (5)　　　1/2 (2) 2/60 (3) 3/90 (1) 4/90 (5) 5/150 (6)
6/159 (7) 7/237 (4) 8/304 (9) 9/304 (10)

Boult 25–9–68–6; Southee 23.2–9–44–3; Wagner 15–3–36–1; Martin 26–10–56–0. *Second Innings*—Boult 29–13–55–1; Southee 30–6–77–2; Martin 39–18–74–0; Wagner 25–8–61–2; Williamson 20–8–44–4.

Umpires: P. R. Reiffel *(Australia)* (4) and R. J. Tucker *(Australia)* (25).
Third umpire: S. J. Davis *(Australia)*. Referee: R. S. Mahanama *(Sri Lanka)* (43).

Close of play: First day, New Zealand 250–1 (Fulton 124, Williamson 83); Second day, England 50–2 (Compton 12, Bell 6); Third day, New Zealand 35–3 (Fulton 14, Brownlie 13); Fourth day, England 90–4 (Bell 8).

SRI LANKA v BANGLADESH 2012–13 (1st Test)

At Galle International Stadium on 8, 9, 10, 11, 12 March, 2013.
Toss: Sri Lanka.   Result: MATCH DRAWN.
Debuts: Sri Lanka – K. D. K. Vithanage. Bangladesh – Anamul Haque, Mominul Haque.
Man of the Match: Mushfiqur Rahim.

Despite conceding a huge total, Bangladesh produced arguably their best overseas performance, forcing their first draw against Sri Lanka after 12 straight defeats, only one of which had reached the fifth day. The meat in Bangladesh's historic reply was supplied by Mohammad Ashraful and Mushfiqur Rahim, who put on 267, their country's highest stand in Tests and only the second above 200. Ashraful seemed poised to score Bangladesh's first double-century, having passed his own national record of 158 not out, but he rushed at Herath on the fourth morning and was caught at slip. Instead it was Mushfiqur who was to celebrate the milestone, shortly after lunch on the fourth day. He did not offer a chance until Kulasekara trapped him the ball after he reached 200. Nasir Hossain pushed on to a maiden century – the first time Bangladesh had had three in the same innings – and past the national-record 556 set against West Indies at Mirpur four months earlier. Before all this, Thirimanne and Chandimal also reached maiden hundreds, before Sangakkara equalled Jayawardene's national record of 31 Test centuries in his first innings since breaking his hand at Melbourne in December. Mathews, Sri Lanka's new captain, declared at 570 for four, little expecting his side would bat again 68 behind. Fifth-day hundreds for Dilshan and Sangakkara – his second of the match – made it plain the pitch had not deteriorated. The match total of eight hundreds equalled the Test record, set by West Indies and South Africa in Antigua in 2004–05.

Sri Lanka

F. D. M. Karunaratne lbw b Sohag Gazi	41	– c Abul Hasan b Shahadat Hossain	3
T. M. Dilshan c Mominul Haque b Sohag Gazi	54	– c Abul Hasan b Mahmudullah	126
K. C. Sangakkara c Jahurul Islam b Sohag Gazi	142	– c Jahurul Islam b Mahmudullah	105
H. D. R. L. Thirimanne not out	155	– (6) not out	2
*A. D. Mathews c and b Abul Hasan	27	– not out	38
†L. D. Chandimal not out	116		
K. D. K. Vithanage (did not bat)		– (4) b Mahmudullah	59
B 8, l-b 17, w 3, n-b 7	35	N-b 2	2
(4 wkts dec, 135 overs)	570	(4 wkts dec, 83 overs)	335

1/114 (2) 2/181 (1) 3/305 (3) 4/367 (5)   1/17 (1) 2/230 (3) 3/249 (2) 4/320 (4)

K. M. D. N. Kulasekara, H. M. R. K. B. Herath, R. M. S. Eranga and B. A. W. Mendis did not bat.

In the first innings Karunaratne, when 15, retired hurt at 46–0 and resumed at 114–1.

Shahadat Hossain 21–2–95–0; Abul Hasan 27–4–112–1; Sohag Gazi 50–6–164–3; Elias Sunny 20–0–89–0; Mohammad Ashraful 4–0–23–0; Mahmudullah 11–1–45–0; Mominul Haque 2–0–17–0. *Second Innings*—Shahadat Hossain 9–1–33–1; Abul Hasan 10–0–45–0; Sohag Gazi 15–1–58–0; Elias Sunny 20–0–76–0; Mominul Haque 5–0–25–0; Mohammad Ashraful 1–0–10–0; Mahmudullah 20–1–70–3; Nasir Hossain 3–0–18–0.

Bangladesh

Jahurul Islam c Chandimal b Eranga	20	– not out	41
Anamul Haque b Mendis	13	– b Eranga	1
Mohammad Ashraful c Mathews b Herath	190	– not out	22
Mominul Haque c Mathews b Kulasekara	55		
Mahmudullah st Chandimal b Herath	0		
*†Mushfiqur Rahim lbw b Kulasekara	200		
Nasir Hossain c Karunaratne b Dilshan	100		
Sohag Gazi c Vithanage b Mendis	21		
Abul Hasan not out	16		
Elias Sunny c Chandimal b Dilshan	0		
Shahadat Hossain b Eranga	13		
B 2, l-b 1, n-b 7	10	B 4, l-b 1, n-b 1	6
(196 overs)	638	(1 wkt, 22 overs)	70

1/23 (1) 2/65 (2) 3/170 (4) 4/177 (5) 5/444 (3) 6/550 (6)   1/2 (2)
7/581 (8) 8/618 (7) 9/618 (10) 10/638 (11)

Kulasekara 27–3–94–2; Eranga 34–4–122–2; Herath 62–11–161–2; Mendis 36–3–152–2; Mathews 9–2–18–0; Dilshan 26–5–75–2; Thirimanne 2–0–13–0. *Second Innings*—Kulasekara 4–1–6–0; Eranga 3–1–10–1; Herath 4–0–15–0; Mendis 7–1–23–0; Dilshan 4–0–11–0.

Umpires: R. K. Illingworth *(England)* (3) and N. J. Llong *(England)* (17).
Third umpire: T. H. Wijewardene *(Sri Lanka)*. Referee: D. C. Boon *(Australia)* (15).

Close of play: First day, Sri Lanka 361–3 (Thirimanne 74, Mathews 25); Second day, Bangladesh 135–2 (Mohammad Ashraful 65, Mominul Haque 35); Third day, Bangladesh 438–4 (Mohammad Ashraful 189, Mushfiqur Rahim 152); Fourth day, Sri Lanka 116–1 (Dilshan 63, Sangakkara 49).

SRI LANKA v BANGLADESH 2012–13 (2nd Test)

At R. Premadasa Stadium, Colombo, on 16, 17, 18, 19 March, 2013.
Toss: Sri Lanka.   Result: SRI LANKA WON BY SEVEN WICKETS.
Debuts: none.
Man of the Match: H. M. R. K. B. Herath. Man of the Series: K. C. Sangakkara.

Sri Lanka salvaged a victory to emerge from the series with their reputation merely bruised rather than broken. Both teams, perhaps dazed by the Galle run-fest, misread the pitch and played only one specialist spinner. And Sri Lanka's twirler triumphed: Herath took 12 for 157, the last four on the fourth morning – his 35th birthday – before his team-mates surged to their target at nearly four an over. Sri Lanka had sent Bangladesh in on a green-tinged pitch. The seamers removed both openers, but Herath then took over to claim five wickets. Mominul Haque had shown his pedigree with 55 on debut at Galle, and now was the only batsman to reach 50. Sri Lanka's batsmen threatened to hand over the advantage as they stumbled to 69 for four on the second morning, before Sangakkara – who hit his third Test hundred in ten days – and Chandimal lifted them out of the mire by adding 195. Once Sangakkara perished, however, the last four wickets added only 30; Mushfiqur Rahim completed his fifth catch of the innings, a Bangladesh record. Sri Lanka's eventual lead was a not-quite-decisive 106, and openers Tamim Iqbal (who had missed the First Test with a wrist injury) and Jahurul Islam came within 15 of wiping that off – but Herath remained effective, eventually reeling in a career-best seven, culminating in his 200th Test wicket (Mushfiqur). Sri Lanka's target was just 160. Dilshan made a brisk 57 in his final Test, while Sangakkara's dismissal for 55 reduced his series average to 110.

Bangladesh

Tamim Iqbal lbw b Kulasekara		10	– b Eranga		59
Jahurul Islam c Chandimal b Eranga		33	– st Chandimal b Herath		48
Mohammad Ashraful run out		16	– b Herath		4
Mominul Haque c Chandimal b Herath		64	– c Karunaratne b Herath		37
Mahmudullah c Mathews b Herath		8	– b Herath		0
*†Mushfiqur Rahim b Herath		7	– c Mathews b Herath		40
Nasir Hossain lbw b Herath		48	– b Herath		0
Sohag Gazi st Chandimal b Herath		32	– c Lakmal b Herath		26
Abul Hasan c Karunaratne b Kulasekara		4	– not out		25
Rubel Hossain c Herath b Kulasekara		0	– b Dilshan		7
Robiul Islam not out		1	– b Eranga		10
L-b 8, w 7, n-b 2		17	B 1, l-b 4, n-b 4		9
(83.3 overs)		240	(100.4 overs)		265

1/16 (1) 2/51 (3) 3/100 (2) 4/128 (5) 5/152 (6)   1/91 (1) 2/96 (3) 3/143 (2) 4/143 (5) 5/160 (4)
6/163 (4) 7/222 (8) 8/232 (9) 9/232 (10) 10/240 (7)   6/171 (7) 7/202 (8) 8/228 (6) 9/239 (10) 10/265 (11)

Kulasekara 18–3–54–3; Lakmal 16–4–44–0; Mathews 3–1–7–0; Eranga 14–2–40–1; Herath 28.3–6–68–5; Dilshan 4–0–19–0. *Second Innings*—Kulasekara 12–0–36–0; Lakmal 9–1–26–0; Herath 36–9–89–7; Dilshan 25–4–62–1; Eranga 15.4–3–39–2; Mathews 3–2–8–0.

Sri Lanka

F. D. M. Karunaratne c Mushfiqur Rahim b Abul Hasan	....	17	– lbw b Robiul Islam		16
T. M. Dilshan c Mushfiqur Rahim b Robiul Islam		0	– b Robiul Islam		57
K. C. Sangakkara c Mushfiqur Rahim b Abul Hasan		139	– b Sohag Gazi		55
H. D. R. L. Thirimanne c Mushfiqur Rahim b Robiul Islam...		0	– not out		13
*A. D. Mathews c Mahmudullah b Sohag Gazi		16	– not out		13
†L. D. Chandimal b Rubel Hossain		102			
K. D. K. Vithanage c Mominul Haque b Rubel Hossain	.....	12			
K. M. D. N. Kulasekara c Mushfiqur Rahim b Sohag Gazi	...	22			
H. M. R. K. B. Herath b Sohag Gazi		3			
R. M. S. Eranga c Mohammad Ashraful b Mahmudullah	...	15			
R. A. S. Lakmal not out		0			
B 2, l-b 2, w 6, n-b 10		20	B 2, l-b 1, n-b 3		6
(111.3 overs)		346	(3 wkts, 41.4 overs)		160

1/7 (2) 2/39 (1) 3/43 (4) 4/69 (5) 5/264 (6) 6/280 (7)
7/316 (3) 8/323 (9) 9/346 (8) 10/346 (10)   1/31 (1) 2/125 (2) 3/135 (3)

Robiul Islam 15–1–52–2; Sohag Gazi 39–4–111–3; Abul Hasan 23–4–80–2; Rubel Hossain 17–5–45–2; Mahmudullah 11.3–1–37–1; Mominul Haque 2–0–6–0; Mohammad Ashraful 2–0–9–0; Nasir Hossain 2–0–2–0. *Second Innings*—Robiul Islam 11–0–42–2; Abul Hasan 4–0–21–0; Sohag Gazi 13–1–47–1; Rubel Hossain 3–0–16–0; Nasir Hossain 4–0–11–0; Mahmudullah 3–0–12–0; Mohammad Ashraful 3.4–0–8–0.

Umpires: R. K. Illingworth *(England)* (4) and N. J. Llong *(England)* (18).
Third umpire: R. S. A. Palliyaguruge *(Sri Lanka)*. Referee: D. C. Boon *(Australia)* (16).

Close of play: First day, Sri Lanka 18–1 (Karunaratne 12, Sangakkara 3); Second day, Sri Lanka 294–6 (Sangakkara 127, Kulasekara 2); Third day, Bangladesh 158–4 (Mominul Haque 36, Mushfiqur Rahim 7).

WEST INDIES v ZIMBABWE 2012–13 (1st Test)

At Kensington Oval, Bridgetown, Barbados, on 12, 13, 14 March, 2013.
Toss: Zimbabwe.   Result: WEST INDIES WON BY NINE WICKETS.
Debuts: Zimbabwe – T. L. Chatara.
Man of the Match: S. Shillingford.

This was only Zimbabwe's fifth Test since returning from exile in August 2011, and their first since a shellacking in New Zealand almost 14 months previously. The effect of such inactivity was obvious. Twice they achieved promising positions: they were 100 for two on the opening day, and later West Indies were 151 for six. But Zimbabwe could not exploit either situation. Batting first, they progressed confidently into the afternoon but, once Mawoyo fell bat–pad to Shillingford after an attractive 50, the innings subsided against spin. Samuels's four wickets, starting with one from his first delivery, were a career-best. Jarvis, swinging the ball at a decent pace, claimed two wickets before the close, despatching Powell and nightwatchman Roach, first ball, to what was in fact the seventh delivery of the seventh over. West Indies sagged further next morning – opening bowler Tendai Chatara claimed a distinguished first Test scalp when Gayle stabbed a lifter to slip – but regained control through Sammy's calculated aggression, with Ramdin in determined support in a stand of 106, although they were helped by Taylor's prolonged trust in Cremer's leg-spin. Sammy lashed four sixes in five overs from him and, when he eventually played on to Masakadza, had faced only 69 balls for his 73. Trailing by 96, Zimbabwe were undone by off-spin for a second time. Shillingford gained bounce from his height and purchase from the pitch for match figures of nine for 107, five of them pouched by close catchers on the leg side.

Zimbabwe

T. M. K. Mawoyo c Powell b Shillingford	50	– c Sammy b Gabriel	9
V. Sibanda b Roach	12	– c and b Shillingford	15
H. Masakadza c Samuels b Roach	17	– c Sammy b Shillingford	1
*B. R. M. Taylor b Gabriel	26	– (5) c Powell b Shillingford	6
C. R. Ervine b Samuels	29	– (6) not out	23
M. N. Waller lbw b Shillingford	9	– (7) c Powell b Shillingford	5
†R. W. Chakabva c Powell b Shillingford	15	– (8) b Shillingford	6
A. G. Cremer c Bravo b Samuels	25	– (9) c Ramdin b Shillingford	14
R. W. Price not out	12	– (4) b Roach	7
K. M. Jarvis c Powell b Samuels	0	– c Ramdin b Gabriel	9
T. L. Chatara c Roach b Samuels	2	– b Gabriel	0
B 4, l-b 10	14	B 8, l-b 2, w 1, n-b 1	12
(76.4 overs)	211	(41.4 overs)	107

1/17 (2) 2/59 (3) 3/100 (1) 4/110 (4) 5/135 (6) 6/158 (5)
7/196 (8) 8/196 (7) 9/197 (10) 10/211 (11)

1/25 (1) 2/26 (3) 3/39 (2) 4/47 (5) 5/47 (4) 6/58 (7)
7/77 (8) 8/97 (9) 9/107 (10) 10/107 (11)

Roach 13–3–31–2; Best 12–3–33–0; Gabriel 14–5–45–1; Sammy 9–5–17–0; Shillingford 22–4–58–3; Samuels 6.4–1–13–4. *Second Innings*—Roach 10–7–12–1; Best 8–2–26–0; Gabriel 7.4–3–10–3; Shillingford 16–4–49–6.

West Indies

C. H. Gayle c Taylor b Chatara	40	– not out	4
K. O. A. Powell lbw b Jarvis	5	– c Cremer b Chatara	6
K. A. J. Roach lbw b Jarvis	0		
D. M. Bravo c Chakabva b Jarvis	11	– (3) not out	1
M. N. Samuels c Chakabva b Masakadza	51		
S. Chanderpaul c Chakabva b Jarvis	26		
†D. Ramdin c Sibanda b Chatara	62		
*D. J. G. Sammy b Masakadza	73		
S. Shillingford c Jarvis b Price	1		
T. L. Best c Cremer b Jarvis	24		
S. T. Gabriel not out	0		
B 9, l-b 3, w 1, n-b 1	14	B 1	1
(84.2 overs)	307	(1 wkt, 5 overs)	12

1/8 (2) 2/8 (3) 3/43 (4) 4/81 (1) 5/144 (5) 6/151 (6)
7/257 (8) 8/268 (9) 9/301 (7) 10/307 (10)   1/8 (2)

Jarvis 17.2–4–54–5; Chatara 19–6–66–2; Cremer 20–0–103–0; Masakadza 10–2–25–2; Price 18–2–47–1. *Second Innings*—Jarvis 3–1–10–0; Chatara 2–1–1–1.

Umpires: R. E. J. Martinesz *(Sri Lanka)* (1) and B. N. J. Oxenford *(Australia)* (13).
Third umpire: A. L. Hill *(New Zealand)*. Referee: J. J. Crowe *(New Zealand)* (61).

Close of play: First day, West Indies 18–2 (Gayle 11, Bravo 0); Second day, Zimbabwe 41–3 (Price 7, Taylor 0).

WEST INDIES v ZIMBABWE 2012–13 (2nd Test)

At Windsor Park, Roseau, Dominica, on 20, 21, 22 March, 2013.
Toss: West Indies.   Result: WEST INDIES WON BY AN INNINGS AND 65 RUNS.
Debuts: Zimbabwe – S. C. Williams.
Man of the Match: S. Shillingford. Man of the Series: S. Shillingford.

Zimbabwe again failed to last beyond tea on the third day as West Indies won the Clive Lloyd Trophy 2–0. Shane Shillingford, the Dominican off-spinner playing his second Test on his home island, repeated his ten-wicket haul against Australia the previous April. After Gabriel triggered the initial crash, pace was virtually redundant. Ervine resisted for 73 balls and Sean Williams – a 26-year-old left-hander making his Test debut after 47 one-day internationals – for 88. Shillingford's impact was immediate: his sixth ball, a doosra, cleaned up Masakadza. A collapse never seemed far away, and the last six tumbled for 34. Jarvis removed Bravo, for his first Test duck in 41 innings (among West Indians, only Clive Lloyd, Basil Butcher and Garry Sobers waited longer for their first), but then Gayle's 15th Test hundred was followed by Chanderpaul's 28th – his first against Zimbabwe – and 86 from Ramdin. Gayle rushed from 81 to 99 with three sixes in four balls, before completing his century with a single, then holed out at long-off: it was Utseya's first Test wicket, almost nine years after his only previous cap. Sammy declared before the start of the third day. Zimbabwe's openers fell to Best and Sammy – their only wickets of the series – then the rest disintegrated against the off-spinners: Samuels ended an unequal contest with two wickets in two balls; no one passed 35 in either innings. Shillingford's 19 wickets were a West Indian record for a two-Test series, beating Courtney Walsh's 16 in New Zealand in 1994–95.

Zimbabwe

T. M. K. Mawoyo b Gabriel	8	– (7) c Sammy b Shillingford	0
V. Sibanda c Roach b Gabriel	32	– (1) lbw b Sammy	35
H. Masakadza b Shillingford	14	– (2) c Ramdin b Best	17
*†B. R. M. Taylor b Shillingford	33	– (3) c Powell b Shillingford	7
C. R. Ervine lbw b Samuels	18	– (4) c Gayle b Shillingford	8
S. C. Williams c Powell b Samuels	31	– (5) c Chanderpaul b Shillingford	6
M. N. Waller c Best b Shillingford	9	– (6) c Sammy b Samuels	20
A. G. Cremer c Powell b Samuels	0	– c Samuels b Shillingford	20
P. Utseya lbw b Shillingford	9	– not out	10
K. M. Jarvis not out	1	– c Sammy b Samuels	1
T. L. Chatara lbw b Shillingford	4	– c Gabriel b Samuels	0
B 10, l-b 4, w 1, n-b 1	16	B 8, l-b 9	17
(60.5 overs)	175	(42.2 overs)	141

1/42 (1) 2/43 (2) 3/64 (3) 4/105 (4) 5/141 (5) 6/158 (7)   1/37 (2) 2/64 (3) 3/64 (1) 4/73 (5) 5/92 (4) 6/96 (7)
7/158 (8) 8/161 (6) 9/171 (9) 10/175 (11)   7/114 (6) 8/138 (8) 9/141 (10) 10/141 (11)

Roach 7–0–30–0; Best 10–0–32–0; Gabriel 8–6–10–2; Sammy 5–1–15–0; Shillingford 21.5–4–59–5; Samuels 9–3–15–3. *Second Innings*—Best 7–2–11–1; Roach 3–0–12–0; Gabriel 3–0–19–0; Shillingford 15–4–34–5; Sammy 5–1–13–1; Samuels 9.2–0–35–3.

West Indies

C. H. Gayle c Jarvis b Utseya	101
K. O. A. Powell b Jarvis	24
D. M. Bravo c Taylor b Jarvis	0
M. N. Samuels b Chatara	26
S. Chanderpaul c Williams b Utseya	108
†D. Ramdin lbw b Cremer	86
*D. J. G. Sammy c Masakadza b Cremer	9
S. Shillingford not out	4
K. A. J. Roach b Utseya	0
T. L. Best not out	11
B 4, l-b 7, w 1	12
(8 wkts dec, 117 overs)	381

1/35 (2) 2/35 (3) 3/114 (4) 4/181 (1) 5/354 (6) 6/366 (7)
7/370 (5) 8/370 (9)

S. T. Gabriel did not bat.

Jarvis 21–3–82–2; Chatara 22–2–69–1; Masakadza 17–6–48–0; Cremer 34–6–102–2; Utseya 22–6–60–3; Williams 1–0–9–0.

Umpires: A. L. Hill *(New Zealand)* (36) and R. E. J. Martinesz *(Sri Lanka)* (2).
Third umpire: B. N. J. Oxenford *(Australia)*. Referee: J. J. Crowe *(New Zealand)* (62).

Close of play: First day, West Indies 114–2 (Gayle 61, Samuels 26); Second day, West Indies 381–8 (Shillingford 4, Best 11).

ZIMBABWE v BANGLADESH 2012–13 (1st Test)

At Harare Sports Club on 17, 18, 19, 20 April, 2013.
Toss: Bangladesh.   Result: ZIMBABWE WON BY 335 RUNS.
Debuts: Zimbabwe – T. Maruma, K. O. Meth, R. Mutumbami.
Man of the Match: B. R. M. Taylor.

Brendan Taylor marked his country's 33rd independence day with the highest score by a Zimbabwe captain, passing Andy Flower's 156 against Pakistan here in 1994–95. Then, once an inadequate Bangladesh reply had fallen 37 runs short of his own 171, Taylor became the first Zimbabwean outside the Flower family to score two hundreds in the same Test. It led to Zimbabwe's tenth Test victory, the sixth against Bangladesh. Things might have been different if Shahriar Nafees, running in from long-off, had held a tough chance in the first innings, when Taylor had 35. Zimbabwe were 94 for three at the time, with Taylor and Waller building cautiously; they added a further 98. The eventual 389 was probably worth an extra 30 runs; the square boundaries were enormous and the outfield slow. Still, Bangladesh reached 102 for one next morning, before rolling over in the most submissive fashion, losing nine for 32 – including the last five without addition, only the fourth such sequence in Test history, and the first not by New Zealand. Despite a lead of 255, Taylor waived the follow-on, a decision which almost backfired when the persistent Robiul Islam took four for 15 in his opening spell. But Taylor withstood the blitz and found enough support to complete his second century early on the fourth morning. Set an implausible 483, the demoralised Bangladeshis lasted less than four hours in their second innings. Jarvis did the early damage, and leg-spinner Cremer took four for four to wrap up the tail.

Zimbabwe

T. Maruma lbw b Robiul Islam		10 – lbw b Robiul Islam	10
V. Sibanda b Robiul Islam	5	– b Robiul Islam	4
H. Masakadza c Mahmudullah b Enamul Haque	25	– c and b Robiul Islam	0
*B. R. M. Taylor c Mushfiqur Rahim b Enamul Haque	171	– not out	102
M. N. Waller b Rubel Hossain	55	– c Nasir Hossain b Robiul Islam	4
E. Chigumbura c and b Rubel Hossain	12	– c Jahurul Islam b Robiul Islam	27
†R. Mutumbami c Mushfiqur Rahim b Robiul Islam	11	– lbw b Robiul Islam	0
A. G. Cremer c Mahmudullah b Sohag Gazi	42	– run out	43
K. O. Meth c Nasir Hossain b Enamul Haque	21	– not out	31
S. W. Masakadza c Jahurul Islam b Sohag Gazi	21		
K. M. Jarvis not out	3		
B 1, l-b 5, w 2, n-b 5	13	L-b 2, w 2, n-b 2	6
(152.3 overs)	389	(7 wkts dec, 64 overs)	227

1/10 (2) 2/22 (1) 3/65 (3) 4/192 (5) 5/223 (6) 6/238 (7)   1/7 (2) 2/9 (3) 3/16 (1) 4/27 (5) 5/84 (6) 6/84 (7)
7/344 (8) 8/344 (4) 9/381 (9) 10/389 (10)   7/163 (8)

Robiul Islam 38–11–84–3; Rubel Hossain 30–6–87–2; Nasir Hossain 5–2–3–0; Enamul Haque 47–5–133–3; Sohag Gazi 22.3–1–55–2; Mahmudullah 3–0–7–0; Shakib Al Hasan 7–3–14–0. *Second Innings*—Robiul Islam 19–1–71–6; Rubel Hossain 10–0–44–0; Shakib Al Hasan 9–2–22–0; Enamul Haque 13–2–45–0; Sohag Gazi 9–0–24–0; Mahmudullah 4–2–19–0.

Bangladesh

Jahurul Islam lbw b Meth		43 – c Mutumbami b S. W. Masakadza	22
Shahriar Nafees c Maruma b Jarvis	29	– b Jarvis	11
Mohammad Ashraful c Waller b S. W. Masakadza	38	– run out	40
Mahmudullah b Meth	3	– c sub (S. C. Williams) b Jarvis	21
Shakib Al Hasan c Sibanda b S. W. Masakadza	5	– c Sibanda b Jarvis	4
*†Mushfiqur Rahim lbw b S. W. Masakadza	3	– c Taylor b Chigumbura	3
Nasir Hossain c Mutumbami b Jarvis	7	– b Cremer	23
Sohag Gazi c Waller b S. W. Masakadza	0	– st Mutumbami b Cremer	4
Enamul Haque, jun. b Jarvis	0	– not out	6
Rubel Hossain b Jarvis	0	– c S. W. Masakadza b Cremer	4
Robiul Islam not out	0	– c Jarvis b Cremer	0
B 4, l-b 1, w 1	6	B 8, n-b 1	9
(54.1 overs)	134	(49.2 overs)	147

1/53 (2) 2/102 (1) 3/112 (4) 4/123 (5) 5/124 (3)   1/21 (2) 2/41 (1) 3/77 (4) 4/81 (5) 5/85 (6) 6/132 (3)
6/134 (6) 7/134 (7) 8/134 (9) 9/134 (10) 10/134 (8)   7/136 (7) 8/139 (8) 9/147 (10) 10/147 (11)

Jarvis 16–8–40–4; Meth 20–6–41–2; S. W. Masakadza 14.1–4–32–4; Chigumbura 3–0–16–0; Cremer 1–1–0–0. *Second Innings*—Jarvis 17–1–75–3; Meth 12–5–16–0; S. W. Masakadza 10–4–26–1; Chigumbura 5–0–18–1; Cremer 5.2–1–4–4.

Umpires: B. F. Bowden *(New Zealand)* (75) and A. L. Hill *(New Zealand)* (37).
Third umpire: T. J. Matibiri *(Zimbabwe)*. Referee: B. C. Broad *(England)* (59).

Close of play: First day, Zimbabwe 217–4 (Taylor 105, Chigumbura 6); Second day, Bangladesh 95–1 (Jahurul Islam 38, Mohammad Ashraful 23); Third day, Zimbabwe 187–7 (Taylor 81, Meth 13).

ZIMBABWE v BANGLADESH 2012–13 (2nd Test)

At Harare Sports Club on 25, 26, 27, 28, 29 April, 2013.
Toss: Zimbabwe.　　　Result: BANGLADESH WON BY 143 RUNS.
Debuts: Bangladesh – Ziaur Rahman.
Man of the Match: Mushfiqur Rahim. Man of the Series: Robiul Islam.

If the First Test was decided by the skill of one player, the Second boiled down to all-round incompetence – with Bangladesh marginally less guilty than Zimbabwe. Catches went down as if in a club match and, when the fielders failed to oblige, batsmen contrived to get themselves out. Taylor bowled first, but the pitch lacked the zest of the First Test. Zimbabwe didn't just bowl poorly; they missed four run-outs and three catches on the first day. Bangladesh in turn gift-wrapped their first five wickets, but still closed on 300 for six – thanks to Shakib Al Hasan and Mushfiqur Rahim, who provided some much-needed sanity while adding 123. Tamim Iqbal could have been run out in the first over of the match or the first after lunch, before he actually was, panicking one short of fifty. Zimbabwe's batsmen then performed equally amateurishly, although Robiul Islam persevered to become the first Bangladesh seamer to take consecutive five-wicket hauls. Chigumbura's counter-attacking Test-best 86 waylaid concerns about the follow-on, and Zimbabwe briefly found themselves back in it, courtesy of some wobbly Bangladesh batting and – with no DRS for cost reasons – questionable umpiring. But once Shakib, Mushfiqur and Nasir had performed a second rescue act, the game was up, despite Hamilton Masakadza's third Test hundred. It was Bangladesh's first victory in Zimbabwe in seven attempts, their first in 18 Tests since beating a weakened West Indies four years earlier, and only their fourth overall out of 79. It was not difficult to see why.

Bangladesh

Tamim Iqbal run out			49	– c Mutumbami b S. W. Masakadza	7
Jahurul Islam c Waller b Meth			24	– c Mutumbami b S. W. Masakadza	2
Mohammad Ashraful c Cremer b S. W. Masakadza	....		4	– lbw b Jarvis	4
Mominul Haque c S. W. Masakadza b Chigumbura			23	– c H. Masakadza b S. W. Masakadza	29
Shakib Al Hasan c Mutumbami b Chigumbura			81	– c Mutumbami b H. Masakadza	59
*†Mushfiqur Rahim lbw b Jarvis			60	– c Sibanda b H. Masakadza	93
Nasir Hossain b Cremer			77	– not out	67
Ziaur Rahman lbw b Meth			14	– st Mutumbami b Cremer	0
Sohag Gazi c Chigumbura b Cremer			21	– c Sibanda b H. Masakadza	11
Sajidul Islam c Mutumbami b Chigumbura			0	– c Mutumbami b S. W. Masakadza	4
Robiul Islam not out			24	– not out	4
B 2, l-b 7, w 1, n-b 4			14	L-b 5, w 2, n-b 4	11
(113.2 overs)			391	(9 wkts dec, 88 overs)	291

1/44 (2) 2/58 (3) 3/102 (1) 4/125 (4) 5/248 (5)　　　1/7 (1) 2/12 (2) 3/18 (3) 4/65 (4) 5/149 (5)
6/280 (6) 7/313 (8) 8/364 (9) 9/367 (7) 10/391 (10)　6/233 (6) 7/234 (8) 8/255 (9) 9/279 (10)

Jarvis 25–4–105–1; Meth 22–7–41–2; S. W. Masakadza 17–2–52–1; Chigumbura 24.2–7–75–3; Cremer 25–3–109–2. *Second Innings*—Jarvis 22–3–80–1; S. W. Masakadza 24–5–58–4; Cremer 17–1–70–1; Chigumbura 14–0–54–0; H. Masakadza 11–1–24–3.

Zimbabwe

V. Sibanda c Mushfiqur Rahim b Robiul Islam			10	– c Sohag Gazi b Shakib Al Hasan	32
R. W. Chakabva c Mushfiqur Rahim b Robiul Islam	...		12	– b Shakib Al Hasan	22
H. Masakadza b Shakib Al Hasan			14	– not out	111
*B. R. M. Taylor c Shakib Al Hasan b Sohag Gazi			36	– lbw b Ziaur Rahman	10
M. N. Waller c Shakib Al Hasan b Sohag Gazi			32	– b Ziaur Rahman	15
E. Chigumbura b Robiul Islam			86	– (7) c Robiul Islam b Sohag Gazi	2
†R. Mutumbami lbw b Robiul Islam			42	– (8) b Ziaur Rahman	12
A. G. Cremer not out			11	– (9) c Nasir Hossain b Ziaur Rahman	3
K. O. Meth c Mushfiqur Rahim b Sohag Gazi			16	– (10) lbw b Robiul Islam	4
S. W. Masakadza c Mushfiqur Rahim b Robiul Islam	.		5	– (6) lbw b Mohammad Ashraful	24
K. M. Jarvis b Sohag Gazi			0	– lbw b Shakib Al Hasan	7
B 5, l-b 11, w 1, n-b 1			18	B 4, l-b 7, n-b 4	15
(96 overs)			282	(95.3 overs)	257

1/23 (2) 2/26 (1) 3/45 (3) 4/97 (4) 5/163 (5) 6/248 (7)　　1/36 (2) 2/66 (1) 3/96 (4) 4/118 (5) 5/164 (6)
7/257 (6) 8/274 (9) 9/281 (10) 10/282 (11)　　　　　　6/169 (7) 7/200 (8) 8/214 (9) 9/219 (10) 10/257 (11)

Robiul Islam 33–11–85–5; Sajidul Islam 16–5–48–0; Ziaur Rahman 7–3–8–0; Shakib Al Hasan 19–4–66–1; Sohag Gazi 19–1–59–4; Mohammad Ashraful 2–2–0–0. *Second Innings*—Robiul Islam 20–5–53–1; Sajidul Islam 3–1–9–0; Shakib Al Hasan 11.3–0–52–3; Sohag Gazi 31–11–56–1; Ziaur Rahman 23–8–63–4; Mohammad Ashraful 7–1–13–1.

Umpires: I. J. Gould *(England)* (34) and A. L. Hill *(New Zealand)* (38).
Third umpire: O. Chirombe *(Zimbabwe)*. Referee: B. C. Broad *(England)* (60).

Close of play: First day, Bangladesh 300–6 (Nasir Hossain 37, Ziaur Rahman 8); Second day, Zimbabwe 158–4 (Waller 30, Chigumbura 45); Third day, Bangladesh 163–5 (Mushfiqur Rahim 50, Nasir Hossain 6); Fourth day, Zimbabwe 138–4 (H. Masakadza 46, S. W. Masakadza 7).

ENGLAND v NEW ZEALAND 2013 (1st Test)

At Lord's, London, on 16, 17, 18, 19 May, 2013.
Toss: England.　　Result: ENGLAND WON BY 170 RUNS.
Debuts: none.
Man of the Match: S. C. J. Broad.

For the first 250 overs, neither side jockeyed ahead of the other. Indeed, after Southee polished England off on the fourth morning – completing only New Zealand's second ten-for in a Lord's Test, after Dion Nash's in 1994 – it was plausible to imagine New Zealand reaching their target of 239. After all, 61 Tests had been won by chasing as many or more, and Taylor and McCullum were arguably the most destructive batsmen on view. England's attack, by contrast, had lacked bite, Anderson excepted. Plausible perhaps – but utterly wrong. Batsman after batsman traipsed out, and writhed in agony briefly before Broad, now butcher-in-chief, despatched them. It was all over in 135 balls, the fourth-shortest Test innings at Lord's; Cook didn't even need to change the bowling, the first time this had happened in a completed Test innings in England since 1924, when South Africa were all out for 30 at Edgbaston. The sudden ending was a shock after three days in which the advantage rocked back and forth like a Newton's Cradle. England managed only 160 from 80 overs (30 maidens) on the first day, and were all out for 232: Prior was out first ball on the way to his first pair in 226 first-class matches. Williamson and Taylor put on 93, but the others struggled against Anderson. And then England struggled too, apart from Root's 71 in his first senior match at Lord's. Without Broad's 26, the total would have been even more modest – but he was just warming up.

England

*A. N. Cook c Watling b Boult	32	– c Brownlie b Boult		21
N. R. D. Compton c Southee b Martin	16	– b Wagner		15
I. J. L. Trott c Brownlie b Boult	39	– b Williamson		56
I. R. Bell c Watling b Wagner	31	– (8) c Brownlie b Southee		6
J. E. Root c Watling b Southee	40	– (4) b Southee		71
J. M. Bairstow c and b Southee	41	– (5) b Southee		5
†M. J. Prior lbw b Southee	0	– (6) c sub (M. J. Guptill) b Southee		0
S. C. J. Broad lbw b Wagner	0	– (9) not out		26
G. P. Swann c Watling b Wagner	5	– (10) c McCullum b Southee		1
S. T. Finn lbw b Southee	4	– (7) c sub (M. J. Guptill) b Southee		6
J. M. Anderson not out	7	– c Southee b Williamson		0
B 1, l-b 9, w 2, n-b 5	17	B 3, w 1, n-b 2		6
(112.2 overs)	232	(68.3 overs)		213

1/43 (2) 2/67 (1) 3/112 (3) 4/157 (4) 5/192 (5) 6/192 (7)　　1/36 (1) 2/36 (2) 3/159 (4) 4/167 (5) 5/171 (6)
7/195 (8) 8/201 (9) 9/221 (10) 10/232 (6)　　6/171 (3) 7/183 (7) 8/200 (8) 9/210 (10) 10/213 (11)

Boult 27–10–48–2; Southee 28.2–8–58–4; Wagner 28–8–70–3; Martin 26–12–38–1; Williamson 3–1–8–0. *Second Innings*—Boult 15–3–56–1; Southee 19–4–50–6; Wagner 13–2–44–1; Martin 13–2–40–0; Williamson 8.3–2–20–2.

New Zealand

P. G. Fulton c Swann b Anderson	2	– c Prior b Broad		1
H. D. Rutherford c Cook b Anderson	4	– b Broad		9
K. S. Williamson c Prior b Anderson	60	– c Finn b Broad		6
L. R. P. L. Taylor lbw b Anderson	66	– c Cook b Broad		0
D. G. Brownlie lbw b Finn	23	– c Cook b Anderson		5
*B. B. McCullum c Prior b Broad	2	– lbw b Broad		8
†B-J. Watling c Prior b Finn	17	– c Trott b Anderson		13
T. G. Southee c Root b Finn	12	– c Root b Broad		7
B. P. Martin b Anderson	0	– (10) b Broad		1
N. Wagner not out	6	– (9) run out		17
T. A. Boult c Anderson b Finn	0	– not out		0
B 4, l-b 8, n-b 3	15	L-b 1		1
(69 overs)	207	(22.3 overs)		68

1/5 (2) 2/7 (1) 3/100 (4) 4/147 (5) 5/155 (6) 6/177 (3)　　1/1 (1) 2/16 (2) 3/16 (4) 4/21 (3) 5/25 (5) 6/29 (6)
7/194 (8) 8/195 (9) 9/207 (7) 10/207 (11)　　7/41 (8) 8/54 (7) 9/67 (10) 10/68 (9)

Anderson 24–11–47–5; Broad 21–4–64–1; Finn 15–3–63–4; Swann 8–0–19–0; Trott 1–0–2–0. *Second Innings*—Anderson 11.3–5–23–2; Broad 11–0–44–7.

Umpires: Aleem Dar *(Pakistan)* (81) and S. J. Davis *(Australia)* (45).
Third umpire: M. Erasmus *(South Africa)*. Referee: D. C. Boon *(Australia)* (17).

Close of play: First day, England 160–4 (Root 25, Bairstow 3); Second day, New Zealand 153–4 (Williamson 44, McCullum 1); Third day, England 180–6 (Finn 6, Bell 0).

ENGLAND v NEW ZEALAND 2013 (2nd Test)

At Headingley, Leeds, on 24 (*no play*), 25, 26, 27, 28 May, 2013.
Toss: England.   Result: ENGLAND WON BY 247 RUNS.
Debuts: none.
Man of the Match: G. P. Swann. Men of the Series: J. E. Root and T. G. Southee.

Less than a week after their Lord's letdown, New Zealand were soon up against it once more: an all-Yorkshire partnership of 124 between Root and Bairstow set up England's imposing first-innings total. New Zealand underperformed again – five made it into the twenties, but none got out the other side as Swann and Finn shared seven wickets. To general surprise, since the forecast was unpromising, Cook waived the follow-on (the loss of the first day meant the margin was 150). As New Zealand's three innings in the series had produced just 449 runs in 135.1 overs, this felt like overkill – and England's second innings suffered from over-caution, too. Compton's desperate search for form ended after 85 minutes with his second single-figure score of the match: he was dropped for the Ashes series that followed. With Cook in good touch the opening stand was still worth 72 – but Trott then played with such self-denial that only 44 runs came in 21 overs before the fourth-day close. The scoring-rate perked up next morning: Cook reached his 25th Test century – the 100th overall at Headingley – but his declaration, which set an impossible 468, was inexplicably delayed beyond lunch. Luckily for Cook the threatened rain kept away, and Swann worked his way through New Zealand, finishing with the best match figures by a spinner at Headingley since Derek Underwood's ten for 82 on the fusarium-infected pitch for the 1972 Ashes Test. Anderson wrapped things up with his 307th wicket, putting him level with Fred Trueman.

England

*A. N. Cook c Brownlie b Bracewell	34	– c Southee b Williamson	130
N. R. D. Compton c Brownlie b Southee	1	– c Rutherford b Williamson	7
I. J. L. Trott c McCullum b Wagner	28	– c McCullum b Wagner	76
I. R. Bell c McCullum b Williamson	30	– c Guptill b Williamson	6
J. E. Root c McCullum b Boult	104	– c Guptill b Wagner	28
J. M. Bairstow c McCullum b Boult	64	– not out	26
†M. J. Prior c Taylor b Southee	39	– not out	4
S. C. J. Broad c McCullum b Boult	0		
G. P. Swann not out	26		
S. T. Finn b Boult	6		
J. M. Anderson c and b Boult	0		
B 9, l-b 7, w 5, n-b 1	22	B 8, l-b 1, w 1	10
(99 overs)	354	(5 wkts dec, 76 overs)	287

1/11 (2) 2/67 (3) 3/67 (1) 4/146 (4) 5/270 (5) 6/279 (6)
7/286 (8) 8/345 (7) 9/354 (10) 10/354 (11)   1/72 (2) 2/206 (1) 3/214 (4) 4/249 (3) 5/268 (5)

Boult 22–4–57–5; Southee 26–6–76–2; Wagner 23–4–73–1; Bracewell 19–3–83–1; Williamson 9–0–49–1. *Second Innings*—Boult 2–1–2–0; Southee 15–4–51–0; Wagner 17–3–67–2; Williamson 24–4–68–3; Bracewell 13–3–49–0; Guptill 5–0–41–0.

New Zealand

P. G. Fulton c and b Finn	28	– c Bell b Broad	5
H. D. Rutherford c Bell b Finn	27	– c Root b Swann	42
K. S. Williamson lbw b Swann	13	– lbw b Swann	3
L. R. P. L. Taylor b Finn	6	– b Swann	70
D. G. Brownlie b Swann	2	– c Bell b Finn	25
M. J. Guptill b Swann	1	– c Trott b Swann	3
*†B. B. McCullum c Prior b Broad	20	– c and b Broad	1
T. G. Southee lbw b Broad	19	– c Trott b Swann	38
D. A. J. Bracewell c Bell b Swann	1	– c Bell b Swann	19
N. Wagner b Anderson	27	– not out	0
T. A. Boult not out	24	– c Prior b Anderson	0
L-b 5, w 1	6	B 2, l-b 11, w 1	14
(43.4 overs)	174	(76.3 overs)	220

1/55 (1) 2/62 (2) 3/72 (4) 4/79 (5) 5/81 (6) 6/82 (3)
7/119 (8) 8/122 (9) 9/122 (7) 10/174 (10)   1/21 (1) 2/40 (3) 3/65 (2) 4/144 (5) 5/153 (6)
6/154 (4) 7/162 (7) 8/218 (8) 9/220 (9) 10/220 (11)

Anderson 7.4–2–34–1; Broad 15–2–57–2; Finn 12–3–36–3; Swann 9–1–42–4. *Second Innings*—Anderson 11.3–4–28–1; Broad 11–3–26–2; Swann 32–12–90–6; Finn 19–5–62–1; Root 3–2–1–0.

Umpires: S. J. Davis (*Australia*) (46) and M. Erasmus (*South Africa*) (18).
Third umpire: Aleem Dar (*Pakistan*). Referee: D. C. Boon (*Australia*) (18).

Close of play: First day, no play; Second day, England 337–7 (Prior 38, Swann 21); Third day, England 116–1 (Cook 88, Trott 11); Fourth day, New Zealand 158–6 (McCullum 0, Southee 4).

ENGLAND v AUSTRALIA 2013 (1st Test)

At Trent Bridge, Nottingham, on 10, 11, 12, 13, 14 July, 2013.
Toss: England.   Result: ENGLAND WON BY 14 RUNS.
Debuts: Australia – A. C. Agar.
Man of the Match: J. M. Anderson.

This was an instant, and very modern, Ashes classic. Australia were boosted by a vegan fast bowler and the joyous strokeplay of a teenage No. 11, but finally suppressed by an Englishman with complete command of reverse swing. England were shot out on the first day by the fiery Siddle, but Australia lost four before stumps, including Cowan and Clarke for ducks. With Anderson in prime form, they lurched to 117 for nine before Ashton Agar – chosen for his left-arm spin, which proved unthreatening – strolled in. Early on he was apparently stumped, but the third umpire disagreed...and Agar, 18, unrolled some superb shots. He and Hughes doubled the score – only the third such instance by a Test last pair – and eventually broke the old tenth-wicket record of 151. Finally Agar fell, with a rueful smile, for 98 – the highest Test score by a No. 11, beating Tino Best's 95 the previous year. Australia somehow led by 65, and England were soon 11 for two. But Cook and Pietersen dug deep, then Bell played beautifully for 109. Broad helped him add 138, despite edging to slip, via Haddin's gloves, but being given not out: Australia had already used up their reviews. Needing 311 in five sessions, Australia started well, but three wickets for three runs set them back. All looked lost at 231 for nine, but Haddin and Pattinson eked out 65, before Hot Spot showed that Haddin had brushed an Anderson off-cutter. Improbably, Australia's last-wicket pairs scored 228 runs in the match.

England

*A. N. Cook c Haddin b Pattinson	13	– c Clarke b Agar		50
J. E. Root b Siddle	30	– c Haddin b Starc		5
I. J. L. Trott b Siddle	48	– lbw b Starc		0
K. P. Pietersen c Clarke b Siddle	14	– b Pattinson		64
I. R. Bell c Watson b Siddle	25	– c Haddin b Starc		109
J. M. Bairstow b Starc	37	– c Haddin b Agar		15
†M. J. Prior c Hughes b Siddle	1	– c Cowan b Siddle		31
S. C. J. Broad c and b Pattinson	24	– c Haddin b Pattinson		65
G. P. Swann c Hughes b Pattinson	1	– c Clarke b Siddle		9
S. T. Finn c Haddin b Starc	0	– not out		2
J. M. Anderson not out	1	– c Hughes b Siddle		0
B 6, l-b 5, w 8, n-b 2	21	B 2, l-b 13, w 1, n-b 9		25
(59 overs)	215	(149.5 overs)		375

1/27 (1) 2/78 (2) 3/102 (4) 4/124 (3) 5/178 (5)
6/180 (7) 7/213 (8) 8/213 (6) 9/213 (10) 10/215 (9)

1/11 (2) 2/11 (3) 3/121 (4) 4/131 (1) 5/174 (6)
6/218 (7) 7/356 (8) 8/371 (5) 9/375 (9) 10/375 (11)

Pattinson 17–2–69–3; Starc 17–5–54–2; Siddle 14–4–50–5; Agar 7–1–24–0; Watson 4–2–7–0. *Second Innings—* Pattinson 34–8–101–2; Starc 32–7–81–3; Agar 35–9–82–2; Siddle 33.5–12–85–3; Watson 15–11–11–0.

Australia

S. R. Watson c Root b Finn	13	– lbw b Broad		46
C. J. L. Rogers lbw b Anderson	16	– c Bell b Anderson		52
E. J. M. Cowan c Swann b Finn	0	– c Trott b Root		14
*M. J. Clarke b Anderson	0	– c Prior b Broad		23
S. P. D. Smith c Prior b Anderson	53	– lbw b Swann		17
P. J. Hughes not out	81	– lbw b Swann		0
†B. J. Haddin b Swann	1	– c Prior b Anderson		71
P. M. Siddle c Prior b Anderson	1	– (10) c Cook b Anderson		11
M. A. Starc c Prior b Anderson	0	– c Cook b Anderson		1
J. L. Pattinson lbw b Swann	2	– (11) not out		25
A. C. Agar c Swann b Broad	98	– (8) c Cook b Anderson		14
L-b 15	15	B 11, l-b 10, n-b 1		22
(64.5 overs)	280	(110.5 overs)		296

1/19 (1) 2/19 (3) 3/22 (4) 4/53 (2) 5/108 (5) 6/113 (7)
7/114 (8) 8/114 (9) 9/117 (10) 10/280 (11)

1/84 (1) 2/111 (3) 3/124 (2) 4/161 (4) 5/161 (5)
6/164 (6) 7/207 (8) 8/211 (9) 9/231 (10) 10/296 (7)

Anderson 24–2–85–5; Finn 15–0–80–2; Swann 19–4–60–2; Broad 6.5–0–40–1. *Second Innings—*Anderson 31.5–11–73–5; Broad 23–7–54–2; Swann 44–10–105–2; Finn 10–3–37–0; Root 2–0–6–1.

Umpires: Aleem Dar *(Pakistan)* (82) and H. D. P. K. Dharmasena *(Sri Lanka)* (16).
Third umpire: M. Erasmus *(South Africa)*. Referee: R. S. Madugalle *(Sri Lanka)* (142).

Close of play: First day, Australia 75–4 (Smith 38, Hughes 7); Second day, England 80–2 (Cook 37, Pietersen 35); Third day, England 326–6 (Bell 95, Broad 47); Fourth day, Australia 174–6 (Haddin 11, Agar 1).

ENGLAND v AUSTRALIA 2013 (2nd Test)

At Lord's, London, on 18, 29, 20, 21 July, 2013.
Toss: England.   Result: ENGLAND WON BY 347 RUNS.
Debuts: none.
Man of the Match: J. E. Root.

This game consisted of three typical Test totals – and one brief and bizarre interlude of almost comical ineptitude. This was Australia's first innings: they were shot out for 128, with Swann taking five wickets, one of them with an outrageous full-toss to Rogers, given as lbw even though it was sailing wide and over the stumps. Australia's coach Darren Lehmann estimated that eight of the wickets were self-inflicted. For England, Cook and Pietersen managed only 27 runs between them, but it didn't matter much: Bell reprised his Nottingham 109 in the first innings – his third hundred in successive Tests against Australia – and Root eased to 180 in the second after Haddin and Clarke allowed an edge to fly between them when he had only four. Root, 22, was the youngest to make an Ashes hundred at Lord's, and the first Yorkshireman to do so since Len Hutton and Willie Watson in 1953. Restarting 582 behind, Australia were soon 36 for three, Swann removing Rogers again, and Hughes for a pair of ones. Khawaja and Clarke settled in for half-centuries before both fell in 11 balls to Root's mild off-spin, but otherwise only Pattinson – soon to return home with back stress fractures – made it past 20, and England completed victory in the last over of the extra hour on the fourth day. It was Australia's sixth successive defeat, one short of their worst run, in the 1880s. England had not won the first two Tests of an Ashes series since 1978–79.

England

*A. N. Cook lbw b Watson	12	– b Siddle	8
J. E. Root lbw b Harris	6	– c Smith b Harris	180
I. J. L. Trott c Khawaja b Harris	58	– b Siddle	0
K. P. Pietersen c Haddin b Harris	2	– c Rogers b Siddle	5
I. R. Bell c Clarke b Smith	109	– (6) c Rogers b Smith	74
J. M. Bairstow c and b Smith	67	– (7) c Haddin b Harris	20
†M. J. Prior c Haddin b Smith	6	– (8) not out	1
T. T. Bresnan c Haddin b Harris	7	– (5) c Rogers b Pattinson	38
J. M. Anderson c Haddin b Harris	12		
S. C. J. Broad c Haddin b Pattinson	33		
G. P. Swann not out	28		
L-b 11, w 4, n-b 6	21	B 15, l-b 8	23
(100.1 overs)	361	(7 wkts dec, 114.1 overs)	349

1/18 (1) 2/26 (2) 3/28 (4) 4/127 (3) 5/271 (5)
6/274 (6) 7/283 (7) 8/289 (8) 9/313 (9) 10/361 (10)

1/22 (1) 2/22 (3) 3/30 (4) 4/129 (5) 5/282 (6)
6/344 (7) 7/349 (2)

Pattinson 20.1–3–95–1; Harris 26–6–72–5; Watson 13–4–45–1; Siddle 22–6–76–0; Agar 13–2–44–0; Smith 6–1–18–3. *Second Innings*—Harris 18.1–4–31–2; Watson 12–5–25–0; Siddle 21–6–65–3; Pattinson 20–8–42–1; Smith 14–0–65–1; Agar 29–5–98–0.

Australia

S. R. Watson lbw b Bresnan	30	– lbw b Anderson	20
C. J. L. Rogers lbw b Swann	15	– b Swann	6
U. T. Khawaja c Pietersen b Swann	14	– c Anderson b Root	54
P. J. Hughes c Prior b Bresnan	1	– lbw b Swann	1
*M. J. Clarke lbw b Broad	28	– c Cook b Root	51
S. P. D. Smith c Bell b Swann	2	– c Prior b Bresnan	1
†B. J. Haddin c Trott b Swann	7	– lbw b Swann	7
A. C. Agar run out	2	– c Prior b Bresnan	16
P. M. Siddle c Swann b Anderson	2	– b Anderson	18
J. L. Pattinson not out	10	– lbw b Swann	35
R. J. Harris c Pietersen b Swann	10	– not out	16
B 4, l-b 1, w 2	7	B 4, l b 5, w 1	10
(53.3 overs)	128	(90.3 overs)	235

1/42 (1) 2/50 (2) 3/53 (4) 4/69 (3) 5/86 (6) 6/91 (5)
7/96 (8) 8/104 (9) 9/104 (7) 10/128 (11)

1/24 (1) 2/32 (2) 3/36 (4) 4/134 (5) 5/135 (3)
6/136 (6) 7/154 (8) 8/162 (7) 9/192 (9) 10/235 (10)

Anderson 14–8–25–1; Broad 11–3–26–1; Bresnan 7–1–28–2; Swann 21.3–5–44–5. *Second Innings*—Anderson 18–2–55–2; Broad 21–4–54–0; Swann 30.3–5–78–4; Bresnan 14–8–30–2; Root 7–3–9–2.

Umpires: H. D. P. K. Dharmasena *(Sri Lanka)* (17) and M. Erasmus *(South Africa)* (19).
Third umpire: A. L. Hill *(New Zealand)*. Referee: R. S. Madugalle *(Sri Lanka)* (143).

Close of play: First day, England 289–7 (Bresnan 7, Anderson 4); Second day, England 31–3 (Root 18, Bresnan 0); Third day, England 333–5 (Root 178, Bairstow 11).

ENGLAND v AUSTRALIA 2013 (3rd Test)

At Old Trafford, Manchester, on 1, 2, 3, 4, 5 August, 2013.
Toss: Australia.   Result: MATCH DRAWN.
Debuts: none.
Man of the Match: M. J. Clarke.

Australia made most of the running in a match in which England – set 332 in 98 overs – were grateful for the rain which eventually ended proceedings soon after tea on the final day. The resultant draw meant England had retained the Ashes in the Third Test of a full series for only the second time, after 1928–29. After winning the toss, Australia ran up 527, initially thanks to Rogers, who looked set for a maiden Test century before, his concentration disturbed by movement in the pavilion (which, for the first time at Old Trafford, was behind the arm), he was lbw for 84. Clarke took over, shrugging off poor form and a dodgy back to purr to 187, his 24th Test century: he eventually played on, Broad's 200th Test wicket 326 balls after the 199th. Australia's seamers then shared nine wickets as England laboured at first, before recovering thanks to Pietersen's 23rd (and, as it turned out, last) Test century, a strutting innings in which he was especially severe on Lyon. Australia still led by 159, but struggled to increase that quickly in indifferent light, although Warner – returning after effectively being suspended for the first two Tests following a late-night incident with Root – moved back to open and made a brisk 41. Cook fell in the third over, trapped by a beauty that swung in from Harris, who soon strangled Trott too. England were 27 for three when Pietersen stomped off after unsuccessfully reviewing a caught-behind… and then it rained.

Australia

S. R. Watson c Cook b Bresnan	19	– (4) c Pietersen b Bresnan		18
C. J. L. Rogers lbw b Swann	84	– (1) c Prior b Broad		12
U. T. Khawaja c Prior b Swann	1	– b Swann		24
*M. J. Clarke b Broad	187	– (5) not out		30
S. P. D. Smith c Bairstow b Swann	89	– (6) run out		19
D. A. Warner c Trott b Swann	5	– (2) c Root b Bresnan		41
†B. J. Haddin not out	65	– c Broad b Anderson		8
P. M. Siddle b Swann	1			
M. A. Starc not out	66	– (8) c Swann b Anderson		11
R. J. Harris (did not bat)		– (9) not out		0
L-b 6, w 2, n-b 2	10	B 4, l-b 2, w 3		9
(7 wkts dec, 146 overs)	527	(7 wkts dec, 36 overs)		172

1/76 (1) 2/82 (3) 3/129 (2) 4/343 (5) 5/365 (6)
6/427 (4) 7/430 (8)

1/23 (1) 2/74 (2) 3/99 (3) 4/103 (4) 5/133 (6)
6/152 (7) 7/172 (8)

N. M. Lyon did not bat.

Anderson 33–6–116–0; Broad 33–6–108–1; Bresnan 32–6–114–1; Swann 43–2–159–5; Root 4–0–18–0; Trott 1–0–6–0. *Second Innings*—Anderson 8–0–37–2; Broad 7–2–30–1; Swann 15–0–74–1; Bresnan 6–0–25–2.

England

*A. N. Cook c Haddin b Starc	62	– lbw b Harris		0
J. E. Root c Haddin b Siddle	8	– not out		13
T. T. Bresnan c Haddin b Siddle	1			
I. J. L. Trott c Clarke b Harris	5	– (3) c Haddin b Harris		11
K. P. Pietersen lbw b Starc	113	– (4) c Haddin b Siddle		8
I. R. Bell b Harris	60	– (5) not out		4
J. M. Bairstow c Watson b Starc	22			
†M. J. Prior c Warner b Siddle	30			
S. C. J. Broad c Haddin b Lyon	32			
G. P. Swann c Haddin b Siddle	11			
J. M. Anderson not out	3			
B 3, l-b 17, n-b 1	21	W 1		1
(139.3 overs)	368	(3 wkts, 20.3 overs)		37

1/47 (2) 2/49 (3) 3/64 (4) 4/110 (1) 5/225 (6) 6/277 (7)
7/280 (5) 8/338 (9) 9/353 (10) 10/368 (8)

1/0 (1) 2/15 (3) 3/27 (4)

Harris 31–9–82–2; Starc 27–5–76–3; Lyon 35–12–95–1; Watson 15–7–26–0; Siddle 29.3–7–63–4; Smith 2–0–6–0. *Second Innings*—Harris 7–3–13–2; Starc 4–2–6–0; Watson 2–2–0–0; Lyon 3–0–8–0; Siddle 3.3–0–8–1; Clarke 1–0–2–0.

Umpires: M. Erasmus *(South Africa)* (20) and A. L. Hill *(New Zealand)* (39).
Third umpire: H. D. P. K. Dharmasena *(Sri Lanka)*. Referee: R. S. Madugalle *(Sri Lanka)* (144).

Close of play: First day, Australia 303–3 (Clarke 125, Smith 70); Second day, England 52–2 (Cook 36, Trott 2); Third day, England 294–7 (Prior 6, Broad 9); Fourth day, Australia 172–7 (Clarke 30, Harris 0).

ENGLAND v AUSTRALIA 2013 (4th Test)

At Riverside Ground, Chester-le-Street, on 9, 10, 11, 12 August, 2013.
Toss: England.   Result: ENGLAND WON BY 74 RUNS.
Debuts: none.
Man of the Match: S. C. J. Broad.

On the fourth evening of a fluctuating Test, Australia were 168 for three, chasing 299 for a victory that would have turned the series finale into an unexpected crack at redemption, if not the urn. And then Cook replaced the misfiring Anderson with Broad, one of the bowlers who had resolved over tea – after pitching too short before – to sort out their lengths. Less than two hours later, the match was over. Broad swept away six for 20 in 45 balls; in all, nine wickets fell in an elongated session, leaving England 3–0 up in an Ashes series for the first time since 1977; Broad's match figures were England's best against Australia since Phil Tufnell took 11 for 93 at The Oval in 1993. The jubilation meant it was easy to forget the batting of Bell, whose third century of the series rescued England from 49 for three in the second innings, a lead of just 17. He shared important stands with Pietersen and Bairstow, before Bresnan and Swann pushed the lead close to 300. For Australia, Rogers completed the century he missed in Manchester, despite being marooned on 96 for 19 deliveries: at 35, he was his country's oldest maiden centurion since Arthur Richardson, who was 12 days short of his 38th birthday when he made 100 at Headingley in 1926. Rogers had scored 60 previous first-class centuries, one short of coach Darren Lehmann's Australian record, and ten shy of the overall mark before making one in a Test, 70 by England's Andy Sandham.

England

*A. N. Cook lbw b Bird	51	– c Haddin b Harris		22
J. E. Root c Haddin b Watson	16	– b Harris		2
I. J. L. Trott c Khawaja b Lyon	49	– c Haddin b Harris		23
K. P. Pietersen c Haddin b Lyon	26	– c Rogers b Lyon		44
I. R. Bell c Harris b Lyon	6	– b Harris		113
J. M. Bairstow lbw b Lyon	14	– c Haddin b Lyon		28
†M. J. Prior lbw b Siddle	17	– (8) b Harris		0
T. T. Bresnan not out	12	– (7) c and b Harris		45
S. C. J. Broad c Warner b Harris	3	– c Smith b Harris		13
G. P. Swann c Lyon b Harris	13	– not out		30
J. M. Anderson b Bird	16	– c Haddin b Lyon		0
B 5, l-b 1, w 3, n-b 6	15	B 4, l-b 5, w 1		10
(92 overs)	238	(95.1 overs)		330

1/34 (2) 2/107 (3) 3/149 (4) 4/153 (1) 5/155 (5)
6/189 (7) 7/193 (6) 8/198 (9) 9/214 (10) 10/238 (11)

1/17 (2) 2/42 (1) 3/49 (3) 4/155 (4) 5/221 (6)
6/251 (5) 7/251 (8) 8/275 (9) 9/317 (7) 10/330 (11)

Harris 19–3–70–2; Bird 22–9–58–2; Watson 13–6–21–1; Siddle 18–6–41–1; Lyon 20–7–42–4. *Second Innings—* Harris 28–2–117–7; Bird 20.3–6–67–0; Watson 6.3–1–22–0; Siddle 17–4–59–0; Lyon 22.1–3–55–3; Smith 1–0–1–0.

Australia

C. J. L. Rogers c Prior b Swann	110	– c Trott b Swann		49
D. A. Warner b Broad	3	– c Prior b Bresnan		71
U. T. Khawaja c Prior b Broad	0	– lbw b Swann		21
*M. J. Clarke c Cook b Broad	6	– b Broad		21
S. P. D. Smith c Prior b Bresnan	17	– b Broad		2
S. R. Watson c Prior b Broad	68	– lbw b Bresnan		2
†B. J. Haddin lbw b Swann	13	– lbw b Broad		4
P. M. Siddle c Cook b Anderson	5	– c Anderson b Broad		23
R. J. Harris lbw b Broad	28	– lbw b Broad		11
N. M. Lyon lbw b Anderson	4	– b Broad		8
J. M. Bird not out	0	– not out		1
B 2, l-b 11, w 1, n-b 2	16	B 6, l-b 5		11
(89.3 overs)	270	(68.3 overs)		224

1/12 (2) 2/12 (3) 3/49 (4) 4/76 (5) 5/205 (6) 6/224 (7)
7/233 (1) 8/245 (8) 9/258 (10) 10/270 (9)

1/109 (1) 2/147 (3) 3/168 (2) 4/174 (4) 5/175 (5)
6/179 (6) 7/181 (7) 8/199 (9) 9/211 (10) 10/224 (8)

Anderson 25–8–65–2; Broad 24.3–7–71–5; Bresnan 19–3–63–1; Swann 18–5–48–2; Trott 3–0–10–0. *Second Innings*—Anderson 16–1–73–0; Broad 18.3–3–50–6; Bresnan 13–2–36–2; Swann 18–6–53–2; Root 3–2–1–0.

Umpires: Aleem Dar *(Pakistan)* (83) and A. L. Hill *(New Zealand)* (40).
Third umpire: M. Erasmus *(South Africa)*. Referee: R. S. Mahanama *(Sri Lanka)* (44).

Close of play: First day, England 238–9 (Bresnan 12, Anderson 16); Second day, Australia 222–5 (Rogers 101, Haddin 12); Third day, England 234–5 (Bell 105, Bresnan 4).

ENGLAND v AUSTRALIA 2013 (5th Test)

At Kennington Oval, London, on 21, 22, 23, 24 (*no play*), 25 August, 2013.
Toss: Australia.   Result: MATCH DRAWN.
Debuts: England – S. C. Kerrigan, C. R. Woakes. Australia – J. P. Faulkner.
Man of the Match: S. R. Watson. Men of the Series: I. R. Bell and R. J. Harris.

A series beset by umpiring controversy ended with one more, when play was called off for bad light at 7.35 with England needing 21 from four overs to complete an unprecedented 4–0 Ashes triumph. A draw was probably the right outcome: Australia scarcely deserved to lose after making all the running. But the strict adherence to the rulebook was bad news for the crowd after a boring third day (England made 215 in 98.3 overs) and a pouring fourth. Australia's big total was set up by Watson's 176 – his first century for 48 innings – and a maiden hundred for Smith, completed with a straight six off Trott (he was the eighth Smith to score a Test ton, edging seven Taylors for clan honours). Watson was especially severe on the debutant slow left-armer Simon Kerrigan. England took their time in reply, hamstrung by Harris: the top seven all reached 25, but the top score was Root's 68. The scoreboard got stuck for a while at 181 for four: such was the scoring-rate that it was some time before anybody noticed. A draw seemed certain after the fourth-day washout, but Australia went for quick runs after England were winkled out; Haddin's final catch was his 29th dismissal of the series, beating Rod Marsh's overall record of 28 in 1982–83. Clarke's tea-time closure left England in 227 in 44 overs. It seemed to have backfired when Pietersen breezed past fifty again. Finally, though, the umpires decided it was too dark to continue.

Australia

C. J. L. Rogers c Trott b Swann	23			
D. A. Warner c Prior b Anderson	6	– (1) c and b Anderson		12
S. R. Watson c Pietersen b Broad	176	– (2) c Pietersen b Swann		26
*M. J. Clarke b Anderson	7	– (5) not out		28
S. P. D. Smith not out	138	– (6) c Swann b Broad		7
P. M. Siddle b Anderson	23			
†B. J. Haddin b Trott	30	– (4) c Prior b Broad		0
J. P. Faulkner c Trott b Woakes	23	– (3) c Prior b Broad		22
M. A. Starc b Swann	13	– (8) not out		13
R. J. Harris c and b Anderson	33	– (7) b Broad		1
N. M. Lyon not out	0			
B 1, l-b 12, w 2, n-b 5	20	L-b 2		2
(9 wkts dec, 128.5 overs)	492	(6 wkts dec, 23 overs)		111

1/11 (2) 2/118 (1) 3/144 (4) 4/289 (3) 5/320 (6)
6/385 (7) 7/422 (8) 8/446 (9) 9/491 (10)   1/34 (1) 2/44 (2) 3/50 (4) 4/67 (3) 5/83 (6) 6/85 (7)

Anderson 29.5–4–95–4; Broad 31–4–128–1; Swann 33–4–95–2; Woakes 24–7–96–1; Kerrigan 8–0–53–0; Trott 3–0–12–1. *Second Innings*—Anderson 6–1–27–1; Broad 10–2–43–4; Swann 7–0–39–1.

England

*A. N. Cook c Haddin b Harris	25	– lbw b Faulkner		34
J. E. Root c Watson b Lyon	68	– c Haddin b Harris		11
I. J. L. Trott lbw b Starc	40	– lbw b Faulkner		59
K. P. Pietersen c Watson b Starc	50	– c Warner b Harris		62
I. R. Bell c Haddin b Faulkner	45	– run out		17
C. R. Woakes c Clarke b Harris	25	– not out		17
†M. J. Prior c Starc b Faulkner	47	– not out		0
S. C. J. Broad b Starc	9			
G. P. Swann b Faulkner	34			
J. M. Anderson c Haddin b Faulkner	4			
S. C. Kerrigan not out	1			
B 11, l-b 10, w 5, n-b 3	29	L-b 4, n-b 2		6
(144.4 overs)	377	(5 wkts, 40 overs)		206

1/68 (1) 2/118 (2) 3/176 (3) 4/217 (4) 5/269 (6)
6/299 (5) 7/315 (8) 8/363 (7) 9/368 (10) 10/377 (9)   1/22 (2) 2/86 (1) 3/163 (4) 4/170 (3) 5/206 (5)

Starc 33–5–92–3; Harris 28–10–64–2; Faulkner 19.4–3–51–4; Siddle 28–7–74–0; Lyon 28–8–59–1; Smith 8–3–16–0. *Second Innings*—Harris 5–0–21–2; Starc 7–0–48–0; Siddle 3–0–16–0; Lyon 10–0–44–0; Clarke 2–0–4–0; Faulkner 8–1–47–2; Watson 5–0–22–0.

Umpires: Aleem Dar *(Pakistan)* (84) and H. D. P. K. Dharmasena *(Sri Lanka)* (18).
Third umpire: A. L. Hill *(New Zealand)*. Referee: R. S. Mahanama *(Sri Lanka)* (45).

Close of play: First day, Australia 307–4 (Smith 66, Siddle 18); Second day, England 32–0 (Cook 17, Root 13); Third day, England 247–4 (Bell 29, Woakes 15); Fourth day, no play.

ZIMBABWE v PAKISTAN 2013–14 (1st Test)

At Harare Sports Club on 3, 4, 5, 6, 7 September, 2013.
Toss: Zimbabwe.　　Result: PAKISTAN WON BY 221 RUNS.
Debuts: Zimbabwe – Sikandar Raza.
Man of the Match: Younis Khan.

It is hardly unprecedented for a team to dominate the first 3½ days of a Test before losing, but for Zimbabwe the scenario was genuinely surprising and hard to stomach. Pakistan would never have won without Saeed Ajmal's 11 wickets, or Younis Khan's hard-earned runs: only after nine hours of studious graft was he able to cut loose and fly, handsomely, to his fourth Test double-century (only Javed Miandad, with six, made more for Pakistan; Mohammad Yousuf and Zaheer Abbas also scored four). Zimbabwe's seamers lacked genuine pace, but bowled with accuracy and patience. Azhar Ali spent almost 4½ hours over 78, but his colleagues were either impatient or careless. Pakistan were in trouble on a good pitch at 182 for eight, before Ajmal cannily ushered the total to semi-respectability. And then Ajmal the bowler undid Zimbabwe's hopes of a decisive lead; his seven wickets included all three half-centurions – one of whom, Pakistan-born Sikandar Raza, was making his debut after Brendan Taylor's wife gave birth. Zimbabwe's lead looked sufficient when Pakistan crashed to 23 for three. Misbah-ul-Haq's rescue attempt ended with a soft drive to cover, and when Asad Shafiq missed Chatara's off-cutter the lead with five wickets left was only 91. But Adnan Akmal made light of the situation by reverse-sweeping with joyous freedom; his stand with Younis, who was twice missed close in, changed the game. The eventual target of 342 was far beyond Zimbabwe, and the spinners wrapped things up just before lunch on the fifth day.

Pakistan

Khurram Manzoor lbw b Panyangara	11	– lbw b Panyangara	5
Mohammad Hafeez c Sibanda b Chatara	5	– c Mawoyo b Chatara	16
Azhar Ali c Sibanda b S. W. Masakadza	78	– lbw b Panyangara	0
Younis Khan b Panyangara	3	– not out	200
*Misbah-ul-Haq c Sibanda b Utseya	53	– c Sibanda b S. W. Masakadza	52
Asad Shafiq c Mawoyo b Utseya	4	– b Chatara	15
†Adnan Akmal b Chatara	18	– run out	64
Abdur Rehman lbw b S. W. Masakadza	7	– lbw b Utseya	9
Saeed Ajmal b Chatara	49	– lbw b Utseya	1
Junaid Khan c Mutumbami b Panyangara	17	– b Utseya	8
Rahat Ali not out	0	– not out	35
L-b 3, w 1	4	B 11, l-b 1, w 2	14
(90.1 overs)	249	(9 wkts dec, 149.3 overs)	419

1/13 (2) 2/21 (1) 3/27 (4) 4/120 (5) 5/132 (6)
6/157 (7) 7/173 (8) 8/182 (3) 9/249 (10) 10/249 (9)

1/17 (1) 2/21 (3) 3/23 (2) 4/139 (5) 5/169 (6)
6/287 (7) 7/309 (8) 8/313 (9) 9/331 (10)

Chatara 22.1–6–64–3; Panyangara 20–2–71–3; S. W. Masakadza 22–8–40–2; Chigumbura 2–0–15–0; Utseya 23–1–55–2; H. Masakadza 1–0–1–0. *Second Innings*—Chatara 33–7–99–2; Panyangara 30–14–42–2; Utseya 37.3–5–137–3; S. W. Masakadza 34–4–100–1; H. Masakadza 15–5–29–0.

Zimbabwe

T. M. K. Mawoyo c Adnan Akmal b Junaid Khan	13	– lbw b Saeed Ajmal	2
V. Sibanda c Adnan Akmal b Junaid Khan	31	– lbw b Junaid Khan	6
*H. Masakadza b Saeed Ajmal	19	– c Azhar Ali b Junaid Khan	1
Sikandar Raza c Misbah-ul-Haq b Saeed Ajmal	60	– c Azhar Ali b Abdur Rehman	24
M. N. Waller c Mohammad Hafeez b Saeed Ajmal	70	– c Rahat Ali b Abdur Rehman	17
E. Chigumbura c Azhar Ali b Saeed Ajmal	69	– c Mohammad Hafeez b Abdur Rehman	28
†R. Mutumbami lbw b Saeed Ajmal	13	– not out	16
P. Utseya b Rahat Ali	16	– b Saeed Ajmal	0
S. W. Masakadza lbw b Saeed Ajmal	14	– lbw b Saeed Ajmal	0
T. Panyangara not out	4	– lbw b Abdur Rehman	6
T. L. Chatara c Younis Khan b Saeed Ajmal	0	– lbw b Saeed Ajmal	13
B 5, l-b 11, w 2	18	B 1, l-b 5, n-b 1	7
(103.3 overs)	327	(46.4 overs)	120

1/25 (1) 2/68 (2) 3/68 (3) 4/195 (5) 5/212 (4)
6/235 (7) 7/278 (8) 8/310 (9) 9/327 (6) 10/327 (11)

1/13 (1) 2/14 (3) 3/19 (2) 4/49 (5) 5/58 (4)
6/89 (6) 7/90 (8) 8/90 (9) 9/101 (10) 10/120 (11)

Junaid Khan 25–8–71–2; Rahat Ali 23–3–70–1; Abdur Rehman 19–5–56–0; Saeed Ajmal 32.3–4–95–7; Younis Khan 4–1–19–0. *Second Innings*—Junaid Khan 10–3–20–2; Rahat Ali 7–1–35–0; Saeed Ajmal 16.4–5–23–4; Abdur Rehman 13–5–36–4.

Umpires: S. J. Davis *(Australia)* (47) and R. E. J. Martinesz *(Sri Lanka)* (3).
Third umpire: T. J. Matibiri *(Zimbabwe)*. Referee: J. Srinath *(India)* (25).

Close of play: First day, Pakistan 249–9 (Saeed Ajmal 49); Second day, Zimbabwe 281–7 (Chigumbura 40, S. W. Masakadza 2); Third day, Pakistan 168–4 (Younis Khan 76, Asad Shafiq 15); Fourth day, Zimbabwe 13–1 (Sibanda 5).

ZIMBABWE v PAKISTAN 2013–14 (2nd Test)

At Harare Sports Club on 10, 11, 12, 13, 14 September, 2013.
Toss: Zimbabwe.   Result: ZIMBABWE WON BY 24 RUNS.
Debuts: none.
Man of the Match: T. L. Chatara. Man of the Series: Younis Khan.

This was more than just a series-levelling victory for Zimbabwe. It was only their fifth win in 82 Tests against the eight leading nations – though their third over Pakistan – and their biggest giant-killing act since beating India here in 2001. It was too close to call on the last morning: Pakistan needed 106, Zimbabwe five wickets. Misbah-ul-Haq held the key – but not even he could pull this one off by himself. He watched in dismay as last man Rahat Ali was run out, sent back after unwisely seeking a single off the final ball of an over. Chatara had completed his first five-for as batsmen struggled to get to grips with an underprepared pitch (this match had been scheduled for Bulawayo, but was shifted to Harare to cut costs). Masakadza and the returning Taylor put on 110 on the first day, and with the last four wickets adding 107, Zimbabwe reached a handy total, unfazed when a stray chicken had to be chased off the field. Younis Khan top-scored again in the reply, passing 7,000 Test runs, but the tail capsized against the lively left-armer Vitori; the last six wickets added only 19. Leading by 64, Zimbabwe were in control at 117 for one late on the third day, than lost three quick wickets before stumps, two of them to Rahat, who finished with five for 52. Khurram Manzoor began the quest for 264 with 11 uncompromising fours in his second half-century of the match, before becoming one of the fourth-day casualties.

Zimbabwe

T. M. K. Mawoyo c Adnan Akmal b Junaid Khan	0	– lbw b Abdur Rehman	58
V. Sibanda b Rahat Ali	14	– (6) c Adnan Akmal b Rahat Ali..........................	10
H. Masakadza c Mohammad Hafeez b Saeed Ajmal...	75	– lbw b Rahat Ali	44
*B. R. M. Taylor lbw b Abdur Rehman	51	– (5) c Azhar Ali b Rahat Ali	27
M. N. Waller c Adnan Akmal b Junaid Khan..............	23	– (7) c Khurram Manzoor b Saeed Ajmal..............	3
E. Chigumbura b Abdur Rehman.................................	15	– (8) c Adnan Akmal b Junaid Khan...................	3
†R. Mutumbami c Adnan Akmal b Junaid Khan	8	– (9) c Abdur Rehman b Saeed Ajmal	29
P. Utseya c Rahat Ali b Junaid Khan..........................	22	– (2) c Asad Shafiq b Rahat Ali	5
T. Panyangara b Rahat Ali..	24	– (4) c Azhar Ali b Abdur Rehman	0
T. L. Chatara lbw b Abdur Rehman	21	– c Adnan Akmal b Rahat Ali	1
B. V. Vitori not out..	19	– not out	0
B 7, l-b 14, w 1..	22	B 3, l-b 11, w 5..............................	19
(109.5 overs)	294	(89.5 overs)	199

1/0 (1) 2/31 (2) 3/141 (3) 4/172 (5) 5/176 (4)   1/13 (2) 2/117 (1) 3/121 (3) 4/121 (4) 5/136 (6)
6/187 (7) 7/203 (6) 8/234 (9) 9/248 (8) 10/294 (10)   6/149 (7) 7/156 (8) 8/177 (5) 9/199 (9) 10/199 (10)

Junaid Khan 33–11–67–4; Rahat Ali 19–7–48–2; Younis Khan 3–0–7–0; Saeed Ajmal 27–6–92–1; Abdur Rehman 23.5–6–47–3; Mohammad Hafeez 4–0–12–0. *Second Innings*—Junaid Khan 19–6–37–1; Rahat Ali 24.5–5–52–5; Saeed Ajmal 22–7–56–2; Abdur Rehman 24–5–40–2.

Pakistan

Khurram Manzoor run out...	51	– c Waller b Utseya	54
Mohammad Hafeez c Masakadza b Vitori....................	22	– c Vitori b Chatara............................	16
Azhar Ali lbw b Panyangara	7	– b Chatara	0
Younis Khan c Mawoyo b Panyangara.........................	77	– b Vitori	29
*Misbah-ul-Haq c Masakadza b Vitori	33	– not out	79
Asad Shafiq b Chatara	10	– c Mutumbami b Utseya........................	14
†Adnan Akmal c Taylor b Vitori	6	– lbw b Chatara	20
Abdur Rehman lbw b Panyangara................................	0	– c Mutumbami b Panyangara..................	16
Saeed Ajmal c Mutumbami b Vitori	7	– lbw b Chatara	2
Junaid Khan b Vitori	3	– c Waller b Chatara	1
Rahat Ali not out..	1	– run out	1
B 4, l-b 6, w 2, n-b 1	13	L-b 2, w 4, n-b 1...........................	7
(104.5 overs)	230	(81 overs)	239

1/29 (2) 2/62 (3) 3/96 (1) 4/182 (5) 5/211 (6)   1/30 (2) 2/46 (3) 3/90 (1) 4/100 (4) 5/133 (6)
6/212 (4) 7/212 (8) 8/224 (7) 9/229 (9) 10/230 (10)   6/163 (7) 7/197 (8) 8/214 (9) 9/238 (10) 10/239 (11)

Panyangara 22–9–43–3; Vitori 26.5–8–61–5; Chatara 27–10–45–1; Masakadza 12–5–24–0; Utseya 12–0–41–0; Chigumbura 5–2–6–0. *Second Innings*—Panyangara 16–3–43–1; Vitori 22–5–69–1; Chatara 23–2–61–5; Utseya 19–2–62–2; Masakadza 1–0–2–0.

Umpires: S. J. Davis *(Australia)* (48) and R. E. J. Martinesz *(Sri Lanka)* (4).
Third umpire: O. Chirombe *(Zimbabwe)*. Referee: J. Srinath *(India)* (26).

Close of play: First day, Zimbabwe 237–8 (Utseya 14, Chatara 0); Second day, Pakistan 163–3 (Younis Khan 52, Misbah-ul-Haq 27); Third day, Zimbabwe 121–4 (Taylor 0); Fourth day, Pakistan 158–5 (Misbah-ul-Haq 26, Adnan Akmal 17).

BANGLADESH v NEW ZEALAND 2013–14 (1st Test)

At Zohur Ahmed Chowdhury Stadium, Chittagong, on 9, 10, 11, 12, 13 October, 2013.
Toss: New Zealand.   Result: MATCH DRAWN.
Debuts: Bangladesh – Marshall Ayub. New Zealand – C. J. Anderson, I. S. Sodhi.
Man of the Match: Sohag Gazi.

Off-spinner Sohag Gazi, 22, became the first to collect a hundred and a hat-trick in the same Test. His hat-trick – Bangladesh's second, after Alok Kapali's at Peshawar in August 2003 – was a pleasant diversion as the game fizzled out. Bowling with the second new ball, Gazi trapped the debutant Corey Anderson with an arm-ball, had Watling caught behind, then Bracewell edged a doosra, which hit Mushfiqur Rahim's right leg but popped up to leg slip. However, Gazi's maiden Test century did more to help Bangladesh avoid defeat against New Zealand for only the second time in ten matches. When he entered they were 168 behind – but his stand of 105 with Robiul Islam helped turn that into an unexpected lead. New Zealand's tail had proved just as stubborn. Watling, caught at gully off a Rubel Hossain no-ball early on, completed his second Test century during a last-wicket stand of 127 with Boult; the fleet-footed Williamson had earlier eased to his fourth Test hundred. Bangladesh were soon eight for two, but the diminutive Mominul Haque, playing only his fourth Test, shot to a 36-ball fifty, almost all of them in front of square, and his maiden century arrived next morning from only 98 deliveries. Mominul, whose 181 included a Bangladesh-record 27 fours, put on 121 with Mushfiqur, saving the follow-on before both departed in the space of six balls. New Zealand still had victory hopes, but rain cut short the fourth day. Bangladesh eventually had 48 overs to survive, and did so with unaccustomed ease.

New Zealand

P. G. Fulton c Mominul Haque b Nasir Hossain	73	– lbw b Sohag Gazi	59
H. D. Rutherford c Abdur Razzak b Sohag Gazi	34	– lbw b Nasir Hossain	32
K. S. Williamson lbw b Shakib Al Hasan	114	– c Anamul Haque b Sohag Gazi	74
L. R. P. L. Taylor c sub (Naeem Islam) b Abdur Razzak	28	– not out	54
*B. B. McCullum lbw b Abdur Razzak	21	– b Sohag Gazi	22
B. P. Martin c Mushfiqur Rahim b Rubel Hossain	1		
C. J. Anderson c Nasir Hossain b Abdur Razzak	1	– (6) lbw b Sohag Gazi	8
†B-J. Watling st Mushfiqur Rahim b Mominul Haque	103	– (7) c Mushfiqur Rahim b Sohag Gazi	0
D. A. J. Bracewell b Sohag Gazi	29	– (8) c Shakib Al Hasan b Sohag Gazi	0
I. S. Sodhi lbw b Shakib Al Hasan	1	– (9) not out	22
T. A. Boult not out	52		
B 4, l-b 6, n-b 2	12	B 11, l-b 4, n-b 1	16
(157.1 overs)	469	(7 wkts dec, 90 overs)	287

1/57 (2) 2/183 (1) 3/244 (4) 4/276 (3) 5/280 (5) 6/282 (6)   1/48 (2) 2/149 (1) 3/200 (3) 4/250 (5)
7/282 (7) 8/339 (9) 9/342 (10) 10/469 (8)   5/260 (6) 6/260 (7) 7/260 (8)

Robiul Islam 13–3–23–0; Rubel Hossain 20–2–77–1; Abdur Razzak 55–10–147–3; Sohag Gazi 32–6–79–2; Shakib Al Hasan 24–5–89–2; Marshall Ayub 2–0–15–0; Nasir Hossain 5–1–19–1; Mominul Haque 6.1–0–10–1. *Second Innings*—Abdur Razzak 32–5–116–0; Rubel Hossain 6–0–21–0; Sohag Gazi 26–4–77–6; Shakib Al Hasan 9–1–19–0; Nasir Hossain 9–4–20–1; Robiul Islam 4–1–9–0; Mominul Haque 4–0–10–0.

Bangladesh

Tamim Iqbal c Williamson b Boult	0	– c Williamson b Martin	46
Anamul Haque lbw b Bracewell	3	– c Anderson b Martin	18
Marshall Ayub c Watling b Anderson	25	– lbw b Sodhi	31
Mominul Haque lbw b Anderson	181	– not out	22
Shakib Al Hasan c Watling b Williamson	19	– not out	50
*†Mushfiqur Rahim c Taylor b Bracewell	67		
Nasir Hossain c Williamson b Sodhi	46		
Sohag Gazi not out	101		
Abdur Razzak lbw b Boult	7		
Robiul Islam c Taylor b Bracewell	33		
Rubel Hossain c Taylor b Sodhi	4		
B 5, l-b 8, w 1, n-b 1	15	B 2, n-b 4	6
(148.5 overs)	501	(3 wkts, 48.2 overs)	173

1/1 (1) 2/8 (2) 3/134 (3) 4/180 (5) 5/301 (4) 6/301 (6)
7/371 (7) 8/387 (9) 9/492 (10) 10/501 (11)   1/39 (2) 2/99 (1) 3/101 (3)

Boult 24–9–50–2; Bracewell 25–2–96–3; Martin 27–3–113–0; Sodhi 28.5–3–112–2; Anderson 17–7–34–2; Williamson 27–4–83–1. *Second Innings*—Boult 4–1–9–0; Bracewell 5–0–14–0; Anderson 2–2–0–0; Williamson 10–3–24–0; Martin 16–4–62–2; Sodhi 10.2–1–57–1; Taylor 1–0–5–0.

Umpires: B. N. J. Oxenford *(Australia)* (14) and S. Ravi *(India)* (1).
Third umpire: Enamul Haque, sen. *(Bangladesh)*. Referee: J. Srinath *(India)* (27).

Close of play: First day, New Zealand 280–5 (Martin 0); Second day, Bangladesh 103–2 (Marshall Ayub 21, Mominul Haque 77); Third day, Bangladesh 380–7 (Sohag Gazi 28, Abdur Razzak 1); Fourth day, New Zealand 117–1 (Fulton 44, Williamson 28).

BANGLADESH v NEW ZEALAND 2013–14 (2nd Test)

At Shere Bangla National Stadium, Mirpur, Dhaka, on 21, 22, 23, 24, 25 (*no play*) October, 2013.
Toss: Bangladesh.　　　Result: MATCH DRAWN.
Debuts: Bangladesh – Al-Amin Hossain.
Man of the Match: Mominul Haque. Man of the Series: Mominul Haque.

The series was on the line heading into the final day, but incessant rain meant not a ball was bowled. Bangladesh emerged the happier, given their history of second-innings vulnerability. New Zealand fielded three left-arm seamers in a Test for the first time; leg-spinner Sodhi completed an unorthodox attack. The change worked: the recalled Wagner, who had toured Bangladesh with the South African academy in 2007–08, bagged his first five-for for his adopted country. Bangladesh were reasonably placed at the first-day close, but lost their last five for 36 next morning, as their old inability to stay at the crease resurfaced: other than Tamim Iqbal no one stayed longer than 80 minutes. Even Tamim was dropped twice, but his luck ran out at 95 when he was cramped up by Wagner, and Williamson took a superb diving catch in the gully. In the second innings, Wagner reduced Bangladesh to 55 for two with a day and a half remaining, and New Zealand smelled victory. Tamim buckled down, and found an ally in the in-form Mominul Haque: they added 157, a Bangladesh third-wicket record. Once again it took a superb catch, one-handed by Taylor above his head at slip, to oust Tamim, after 70 from 218 deliveries, his slowest 50-plus score. Mominul completed back-to-back hundreds when, after 12 balls on 99, he bashed Wagner back over his head for four. New Zealand's commanding position had been built on an unflashy stand between Williamson and Anderson, who scored his maiden century in his second Test.

Bangladesh

Tamim Iqbal c Williamson b Wagner	95	– c Taylor b Williamson	70
Anamul Haque c Williamson b Boult	7	– c Fulton b Wagner	22
Marshall Ayub b Wagner	41	– c Taylor b Wagner	9
Mominul Haque c Watling b Anderson	47	– not out	126
Shakib Al Hasan lbw b Sodhi	20	– not out	32
*†Mushfiqur Rahim c Fulton b Wagner	18		
Nasir Hossain c Taylor b Sodhi	19		
Sohag Gazi c Williamson b Wagner	14		
Abdur Razzak b Sodhi	13		
Rubel Hossain c Watling b Wagner	4		
Al-Amin Hossain not out	0		
B 2, l-b 1, w 1	4	B 8, l-b 1, n-b 1	10
(74.5 overs)	282	(3 wkts, 89 overs)	269

1/23 (2) 2/90 (3) 3/166 (4) 4/208 (1) 5/228 (5) 6/246 (6)
7/252 (7) 8/266 (8) 9/274 (10) 10/282 (9)　　　　1/39 (2) 2/55 (3) 3/212 (1)

Boult 16–2–55–1; Bracewell 14–1–57–0; Wagner 19–5–64–5; Sodhi 18.5–3–59–3; Williamson 4–0–30–0; Anderson 3–0–14–1. *Second Innings*—Boult 16–2–62–0; Bracewell 14–2–47–0; Wagner 18–4–52–2; Sodhi 14–2–37–0; Anderson 9–2–18–0; Williamson 18–4–44–1.

New Zealand

P. G. Fulton lbw b Shakib Al Hasan	14
H. D. Rutherford c Mominul Haque b Shakib Al Hasan	13
K. S. Williamson c Tamim Iqbal b Abdur Razzak	62
L. R. P. L. Taylor c Nasir Hossain b Shakib Al Hasan	53
*B. B. McCullum c Rubel Hossain b Shakib Al Hasan	11
C. J. Anderson c Sohag Gazi b Al-Amin Hossain	116
†B-J. Watling not out	70
D. A. J. Bracewell c Mushfiqur Rahim b Shakib Al Hasan	17
N. Wagner c Marshall Ayub b Nasir Hossain	8
I. S. Sodhi run out	58
T. A. Boult lbw b Abdur Razzak	4
B 4, l-b 4, w 2, n-b 1	11
(140 overs)	437

1/31 (2) 2/32 (1) 3/101 (5) 4/127 (4) 5/267 (3) 6/287 (6)
7/318 (8) 8/335 (9) 9/428 (10) 10/437 (11)

Williamson, when 27, retired hurt at 76–2 and resumed at 101–3.

Al-Amin Hossain 16–3–58–1; Sohag Gazi 34–8–77–0; Shakib Al Hasan 43–13–103–5; Abdur Razzak 23–1–96–2; Rubel Hossain 18–1–81–0; Nasir Hossain 3–1–7–1; Mominul Haque 3–0–7–0.

Umpires: R. K. Illingworth *(England)* (5) and B. N. J. Oxenford *(Australia)* (15).
Third umpire: Sharfuddoula *(Bangladesh)*. Referee: J. Srinath *(India)* (28).

Close of play: First day, Bangladesh 228–5 (Mushfiqur Rahim 14); Second day, New Zealand 107–3 (Taylor 37, Williamson 28); Third day, New Zealand 419–8 (Watling 59, Sodhi 55); Fourth day, Bangladesh 269–3 (Mominul Haque 126, Shakib Al Hasan 32).

PAKISTAN v SOUTH AFRICA 2013–14 (1st Test)

At Sheikh Zayed Stadium Abu Dhabi, on 14, 15, 16, 17 October, 2013.
Toss: South Africa.   Result: PAKISTAN WON BY SEVEN WICKETS.
Debuts: Pakistan – Shan Masood, Zulfiqar Babar.
Man of the Match: Khurram Manzoor.

Pakistan had just lost their previous Test, to Zimbabwe; their administration was in turmoil after disputed elections; and Saeed Ajmal had questioned the need for a foreign coach. Out of chaos came a convincing victory. It started with South Africa's inadequate first innings, in which Amla – imperious off the back foot – stood alone for his 20th Test century. There were three wickets apiece for the lofty Mohammad Irfan and slow left-armer Zulfiqar Babar, Pakistan's fourth-oldest debutant at nearly 35. De Villiers was carelessly run out after stretching forward; he had dragged his back foot out of the crease and Younis Khan threw the stumps down from slip. Pakistan's sixth opening pair in seven Tests then provided their first century start for 21 months. Khurram Manzoor extended his maiden hundred to Pakistan's highest score against South Africa (previously Azhar Mahmood's 136 at Johannesburg in 1997–98), while Shan Masood made 75. The third Test player born in nearby Kuwait, after Shakeel Ahmed and Tanvir Ahmed, Masood also became only the 12th to make his Test debut on his birthday, his 24th. Misbah-ul-Haq inflated the lead with a resolute 100, his first for 2½ years: at 39 he was the oldest Test centurion since Graham Gooch in 1994. South Africa were soon sunk at 133 for seven. Junaid Khan removed Kallis cheaply for the second time, and only de Villiers's accomplished 90 delayed matters. Needing only 40, Pakistan plunged to seven for three, but Misbah sealed a notable win by launching Peterson into the sightscreen.

South Africa

A. N. Petersen c Shan Masood b Mohammad Irfan.....	3	– (2) c Adnan Akmal b Mohammad Irfan.............	17
*G. C. Smith c Adnan Akmal b Mohammad Irfan......	15	– (1) st Adnan Akmal b Saeed Ajmal....................	32
H. M. Amla c Younis Khan b Mohammad Irfan..........	118	– c Adnan Akmal b Zulfiqar Babar.......................	10
J. H. Kallis c Adnan Akmal b Junaid Khan................	5	– lbw b Junaid Khan	0
†A. B. de Villiers run out	19	– c Shan Masood b Junaid Khan..........................	90
J-P. Duminy c Asad Shafiq b Zulfiqar Babar..............	57	– (7) lbw b Junaid Khan......................................	0
F. du Plessis c Asad Shafiq b Zulfiqar Babar.............	1	– (8) c and b Saeed Ajmal...................................	9
R. J. Peterson b Zulfiqar Babar................................	5	– (9) not out...	47
V. D. Philander lbw b Saeed Ajmal	3	– (10) c Adnan Akmal b Saeed Ajmal..................	10
D. W. Steyn st Adnan Akmal b Saeed Ajmal..............	15	– (6) b Zulfiqar Babar...	7
M. Morkel not out	2	– c and b Saeed Ajmal...	0
B 1, l-b 4, n-b 1	6	B 4, l-b 4, n-b 2	10
(93.1 overs)	249	(82.4 overs)	232

1/6 (1) 2/19 (2) 3/43 (4) 4/104 (5) 5/199 (6) 6/205 (7)
7/217 (8) 8/222 (9) 9/245 (3) 10/249 (10)

1/38 (2) 2/57 (1) 3/58 (4) 4/72 (3) 5/104 (6) 6/109 (7)
7/133 (8) 8/190 (5) 9/232 (10) 10/232 (11)

Mohammad Irfan 18.2–4–44–3; Junaid Khan 18.4–2–52–1; Zulfiqar Babar 27–2–89–3; Saeed Ajmal 29.1–6–59–2. *Second Innings*—Mohammad Irfan 13–1–42–1; Junaid Khan 18–1–57–3; Saeed Ajmal 32.4–7–74–4; Zulfiqar Babar 19–6–51–2.

Pakistan

Khurram Manzoor c Kallis b Philander........................	146	– c de Villiers b Philander.................................	4
Shan Masood lbw b Duminy....................................	75	– c de Villiers b Philander.................................	0
Azhar Ali c de Villiers b Philander	11	– c Kallis b Steyn	3
Younis Khan c Petersen b Morkel.............................	1	– not out...	9
*Misbah-ul-Haq lbw b Steyn....................................	100	– not out...	28
Asad Shafiq c Petersen b Duminy	54		
†Adnan Akmal b Steyn...	32		
Saeed Ajmal c de Villiers b Philander........................	13		
Zulfiqar Babar run out..	2		
Junaid Khan c Morkel b Steyn.................................	3		
Mohammad Irfan not out	0		
L-b 4, n-b 1	5	L-b 1..	1
(138.4 overs)	442	(3 wkts, 13.5 overs).........................	45

1/135 (2) 2/173 (3) 3/178 (4) 4/290 (1) 5/372 (6)
6/394 (5) 7/423 (8) 8/429 (9) 9/437 (10) 10/442 (7)

1/4 (2) 2/7 (3) 3/7 (1)

Steyn 28.4–5–88–3; Philander 26–5–84–3; Morkel 23–5–35–1; Kallis 13–2–44–0; Peterson 27–2–111–0; Duminy 19–1–68–2; du Plessis 2–0–8–0. *Second Innings*—Steyn 5–3–7–1; Philander 5–1–11–2; Morkel 2–0–12–0; Peterson 1.5–0–14–0.

Umpires: P. R. Reiffel *(Australia)* (5) and R. J. Tucker *(Australia)* (26).
Third umpire: I. J. Gould *(England)*. Referee: D. C. Boon *(Australia)* (19).

Close of play: First day, South Africa 245–8 (Amla 118, Steyn 13); Second day, Pakistan 263–3 (Khurram Manzoor 131, Misbah-ul-Haq 44); Third day, South Africa 72–4 (de Villiers 11, Steyn 0).

PAKISTAN v SOUTH AFRICA 2013–14 (2nd Test)

At Dubai International Cricket Stadium on 23, 24, 25, 26 October, 2013.
Toss: Pakistan.   Result: SOUTH AFRICA WON BY AN INNINGS AND 92 RUNS.
Debuts: none.
Man of the Match: G. C. Smith. Man of the Series: A. B. de Villiers.

South Africa maintained their unbeaten record in overseas Test series since 2006, although their comprehensive victory was tarnished somewhat by a five-run penalty for ball-tampering – du Plessis was fined half his match fee for rubbing it vigorously on his trouser-pocket zip. Pakistan grumbled about leniency: Shahid Afridi had been banned for two one-day games after biting the ball in 2010. Pakistan had started badly, gifting five wickets to their former countryman Imran Tahir; he wasn't complaining, as he had been mauled for figures of 37–1–260–0 in his previous Test, at Adelaide 11 months before. Pakistan had also been dismissed for 99 in their last Test at Dubai, against England in 2011–12. They bounced back to win that one, but Smith made sure there was no repeat, extending his 27th and last Test century to his fifth double. He battled for 627 minutes, and hit only 16 fours. South Africa were ahead by the end of the first day, and Smith and de Villiers – dropped first ball by Adnan Akmal off Mohammad Irfan – batted almost throughout the second, eventually adding 338. Pakistan's openers went for ducks – Khurram Manzoor completing a pair – but Misbah-ul-Haq and Asad Shafiq staved off embarrassment in a stand of 197. However, South Africa's spinners worked their way through. Amla missed the match as he had flown home for the birth of his first child. This was the only Test match in 2013 won by the away team, apart from victories by Bangladesh and Pakistan in Zimbabwe.

Pakistan

Khurram Manzoor c du Plessis b Steyn	0	– (2) c Kallis b Philander		0
Shan Masood b Imran Tahir	21	– (1) lbw b Steyn		0
Azhar Ali lbw b Morkel	19	– lbw b Duminy		19
Younis Khan c de Villiers b Steyn	10	– b Imran Tahir		36
*Misbah-ul-Haq lbw b Imran Tahir	2	– c Kallis b Elgar		88
Asad Shafiq b Imran Tahir	10	– st de Villiers b Duminy		130
†Adnan Akmal b Imran Tahir	0	– lbw b Imran Tahir		5
Saeed Ajmal run out	0	– lbw b Imran Tahir		9
Zulfiqar Babar not out	25	– absent hurt		
Mohammad Irfan b Imran Tahir	0	– (9) b Duminy		14
Junaid Khan b Steyn	4	– (10) not out		2
B 5, l-b 3	8	B 10, l-b 5, w 1, n-b 2, p 5		23
(36.4 overs)	99	(135.1 overs)		326

1/0 (1) 2/38 (3) 3/52 (2) 4/60 (4) 5/60 (5) 6/60 (7)
7/64 (8) 8/76 (6) 9/76 (10) 10/99 (11)

1/0 (1) 2/2 (2) 3/48 (3) 4/70 (4) 5/267 (5)
6/278 (7) 7/301 (8) 8/323 (9) 9/326 (6)

Steyn 13.4–2–38–3; Philander 5–2–9–0; Morkel 5–1–12–1; Imran Tahir 13–3–32–5. *Second Innings*—Steyn 22–9–48–1; Philander 19–7–34–1; Morkel 22–7–47–0; Imran Tahir 42–14–98–3; Kallis 7–3–9–0; Duminy 21.1–3–67–3; Elgar 2–0–3–1.

South Africa

A. N. Petersen lbw b Zulfiqar Babar	26
*G. C. Smith c Younis Khan b Saeed Ajmal	234
D. Elgar c Azhar Ali b Saeed Ajmal	23
J. H. Kallis lbw b Saeed Ajmal	7
D. W. Steyn b Mohammad Irfan	7
†A. B. de Villiers c Adnan Akmal b Mohammad Irfan	164
J-P. Duminy b Mohammad Irfan	7
F. du Plessis not out	17
V. D. Philander b Saeed Ajmal	8
M. Morkel c Younis Khan b Saeed Ajmal	7
Imran Tahir c Misbah-ul-Haq b Saeed Ajmal	2
B 5, l-b 8, w 2	15
(163.1 overs)	517

1/37 (1) 2/91 (3) 3/119 (4) 4/134 (5) 5/472 (6) 6/478 (2)
7/486 (7) 8/505 (9) 9/515 (10) 10/517 (11)

Mohammad Irfan 34.3–5–102–3; Junaid Khan 31.3–2–105–0; Saeed Ajmal 55.5–8–151–6; Zulfiqar Babar 36.2–2–124–1; Azhar Ali 5–0–22–0.

Umpires: I. J. Gould *(England)* (35) and R. J. Tucker *(Australia)* (27).
Third umpire: P. R. Reiffel *(Australia)*. Referee: D. C. Boon *(Australia)* (20).

Close of play: First day, South Africa 128–3 (Smith 67, Steyn 3); Second day, South Africa 460–4 (Smith 227, de Villiers 157); Third day, Pakistan 132–4 (Misbah-ul-Haq 42, Asad Shafiq 28).

INDIA v WEST INDIES 2013–14 (1st Test)

At Eden Gardens, Kolkata, on 6, 7, 8 November, 2013.
Toss: West Indies.   Result: INDIA WON BY AN INNINGS AND 51 RUNS.
Debuts: India – Mohammed Shami, R. G. Sharma. West Indies – S. S. Cottrell.
Man of the Match: R. G. Sharma.

This series was arranged at short notice, primarily to give Sachin Tendulkar a fond farewell at home after he decided to retire, aged 40, after 24 years of international cricket. West Indies' planned 2014–15 visit was advanced by 12 months, and the ensuing South African tour shortened. This match did not go by the script at first: at 83 for five on the second morning, India were in a spot of bother, with Shillingford finding bounce and turn to take four wickets, including Tendulkar, lbw after being hit on the thigh. Vijay had earlier become Shillingford's 50th wicket in just 11 matches. But Rohit Sharma – finally winning his first Test cap after a record 111 one-day internationals, crafted a fine 177, and put on 280 in 72 overs with Ashwin, the third-highest for the seventh wicket in all Tests. Sharma, the 14th Indian to make a century on Test debut, cuffed 23 fours and a six from 301 balls. A lead of 219 proved more than enough when West Indies batted poorly for the second time in the match. Gayle was twice an easy victim for the bustling Bhuvneshwar Kumar, while Bravo first ran himself out then cut loosely to point. Chanderpaul was left high and dry in the second innings as the pacy Mohammed Shami, a local boy, claimed a five-for on debut: his match figures had been bettered for Indian seamers at home only by Javagal Srinath and Kapil Dev (twice). Six of Shami's nine victims were bowled.

West Indies

C. H. Gayle c Vijay b Bhuvneshwar Kumar	18	– c Kohli b Bhuvneshwar Kumar	33
K. O. A. Powell c Bhuvneshwar Kumar b Mohammed Shami	28	– lbw b Ashwin	36
D. M. Bravo run out	23	– c Sharma b Ashwin	37
M. N. Samuels b Mohammed Shami	65	– lbw b Mohammed Shami	4
S. Chanderpaul b Ashwin	36	– not out	31
†D. Ramdin b Mohammed Shami	4	– c Vijay b Mohammed Shami	1
*D. J. G. Sammy c Bhuvneshwar Kumar b Ojha	16	– b Mohammed Shami	8
S. Shillingford lbw b Tendulkar	5	– b Mohammed Shami	0
V. Permaul c and b Ashwin	14	– run out	0
T. L. Best not out	14	– c Ojha b Ashwin	3
S. S. Cottrell b Mohammed Shami	0	– b Mohammed Shami	5
B 4, l-b 7	11	L-b 10	10
(78 overs)	234	(54.1 overs)	168

1/34 (1) 2/47 (2) 3/138 (4) 4/138 (3) 5/143 (6)
6/172 (7) 7/192 (8) 8/211 (9) 9/233 (5) 10/234 (11)

1/33 (1) 2/101 (2) 3/110 (4) 4/120 (3) 5/125 (6)
6/152 (7) 7/152 (8) 8/152 (9) 9/159 (10) 10/168 (11)

Bhuvneshwar Kumar 14–6–33–1; Mohammed Shami 17–2–71–4; Ashwin 21–9–52–2; Ojha 24–6–62–1; Tendulkar 2–1–5–1. *Second Innings*—Bhuvneshwar Kumar 6–1–20–1; Mohammed Shami 13.1–0–47–5; Ashwin 19–2–46–3; Ojha 13–3–27–0; Tendulkar 3–0–18–0.

India

S. Dhawan b Shillingford	23
M. Vijay st Ramdin b Shillingford	26
C. A. Pujara c Ramdin b Cottrell	17
S. R. Tendulkar lbw b Shillingford	10
V. Kohli c Powell b Shillingford	3
R. G. Sharma lbw b Permaul	177
*†M. S. Dhoni c Ramdin b Best	42
R. Ashwin b Shillingford	124
Bhuvneshwar Kumar c Gayle b Shillingford	12
Mohammed Shami st Ramdin b Permaul	1
P. P. Ojha not out	2
B 4, l-b 8, w 1, n-b 3	16
(129.4 overs)	453

1/42 (1) 2/57 (2) 3/79 (3) 4/82 (4) 5/83 (5) 6/156 (7)
7/436 (6) 8/444 (8) 9/451 (9) 10/453 (10)

Best 17–0–71–1; Cottrell 18–3–72–1; Shillingford 55–9–167–6; Permaul 23.4–2–67–2; Sammy 12–1–52–0; Samuels 4–0–12–0.

Umpires: R. A. Kettleborough *(England)* (15) and N. J. Llong *(England)* (19).
Third umpire: V. A. Kulkarni *(India)*. Referee: A. J. Pycroft *(Zimbabwe)* (23).

Close of play: First day, India 37–0 (Dhawan 21, Vijay 16); Second day, India 354–6 (Sharma 127, Ashwin 92).

INDIA v WEST INDIES 2013–14 (2nd Test)

At Wankhede Stadium, Mumbai, on 14, 15, 16 November, 2013.
Toss: India.   Result: WEST INDIES WON BY AN INNINGS AND 126 RUNS.
Debuts: none.
Man of the Match: P. P. Ojha. Man of the Series: R. G. Sharma.

Sachin Tendulkar's 200th and final Test, in front of his home crowd in Mumbai, was never going to be a tearless farewell, although the brevity of the match meant there were fewer waterworks than expected. As soon as he walked out to bat late on the first day, anxiety set in. His every move was watched, noted, and interpreted… the story of his career, really. The second day marked precisely 24 years since Tendulkar's Test debut at Karachi, aged 16. Hearts were in mouths when, at 48, he tried to upper-cut Best, but missed by some distance. Finally, at 74 Tendulkar attempted to cut Deonarine's off-spin, and Sammy clasped a smart catch with both hands in front of his face. It took a few seconds for the crowd to react. Then they stood as one and gave their man a rousing ovation. Tendulkar walked off with 15,921 Test runs at 53.78, and 51 centuries – figures which may never be approached in the Twenty20 age. Rather like Don Bradman at The Oval in 1948, it was unlikely he would have to bat again: West Indies had already been despatched for 182. Pujara collected a calm century, and Sharma another to go with his debut 177 at Kolkata. West Indies dipped again to 89 for six, before a brief rally from Chanderpaul (in his 150th Test) and Ramdin. Dhoni gave Tendulkar a bowl, but he couldn't break through: instead it was Ojha, with ten wickets in the match, who took the bowling honours.

West Indies

C. H. Gayle c Sharma b Mohammed Shami	11	– c Dhoni b Ojha	35
K. O. A. Powell c Dhawan b Ojha	48	– c Mohammed Shami b Ashwin	9
D. M. Bravo c Dhoni b Ashwin	29	– (4) c Vijay b Ashwin	11
M. N. Samuels c Vijay b Ojha	19	– (5) st Dhoni b Ojha	11
S. Chanderpaul c Ashwin b Bhuvneshwar Kumar	25	– (6) lbw b Ashwin	41
N. Deonarine c Vijay b Ashwin	21	– (7) c and b Ojha	0
†D. Ramdin not out	12	– (8) not out	53
*D. J. G. Sammy c Sharma b Ashwin	0	– (9) lbw b Ojha	1
S. Shillingford lbw b Ojha	0	– (10) lbw b Ashwin	8
T. L. Best c Dhoni b Ojha	0	– (3) lbw b Ojha	9
S. T. Gabriel c Dhoni b Ojha	1	– b Mohammed Shami	0
B 8, l-b 8	16	B 4, l-b 5	9
(55.2 overs)	182	(47 overs)	187

1/25 (1) 2/86 (3) 3/97 (2) 4/140 (4) 5/148 (5)
6/162 (6) 7/162 (8) 8/162 (9) 9/172 (10) 10/182 (11)

1/15 (2) 2/28 (3) 3/43 (4) 4/74 (5) 5/87 (1)
6/89 (7) 7/157 (6) 8/162 (9) 9/185 (10) 10/187 (11)

Bhuvneshwar Kumar 17–2–45–1; Mohammed Shami 12–2–36–1; Ashwin 15–2–45–3; Ojha 11.2–2–40–5. *Second Innings*—Bhuvneshwar Kumar 3–0–4–0; Mohammed Shami 7–0–28–1; Ashwin 17–4–89–4; Ojha 18–6–49–5; Tendulkar 2–0–8–0.

India

M. Vijay c Sammy b Shillingford	43
S. Dhawan c Chanderpaul b Shillingford	33
C. A. Pujara c and b Shillingford	113
S. R. Tendulkar c Sammy b Deonarine	74
V. Kohli c Sammy b Shillingford	57
R. G. Sharma not out	111
*†M. S. Dhoni c Sammy b Best	4
R. Ashwin c and b Gabriel	30
Bhuvneshwar Kumar c Sammy b Shillingford	4
P. P. Ojha run out	0
Mohammed Shami c Best b Deonarine	11
B 8, l-b 2, w 2, n-b 3	15
(108 overs)	495

1/77 (2) 2/77 (1) 3/221 (4) 4/315 (5) 5/354 (3)
6/365 (7) 7/409 (8) 8/414 (9) 9/415 (10) 10/495 (11)

Sammy 9–1–41–0; Gabriel 16–0–85–1; Shillingford 43–6–179–5; Best 18–0–93–1; Samuels 11–0–42–0; Deonarine 11–0–45–2.

Umpires: R. A. Kettleborough *(England)* (16) and N. J. Llong *(England)* (20).
Third umpire: V. A. Kulkarni *(India)*. Referee: A. J. Pycroft *(Zimbabwe)* (24).

Close of play: First day, India 157–2 (Pujara 34, Tendulkar 38); Second day, West Indies 43–3 (Gayle 6).

AUSTRALIA v ENGLAND 2013–14 (1st Test)

At Woolloongabba, Brisbane, on 21, 22, 23, 24 November, 2013.
Toss: Australia.   Result: AUSTRALIA WON BY 381 RUNS.
Debuts: Australia – G. J. Bailey.
Man of the Match: M. G. Johnson.

When Australia dipped to 132 for six on the first day, it was generally assumed that England's dominance of the three most recent Ashes series would continue. Even when Haddin led a recovery to 295, there were those who thought it would soon be business as (recently) usual. But Haddin's partner in a seventh-wicket stand of 114 was Johnson who, buoyed by his brisk 64, bowled with fire and venom to take nine wickets in the match, including Trott in both innings: he returned home shortly afterwards with a stress-related disorder. England were bundled out in their first innings for 136, and were then pummelled by Warner and Clarke in a stand of 158 in 29 overs. Clarke, who made his 25th Test century, declared not long after Swann had taken his 250th Test wicket (Bailey), uniquely within five years of his debut. Set 561 – roughly what they had scored for the loss of one wicket on this ground in 2010–11 – England soon slipped to ten for two, and never looked like recovering. Pietersen, in his 100th Test, was caught at long leg by Chris Sabburg, a local substitute with no first-class experience who was only on the field for two balls, briefly replacing Harris. This was the first time since 1975 that England and Australia had played back-to-back Ashes series: in all the teams contested ten Tests in less than six months. It was the tenth time England had lost the first Test in their last 15 overseas series.

Australia

C. J. L. Rogers c Bell b Broad		1	– c Carberry b Broad	16
D. A. Warner c Pietersen b Broad	49		– c Prior b Broad	124
S. R. Watson c Swann b Broad	22		– c Broad b Tremlett	6
*M. J. Clarke c Bell b Broad		1	– b Swann	113
S. P. D. Smith c Cook b Tremlett	31		– c Prior b Tremlett	0
G. J. Bailey c Cook b Anderson		3	– b Swann	34
†B. J. Haddin run out		94	– c Anderson b Tremlett	53
M. G. Johnson b Broad		64	– not out	39
P. M. Siddle c Cook b Anderson		7	– not out	4
R. J. Harris c Prior b Broad	9			
N. M. Lyon not out	1			
L-b 11, w 1, n-b 1	13		B 4, l-b 8	12
(97.1 overs)	295		(7 wkts dec, 94 overs)	401

1/12 (1) 2/71 (3) 3/73 (4) 4/83 (2) 5/100 (6) 6/132 (5)
7/246 (8) 8/265 (9) 9/282 (10) 10/295 (7)

1/67 (1) 2/75 (3) 3/233 (2) 4/242 (5) 5/294 (4)
6/305 (6) 7/395 (7)

Anderson 25.1–5–67–2; Broad 24–3–81–6; Tremlett 19–3–51–1; Swann 26–4–80–0; Root 3–1–5–0. *Second Innings*—Anderson 19–2–73–0; Broad 16–4–55–2; Tremlett 17–2–69–3; Swann 27–2–135–2; Root 15–2–57–0.

England

*A. N. Cook c Haddin b Harris		13	– c Haddin b Lyon	65
M. A. Carberry c Watson b Johnson		40	– b Harris	0
I. J. L. Trott c Haddin b Johnson		10	– c Lyon b Johnson	9
K. P. Pietersen c Bailey b Harris		18	– c sub (C. J. M. Sabburg) b Johnson	26
I. R. Bell c Smith b Lyon		5	– c Haddin b Siddle	32
J. E. Root c Smith b Johnson		2	– not out	26
†M. J. Prior c Smith b Lyon		0	– c Warner b Lyon	4
S. C. J. Broad c Rogers b Siddle		32	– c Haddin b Johnson	4
G. P. Swann c Bailey b Johnson		0	– c Smith b Johnson	0
C. T. Tremlett c Lyon b Harris		8	– c Bailey b Harris	7
J. M. Anderson not out		2	– c and b Johnson	2
B 4, l-b 2	6		L-b 2, w 1, n-b 1	4
(52.4 overs)	136		(81.1 overs)	179

1/28 (1) 2/55 (3) 3/82 (4) 4/87 (2) 5/87 (5) 6/87 (7)
7/89 (6) 8/91 (9) 9/110 (10) 10/136 (8)

1/1 (2) 2/10 (3) 3/72 (4) 4/130 (5) 5/142 (1)
6/146 (7) 7/151 (8) 8/151 (9) 9/172 (10) 10/179 (11)

Harris 15–5–28–3; Johnson 17–2–61–4; Siddle 11.4–3–24–1; Lyon 9–4–17–2. *Second Innings*—Harris 19–4–49–2; Johnson 21.1–7–42–5; Siddle 15–3–25–1; Lyon 20–6–46–2; Smith 4–1–15–0; Watson 2–2–0–0.

Umpires: Aleem Dar *(Pakistan)* (85) and H. D. P. K. Dharmasena *(Sri Lanka)* (19).
Third umpire: M. Erasmus *(South Africa)*. Referee: J. J. Crowe *(New Zealand)* (63).

Close of play: First day, Australia 273–8 (Haddin 78, Harris 4); Second day, Australia 65–0 (Rogers 15, Warner 45); Third day, England 24–2 (Cook 11, Pietersen 3).

AUSTRALIA v ENGLAND 2013–14 (2nd Test)

At Adelaide Oval on 5, 6, 7, 8, 9 December, 2013.
Toss: Australia.   Result: AUSTRALIA WON BY 218 RUNS.
Debuts: England – B. A. Stokes.
Man of the Match: M. G. Johnson.

If the First Test had been a rude awakening, what followed was even harder for England to bear. Australia's most docile surface offered an opportunity to regroup after their hounding at Brisbane: instead they lost heavily again, Johnson's fearsome pace once more the decisive factor. England were blown away for 172 – only Carberry and Bell managed more than 15 – as Johnson, twice on a hat-trick, produced a spell of six for 16 in 26 balls. The confusion was epitomised by Broad, who spent seven minutes fussing about the sightscreen before Johnson ripped out his leg stump, first ball. England's inadequate total was in response to Australia's towering 570, which featured another hundred from Clarke, and one from Haddin (containing five sixes) to make up for his near-miss at Brisbane. The total was swelled by a half-century from Harris, on the ground where he bagged a king pair in the 2010–11 Ashes. Clarke waived the follow-on, and extended an already formidable lead to 531 then declared shortly before the fourth day started. As England had not scored that many in their last three innings put together, defeat seemed inevitable – and so it was, although Root and Pietersen saved some face. Ben Stokes, on his debut, resisted for two hours, although he and Johnson were lucky to escape fines after a mid-pitch confrontation. Prior counter-attacked on the final morning, but soon became Siddle's fourth victim (he also broke one of Anderson's ribs), before Harris removed the hapless Panesar, who was thenceforth dropped.

Australia

C. J. L. Rogers c Prior b Swann	72	– c Prior b Anderson	2
D. A. Warner c Carberry b Broad	29	– not out	83
S. R. Watson c and b Anderson	51	– c Carberry b Anderson	0
*M. J. Clarke c Anderson b Stokes	148	– b Panesar	22
S. P. D. Smith b Panesar	6	– not out	23
G. J. Bailey c Swann b Broad	53		
†B. J. Haddin c Prior b Broad	118		
M. G. Johnson c Broad b Swann	5		
P. M. Siddle c Prior b Stokes	2		
R. J. Harris not out	55		
N. M. Lyon not out	17		
B 8, l-b 1, w 1, n-b 4	14	B 1, l-b 1	2
(9 wkts dec, 158 overs)	570	(3 wkts dec, 39 overs)	132

1/34 (2) 2/155 (3) 3/155 (1) 4/174 (5) 5/257 (6)
6/457 (4) 7/474 (8) 8/483 (9) 9/529 (7)   1/4 (1) 2/4 (3) 3/65 (4)

Anderson 30–10–85–1; Broad 30–3–98–3; Swann 36–4–151–2; Panesar 44–7–157–1; Stokes 18–2–70–2. *Second Innings*—Anderson 7–1–19–2; Broad 6–0–19–0; Swann 9–3–31–0; Stokes 7–3–20–0; Panesar 10–0–41–1.

England

*A. N. Cook b Johnson	3	– c Harris b Johnson	1
M. A. Carberry c Warner b Watson	60	– c Lyon b Siddle	14
J. E. Root c Rogers b Lyon	15	– c Haddin b Lyon	87
K. P. Pietersen c Bailey b Siddle	4	– b Siddle	53
I. R. Bell not out	72	– c Johnson b Smith	6
B. A. Stokes lbw b Johnson	1	– c Clarke b Harris	28
†M. J. Prior c Haddin b Johnson	0	– c Harris b Siddle	69
S. C. J. Broad b Johnson	0	– c Lyon b Siddle	29
G. P. Swann c Clarke b Johnson	7	– c Clarke b Harris	6
J. M. Anderson b Johnson	0	– not out	13
M. S. Panesar b Johnson	2	– c Rogers b Harris	0
L-b 3, w 2, n-b 3	8	L-b 1, w 4, n-b 1	6
(68.2 overs)	172	(101.4 overs)	312

1/9 (1) 2/57 (3) 3/66 (4) 4/111 (2) 5/117 (6)   1/1 (1) 2/20 (2) 3/131 (4) 4/143 (5) 5/171 (3)
6/117 (7) 7/117 (8) 8/135 (9) 9/135 (10) 10/172 (11)   6/210 (6) 7/255 (8) 8/293 (9) 9/301 (7) 10/312 (11)

Johnson 17.2–8–40–7; Harris 14–8–31–0; Lyon 20–5–64–1; Siddle 14–4–34–1; Watson 3–3–0–1. *Second Innings*—Harris 19.4–3–54–3; Johnson 24–8–73–1; Siddle 19–4–57–4; Lyon 26–7–78–1; Watson 6–3–6–0; Smith 7–0–43–1.

Umpires: H. D. P. K. Dharmasena *(Sri Lanka)* (20) and M. Erasmus *(South Africa)* (21).
Third umpire: A. L. Hill *(New Zealand)*. Referee: J. J. Crowe *(New Zealand)* (64).

Close of play: First day, Australia 273–5 (Clarke 48, Haddin 7); Second day, England 35–1 (Carberry 20, Root 9); Third day, Australia 132–3 (Warner 83, Smith 23); Fourth day, England 247–6 (Prior 31, Broad 22).

AUSTRALIA v ENGLAND 2013–14 (3rd Test)

At W. A. C. A. Ground, Perth, on 13, 14, 15, 16, 17 December, 2013.
Toss: Australia.　　　Result: AUSTRALIA WON BY 150 RUNS.
Debuts: none.
Man of the Match: S. P. D. Smith.

Australia recaptured the Ashes, in English hands since 2009, with another comprehensive victory on England's least favourite ground – they have lost nine and won only one (in 1978–79) of their 13 Tests at Perth, and this was their seventh successive defeat there. Things had looked a little brighter when Australia dipped to 143 for five on the first day, but the seemingly unstoppable Haddin made 55, and put on 124 with Smith, who went on to his second Test hundred. Cook and Carberry started with 85 for England, but it was downhill from there. Root was aghast when his caught-behind review proved inconclusive, and later Bell was given out lbw by Hawk-Eye. Only Bresnan passed 20 as England conceded a lead of 134. Warner gave Australia's second innings a turbocharged start, first out for 112 in a stand of 157 with Rogers; Watson added a rapid century, and Bailey applied the coup de grace by smashing 28, to equal the Test record, off the last over before the declaration. The bowler, Swann, announced his immediate retirement after the match, finishing with 255 Test wickets. Once again England had a mountain to climb. It became steeper when Harris's first ball swung in, moved away off the pitch, and flicked the top of Cook's off stump. Pietersen and Bell fought well, then Stokes made a pugnacious century in only his second Test, but it was 3–0 shortly after lunch on the final day. Both captains were playing in their 100th Tests.

Australia

C. J. L. Rogers run out		11	– c Carberry b Bresnan	54
D. A. Warner c Carberry b Swann	60		– c Stokes b Swann	112
S. R. Watson c Swann b Broad	18		– run out	103
*M. J. Clarke c Cook b Swann	24		– b Stokes	23
S. P. D. Smith c Prior b Anderson	111		– c sub (J. M. Bairstow) b Stokes	15
G. J. Bailey c Pietersen b Broad	7		– not out	39
†B. J. Haddin c Anderson b Stokes	55		– c Swann b Bresnan	5
M. G. Johnson c Prior b Broad	39		– not out	0
P. M. Siddle c Prior b Bresnan	21			
R. J. Harris c Root b Anderson	12			
N. M. Lyon not out	17			
L-b 6, w 3, n-b 1	10		B 8, l-b 5, w 5	18
(103.3 overs)	385		(6 wkts dec, 87 overs)	369

1/13 (1) 2/52 (3) 3/106 (4) 4/129 (2) 5/143 (6) 6/267 (7)
7/326 (8) 8/338 (5) 9/354 (10) 10/385 (9)

1/157 (1) 2/183 (2) 3/223 (4) 4/301 (5) 5/331 (3)
6/340 (7)

Anderson 23–5–60–2; Broad 22–2–100–3; Bresnan 23.3–4–81–1; Stokes 17–3–63–1; Swann 17–0–71–2; Root 1–0–4–0. *Second Innings*—Anderson 19–5–105–0; Bresnan 14–3–53–2; Stokes 18–1–82–2; Swann 27–8–92–1; Root 9–1–24–0.

England

*A. N. Cook c Warner b Lyon	72		– b Harris	0
M. A. Carberry b Harris	43		– lbw b Watson	31
J. E. Root c Haddin b Watson	4		– c Haddin b Johnson	19
K. P. Pietersen c Johnson b Siddle	19		– c Harris b Lyon	45
I. R. Bell lbw b Harris	15		– c Haddin b Siddle	60
B. A. Stokes c Haddin b Johnson	18		– c Haddin b Lyon	120
†M. J. Prior c Haddin b Siddle	8		– c Haddin b Johnson	26
T. T. Bresnan c Haddin b Harris	21		– c Rogers b Johnson	12
S. C. J. Broad lbw b Johnson	5		– (10) not out	2
G. P. Swann not out	19		– (9) c Smith b Lyon	4
J. M. Anderson c Bailey b Siddle	2		– c Bailey b Johnson	2
B 11, l-b 7, w 5, n-b 2	25		B 13, l-b 13, w 6	32
(88 overs)	251		(103.2 overs)	353

1/85 (2) 2/90 (3) 3/136 (1) 4/146 (4) 5/190 (5)
6/198 (6) 7/207 (7) 8/229 (9) 9/233 (8) 10/251 (11)

1/0 (1) 2/62 (2) 3/76 (3) 4/121 (4) 5/220 (5)
6/296 (7) 7/336 (6) 8/347 (9) 9/349 (8) 10/353 (11)

Harris 22–10–48–3; Johnson 22–7–62–2; Watson 12–3–48–1; Siddle 16–5–36–3; Lyon 16–6–39–1. *Second Innings*—Harris 19–2–73–1; Johnson 25.2–6–78–4; Lyon 22–5–70–3; Siddle 26–11–67–1; Watson 11–1–39–1.

Umpires: B. F. Bowden *(New Zealand)* (76) and M. Erasmus *(South Africa)* (22).
Third umpire: A. L. Hill *(New Zealand)*. Referee: J. J. Crowe *(New Zealand)* (65).

Close of play: First day, Australia 326–6 (Smith 103, Johnson 39); Second day, England 180–4 (Bell 9, Stokes 14); Third day, Australia 235–3 (Watson 29, Smith 5); Fourth day, England 251–5 (Stokes 72, Prior 7).

AUSTRALIA v ENGLAND 2013–14 (4th Test)

At Melbourne Cricket Ground on 26, 27, 28, 29 December, 2013.
Toss: Australia.   Result: AUSTRALIA WON BY EIGHT WICKETS.
Debuts: none.
Man of the Match: M. G. Johnson.

This was a close-fought match, but the result was the same: Australia made light of a potentially tricky target, and gambolled to an eight-wicket victory. Rogers took them almost home with his second Test hundred, unshackled by the retirement of Swann, who had dismissed him in seven of his previous 16 innings. Australia had to come behind to win this one – the first time they had done this in a Test since Barbados in April 2012 – after Anderson and Broad shared seven wickets: even Haddin's customary half-century could not prevent England taking a lead of 51. Pietersen had top-scored with 71, opening out after a cautious start in which he made only six from his first 44 balls, before doubling that when the substitute Nathan Coulter-Nile made a mess of a catch at fine leg. But England's strong position was once again undone by Johnson, with a vicious spell of five for 18 with the second new ball. Then in their second innings, England lost wickets in grisly clumps – three for one, then five for six at the end. Cook reached 8,000 Test runs in the first innings, at 29 years three days the youngest to get there (edging Sachin Tendulkar by 24 days); Clarke, 32, reached the same landmark later in the match (Pietersen, 33, had reached 8,000 in the previous Test). The first day was witnessed by 91,112 people, the official record for any day's Test cricket; the overall attendance of 271,865 was a record for a four-day match.

England

*A. N. Cook c Clarke b Siddle	27	– lbw b Johnson	51
M. A. Carberry b Watson	38	– lbw b Siddle	12
J. E. Root c Haddin b Harris	24	– run out	15
K. P. Pietersen b Johnson	71	– c Harris b Lyon	49
I. R. Bell c Haddin b Harris	27	– c Johnson b Lyon	0
B. A. Stokes c Watson b Johnson	14	– c Smith b Lyon	19
†J. M. Bairstow b Johnson	10	– c Haddin b Johnson	21
T. T. Bresnan c Bailey b Johnson	1	– b Lyon	0
S. C. J. Broad lbw b Johnson	11	– c Clarke b Lyon	0
J. M. Anderson not out	11	– not out	1
M. S. Panesar b Lyon	2	– lbw b Johnson	0
B 10, l-b 7, w 1, n-b 1	19	B 5, l-b 6	11
(100 overs)	255	(61 overs)	179

1/48 (1) 2/96 (2) 3/106 (3) 4/173 (5) 5/202 (6)
6/216 (7) 7/230 (8) 8/231 (4) 9/242 (9) 10/255 (11)

1/65 (1) 2/86 (2) 3/86 (3) 4/87 (5) 5/131 (6)
6/173 (7) 7/174 (8) 8/174 (9) 9/179 (4) 10/179 (11)

Harris 24–8–47–2; Johnson 24–4–63–5; Siddle 23–7–50–1; Lyon 22.2–3–67–1; Watson 6.4–2–11–1. *Second Innings*—Harris 10–1–34–0; Johnson 15–5–25–3; Lyon 17–3–50–5; Siddle 15–6–46–1; Watson 4–2–13–0.

Australia

C. J. L. Rogers c Pietersen b Bresnan	61	– c Bairstow b Panesar	116
D. A. Warner c Bairstow b Anderson	9	– c Bairstow b Stokes	25
S. R. Watson c Bairstow b Stokes	10	– not out	83
*M. J. Clarke b Anderson	10	– not out	6
S. P. D. Smith c Bell b Broad	19		
G. J. Bailey c Bairstow b Anderson	0		
†B. J. Haddin c Bairstow b Anderson	65		
M. G. Johnson c Anderson b Bresnan	2		
R. J. Harris c Root b Broad	6		
P. M. Siddle c Bresnan b Broad	0		
N. M. Lyon not out	18		
L-b 4	4	N-b 1	1
(82.2 overs)	204	(2 wkts, 51.5 overs)	231

1/19 (2) 2/36 (3) 3/62 (4) 4/110 (5) 5/112 (1)
6/122 (6) 7/151 (8) 8/162 (9) 9/164 (10) 10/204 (7)

1/64 (2) 2/200 (1)

Anderson 20.2–4–67–4; Broad 20–6–45–3; Stokes 15–4–46–1; Bresnan 18–6–24–2; Panesar 9–2–18–0. *Second Innings*—Anderson 11–2–26–0; Broad 10–0–58–0; Panesar 7.5–0–41–1; Stokes 12–0–50–1; Root 4–1–8–0; Bresnan 7–1–48–0.

Umpires: Aleem Dar *(Pakistan)* (86) and H. D. P. K. Dharmasena *(Sri Lanka)* (21).
Third umpire: B. F. Bowden *(New Zealand)*. Referee: R. S. Madugalle *(Sri Lanka)* (145).

Close of play: First day, England 226–6 (Pietersen 67, Bresnan 1); Second day, Australia 164–9 (Haddin 43); Third day, Australia 30–0 (Rogers 18, Warner 12).

AUSTRALIA v ENGLAND 2013–14 (5th Test)

At Sydney Cricket Ground on 3, 4, 5 January, 2014.
Toss: England.　　　Result: AUSTRALIA WON BY 281 RUNS.
Debuts: England – G. S. Ballance, S. G. Borthwick, W. B. Rankin.
Man of the Match: R. J. Harris. Man of the Series: M. G. Johnson.

Unchanged through a five-match series for the first time, Australia romped to victory inside three days, to complete only the third 5–0 Ashes whitewash after similar triumphs in 1920–21 and 2006–07. England, battered and bewildered, were bedevilled for one last time by Johnson, who finished with 37 wickets (at 13.97), equalling the series record for any left-arm bowler, by the Australian seamer Bill Whitty at home to South Africa in 1910–11. Again England had made a good start, reducing Australia to 97 for five before Haddin performed yet another salvage job, becoming the first No. 7 to pass 50 in each Test of a five-match series. Smith added his third hundred in six Tests, and the last five wickets put on 229 in all. England were soon 23 for five: the combative Stokes made 47, but it was left to the last pair to avoid the follow-on. Rogers's second successive century underpinned Australia's second innings; he was not dismissed until the lead reached 426. Three late wickets for leg-spinner Scott Borthwick – one of three debutants – meant England had 236 overs to survive. They actually lasted 31.4, their sixth-shortest innings in the previous 100 years. Only Stokes, who took 20 off a Lyon over, and Broad stood up with their jaws jutting: Broad's four sixes took the series total to 65, 14 more than the previous record, set during the 2005 Ashes. Pietersen was jettisoned by England after this match, despite having been their leading scorer in the series (294 runs).

Australia

C. J. L. Rogers b Stokes	11	– c and b Borthwick	119
D. A. Warner b Broad	16	– lbw b Anderson	16
S. R. Watson lbw b Anderson	43	– c Bairstow b Anderson	9
*M. J. Clarke c Bell b Stokes	10	– c Bairstow b Broad	6
S. P. D. Smith c sub (J. E. Root) b Stokes	115	– c Cook b Stokes	7
G. J. Bailey c Cook b Broad	1	– c Borthwick b Broad	46
†B. J. Haddin c Cook b Stokes	75	– b Borthwick	28
M. G. Johnson c sub (J. E. Root) b Borthwick	12	– b Stokes	4
R. J. Harris c Anderson b Stokes	22	– c Carberry b Borthwick	13
P. M. Siddle c Bairstow b Stokes	0	– c Bairstow b Rankin	4
N. M. Lyon not out	1	– not out	6
B 10, l-b 2, w 2, n-b 6	20	L-b 14, w 2, n-b 2	18
(76 overs)	326	(61.3 overs)	276

1/22 (2) 2/51 (1) 3/78 (4) 4/94 (3) 5/97 (6) 6/225 (7)　　　1/27 (2) 2/47 (3) 3/72 (4) 4/91 (5) 5/200 (6)
7/269 (8) 8/325 (9) 9/325 (10) 10/326 (5)　　　6/239 (7) 7/244 (8) 8/255 (1) 9/266 (9) 10/276 (10)

Anderson 21–3–67–1; Broad 19.5–5–65–2; Stokes 19.5–1–99–6; Rankin 8.2–0–34–0; Borthwick 7–0–49–1. *Second Innings*—Anderson 15–6–46–2; Broad 14–1–57–2; Rankin 12.3–0–47–1; Stokes 10–0–62–2; Borthwick 6–0–33–3; Pietersen 4–1–17–0.

England

*A. N. Cook lbw b Harris	7	– c Haddin b Johnson	7
M. A. Carberry c Lyon b Johnson	0	– c Haddin b Johnson	43
J. M. Anderson c Clarke b Johnson	7	– (10) not out	1
I. R. Bell c Haddin b Siddle	2	– (3) c Warner b Harris	16
K. P. Pietersen c Watson b Harris	3	– (4) c Bailey b Harris	6
G. S. Ballance c Haddin b Lyon	18	– (5) lbw b Johnson	7
B. A. Stokes b Siddle	47	– (6) b Harris	32
†J. M. Bairstow c Bailey b Siddle	18	– (7) c Bailey b Lyon	0
S. G. Borthwick c Smith b Harris	1	– c Clarke b Lyon	4
S. C. J. Broad not out	30	– (9) b Harris	42
W. B. Rankin b Johnson	13	– c Clarke b Harris	0
L-b 1, w 5, n-b 3	9	B 5, l-b 2, n-b 1	8
(58.5 overs)	155	(31.4 overs)	166

1/6 (2) 2/8 (1) 3/14 (3) 4/17 (5) 5/23 (4) 6/62 (6)　　　1/7 (1) 2/37 (3) 3/57 (4) 4/87 (2) 5/90 (5)
7/111 (8) 8/112 (7) 9/125 (9) 10/155 (11)　　　6/91 (7) 7/95 (8) 8/139 (6) 9/166 (9) 10/166 (11)

Harris 14–5–36–3; Johnson 13.5–3–33–3; Siddle 13–4–23–3; Watson 3–1–5–0; Lyon 15–3–57–1. *Second Innings*—Harris 9.4–4–25–5; Johnson 9–1–40–3; Siddle 4–1–24–0; Lyon 9–0–70–2.

Umpires: Aleem Dar *(Pakistan)* (87) and M. Erasmus *(South Africa)* (23).
Third umpire: A. L. Hill *(New Zealand)*. Referee: R. S. Madugalle *(Sri Lanka)* (146).

Close of play: First day, England 8–1 (Cook 7, Anderson 1); Second day, Australia 140–4 (Rogers 73, Bailey 20).

NEW ZEALAND v WEST INDIES 2013–14 (1st Test)

At University Oval, Dunedin, on 3, 4, 5, 6, 7 December, 2013.
Toss: West Indies.　　　Result: MATCH DRAWN.
Debuts: none.
Man of the Match: L. R. P. L. Taylor.

Eight months after being denied by England's last pair at Auckland, New Zealand again drew when victory had appeared certain. This time weather played a part, curtailing their unconvincing run-chase five minutes before tea on the final day. However, West Indies showed incredible resolve after following on. Having spent more than eight hours watching Taylor compile his maiden double-hundred, Darren Bravo spent 9½ over his own. Rutherford had made his first Test fifty since scoring 171 on debut against England earlier in the year, then Taylor and McCullum – with his first Test century for three years – added 195 as New Zealand reached 600 for the fourth time (for the fourth time they would be denied victory). West Indies began badly against Boult and Southee; only Chanderpaul resisted for long, and they followed on nearly 400 behind. And when next morning the score dipped to 185 for four, bags were being packed. But over by over, hour by hour, session by session, Bravo ploughed on, finally succumbing to a grubber from Boult after 572 minutes, 416 balls and 31 fours. It was his sixth Test hundred, all away from home. Sammy was left to edge the advantage over 100 as the weather worsened. New Zealand began slowly, and were still 33 short when the rain started. McCullum's expression was as drawn as the match itself: exactly a year on from his appointment as captain, he was still awaiting his first victory. After so much hard work, New Zealand were left cursing the win that got away.

New Zealand

P. G. Fulton c Edwards b Sammy	61	– c Ramdin b Shillingford	3
H. D. Rutherford c Deonarine b Shillingford	62	– c Gabriel b Shillingford	20
A. J. Redmond c Samuels b Best	20	– c Deonarine b Shillingford	6
L. R. P. L. Taylor not out	217	– not out	16
*B. B. McCullum b Sammy	113	– c Ramdin b Shillingford	9
C. J. Anderson c Ramdin b Best	0	– not out	20
†B-J. Watling c Edwards b Best	41		
T. G. Southee c Bravo b Deonarine	2		
I. S. Sodhi c and b Deonarine	35		
N. Wagner run out	37		
B 10, l-b 10, n-b 1	21	B 1, l-b 3, w 1	5
(9 wkts dec, 153.1 overs)	609	(4 wkts, 30 overs)	79

1/95 (2) 2/117 (3) 3/185 (1) 4/380 (5) 5/385 (6)
6/469 (7) 7/472 (8) 8/548 (9) 9/609 (10)　　　1/3 (1) 2/15 (3) 3/31 (2) 4/44 (5)

T. A. Boult did not bat.

Best 34.1–5–148–3; Gabriel 27.5–4–148–0; Sammy 23.1–4–79–2; Shillingford 46–7–138–1; Deonarine 22–0–76–2. *Second Innings*—Best 8–1–26–0; Shillingford 15–5–26–4; Gabriel 5–1–16–0; Deonarine 2–0–7–0.

West Indies

K. A. Edwards c Fulton b Boult	0	– lbw b Sodhi	59
K. O. A. Powell c Watling b Southee	7	– c Southee b Boult	14
D. M. Bravo c McCullum b Southee	40	– b Boult	218
M. N. Samuels c Taylor b Southee	14	– c and b Southee	23
S. Chanderpaul lbw b Boult	76	– lbw b Wagner	1
N. Deonarine c Taylor b Southee	15	– c Watling b Anderson	52
†D. Ramdin c Watling b Boult	12	– b Sodhi	24
*D. J. G. Sammy not out	27	– c Sodhi b Southee	80
S. Shillingford b Sodhi	9	– c Taylor b Wagner	15
T. L. Best run out	0	– c Taylor b Wagner	3
S. T. Gabriel lbw b Sodhi	0	– not out	0
L-b 11, w 1, n-b 1	13	B 4, l-b 7, w 5, n-b 2	18
(62.1 overs)	213	(162.1 overs)	507

1/4 (1) 2/24 (2) 3/70 (3) 4/73 (4) 5/106 (6) 6/174 (7)　　　1/18 (2) 2/135 (1) 3/178 (4) 4/185 (5) 5/307 (6)
7/183 (5) 8/202 (9) 9/205 (10) 10/213 (11)　　　6/363 (7) 7/453 (3) 8/491 (9) 9/507 (10) 10/507 (8)

Boult 18–5–40–3; Southee 16–1–52–4; Wagner 13–2–47–0; Sodhi 15.1–2–63–2. *Second Innings*—Southee 29.1–4–101–2; Boult 35–11–81–2; Wagner 30–3–112–3; Anderson 14–2–29–1; Sodhi 49–7–155–2; Redmond 5–1–18–0.

Umpires: N. J. Llong *(England)* (21) and P. R. Reiffel *(Australia)* (6).
Third umpire: I. J. Gould *(England)*. Referee: R. S. Mahanama *(Sri Lanka)* (46).

Close of play: First day, New Zealand 367–3 (Taylor 103, McCullum 109); Second day, West Indies 67–2 (Bravo 37, Samuels 14); Third day, West Indies 168–2 (Bravo 72, Samuels 17); Fourth day, West Indies 443–6 (Bravo 210, Sammy 44).

NEW ZEALAND v WEST INDIES 2013–14 (2nd Test)

At Basin Reserve, Wellington, on 11, 12, 13 December, 2013.
Toss: West Indies.   Result: NEW ZEALAND WON BY AN INNINGS AND 73 RUNS.
Debuts: none.
Man of the Match: T. A. Boult.

After the frustration of Dunedin, New Zealand secured their first home win in nine attempts. Sixteen wickets fell on the third day, with Boult bagging New Zealand's second-best match figures against West Indies, after Richard Hadlee's 11 for 102 at Dunedin in 1979–80. He was helped by a feeble all-round performance from West Indies. For the first time, their last four batsmen were dismissed for ducks, then in the second innings all ten wickets clattered for 101 after a useful start. For New Zealand, Fulton was given lbw to the match's first ball, but was saved when DRS showed an inside edge. Still, it would have been 26 for three if Taylor had not been dropped at third slip before scoring. Instead, he skipped to his tenth Test hundred: a first-day total of 307 for six was well above par, then the first session next day produced 134 runs in 25 overs. West Indies scored freely as the bowlers pitched up, but could not form substantial partnerships. Deonarine's departure opened the floodgates; the last six wickets crumbled for 18, five to Boult in the space of 15 balls. McCullum enforced the follow-on, despite the experience of the previous week. He may have been nervous as the openers added 74, but after lunch Southee claimed three for 19 in an impressive nine-over burst, then Boult ran through the lower order, adding a breathtaking catch at backward point to intercept Ramdin's cut. Sammy's pair – and defeat – made it a bad Friday 13th for him.

New Zealand

P. G. Fulton c Ramdin b Sammy		6
H. D. Rutherford c Ramdin b Best		11
K. S. Williamson c Sammy b Best		45
L. R. P. L. Taylor c Shillingford b Gabriel		129
*B. B. McCullum c Edwards b Deonarine		37
C. J. Anderson c Powell b Shillingford		38
†B-J. Watling b Gabriel		65
T. G. Southee c Bravo b Sammy		21
I. S. Sodhi c Ramdin b Best		27
N. Wagner c Sammy b Best		0
T. A. Boult not out		38
B 16, l-b 6, n-b 2		24
(115.1 overs)		441

1/14 (1) 2/24 (2) 3/112 (3) 4/189 (5) 5/257 (6)
6/296 (4) 7/334 (8) 8/383 (9) 9/383 (10) 10/441 (7)

Best 21–1–110–4; Gabriel 25.1–5–86–2; Sammy 25–3–92–2; Shillingford 28–4–92–1; Deonarine 16–2–39–1.

West Indies

K. A. Edwards c Rutherford b Anderson	55	– c Williamson b Southee	35
K. O. A. Powell lbw b Southee	21	– b Southee	36
D. M. Bravo c Fulton b Anderson	4	– c Watling b Wagner	0
M. N. Samuels c Watling b Boult	60	– c Anderson b Southee	12
S. Chanderpaul c Anderson b Boult	6	– not out	31
N. Deonarine c Taylor b Boult	22	– b Boult	12
†D. Ramdin not out	12	– c Boult b Anderson	19
*D. J. G. Sammy b Boult	0	– lbw b Boult	0
S. Shillingford b Boult	0	– c Taylor b Wagner	1
T. L. Best b Boult	0	– c Fulton b Boult	21
S. T. Gabriel b Southee	0	– b Boult	0
L-b 8, w 1, n-b 4	13	L-b 6, w 1, n-b 1	8
(49.5 overs)	193	(54.5 overs)	175

1/46 (2) 2/67 (3) 3/103 (1) 4/119 (5) 5/175 (6)   1/74 (2) 2/75 (3) 3/85 (1) 4/94 (4) 5/117 (6)
6/182 (4) 7/182 (8) 8/188 (9) 9/188 (10) 10/193 (11)   6/146 (7) 7/147 (8) 8/148 (9) 9/175 (10) 10/175 (11)

Boult 15–5–40–6; Southee 15.5–2–58–2; Wagner 7–1–37–0; Anderson 7–1–20–2; Sodhi 3–1–18–0; Williamson 2–0–12–0. *Second Innings*—Boult 12.5–2–40–4; Southee 11–2–24–3; Wagner 17–2–67–2; Anderson 11–1–29–1; Williamson 3–1–9–0.

Umpires: I. J. Gould *(England)* (36) and P. R. Reiffel *(Australia)* (7).
Third umpire: N. J. Llong *(England)*. Referee: R. S. Mahanama *(Sri Lanka)* (47).

Close of play: First day, New Zealand 307–6 (Watling 8, Southee 9); Second day, West Indies 158–4 (Samuels 50, Deonarine 11).

NEW ZEALAND v WEST INDIES 2013–14 (3rd Test)

At Seddon Park, Hamilton, on 19, 20, 21, 22 December, 2013.
Toss: New Zealand.   Result: NEW ZEALAND WON BY EIGHT WICKETS.
Debuts: none.
Man of the Match: L. R. P. L. Taylor.

When New Zealand were dismissed on the third afternoon for 349, a deficit of 18 on a dry pitch offering considerable help to Narine, the match was on a knife-edge. But less than 32 overs later the series had been decided, after another inept West Indian batting performance. They were dismantled by the seamers and shot out so quickly that New Zealand were batting again before the close. It was their first series victory over anyone other than Bangladesh or Zimbabwe for eight years, since beating West Indies at home in 2005–06. For the tenth Test in succession in New Zealand, the captain winning the toss had bowled first, although McCullum later admitted this was a mistake. West Indies still slid to 86 for five, but Chanderpaul (who compiled his 29th century, and passed Allan Border's 11,174 Test runs) and Ramdin then added exactly 200. After the openers went cheaply, Taylor became the second New Zealander after Mark Burgess (1969–72) to score hundreds in three successive Tests. Narine – recalled as Shane Shillingford had been suspended by the ICC for a suspect action – took his second five-for (both against New Zealand) to give West Indies a slender advantage… but they threw that away, seven wickets being shared by the increasingly impressive new-ball pair of Boult and Southee, who took his 100th Test wicket when he dismissed Permaul. New Zealand needed only 122 to win 2–0: Taylor's brief stay took him to 495 runs in the three-match series.

West Indies

K. C. Brathwaite c Williamson b Southee	45 – b Boult	7
K. O. A. Powell c Watling b Wagner	26 – (3) c Southee b Boult	0
K. A. Edwards c Watling b Southee	6 – (2) c Watling b Boult	1
M. N. Samuels c Williamson b Anderson	0 – c Watling b Anderson	8
S. Chanderpaul not out	122 – c Williamson b Wagner	20
N. Deonarine lbw b Anderson	2 – c Taylor b Wagner	13
†D. Ramdin c Watling b Anderson	107 – lbw b Boult	18
*D. J. G. Sammy c Watling b Southee	3 – c Watling b Southee	24
S. P. Narine b Boult	2 – not out	0
V. Permaul c Fulton b Southee	20 – lbw b Southee	0
T. L. Best c Watling b Sodhi	25 – lbw b Southee	0
B 2, l-b 6, w 1	9 L-b 12	12
(116.2 overs)	367 (31.5 overs)	103

1/41 (2) 2/77 (1) 3/78 (3) 4/82 (4) 5/86 (6) 6/286 (7)   1/12 (1) 2/12 (3) 3/13 (2) 4/40 (4) 5/46 (5)
7/296 (8) 8/307 (9) 9/332 (10) 10/367 (11)   6/75 (6) 7/91 (7) 8/103 (8) 9/103 (10) 10/103 (11)

Boult 26–2–84–1; Southee 28–3–79–4; Wagner 21–4–67–1; Anderson 19–3–47–3; Williamson 5–0–17–0; Sodhi 17.2–0–65–1. *Second Innings*—Boult 10–4–23–4; Southee 8.5–5–12–3; Anderson 6–0–22–1; Wagner 7–1–34–2.

New Zealand

P. G. Fulton c Sammy b Narine	11 – c and b Sammy	10
H. D. Rutherford c and b Sammy	10 – not out	48
K. S. Williamson lbw b Narine	58 – b Permaul	56
L. R. P. L. Taylor c Samuels b Best	131 – not out	2
*B. B. McCullum c Sammy b Narine	12	
C. J. Anderson c Deonarine b Permaul	39	
†B-J. Watling c Ramdin b Sammy	20	
T. G. Southee lbw b Narine	18	
I. S. Sodhi b Narine	9	
N. Wagner c Edwards b Narine	22	
T. A. Boult not out	1	
B 6, l-b 8, n-b 4	18 B 7, n-b 1	8
(117.3 overs)	349 (2 wkts, 40.4 overs)	124

1/18 (2) 2/43 (1) 3/138 (3) 4/174 (5) 5/224 (6) 6/269 (7)
7/306 (4) 8/317 (8) 9/332 (9) 10/349 (10)   1/33 (1) 2/116 (3)

Best 14–1–63–1; Sammy 23–8–69–2; Permaul 35–6–103–1; Narine 42.3–17–91–6; Deonarine 3–0–9–0. *Second Innings*—Best 7–3–22–0; Narine 16–6–39–0; Sammy 9–3–21–1; Permaul 7–1–29–1; Deonarine 1.4–0–6–0.

Umpires: I. J. Gould *(England)* (37) and N. J. Llong *(England)* (22).
Third umpire: P. R. Reiffel *(Australia)*. Referee: R. S. Mahanama *(Sri Lanka)* (48).

Close of play: First day, West Indies 289–6 (Chanderpaul 94, Sammy 0); Second day, New Zealand 156–3 (Taylor 56, McCullum 11); Third day, New Zealand 6–0 (Fulton 4, Rutherford 0).

SOUTH AFRICA v INDIA 2013–14 (1st Test)

At The Wanderers, Johannesburg, on 18, 19, 20, 21, 22 December, 2013.
Toss: India.   Result: MATCH DRAWN.
Debuts: none.
Man of the Match: V. Kohli.

An astonishing match had the tamest of endings. When du Plessis was out, South Africa – asked to score a world-record 458 to win – needed 16 off 19 balls; India needed three wickets. Philander and Steyn blocked three of the remaining deliveries, left three, declined three singles… and were booed off. Before the Test, India's first since the retirement of Sachin Tendulkar, the focus had been on his heir apparent – and Kohli did not disappoint, following a chanceless 119 with 96 in the second innings, when his partnership of 222 with Pujara allowed India to set that huge target. Earlier, Dhawan had become Philander's 100th wicket in his 19th Test, a South African record. South Africa also lost five for 16, including Kallis first ball: Philander's late fusillade limited the deficit to 36. In the chase their openers put on 108, but after Zaheer Khan became the fourth Indian to 300 Test wickets (thanks to an lbw which Kallis clearly edged) du Plessis and de Villiers shared a pulsating stand of 205. They weren't separated until the score was past 400, but with history in sight du Plessis was beaten by Rahane's direct hit from mid-off – and down came the shutters. This was the first Test in which both wicketkeepers bowled; Dhoni did so in his 50th Test as captain, breaking Sourav Ganguly's Indian record. This series was controversially reduced to two matches after the late arrangement of India's series against West Indies, which had allowed Tendulkar to play his 200th and final Test at home.

India

M. Vijay c de Villiers b Morkel	6	– (2) c de Villiers b Kallis	39
S. Dhawan c Imran Tahir b Steyn	13	– (1) c Kallis b Philander	15
C. A. Pujara run out	25	– c de Villiers b Kallis	153
V. Kohli c Duminy b Kallis	119	– c de Villiers b Duminy	96
R. G. Sharma c de Villiers b Philander	14	– b Kallis	6
A. M. Rahane c de Villiers b Philander	47	– c Smith b Duminy	15
*†M. S. Dhoni c de Villiers b Morkel	19	– c sub (D. Elgar) b Philander	29
R. Ashwin not out	11	– c du Plessis b Philander	7
Zaheer Khan lbw b Philander	0	– not out	29
I. Sharma b Philander	0	– lbw b Imran Tahir	4
Mohammed Shami b Morkel	0	– b Imran Tahir	4
B 4, l-b 6, w 14, n-b 2	26	B 9, l-b 7, w 8	24
(103 overs)	280	(120.4 overs)	421

1/17 (2) 2/24 (1) 3/113 (3) 4/151 (5) 5/219 (4)
6/264 (7) 7/264 (6) 8/264 (9) 9/278 (10) 10/280 (11)

1/23 (1) 2/93 (2) 3/315 (3) 4/325 (5) 5/327 (4)
6/358 (6) 7/369 (8) 8/384 (7) 9/405 (10) 10/421 (11)

Steyn 26–7–61–1; Philander 27–6–61–4; Morkel 23–12–34–3; Kallis 14–4–37–1; Imran Tahir 8–0–47–0; Duminy 5–0–30–0. *Second Innings*—Steyn 30–5–104–0; Philander 28–10–68–3; Morkel 2–1–4–0; Kallis 20–5–68–3; Imran Tahir 15.4–1–69–2; de Villiers 1–0–5–0; Duminy 24–0–87–2.

South Africa

*G. C. Smith lbw b Zaheer Khan	68	– (2) run out	44
A. N. Petersen lbw b I. Sharma	21	– (1) b Mohammed Shami	76
H. M. Amla b I. Sharma	36	– b Mohammed Shami	4
J. H. Kallis lbw b I. Sharma	0	– (5) lbw b Zaheer Khan	34
†A. B. de Villiers lbw b Mohammed Shami	13	– (6) b I. Sharma	103
J-P. Duminy c Vijay b Mohammed Shami	2	– (7) b Mohammed Shami	5
F. du Plessis c Dhoni b Zaheer Khan	20	– (4) run out	134
V. D. Philander c Ashwin b Zaheer Khan	59	– not out	25
D. W. Steyn c R. G. Sharma b I. Sharma	10	– not out	6
M. Morkel b Zaheer Khan	7		
Imran Tahir not out	0		
L-b 4, w 1, n-b 3	8	B 2, l-b 7, w 8, n-b 2	19
(75.3 overs)	244	(7 wkts, 136 overs)	450

1/37 (2) 2/130 (3) 3/130 (4) 4/130 (1) 5/145 (6)
6/146 (5) 7/226 (8) 8/237 (9) 9/239 (7) 10/244 (10)

1/108 (2) 2/118 (3) 3/143 (1) 4/197 (5) 5/402 (6)
6/407 (7) 7/442 (4)

Zaheer Khan 26.3–6–88–4; Mohammed Shami 18–3–48–2; I. Sharma 25–5–79–4; Ashwin 6–0–25–0. *Second Innings*—Zaheer Khan 34–1–135–1; I. Sharma 29–4–91–1; Mohammed Shami 28–5–107–3; Ashwin 36–5–83–0; Vijay 1–0–3–0; Dhoni 2–0–4–0; Kohli 6–0–18–0.

Umpires: S. J. Davis *(Australia)* (49) and R. J. Tucker *(Australia)* (28).
Third umpire: S. George *(South Africa)*. Referee: A. J. Pycroft *(Zimbabwe)* (25).

Close of play: First day, India 255–5 (Rahane 43, Dhoni 17); Second day, South Africa 213–6 (du Plessis 17, Philander 48); Third day, India 284–2 (Pujara 135, Kohli 77); Fourth day, South Africa 138–2 (Petersen 76, du Plessis 10).

SOUTH AFRICA v INDIA 2013–14 (2nd Test)

At Kingsmead, Durban, on 26, 27, 28, 29, 30 December, 2013.
Toss: India.   Result: SOUTH AFRICA WON BY TEN WICKETS.
Debuts: none.
Man of the Match: D. W. Steyn. Man of the Series: A. B. de Villiers.

South Africans were given an unwanted Christmas present when Jacques Kallis announced that his 166th Test would be his last. He left with another hundred and one last victory. India did well on a first day reduced to 61 overs by bad light, Vijay and Pujara enjoying themselves on an Indian-style pitch, on which South Africa had lost their four previous Tests. Things changed next day: Steyn, without a wicket for 69 overs, ended the stand at 157, and finished with six as the last five wickets added only 14. After another good start from Smith and Petersen, all eyes were on Kallis: greeted by an Indian guard of honour, he was 16 balls on nought, but reached the close ominously unbeaten on 78. Next morning, Kallis dabbed Jadeja to midwicket for a single to bring up his seventh century against India, his fifth at Durban. Dhoni refused to accept the new ball until the seam split on the old one after 146 overs, a factor in Jadeja's Test-best haul, although he also found biting turn. South Africa led by 166: Kohli was adjudged caught behind first ball of the final day, although it came off his sleeve, then Steyn defeated Pujara with one that zapped back off a crack. Rahane made 96, but Peterson mopped up the tail to leave a target of just 58, which the openers knocked off – disappointing those who wanted one last sight of Kallis. Instead he finished with 13,289 runs, 45 centuries, 292 wickets and exactly 200 catches.

India

S. Dhawan c Petersen b Morkel	29	– c du Plessis b Peterson	19
M. Vijay c de Villiers b Steyn	97	– c Smith b Philander	6
C. A. Pujara c de Villiers b Steyn	70	– b Steyn	32
V. Kohli c de Villiers b Morkel	46	– c de Villiers b Steyn	11
R. G. Sharma b Steyn	0	– lbw b Philander	25
A. M. Rahane not out	51	– b Philander	96
*†M. S. Dhoni c Smith b Steyn	24	– c Petersen b Peterson	15
R. A. Jadeja c Kallis b Duminy	0	– c Morkel b Peterson	8
Zaheer Khan c de Villiers b Steyn	0	– lbw b Peterson	3
I. Sharma c de Villiers b Steyn	4	– c de Villiers b Steyn	1
Mohammed Shami c Smith b Morkel	1	– not out	1
L-b 7, w 4, n-b 1	12	B 4, w 2	6
(111.3 overs)	334	(86 overs)	223

1/41 (1) 2/198 (3) 3/199 (2) 4/199 (5) 5/265 (4) 6/320 (7)   1/8 (2) 2/53 (1) 3/68 (4) 4/71 (3) 5/104 (5)
7/321 (8) 8/322 (9) 9/330 (10) 10/334 (11)   6/146 (7) 7/154 (8) 8/189 (9) 9/206 (10) 10/223 (6)

Steyn 30–9–100–6; Philander 21–6–56–0; Morkel 23.3–6–50–3; Kallis 11–1–36–0; Peterson 22–2–75–0; Duminy 4–0–10–1. *Second Innings*—Steyn 21–8–47–3; Philander 16–4–43–3; Morkel 16–6–34–0; Peterson 24–3–74–4; Duminy 8–2–20–0; du Plessis 1–0–1–0.

South Africa

*G. C. Smith c Dhawan b Jadeja	47	– (2) not out	27
A. N. Petersen c Vijay b Jadeja	62	– (1) not out	31
H. M. Amla b Mohammed Shami	3		
J. H. Kallis c Dhoni b Jadeja	115		
†A. B. de Villiers c Kohli b Jadeja	74		
J-P. Duminy lbw b Jadeja	28		
D. W. Steyn c Dhoni b Zaheer Khan	44		
F. du Plessis run out	43		
R. J. Peterson c Vijay b Zaheer Khan	61		
V. D. Philander not out	0		
M. Morkel c and b Jadeja	0		
B 3, l-b 15, w 2, n-b 3	23	W 1	1
(155.2 overs)	500	(no wkt, 11.4 overs)	59

1/103 (1) 2/113 (3) 3/113 (2) 4/240 (5) 5/298 (6)
6/384 (4) 7/387 (7) 8/497 (9) 9/500 (8) 10/500 (11)

Zaheer Khan 28–4–97–2; Mohammed Shami 27–2–104–1; I. Sharma 31–7–114–0; Jadeja 58.2–15–138–6; R. G. Sharma 11–1–29–0. *Second Innings*—Mohammed Shami 2–1–4–0; I. Sharma 5–1–29–0; Jadeja 4–0–16–0; R. G. Sharma 0.4–0–10–0.

Umpires: S. J. Davis *(Australia)* (50) and R. J. Tucker *(Australia)* (29).
Third umpire: A. T. Holdstock *(South Africa)*. Referee: A. J. Pycroft *(Zimbabwe)* (26).

Close of play: First day, India 181–1 (Vijay 91, Pujara 58); Second day, South Africa 82–0 (Smith 35, Petersen 46); Third day, South Africa 299–5 (Kallis 78, Steyn 0); Fourth day, India 68–2 (Pujara 32, Kohli 11).

PAKISTAN v SRI LANKA 2013–14 (1st Test)

At Sheikh Zayed Stadium, Abu Dhabi, on 31 December, 2013, 1, 2, 3, 4 January, 2014.
Toss: Pakistan.   Result: MATCH DRAWN.
Debuts: Pakistan – Ahmed Shehzad, Bilawal Bhatti. Sri Lanka – S. M. S. M. Senanayake.
Man of the Match: A. D. Mathews.

Sri Lanka showed great resilience to escape with a draw. By the third-day close, they were four down and only seven runs ahead; but 24 hours later, it was Pakistan who were under the pump. Sri Lanka lost only one wicket all day, and wicketkeeper Adnan Akmal had broken a finger. Pakistan finally cut their losses and batted out time. Sri Lanka, put in, lost only one wicket in the first session, but seven in a disastrous passage after lunch. Jayawardene nicked a rising beauty from the debutant Bilawal Bhatti, but was spared when replays showed the bowler had overstepped; next ball, Jayawardene edged a legitimate yorker. Junaid Khan collected his fourth Test five-for – all against Sri Lanka. From 83 for three before lunch on New Year's Day – this was the first Test to span two calendar years since 1984–85 – Younis Khan put on 218 with Misbah-ul-Haq, who was last out as the last six wickets tumbled on the third morning. Silva and Sangakkara clawed Sri Lanka back into the match but, soon after the last drinks break of the evening, Younis took a smart low catch to remove Sangakkara and, first ball, Jayawardene edged Bhatti for the third delivery in a row. But Mathews's 116 led the way next day. Saeed Ajmal was tamed to the extent that he bowled 49 overs without taking a wicket. Both sides named six players with fewer than 15 Test caps; Sri Lanka included four reasonably regular wicketkeepers, which did little for their fill-in bowling.

Sri Lanka

F. D. M. Karunaratne c Asad Shafiq b Junaid Khan	38	– b Junaid Khan	24
J. K. Silva c Mohammad Hafeez b Bilawal Bhatti	20	– c Adnan Akmal b Junaid Khan	81
K. C. Sangakkara c Ahmed Shehzad b Junaid Khan	16	– c Younis Khan b Bilawal Bhatti	55
D. P. M. D. Jayawardene c Adnan Akmal b Bilawal Bhatti	5	– c Asad Shafiq b Bilawal Bhatti	0
L. D. Chandimal c Mohammad Hafeez b Bilawal Bhatti	0	– c Rahat Ali b Junaid Khan	89
*A. D. Mathews st Adnan Akmal b Saeed Ajmal	91	– not out	157
†H. A. P. W. Jayawardene c Adnan Akmal b Junaid Khan	5	– not out	63
S. M. S. M. Senanayake c Adnan Akmal b Junaid Khan	5		
H. M. R. K. B. Herath b Junaid Khan	0		
R. M. S. Eranga c Adnan Akmal b Saeed Ajmal	14		
R. A. S. Lakmal not out	1		
B 4, l-b 4, n-b 1	9	B 4, l-b 7	11
(65 overs)	204	(5 wkts dec, 168.3 overs)	480

1/57 (1) 2/67 (2) 3/76 (4) 4/76 (5) 5/82 (3) 6/104 (7)
7/124 (8) 8/124 (9) 9/185 (10) 10/204 (6)

1/47 (1) 2/146 (3) 3/150 (4) 4/186 (2)
5/324 (5)

Junaid Khan 20–4–58–5; Rahat Ali 16–3–41–0; Bilawal Bhatti 15–1–65–3; Saeed Ajmal 14–3–32–2. *Second Innings*—Junaid Khan 36–3–93–3; Rahat Ali 38.3–9–92–0; Bilawal Bhatti 36–8–146–2; Saeed Ajmal 49–10–115–0; Mohammad Hafeez 9–1–23–0.

Pakistan

Khurram Manzoor run out	21	– c H. A. P. W. Jayawardene b Lakmal	8
Ahmed Shehzad c Karunaratne b Eranga	38	– lbw b Herath	55
Mohammad Hafeez c Silva b Lakmal	11	– not out	80
Younis Khan b Eranga	136	– not out	13
*Misbah-ul-Haq c Sangakkara b Herath	135		
Asad Shafiq c Silva b Lakmal	13		
†Adnan Akmal c Senanayake b Eranga	6		
Bilawal Bhatti c H. A. P. W. Jayawardene b Mathews	14		
Saeed Ajmal lbw b Herath	0		
Rahat Ali b Herath	0		
Junaid Khan not out	4		
L-b 2, w 1, n-b 2	5	L-b 1, n-b 1	2
(129.1 overs)	383	(2 wkts, 52 overs)	158

1/46 (1) 2/59 (3) 3/83 (2) 4/301 (4) 5/329 (6)
6/342 (7) 7/369 (8) 8/378 (9) 9/378 (10) 10/383 (5)

1/24 (1) 2/125 (2)

Lakmal 33–9–99–2; Mathews 13–1–43–1; Eranga 30–6–80–3; Herath 35.1–9–93–3; Senanayake 18–2–66–0. *Second Innings*—Lakmal 13–1–43–1; Eranga 11–0–38–0; Herath 21–8–37–1; Mathews 2–0–9–0; Senanayake 5–0–30–0.

Umpires: R. A. Kettleborough *(England)* (17) and B. N. J. Oxenford *(Australia)* (16).
Third umpire: S. Ravi *(India)*. Referee: J. Srinath *(India)* (29).

Close of play: First day, Pakistan 46–1 (Ahmed Shehzad 25); Second day, Pakistan 327–4 (Misbah-ul-Haq 105, Asad Shafiq 12); Third day, Sri Lanka 186–4 (Chandimal 24); Fourth day, Sri Lanka 420–5 (Mathews 116, H. A. P. W. Jayawardene 48).

PAKISTAN v SRI LANKA 2013–14 (2nd Test)

At Dubai International Cricket Stadium on 8, 9, 10, 11, 12 January, 2014.
Toss: Sri Lanka.   Result: SRI LANKA WON BY NINE WICKETS.
Debuts: none.
Man of the Match: D. P. M. D. Jayawardene.

Pakistan paid a heavy price for inept batting on the opening day. They were surprised by an unusually grassy surface, and could not adapt their leaden-footed strokeplay. The upshot was their second Test defeat of the winter at Dubai, and the feeling that their dominion in this part of the world was loosening a little. It was a landmark win for Sri Lanka – just their second victory overseas in 19 attempts. Mathews's decision to bowl was unprecedented here, but not a complete surprise given Pakistan's recent collapses for 99 against England and South Africa in Dubai. Khurram Manzoor played well for 73, but the last eight wickets mustered only 58. Jayawardene, down at No. 5 after a poor run and a hand injury, then played himself back into form, scoring his 32nd Test century – 18 innings after the 31st – and putting on 139 with Silva, who just missed a maiden ton. Pakistan, starting 223 adrift, were as good as buried at 19 for three. Misbah-ul-Haq embarked on another rescue mission with Younis Khan and, helped by a ball change in the 13th over that seemed to reduce the swing, they added 129. Misbah had just taken Pakistan into the lead, and was within three of back-to-back hundreds, when Herath turned one past his forward prod. Sarfraz Ahmed fought hard for a maiden fifty, but Pakistan were dismissed 75 minutes into the final day, leaving a modest target. Only six times before had Sri Lankan seamers taken as many as 15 wickets in a Test.

Pakistan

Khurram Manzoor c H. A. P. W. Jayawardene b Lakmal.....	73	– c H. A. P. W. Jayawardene b Fernando	6
Ahmed Shehzad lbw b Fernando	3	– c H. A. P. W. Jayawardene b Herath	9
Mohammad Hafeez b Fernando.................................	21	– c H. A. P. W. Jayawardene b Fernando	1
Younis Khan c H. A. P. W. Jayawardene b Eranga	13	– c H. A. P. W. Jayawardene b Lakmal	77
*Misbah-ul-Haq c H. A. P. W. Jayawardene b Eranga.......	1	– b Herath..	97
Asad Shafiq c Silva b Lakmal..	6	– c Karunaratne b Eranga.................................	23
†Sarfraz Ahmed c H. A. P. W. Jayawardene b Fernando ...	7	– b Lakmal	74
Bilawal Bhatti not out	24	– b Eranga	32
Saeed Ajmal c Silva b Herath	8	– b Lakmal	21
Rahat Ali lbw b Herath...	0	– c H. A. P. W. Jayawardene b Lakmal	8
Junaid Khan lbw b Herath...	2	– not out	2
L-b 7..	7	B 1, l-b 8	9
(63.5 overs)	165	(137.3 overs)	359

1/28 (2) 2/78 (3) 3/107 (4) 4/109 (5) 5/118 (1)   1/11 (2) 2/12 (3) 3/19 (1) 4/148 (4) 5/200 (6)
6/127 (6) 7/129 (7) 8/151 (9) 9/151 (10) 10/165 (11)   6/245 (5) 7/312 (8) 8/334 (7) 9/354 (10) 10/359 (9)

Lakmal 21–6–45–2; Eranga 14–4–25–2; Fernando 18–2–62–3; Herath 10.5–3–26–3. *Second Innings*—Lakmal 28.3–4–78–4; Fernando 19–3–50–2; Herath 48–10–132–2; Eranga 36–9–74–2; Mathews 5–1–9–0; Sangakkara 1–0–7–0.

Sri Lanka

F. D. M. Karunaratne lbw b Junaid Khan........................	32	– not out	62
J. K. Silva lbw b Mohammad Hafeez..............................	95	– lbw b Saeed Ajmal	58
K. C. Sangakkara lbw b Rahat Ali	26	– not out	9
L. D. Chandimal c Rahat Ali b Junaid Khan....................	12		
D. P. M. D. Jayawardene b Saeed Ajmal.........................	129		
*A. D. Mathews c Sarfraz Ahmed b Rahat Ali	42		
†H. A. P. W. Jayawardene b Junaid Khan	9		
H. M. R. K. B. Herath run out.......................................	6		
R. M. S. Eranga b Bilawal Bhatti...................................	14		
R. A. S. Lakmal not out..	10		
A. N. P. R. Fernando lbw b Saeed Ajmal	3		
B 1, l-b 7, w 1, n-b 1	10	B 3, l-b 4, n-b 1	8
(134 overs)	388	(1 wkt, 46.2 overs)	137

1/40 (1) 2/75 (3) 3/88 (4) 4/227 (2) 5/320 (6)   1/124 (2)
6/341 (7) 7/348 (8) 8/365 (5) 9/377 (9) 10/388 (11)

Junaid Khan 36–7–102–3; Rahat Ali 36–6–131–2; Saeed Ajmal 34–11–56–2; Bilawal Bhatti 22–3–80–1; Mohammad Hafeez 6–1–11–1. *Second Innings*—Mohammad Hafeez 8–3–22–0; Junaid Khan 10–2–34–0; Rahat Ali 11–1–29–0; Saeed Ajmal 17.2–5–45–1.

Umpires: B. N. J. Oxenford *(Australia)* (17) and S. Ravi *(India)* (2).
Third umpire: R. A. Kettleborough *(England)*. Referee: J. Srinath *(India)* (30).

Close of play: First day, Sri Lanka 57–1 (Silva 12, Sangakkara 12); Second day, Sri Lanka 318–4 (D. P. M. D. Jayawardene 106, Mathews 42); Third day, Pakistan 132–3 (Younis Khan 62, Misbah-ul-Haq 53); Fourth day, Pakistan 330–7 (Sarfraz Ahmed 70, Saeed Ajmal 7).

PAKISTAN v SRI LANKA 2013–14 (3rd Test)

At Sharjah C. A. Stadium on 16, 17, 18, 19, 20 January, 2014.
Toss: Sri Lanka.   Result: PAKISTAN WON BY FIVE WICKETS.
Debuts: Sri Lanka – M. D. K. Perera.
Man of the Match: Azhar Ali. Man of the Series: A. D. Mathews.

The first 4½ days contained some of the dreariest cricket imaginable – but the last session and a half was stuff from the firmament. Pakistan needed 302 in 59 overs to preserve an unbeaten home Test-series record stretching back to 2007–08. Their second-innings run-rate of 5.25, ending in an astonishing victory, was the fastest of any 300-plus chase in Test history. Sri Lanka had taken 101.4 overs to score 214 in their second innings, which finished before lunch on the last day. The truth was that, after Mathews's otherwise superb series with the bat, it was his 99-ball crawl to 14 on the fourth day that gave Pakistan a sniff. By tea on the final day, they still required 195 from 35 overs – but the promoted Sarfraz Ahmed clumped 48 from 46 balls then, with all nine fielders on the ropes, Azhar Ali and Misbah-ul-Haq calmly milked the ones and twos. In the last half-hour, Sri Lanka began resorting to delaying tactics, but the umpires turned a blind eye to the fading light. Azhar sprinted off after a stupendous 103, and in the next over, with just nine balls left, Misbah tapped the single that completed one of Pakistan's most famous victories to square the series. All this had looked unlikely as Sri Lanka used up the first two days in scoring 428, Mathews and the debutant Dilruwan Perera just missing centuries. Ahmed Shehzad's 5½-hour 147 – his maiden Test hundred – took Pakistan to within 87, then Sri Lanka crawled along at little more than two an over.

Sri Lanka

F. D. M. Karunaratne c Younis Khan b Abdur Rehman	34	– b Mohammad Talha......................................	8		
J. K. Silva c Sarfraz Ahmed b Mohammad Talha	17	– b Abdur Rehman	36		
K. C. Sangakkara c Khurram Manzoor b Junaid Khan	52	– c Khurram Manzoor b Abdur Rehman	8		
D. P. M. D. Jayawardene c Azhar Ali b Saeed Ajmal	47	– c Azhar Ali b Saeed Ajmal............................	46		
L. D. Chandimal c Asad Shafiq b Saeed Ajmal	11	– b Mohammad Talha.......................................	13		
*A. D. Mathews c Ahmed Shehzad b Junaid Khan	91	– c Khurram Manzoor b Mohammad Talha......	31		
†H. A. P. W. Jayawardene c Junaid Khan					
b Mohammad Talha	35	– c Azhar Ali b Saeed Ajmal............................	49		
M. D. K. Perera c Junaid Khan b Mohammad Talha........	95	– c Azhar Ali b Abdur Rehman	8		
H. M. R. K. B. Herath lbw b Junaid Khan	0	– c Younis Khan b Abdur Rehman	0		
R. M. S. Eranga not out......................................	25	– c Abdur Rehman b Saeed Ajmal	3		
R. A. S. Lakmal not out......................................	3	– not out	2		
B 5, l-b 11, n-b 2	18	B 2, l-b 4, w 2, n-b 2	10		
(9 wkts dec, 172 overs)	428	(101.4 overs)	214		

1/31 (2) 2/65 (1) 3/125 (3) 4/159 (4) 5/166 (5)   1/13 (1) 2/37 (3) 3/66 (2) 4/89 (5) 5/127 (4)
6/239 (7) 7/351 (6) 8/351 (9) 9/423 (8)   6/189 (6) 7/203 (8) 8/203 (9) 9/209 (7) 10/214 (10)

Junaid Khan 32–5–81–3; Mohammad Talha 32–3–99–3; Saeed Ajmal 55–16–120–2; Abdur Rehman 50–14–101–1; Azhar Ali 3–0–11–0. *Second Innings*—Junaid Khan 20–6–34–0; Mohammad Talha 23–2–65–3; Abdur Rehman 33–10–56–4; Saeed Ajmal 25.4–7–53–3.

Pakistan

Khurram Manzoor c H. A. P. W. Jayawardene b Eranga ...	52	– c H. A. P. W. Jayawardene b Lakmal	21		
Ahmed Shehzad b Herath	147	– c Karunaratne b Lakmal................................	21		
Azhar Ali c Mathews b Perera	8	– c H. A. P. W. Jayawardene b Lakmal.............	103		
Younis Khan c H. A. P. W. Jayawardene b Herath.............	17	– c Sangakkara b Mathews................................	29		
*Misbah-ul-Haq c Chandimal b Herath..........................	63	– (6) not out..	68		
Asad Shafiq lbw b Eranga	18	– (7) not out..	1		
†Sarfraz Ahmed c H. A. P. W. Jayawardene b Herath	5	– (5) c H. A. P. W. Jayawardene b Eranga	48		
Abdur Rehman c H. A. P. W. Jayawardene b Eranga	2				
Mohammad Talha lbw b Eranga	2				
Saeed Ajmal not out.......................................	0				
Junaid Khan c Chandimal b Herath	16				
B 3, l-b 6, w 1, n-b 1	11	B 6, l-b 1, w 3, n-b 1	11		
(109.1 overs)	341	(5 wkts, 57.3 overs)....................	302		

1/114 (1) 2/149 (3) 3/189 (4) 4/245 (2) 5/274 (6)
6/291 (7) 7/294 (8) 8/300 (9) 9/325 (5) 10/341 (11)   1/35 (2) 2/48 (1) 3/97 (4) 4/186 (5) 5/295 (3)

Herath 38.1–8–125–5; Lakmal 23–4–61–0; Perera 17–1–71–1; Eranga 24–5–60–4; Mathews 7–3–15–0. *Second Innings*—Lakmal 12–0–79–3; Eranga 15.3–0–68–1; Herath 19–0–100–0; Mathews 11–0–48–1.

Umpires: R. A. Kettleborough *(England)* (18) and S. Ravi *(India)* (3).
Third umpire: B. N. J. Oxenford *(Australia)*. Referee: J. Srinath *(India)* (31).

Close of play: First day, Sri Lanka 220–5 (Mathews 24, H. A. P. W. Jayawardene 28); Second day, Pakistan 19–0 (Khurram Manzoor 14, Ahmed Shehzad 5); Third day, Pakistan 291–6 (Misbah-ul-Haq 36); Fourth day, Sri Lanka 133–5 (Mathews 14, H. A. P. W. Jayawardene 6).

BANGLADESH v SRI LANKA 2013–14 (1st Test)

At Shere Bangla National Stadium, Mirpur, Dhaka, on 27, 28, 29, 30 January, 2014.
Toss: Sri Lanka.   Result: SRI LANKA WON BY AN INNINGS AND 248 RUNS.
Debuts: Bangladesh – Shamsur Rahman.
Man of the Match: D. P. M. D. Jayawardene.

On a sluggish surface Bangladesh were once again overwhelmed, falling well short in two innings of what Sri Lanka amassed in one. Kaushal Silva, who was dropped three times, and Kithuruwan Vithanage made their first Test centuries, while Jayawardene extended his 33rd into his seventh double. Sri Lanka's fourth-biggest total set up their second-largest win (they beat Zimbabwe by an innings and 254 at Bulawayo in May 2004). Bangladesh's resistance was tepid: the batsmen appeared keener to entertain than endure, thrashing attractive boundaries but displaying none of the grit that might have made a game of it. Tamim Iqbal top-edged a pull to fine leg, the first of three wickets in three overs, and although Shakib Al Hasan and Mushfiqur Rahim steadied them, the comeback was not sustained. A run-rate of 3.63 in a total of 232 suggested a glaring lack of application, which was then shown up by Sri Lanka's massive response. It was no better second time around. Tamim was out on the third evening, but next morning the batsmen seemed to decide there was no hope of a draw. This time they galloped along at 4.82 an over; four of the top seven perished playing attacking strokes, and only Mominul Haque reached 50. Off-spinner Dilruwan Perera wrapped up victory with a maiden five-for in his second Test, and by mid-afternoon the Sri Lankans – perhaps in search of something a little more competitive – were playing football. Bangladesh's 82nd Test had ended in their 68th defeat, 36 of them by an innings.

Bangladesh

Tamim Iqbal c Lakmal b Eranga			6 – c Perera b Herath	11
Shamsur Rahman c Perera b Eranga	33		– c Chandimal b Eranga	9
Marshall Ayub lbw b Mathews	1		– c Silva b Lakmal	18
Mominul Haque c Vithanage b Lakmal	8		– lbw b Perera	50
Shakib Al Hasan lbw b Herath	55		– lbw b Perera	25
*†Mushfiqur Rahim lbw b Lakmal	61		– b Perera	14
Nasir Hossain c Chandimal b Eranga	4		– c Herath b Perera	29
Sohag Gazi c Eranga b Lakmal	42		– lbw b Lakmal	23
Robiul Islam c Perera b Eranga	5		– lbw b Lakmal	1
Rubel Hossain b Herath	2		– c Silva b Perera	17
Al-Amin Hossain not out	6		– not out	32
L-b 4, n-b 5	9		B 9, l-b 10, n-b 2	21
(63.5 overs)	232		(51.5 overs)	250

1/35 (1) 2/40 (3) 3/40 (2) 4/59 (4) 5/145 (5) 6/150 (7)   1/15 (1) 2/35 (2) 3/50 (3) 4/102 (5) 5/133 (4)
7/203 (6) 8/219 (8) 9/222 (10) 10/232 (9)   6/150 (6) 7/183 (8) 8/197 (9) 9/197 (7) 10/250 (10)

Lakmal 18.1–3–66–3; Eranga 17.4–2–49–4; Mathews 6–3–18–1; Perera 11–2–45–0; Herath 11–1–50–2. *Second Innings*—Lakmal 14–4–39–3; Eranga 6–1–26–1; Herath 9–3–47–1; Perera 19.5–0–109–5; Mathews 3–0–10–0.

Sri Lanka

F. D. M. Karunaratne c Robiul Islam b Shakib Al Hasan .	53
J. K. Silva lbw b Shakib Al Hasan	139
K. C. Sangakkara c Nasir Hossain b Al-Amin Hossain....	75
D. P. M. D. Jayawardene not out	203
†L. D. Chandimal b Shakib Al Hasan	40
R. A. S. Lakmal c Nasir Hossain b Sohag Gazi	0
*A. D. Mathews c Marshall Ayub b Sohag Gazi	86
K. D. K. Vithanage not out	103
B 12, w 12, n-b 7	31
(6 wkts dec, 187.5 overs)	730

1/118 (1) 2/273 (3) 3/302 (2) 4/374 (5) 5/375 (6)
6/554 (7)

M. D. K. Perera, R. M. S. Eranga and H. M. R. K. B. Herath did not bat.

Robiul Islam 29–2–109–0; Al-Amin Hossain 32–3–118–1; Rubel Hossain 20–0–84–0; Sohag Gazi 39–5–130–2; Shakib Al Hasan 43–6–159–3; Mominul Haque 6–0–20–0; Nasir Hossain 10.5–0–60–0; Marshall Ayub 8–0–38–0.

Umpires: N. J. Llong *(England)* (23) and P. R. Reiffel *(Australia)* (8).
Third umpire: Sharfuddoula *(Bangladesh)*. Referee: J. Srinath *(India)* (32).

Close of play: First day, Sri Lanka 60–0 (Karunaratne 28, Silva 30); Second day, Sri Lanka 375–5 (Jayawardene 42); Third day, Bangladesh 35–1 (Shamsur Rahman 9, Marshall Ayub 11).

BANGLADESH v SRI LANKA 2013–14 (2nd Test)

At Zohur Ahmed Chowdhury Stadium, Chittagong, on 4, 5, 6, 7, 8 February, 2014.
Toss: Sri Lanka.   Result: MATCH DRAWN.
Debuts: none.
Man of the Match: K. C. Sangakkara. Man of the Series: K. C. Sangakkara.

Sangakkara had missed out, relatively speaking, in the First Test – but cashed in now, becoming only the second batsman, after Graham Gooch for England against India at Lord's in 1990, to make a triple-century and a hundred in the same first-class match. Sangakkara's 319, his 35th century and ninth double, came from 482 balls in 551 minutes: he hit 32 fours and eight sixes, two in succession off Shakib Al Hasan to take him to Sri Lanka's third Test triple-hundred. He entered after 16 overs, and was last out in the 157th. For once Bangladesh did not cave in, on a pitch that stayed slow and low. Although Tamim Iqbal fell fourth ball, Shamsur Rahman (in his second Test) and Imrul Kayes both scored maiden centuries during a stand of 232, a national second-wicket record, and the rest ensured the follow-on was avoided. With the series in the bag, Mathews batted on to set a lofty target of 468: Chandimal made his third Test hundred (all against Bangladesh), and Sangakkara added a further 105, his seventh century against them. Only Gooch (456 in 1990) and Mark Taylor (426 for Australia v Pakistan at Peshawar in 1998–99) had scored more runs in a Test than his 424. Bangladesh were left with just over a day to survive (or chase 467, which was never very likely). Showing much more resolution than previously, they easily held out for the draw, with the diminutive Mominul Haque completing his third century in just 13 innings.

Sri Lanka

F. D. M. Karunaratne c Mahmudullah b Al-Amin Hossain..	31	– c Nasir Hossain b Mahmudullah		15
J. K. Silva lbw b Sohag Gazi	11	– lbw b Mahmudullah		29
K. C. Sangakkara c Sohag Gazi b Nasir Hossain	319	– b Sohag Gazi		105
D. P. M. D. Jayawardene lbw b Mahmudullah	72	– lbw b Shakib Al Hasan		11
†L. D. Chandimal c Imrul Kayes b Shakib Al Hasan	27	– not out		100
*A. D. Mathews b Shakib Al Hasan	5	– not out		43
K. D. K. Vithanage lbw b Nasir Hossain	35			
M. D. K. Perera lbw b Shakib Al Hasan	1			
B. A. W. Mendis lbw b Shakib Al Hasan	47			
R. A. S. Lakmal lbw b Shakib Al Hasan	0			
A. N. P. R. Fernando not out	4			
B 21, l-b 6, w 2, n-b 1, p 5	35	L-b 2		2
(156.4 overs)	587	(4 wkts dec, 75.5 overs)		305

1/39 (2) 2/49 (1) 3/227 (4) 4/294 (5) 5/312 (6)
6/402 (7) 7/405 (8) 8/505 (9) 9/533 (10) 10/587 (3)   1/36 (1) 2/49 (2) 3/78 (4) 4/223 (3)

Al-Amin Hossain 25–5–81–1; Sohag Gazi 48–4–181–1; Abdur Razzak 4–1–6–0; Shakib Al Hasan 34–3–148–5; Mahmudullah 34–2–110–1; Nasir Hossain 6.4–0–16–2; Shamsur Rahman 1–0–5–0; Mominul Haque 4–0–8–0. *Second Innings*—Al-Amin Hossain 7–1–31–0; Sohag Gazi 18.5–1–87–1; Shakib Al Hasan 22–2–80–1; Mahmudullah 18–4–46–2; Mominul Haque 7–0–46–0; Nasir Hossain 3–0–13–0.

Bangladesh

Tamim Iqbal b Lakmal	0	– b Vithanage		31
Shamsur Rahman b Mendis	106	– b Perera		45
Imrul Kayes b Mendis	115	– lbw b Perera		25
Mominul Haque lbw b Perera	13	– not out		100
Shakib Al Hasan c Karunaratne b Perera	50	– not out		43
*†Mushfiqur Rahim c Silva b Perera	20			
Nasir Hossain c Chandimal b Mendis	42			
Mahmudullah c Silva b Mendis	30			
Sohag Gazi lbw b Mendis	0			
Al-Amin Hossain b Mendis	9			
Abdur Razzak not out	11			
B 8, l-b 1, n-b 21	30	B 12, l-b 2, n-b 13		27
(119.5 overs)	426	(3 wkts, 84.4 overs)		271

1/0 (1) 2/232 (2) 3/252 (4) 4/259 (3) 5/319 (6)
6/350 (5) 7/396 (7) 8/396 (9) 9/409 (8) 10/426 (10)   1/71 (1) 2/81 (2) 3/151 (3)

Lakmal 25–6–70–1; Fernando 15–2–96–0; Mendis 29.5–3–99–6; Perera 39–4–119–3; Mathews 11–1–33–0. *Second Innings*—Lakmal 13–5–30–0; Perera 28–7–55–2; Mendis 16–0–61–0; Fernando 9.4–1–33–0; Vithanage 16–0–73–1; Karunaratne 2–0–5–0.

Umpires: N. J. Llong *(England)* (24) and P. R. Reiffel *(Australia)* (9).
Third umpire: Anisur Rahman *(Bangladesh)*. Referee: D. C. Boon *(Australia)* (21).

Close of play: First day, Sri Lanka 314–5 (Sangakkara 160, Vithanage 0); Second day, Bangladesh 86–1 (Shamsur Rahman 45, Imrul Kayes 36); Third day, Bangladesh 409–8 (Mahmudullah 30, Al-Amin Hossain 3); Fourth day, Bangladesh 12–0 (Tamim Iqbal 7, Shamsur Rahman 4).

NEW ZEALAND v INDIA 2013–14 (1st Test)

At Eden Park, Auckland, on 6, 7, 8, 9 February, 2014.
Toss: India.   Result: NEW ZEALAND WON BY 40 RUNS.
Debuts: none.
Man of the Match: B. B. McCullum.

A riveting storyline contained several engaging subplots: McCullum's second Test double-century, an all-too-familiar third-innings collapse by New Zealand after they had waived the follow-on, and a fourth and final day in which the match hung in the balance. The upshot was New Zealand's first Test win over India since December 2002 – but they were made to fight. Sent in on a green drop-in pitch, New Zealand were soon 30 for three, but were rescued by McCullum, who put on 221 with Williamson in a stand full of textbook strokes, and a further 133 with Anderson before being last out one short of his career-best at the time, 225 against India at Hyderabad in 2010–11. Ishant Sharma persevered for six for 134 – but his colleagues managed only four for 363 between them. India made an even worse start, and their recovery was less successful, despite Rohit Sharma's 72. McCullum batted again… and New Zealand were soon 25 for four. It was left to the last-wicket pair to raise the hundred – but New Zealand still led by 406. India had knocked off 87 of those by the end of a third day in which 17 wickets fell for 264. While Dhawan and Kohli were together a miracle seemed just possible, but regular wickets fell after that – although Dhoni and Jadeja jangled more home nerves while putting on 54. New Zealand's feisty seamers took all ten wickets, while wicketkeeper Watling finished with six catches, a record for the fourth innings of any Test.

New Zealand

P. G. Fulton lbw b Zaheer Khan	13	– c Jadeja b Mohammed Shami	5
H. D. Rutherford c Rahane b I. Sharma	6	– lbw b Mohammed Shami	0
K. S. Williamson c Dhoni b Zaheer Khan	113	– c Jadeja b Zaheer Khan	3
L. R. P. L. Taylor c Jadeja b I. Sharma	3	– c Rahane b Zaheer Khan	41
*B. B. McCullum c Jadeja b I. Sharma	224	– run out	1
C. J. Anderson lbw b I. Sharma	77	– b Mohammed Shami	2
†B-J. Watling c Dhawan b I. Sharma	1	– b I. Sharma	11
T. G. Southee b Mohammed Shami	28	– c Pujara b Jadeja	14
I. S. Sodhi c R. G. Sharma b I. Sharma	23	– c R. G. Sharma b I. Sharma	0
N. Wagner c Kohli b Jadeja	0	– c Jadeja b I. Sharma	14
T. A. Boult not out	1	– not out	7
B 1, l-b 5, w 5, n-b 3	14	B 4, w 1, n-b 2	7
(121.4 overs)	503	(41.2 overs)	105

1/19 (2) 2/23 (1) 3/30 (4) 4/251 (3) 5/384 (6)   1/1 (2) 2/9 (1) 3/11 (3) 4/15 (5) 5/25 (6)
6/398 (7) 7/434 (8) 8/490 (9) 9/495 (10) 10/503 (5)   6/63 (4) 7/78 (8) 8/78 (7) 9/80 (9) 10/105 (10)

Mohammed Shami 28–6–95–1; Zaheer Khan 30–2–132–2; I. Sharma 33.4–4–134–6; Jadeja 26–1–120–1; Kohli 1–0–4–0; R. G. Sharma 3–0–12–0. *Second Innings*—Mohammed Shami 12–1–37–3; Zaheer Khan 9–2–23–2; I. Sharma 10.2–3–28–3; Jadeja 9–4–10–1; R. G. Sharma 1–0–3–0.

India

S. Dhawan c Williamson b Boult	0	– (2) c Watling b Wagner	115
M. Vijay b Wagner	26	– (1) c Watling b Southee	13
C. A. Pujara c Watling b Boult	1	– c Watling b Southee	23
V. Kohli c Fulton b Southee	4	– c Watling b Wagner	67
R. G. Sharma b Boult	72	– c Watling b Southee	19
A. M. Rahane c Taylor b Southee	26	– lbw b Boult	18
*†M. S. Dhoni c Watling b Wagner	10	– b Wagner	39
R. A. Jadeja not out	30	– c Sodhi b Boult	26
Zaheer Khan c Watling b Wagner	14	– c Taylor b Wagner	17
I. Sharma c Boult b Southee	0	– c Watling b Boult	4
Mohammed Shami c Fulton b Wagner	2	– not out	0
B 5, l-b 6, w 3, n-b 3	17	B 12, l-b 7, w 2, n-b 4	25
(60 overs)	202	(96.3 overs)	366

1/1 (1) 2/3 (3) 3/10 (4) 4/51 (2) 5/138 (6)   1/36 (1) 2/96 (3) 3/222 (4) 4/248 (2) 5/268 (6)
6/138 (5) 7/167 (7) 8/188 (9) 9/189 (10) 10/202 (11)   6/270 (5) 7/324 (8) 8/349 (9) 9/362 (7) 10/366 (10)

Boult 17–2–38–3; Southee 19–6–38–3; Anderson 5–0–29–0; Wagner 11–0–64–4; Sodhi 6–0–13–0; Williamson 2–0–9–0. *Second Innings*—Boult 23.3–2–86–3; Southee 23–4–81–3; Wagner 25–8–62–4; Anderson 7–1–22–0; Sodhi 15–2–78–0; Williamson 3–0–18–0.

Umpires: S. J. Davis *(Australia)* (51) and R. A. Kettleborough *(England)* (19).
Third umpire: G. A. V. Baxter *(New Zealand)*. Referee: R. S. Madugalle *(Sri Lanka)* (147).

Close of play: First day, New Zealand 329–4 (McCullum 143, Anderson 42); Second day, India 130–4 (R. G. Sharma 67, Rahane 23); Third day, India 87–1 (Dhawan 49, Pujara 22).

NEW ZEALAND v INDIA 2013–14 (2nd Test)

At Basin Reserve, Wellington, on 14, 15, 16, 17, 18 February, 2014.
Toss: India. Result: MATCH DRAWN.
Debuts: New Zealand – T. W. M. Latham, J. D. S. Neesham.
Man of the Match: B. B. McCullum.

When Watling joined McCullum shortly after lunch on the third day, New Zealand were still 152 short of avoiding an innings defeat. Nearly two days later, McCullum reached their first Test triple-century, and several long-standing records had been obliterated after a fantastic salvage operation. Put in, New Zealand had subsided on an emerald-tinged strip. India then cantered to a big lead, thanks to 98 from Dhawan and Rahane's maiden century. They looked sure to square the series at 94 for five, but McCullum and Watling dug in for 8½ hours and the highest sixth-wicket partnership in Tests, edging by one the 351 of Mahela and Prasanna Jayawardene for Sri Lanka against India at Ahmedabad in 2009–10. After Watling was finally lbw, left-hander Jimmy Neesham – who had been padded up for 123 overs – marked his debut with an undefeated 137. After becoming the fourth New Zealander to complete 5,000 Test runs, McCullum started the final day with 281, and eventually cut Zaheer Khan for the four that erased Martin Crowe's agonising near-miss national-record 299; it was only the second Test triple in the second innings, after Hanif Mohammad's 337 for Pakistan against West Indies at Bridgetown in 1957–58. In all McCullum hit 32 fours and four sixes in 775 minutes, but delayed his declaration until New Zealand's record 671 from Crowe's 1990–91 Wellington match against Sri Lanka was also surpassed. With a draw certain, Kohli made an untroubled sixth Test century. It was only the second time – after 1989–90 – New Zealand had won two series in a home summer.

New Zealand

P. G. Fulton lbw b I. Sharma	13	– lbw b Zaheer Khan	1
H. D. Rutherford c Vijay b I. Sharma	12	– c Dhoni b Zaheer Khan	35
K. S. Williamson c R. G. Sharma b Mohammed Shami	47	– c Dhoni b Zaheer Khan	7
T. W. M. Latham c Dhoni b I. Sharma	0	– c Dhoni b Mohammed Shami	29
*B. B. McCullum c Jadeja b Mohammed Shami	8	– c Dhoni b Zaheer Khan	302
C. J. Anderson c Kohli b I. Sharma	24	– c and b Jadeja	2
†B-J. Watling c R. G. Sharma b I. Sharma	0	– lbw b Mohammed Shami	124
J. D. S. Neesham c Dhoni b Mohammed Shami	33	– not out	137
T. G. Southee c Vijay b I. Sharma	32	– c Pujara b Zaheer Khan	11
N. Wagner not out	5	– not out	2
T. A. Boult c Pujara b Mohammed Shami	2		
L-b 2, w 8, n-b 6	16	B 9, l-b 12, w 2, n-b 7	30
(52.5 overs)	192	(8 wkts dec, 210 overs)	680

1/23 (2) 2/26 (1) 3/26 (4) 4/45 (5) 5/84 (6) 6/86 (7)   1/1 (1) 2/27 (3) 3/52 (2) 4/87 (4) 5/94 (6) 6/446 (7)
7/133 (8) 8/165 (8) 9/184 (9) 10/192 (11)   7/625 (5) 8/639 (9)

Zaheer Khan 17–3–57–0; Mohammed Shami 16.5–4–70–4; I. Sharma 17–3–51–6; Jadeja 2–1–12–0. *Second Innings*—I. Sharma 45–4–164–0; Zaheer Khan 51–13–170–5; Mohammed Shami 43–6–149–2; Jadeja 52–11–115–1; R. G. Sharma 11–0–40–0; Kohli 6–1–13–0; Dhoni 1–0–5–0; Dhawan 1–0–3–0.

India

S. Dhawan c Watling b Southee	98	– (2) lbw b Boult	2
M. Vijay c Watling b Southee	2	– (1) c Anderson b Southee	7
C. A. Pujara lbw b Boult	19	– c Watling b Southee	17
I. Sharma c Watling b Boult	26		
V. Kohli c Rutherford b Wagner	38	– (4) not out	105
R. G. Sharma b Neesham	0	– (5) not out	31
A. M. Rahane c Boult b Southee	118		
*†M. S. Dhoni c Watling b Boult	68		
R. A. Jadeja c Fulton b Wagner	26		
Zaheer Khan c Watling b Wagner	22		
Mohammed Shami not out	0		
B 8, 1 b 4, w 7, n-b 2	21	W 2, n-b 2	4
(102.4 overs)	438	(3 wkts, 52 overs)	166

1/2 (2) 2/89 (3) 3/141 (4) 4/162 (1) 5/165 (6) 6/228 (5)
7/348 (8) 8/385 (9) 9/423 (7) 10/438 (10)   1/10 (2) 2/10 (1) 3/54 (3)

Boult 26–7–99–3; Southee 20–0–93–3; Wagner 22.4–3–106–3; Anderson 16–2–66–0; Neesham 18–2–62–1. *Second Innings*—Boult 16–5–47–1; Southee 16–3–50–2; Wagner 11–3–38–0; Neesham 5–0–25–0; Anderson 4–1–6–0.

Umpires: S. J. Davis *(Australia)* (52) and R. A. Kettleborough *(England)* (20).
Third umpire: D. J. Walker *(New Zealand)*. Referee: R. S. Madugalle *(Sri Lanka)* (148).

Close of play: First day, India 100–2 (Dhawan 71, I. Sharma 3); Second day, New Zealand 24–1 (Rutherford 18, Williamson 4); Third day, New Zealand 252–5 (McCullum 114, Watling 52); Fourth day, New Zealand 571–6 (McCullum 281, Neesham 67).

SOUTH AFRICA v AUSTRALIA 2013–14 (1st Test)

At Centurion Park, Pretoria, on 12, 13, 14, 15 February, 2014.
Toss: South Africa.　　　Result: AUSTRALIA WON BY 281 RUNS.
Debuts: Australia – A. J. Doolan.
Man of the Match: M. G. Johnson.

After flattening England on his own soil, Mitchell Johnson now obliterated the No. 1 Test nation on theirs. Generating vicious pace and hostility, he twice cut a swathe through the batting, claiming a dozen wickets and hastening an emphatic defeat, South Africa's first at home for more than two years. They had lost only once in 18 previous matches at Centurion, and that in the now-tainted game against England in 1999–2000 when Hansie Cronje manufactured a result. Smith had twice previously put the opposition in here and won by an innings, but now centuries from Marsh – a surprise reinforcement to replace the injured Watson – and Smith set up a total of 397. That looked much bigger as South Africa dipped to 23 for three, all to the fiery Johnson. De Villiers mounted a brave and skilful counter-attack, but South Africa never recovered from that opening blast: Johnson finished with seven for 68, and Australia with a lead of 191. Warner and the debutant Alex Doolan swelled that with a second-wicket partnership of 205, and the eventual target was 482. That soon looked notional as Johnson again ripped out the openers – including Petersen, his 250th Test wicket – and he returned later to disrupt the middle order too, dismissing McLaren after clonking him on the helmet so hard he missed the next Test. Only Clarrie Grimmett (twice) had recorded better match figures for Australia against South Africa than Johnson's 12 for 127; he had taken 49 wickets in his last six Tests.

Australia

C. J. L. Rogers c Duminy b Morkel	4	– b Steyn	1
D. A. Warner b Steyn	12	– c Smith b Peterson	115
A. J. Doolan c Peterson b McLaren	27	– c de Villiers b Duminy	89
S. E. Marsh c Smith b Philander	148	– c de Villiers b Steyn	44
*M. J. Clarke c Philander b Steyn	23	– not out	17
S. P. D. Smith c Petersen b McLaren	100		
†B. J. Haddin lbw b Peterson	0		
M. G. Johnson b Peterson	33		
R. J. Harris b Steyn	19		
P. M. Siddle b Steyn	2		
N. M. Lyon not out	4		
B 4, l-b 8, w 11, n-b 2	25	B 3, l-b 14, w 7	24
(122 overs)	397	(4 wkts dec, 72.2 overs)	290

1/15 (2) 2/24 (1) 3/72 (3) 4/98 (5) 5/331 (6) 6/332 (7)
7/348 (4) 8/391 (9) 9/391 (8) 10/397 (10)　　　1/1 (1) 2/206 (2) 3/243 (3) 4/290 (4)

Steyn 29–6–78–4; Philander 24–5–69–1; Morkel 22–5–73–1; McLaren 20–4–72–2; Peterson 15–0–49–2; Duminy 12–1–44–0. *Second Innings*—Philander 11–2–28–0; Steyn 14.2–2–61–2; McLaren 11–0–47–0; Morkel 13–4–38–0; Peterson 19–0–87–1; Duminy 4–0–12–1.

South Africa

*G. C. Smith c Marsh b Johnson	10	– (2) c Doolan b Johnson	4
A. N. Petersen c Haddin b Johnson	2	– (1) c Haddin b Johnson	1
H. M. Amla lbw b Siddle	17	– c Marsh b Harris	35
F. du Plessis c Clarke b Johnson	3	– lbw b Siddle	18
†A. B. de Villiers c Warner b Johnson	91	– c Smith b Johnson	48
J-P. Duminy c Johnson b Lyon	25	– c Doolan b Johnson	10
R. McLaren b Johnson	8	– c Haddin b Johnson	6
R. J. Peterson c Clarke b Johnson	10	– b Siddle	21
V. D. Philander lbw b Lyon	15	– not out	26
D. W. Steyn not out	7	– c Clarke b Harris	3
M. Morkel c Haddin b Johnson	0	– run out	1
B 14, l-b 2, w 1, n-b 1	18	B 10, l-b 5, w 11, n-b 1	27
(61.1 overs)	206	(59.4 overs)	200

1/11 (1) 2/15 (2) 3/23 (4) 4/43 (3) 5/110 (6)　　　1/6 (1) 2/12 (2) 3/49 (4) 4/97 (3) 5/128 (6)
6/126 (7) 7/140 (8) 8/189 (9) 9/202 (5) 10/206 (11)　　　6/140 (7) 7/151 (5) 8/165 (8) 9/178 (10) 10/200 (11)

Harris 17–3–51–0; Johnson 17.1–1–68–7; Siddle 13–1–33–1; Lyon 14–0–38–2. *Second Innings*—Harris 12.4–5–35–2; Johnson 16–3–59–5; Siddle 16–6–55–2; Warner 2–0–3–0; Lyon 13–1–33–0.

Umpires: Aleem Dar *(Pakistan)* (88) and R. K. Illingworth *(England)* (6).
Third umpire: I. J. Gould *(England)*. Referee: R. S. Mahanama *(Sri Lanka)* (49).

Close of play: First day, Australia 297–4 (Marsh 122, Smith 91); Second day, South Africa 140–6 (de Villiers 52, Peterson 10); Third day, Australia 288–3 (Marsh 44, Clarke 17).

SOUTH AFRICA v AUSTRALIA 2013–14 (2nd Test)

At St George's Park, Port Elizabeth, on 20, 21, 22, 23 February, 2014.
Toss: South Africa.   Result: SOUTH AFRICA WON BY 231 RUNS.
Debuts: South Africa – Q. de Kock.
Man of the Match: J-P. Duminy.

South Africa bounced back to square the series, as the Australians were first neutralised by a subcontinental pitch then splintered by reverse swing. Johnson managed only one wicket as South Africa dug deep for 423, with centuries for de Villiers (his 19th) and Duminy, who added 149 for the sixth wicket. Earlier Elgar, replacing the unwell Petersen, made 83. Warner cracked a flashy 70, but Marsh and Doolan fell in the first three balls from the waspish Parnell, in his first Test for four years (he later broke down with a groin strain). South Africa's lead was a healthy 177, and Amla's dominant century – Harris said later he felt like a bowling machine – extended that to 447. For 29 overs, Rogers and Warner made the declaration appear optimistic. But Warner was winkled out by Duminy, and the runs dried up. Doolan laboured to five before snicking his 43rd ball into the slips, then Steyn swerved through Clarke, Smith and Haddin in a matter of minutes. The match ended in the extra half-hour on the fourth day, when Lyon was given out lbw despite edging the ball (Australia had exhausted their reviews). Rogers was ninth out, trying to farm the strike after a century of great poise and good sense: he and Warner made 88.71% of the runs off the bat, the greatest percentage by a pair of batsmen in any completed Test innings (previously 81.07% by Gautam Gambhir and Virender Sehwag for India against Sri Lanka at Galle in 2008).

South Africa

*G. C. Smith lbw b Harris	9	– b Johnson		14
D. Elgar c Harris b Lyon	83	– c Haddin b Siddle		16
H. M. Amla lbw b Johnson	0	– not out		127
F. du Plessis c Smith b Lyon	55	– c Haddin b Siddle		24
†A. B. de Villiers c and b Lyon	116	– c Haddin b Johnson		29
Q. de Kock c sub (M. C. Henriques) b Smith	7	– c Clarke b Lyon		34
J-P. Duminy lbw b Lyon	123	– not out		18
V. D. Philander c and b Clarke	6			
W. D. Parnell c Haddin b Lyon	10			
D. W. Steyn not out	4			
M. Morkel run out	1			
B 4, l-b 4, w 1	9	B 2, l-b 6		8
(150.5 overs)	423	(5 wkts dec, 64 overs)		270

1/10 (1) 2/11 (3) 3/123 (4) 4/181 (2) 5/200 (6)
6/349 (5) 7/378 (8) 8/413 (9) 9/420 (7) 10/423 (11)   1/20 (1) 2/42 (2) 3/112 (4) 4/167 (5) 5/231 (6)

Harris 27–6–63–1; Johnson 25–5–70–1; Siddle 34–9–96–0; Lyon 46–7–130–5; Warner 3–0–10–0; Smith 8–0–30–1; Clarke 7.5–2–16–1. *Second Innings*—Johnson 15–1–51–2; Harris 13–1–74–0; Lyon 17–2–48–1; Siddle 19–2–89–2.

Australia

C. J. L. Rogers lbw b Philander	5	– run out		107
D. A. Warner c Smith b Philander	70	– lbw b Duminy		66
A. J. Doolan c de Villiers b Parnell	8	– c Smith b Morkel		5
S. E. Marsh c de Villiers b Parnell	0	– lbw b Philander		0
*M. J. Clarke c Elgar b Philander	19	– c du Plessis b Steyn		1
N. M. Lyon b Morkel	15	– (11) lbw b Elgar		0
S. P. D. Smith c de Villiers b Morkel	49	– (6) lbw b Steyn		0
†B. J. Haddin b Steyn	9	– (7) b Steyn		1
M. G. Johnson b Duminy	27	– (8) lbw b Philander		6
R. J. Harris c du Plessis b Morkel	26	– (9) lbw b Steyn		6
P. M. Siddle not out	11	– (10) not out		3
L-b 4, w 2, n-b 1	7	B 2, l-b 17, w 2		21
(57 overs)	246	(73.4 overs)		216

1/7 (1) 2/41 (3) 3/41 (4) 4/81 (5) 5/120 (2)
6/128 (6) 7/168 (8) 8/205 (9) 9/209 (7) 10/246 (10)   1/126 (2) 2/152 (3) 3/153 (4) 4/156 (5) 5/156 (6)
6/166 (7) 7/197 (8) 8/209 (9) 9/214 (1) 10/216 (11)

Steyn 13–3–55–1; Philander 13–0–68–3; Morkel 17–0–63–3; Parnell 8.3–2–31–2; Elgar 0.3–0–1–0; Duminy 5–0–24–1. *Second Innings*—Steyn 20–5–55–4; Philander 17–3–39–2; Morkel 15–6–46–1; Duminy 14–3–33–1; Elgar 7.4–0–24–1.

Umpires: H. D. P. K. Dharmasena *(Sri Lanka)* (22) and R. K. Illingworth *(England)* (7).
Third umpire: Aleem Dar *(Pakistan)*. Referee: R. S. Mahanama *(Sri Lanka)* (50).

Close of play: First day, South Africa 214–5 (de Villiers 51, Duminy 2); Second day, Australia 112–4 (Warner 65, Lyon 12); Third day, South Africa 192–4 (Amla 93, de Kock 9).

SOUTH AFRICA v AUSTRALIA 2013–14 (3rd Test)

At Newlands, Cape Town, on 1, 2, 3, 4, 5 March, 2014.
Toss: Australia.   Result: AUSTRALIA WON BY 245 RUNS.
Debuts: none.
Man of the Match: D. A. Warner. Man of the Series: D. A. Warner.

Little more than two years previously, Australia had been humiliated for 47 here. But now they inflicted a tense defeat on Graeme Smith in his last Test. After Clarke won an invaluable toss, Warner took advantage of Steyn's sore hamstring to make 135. Clarke was battered by Morkel – his shoulder was broken by a bouncer – but survived; becalmed on 99 for 24 balls, he extended his 27th Test hundred to an undefeated 161. Harris and Johnson then shattered South Africa, although du Plessis organised a handy rearguard – and was abused at one point for picking up the ball. He likened the Australians to "a pack of dogs", which provoked mock barking when he departed in the second innings. Clarke waived the follow-on, instead unleashing Warner again: he obliged with his fourth hundred in six Tests against South Africa, the 20th time an Australian had scored two in the same Test. South Africa needed a monumental 511 in 131 overs, and were soon 15 for three. But the middle order dug in – de Villiers batted for 5½ hours – and a draw looked likely until Johnson removed Duminy. Still, there were only five overs remaining when the weary Harris returned – and yorked Steyn with his first ball and zipped through Morkel with his third. Australia's 2–1 victory ended South Africa's run of 14 unbeaten series stretching back to December 2009. Smith followed his mate Jacques Kallis into retirement after 9,265 runs in 117 Tests, with 27 centuries; he won 53 of 109 Tests as captain (both records).

Australia

C. J. L. Rogers c Smith b Steyn	25	– run out	39
D. A. Warner c de Villiers b Duminy	135	– c de Villiers b Abbott	145
A. J. Doolan c Steyn b Philander	20	– c Abbott b Morkel	37
*M. J. Clarke not out	161	– (5) c sub (Q. de Kock) b Abbott	0
S. P. D. Smith b Elgar	84	– (6) not out	36
S. R. Watson c Amla b Duminy	40	– (4) c Duminy b Abbott	25
†B. J. Haddin c Amla b Duminy	13	– not out	3
M. G. Johnson c de Villiers b Duminy	0		
R. J. Harris not out	4		
W 6, n-b 6	12	B 3, l-b 12, n-b 3	18
(7 wkts dec, 127.4 overs)	494	(5 wkts dec, 58 overs)	303

1/65 (1) 2/138 (3) 3/217 (2) 4/401 (5) 5/456 (6)
6/489 (7) 7/489 (8)

1/123 (1) 2/188 (3) 3/245 (4) 4/257 (5) 5/290 (2)

J. L. Pattinson and N. M. Lyon did not bat.

Steyn 10.1–0–44–1; Philander 26.4–2–116–1; Morkel 23.5–2–94–0; Duminy 17–0–73–4; Abbott 28–11–68–0; Elgar 22–0–99–1. *Second Innings*—Morkel 13–1–67–1; Abbott 14–2–61–3; Philander 6–0–42–0; Duminy 19–3–76–0; Steyn 3–1–24–0; Elgar 3–0–18–0.

South Africa

*G. C. Smith c Haddin b Harris	5	– (2) c Doolan b Johnson	3
A. N. Petersen c Haddin b Johnson	53	– (1) lbw b Harris	9
D. Elgar c Haddin b Pattinson	11	– b Johnson	0
H. M. Amla b Harris	38	– lbw b Pattinson	41
†A. B. de Villiers c Clarke b Johnson	14	– c Haddin b Harris	43
F. du Plessis c Warner b Johnson	67	– (7) lbw b Smith	47
J-P. Duminy c Haddin b Harris	4	– (8) c Lyon b Johnson	43
V. D. Philander not out	37	– (9) not out	51
K. J. Abbott b Watson	3	– (6) b Pattinson	7
D. W. Steyn c Watson b Johnson	28	– b Harris	1
M. Morkel c Watson b Pattinson	7	– b Harris	0
B 8, l-b 3, w 6, n-b 3	20	B 8, l-b 5, w 2, n-b 5	20
(82.5 overs)	287	(134.3 overs)	265

1/7 (1) 2/42 (3) 3/95 (2) 4/121 (4) 5/133 (5)
6/146 (7) 7/241 (6) 8/249 (9) 9/279 (10) 10/287 (11)

1/12 (1) 2/12 (3) 3/15 (3) 4/68 (4) 5/95 (6)
6/136 (5) 7/173 (7) 8/246 (8) 9/265 (10) 10/265 (11)

Harris 22–9–63–3; Johnson 19–5–42–4; Pattinson 18.5–4–77–2; Watson 9–1–34–1; Lyon 12–1–53–0; Smith 2–0–7–0. *Second Innings*—Harris 24.3–15–32–4; Johnson 34–11–92–3; Pattinson 27–10–62–2; Lyon 22–17–10–0; Watson 9–6–6–0; Smith 13–3–43–1; Clarke 5–2–7–0.

Umpires: Aleem Dar *(Pakistan)* (89) and H. D. P. K. Dharmasena *(Sri Lanka)* (23).
Third umpire: R. K. Illingworth *(England)*. Referee: R. S. Mahanama *(Sri Lanka)* (51).

Close of play: First day, Australia 331–3 (Clarke 92, Smith 50); Second day, Australia 494–7 (Clarke 161, Harris 4); Third day, Australia 27–0 (Rogers 1, Warner 25); Fourth day, South Africa 71–4 (de Villiers 16, Abbott 1).

WEST INDIES v NEW ZEALAND 2014 (1st Test)

At Sabina Park, Kingston, Jamaica, on 8, 9, 10, 11 June, 2014.
Toss: New Zealand.　　　Result: NEW ZEALAND WON BY 186 RUNS.
Debuts: New Zealand – M. D. Craig.
Man of the Match: M. D. Craig.

New Zealand were on top almost throughout their second Test victory in the Caribbean, after Barbados in 2002; McCullum hailed it as "nigh on the perfect Test for us". His batsmen steadily accumulated a daunting total over the first two days, then a varied bowling attack twice exposed West Indies' batting frailties. After Latham added 165 with Williamson, who batted for 370 minutes, Neesham made his second century in his second Test, and put on 201 for the sixth wicket in 70 overs with Watling. Gayle, playing his 100th Test in his native Jamaica, made a subdued 64, but the only other resistance came from Chanderpaul and Ramdin, in his first match as captain after replacing Darren Sammy (who retired from Tests after being sidelined). There were four wickets apiece for Southee and Mark Craig, the debutant off-spinner, who later became the first man ever to hit his first ball in a Test for six. That came at the end of an undistinguished second innings, in which Jerome Taylor (in his first Test for five years) helped scupper New Zealand's search for quick runs. West Indies needed 403 in a day and a half – but were bundled out in the half. The margin would have been even wider but for Shillingford, returning after his action was cleared by the ICC. He smashed five sixes to reach a 25-ball fifty, the fastest by a West Indian; it was only the tenth time the No. 11 had top-scored in a Test innings.

New Zealand

T. W. M. Latham c and b Shillingford	83	– (2) c Gayle b Roach	73
P. G. Fulton c Ramdin b Taylor	1	– (1) c Ramdin b Taylor	0
K. S. Williamson b Benn	113	– b Roach	2
L. R. P. L. Taylor c Edwards b Shillingford	55	– (5) lbw b Taylor	0
*B. B. McCullum c Gayle b Benn	7	– (6) b Shillingford	17
J. D. S. Neesham c Ramdin b Benn	107	– (7) c sub (K. C. Brathwaite) b Shillingford	20
†B-J. Watling c Powell b Shillingford	89	– (8) not out	22
T. G. Southee not out	21	– (9) c Bravo b Benn	3
I. S. Sodhi (did not bat)		– (4) lbw b Taylor	4
M. D. Craig (did not bat)		– not out	7
B 19, l-b 6, w 5, n-b 2	32	L-b 8	8
(7 wkts dec, 174.3 overs)	508	(8 wkts dec, 60.5 overs)	156

1/9 (2) 2/174 (1) 3/259 (3) 4/277 (4) 5/279 (5)　　　　1/0 (1) 2/7 (3) 3/14 (4) 4/14 (5) 5/55 (6)
6/480 (6) 7/508 (7)　　　　　　　　　　　　　　　　　　6/118 (7) 7/143 (2) 8/146 (9)

T. A. Boult did not bat.

Taylor 26–11–37–1; Roach 29–6–85–0; Bravo 1–0–2–0; Benn 52–14–142–3; Samuels 15–1–55–0; Shillingford 46.3–7–145–3; Gayle 5–0–17–0. *Second Innings*—Taylor 12–4–28–3; Roach 12–6–12–2; Benn 17.5–3–47–1; Shillingford 13–0–39–2; Samuels 6–1–22–0.

West Indies

C. H. Gayle c Watling b Southee	64	– c Watling b Southee	10
K. O. A. Powell lbw b Craig	28	– c Latham b Southee	0
K. A. Edwards c Taylor b Craig	0	– c Neesham b Craig	14
D. M. Bravo c and b Sodhi	0	– c Watling b Craig	12
S. Chanderpaul not out	84	– lbw b Sodhi	24
M. N. Samuels lbw b Southee	0	– c Latham b Craig	0
*†D. Ramdin c Watling b Southee	39	– b Sodhi	34
K. A. J. Roach c Fulton b Craig	4	– c Watling b Craig	19
J. E. Taylor c McCullum b Boult	7	– c Watling b Sodhi	18
S. J. Benn b Craig	17	– c Watling b Williamson	25
S. Shillingford c Watling b Southee	14	– not out	53
L-b 2, w 1, n-b 2	5	B 4, l-b 2, w 1	7
(81.2 overs)	262	(47.4 overs)	216

1/60 (2) 2/60 (3) 3/61 (4) 4/104 (1) 5/104 (6)　　　　1/8 (2) 2/11 (1) 3/30 (4) 4/54 (4) 5/54 (6)
6/176 (7) 7/185 (8) 8/194 (9) 9/223 (10) 10/262 (11)　　6/76 (5) 7/115 (8) 8/121 (7) 9/134 (9) 10/216 (10)

Boult 19–3–67–1; Southee 16.2–9–19–4; Craig 24–3–91–4; Neesham 6–1–14–0; Sodhi 16–1–69–1. *Second Innings*—Boult 10–3–29–0; Southee 9–2–32–2; Craig 15–2–97–4; Neesham 2–0–9–0; Sodhi 11–1–42–3; Williamson 0.4–0–1–1.

Umpires: R. K. Illingworth *(England)* (8) and R. J. Tucker *(Australia)* (30).
Third umpire: I. J. Gould *(England)*. Referee: B. C. Broad *(England)* (61).

Close of play: First day, New Zealand 240–2 (Williamson 105, Taylor 34); Second day, West Indies 19–0 (Gayle 8, Powell 11); Third day, New Zealand 14–2 (Latham 8, Sodhi 4).

WEST INDIES v NEW ZEALAND 2014 (2nd Test)

At Queen's Park Oval, Port-of-Spain, Trinidad, on 16, 17, 18, 19, 20 June, 2014.
Toss: New Zealand.   Result: WEST INDIES WON BY TEN WICKETS.
Debuts: West Indies – J. Blackwood.
Man of the Match: K. C. Brathwaite.

In an extraordinary turnaround, West Indies levelled the series after losing five of their previous six Tests heavily, three of them to New Zealand. They were denied an innings victory only by a ninth-wicket stand of 99 between Watling, who survived 6½ hours, and No. 10 Craig, whose 67 occupied 184 minutes. After New Zealand were rolled in their first innings for a below-par 221 – opener Latham made his second 80 in successive Tests – West Indies were put in front by a determined maiden century from Kraigg Brathwaite. Only four younger men had made hundreds for West Indies: Adrian Barath (19), George Headley and Dwayne Smith (20), and Carl Hooper (also 21). Brathwaite put on 182 with Bravo, whose own century (his sixth in Tests but first in the Caribbean) was a rather more rumbustious affair, containing four sixes. The Jamaican debutant Jermaine Blackwood – down at No. 8 after two nightwatchmen were used – showed the strokeplay which had made him the leading scorer of the domestic season in an attractive 63, which lifted his side towards a lead of 239. That looked like enough when New Zealand sank to 212 for eight, despite long innings from Latham and Williamson, who both batted for over three hours. But the admirable resistance of Watling and Craig prolonged the match into the final day – when a requirement of 95 allowed Gayle to switch into Twenty20 mode, and hammer six sixes and seven fours from 46 balls as the target was overhauled in double-quick time.

New Zealand

T. W. M. Latham c Benn b Roach	82	– c Brathwaite b Benn	36
H. D. Rutherford c Gayle b Taylor	3	– (7) lbw b Taylor	13
K. S. Williamson c sub (J. O. Holder) b Gabriel	42	– c Ramdin b Roach	52
L. R. P. L. Taylor not out	45	– c Ramdin b Gabriel	36
*B. B. McCullum lbw b Benn	4	– (2) lbw b Taylor	3
J. D. S. Neesham c Gayle b Taylor	15	– (5) c and b Benn	7
†B-J. Watling c Ramdin b Taylor	0	– (6) not out	66
I. S. Sodhi c Gayle b Taylor	0	– c Ramdin b Roach	14
T. G. Southee lbw b Benn	10	– c Edwards b Roach	15
M. D. Craig c Bravo b Gabriel	4	– c Ramdin b Roach	67
T. A. Boult lbw b Benn	1	– c Ramdin b Gabriel	8
B 4, l-b 6, w 2, n-b 3	15	B 9, l-b 2, w 1, n-b 2	14
(74.4 overs)	221	(152.2 overs)	331

1/16 (2) 2/120 (3) 3/146 (1) 4/161 (5) 5/192 (6)
6/198 (7) 7/199 (8) 8/210 (9) 9/215 (10) 10/221 (11)

1/9 (2) 2/84 (1) 3/108 (3) 4/121 (5) 5/153 (4)
6/176 (7) 7/193 (8) 8/212 (9) 9/311 (10) 10/331 (11)

Taylor 17–5–34–4; Roach 17–1–61–1; Gabriel 12–2–43–2; Benn 28.4–6–73–3. *Second Innings*—Taylor 30–8–73–2; Roach 28–6–74–4; Gabriel 23.2–3–66–2; Benn 58–20–78–2; Gayle 13–3–29–0.

West Indies

C. H. Gayle b Boult	1	– not out	80
K. C. Brathwaite c and b Boult	129	– not out	14
S. J. Benn b Southee	4		
K. A. Edwards c Watling b Sodhi	55		
D. M. Bravo c Craig b Williamson	109		
S. Chanderpaul lbw b Sodhi	47		
K. A. J. Roach c Neesham b Boult	6		
J. Blackwood c Taylor b Sodhi	63		
*†D. Ramdin c Taylor b Neesham	32		
J. E. Taylor c Craig b Sodhi	4		
S. T. Gabriel not out	0		
L-b 6, w 3, n-b 1	10	L-b 1	1
(137.1 overs)	460	(no wkt, 13.2 overs)	95

1/4 (1) 2/16 (3) 3/109 (4) 4/291 (5) 5/310 (2) 6/333 (7)
7/380 (6) 8/456 (8) 9/460 (9) 10/460 (10)

Boult 30–6–75–3; Southee 30–9–69–1; Craig 29–4–111–0; Neesham 15–1–68–1; Sodhi 19.1–2–96–4; Williamson 14–2–35–1. *Second Innings*—Southee 4–1–21–0; Boult 3–0–27–0; Sodhi 2–0–21–0; Craig 3–0–17–0; Williamson 1.2–0–8–0.

Umpires: I. J. Gould *(England)* (38) and R. J. Tucker *(Australia)* (31).
Third umpire: R. K. Illingworth *(England)*. Referee: B. C. Broad *(England)* (62).

Close of play: First day, West Indies 6–1 (Brathwaite 5, Benn 0); Second day, West Indies 310–5 (Chanderpaul 4, Roach 0); Third day, New Zealand 73–1 (Latham 30, Williamson 38); Fourth day, New Zealand 257–8 (Watling 38, Craig 29).

WEST INDIES v NEW ZEALAND 2014 (3rd Test)

At Kensington Oval, Bridgetown, Barbados, on 26, 27, 28, 29, 30 June, 2014.
Toss: New Zealand.   Result: NEW ZEALAND WON BY 53 RUNS.
Debuts: West Indies – J. O. Holder.
Man of the Match: K. S. Williamson. Man of the Series: K. S. Williamson.

The decider provided a contest of riveting twists and turns. New Zealand prevailed principally because they performed with more intensity and confidence than West Indies, to complete their first overseas series victory (outside Bangladesh and Zimbabwe) since 2002 and their only previous triumph in the Caribbean. McCullum won the toss for the third time running, but New Zealand's early batting was unimpressive, as it had been in the first innings of the previous Test, before Neesham and Craig rescued them from an unsteady 194 for seven. West Indies, at 169 for two, were replying with their usual aggressive intent before the first significant rainfall in three months ended the second day shortly after lunch – but the loss of the remaining eight wickets for 148 next day left them with a negligible lead. Still, with New Zealand 135 for four early on the fourth morning, the match was back in the balance – but it swung steadily back their way, through Williamson's second high-quality hundred of the series (although he was dropped twice by Ramdin) and his partnerships with Neesham and Watling, which yielded 170. McCullum spotted West Indies' vulnerability: his overnight declaration, which offered 308 to win at 3.14 an over on a decent pitch, was more conviction than gamble. The top order misfired, and after Chanderpaul was stumped for the first time in 266 Test innings only two brief rain-breaks and the lofty debutant Jason Holder's eighth-wicket partnership of 77 with Shillingford delayed the end until midway through the final session.

New Zealand

T. W. M. Latham lbw b Roach	14	– c Shillingford b Roach		0
H. D. Rutherford c Chanderpaul b Roach	4	– c Ramdin b Roach		19
K. S. Williamson c Bravo b Benn	43	– not out		161
L. R. P. L. Taylor c Benn b Roach	45	– c Bravo b Holder		6
*B. B. McCullum c Bravo b Benn	31	– lbw b Roach		25
J. D. S. Neesham run out	78	– c Brathwaite b Holder		51
†B-J. Watling c Gayle b Benn	1	– c Holder b Roach		29
T. G. Southee b Benn	6	– c and b Taylor		7
M. D. Craig not out	46	– not out		4
N. Wagner c Ramdin b Roach	2			
T. A. Boult st Ramdin b Benn	12			
B 5, l-b 2, w 1, n-b 3	11	B 20, l-b 1, w 7, n-b 1		29
(78.2 overs)	293	(7 wkts dec, 89.1 overs)		331

1/17 (2) 2/28 (1) 3/102 (3) 4/114 (4) 5/168 (5)
6/172 (7) 7/194 (8) 8/258 (6) 9/277 (10) 10/293 (11)

1/1 (1) 2/56 (2) 3/68 (4) 4/135 (5) 5/226 (6)
6/305 (7) 7/327 (8)

Taylor 11–2–55–0; Roach 18–2–61–4; Holder 10–4–24–0; Benn 26.2–1–93–5; Shillingford 13–0–53–0. *Second Innings*—Taylor 16–4–54–1; Roach 19.1–4–55–4; Benn 26–1–94–0; Holder 10–2–26–2; Shillingford 18–2–81–0.

West Indies

C. H. Gayle c Rutherford b Craig	42	– b Southee		11
K. C. Brathwaite c Southee b Wagner	68	– b Boult		6
K. A. Edwards c Rutherford b Southee	58	– c Taylor b Boult		10
D. M. Bravo c Williamson b Wagner	24	– (5) c Williamson b Southee		40
S. Chanderpaul c Watling b Wagner	15	– (4) st Watling b Craig		25
*†D. Ramdin lbw b Boult	45	– c Taylor b Southee		29
J. O. Holder c Watling b Neesham	38	– b Craig		52
K. A. J. Roach c Watling b Boult	0	– c Latham b Craig		7
S. Shillingford not out	10	– not out		30
S. J. Benn b Wagner	1	– c Southee b Wagner		10
J. E. Taylor b Neesham	1	– lbw b Boult		12
B 2, l-b 4, w 7, n-b 2	15	B 4, l-b 15, w 1, n-b 2		22
(97.1 overs)	317	(82.2 overs)		254

1/79 (1) 2/153 (2) 3/197 (4) 4/205 (3) 5/240 (5)
6/277 (6) 7/277 (8) 8/313 (7) 9/316 (10) 10/317 (11)

1/7 (2) 2/23 (3) 3/31 (1) 4/81 (4) 5/122 (6)
6/129 (5) 7/144 (8) 8/221 (7) 9/232 (10) 10/254 (11)

Boult 23–5–71–2; Southee 21–8–63–1; Craig 18–2–90–1; Wagner 27–7–64–4; Williamson 2–0–11–0; Neesham 6.1–1–12–2. *Second Innings*—Boult 16.2–1–48–3; Southee 16–4–28–3; Craig 28–7–84–3; Wagner 16–3–50–1; Neesham 3–1–9–0; Williamson 3–0–16–0.

Umpires: I. J. Gould *(England)* (39) and R. K. Illingworth *(England)* (9).
Third umpire: R. J. Tucker *(Australia)*. Referee: J. Srinath *(India)* (33).

Close of play: First day, West Indies 32–0 (Gayle 18, Brathwaite 11); Second day, West Indies 169–2 (Edwards 42, Bravo 8); Third day, New Zealand 123–3 (Williamson 58, McCullum 23); Fourth day, New Zealand 331–7 (Williamson 161, Craig 4).

ENGLAND v SRI LANKA 2014 (1st Test)

At Lord's, London, on 12, 13, 14, 15, 16 June, 2014.
Toss: Sri Lanka.   Result: MATCH DRAWN.
Debuts: England – M. M. Ali, C. J. Jordan, S. D. Robson.
Man of the Match: J. E. Root.

When Nuwan Pradeep Fernando was adjudged lbw to the penultimate ball of the match, England thought they had won – but replays showed an edge, and Fernando was reprieved; he survived Broad's final ball too, edging just short of second slip. And so it was a draw – no surprise to anyone who had dozed off at tea, when Sri Lanka were 164 for three. But Anderson was getting the old ball to reverse, and the new one was imminent: eventually England needed four wickets in 11 overs. The ninth fell to the first ball of the last one, but Fernando hung on. England fielded three debutants for the second match running, for the first time since 1938, and overall made six changes from Sydney in January. Plunkett returned after seven years and 85 Tests. Root repaired an uncertain start with his maiden double-century; Prior, a fellow returnee, smacked 86 after narrowly surviving a second-ball lbw shout. England scored quickly (4.4 an over) but, after Karunaratne fell to Jordan's third ball in Tests, Sangakkara made a serene first Test century at Lord's (his 36th overall), as did Mathews. Looking to build on a lead of 124, England slipped to 121 for six, but were rescued by Ballance, in only his second Test: he slog-swept Herath for six to reach his maiden century in the last over of the fourth day. Cook's overnight declaration left Sri Lanka 390 to win – they never approached that, but looked set to survive comfortably until their last-session wobble.

England

*A. N. Cook b Kulasekara	17	– (2) c H. A. P. W. Jayawardene b Eranga	28
S. D. Robson c H. A. P. W. Jayawardene b Fernando ...	1	– (1) b Eranga	19
G. S. Ballance c H. A. P. W. Jayawardene b Fernando....	23	– not out	104
I. R. Bell lbw b Eranga	56	– b Eranga	9
J. E. Root not out	200	– lbw b Herath	15
M. M. Ali c D. P. M. D. Jayawardene b Herath	48	– b Herath	4
†M. J. Prior c Silva b Eranga	86	– c Thirimanne b Kulasekara	16
C. J. Jordan c H. A. P. W. Jayawardene b Eranga	19	– c Sangakkara b Herath	35
S. C. J. Broad c Karunaratne b Fernando	47	– c and b Herath	24
L. E. Plunkett c Silva b Fernando	39	– not out	2
J. M. Anderson not out	9		
B 12, l-b 12, n-b 6	30	B 3, l-b 4, w 2, n-b 2	11
(9 wkts dec, 130.3 overs)	575	(8 wkts dec, 69 overs)	267

1/14 (2) 2/22 (1) 3/74 (3) 4/120 (4) 5/209 (6)   1/46 (2) 2/51 (1) 3/69 (4) 4/98 (5) 5/102 (6)
6/380 (7) 7/402 (8) 8/466 (9) 9/547 (10)   6/121 (7) 7/199 (8) 8/256 (9)

Kulasekara 22–3–83–1; Fernando 29–2–123–4; Eranga 30–3–163–3; Mathews 11–2–39–0; Herath 37.3–2–136–1; Thirimanne 1–0–7–0. *Second Innings*—Kulasekara 15–2–65–1; Fernando 13–3–37–0; Eranga 18–7–63–3; Herath 23–2–95–4.

Sri Lanka

F. D. M. Karunaratne c Prior b Jordan	38	– c Robson b Broad	16
J. K. Silva c Prior b Anderson	63	– c Prior b Jordan	57
K. C. Sangakkara c Prior b Ali	147	– b Anderson	61
D. P. M. D. Jayawardene lbw b Broad	55	– c Prior b Anderson	18
H. D. R. L. Thirimanne c Robson b Anderson	2	– c Jordan b Anderson	2
*A. D. Mathews lbw b Plunkett	102	– c Cook b Anderson	18
†H. A. P. W. Jayawardene c Bell b Plunkett	6	– lbw b Jordan	8
K. M. D. N. Kulasekara c Prior b Jordan	9	– lbw b Broad	1
H. M. R. K. B. Herath b Anderson	2	– c Prior b Broad	1
R. M. S. Eranga not out	5	– not out	0
A. N. P. R. Fernando hit wkt b Jordan	4	– not out	0
B 7, l-b 5, w 6, n-b 2	20	B 11, l-b 7, n-b 1	19
(138.4 overs)	453	(9 wkts, 90 overs)	201

1/54 (1) 2/151 (2) 3/277 (4) 4/289 (5) 5/385 (3)   1/25 (1) 2/123 (2) 3/159 (4) 4/169 (3) 5/170 (5)
6/400 (7) 7/413 (8) 8/430 (9) 9/442 (6) 10/453 (11)   6/194 (7) 7/199 (8) 8/201 (6) 9/201 (9)

Anderson 31–7–93–3; Broad 29–8–67–1; Jordan 27.4–4–102–3; Plunkett 32–2–116–2; Ali 16–2–56–1; Root 3–1–7–0. *Second Innings*—Anderson 19–10–25–4; Broad 21–9–43–3; Jordan 18–10–34–2; Plunkett 16–5–39–0; Ali 12–2–35–0; Root 4–3–7–0.

Umpires: B. F. Bowden *(New Zealand)* (77) and P. R. Reiffel *(Australia)* (10).
Third umpire: S. J. Davis *(Australia)*. Referee: A. J. Pycroft *(Zimbabwe)* (27).

Close of play: First day, England 344–5 (Root 102, Prior 76); Second day, Sri Lanka 140–1 (Silva 62, Sangakkara 32); Third day, Sri Lanka 415–7 (Mathews 79, Herath 0); Fourth day, England 267–8 (Ballance 104, Plunkett 2).

ENGLAND v SRI LANKA 2014 (2nd Test)

At Headingley, Leeds, on 20, 21, 22, 23, 24 June, 2014.
Toss: England.   Result: SRI LANKA WON BY 100 RUNS.
Debuts: none.
Man of the Match: A. D. Mathews. Men of the Series: J. M. Anderson and A. D. Mathews.

For the second time in nine days, the teams took a Test to the wire. At the end of a draining final session, England were two balls away from a draw that had looked impossible – no side had ever saved a Test after being five down going into the final day. But Eranga speared one in at last man Anderson's throat: in an instinctive act of self-preservation, he threw up his hands. The ball looped off his bat to short backward square, and Sri Lanka had won their first Test series in England. Anderson was in tears after surviving for 81 minutes before succumbing to his 55th ball. At the other end, Moeen Ali had survived for 385 minutes, and a valiant maiden century, in only his second Test. Earlier Robson, England's Sydney-born opener, had made a hundred in his second Test too. That underpinned England's solid response to Sri Lanka's below-par 257, in which Plunkett took his maiden Test five-for, and Broad claimed his second hat-trick, although he didn't realise it at first, as it was split across two overs. In the second innings the departures of Sangakkara and Thirimanne (for a pair) put England on top, but Jayawardene dug deep, then Mathews took advantage of Cook's eagerness to get at No. 9 Herath to motor to 160, dominating a stand of 149. From a position of relative dominance England now needed 350 – and, when they slid to 57 for five, faced disgrace as well as defeat. But, led by Ali, they nearly pulled off one of Test cricket's greatest escapes.

Sri Lanka

F. D. M. Karunaratne b Plunkett	28	– c Prior b Plunkett			45
J. K. Silva c Prior b Anderson	13	– c Prior b Plunkett			13
K. C. Sangakkara c Bell b Broad	79	– lbw b Ali			55
D. P. M. D. Jayawardene c Jordan b Plunkett	22	– c Prior b Anderson			79
H. D. R. L. Thirimanne c Robson b Plunkett	0	– b Ali			0
*A. D. Mathews c Ballance b Anderson	26	– c Ali b Anderson			160
†L. D. Chandimal c Cook b Broad	45	– c Ballance b Plunkett			7
K. T. G. D. Prasad c Prior b Plunkett	0	– c Root b Plunkett			0
H. M. R. K. B. Herath not out	14	– run out			48
R. M. S. Eranga c Prior b Broad	0	– not out			20
A. N. P. R. Fernando c Prior b Plunkett	13	– b Anderson			0
B 8, l-b 7, w 2	17	B 5, l-b 10, w 10, n-b 5			30
(69.5 overs)	257	(132.5 overs)			457

1/37 (2) 2/56 (1) 3/108 (4) 4/108 (5) 5/161 (6)
6/228 (3) 7/229 (8) 8/229 (7) 9/229 (10) 10/257 (11)

1/40 (2) 2/93 (1) 3/172 (3) 4/176 (5) 5/268 (4)
6/277 (7) 7/277 (8) 8/426 (9) 9/437 (6) 10/457 (11)

Anderson 19–5–49–2; Broad 15–3–46–3; Jordan 16–4–58–0; Plunkett 15.5–2–64–5; Ali 3–0–16–0; Root 1–0–9–0.
Second Innings—Anderson 25.5–5–91–3; Broad 29–6–86–0; Jordan 28–8–79–0; Plunkett 29–2–112–4; Ali 21–0–74–2.

England

*A. N. Cook c Sangakkara b Prasad	17	– (2) b Prasad			16
S. D. Robson b Fernando	127	– (1) c Jayawardene b Prasad			24
G. S. Ballance c Chandimal b Mathews	74	– lbw b Prasad			0
I. R. Bell c Chandimal b Eranga	64	– b Prasad			8
J. E. Root c Chandimal b Mathews	13	– c Thirimanne b Fernando			31
M. M. Ali c Chandimal b Eranga	2	– (7) not out			108
†M. J. Prior not out	27	– (8) c Silva b Prasad			10
C. J. Jordan c Jayawardene b Eranga	17	– (9) lbw b Herath			21
S. C. J. Broad c Thirimanne b Mathews	4	– (10) lbw b Herath			0
L. E. Plunkett b Mathews	2	– (6) c Fernando b Herath			0
J. M. Anderson c and b Eranga	0	– c Herath b Eranga			0
L-b 2, w 3, n-b 13	18	B 11, l-b 7, w 4, n-b 9			31
(115.5 overs)	365	(116.5 overs)			249

1/49 (1) 2/191 (3) 3/278 (2) 4/311 (4) 5/311 (5)
6/313 (6) 7/338 (8) 8/344 (9) 9/350 (10) 10/365 (11)

1/39 (2) 2/39 (3) 3/50 (1) 4/52 (4) 5/57 (6)
6/124 (5) 7/160 (8) 8/212 (9) 9/228 (10) 10/249 (11)

Fernando 22–3–90–1; Eranga 32.5–10–93–4; Herath 25–3–61–0; Prasad 20–3–75–1; Mathews 16–4–44–4.
Second Innings—Fernando 13–2–55–1; Eranga 23.5–10–38–1; Herath 42–16–59–3; Mathews 10–3–16–0; Prasad 22–5–50–5; Jayawardene 6–2–13–0.

Umpires: B. F. Bowden *(New Zealand)* (78) and S. J. Davis *(Australia)* (53).
Third umpire: P. R. Reiffel *(Australia)*. Referee: A. J. Pycroft *(Zimbabwe)* (28).

Close of play: First day, England 36–0 (Cook 14, Robson 21); Second day, England 320–6 (Prior 3, Jordan 4); Third day, Sri Lanka 214–4 (Jayawardene 55, Mathews 24); Fourth day, England 57–5 (Root 6).

ENGLAND v INDIA 2014 (1st Test)

At Trent Bridge, Nottingham, on 9, 10, 11, 12, 13 July, 2014.
Toss: India.   Result: MATCH DRAWN.
Debuts: India – S. T. R. Binny.
Man of the Match: J. M. Anderson.

A benign pitch ultimately led to the first draw in 11 Tests at Trent Bridge since 2002 – although a flurry of three for 17 on the final morning briefly gave England hope before Stuart Binny's debut 78 effectively saved the match. He put on 91 with Bhuvneshwar Kumar, who became only the second No. 9 to make two half-centuries in a Test, after Australia's Peter Siddle against India at Delhi in 2012–13. India's first innings was dominated by Vijay, who batted for 468 minutes, before Kumar and Mohammed Shami – who both made maiden fifties – shared India's second-highest last-wicket stand. England then struggled against India's pacemen – Kumar added a five-for – and looked set for a big deficit before their own last-wicket pair shattered the Test record of 163, set here the previous year by Phil Hughes and Ashton Agar of Australia. Root had only 50 when the ninth wicket fell, but added 198 with Anderson, who had never previously made a half-century in any form of cricket. Perhaps dazzled by the prospect of a hundred, he was out shortly after lunch on the fourth day, having hit 17 fours in 230 minutes. Anderson also equalled Fred Trueman's record of 229 Test wickets in England, and collected his sixth match award, the fourth at Nottingham. Less happily, he was embroiled in a spat with Jadeja, which rumbled on for the rest of the series, as they left the field at lunch on the second day; both players were charged but escaped bans.

India

M. Vijay lbw b Anderson	146	– c Prior b Ali	52
S. Dhawan c Prior b Anderson	12	– c and b Ali	29
C. A. Pujara c Bell b Anderson	38	– c Stokes b Plunkett	55
V. Kohli c Bell b Broad	1	– lbw b Broad	8
A. M. Rahane c Cook b Plunkett	32	– c Prior b Broad	24
*†M. S. Dhoni run out	82	– b Plunkett	11
R. A. Jadeja c Prior b Stokes	25	– c Prior b Anderson	31
S. T. R. Binny c Root b Stokes	1	– lbw b Ali	78
Bhuvneshwar Kumar c Root b Ali	58	– not out	63
I. Sharma b Broad	1	– c Prior b Cook	13
Mohammed Shami not out	51	– not out	4
B 1, l-b 8, w 1	10	B 9, l-b 7, n-b 7	23
(161 overs)	457	(9 wkts dec, 123 overs)	391

1/33 (2) 2/106 (3) 3/107 (4) 4/178 (5) 5/304 (1)
6/344 (7) 7/345 (6) 8/345 (8) 9/346 (10) 10/457 (9)

1/49 (2) 2/140 (1) 3/140 (3) 4/168 (4) 5/173 (5)
6/184 (6) 7/249 (7) 8/340 (8) 9/387 (10)

Anderson 38–10–123–3; Broad 33–13–53–2; Stokes 34–6–81–2; Plunkett 37–8–88–1; Ali 18–0–97–1; Root 1–0–6–0. *Second Innings*—Anderson 21–8–47–1; Broad 21–7–50–2; Plunkett 20–1–85–2; Ali 28–4–105–3; Stokes 18–3–60–0; Root 12–4–22–0; Cook 2–0–6–1; Ballance 1–1–0–0.

England

*A. N. Cook b Mohammed Shami	5
S. D. Robson lbw b Sharma	59
G. S. Ballance lbw b Sharma	71
I. R. Bell c Dhoni b Sharma	25
J. E. Root not out	154
M. M. Ali c Dhawan b Mohammed Shami	14
†M. J. Prior c Dhoni b Bhuvneshwar Kumar	5
B. A. Stokes c Dhoni b Bhuvneshwar Kumar	0
S. C. J. Broad lbw b Bhuvneshwar Kumar	47
L. E. Plunkett b Bhuvneshwar Kumar	7
J. M. Anderson c Dhawan b Bhuvneshwar Kumar	81
B 6, l-b 5, w 4, n-b 13	28
(144.5 overs)	496

1/9 (1) 2/134 (2) 3/154 (3) 4/172 (4) 5/197 (6)
6/202 (7) 7/202 (8) 8/280 (9) 9/298 (10) 10/496 (11)

Bhuvneshwar Kumar 30.5–8–82–5; Mohammed Shami 29–3–128–2; Sharma 38–3–150–3; Jadeja 35–5–80–0; Binny 10–0–37–0; Vijay 2–0–8–0.

Umpires: H. D. P. K. Dharmasena *(Sri Lanka)* (24) and B. N. J. Oxenford *(Australia)* (18).
Third umpire: I. J. Gould *(England)*. Referee: D. C. Boon *(Australia)* (22).

Close of play: First day, India 259–4 (Vijay 122, Dhoni 50); Second day, England 43–1 (Robson 20, Ballance 15); Third day, England 352–9 (Root 78, Anderson 23); Fourth day, India 167–3 (Kohli 8, Rahane 18).

ENGLAND v INDIA 2014 (2nd Test)

At Lord's, London, on 17, 18, 19, 20, 21 July, 2014.
Toss: England.　　Result: INDIA WON BY 95 RUNS.
Debuts: none.
Man of the Match: I. Sharma.

On the greenest surface at Lord's in living memory, India lost the toss and had to face England's swing-masters, Anderson and Broad. But the Indians batted and bowled better, and ended up with only their second win at Lord's in 17 attempts, their first overseas in 16 since beating West Indies at Kingston in June 2011. England batted brainlessly on the final afternoon, after bowling poorly on the first day. Even so, India were 145 for seven before Rahane's composed century rescued them. Anderson annexed several records: Dhawan was his 230th Test wicket in England (passing Fred Trueman), Kohli his 63rd against India (beating Derek Underwood and Bob Willis) and his 70th at Lord's (eclipsing Ian Botham). But then India's seamers showed how to bowl on this pitch: Kumar pitched it up, wobbled it around, and took six wickets. Ballance made a measured century, but England were still behind before the last pair nudged them ahead. Vijay anchored India's second innings, although his departure for 95 put the game back in the balance – only for Jadeja and Kumar to reclaim the initiative. England, needing 319, were soon an indifferent 72 for four. But Root and Ali batted responsibly until shortly before lunch on the final day, when Dhoni – in some desperation – told Sharma to bang it in from round the wicket. Ali gloved the last ball to short leg, then after the interval three batsmen obligingly hooked straight to boundary fielders. Sharma finished with India's best figures at Lord's, improving Kumar's first-innings effort.

India

M. Vijay c Ballance b Plunkett	24	– c Prior b Anderson	95
S. Dhawan c Ballance b Anderson	7	– c Root b Stokes	31
C. A. Pujara b Stokes	28	– c Prior b Plunkett	43
V. Kohli c Prior b Anderson	25	– b Plunkett	0
A. M. Rahane c and b Anderson	103	– c Prior b Broad	5
*†M. S. Dhoni c Prior b Broad	1	– c Bell b Plunkett	19
R. A. Jadeja lbw b Ali	3	– (8) c Cook b Stokes	68
S. T. R. Binny lbw b Anderson	9	– (7) c Cook b Ali	0
Bhuvneshwar Kumar b Broad	36	– c Bell b Stokes	52
Mohammed Shami c Cook b Stokes	19	– c Prior b Ali	0
I. Sharma not out	12	– not out	0
B 17, l-b 10, n-b 1	28	B 19, l-b 9, w 1	29
(91.4 overs)	295	(103.1 overs)	342

1/11 (2) 2/48 (1) 3/86 (4) 4/113 (3) 5/123 (6)
6/128 (7) 7/145 (8) 8/235 (9) 9/275 (5) 10/295 (10)

1/40 (2) 2/118 (3) 3/118 (4) 4/123 (5) 5/202 (6)
6/203 (7) 7/235 (1) 8/334 (8) 9/338 (10) 10/342 (9)

Anderson 23–7–60–4; Broad 22–5–79–2; Plunkett 15–5–51–1; Stokes 17.4–5–40–2; Ali 14–2–38–1. *Second Innings*—Anderson 29–11–77–1; Broad 23–6–93–1; Stokes 18.1–2–51–3; Plunkett 22–6–65–3; Ali 11–3–28–2.

England

*A. N. Cook c Dhoni b Bhuvneshwar Kumar	10	– (2) c Dhoni b Sharma	22
S. D. Robson c Dhoni b Bhuvneshwar Kumar	17	– (1) lbw b Jadeja	7
G. S. Ballance c Dhoni b Bhuvneshwar Kumar	110	– c Dhoni b Mohammed Shami	27
I. R. Bell c Jadeja b Bhuvneshwar Kumar	16	– b Sharma	1
J. E. Root lbw b Jadeja	13	– c Binny b Sharma	66
M. M. Ali lbw b Vijay	32	– c Pujara b Sharma	39
L. E. Plunkett not out	55	– (10) not out	7
†M. J. Prior c Dhawan b Mohammed Shami	23	– (7) c Vijay b Sharma	12
B. A. Stokes b Bhuvneshwar Kumar	0	– (8) c Pujara b Sharma	0
S. C. J. Broad c Dhawan b Bhuvneshwar Kumar	4	– (9) c Dhoni b Sharma	8
J. M. Anderson c Rahane b Jadeja	19	– run out	2
B 5, l-b 10, w 2, n-b 3	20	B 13, l-b 16, w 1, n-b 2	32
(105.5 overs)	319	(88.2 overs)	223

1/22 (1) 2/31 (2) 3/70 (4) 4/113 (5) 5/211 (6)
6/214 (3) 7/265 (8) 8/276 (9) 9/280 (10) 10/319 (11)

1/12 (1) 2/70 (3) 3/71 (4) 4/72 (2) 5/173 (6)
6/198 (7) 7/201 (8) 8/201 (5) 9/216 (9) 10/223 (11)

Bhuvneshwar Kumar 31–10–82–6; Mohammed Shami 19–5–58–1; Sharma 24–5–61–0; Binny 10–0–45–0; Jadeja 18.5–1–46–2; Vijay 3–0–12–1. *Second Innings*—Bhuvneshwar Kumar 16–7–21–0; Mohammed Shami 11–3–33–1; Sharma 23–6–74–7; Jadeja 32.2–7–53–1; Vijay 4–1–11–0; Dhawan 2–0–2–0.

Umpires: H. D. P. K. Dharmasena *(Sri Lanka)* (25) and B. N. J. Oxenford *(Australia)* (19).
Third umpire: R. K. Illingworth *(England)*. Referee: D. C. Boon *(Australia)* (23).

Close of play: First day, India 290–9 (Mohammed Shami 14, Sharma 12); Second day, England 219–6 (Plunkett 4, Prior 2); Third day, India 169–4 (Vijay 59, Dhoni 12); Fourth day, England 105–4 (Root 14, Ali 15).

ENGLAND v INDIA 2014 (3rd Test)

At the Rose Bowl, Southampton, on 27, 28, 29, 30, 31 July, 2014.
Toss: England.   Result: ENGLAND WON BY 266 RUNS.
Debuts: England – J. C. Buttler. India – Pankaj Singh.
Man of the Match: J. M. Anderson.

Cook received severe criticism, and numerous calls to resign, after England's performance at Lord's and the earlier loss to Sri Lanka. He resolved to carry on – but might not have survived had Jadeja at third slip held a regulation chance off the debutant Pankaj Singh when he had 14. Cook pressed on to 95, while the luckless Pankaj toiled through 47 wicketless overs in the Rose Bowl's second Test. Cook put on 158 with Ballance, who then added 142 with Root. Finally Jos Buttler – called up in place of Matt Prior, who stood down to rest various injuries after an undistinguished Lord's Test – hit a rapid 85 after seemingly being caught at slip by Rahane before he had scored; replays were inconclusive, and Buttler survived to clump nine fours and three sixes as England sprinted past 550. Anderson and Broad then rediscovered the lines mislaid at Lord's, working their way through the batting: for once there was little tail-end resistance, and England claimed a lead of 239, which was swelled at four an over through sprightly innings from Cook and Root. India never got close to their target of 445, once their most solid batsmen Vijay and Pujara departed in successive overs. Rahane batted attractively again, but the rest fell to an unlikely destroyer: Ali finished with the best figures by an off-spinner against India in England after Ray Illingworth's six for 29 at Lord's in 1967. England's first win for 11 Tests was, according to Cook, "the perfect game".

England

*A. N. Cook c Dhoni b Jadeja	95	– (2) not out	70
S. D. Robson c Jadeja b Mohammed Shami	26	– (1) c Dhawan b Bhuvneshwar Kumar	13
G. S. Ballance c Dhoni b Sharma	156	– c Pujara b Jadeja	38
I. R. Bell c Pankaj Singh b Bhuvneshwar Kumar	167	– b Jadeja	23
J. E. Root c Dhoni b Bhuvneshwar Kumar	3	– b Jadeja	56
M. M. Ali c Rahane b Bhuvneshwar Kumar	12		
†J. C. Buttler b Jadeja	85		
C. R. Woakes not out	7		
B 5, l-b 11, w 2	18	B 4, w 1	5
(7 wkts dec, 163.4 overs)	569	(4 wkts dec, 40.4 overs)	205

1/55 (2) 2/213 (1) 3/355 (3) 4/378 (5) 5/420 (6)
6/526 (4) 7/569 (7)   1/22 (1) 2/80 (3) 3/106 (4) 4/205 (5)

C. J. Jordan, S. C. J. Broad and J. M. Anderson did not bat.

Bhuvneshwar Kumar 37–10–101–3; Mohammed Shami 33–4–123–1; Pankaj Singh 37–8–146–0; Sharma 9–0–26–1; Jadeja 45.4–10–153–2; Dhawan 2–0–4–0. *Second Innings*—Bhuvneshwar Kumar 10–0–59–1; Pankaj Singh 10–4–33–0; Mohammed Shami 4–0–24–0; Sharma 5–0–32–0; Jadeja 10.4–1–52–3; Vijay 1–0–1–0.

India

M. Vijay b Broad	35	– run out	12
S. Dhawan c Cook b Anderson	6	– c Jordan b Root	37
C. A. Pujara c Buttler b Broad	24	– c Jordan b Ali	2
V. Kohli c Cook b Anderson	39	– c Buttler b Ali	28
A. M. Rahane c sub (S. P. Terry) b Ali	54	– not out	52
R. G. Sharma c Broad b Ali	28	– c Buttler b Anderson	6
*†M. S. Dhoni c Buttler b Anderson	50	– c Buttler b Anderson	6
R. A. Jadeja lbw b Anderson	31	– b Ali	15
Bhuvneshwar Kumar c Ballance b Broad	19	– c Anderson b Ali	0
Mohammed Shami c Buttler b Anderson	5	– b Ali	0
Pankaj Singh not out	1	– b Ali	9
B 16, l-b 14, w 8	38	B 4, l-b 6, w 1	11
(106.1 overs)	330	(66.4 overs)	178

1/17 (2) 2/56 (3) 3/88 (1) 4/136 (4) 5/210 (6)   1/26 (1) 2/29 (3) 3/80 (2) 4/89 (4) 5/112 (6)
6/217 (5) 7/275 (8) 8/313 (9) 9/329 (7) 10/330 (10)   6/120 (7) 7/152 (8) 8/152 (9) 9/154 (10) 10/178 (11)

Anderson 26.1–10–53–5; Broad 25–7–66–3; Jordan 17–4–59–0; Woakes 20–8–60–0; Ali 18–0–62–2. *Second Innings*—Anderson 14–5–24–2; Broad 13–6–22–0; Woakes 11–3–23–0; Ali 20.4–4–67–6; Jordan 5–0–22–0; Root 2–0–5–1; Ballance 1–0–5–0.

Umpires: M. Erasmus *(South Africa)* (24) and R. J. Tucker *(Australia)* (32).
Third umpire: R. J. Bailey *(England)*. Referee: D. C. Boon *(Australia)* (24).

Close of play: First day, England 247–2 (Ballance 104, Bell 16); Second day, India 25–1 (Vijay 11, Pujara 4); Third day, India 323–8 (Dhoni 50, Mohammed Shami 4); Fourth day, India 112–4 (Rahane 18, Sharma 6).

ENGLAND v INDIA 2014 (4th Test)

At Old Trafford, Manchester, on 7, 8, 9 August, 2014.
Toss: India.   Result: ENGLAND WON BY AN INNINGS AND 54 RUNS.
Debuts: none.
Man of the Match: S. C. J. Broad.

The remarkable turnaround continued: after looking likely to lose their captain following their Lord's meltdown, England now rattled to victory inside three days, even though around half the second day was lost to rain. The match total of 195.1 overs was the lowest in any England–India Test that produced a result. India were soon tottering at eight for four, and were indebted to Dhoni and Ashwin, who doubled the score from 63 for six. Still, England were closing in on the lead by the first-day close, and although they too wobbled next day – to an uncertain 170 for six – they were yanked in front by a seventh-wicket stand of 134 between Root and Buttler, who looked comfortable with the bat at Test level and also kept wicket well. Facing a deficit of 215, India struggled again: Anderson, despite feeling ill, continued his personal hold over Kohli, who endured a nightmare series, then Ali's friendly-looking off-spin accounted for three victims as India slid to 66 for six. Dhoni counterattacked for 27 off 22 balls, but once he also fell to Ali only Ashwin held England up for long. In all, nine wickets fell after tea, including a spell of five for 13 in 29 balls. It was a particularly tame surrender by India, as the weather forecast for the fourth day was dire, and England were lacking Broad, whose nose had been broken when a bouncer from the pacy Aaron crashed through his helmet-grille. Pankaj Singh finally collected a Test wicket, in his 70th over.

India

M. Vijay c Cook b Anderson	0	– lbw b Woakes	18
G. Gambhir c Root b Broad	4	– c Buttler b Anderson	18
C. A. Pujara c Jordan b Broad	0	– lbw b Ali	17
V. Kohli c Cook b Anderson	0	– c Bell b Anderson	7
A. M. Rahane c Bell b Jordan	24	– c and b Ali	1
*†M. S. Dhoni c Jordan b Broad	71	– c Ballance b Ali	27
R. A. Jadeja lbw b Anderson	0	– c Jordan b Ali	4
R. Ashwin c Robson b Broad	40	– not out	46
Bhuvneshwar Kumar b Broad	0	– run out	10
V. R. Aaron not out	1	– c Buttler b Jordan	9
Pankaj Singh b Broad	0	– b Jordan	0
B 10, l-b 1, w 1	12	B 1, l-b 1, w 1, n-b 1	4
(46.4 overs)	152	(43 overs)	161

1/8 (2) 2/8 (1) 3/8 (4) 4/8 (3) 5/62 (5) 6/63 (7)   1/26 (1) 2/53 (2) 3/53 (3) 4/61 (5) 5/61 (4)
7/129 (8) 8/137 (9) 9/152 (6) 10/152 (11)   6/66 (7) 7/105 (6) 8/133 (9) 9/161 (10) 10/161 (11)

Anderson 14–3–46–3; Broad 13.4–6–25–6; Woakes 10–1–43–0; Jordan 9–4–27–1. *Second Innings*—Anderson 9–4–18–2; Woakes 9–2–37–1; Jordan 12–1–65–2; Ali 13–3–39–4.

England

*A. N. Cook c Pankaj Singh b Aaron	17
S. D. Robson b Bhuvneshwar Kumar	6
G. S. Ballance lbw b Aaron	37
I. R. Bell c Dhoni b Bhuvneshwar Kumar	58
C. J. Jordan c Aaron b Bhuvneshwar Kumar	13
J. E. Root c Dhoni b Pankaj Singh	77
M. M. Ali b Aaron	13
†J. C. Buttler c Pujara b Pankaj Singh	70
C. R. Woakes not out	26
S. C. J. Broad retired hurt	12
J. M. Anderson lbw b Jadeja	9
B 5, l-b 12, w 6, n-b 6	29
(105.3 overs)	367

1/21 (2) 2/36 (1) 3/113 (3) 4/136 (5) 5/140 (4)
6/170 (7) 7/304 (6) 8/325 (8) 9/367 (11)

Broad retired hurt at 338–8.

Bhuvneshwar Kumar 24–7–75–3; Pankaj Singh 28–5–113–2; Aaron 26–4–97–3; Ashwin 14–1–29–0; Jadeja 13.3–1–36–1.

Umpires: M. Erasmus *(South Africa)* (25) and R. J. Tucker *(Australia)* (33).
Third umpire: R. A. Kettleborough *(England)*. Referee: R. S. Madugalle *(Sri Lanka)* (149).

Close of play: First day, England 113–3 (Bell 45, Jordan 0); Second day, England 237–6 (Root 48, Buttler 22).

ENGLAND v INDIA 2014 (5th Test)

At Kennington Oval, London, on 15, 16, 17 August, 2014.
Toss: England.   Result: ENGLAND WON BY AN INNINGS AND 244 RUNS.
Debuts: none.
Man of the Match: J. E. Root. Men of the Series: J. M. Anderson and B. Kumar.

Another tame Indian performance handed England the series, only the tenth time a team had come from behind to win 3–1 or better. As at Manchester, it was all over inside three days; again India were twice 66 for six. Put in, they were 43 for five by lunch, and things didn't improve much. Dhoni lashed 15 fours and a six in a defiant 82, but no one else made more than 18. Jordan, who had ended the previous Test with two wickets in two balls, started with two for none from his first 12 deliveries. England swept into the lead well before lunch on the second day. Cook again fell within sight of three figures, but Root had no such trouble, motoring to his third unbeaten hundred of the summer. In all he amassed 777 runs in the seven home Tests, including 518 in this series; his county colleague Ballance also passed 500 against India, and 700 overall. With Broad hitting out defiantly despite wearing a mask to protect his broken nose – he was briefly in line for the fastest Test fifty, before holing out for 37 off 21 balls – England stormed to a huge lead. India's subsequent demise was shockingly sudden even given their recent poor form: all out in 29.2 overs for 94, their 24th double-figure total in Tests, and their third-heaviest defeat. Kohli took his series aggregate to just 134 runs in ten innings. This was only India's second five-Test series in England, after 1959 when they lost 5–0.

India

M. Vijay c Root b Woakes	18	– lbw b Anderson		2
G. Gambhir c Buttler b Anderson	0	– run out		3
C. A. Pujara b Broad	4	– c Buttler b Anderson		11
V. Kohli lbw b Jordan	6	– c Cook b Jordan		20
A. M. Rahane c and b Jordan	0	– c Ballance b Broad		4
*†M. S. Dhoni c Woakes b Broad	82	– c Robson b Woakes		0
S. T. R. Binny c Cook b Anderson	5	– not out		25
R. Ashwin c Root b Woakes	13	– c Bell b Jordan		7
Bhuvneshwar Kumar c Buttler b Jordan	5	– c Bell b Jordan		4
V. R. Aaron c and b Woakes	1	– run out		1
I. Sharma not out	7	– c Ali b Jordan		2
B 6, l-b 1	7	B 8, l-b 6, w 1		15
(61.1 overs)	148	(29.2 overs)		94

1/3 (2) 2/10 (3) 3/26 (4) 4/28 (5) 5/36 (1) 6/44 (7)
7/68 (8) 8/79 (9) 9/90 (10) 10/148 (6)

1/6 (1) 2/9 (2) 3/30 (3) 4/45 (5) 5/46 (6)
6/62 (4) 7/70 (8) 8/74 (9) 9/84 (10) 10/94 (11)

Anderson 17–4–51–2; Broad 15.1–4–27–2; Jordan 14–7–32–3; Woakes 14–7–30–3; Ali 1–0–1–0. *Second Innings*—Anderson 8–3–16–2; Broad 10–2–22–1; Woakes 7–0–24–1; Jordan 4.2–0–18–4.

England

*A. N. Cook c Vijay b Aaron	79
S. D. Robson b Aaron	37
G. S. Ballance c Pujara b Ashwin	64
I. R. Bell c Dhoni b Sharma	7
J. E. Root not out	149
M. M. Ali b Ashwin	14
†J. C. Buttler c Ashwin b Sharma	45
C. R. Woakes c Dhoni b Bhuvneshwar Kumar	0
C. J. Jordan c Dhoni b Sharma	20
S. C. J. Broad c Kohli b Sharma	37
J. M. Anderson lbw b Ashwin	1
B 18, l-b 3, w 1, n-b 11	33
(116.3 overs)	486

1/66 (2) 2/191 (1) 3/201 (3) 4/204 (4) 5/229 (6)
6/309 (7) 7/318 (8) 8/400 (9) 9/463 (10) 10/486 (11)

Bhuvneshwar Kumar 24–3–86–1; Sharma 30–8–96–4; Aaron 29–1–153–2; Binny 12–0–58–0; Ashwin 21.3–2–72–3.

Umpires: H. D. P. K. Dharmasena *(Sri Lanka)* (26) and P. R. Reiffel *(Australia)* (11).
Third umpire: R. T. Robinson *(England)*. Referee: R. S. Madugalle *(Sri Lanka)* (150).

Close of play: First day, England 62–0 (Cook 24, Robson 33); Second day, England 385–7 (Root 92, Jordan 19).

SRI LANKA v SOUTH AFRICA 2014 (1st Test)

At Galle International Stadium on 16, 17, 18, 19, 20 July, 2014.
Toss: South Africa.   Result: SOUTH AFRICA WON BY 153 RUNS.
Debuts: none.
Man of the Match: D. W. Steyn.

Hashim Amla's first Test as captain ended in victory – only South Africa's third in Sri Lanka, and their first since 2000. Amla's return with the bat was modest, but his reshaped team did him proud: Elgar, handed the tough task of replacing Graeme Smith at the top of the order, made a four-hour century, adding 125 with du Plessis, up at No. 3 after the retirement of Jacques Kallis. Then Duminy chipped in with his fourth Test century, and South Africa reached 455 on an atypical Galle pitch. Tharanga, in his first Test for 6½ years, made a fluent 83, but otherwise only Mathews defied the pacemen. South Africa built on their lead of 163 at four an over on the fourth day, before Amla's declaration left a distant target of 370. Sangakkara propped the innings up with 76 – his eighth score of 50-plus in his last nine innings – and completed 1,000 Test runs in a calendar year for the fifth time (only Sachin Tendulkar, six, did it more often). However, Sri Lanka slid to defeat after he pulled a long-hop from Duminy straight to short midwicket. Steyn and Morkel improved the previous-best innings and match figures by fast bowlers at Galle, usually a haven for the spinners (Herath, who had previously claimed 57 wickets here at 23.80, took three for 232 in this game). Quinton de Kock made nine dismissals in his first Test as wicketkeeper; he had won one previous cap as a batsman earlier in the year.

South Africa

A. N. Petersen lbw b Perera	34	– (2) c Chandimal b Perera	32
D. Elgar c Chandimal b Lakmal	103	– (1) c Chandimal b Herath	12
F. du Plessis c Silva b Perera	80	– b Herath	37
*H. M. Amla c Perera b Herath	11	– c Tharanga b Perera	22
A. B. de Villiers b Lakmal	21	– b Perera	51
†Q. de Kock c Jayawardene b Perera	51	– c and b Perera	36
D. W. Steyn b Lakmal	3		
J-P. Duminy not out	100	– (7) not out	8
V. D. Philander lbw b Mathews	27		
M. Morkel b Perera	22		
L-b 2, n-b 1	3	B 4, l-b 4	8
(9 wkts dec, 166.2 overs)	455	(6 wkts dec, 50.2 overs)	206

1/70 (1) 2/195 (2) 3/220 (4) 4/246 (3) 5/266 (5)   1/33 (1) 2/54 (2) 3/88 (4) 4/131 (3) 5/193 (5)
6/290 (7) 7/314 (6) 8/389 (9) 9/455 (10)   6/206 (6)

Imran Tahir did not bat.

Lakmal 33–12–75–3; Eranga 9–4–32–0; Herath 60–12–148–1; Mathews 11–1–36–1; Perera 53.2–8–162–4. *Second Innings*—Lakmal 9–0–35–0; Herath 22–2–84–2; Perera 19.2–1–79–4.

Sri Lanka

J. K. Silva c Philander b Steyn	8	– (2) c de Kock b Steyn	38
W. U. Tharanga st de Kock b Duminy	83	– (1) c de Kock b Steyn	14
K. C. Sangakkara b Morkel	24	– c Amla b Duminy	76
D. P. M. D. Jayawardene lbw b Steyn	3	– c de Kock b Morkel	10
H. D. R. L. Thirimanne c de Kock b Steyn	38	– c de Villiers b Steyn	12
*A. D. Mathews b Imran Tahir	89	– not out	27
†L. D. Chandimal c Petersen b Steyn	6	– c de Kock b Morkel	1
M. D. K. Perera c de Kock b Steyn	0	– c de Kock b Steyn	0
H. M. R. K. B. Herath c de Villiers b Morkel	19	– c de Villiers b Duminy	20
R. A. S. Lakmal c de Kock b Morkel	6	– c Imran Tahir b Morkel	12
R. M. S. Eranga not out	1	– c Elgar b Morkel	0
B 4, l-b 7, w 3, n-b 1	15	L-b 5, n-b 1	6
(104.5 overs)	292	(71.3 overs)	216

1/39 (1) 2/98 (3) 3/104 (4) 4/136 (2) 5/190 (5) 6/200 (7)   1/14 (1) 2/118 (2) 3/138 (4) 4/149 (3) 5/153 (5)
7/201 (8) 8/272 (6) 9/283 (10) 10/292 (9)   6/158 (7) 7/161 (8) 8/190 (9) 9/216 (10) 10/216 (11)

Steyn 23–8–54–5; Philander 15–6–31–0; Morkel 18.5–8–49–3; Imran Tahir 26–5–75–1; Duminy 15–4–47–1; Elgar 7–1–25–0. *Second Innings*—Steyn 17–4–45–4; Philander 11–4–34–0; Morkel 13.3–6–29–4; Imran Tahir 19–3–64–0; Duminy 10–4–38–2; Elgar 1–0–1–0.

Umpires: B. F. Bowden *(New Zealand)* (79) and R. A. Kettleborough *(England)* (21).
Third umpire: N. J. Llong *(England)*. Referee: J. J. Crowe *(New Zealand)* (66).

Close of play: First day, South Africa 268–5 (de Kock 17, Steyn 0); Second day, Sri Lanka 30–0 (Silva 8, Tharanga 20); Third day, Sri Lanka 283–9 (Herath 12); Fourth day, Sri Lanka 110–1 (Silva 37, Sangakkara 58).

SRI LANKA v SOUTH AFRICA 2014 (2nd Test)

At Sinhalese Sports Club, Colombo, on 24, 25, 26, 27, 28 July, 2014.
Toss: Sri Lanka.　　　Result: MATCH DRAWN.
Debuts: Sri Lanka – D. P. D. N. Dickwella.
Man of the Match: D. P. M. D. Jayawardene. Man of the Series: M. D. K. Perera.

Sri Lanka looked set to square the series when South Africa dipped to 110 for six on the final afternoon, with 32.2 overs remaining. But Duminy, who had made three in 68 minutes in the first innings, now gritted out three singles in 63 minutes, Philander resisted for 105, and Steyn and Imran Tahir for half-an-hour apiece – enabling South Africa to get out of jail. A superb 165 in 456 minutes from Jayawardene, his 11th Test century on his favourite ground, lifted Sri Lanka towards an imposing total, one which had looked unlikely when Sangakkara fell first ball to make it 16 for two. Amla responded with a tour de force of his own, an unbeaten 139 in 486 minutes, from 382 balls. With support from the tail he inched the total upwards, but South Africa still trailed by 139. It was Jayawardene's turn for a duck in the second innings, but Sangakkara and Mathews took the lead towards 368 on a weather-shortened fourth day, during which Morkel took his 200th Test wicket (Vithanage). South Africa managed only 121 runs from 94 overs on the last day – but Amla, whose own 25 occupied 170 minutes, wasn't complaining after his side's first series win in Sri Lanka since their first visit in 1993–94 put them back on top of the ICC's Test rankings. Jayawardene's catch to dismiss du Plessis made him the third outfielder to take 200 in Tests, after Rahul Dravid (210) and Jacques Kallis (200). Jayawardene would finish with 205.

Sri Lanka

W. U. Tharanga c de Kock b Steyn	11	– c de Kock b Steyn	30
J. K. Silva c de Villiers b Duminy	44	– c Philander b Morkel	26
K. C. Sangakkara c Imran Tahir b Steyn	0	– c de Kock b Morkel	72
D. P. M. D. Jayawardene run out	165	– c Elgar b Imran Tahir	0
*A. D. Mathews c de Kock b Duminy	63	– not out	63
K. D. K. Vithanage c de Villiers b Morkel	13	– c du Plessis b Morkel	7
†D. P. D. N. Dickwella run out	72	– c de Villiers b Steyn	16
M. D. K. Perera c Amla b Imran Tahir	12	– b Imran Tahir	7
H. M. R. K. B. Herath not out	7	– c de Villiers b Morkel	4
B. A. W. Mendis c de Kock b Philander	2		
R. A. S. Lakmal c de Kock b Philander	4		
B 11, l-b 14, n-b 3	28	B 1, l-b 2, n-b 1	4
(121.4 overs)	421	(8 wkts dec, 53.4 overs)	229

1/16 (1) 2/16 (3) 3/115 (2) 4/246 (5) 5/285 (6) 6/385 (4) 7/404 (8) 8/409 (7) 9/415 (10) 10/421 (11).

1/38 (1) 2/82 (2) 3/83 (4) 4/164 (3) 5/174 (6) 6/203 (7) 7/214 (8) 8/229 (9)

Steyn 22–5–69–2; Philander 21.4–7–52–2; Morkel 26–6–69–1; Imran Tahir 33–4–121–1; Duminy 18–1–80–2; Elgar 1–0–5–0. *Second Innings*—Steyn 13–1–59–2; Philander 11–3–35–0; Imran Tahir 18–0–76–2; Morkel 9.4–1–45–4; Elgar 1–0–9–0; Duminy 1–0–2–0.

South Africa

A. N. Petersen c and b Herath	2	– c Vithanage b Herath	0
D. Elgar c Silva b Perera	1	– b Perera	13
F. du Plessis c Dickwella b Lakmal	36	– (6) c Jayawardene b Herath	10
*H. M. Amla not out	139	– c Jayawardene b Perera	25
A. B. de Villiers lbw b Perera	37	– b Herath	12
†Q. de Kock b Perera	0	– (3) c Vithanage b Herath	37
J-P. Duminy st Dickwella b Herath	3	– lbw b Perera	3
V. D. Philander b Perera	9	– not out	27
D. W. Steyn c Sangakkara b Herath	30	– c Dickwella b Herath	6
Imran Tahir c Tharanga b Herath	15	– not out	4
M. Morkel c Silva b Perera	0		
L-b 3, w 1, n-b 6	10	B 5, l-b 14, n-b 3	22
(134.5 overs)	282	(8 wkts, 111 overs)	159

1/3 (1) 2/13 (2) 3/71 (3) 4/150 (5) 5/150 (6) 6/175 (7) 7/204 (8) 8/251 (9) 9/279 (10) 10/282 (11).

1/4 (1) 2/47 (2) 3/68 (3) 4/93 (5) 5/105 (4) 6/110 (6) 7/130 (7) 8/148 (9)

Lakmal 23–7–54–1; Herath 45–17–71–4; Perera 41.5–11–69–5; Mendis 21–1–68–0; Vithanage 4–0–17–0. *Second Innings*—Herath 45–30–40–5; Perera 44–24–60–3; Mendis 13–8–17–0; Lakmal 4–1–11–0; Vithanage 5–1–12–0.

Umpires: R. A. Kettleborough *(England)* (22) and N. J. Llong *(England)* (25).
Third umpire: B. F. Bowden *(New Zealand)*. Referee: J. J. Crowe *(New Zealand)* (67).

Close of play: First day, Sri Lanka 305–5 (Jayawardene 140, Dickwella 12); Second day, South Africa 98–3 (Amla 46, de Villiers 11); Third day, Sri Lanka 11–0 (Tharanga 6, Silva 5); Fourth day, South Africa 38–1 (Elgar 13, de Kock 21).

SRI LANKA v PAKISTAN 2014 (1st Test)

At Galle International Stadium on 6, 7, 8, 9, 10 August, 2014.
Toss: Pakistan.　　　Result: SRI LANKA WON BY SEVEN WICKETS.
Debuts: none.
Man of the Match: H. M. R. K. B. Herath.

Sri Lanka bounced back from series defeat by South Africa with a convincing win over Pakistan, one which had looked unlikely when the tourists occupied most of the first two days in racking up 451. Younis Khan batted for 496 minutes for 177, his 24th Test century, after entering at 19 for two. On a pitch more typical of Galle than the one on which South Africa emerged victorious the previous month, off-spinner Perera took five wickets and slow left-armer Herath three. A massive 221 in 698 minutes from Sangakkara, his 37th Test hundred and tenth double – only Don Bradman (12) made more – eased Sri Lanka in front. He hit 24 fours, and shared century stands with Silva, Jayawardene and Mathews. Saeed Ajmal's five-for restricted the advantage to 82, but Pakistan lost four men clearing the deficit, then crucially surrendered the key wickets of Azhar Ali and Misbah-ul-Haq in the space of three balls from Herath (who finished with six wickets) and Perera. Sarfraz Ahmed's second half-century of the match stretched the lead to 98, but under threatening skies Sri Lanka charged home at more than six an over. Mathews completed victory by tapping a quick single into the covers with 4.4 overs remaining, just before the heavens opened. More bad news followed for Pakistan: off-spinner Ajmal was reported for a suspect action, and was subsequently banned from bowling in international cricket when tests showed he routinely flexed his elbow by around 40 degrees, over twice the legal limit of 15.

Pakistan

Khurram Manzoor lbw b Prasad	3	– c Dickwella b Herath		3
Ahmed Shehzad b Prasad	4	– lbw b Perera		16
Azhar Ali b Herath	30	– (4) c Dickwella b Herath		41
Younis Khan c Vithanage b Perera	177	– (5) b Herath		13
*Misbah-ul-Haq c Dickwella b Herath	31	– (6) lbw b Perera		28
Asad Shafiq lbw b Herath	75	– (7) lbw b Herath		8
†Sarfraz Ahmed c Mathews b Perera	55	– (8) not out		52
Abdur Rehman c Sangakkara b Perera	50	– (9) c Dickwella b Eranga		1
Saeed Ajmal c Jayawardene b Perera	12	– (3) c Dickwella b Prasad		4
Mohammad Talha not out	9	– c Dickwella b Herath		4
Junaid Khan c Jayawardene b Perera	0	– lbw b Herath		0
L-b 4, n-b 1	5	B 7, l-b 3		10
(140.5 overs)	451	(80.2 overs)		180

1/4 (2) 2/19 (1) 3/56 (3) 4/156 (5) 5/293 (6) 6/359 (4)　　　1/3 (1) 2/11 (3) 3/39 (2) 4/55 (5) 5/111 (4)
7/388 (7) 8/424 (9) 9/451 (8) 10/451 (11)　　　6/111 (6) 7/133 (7) 8/153 (9) 9/178 (10) 10/180 (11)

Eranga 31–13–78–0; Prasad 24–3–81–2; Mathews 15–7–25–0; Herath 38–9–116–3; Perera 31.5–1–137–5; Vithanage 1–0–10–0. *Second Innings*—Herath 30.2–11–48–6; Eranga 14–5–44–1; Perera 28–6–68–2; Prasad 8–3–10–1.

Sri Lanka

W. U. Tharanga lbw b Junaid Khan	19	– b Junaid Khan		12
J. K. Silva c Sarfraz Ahmed b Mohammad Talha	64			
K. C. Sangakkara st Sarfraz Ahmed b Abdur Rehman	221	– c Khurram Manzoor b Mohammad Talha		21
D. P. M. D. Jayawardene lbw b Junaid Khan	59	– (2) b Junaid Khan		26
*A. D. Mathews c Younis Khan b Saeed Ajmal	91	– (4) not out		25
K. D. K. Vithanage c Asad Shafiq b Saeed Ajmal	5	– (5) not out		11
†D. P. D. N. Dickwella c Asad Shafiq b Saeed Ajmal	5			
M. D. K. Perera c Junaid Khan b Saeed Ajmal	5			
K. T. G. D. Prasad st Sarfraz Ahmed b Saeed Ajmal	31			
H. M. R. K. B. Herath not out	6			
B 5, l-b 11, w 7, n-b 4	27	L-b 3, w 1		4
(9 wkts dec, 163.1 overs)	533	(3 wkts, 16.2 overs)		99

1/24 (1) 2/144 (2) 3/257 (4) 4/438 (5) 5/450 (6) 6/458 (7)
7/475 (8) 8/511 (3) 9/533 (9)　　　1/28 (1) 2/59 (2) 3/73 (3)

R. M. S. Eranga did not bat.

Junaid Khan 33–9–104–2; Mohammad Talha 27–4–104–1; Saeed Ajmal 59.1–8–166–5; Abdur Rehman 39–2–123–1; Ahmed Shehzad 5–0–20–0. *Second Innings*—Saeed Ajmal 6–0–29–0; Junaid Khan 8–0–55–2; Mohammad Talha 2.2–0–12–1.

Umpires: I. J. Gould *(England)* (40) and B. N. J. Oxenford *(Australia)* (20).
Third umpire: R. K. Illingworth *(England)*. Referee: A. J. Pycroft *(Zimbabwe)* (29).

Close of play: First day, Pakistan 261–4 (Younis Khan 133, Asad Shafiq 55); Second day, Sri Lanka 99–1 (Silva 38, Sangakkara 36); Third day, Sri Lanka 252–2 (Sangakkara 102, Jayawardene 55); Fourth day, Pakistan 4–1 (Ahmed Shehzad 1, Saeed Ajmal 0).

SRI LANKA v PAKISTAN 2014 (2nd Test)

At Sinhalese Sports Club, Colombo, on 14, 15, 16, 17, 18 August, 2014.
Toss: Sri Lanka.   Result: SRI LANKA WON BY 105 RUNS.
Debuts: none.
Man of the Match: H. M. R. K. B. Herath. Man of the Series: H. M. R. K. B. Herath.

Rangana Herath took 14 wickets in the match to guide Sri Lanka to a 2–0 series victory. That included the 18th (if most costly) instance of a bowler taking nine or more in an innings, the third for Sri Lanka after two by Muttiah Muralitharan. Herath's heroics – and five catches by the new wicketkeeper Niroshan Dickwella – restricted Pakistan to a narrow lead despite Sarfraz Ahmed's maiden Test century; Tharanga had just missed a hundred of his own in the first innings, as consistent scoring down the order lifted Sri Lanka to 320 despite eight wickets for the left-arm opening pair of Junaid Khan and Wahab Riaz. In all, 29 wickets would fall to left-arm bowlers in the match, a Test record (beating 28 by South Africa and England at Cape Town in 1888–89). When Sri Lanka batted again, Sangakkara and Jayawardene made one final century partnership – their 19th in Tests – but after that three wickets for Riaz, and two run-outs, left Mathews high and dry with 43. Pakistan needed only 271 to win, but Prasad removed the openers then Herath got stuck in again. Pakistan were all but sunk at 50 for five, and although Sarfraz completed his fourth half-century of the series on the final morning Herath soon wrapped things up. It was a fitting end to the career of Mahela Jayawardene, who bowed out on his home ground with 11,814 Test runs at 49.84, with 34 centuries, in 149 Tests. At the SSC alone he made 2,921 runs, a record for a single Test venue.

Sri Lanka

W. U. Tharanga c Azhar Ali b Wahab Riaz	92	– b Abdur Rehman		45
J. K. Silva c Sarfraz Ahmed b Junaid Khan	41	– c Younis Khan b Abdur Rehman		17
K. C. Sangakkara b Wahab Riaz	22	– c Azhar Ali b Saeed Ajmal		59
D. P. M. D. Jayawardene lbw b Saeed Ajmal	4	– c Ahmed Shehzad b Saeed Ajmal		54
*A. D. Mathews c Sarfraz Ahmed b Wahab Riaz	39	– not out		43
H. D. R. L. Thirimanne c Sarfraz Ahmed b Junaid Khan	20	– b Saeed Ajmal		10
†D. P. D. N. Dickwella lbw b Junaid Khan	24	– lbw b Wahab Riaz		21
M. D. K. Perera lbw b Junaid Khan	0	– lbw b Wahab Riaz		0
K. T. G. D. Prasad lbw b Junaid Khan	13	– run out		19
H. M. R. K. B. Herath c Younis Khan b Abdur Rehman	17	– b Wahab Riaz		0
U. W. M. B. C. A. Welagedara not out	27	– run out		0
B 8, l-b 7, n-b 6	21	B 10, l-b 2, w 1, n-b 1		14
(99.3 overs)	320	(109 overs)		282

1/79 (2) 2/144 (3) 3/167 (4) 4/177 (1) 5/215 (6) 6/249 (7) 7/249 (8) 8/261 (5) 9/284 (9) 10/320 (10)

1/54 (1) 2/79 (2) 3/186 (3) 4/189 (4) 5/212 (6) 6/247 (7) 7/247 (8) 8/278 (9) 9/282 (10) 10/282 (11)

Junaid Khan 27–6–87–5; Wahab Riaz 20–3–88–3; Abdur Rehman 19.3–4–53–1; Saeed Ajmal 33–5–77–1. *Second Innings*—Wahab Riaz 25–3–76–3; Abdur Rehman 35–3–97–2; Saeed Ajmal 46–10–89–3; Ahmed Shehzad 3–0–8–0.

Pakistan

Khurram Manzoor c Dickwella b Herath	23	– c Dickwella b Prasad		10
Ahmed Shehzad c Dickwella b Perera	58	– lbw b Prasad		8
Azhar Ali c Mathews b Herath	32	– c Jayawardene b Herath		10
Younis Khan c Dickwella b Herath	13	– lbw b Herath		8
*Misbah-ul-Haq c Dickwella b Herath	5	– c Jayawardene b Herath		3
Asad Shafiq b Herath	42	– st Dickwella b Herath		32
†Sarfraz Ahmed c Dickwella b Herath	103	– c Sangakkara b Welagedara		55
Abdur Rehman c Jayawardene b Herath	16	– lbw b Perera		5
Wahab Riaz c Welagedara b Herath	17	– c Silva b Herath		17
Saeed Ajmal b Herath	4	– not out		3
Junaid Khan not out	13	– absent hurt		
L-b 3, n-b 3	6	B 4, l-b 7, n-b 3		14
(93.1 overs)	332	(52.1 overs)		165

1/47 (1) 2/110 (3) 3/122 (2) 4/131 (4) 5/140 (5) 6/233 (6) 7/273 (8) 8/301 (9) 9/315 (7) 10/332 (10)

1/17 (1) 2/21 (2) 3/31 (3) 4/39 (5) 5/50 (4) 6/105 (6) 7/122 (8) 8/151 (7) 9/165 (9)

Prasad 16–4–53–0; Welagedara 18–2–65–0; Herath 33.1–3–127–9; Mathews 9–1–21–0; Perera 17–1–63–1. *Second Innings*—Welagedara 9–4–22–1; Prasad 8–0–29–2; Herath 22.1–2–57–5; Perera 13–1–46–1.

Umpires: I. J. Gould *(England)* (41) and R. K. Illingworth *(England)* (10).
Third umpire: B. N. J. Oxenford *(Australia)*. Referee: A. J. Pycroft *(Zimbabwe)* (30).

Close of play: First day, Sri Lanka 261–8 (Prasad 4); Second day, Pakistan 244–6 (Sarfraz Ahmed 66, Abdur Rehman 1); Third day, Sri Lanka 177–2 (Sangakkara 54, Jayawardene 49); Fourth day, Pakistan 127–7 (Sarfraz Ahmed 38, Wahab Riaz 2).

ZIMBABWE v SOUTH AFRICA 2014 (Only Test)

At Harare Sports Club on 9, 10, 11, 12 August, 2014.
Toss: Zimbabwe.   Result: SOUTH AFRICA WON BY NINE WICKETS.
Debuts: Zimbabwe – J. C. Nyumbu, D. T. Tiripano. South Africa – D. L. Piedt.
Man of the Match: D. L. Piedt.

Zimbabwe's first Test against South Africa for 9½ years ended predictably in defeat – the seventh in their eight meetings, to go with a draw in 2001–02 – but the match was not entirely one-sided. Zimbabwe countered a fearsome pace attack reasonably well on the first day, with Taylor holing out on the midwicket boundary after a responsible four-hour 93. He was one of four wickets for off-spinner Dane Piedt, who became only the second South African (after Ernie Vogler in 1905–06) to take a wicket with his first ball in a Test. His lbw victim, 35-year-old Mark Vermeulen, was returning to Test cricket after more than ten years, an eventful period which included his arrest for trying to burn down the Zimbabwe cricket academy. South Africa progressed serenely to 132 for one, before three quick wickets gave Zimbabwe hope. But du Plessis hung on for almost six hours, adding 119 with de Kock, then Duminy marshalled the tail in assembling a lead of 141. Off-spinner John Nyumbu persevered for five expensive wickets, only Zimbabwe's second debut five-for after Andy Blignaut's in 2000–01 (John Traicos took five for 86 in Zimbabwe's inaugural Test, against India in 1992–93, but had previously played for South Africa). Seasoned Zimbabwe-watchers feared a collapse, and it duly came: a handy 98 for two became a disastrous 124 for seven. Mutumbami avoided the innings defeat, but South Africa were left only 41 to win. Steyn took eight wickets in the match, as did the debutant Piedt.

Zimbabwe

V. Sibanda c Petersen b Steyn	0	– (2) c and b Piedt		45
H. Masakadza b Piedt	45	– (1) c de Villiers b Morkel		19
M. A. Vermeulen lbw b Piedt	14	– (4) lbw b Steyn		21
*B. R. M. Taylor c Duminy b Piedt	93	– (5) c Elgar b Piedt		5
R. W. Chakabva c Amla b Piedt	0	– (6) b Morkel		15
S. C. Williams c de Kock b Steyn	24	– (7) c Duminy b Morkel		3
†R. Mutumbami lbw b Steyn	21	– (8) c de Kock b Steyn		43
T. Panyangara c de Kock b Philander	12	– (11) b Steyn		2
D. T. Tiripano not out	15	– (3) b Piedt		5
T. L. Chatara c de Kock b Steyn	22	– not out		0
J. C. Nyumbu c de Kock b Steyn	2	– (9) c and b Piedt		13
L-b 4, w 2, n-b 2	8	B 2, l-b 7, n-b 1		10
(92.4 overs)	256	(76.2 overs)		181

1/0 (1) 2/33 (3) 3/90 (2) 4/90 (5) 5/120 (6) 6/179 (7)   1/25 (1) 2/58 (3) 3/98 (4) 4/98 (2) 5/113 (5)
7/204 (8) 8/220 (4) 9/246 (10) 10/256 (11)   6/121 (6) 7/124 (7) 8/178 (8) 9/178 (9) 10/181 (11)

Steyn 22.4–11–46–5; Philander 18–5–51–1; Morkel 19–3–39–0; Piedt 24–1–90–4; Duminy 9–0–26–0. *Second Innings*—Steyn 21.2–9–38–3; Philander 10–3–25–0; Morkel 15–9–15–3; Piedt 25–3–62–4; Duminy 2–1–12–0; Elgar 3–0–20–0.

South Africa

D. Elgar c Mutumbami b Tiripano	61	– b Chatara	21
A. N. Petersen c Mutumbami b Nyumbu	32	– not out	17
F. du Plessis c Chakabva b Nyumbu	98	– not out	5
*H. M. Amla c Sibanda b Chatara	4		
A. B. de Villiers c Sibanda b Nyumbu	7		
†Q. de Kock c Sibanda b Williams	81		
J-P. Duminy c Taylor b Nyumbu	55		
V. D. Philander b Williams	17		
D. W. Steyn c Tiripano b Nyumbu	19		
D. L. Piedt lbw b Tiripano	13		
M. Morkel not out	2		
B 3, l-b 4, n-b 1	8	L-b 1	1
(158.3 overs)	397	(1 wkt, 10.4 overs)	44

1/57 (2) 2/132 (1) 3/146 (4) 4/157 (5) 5/276 (3)
6/292 (6) 7/334 (8) 8/367 (9) 9/395 (10) 10/397 (7)   1/39 (1)

Panyangara 30–12–39–0; Tiripano 26–8–65–2; Nyumbu 49.3–7–157–5; Chatara 27–12–34–1; Williams 26–2–95–2. *Second Innings*—Nyumbu 4–0–24–0; Panyangara 3–1–5–0; Chatara 2–1–5–1; Williams 1.4–0–9–0.

Umpires: Aleem Dar *(Pakistan)* (90) and C. B. Gaffaney *(New Zealand)* (1).
Third umpire: T. J. Matibiri *(Zimbabwe)*. Referee: R. S. Mahanama *(Sri Lanka)* (52).

Close of play: First day, Zimbabwe 248–9 (Tiripano 9, Nyumbu 0); Second day, South Africa 201–4 (du Plessis 69, de Kock 27); Third day, Zimbabwe 28–1 (Sibanda 8, Tiripano 1).

WEST INDIES v BANGLADESH 2014 (1st Test)

At Arnos Vale, Kingstown, St Vincent, on 5, 6, 7, 8, 9 September, 2014.
Toss: Bangladesh.   Result: WEST INDIES WON BY TEN WICKETS.
Debuts: Bangladesh – Shuvagata Hom, Taijul Islam.
Man of the Match: K. C. Brathwaite.

Bangladesh had won both Tests on their previous tour of the Caribbean, in 2009, admittedly against a side severely depleted by a contracts dispute. This time it was Bangladesh who were weakened; star all-rounder Shakib Al Hasan had been suspended by his board for various bouts of "serious misbehaviour". Mushfiqur Rahim decided to bowl, saying he thought the pitch would help his seamers – then gave off-spinner Mahmudullah the fifth over. One of those seamers, Al-Amin Hossain, was later reported for a suspect action. On a surface that turned out to be lifeless, West Indies laid the foundations for victory with a formidable total, though their plodding batting on a truncated second day – Brathwaite and Chanderpaul put on 143 in 56 overs – was trying for a sparse crowd. Brathwaite hit only 14 fours in his 212: not quite 22, he was West Indies' third-youngest Test double-centurion, after George Headley (1929–30) and Garry Sobers (1957–58). Off-spinner Taijul Islam persevered for a debut five-for. Bangladesh were saved from indignity by Mominul Haque and Mushfiqur Rahim – and by poor catching, although Bravo did manage to cling on to five chances, equalling the West Indian record for a fielder set by Darren Sammy at Mumbai in November 2013. Following on 302 behind, Bangladesh did better: after Tamim Iqbal knuckled down for 143 minutes, Mahmudullah put on 130 with Mushfiqur, who batted for 327 minutes in all and reached his third Test century. It at least ensured West Indies had to bat again, although they won before lunch on the final day.

West Indies

C. H. Gayle lbw b Shuvagata Hom	64	– not out	9
K. C. Brathwaite c Mominul Haque b Taijul Islam	212	– not out	4
K. A. Edwards c Mominul Haque b Taijul Islam	10		
D. M. Bravo c Mahmudullah b Taijul Islam	62		
S. Chanderpaul not out	85		
J. Blackwood lbw b Rubel Hossain	10		
*†D. Ramdin c Rubel Hossain b Taijul Islam	5		
J. E. Taylor c Shuvagata Hom b Taijul Islam	10		
K. A. J. Roach not out	2		
B 5, l-b 18, n-b 1	24		
(7 wkts dec, 160 overs)	484	(no wkt, 2.4 overs)	13

1/116 (1) 2/133 (3) 3/261 (4) 4/422 (2) 5/451 (6)
6/466 (7) 7/479 (8)

S. J. Benn and S. T. Gabriel did not bat.

Al-Amin Hossain 22–12–43–0; Rubel Hossain 30–1–110–1; Mahmudullah 19–0–64–0; Shuvagata Hom 37–6–104–1; Taijul Islam 47–9–135–5; Nasir Hossain 4–1–4–0; Mominul Haque 1–0–1–0. *Second Innings*—Al-Amin Hossain 1.4–0–9–0; Taijul Islam 1–0–4–0.

Bangladesh

Tamim Iqbal c Bravo b Roach	1	– b Benn	53
Shamsur Rahman c Bravo b Benn	35	– c Ramdin b Roach	4
Imrul Kayes c Bravo b Taylor	9	– c Edwards b Gayle	25
Mominul Haque c Ramdin b Gabriel	51	– c Ramdin b Benn	12
Mahmudullah lbw b Blackwood	7	– c Ramdin b Roach	66
*†Mushfiqur Rahim not out	48	– c Bravo b Taylor	116
Nasir Hossain c Benn b Blackwood	2	– c Gabriel b Roach	19
Shuvagata Hom c and b Benn	16	– lbw b Roach	0
Taijul Islam c Bravo b Benn	2	– b Gabriel	0
Rubel Hossain c Ramdin b Benn	1	– b Gabriel	0
Al-Amin Hossain c Bravo b Benn	5	– not out	0
L-b 2, w 2, n-b 1	5	B 12, l-b 4, w 2, n-b 1	19
(71.4 overs)	182	(113.3 overs)	314

1/1 (1) 2/18 (3) 3/80 (2) 4/105 (4) 5/110 (5)
6/118 (7) 7/147 (8) 8/155 (9) 9/166 (10) 10/182 (11)

1/11 (2) 2/81 (3) 3/104 (4) 4/107 (1) 5/237 (5)
6/279 (7) 7/291 (8) 8/292 (9) 9/292 (10) 10/314 (6)

Taylor 15–4–46–1; Roach 13–4–31–1; Gabriel 13–2–50–1; Benn 24.4–8–39–5; Blackwood 6–1–14–2. *Second Innings*—Taylor 17.3–3–64–1; Roach 22–6–64–4; Gabriel 17–9–25–2; Blackwood 12–1–51–0; Benn 28–8–44–2; Gayle 17–3–50–1.

Umpires: M. Erasmus *(South Africa)* (26) and R. K. Illingworth *(England)* (11).
Third umpire: S. J. Davis *(Australia)*. Referee: R. S. Mahanama *(Sri Lanka)* (53).

Close of play: First day, West Indies 264–3 (Brathwaite 123, Chanderpaul 1); Second day, West Indies 407–3 (Brathwaite 205, Chanderpaul 51); Third day, Bangladesh 182; Fourth day, Bangladesh 256–5 (Mushfiqur Rahim 70, Nasir Hossain 7).

WEST INDIES v BANGLADESH 2014 (2nd Test)

At Beausejour Stadium, Gros Islet, St Lucia, on 13, 14, 15, 16 September, 2014.
Toss: Bangladesh.   Result: WEST INDIES WON BY 296 RUNS.
Debuts: West Indies – L. R. Johnson.
Man of the Match: S. Chanderpaul. Man of the Series: K. C. Brathwaite.

West Indies duly completed a 2–0 series victory. again based on a sizeable first-innings total, which started with an opening stand of 143 and was then underpinned by the inevitable Chanderpaul, whose late stands with Taylor and Benn boosted the score to 380. Tamim Iqbal made a brisk 48, but wickets tumbled at the other end as Roach proved too hot to handle. Mahmudullah's responsible 53 still left Bangladesh 219 behind, but Ramdin waived the follow-on. West Indies stumbled slightly to 100 for four, before 40-year-old Chanderpaul, in his 159th Test, and Blackwood, in his third, took them out of sight with a stand of 169. Ramdin declared once Chanderpaul reached his 30th Test century early on the fourth morning. Bangladesh made a decent start: Shamsur Rahman zoomed to 39 off 27 balls, then Tamim and Mominul Haque took the score to 158 for two. But then Tamim top-edged an ugly swipe against Benn, starting a collapse in which the last eight wickets cascaded for 34. It was all over just before the scheduled fourth-day close, Taylor taking his 100th Test wicket (Robiul Islam) and Benn his third five-for in successive matches since his comeback after nearly four years. The absence of Gayle, resting a suspect back, meant that Guyana's Leon Johnson became West Indies' 300th player, in their 500th Test. This was their 163rd win, to go with 168 defeats and 168 draws (and one tie). For Bangladesh, though, it was a 70th defeat in 85 Tests.

West Indies

K. C. Brathwaite c Taijul Islam b Shafiul Islam	63	– c Shamsur Rahman b Mahmudullah	45
L. R. Johnson lbw b Taijul Islam	66	– b Taijul Islam	41
K. A. Edwards c Shamsur Rahman b Mahmudullah	16	– c Shamsur Rahman b Shafiul Islam	2
D. M. Bravo c Mushfiqur Rahim b Robiul Islam	46	– b Mahmudullah	7
S. Chanderpaul not out	84	– not out	101
J. Blackwood c Anamul Haque b Al-Amin Hossain	8	– not out	66
*†D. Ramdin c Mushfiqur Rahim b Al-Amin Hossain	0		
K. A. J. Roach c Mushfiqur Rahim b Shafiul Islam	0		
J. E. Taylor c Mahmudullah b Taijul Islam	40		
S. J. Benn c Shafiul Islam b Al-Amin Hossain	25		
S. T. Gabriel b Robiul Islam	4		
B 8, l-b 4, w 10, n-b 6	28	L-b 5, w 2	7
(124 overs)	380	(4 wkts dec, 77 overs)	269

1/143 (1) 2/145 (2) 3/185 (3) 4/251 (4) 5/268 (6)
6/268 (7) 7/269 (8) 8/323 (9) 9/375 (10) 10/380 (11)   1/76 (2) 2/81 (3) 3/97 (4) 4/100 (1)

Al-Amin Hossain 31–6–80–3; Shafiul Islam 27–7–80–2; Robiul Islam 26–7–63–2; Taijul Islam 22–4–89–2; Mahmudullah 16–2–49–1; Nasir Hossain 2–0–7–0. *Second Innings*—Taijul Islam 28–5–81–1; Al-Amin Hossain 4–0–18–0; Robiul Islam 12–3–42–0; Shafiul Islam 13–1–42–1; Mahmudullah 16–2–64–2; Mominul Haque 4–0–17–0.

Bangladesh

Tamim Iqbal c Ramdin b Roach	48	– c Gabriel b Benn	64
Shamsur Rahman c Ramdin b Roach	1	– c Edwards b Taylor	39
Anamul Haque c Bravo b Roach	9	– c Ramdin b Benn	0
Mominul Haque c Blackwood b Taylor	3	– c Gabriel b Benn	56
*†Mushfiqur Rahim b Taylor	4	– (6) b Taylor	11
Mahmudullah c Ramdin b Benn	53	– (5) lbw b Gabriel	0
Nasir Hossain c Ramdin b Roach	1	– lbw b Benn	2
Taijul Islam c Gabriel b Roach	12	– c and b Benn	4
Shafiul Islam c Ramdin b Gabriel	10	– b Roach	14
Robiul Islam lbw b Benn	0	– lbw b Taylor	0
Al-Amin Hossain not out	7	– not out	0
L-b 10, w 1, n-b 2	13	L-b 1, w 1	2
(62.3 overs)	161	(77.4 overs)	192

1/14 (2) 2/43 (3) 3/62 (1) 4/65 (4) 5/68 (5)   1/47 (2) 2/48 (3) 3/158 (1) 4/160 (5) 5/160 (4)
6/69 (7) 7/89 (8) 8/134 (9) 9/154 (6) 10/161 (10)   6/167 (7) 7/173 (8) 8/188 (6) 9/188 (10) 10/192 (9)

Taylor 19–5–41–2; Roach 20–5–42–5; Gabriel 15–1–49–1; Benn 8.3–2–19–2. *Second Innings*—Taylor 13–4–39–3; Roach 15.4–1–43–1; Benn 32–6–72–5; Blackwood 2–0–4–0; Gabriel 11–2–24–1; Johnson 4–0–9–0.

Umpires: S. J. Davis (*Australia*) (54) and R. K. Illingworth (*England*) (12).
Third umpire: M. Erasmus (*South Africa*). Referee: R. S. Mahanama (*Sri Lanka*) (54).

Close of play: First day, West Indies 246–3 (Bravo 44, Chanderpaul 34); Second day, Bangladesh 104–7 (Mahmudullah 13, Shafiul Islam 6); Third day, West Indies 208–4 (Chanderpaul 63, Blackwood 43).

Individual Test Career Records

Compiled by Philip Bailey

These career records for all players appearing in official Test matches are complete to
21 October, 2014.

Symbols: * not out; † in the Innings column denotes a left-hand batsman, in the
Balls column a left-arm bowler; ‡ marks a player who appeared in official Test matches
for more than one team (his record for each team is given under that country,
while combined totals are shown at the end of this section).

INDIVIDUAL CAREER RECORDS – ENGLAND

			BATTING AND FIELDING										BOWLING						
	First Test	Last Test	Tests	Inns	NO	Runs	HS	Avge	100	50	Ct	St	Balls	Runs	Wkts	Avge	BB	5wI	10wM
Abel, R.	1888	1902	13	22	2	744	132*	37.20	2	2	13	–	–							
Absolom, C.A.	1878-79	1878-79	1	2	0	58	52	29.00	–	1	–	–	–							
Adams, C.J.	1999-2000	1999-2000	5	8	1	104	31	13.00	–	–	6	–	120	59	1	59.00	1-42	–	–
Afzaal, U.	2001	2001	3	6†	1	83	54	16.60	–	1	–	–	54†	49	1	49.00	1-49	–	–
Agnew, J.P.	1984	1985	3	4	3	10	5	10.00	–	–	–	–	552	373	4	93.25	2-51	–	–
Ali, K.	2003	2003	1	2	0	10	9	5.00	–	–	–	–	216	136	5	27.20	3-80	–	–
Ali, M.M.	2014	2014	7	10†	1	286	108*	31.77	1	5	4	–	1054	618	22	28.09	6-67	1	–
Allen, D.A.	1959-60	1966	39	51	15	918	88	25.50	–	5	10	–	11297	3779	122	30.97	5-30	4	–
Allen, G.O.B.	1930	1947-48	25	33	2	750	122	24.19	1	3	20	–	4386	2379	81	29.37	7-80	5	1
Allom, M.J.C.	1929-30	1930-31	5	3	3	14	8*	14.00	–	–	–	–	817	265	14	18.92	5-38	1	–
Allott, P.J.W.	1981	1985	13	18	3	213	52*	14.20	–	1	4	–	2225	1084	26	41.69	6-61	1	–
Ambrose, T.R.	2007-08	2008-09	11	16	1	447	102	29.80	1	3	31	–	–							
Ames, L.E.G.	1929	1938-39	47	72	12	2434	149	40.56	8	7	74	23	–							
Amiss, D.L.	1966	1977	50	88	10	3612	262*	46.30	11	11	24	–	–							
Anderson, J.M.	2003	2014	99	135†	48	949	81	10.90	–	1	57	–	22114	11295	380	29.72	7-43	16	2
Andrew, K.V.	1954-55	1963	2	4	1	29	15	9.66	–	–	1	–	–							
Appleyard, R.	1954	1956	9	9	6	51	19*	17.00	–	–	4	–	1596	554	31	17.87	5-51	1	–
Archer, A.G.	1898-99	1898-99	1	2	0	31	24*	31.00	–	–	–	–	–							
Armitage, T.	1876-77	1876-77	2	3	0	33	21	11.00	–	–	–	–	12	15	0	–	–	–	–
Arnold, E.G.	1903-04	1907	10	15	3	160	40	13.33	–	–	8	–	1677	788	31	25.41	5-37	1	–
Arnold, G.G.	1967	1975	34	46	11	421	59	12.02	–	1	9	–	7650	3254	115	28.29	6-45	6	–
Arnold, J.	1931	1931	1	2	0	34	34	17.00	–	–	–	–	–							
Astill, W.E.	1927-28	1929-30	9	15	0	190	40	12.66	–	–	7	–	2182	856	25	34.24	4-58	–	–
Atherton, M.A.	1989	2001	115	212	7	7728	185*	37.69	16	46	83	–	408	302	2	151.00	1-20	–	–
Athey, C.W.J.	1980	1988	23	41	1	919	123	22.97	–	4	13	–	–							
Attewell, W.	1884-85	1891-92	10	15	6	150	43*	16.66	–	–	9	–	2850	626	28	22.35	4-42	–	–
Bailey, R.J.	1988	1989-90	4	8	0	119	43	14.87	–	–	–	–	–							
Bailey, T.E.	1949	1958-59	61	91	14	2290	134*	29.74	1	10	32	–	9712	3856	132	29.21	7-34	5	1
Bairstow, D.L.	1979	1980-81	4	7	1	125	59	20.83	–	1	12	1	–							
Bairstow, J.M.	2012	2013-14	14	24	2	593	95	26.95	–	4	16	–	–							
Bakewell, A.H.	1931	1935	6	9	0	409	107	45.44	1	3	3	–	18	8	0	–	–	–	–
Balderstone, J.C.	1976	1976	2	4	0	39	35	9.75	–	–	1	–	96†	80	1	80.00	1-80	–	–
Ballance, G.S.	2013-14	2014	8	13†	1	729	156	60.75	3	3	7	–	12	5	0	–	–	–	–
Barber, R.W.	1960	1968	28	45†	3	1495	185	35.59	1	9	21	–	3426	1806	42	43.00	4-132	–	–
Barber, W.	1935	1935	2	4	0	83	44	20.75	–	–	1	–	2	0	1	0.00	1-0	–	–
Barlow, G.D.	1976-77	1977	3	5†	1	17	7*	4.25	–	–	–	–	–							
Barlow, R.G.	1881-82	1886-87	17	30	4	591	62	22.73	–	2	14	–	2456†	767	34	22.55	7-40	3	–

INDIVIDUAL CAREER RECORDS – ENGLAND *continued*

	First Test	Last Test	Tests	Inns	NO	Runs	HS	Avge	100	50	Ct	St	Balls	Runs	Wkts	Avge	BB	5wI	10wM
Barnes, S.F.	1901–02	1913–14	27	39	9	242	38*	8.06	–	1	12	–	7873	3106	189	16.43	9-103	24	7
Barnes, W.	1880	1890	21	33	2	725	134	23.38	1	5	19	–	2289	793	51	15.54	6-28	3	–
Barnett, C.J.	1933	1948	20	35	4	1098	129	35.41	2	5	14	–	256	93	0	–	–	–	–
Barnett, K.J.	1988	1989	4	7	0	207	80	29.57	–	2	1	–	36	32	0	–	–	–	–
Barratt, F.	1929	1929–30	5	4	1	28	17	9.33	–	–	2	–	750	235	5	47.00	1-8	–	–
Barrington, K.F.	1955	1968	82	131	15	6806	256	58.67	20	35	58	–	2715	1300	29	44.82	3-4	–	–
Barton, V.A.	1891–92	1891–92	1	1	0	23	23	23.00	–	–	–	–							
Bates, W.	1881–82	1886–87	15	26	2	656	64	27.33	–	5	9	–	2364	821	50	16.42	7-28	4	1
Batty, G.J.	2003–04	2005	7	8	1	144	38	20.57	–	–	3	–	1394	733	11	66.63	3-55	–	–
Bean, G.	1891–92	1891–92	3	5	0	92	50	18.40	–	1	4	–							
Bedser, A.V.	1946	1955	51	71	15	714	79	12.75	–	1	26	–	15918	5876	236	24.89	7-44	15	5
Bell, I.R.	2004	2014	105	181	22	7156	235	45.00	21	42	88	–	108	76	1	76.00	1-33	–	–
Benjamin, J.E.	1994	1994	1	1	0	0	0	0.00	–	–	–	–	168	80	4	20.00	4-42	–	–
Benson, M.R.	1986	1986	1	2†	0	51	30	25.50	–	–	–	–							
Berry, R.	1950	1950	2	4†	2	6	4*	3.00	–	–	2	–	653†	228	9	25.33	5-63	1	–
Bicknell, M.P.	1993	2003	4	7	0	45	15	6.42	–	–	2	–	1080	543	14	38.78	4-84	–	–
Binks, J.G.	1963–64	1963–64	2	4	0	91	55	22.75	–	1	8	–							
Bird, M.C.	1909–10	1913–14	10	16	1	280	61	18.66	–	2	5	–	259	120	8	15.00	3-11	–	–
Birkenshaw, J.	1972–73	1973–74	5	7†	1	148	64	21.14	–	1	3	–	1017	469	13	36.07	5-57	1	–
Blackwell, I.D.	2005–06	2005–06	1	1†	0	4	4	4.00	–	–	2	–	114†	71	0	–	–	–	–
Blakey, R.J.	1992–93	1992–93	2	4	0	7	6	1.75	–	–	2	–							
Bligh, Hon I.F.W.	1882–83	1882–83	4	7	1	62	19	10.33	–	–	7	–							
Blythe, C.	1901–02	1909–10	19	31	12	183	27	9.63	–	–	6	–	4546†	1863	100	18.63	8-59	9	4
Board, J.H.	1898–99	1905–06	6	12	1	108	29	10.80	–	–	8	3							
Bolus, J.B.	1963	1963–64	7	12	0	496	88	41.33	–	4	2	–	18†	16	0	–	–	–	–
Booth, M.W.	1913–14	1913–14	2	2	0	46	32	23.00	–	–	6	–	312	130	7	18.57	4-49	–	–
Bopara, R.S.	2007–08	2012	13	19	1	575	143	31.94	3	–	6	–	434	290	1	290.00	1-39	–	–
Borthwick, S.G.	2013–14	2013–14	1	2†	0	5	4	2.50	–	–	2	–	78	82	4	20.50	3-33	–	–
Bosanquet, B.J.T.	1903–04	1905	7	14	3	147	27	13.36	–	–	9	–	970	604	25	24.16	8-107	2	–
Botham, I.T.	1977	1992	102	161	6	5200	208	33.54	14	22	120	–	21815	10878	383	28.40	8-34	27	4
Bowden, M.P.	1888–89	1888–89	2	2	0	25	25	12.50	–	–	1	–							
Bowes, W.E.	1932	1946	15	11	5	28	10*	4.66	–	–	2	–	3655	1519	68	22.33	6-33	6	–
Bowley, E.H.	1929	1929–30	5	7	0	252	109	36.00	1	–	2	–	252	116	0	–	–	–	–
Boycott, G.	1964	1981–82	108	193	23	8114	246*	47.72	22	42	33	–	944	382	7	54.57	3-47	–	–
Bradley, W.M.	1899	1899	2	2	1	23	23*	23.00	–	–	–	–	625	233	6	38.83	5-67	1	–
Braund, L.C.	1901–02	1907–08	23	41	3	987	104	25.97	3	2	39	–	3805	1810	47	38.51	8-81	3	–
Brearley, J.M.	1976	1981	39	66	3	1442	91	22.88	–	9	52	–							
Brearley, W.	1905	1912	4	5	2	21	11*	7.00	–	–	–	–	705	359	17	21.11	5-110	1	–

INDIVIDUAL CAREER RECORDS – ENGLAND continued

	First Test	Last Test	Tests	Inns	NO	Runs	HS	Avge	100	50	Ct	St	Balls	Runs	Wkts	Avge	BB	5wI	10wM
						BATTING AND FIELDING									BOWLING				
Brennan, D.V.	1951	1951	2	2	0	16	16	8.00	–	–	–	1	–	–	–	–	–	–	–
Bresnan, T.T.	2009	2013–14	23	26	4	575	91	26.13	–	3	8	–	4674	2357	72	32.73	5-48	1	–
Briggs, J.	1884–85	1899	33	50	5	815	121	18.11	–	2	12	–	5332†	2095	118	17.75	8-11	9	4
Broad, B.C.	1984	1989	25	44†	2	1661	162	39.54	6	6	10	–	6	4	0	–	–	–	–
Broad, S.C.J.	2007–08	2014	74	104†	13	2193	169	24.09	1	10	21	–	15515	7894	264	29.90	7-44	12	2
Brockwell, W.	1893	1899	7	12	0	202	49	16.83	–	1	6	–	582	309	5	61.80	3-33	–	–
Bromley-Davenport, H.R.	1895–96	1898–99	4	6	0	128	84	21.33	–	1	1	–	155†	98	4	24.50	2-46	–	–
Brookes, D.	1947–48	1947–48	1	2	0	17	10	8.50	–	–	1	–	–	–	–	–	–	–	–
Brown, A.	1961–62	1961–62	2	1	1	3	3*	–	–	–	1	–	323	150	3	50.00	3-27	–	–
Brown, D.J.	1965	1969	26	34	5	342	44*	11.79	–	–	7	–	5098	2237	79	28.31	5-42	2	–
Brown, F.R.	1931	1953	22	30	1	734	79	25.31	–	5	22	–	3260	1398	45	31.06	5-49	1	–
Brown, G.	1921	1922–23	7	12†	2	299	84	29.90	–	2	9	3	–	–	–	–	–	–	–
Brown, J.T.	1894–95	1899	8	16	3	470	140	36.15	1	1	7	–	35	22	0	–	–	–	–
Brown, S.J.E.	1996	1996	1	2	1	11	10*	11.00	–	–	–	–	198†	138	2	69.00	1-60	–	–
Buckenham, C.P.	1909–10	1909–10	4	7	0	43	17	6.14	–	–	2	–	1182	593	21	28.23	5-115	1	–
Butcher, A.R.	1979	1979	1	2†	0	34	20	17.00	–	–	–	–	12†	9	0	–	–	–	–
Butcher, M.A.	1997	2004–05	71	131†	7	4288	173*	34.58	8	23	61	–	901	541	15	36.06	4-42	–	–
Butcher, R.O.	1980–81	1980–81	3	5	0	71	32	14.20	–	–	3	–	–	–	–	–	–	–	–
Butler, H.J.	1947	1947–48	2	2	1	15	15*	15.00	–	–	1	–	552	215	12	17.91	4-34	–	–
Butt, H.R.	1895–96	1895–96	3	4	1	22	13	7.33	–	–	1	1	–	–	–	–	–	–	–
Buttler, J.C.	2014	2014	3	3	0	200	85	66.66	–	2	11	–	–	–	–	–	–	–	–
Caddick, A.R.	1993	2002–03	62	95	12	861	49*	10.37	–	–	21	–	13558	6999	234	29.91	7-46	13	1
Calthorpe, Hon F.S.G.	1929–30	1929–30	4	7	0	129	49	18.42	–	–	3	–	204	91	1	91.00	1-38	–	–
Capel, D.J.	1987	1989–90	15	25	1	374	98	15.58	–	2	6	–	2000	1064	21	50.66	3-88	–	–
Carberry, M.A.	2009–10	2013–14	6	12†	0	345	60	28.75	–	1	7	–	–	–	–	–	–	–	–
Carr, A.W.	1922–23	1929	11	13	1	237	63	19.75	–	1	3	–	–	–	–	–	–	–	–
Carr, D.B.	1951–52	1951–52	2	4	0	135	76	33.75	–	1	–	–	210†	140	2	70.00	2-84	–	–
Carr, D.W.	1909	1909	1	1	1	0	0	0.00	–	–	–	–	414	282	7	40.28	5-146	1	–
Cartwright, T.W.	1964	1965	5	7	2	26	9	5.20	–	–	2	–	1611	544	15	36.26	6-94	1	–
Chapman, A.P.F.	1924	1930–31	26	36†	4	925	121	28.90	1	5	32	–	40†	20	0	–	–	–	–
Charlwood, H.R.J.	1876–77	1876–77	2	4	0	63	36	15.75	–	–	1	–	–	–	–	–	–	–	–
Chatterton, W.	1891–92	1891–92	1	1	0	48	48	48.00	–	–	1	–	–	–	–	–	–	–	–
Childs, J.H.	1988	1988	2	4†	4	2	2*	–	–	–	1	–	516†	183	3	61.00	1-13	–	–
Christopherson, S.	1884	1884	1	1	0	17	17	17.00	–	–	1	–	136	69	1	69.00	1-52	–	–
Clark, E.W.	1929	1934	8	9†	5	36	10	9.00	–	–	1	–	1931†	899	32	28.09	5-98	1	–
Clarke, R.	2003–04	2003–04	2	3	0	96	55	32.00	–	1	1	–	174	60	4	15.00	2-7	–	–
Clay, J.C.	1935	1935	1	–	–	–	–	–	–	–	1	–	192	75	0	–	–	–	–

INDIVIDUAL CAREER RECORDS – ENGLAND *continued*

	First Test	Last Test	Tests	Inns	NO	Runs	HS	Avge	100	50	Ct	St	Balls	Runs	Wkts	Avge	BB	5wI	10wM
						BATTING AND FIELDING									*BOWLING*				
Close, D.B.	1949	1976	22	37†	2	887	70	25.34	–	4	24	–	1212	532	18	29.55	4-35	1	–
Coldwell, L.J.	1962	1964	7	7	5	9	6*	4.50	–	–	1	–	1668	610	22	27.72	6-85	1	–
Collingwood, P.D.	2003–04	2010–11	68	115	10	4259	206	40.56	10	20	96	–	1905	1018	17	59.88	3-23	–	–
Compton, D.C.S.	1937	1956–57	78	131	15	5807	278	50.06	17	28	49	–	2710†	1410	25	56.40	5-70	1	–
Compton, N.R.D.	2012–13	2013	9	17	2	479	117	31.93	2	1	4	–	–	–	–	–	–	–	–
Cook, A.N.	2005–06	2014	109	194†	11	8423	294	46.02	25	38	108	–	18	7	1	7.00	1-6	–	–
Cook, C.	1947	1947	1	2	0	4	4	2.00	–	–	–	–	180†	127	0	–	–	–	–
Cook, G.	1981–82	1982–83	7	13	0	203	66	15.61	–	2	9	–	42†	27	0	–	–	–	–
Cook, N.G.B.	1983	1989	15	25	4	179	31	8.52	–	–	5	–	4174†	1689	52	32.48	6-65	4	1
Cope, G.A.	1977–78	1977–78	3	3	1	40	22	13.33	–	–	1	–	864	277	8	34.62	3-102	1	–
Copson, W.H.	1939	1947	3	1	0	6	6	6.00	–	–	1	–	762	297	15	19.80	5-85	1	–
Cork, D.G.	1995	2002	37	56	8	864	59	18.00	–	3	18	–	7678	3906	131	29.81	7-43	5	–
Cornford, W.L.	1929–30	1929–30	4	4	0	36	18	9.00	–	–	5	3	–	–	–	–	–	–	–
Cottam, R.M.H.	1968–69	1972–73	4	5	1	27	13	6.75	–	–	2	–	903	327	14	23.35	4-50	–	–
Coventry, Hon C.J.	1888–89	1888–89	2	2	1	13	12	13.00	–	–	–	–	–	–	–	–	–	–	–
Cowans, N.G.	1982–83	1985	19	29	7	175	36	7.95	–	–	9	–	3452	2003	51	39.27	6-77	2	–
Cowdrey, C.S.	1984–85	1988	6	8	1	101	38	14.42	–	–	5	–	399	309	4	77.25	2-65	–	–
Cowdrey, M.C.	1954–55	1974–75	114	188	15	7624	182	44.06	22	38	120	–	119	104	0	–	–	–	–
Coxon, A.	1948	1948	1	2†	0	19	19	9.50	–	–	1	–	378	172	3	57.33	2-90	–	–
Cranston, J.	1890	1890	1	2	0	31	16	15.50	–	–	1	–	–	–	–	–	–	–	–
Cranston, K.	1947	1948	8	14	0	209	45	14.92	–	–	3	–	1010	461	18	25.61	4-12	–	–
Crapp, J.F.	1948–49	1948	7	13†	2	319	56	29.00	–	3	7	–	–	–	–	–	–	–	–
Crawford, J.N.	1905–06	1907–08	12	23	2	469	74	22.33	–	2	13	–	2203	1150	39	29.48	5-48	3	–
Crawley, J.P.	1994	2002–03	37	61	9	1800	156*	34.61	4	9	29	–	–	–	–	–	–	–	–
Croft, R.D.B.	1996	2001	21	34	8	421	37*	16.19	–	–	10	–	4619	1825	49	37.24	5-95	1	–
Curtis, T.S.	1988	1989	5	9	0	140	41	15.55	–	–	3	–	18	7	0	–	–	–	–
Cuttell, W.R.	1898–99	1898–99	2	4	0	65	21	16.25	–	–	2	–	285	73	6	12.16	3-17	–	–
Dawson, E.W.	1927–28	1929–30	5	9	0	175	55	19.44	–	1	3	–	–	–	–	–	–	–	–
Dawson, R.K.J.	2001–02	2002–03	7	13	3	114	19*	11.40	–	–	2	–	1116	677	11	61.54	4-134	–	–
Dean, H.	1912	1912	3	4†	2	10	8	5.00	–	–	2	–	447†	153	11	13.90	4-19	–	–
DeFreitas, P.A.J.	1986–87	1995	44	68	5	934	88	14.82	–	4	14	–	9838	4700	140	33.57	7-70	4	–
Denness, M.H.	1969	1975	28	45	3	1667	188	39.69	4	7	28	–	–	–	–	–	–	–	–
Denton, D.	1905	1909–10	11	22	1	424	104	20.19	1	1	8	–	–	–	–	–	–	–	–
Dewes, J.G.	1948	1950–51	5	10†	1	121	67	12.10	–	1	–	–	–	–	–	–	–	–	–
Dexter, E.R.	1958	1968	62	102	8	4502	205	47.89	9	27	29	–	5317	2306	66	34.93	4-10	–	–
Dilley, G.R.	1979–80	1989	41	58†	19	521	56	13.35	–	2	10	–	8192	4107	138	29.76	6-38	6	–
Dipper, A.E.	1921	1921	1	2	0	51	40	25.50	–	–	–	–	–	–	–	–	–	–	–

INDIVIDUAL CAREER RECORDS – ENGLAND continued

					BATTING AND FIELDING									BOWLING					
	First Test	Last Test	Tests	Inns	NO	Runs	HS	Avge	100	50	Ct	St	Balls	Runs	Wkts	Avge	BB	5wI	10wM
Doggart, G.H.G.	1950	1950	2	4	0	76	29	19.00	–	–	3	–	–					–	–
D'Oliveira, B.L.	1966	1972	44	70	8	2484	158	40.06	5	15	29	–	5706	1859	47	39.55	3-46	–	–
Dollery, H.E.	1947	1950	4	7	0	72	37	10.28	–	–	1	–							
Dolphin, A.	1920–21	1920–21	1	2	0	1	1	0.50	–	–	1	–	–					–	–
Douglas, J.W.H.T.	1911–12	1924–25	23	35	2	962	119	29.15	1	6	9	–	2812	1486	45	33.02	5-46	1	–
Downton, P.R.	1980–81	1988	30	48	8	785	74	19.62	–	4	70	5	–					–	–
Druce, N.F.	1897–98	1897–98	5	9	0	252	64	28.00	–	1	5	–	–						
Ducat, A.	1921	1921	1	2	0	5	3	2.50	–	–	1	–	–						
Duckworth, G.	1924	1936	24	28	12	234	39*	14.62	–	–	45	15	6	7	0	–	–	–	–
Duleepsinhji, K.S.	1929	1931	12	19	2	995	173	58.52	3	5	10	–						–	–
Durston, F.J.	1921	1921	1	2	1	8	6*	8.00	–	–	–	–	202	136	5	27.20	4-102	–	–
Ealham, M.A.	1996	1998	8	13	3	210	53*	21.00	–	2	4	–	1060	488	17	28.70	4-21	–	–
Edmonds, P.H.	1975	1987	51	65	15	875	64	17.50	–	2	42	–	12028†	4273	125	34.18	7-66	2	–
Edrich, J.H.	1963	1976	77	127†	9	5138	310*	43.54	12	24	43	–	30	23	0	–	–	–	–
Edrich, W.J.	1938	1954–55	39	63	2	2440	219	40.00	6	13	39	–	3234	1693	41	41.29	4-68	–	–
Elliott, H.	1927–28	1933–34	4	5	1	61	37*	15.25	–	–	8	3							
Ellison, R.M.	1984	1986	11	16†	5	202	41	13.46	–	–	2	–	2264	1048	35	29.94	6-77	3	1
Emburey, J.E.	1978	1995	64	96	20	1713	75	22.53	–	10	34	–	15391	5646	147	38.40	7-78	6	–
Emmett, G.M.	1948	1948	1	2	0	10	10	5.00	–	–	–	–	–						
Emmett, T.	1876–77	1881–82	7	13†	1	160	48	13.33	–	–	9	–	728†	284	9	31.55	7-68	1	–
Evans, A.J.	1921	1921	1	2	0	18	14	9.00	–	–	–	–	–						
Evans, T.G.	1946	1959	91	133	14	2439	104	20.49	2	8	173	46	–						
Fagg, A.E.	1936	1939	5	8	0	150	39	18.75	–	–	5	–	–					–	
Fairbrother, N.H.	1987	1992–93	10	15†	1	219	83	15.64	–	1	4	–	12†	9	0	–	–	–	
Fane, F.L.	1905–06	1909–10	14	27	1	682	143	26.23	1	3	6	–	–						
Farnes, K.	1934	1938–39	15	17	5	58	20	4.83	–	–	1	–	3932	1719	60	28.65	6-96	3	1
Farrimond, W.	1930–31	1935	4	7	0	116	35	16.57	–	–	5	2	–						
Fender, P.G.H.	1920–21	1929	13	21	1	380	60	19.00	–	2	14	–	2178	1185	29	40.86	5-90	2	1
Ferris, J.J. ‡	1891–92	1891–92	1	1†	0	16	16	16.00	–	–	–	–	272†	91	13	7.00	7-37	2	1
Fielder, A.	1903–04	1907–08	6	12	5	78	20	11.14	–	–	4	–	1491	711	26	27.34	6-82	1	–
Finn, S.T.	2009–10	2013	23	29	14	169	56	11.26	–	1	6	–	4348	2646	90	29.40	6-125	4	–
Fishlock, L.B.	1936	1946–47	4	5†	1	47	19*	11.75	–	–	1	–	–						
Flavell, J.A.	1961	1964	4	6†	2	31	14	7.75	–	–	–	–	792	367	7	52.42	2-65	–	–
Fletcher, K.W.R.	1968	1981–82	59	96	14	3272	216	39.90	7	19	54	–	285	193	2	96.50	1-6	–	–
Flintoff, A. ‡	1998	2009	78	128	9	3795	167	31.89	5	26	52	–	14747	7303	219	33.34	5-58	3	–
Flowers, W.	1884–85	1893	8	14	0	254	56	18.14	–	1	2	–	858	296	14	21.14	5-46	1	–

	First Test	Last Test	Tests	Inns	NO	Runs	HS	Avge	100	50	Ct	St	Balls	Runs	Wkts	Avge	BB	5wI	10wM
Ford, F.G.J.	1894-95	1894-95	5	9†	0	168	48	18.66	–	–	5	–	204†	129	1	129.00	1-47	–	–
Foster, F.R.	1911-12	1912	11	15	1	330	71	23.57	–	3	11	–	2447†	926	45	20.57	6-91	4	–
Foster, J.S.	2001-02	2002-03	7	12	3	226	48	25.11	–	–	17	1	–						
Foster, N.A.	1983	1993	29	45	7	446	39	11.73	–	1	7	–	6261	2891	88	32.85	8-107	5	1
Foster, R.E.	1903-04	1907	8	14	1	602	287	46.30	1	1	13	–	–						
Fothergill, A.J.	1888-89	1888-89	2	2†	0	33	32	16.50	–	–	–	–	321†	90	8	11.25	4-19	–	–
Fowler, G.	1982	1984-85	21	37†	15	1307	201	35.32	3	8	10	–	18	11	0	–	–	–	–
Fraser, A.R.C.	1989	1998-99	46	67	15	388	32	7.46	–	1	9	–	10876	4836	177	27.32	8-53	13	2
Freeman, A.P.	1924-25	1929	12	16	5	154	50*	14.00	–	1	4	–	3732	1707	66	25.86	7-71	5	3
French, B.N.	1986	1987-88	16	21	4	308	59	18.11	–	1	38	1	–						
Fry, C.B.	1895-96	1912	26	41	3	1223	144	32.18	2	7	17	–	10	3	0	–	–	–	–
Gallian, J.E.R.	1995	1995-96	3	6	0	74	28	12.33	–	–	1	–	84	62	0	–	–	–	–
Gatting, M.W.	1977-78	1994-95	79	138	14	4409	207	35.55	10	21	59	–	752	317	4	79.25	1-14	–	–
Gay, L.H.	1894-95	1894-95	1	2	0	37	33	18.50	–	–	3	1	–						
Geary, G.	1924	1934	14	20	4	249	66	15.56	–	2	13	–	3810	1353	46	29.41	7-70	4	1
Gibb, P.A.	1938-39	1946-47	8	13	0	581	120	44.69	2	3	3	1	–						
Giddins, E.S.H.	1999	2000	4	7	3	10	7	2.50	–	–	–	–	444	240	12	20.00	5-15	1	–
Gifford, N.	1964	1973	15	20†	9	179	25*	16.27	–	–	8	–	3084†	1026	33	31.09	5-55	1	–
Giles, A.F.	1998	2006-07	54	81	13	1421	59	20.89	–	4	33	–	12180†	5806	143	40.60	5-57	5	1
Gilligan, A.E.R.	1922-23	1924-25	11	16	3	209	39*	16.07	–	–	3	–	2404	1046	36	29.05	6-7	2	1
Gilligan, A.H.H.	1929-30	1929-30	4	4	0	71	32	17.75	–	–	–	–	–						
Gimblett, H.	1936	1939	3	5	1	129	67*	32.25	–	1	1	–	–						
Gladwin, C.	1947	1949	8	11	5	170	51*	28.33	–	1	2	–	2129	571	15	38.06	3-21	–	–
Goddard, T.W.J.	1930	1939	8	5	3	13	8	6.50	–	–	3	–	1563	588	22	26.72	6-29	1	–
Gooch, G.A.	1975	1994-95	118	215	6	8900	333	42.58	20	46	103	–	2655	1069	23	46.47	3-39	–	–
Gough, D.	1994	2003	58	86	18	855	65	12.57	–	2	13	–	11821	6503	229	28.39	6-42	9	–
Gover, A.R.	1936	1946	4	1	0	2	2*	–	–	–	1	–	816	359	8	44.87	3-85	–	–
Gower, D.I.	1978	1992	117	204†	18	8231	215	44.25	18	39	74	–	36	20	1	20.00	1-1	–	–
Grace, E.M.	1880	1880	1	2	0	36	36	18.00	–	–	1	–	–						
Grace, G.F.	1880	1880	1	2	0	0	0	0.00	–	–	2	–	–						
Grace, W.G.	1880	1899	22	36	2	1098	170	32.29	2	5	39	–	666	236	9	26.22	2-12	–	–
Graveney, T.W.	1951	1969	79	123	13	4882	258	44.38	11	20	80	–	260	167	1	167.00	1-34	–	–
Greenhough, T.	1959	1960	4	4	1	4	2	1.33	–	–	1	–	1129	357	16	22.31	5-35	1	–
Greenwood, A.	1876-77	1876-77	2	4	0	77	49	19.25	–	–	2	–	–						
Greig, A.W.	1972	1977	58	93	4	3599	148	40.43	8	20	87	–	9802	4541	141	32.20	8-86	6	2
Greig, I.A.	1982	1982	2	4	0	26	14	6.50	–	–	–	–	188	114	4	28.50	4-53	–	–
Grieve, B.A.F.	1888-89	1888-89	2	3	2	40	14*	40.00	–	–	–	–	–						

215

INDIVIDUAL CAREER RECORDS – ENGLAND continued

| | | | | BATTING AND FIELDING | | | | | | | | | | BOWLING | | | | | |
	First Test	Last Test	Tests	Inns	NO	Runs	HS	Avge	100	50	Ct	St	Balls	Runs	Wkts	Avge	BB	5wI	10wM
Griffith, S.C.	1947-48	1948-49	3	5	0	157	140	31.40	1	–	5	–	12	8	0	–	–	–	–
Gunn, G.	1907-08	1929-30	15	29	1	1120	122*	40.00	2	7	15	–	999†	387	18	21.50	5-76	1	–
Gunn, J.R.	1901-02	1905	6	10†	2	85	24	10.62	–	1	3	–	–	–	–	–	–	–	–
Gunn, W.	1886-87	1899	11	20	2	392	102*	21.77	1	1	5	–	–	–	–	–	–	–	–
Habib, A.	1999	1999	2	3	0	26	19	8.66	–	–	–	–	–	–	–	–	–	–	–
Haig, N.E.	1921	1929-30	5	9	0	126	47	14.00	–	–	4	–	1026	448	13	34.46	3-73	–	–
Haigh, S.	1898-99	1912	11	18	3	113	25	7.53	–	–	8	–	1294	622	24	25.91	6-11	1	1
Hallows, C.	1921	1928	2	2†	1	42	26	42.00	–	–	–	–	–	–	–	–	–	–	–
Hamilton, G.M.	1999-2000	1999-2000	1	2†	0	0	0	0.00	–	–	–	–	90	63	0	–	–	–	–
Hammond, W.R.	1927-28	1946-47	85	140	16	7249	336*	58.45	22	24	110	–	7969	3138	83	37.80	5-36	2	–
Hampshire, J.H.	1969	1975	8	16	1	403	107	26.86	1	2	9	–	–	–	–	–	–	–	–
Hardinge, H.T.W.	1921	1921	1	2	0	30	25	15.00	–	–	1	–	–	–	–	–	–	–	–
Hardstaff, J., sen.	1907-08	1907-08	5	10	0	311	72	31.10	–	3	1	–	–	–	–	–	–	–	–
Hardstaff, J., jun.	1935	1948	23	38	3	1636	205*	46.74	4	10	9	–	–	–	–	–	–	–	–
Harmison, S.J. ‡	2002	2009	62	84	23	742	49*	12.16	–	1	7	–	13192	7091	222	31.94	7-12	8	1
Harris, Lord	1878-79	1884	4	6	1	145	52	29.00	–	1	2	–	32	29	0	–	–	–	–
Hartley, J.C.	1905-06	1905-06	2	4	0	15	9	3.75	–	–	2	–	192	115	1	115.00	1-62	–	–
Hawke, Lord	1895-96	1898-99	5	8	1	55	30	7.85	–	–	3	–	–	–	–	–	–	–	–
Hayes, E.G.	1905-06	1912	5	9	1	86	35	10.75	–	–	2	–	90	52	1	52.00	1-28	–	–
Hayes, F.C.	1973	1976	9	17	1	244	106*	15.25	1	–	7	–	–	–	–	–	–	–	–
Hayward, T.W.	1895-96	1909	35	60	2	1999	137	34.46	3	12	19	–	893	514	14	36.71	4-22	–	–
Headley, D.W.	1997	1999	15	26	4	186	31	8.45	–	–	7	–	3026	1671	60	27.85	6-60	1	–
Hearne, A.	1891-92	1891-92	1	1	0	9	9	9.00	–	–	1	–	–	–	–	–	–	–	–
Hearne, F. ‡	1888-89	1888-89	2	2	0	47	27	23.50	–	–	1	–	–	–	–	–	–	–	–
Hearne, G.G.	1891-92	1891-92	1	1†	0	0	0	0.00	–	–	–	–	–	–	–	–	–	–	–
Hearne, J.T.	1891-92	1899	12	18	4	126	40	9.00	–	–	4	–	2976	1082	49	22.08	6-41	4	1
Hearne, J.W.	1911-12	1926	24	36	5	806	114	26.00	1	2	13	–	2926	1462	30	48.73	5-49	1	–
Hegg, W.K.	1998-99	1998-99	2	4	4	30	15	7.50	–	–	8	–	–	–	–	–	–	–	–
Hemmings, E.E.	1982	1990-91	16	21	4	383	95	22.52	–	2	5	–	4437	1825	43	42.44	6-58	1	–
Hendren, E.H.	1920-21	1934-35	51	83	9	3525	205*	47.63	7	21	33	–	47	31	1	31.00	1-27	–	–
Hendrick, M.	1974	1981	30	35	15	128	15	6.40	–	–	25	–	6208	2248	87	25.83	4-28	–	–
Heseltine, C.	1895-96	1895-96	2	2	0	18	18	9.00	–	–	3	–	157	84	5	16.80	5-38	1	–
Hick, G.A.	1991	2000-01	65	114	6	3383	178	31.32	6	18	90	–	3057	1306	23	56.78	4-126	–	–
Higgs, K.	1965	1968	15	19†	3	185	63	11.56	–	1	4	–	4112	1473	71	20.74	6-91	2	–
Hill, A.	1876-77	1876-77	2	4	2	101	49	50.50	–	1	1	–	340	130	7	18.57	4-27	–	–
Hill, A.J.L.	1895-96	1895-96	3	4	0	251	124	62.75	1	1	1	–	40	8	4	2.00	4-8	–	–
Hilton, M.J.	1950	1951-52	4	6	1	37	15	7.40	–	–	1	–	1244†	477	14	34.07	5-61	1	–

INDIVIDUAL CAREER RECORDS – ENGLAND *continued*

						BATTING AND FIELDING								BOWLING					
	First Test	Last Test	Tests	Inns	NO	Runs	HS	Avge	100	50	Ct	St	Balls	Runs	Wkts	Avge	BB	5wI	10wM
Hirst, G.H.	1897–98	1909	24	38	3	790	85	22.57	–	5	18	–	4010†	1770	59	30.00	5-48	3	–
Hitch, J.W.	1911–12	1921	7	10	3	103	51*	14.71	–	1	4	–	462	325	7	46.42	2-31	–	–
Hobbs, J.B.	1907–08	1930	61	102	7	5410	211	56.94	15	28	17	–	376	165	1	165.00	1-19	–	–
Hobbs, R.N.S.	1967	1971	7	8	3	34	15*	6.80	–	–	8	–	1291	481	12	40.08	3-25	–	–
Hoggard, M.J.	2000	2007–08	67	92	27	473	38	7.27	–	–	24	–	13909	7564	248	30.50	7-61	7	1
Hollies, W.E.	1934–35	1950	13	15	8	37	18*	5.28	–	–	2	–	3554	1332	44	30.27	7-50	5	–
Hollioake, A.J.	1997	1997–98	4	6	0	65	45	10.83	–	–	4	–	144	67	2	33.50	2-31	–	–
Hollioake, B.C.	1997	1998	2	4	0	44	28	11.00	–	–	2	–	252	199	4	49.75	2-105	–	–
Holmes, E.R.T.	1934–35	1935	5	9	2	114	85*	16.28	–	1	4	–	108	76	2	38.00	1-10	–	–
Holmes, P.	1921	1932	7	14	1	357	88	27.46	–	4	3	–	–						
Hone, L.	1878–79	1878–79	1	2	0	13	7	6.50	–	–	2	3							
Hopwood, J.L.	1934	1934	2	3	1	12	8	6.00	–	–	2	–	462†	155	0	–	–	–	–
Hornby, A.N.	1878–79	1884	3	6	0	21	9	3.50	–	–	–	–	28	0	1	0.00	1-0	–	–
Horton, M.J.	1959	1959	2	2	0	60	58	30.00	–	1	2	–	238	59	2	29.50	2-24	–	–
Howard, N.D.	1951–52	1951–52	4	6	1	86	23	17.20	–	–	4	–	–						
Howell, H.	1920–21	1924	5	8	6	15	5	7.50	–	–	–	–	918	559	7	79.85	4-115	–	–
Howorth, R.	1947	1947–48	5	10†	2	145	45*	18.12	–	–	2	–	1536†	635	19	33.42	6-124	1	–
Humphries, J.	1907–08	1907–08	3	6	1	44	16	8.80	–	–	7	–	–						
Hunter, J.	1884–85	1884–85	5	7	2	93	39*	18.60	–	–	8	3	–						
Hussain, N.	1989–90	2004	96	171	16	5764	207	37.18	14	33	67	–	30	15	0	–	–	–	–
Hutchings, K.L.	1907–08	1909	7	12	0	341	126	28.41	1	1	9	–	90	81	1	81.00	1-5	–	–
Hutton, L.	1937	1954–55	79	138	15	6971	364	56.67	19	33	57	–	260	232	3	77.33	1-2	–	–
Hutton, R.A.	1971	1971	5	8	2	219	81	36.50	–	2	9	–	738	257	9	28.55	3-72	–	–
Iddon, J.	1934–35	1935	5	7	1	170	73	28.33	–	2	–	–	66†	27	0	–	–	–	–
Igglesden, A.P.	1989	1993–94	3	5	3	6	3*	3.00	–	–	1	–	555	329	6	54.83	2-91	–	–
Ikin, J.T.	1946	1955	18	31†	3	606	60	20.89	–	3	31	–	572	354	3	118.00	1-38	–	–
Illingworth, R.	1958	1973	61	90	11	1836	113	23.24	2	5	45	–	11934	3807	122	31.20	6-29	3	–
Illingworth, R.K.	1991	1995–96	9	14	7	128	28	18.28	–	–	5	–	1485†	615	19	32.36	4-96	–	–
Ilott, M.C.	1993	1995–96	5	6	2	28	15	7.00	–	–	–	–	1042†	542	12	45.16	3-48	–	–
Insole, D.J.	1950	1957	9	17	1	408	110*	27.20	1	1	8	–	–						
Irani, R.C.	1996	1999	3	5	0	86	41	17.20	–	–	2	–	192	112	3	37.33	1-22	–	–
Jackman, R.D.	1980–81	1982	4	6	0	42	17	7.00	–	–	–	–	1070	445	14	31.78	4-110	–	–
Jackson, Hon. F.S.	1893	1905	20	33	4	1415	144*	48.79	5	6	10	–	1587	799	24	33.29	5-52	1	–
Jackson, H.L.	1949	1961	2	2	1	15	8	15.00	–	–	1	–	498	155	7	22.14	2-26	–	–
James, S.P.	1998	1998	2	4	0	71	36	17.75	–	–	–	–	–						
Jameson, J.A.	1971	1973–74	4	8	0	214	82	26.75	–	1	–	–	42	17	1	17.00	1-17	–	–

INDIVIDUAL CAREER RECORDS – ENGLAND *continued*

	First Test	Last Test	Tests	Inns	NO	Runs	HS	Avge	100	50	Ct	St	Balls	Runs	Wkts	Avge	BB	5wI	10wM
						BATTING AND FIELDING									*BOWLING*				
Jardine, D.R.	1928	1933–34	22	33	6	1296	127	48.00	1	10	26	–	6	10	0	–	–	–	–
Jarvis, P.W.	1987–88	1992–93	9	15	2	132	29*	10.15	–	–	2	–	1912	965	21	45.95	4-107	–	–
Jenkins, R.O.	1948–49	1952	9	12	1	198	39	18.00	–	–	4	–	2118	1098	32	34.31	5-116	1	–
Jessop, G.L.	1899	1912	18	26	0	569	104	21.88	1	3	11	–	732	354	10	35.40	4-68	–	–
Johnson, R.L.	2003	2003–04	3	4	0	59	26	14.75	–	–	–	–	547	275	16	17.18	6-33	2	–
Jones, A.O.	1899	1909	12	21	0	291	34	13.85	–	–	15	–	228	133	3	44.33	3-73	–	–
Jones, G.O.	2003–04	2006–07	34	53	4	1172	100	23.91	1	6	128	5	–	–	–	–	–	–	–
Jones, I.J.	1963–64	1967–68	15	17	9	38	16	4.75	–	–	4	–	3546†	1769	44	40.20	6-118	1	–
Jones, S.P.	2002	2005	18	18†	5	205	44	15.76	–	–	4	–	2821	1666	59	28.23	6-53	3	–
Jordan, C.J.	2014	2014	5	6	0	125	35	20.83	–	1	8	–	906	496	15	33.06	4-18	–	–
Jupp, H.	1876–77	1876–77	2	4	0	68	63	17.00	–	1	2	–	–	–	–	–	–	–	–
Jupp, V.W.C.	1921	1928	8	13	1	208	38	17.33	–	–	5	–	1301	616	28	22.00	4-37	–	–
Keeton, W.W.	1934	1939	2	4	0	57	25	14.25	–	–	–	–	–	–	–	–	–	–	–
Kennedy, A.S.	1922–23	1922–23	5	8	2	93	41*	15.50	–	–	5	–	1683	599	31	19.32	5-76	2	–
Kenyon, D.	1951–52	1955	8	15	0	192	87	12.80	–	1	5	–	–	–	–	–	–	–	–
Kerrigan, S.C.	2013	2013	1	1	0	1	1*	–	–	–	–	–	48†	53	0	–	–	–	–
Key, R.W.T.	2002	2004–05	15	26	1	775	221	31.00	1	3	11	–	–	–	–	–	–	–	–
Khan, A.	2008–09	2008–09	1	–	–	–	–	–	–	–	–	–	174	122	1	122.00	1-111	–	–
Killick, E.T.	1929	1929	2	4	0	81	31	20.25	–	–	2	–	–	–	–	–	–	–	–
Kilner, R.	1924	1926	9	8†	1	233	74	33.28	–	2	6	–	2368†	734	24	30.58	4-51	–	–
King, J.H.	1909	1909	1	2†	0	64	60	32.00	–	1	–	–	162†	99	1	99.00	1-99	–	–
Kinneir, S.	1911–12	1911–12	1	2†	0	52	30	26.00	–	–	–	–	–	–	–	–	–	–	–
Kirtley, R.J.	2003	2003–04	4	7	1	32	12	5.33	–	–	3	–	1079	561	19	29.52	6-34	1	–
Knight, A.E.	1903–04	1903–04	3	6	1	81	70*	16.20	–	1	1	–	–	–	–	–	–	–	–
Knight, B.R.	1961–62	1969	29	38	7	812	127	26.19	2	2	14	–	5377	2223	70	31.75	4-38	–	–
Knight, D.J.	1921	1921	2	4	0	54	38	13.50	–	–	1	–	–	–	–	–	–	–	–
Knight, N.V.	1995	2001	17	30†	0	719	113	23.96	1	4	26	–	–	–	–	–	–	–	–
Knott, A.P.E.	1967	1981	95	149	15	4389	135	32.75	5	30	250	19	–	–	–	–	–	–	–
Knox, N.A.	1907	1907	2	4	1	24	8*	8.00	–	–	–	–	126	105	3	35.00	2-39	–	–
Laker, J.C.	1947–48	1958–59	46	63	15	676	63	14.08	–	2	12	–	12027	4101	193	21.24	10-53	9	3
Lamb, A.J.	1982	1992	79	139	10	4656	142	36.09	14	18	75	–	30	23	1	23.00	1-6	–	–
Langridge, J.	1933	1946	8	9†	1	242	70	26.88	–	1	6	–	1074†	413	19	21.73	7-56	2	–
Larkins, W.	1979–80	1990–91	13	25	1	493	64	20.54	–	3	8	–	–	–	–	–	–	–	–
Larter, J.D.F.	1962	1965	10	7	2	16	10	3.20	–	–	5	–	2172	941	37	25.43	5-57	2	–
Larwood, H.	1926	1932–33	21	28	3	485	98	19.40	–	2	15	–	4969	2212	78	28.35	6-32	4	1
Lathwell, M.N.	1993	1993	2	4	0	78	33	19.50	–	–	–	–	–	–	–	–	–	–	–

	First Test	Last Test	Tests	BATTING AND FIELDING									BOWLING						
				Inns	NO	Runs	HS	Avge	100	50	Ct	St	Balls	Runs	Wkts	Avge	BB	5wI	10wM
Lawrence, D.V.	1988	1991-92	5	6	0	60	34	10.00	–	–	–	–	1089	676	18	37.55	5-106	1	–
Leadbeater, E.	1951-52	1951-52	2	2	0	40	38	20.00	–	–	3	–	289	218	2	109.00	1-38	–	–
Lee, H.W.	1930-31	1930-31	1	2	0	19	18	9.50	–	–	–	–						–	–
Lees, W.S.	1905-06	1905-06	5	9	3	66	25*	11.00	–	–	2	–	1256	467	26	17.96	6-78	2	–
Legge, G.B.	1927-28	1929-30	5	7	1	299	196	49.83	1	1	1	–	30	34	0	–	–	–	–
Leslie, C.F.H.	1882-83	1882-83	4	7	0	106	54	15.14	–	1	1	–	96	44	4	11.00	3-31	–	–
Lever, J.K.	1986	1986	21	31	5	306	53	11.76	–	1	11	–	4433†	1951	73	26.72	7-46	3	1
Lever, P.	1970-71	1975	17	18	2	350	88*	21.87	–	2	11	–	3571	1509	41	36.80	6-38	2	–
Leveson Gower, H.D.G.	1909-10	1909-10	3	6	2	95	31	23.75	–	–	1	–						–	–
Levett, W.H.V.	1933-34	1933-34	1	2	1	7	5	7.00	–	–	3	–						–	–
Lewis, A.R.	1972-73	1973	9	16	2	457	125	32.64	1	3	–	–						–	–
Lewis, C.C.	1990	1996	32	51	3	1105	117	23.02	1	4	25	–	6852	3490	93	37.52	6-111	3	–
Lewis, J.	2006	2006	1	2	0	27	20	13.50	–	–	–	–	246	122	3	40.66	3-68	–	–
Leyland, M.	1928	1938	41	65†	5	2764	187	46.06	9	10	13	–	1103†	585	6	97.50	3-91	–	–
Lilley, A.F.A.	1896	1909	35	52	8	903	84	20.52	–	4	70	22	25	23	1	23.00	1-23	–	–
Lillywhite, J.	1876-77	1876-77	2	3†	1	16	10	8.00	–	–	1	–	340†	126	8	15.75	4-70	–	–
Lloyd, D.	1974	1974-75	9	15†	2	552	214*	42.46	1	–	11	–	24†	17	0	–	–	–	–
Lloyd, T.A.	1984	1984	1	1†	1	10	10*	–	–	–	–	–						–	–
Loader, P.J.	1954	1958-59	13	19	6	76	17	5.84	–	–	2	–	2662	878	39	22.51	6-36	1	–
Lock, G.A.R.	1952	1967-68	49	63	9	742	89	13.74	–	3	59	–	13147†	4451	174	25.58	7-35	9	3
Lockwood, W.H.	1893	1902	12	16	3	231	52*	17.76	–	1	4	–	1973	883	43	20.53	7-71	5	1
Lohmann, G.A.	1886	1896	18	26	2	213	62*	8.87	–	1	28	–	3830	1205	112	10.75	9-28	9	5
Lowson, F.A.	1951	1955	7	13	0	245	68	18.84	–	2	5	–						–	–
Lucas, A.P.	1878-79	1884	5	9	1	157	55	19.62	–	1	1	–	120	54	0	–	–	–	–
Luckhurst, B.W.	1970-71	1974-75	21	41	5	1298	131	36.05	4	5	14	–	57†	32	1	32.00	1-9	–	–
Lyttelton, Hon. A.	1880	1884	4	7	1	94	31	15.66	–	–	2	–	48	19	4	4.75	4-19	–	–
Macaulay, G.G.	1922-23	1933	8	10	4	112	76	18.66	–	1	5	–	1701	662	24	27.58	5-64	1	–
MacBryan, J.C.W.	1924	1924	1	–	–	–	–	–	–	–	–	–						–	–
McCague, M.J.	1993	1994-95	3	5	0	21	11	4.20	–	–	1	–	593	390	6	65.00	4-121	–	–
McConnon, J.E.	1954	1954	2	3	1	18	11	9.00	–	–	4	–	216	74	4	18.50	3-19	–	–
McGahey, C.P.	1901-02	1901-02	2	4	0	38	18	9.50	–	–	1	–						–	–
McGrath, A.	2003	2003	4	5	0	201	81	40.20	–	2	3	–	102	56	4	14.00	3-16	–	–
MacGregor, G.	1890	1893	8	11	3	96	31	12.00	–	–	14	3						–	–
McIntyre, A.J.W.	1950	1955	3	6	0	19	7	3.16	–	–	8	–						–	–
MacKinnon, F.A.	1878-79	1878-79	1	2	0	5	5	2.50	–	–	–	–						–	–
MacLaren, A.C.	1894-95	1909	35	61	4	1931	140	33.87	5	8	29	–						–	–
McMaster, J.E.P.	1888-89	1888-89	1	1	0	0	0	0.00	–	–	–	–						–	–

INDIVIDUAL CAREER RECORDS – ENGLAND continued

	First Test	Last Test	Tests	Inns	NO	Runs	HS	Avge	100	50	Ct	St	Balls	Runs	Wkts	Avge	BB	5wI	10wM
Maddy, D.L.	1999	1999–2000	3	4	0	46	24	11.50	–	–	4	–	84	40	0	–	–	–	–
Mahmood, S.I.	2006	2006–07	8	11	1	81	34	8.10	–	–	–	–	1130	762	20	38.10	4-22	–	–
Makepeace, J.W.H.	1920–21	1920–21	4	8	0	279	117	34.87	1	2	–	–	–	–	–	–	–	–	–
Malcolm, D.E.	1989	1997	40	58	19	236	29	6.05	–	–	7	–	8480	4748	128	37.09	9-57	5	2
Mallender, N.A.	1992	1992	2	3	2	8	4	2.66	–	–	–	–	449	215	10	21.50	5-50	1	–
Mann, F.G.	1948–49	1949	7	12	2	376	136*	37.60	1	2	3	–	–	–	–	–	–	–	–
Mann, F.T.	1922–23	1922–23	5	9	1	281	84	35.12	–	2	4	–	–	–	–	–	–	–	–
Marks, V.J.	1982	1983–84	6	10	1	249	83	27.66	–	3	1	–	1082	484	11	44.00	3-78	–	–
Marriott, C.S.	1933	1933	1	1	0	0	0	0.00	–	–	1	–	247	96	11	8.72	6-59	2	1
Martin, F.	1890	1891–92	2	2†	0	14	13	7.00	–	–	2	–	410†	141	14	10.07	6-50	2	1
Martin, J.W.	1947	1947	1	2	0	26	26	13.00	–	–	–	–	270	129	1	129.00	1-111	–	–
Martin, P.J.	1995	1997	8	13	0	115	29	8.84	–	–	6	–	1452	580	17	34.11	4-60	–	–
Mason, J.R.	1897–98	1897–98	5	10	0	129	32	12.90	–	–	3	–	324	149	2	74.50	1-8	–	–
Matthews, A.D.G.	1937	1937	1	1	1	2	2*	–	–	–	1	–	180	65	2	32.50	1-13	–	–
May, P.B.H.	1951	1961	66	106	9	4537	285*	46.77	13	22	42	–	–						
Maynard, M.P.	1988	1993–94	4	8	0	87	35	10.87	–	–	3	–	–						
Mead, C.P.	1911–12	1928–29	17	26†	2	1185	182*	49.37	4	3	4	–	–						
Mead, W.	1899	1899	1	2	0	7	7	3.50	–	–	1	–	265	91	1	91.00	1-91	–	–
Midwinter, W.E. ‡	1881–82	1881–82	4	7	0	95	36	13.57	–	2	5	–	776	272	10	27.20	4-81	–	–
Milburn, C.	1966	1968–69	9	16	2	654	139	46.71	2	2	7	–	–						
Miller, A.M.	1895–96	1895–96	1	2	2	24	20*	–	–	–	–	–	–						
Miller, G.	1976	1984	34	51	4	1213	98*	25.80	–	7	17	–	5149	1859	60	30.98	5-44	1	–
Milligan, F.W.	1898–99	1898–99	2	4	0	58	38	14.50	–	–	1	–	45	29	0	–	–	–	–
Millman, G.	1961–62	1962	6	7	2	60	32*	12.00	–	–	13	2	–						
Milton, C.A.	1958	1959	6	9	1	204	104*	25.50	1	–	5	–	24	12	0	–	–	–	–
Mitchell, A.	1933–34	1936	6	10	0	298	72	29.80	–	2	9	–	6	4	0	–	–	–	–
Mitchell, F. ‡	1898–99	1898–99	2	4	0	88	41	22.00	–	–	2	–	–						
Mitchell, T.B.	1932–33	1935	5	6	2	20	9	5.00	–	–	1	–	894	498	8	62.25	2-49	–	–
Mitchell-Innes, N.S.	1935	1935	1	1	0	5	5	5.00	–	–	–	–	–						
Mold, A.W.	1893	1893	3	3	1	0	0*	0.00	–	–	1	–	491	234	7	33.42	3-44	–	–
Moon, L.J.	1905–06	1905–06	4	8	0	182	36	22.75	–	–	4	–	–						
Morgan, E.J.G.	2010	2011–12	16	24†	1	700	130	30.43	2	3	11	–	–						
Morley, F.	1880	1882–83	4	6†	2	6	2*	1.50	–	–	4	–	972†	296	16	18.50	5-56	1	–
Morris, H.	1991	1991	3	6†	0	115	44	19.16	–	–	3	–	–						
Morris, J.E.	1990	1990	3	5	2	71	32	23.66	–	–	3	–	–						
Mortimore, J.B.	1958–59	1964	9	12	2	243	73*	24.30	–	1	3	–	2162	733	13	56.38	3-36	–	–
Moss, A.E.	1953–54	1960	9	7	1	61	26	10.16	–	–	1	–	1657	626	21	29.80	4-35	–	–
Moxon, M.D.	1986	1989	10	17	1	455	99	28.43	–	3	10	–	48	30	0	–	–	–	–

INDIVIDUAL CAREER RECORDS – ENGLAND *continued*

	First Test	Last Test	Tests	Inns	NO	Runs	HS	Avge	100	50	Ct	St	Balls	Runs	Wkts	Avge	BB	5wI	10wM
						BATTING AND FIELDING										*BOWLING*			
Mullally, A.D.	1996	2001	19	27	4	127	24	5.52	–	–	6	–	4525†	1812	58	31.24	5-105	1	–
Munton, T.A.	1992	1992	2	2	1	25	25*	25.00	–	–	–	–	405	200	4	50.00	2-22	–	–
Murdoch, W.L. ‡	1891-92	1891-92	1	1	0	12	12	12.00	–	–	–	1	–						
Murray, J.T.	1961	1967	21	28	5	506	112	22.00	1	2	52	3	–						
Newham, W.	1887-88	1887-88	1	2	0	26	17	13.00	–	–	–	–	–	–					
Newport, P.J.	1988	1990-91	3	5	1	110	40*	27.50	–	–	1	–	669	417	10	41.70	4-87	–	–
Nichols, M.S.	1929-30	1939	14	19†	7	355	78*	29.58	–	2	11	–	2565	1152	41	28.09	6-35	2	–
Oakman, A.S.M.	1956	1956	2	2	0	14	10	7.00	–	–	7	–	48	21	0	–	–	–	–
O'Brien, T.C.	1884	1895-96	5	8	0	59	20	7.37	–	–	4	–	–						
O'Connor, J.	1929	1929-30	4	7	0	153	51	21.85	–	1	2	–	162	72	1	72.00	1-31	–	–
Old, C.M.	1972-73	1981	46	66†	9	845	65	14.82	–	2	22	–	8858	4020	143	28.11	7-50	4	–
Oldfield, N.	1939	1939	1	2	0	99	80	49.50	–	1	–	–	–						
Onions, G.	2009	2012	9	10	7	30	17*	10.00	–	–	–	–	1606	957	32	29.90	5-38	1	–
Ormond, J.	2001	2001-02	2	4	1	38	18	12.66	–	–	–	–	372	185	2	92.50	1-70	–	–
Padgett, D.E.V.	1960	1960	2	4	0	51	31	12.75	–	–	–	–	12	8	0	–	–	–	–
Paine, G.A.E.	1934-35	1934-35	4	7	1	97	49	16.16	–	–	5	–	1044†	467	17	27.47	5-168	1	–
Palairet, L.C.H.	1902	1902	2	4	0	49	20	12.25	–	–	2	–	–						
Palmer, C.H.	1953-54	1953-54	1	1	0	22	22	11.00	–	–	–	–	30	15	0	–	–	–	–
Palmer, K.E.	1964-65	1964-65	1	1	0	10	10	10.00	–	–	–	–	378	189	1	189.00	1-113	–	–
Panesar, M.S.	2005-06	2013-14	50	68†	23	220	26	4.88	–	–	10	–	12475†	5797	167	34.71	6-37	12	2
Parfitt, P.H.	1961-62	1972	37	52†	6	1882	131*	40.91	7	6	42	–	1326	574	12	47.83	2-5	–	–
Parker, C.W.L.	1921	1921	1	1	1	3	3*	–	–	–	–	–	168†	32	2	16.00	2-32	–	–
Parker, P.W.G.	1981	1981	1	2	0	13	13	6.50	–	–	–	–	–						
Parkhouse, W.G.A.	1950	1959	7	13	0	373	78	28.69	–	2	3	–	–						
Parkin, C.H.	1920-21	1924	10	16	3	160	36	12.30	–	–	3	–	2095	1128	32	35.25	5-38	2	–
Parks, J.H.	1937	1937	1	2	0	29	22	14.50	–	–	–	–	126	36	3	12.00	2-26	–	–
Parks, J.M.	1954	1967-68	46	68	7	1962	108*	32.16	2	9	103	11	54	51	1	51.00	1-43	–	–
Pataudi, Nawab of, sen. ‡	1932-33	1934	3	5	0	144	102	28.80	1	–	–	–	–						
Patel, M.M.	1996	1996	2	2	0	45	27	22.50	–	–	2	–	276†	180	1	180.00	1-101	–	–
Patel, S.R.	2011-12	2012-13	5	7	0	109	33	15.57	–	–	2	–	606†	257	4	64.25	2-27	–	–
Pattinson, D.J.	2008	2008	1	1	0	21	13	10.50	–	–	–	–	181	96	2	48.00	2-95	–	–
Paynter, E.	1931	1939	20	31†	5	1540	243	59.23	4	7	7	–	–						
Peate, E.	1881-82	1886	9	14†	8	70	13	11.66	–	–	2	–	2096†	683	31	22.03	6-85	2	–
Peebles, I.A.R.	1927-28	1931	13	17	8	98	26	10.88	–	–	5	–	2882	1391	45	30.91	6-63	3	–
Peel, R.	1884-85	1896	20	33†	4	427	83	14.72	–	3	17	–	5216†	1715	101	16.98	7-31	5	1

INDIVIDUAL CAREER RECORDS – ENGLAND continued

	First Test	Last Test	Tests	Inns	NO	Runs	HS	Avge	100	50	Ct	St	BOWLING Balls	Runs	Wkts	Avge	BB	5wI	10wM
Penn, F.	1880	1880	1	2	1	50	27*	50.00	–	–	1	–	12	2	0	–	–	–	–
Perks, R.T.D.	1938–39	1939	2	2†	2	3	2*	–	–	–	1	–	829	355	11	32.27	5-100	2	–
Philipson, H.	1891–92	1894–95	5	8	1	63	30	9.00	–	–	8	3	–	–	–	–	–	–	–
Pietersen, K.P.	2005	2013–14	104	181	8	8181	227	47.28	23	35	62	–	1311	886	10	88.60	3-52	–	–
Pigott, A.C.S.	1983–84	1983–84	1	2	1	12	8*	12.00	–	–	–	–	102	75	2	37.50	2-75	–	–
Pilling, R.	1881–82	1888	8	13	1	91	23	7.58	–	–	10	4	–	–	–	–	–	–	–
Place, W.	1947–48	1947–48	3	6	1	144	107	28.80	1	–	–	–	–	–	–	–	–	–	–
Plunkett, L.E.	2005–06	2014	13	20	5	238	55*	15.86	–	1	3	–	2659	1536	41	37.46	5-64	1	–
Pocock, P.I.	1967–68	1984–85	25	37	4	206	33	6.24	–	–	15	–	6650	2976	67	44.41	6-79	3	–
Pollard, R.	1946	1948	4	3	2	13	10*	13.00	–	–	3	–	1102	378	15	25.20	5-24	1	–
Poole, C.J.	1951–52	1951–52	3	5†	1	161	69*	40.25	–	2	1	–	30†	9	0	–	–	–	–
Pope, G.H.	1947	1947	1	1	1	8	8*	–	–	–	–	–	218	85	1	85.00	1-49	–	–
Pougher, A.D.	1891–92	1891–92	1	1	0	17	17	17.00	–	–	2	–	105	26	3	8.66	3-26	–	–
Price, J.S.E.	1963–64	1972	15	15†	6	66	32	7.33	–	–	7	–	2724	1401	40	35.02	5-73	1	–
Price, W.F.F.	1938	1938	1	2	0	6	6	3.00	–	–	2	–	–	–	–	–	–	–	–
Prideaux, R.M.	1968	1968–69	3	6	1	102	64	20.40	–	1	–	–	12	0	0	–	–	–	–
Pringle, D.R.	1982	1992	30	50	4	695	63	15.10	–	1	10	–	5287	2518	70	35.97	5-95	3	–
Prior, M.J.	2007	2014	79	123	21	4099	131*	40.18	7	28	243	13	–	–	–	–	–	–	–
Pullar, G.	1959	1962–63	28	49†	4	1974	175	43.86	4	12	2	–	66	37	1	37.00	1-1	–	–
Quaife, W.G.	1899	1901–02	7	13	1	228	68	19.00	–	1	4	–	15	6	0	–	–	–	–
Radford, N.V.	1986	1987–88	3	4	1	21	12*	7.00	–	–	–	–	678	351	4	87.75	2-131	–	–
Radley, C.T.	1977–78	1978	8	10	0	481	158	48.10	2	2	4	–	–	–	–	–	–	–	–
Ramprakash, M.R.	1991	2001–02	52	92	6	2350	154	27.32	2	12	39	–	895	477	4	119.25	1-2	–	–
Randall, D.W.	1976–77	1984	47	79	5	2470	174	33.37	7	12	31	–	16	3	0	–	–	–	–
Ranjitsinhji, K.S.	1896	1902	15	26	4	989	175	44.95	2	6	13	–	97	39	1	39.00	1-23	–	–
Rankin, W.B.	2013–14	2013–14	1	2†	0	13	13	6.50	–	–	–	–	125	81	1	81.00	1-47	–	–
Read, C.M.W.	1999	2006–07	15	23	4	360	55	18.94	–	1	48	6	–	–	–	–	–	–	–
Read, H.D.	1935	1935	1	–	–	–	–	–	–	–	–	–	270	200	6	33.33	4-136	–	–
Read, J.M.	1882	1893	17	29	2	461	57	17.07	–	2	8	–	60	63	0	–	–	–	–
Read, W.W.	1882–83	1893	18	27	1	720	117	27.69	1	5	16	–	149	60	2	30.00	1-4	–	–
Reeve, D.A.	1991–92	1991–92	3	5	0	124	59	24.80	–	1	1	–	1764	624	25	24.96	5-85	1	–
Relf, A.E.	1903–04	1913–14	13	21	3	416	63	23.11	–	1	14	–	449	244	9	27.11	4-50	–	–
Rhodes, H.J.	1959	1959	2	1	1	0	0*	–	–	–	–	–	–	–	–	–	–	–	–
Rhodes, S.J.	1994	1994	11	17	5	294	65*	24.50	–	1	46	3	–	–	–	–	–	–	–
Rhodes, W.	1899	1929–30	58	98	21	2325	179	30.19	2	11	60	–	8225†	3425	127	26.96	8-68	6	1
Richards, C.J.	1986–87	1988	8	13	0	285	133	21.92	1	–	20	1	–	–	–	–	–	–	–

INDIVIDUAL CAREER RECORDS – ENGLAND *continued*

				BATTING AND FIELDING									BOWLING						
	First Test	Last Test	Tests	Inns	NO	Runs	HS	Avge	100	50	Ct	St	Balls	Runs	Wkts	Avge	BB	5wI	10wM
Richardson, D.W.	1957	1957	1	1†	0	33	33	33.00	–	–	1	–	120	48	3	16.00	2-10	–	–
Richardson, P.E.	1956	1963	34	56†	1	2061	126	37.47	5	9	6	–	–	–	–	–	–	–	–
Richardson, T.	1893	1897-98	14	24	8	177	25*	11.06	–	–	5	–	4498	2220	88	25.22	8-94	11	4
Richmond, T.L.	1921	1921	1	2	0	6	4	3.00	–	–	–	–	114	86	2	43.00	2-69	–	–
Ridgway, F.	1951-52	1951-52	5	6	0	49	24	8.16	–	–	3	–	793	379	7	54.14	4-83	–	–
Robertson, J.D.B.	1947	1951-52	11	21	2	881	133	46.36	2	6	6	–	138	58	2	29.00	2-17	–	–
Robins, R.W.V.	1929	1937	19	27	4	612	108	26.60	1	4	12	–	3318	1758	64	27.46	6-32	–	–
Robinson, R.T.	1984-85	1989	29	49	5	1601	175	36.38	4	6	8	–	–	–	–	–	–	–	–
Robson, S.D.	2014	2014	7	11	0	336	127	30.54	1	1	5	–	6	0	0	–	–	–	–
Roope, G.R.J.	1972-73	1978	21	32	4	860	77	30.71	–	7	35	–	172	76	0	–	–	–	–
Root, C.F.	1926	1926	3	–	–	–	–	–	–	–	1	–	642	194	8	24.25	4-84	–	–
Root, J.E.	2012-13	2014	22	40	6	1732	200*	50.94	5	7	15	–	510	225	4	56.25	2-9	–	–
Rose, B.C.	1977-78	1980-81	9	16†	2	358	70	25.57	–	2	4	–	16	6	0	–	–	–	–
Royle, V.P.F.A.	1878-79	1878-79	1	2	0	21	18	10.50	–	–	2	–	–	–	–	–	–	–	–
Rumsey, F.E.	1964	1965	5	5	3	30	21*	15.00	–	–	–	–	1145†	461	17	27.11	4-25	–	–
Russell, C.A.G.	1920-21	1922-23	10	18	2	910	140	56.87	5	2	8	–	–	–	–	–	–	–	–
Russell, R.C.	1988	1997-98	54	86†	16	1897	128*	27.10	2	6	153	12	–	–	–	–	–	–	–
Russell, W.E.	1961-62	1967	10	18	1	362	70	21.29	–	2	4	–	144	44	0	–	–	–	–
Saggers, M.J.	2003-04	2004	3	3	0	1	1	0.33	–	–	–	–	493	247	7	35.28	2-29	–	–
Salisbury, I.D.K.	1992	2000-01	15	25	3	368	50	16.72	–	1	5	–	2492	1539	20	76.95	4-163	–	–
Sandham, A.	1921	1929-30	14	23	0	879	325	38.21	2	3	4	–	–	–	–	–	–	–	–
Schofield, C.P.	2000	2000	2	3†	0	67	57	22.33	–	1	–	–	108	73	0	–	–	–	–
Schultz, S.S.	1878-79	1878-79	1	2	1	20	20	20.00	–	–	–	–	34	26	1	26.00	1-16	–	–
Scotton, W.H.	1881-82	1886-87	15	25†	2	510	90	22.17	–	3	4	–	20†	20	0	–	–	–	–
Selby, J.	1876-77	1881-82	6	12	1	256	70	23.27	–	2	1	–	–	–	–	–	–	–	–
Selvey, M.W.W.	1976	1976-77	3	5	3	15	5*	7.50	–	–	1	–	492	343	6	57.16	4-41	–	–
Shackleton, D.	1950	1963	7	13	7	113	42	18.83	–	–	1	–	2078	768	18	42.66	4-72	–	–
Shah, O.A.	2005-06	2008-09	6	10	0	269	88	26.90	–	2	2	–	30	31	0	–	–	–	–
Shahzad, A.	2010	2010	1	1	0	5	5	5.00	–	–	–	–	102	63	4	15.75	3-45	–	–
Sharp, J.	1909	1909	3	6	2	188	105	47.00	1	1	2	–	183†	111	3	37.00	3-67	–	–
Sharpe, J.W.	1890	1891-92	3	6	4	44	26	22.00	–	–	2	–	975	305	11	27.72	6-84	1	–
Sharpe, P.J.	1963	1969	12	21	4	786	111	46.23	1	4	17	–	–	–	–	–	–	–	–
Shaw, A.	1876-77	1881-82	7	12	1	111	40	10.09	–	–	4	–	1096	285	12	23.75	5-38	1	–
Sheppard, D.S.	1950	1962-63	22	33	2	1172	119	37.80	3	6	12	–	–	–	–	–	–	–	–
Sherwin, M.	1886-87	1888	3	6	4	30	21*	15.00	–	–	5	2	–	–	–	–	–	–	–
Shrewsbury, A.	1881-82	1893	23	40	4	1277	164	35.47	3	4	29	–	12	2	0	–	–	–	–
Shuter, J.	1888	1888	1	1	0	28	28	28.00	–	–	–	–	–	–	–	–	–	–	–

INDIVIDUAL CAREER RECORDS – ENGLAND continued

	First Test	Last Test	Tests	Inns	NO	Runs	HS	Avge	100	50	Ct	St	Balls	Runs	Wkts	Avge	BB	5wI	10wM
						BATTING AND FIELDING									BOWLING				
Shuttleworth, K.	1970-71	1971	5	6	0	46	21	7.66	–	–	1	–	1071	427	12	35.58	5-47	1	–
Sidebottom, A.	1985	1985	1	1	0	2	2	2.00	–	–	–	–	112	65	1	65.00	1-65	–	–
Sidebottom, R.J.	2001	2009-10	22	31†	11	313	31	15.65	–	–	5	–	4812†	2231	79	28.24	7-47	5	1
Silverwood, C.E.W.	1996-97	2002-03	6	7	3	29	10	7.25	–	–	2	–	828	444	11	40.36	5-91	1	–
Simpson, R.T.	1948-49	1954-55	27	45	3	1401	156*	33.35	4	6	5	–	45	22	2	11.00	2-4	–	–
Simpson-Hayward, G.H.T.	1909-10	1909-10	5	8	1	105	29*	15.00	–	–	1	–	898	420	23	18.26	6-43	2	–
Sims, J.M.	1935	1936-37	4	4	0	16	12	4.00	–	–	6	–	887	480	11	43.63	5-73	1	–
Sinfield, R.A.	1938	1938	1	1	0	6	6	6.00	–	–	–	–	378	123	2	61.50	1-51	–	–
Slack, W.N.	1985-86	1986	3	6†	0	81	52	13.50	–	1	3	–	–	–	–	–	–	–	–
Smailes, T.F.	1946	1946	1	1†	0	25	25	25.00	–	–	–	–	120	62	3	20.66	3-44	–	–
Small, G.C.	1986	1990-91	17	24	7	263	59	15.47	–	1	9	–	3927	1871	55	34.01	5-48	2	–
Smith, A.C.	1962-63	1962-63	6	7	3	118	69*	29.50	–	1	20	–	–	–	–	–	–	–	–
Smith, A.M.	1997	1997	1	2	1	4	4*	4.00	–	–	–	–	138†	89	0	–	–	–	–
Smith, C.A.	1888-89	1888-89	1	1	0	3	3	3.00	–	–	1	–	154	61	7	8.71	5-19	1	–
Smith, C.I.J.	1934-35	1937	5	10	0	102	27	10.20	–	–	1	–	930	393	15	26.20	5-16	1	–
Smith, C.L.	1983	1986	8	14	1	392	91	30.15	–	2	5	–	102	39	3	13.00	2-31	–	–
Smith, D.	1935	1935	2	4†	0	128	57	32.00	–	1	1	–	–	–	–	–	–	–	–
Smith, D.M.	1985-86	1985-86	2	4†	0	80	47	20.00	–	–	–	–	–	–	–	–	–	–	–
Smith, D.R.	1961-62	1961-62	5	5	1	38	34	9.50	–	–	2	–	972	359	6	59.83	2-60	–	–
Smith, D.V.	1957	1957	3	4†	1	25	16*	8.33	–	–	–	–	270†	97	1	97.00	1-12	–	–
Smith, E.J.	1911-12	1913-14	11	14	1	113	22	8.69	–	–	17	3	–	–	–	–	–	–	–
Smith, E.T.	2003	2003	3	5	0	87	64	17.40	–	1	5	–	–	–	–	–	–	–	–
Smith, H.	1928	1928	1	1	0	7	7	7.00	–	–	1	–	–	–	–	–	–	–	–
Smith, M.J.K.	1958	1972	50	78	6	2278	121	31.63	3	11	53	–	214	128	1	128.00	1-10	–	–
Smith, R.A.	1988	1995-96	62	112	15	4236	175	43.67	9	28	39	–	24	6	0	–	–	–	–
Smith, T.P.B.	1946	1946-47	4	3†	0	33	24	6.60	–	–	1	–	538	319	3	106.33	2-172	–	–
Smithson, G.A.	1947-48	1947-48	2	3†	0	70	35	23.33	–	–	–	–	–	–	–	–	–	–	–
Snow, J.A.	1965	1976	49	71	14	772	73	13.54	–	2	16	–	12021	5387	202	26.66	7-40	8	1
Southerton, J.	1876-77	1876-77	2	3	1	7	6	3.50	–	–	2	–	263	107	7	15.28	4-46	–	–
Spooner, R.H.	1905	1912	10	15	0	481	119	32.06	1	4	4	–	–	–	–	–	–	–	–
Spooner, R.T.	1951-52	1955	7	14†	1	354	92	27.23	–	3	10	2	–	–	–	–	–	–	–
Stanyforth, R.T.	1927-28	1927-28	4	6	1	13	6*	2.60	–	–	7	2	–	–	–	–	–	–	–
Staples, S.J.	1927-28	1927-28	3	5	0	65	39	13.00	–	–	–	–	1149	435	15	29.00	3-50	–	–
Statham, J.B.	1950-51	1965	70	87†	28	675	38	11.44	–	–	28	–	16056	6261	252	24.84	7-39	9	1
Steel, A.G.	1880	1888	13	20	3	600	148	35.29	2	–	5	–	1360	605	29	20.86	3-27	–	–
Steele, D.S.	1975	1976	8	16	0	673	106	42.06	1	5	7	–	88†	39	2	19.50	1-1	–	–
Stephenson, J.P.	1989	1989	1	2	0	36	25	18.00	–	–	–	–	–	–	–	–	–	–	–
Stevens, G.T.S.	1922-23	1929-30	10	17	0	263	69	15.47	–	1	9	–	1186	648	20	32.40	5-90	2	1

INDIVIDUAL CAREER RECORDS – ENGLAND *continued*

	First Test	Last Test	Tests	Inns	NO	Runs	HS	Avge	100	50	Ct	St	Balls	Runs	Wkts	Avge	BB	5wI	10wM
Stevenson, G.B.	1979-80	1980-81	2	2	1	28	27*	28.00	–	–	–	–	312	183	5	36.60	3-111	–	–
Stewart, A.J.	1989-90	2003	133	235	21	8463	190	39.54	15	45	263	14	20	13	0	–	–	–	–
Stewart, M.J.	1962	1963-64	8	12	0	385	87	35.00	–	2	6	–							
Stoddart, A.E.	1887-88	1897-98	16	30	2	996	173	35.57	2	3	6	–	162	94	2	47.00	1-10	–	–
Stokes, B.A.	2013-14	2014	6	11†	0	279	120	25.36	1	1	2	–	1228	724	22	32.90	6-99	1	–
Storer, W.	1897-98	1899	6	11	0	215	51	19.54	–	1	11	–	168	108	2	54.00	1-24	–	–
Strauss, A.J.	2004	2012	100	178†	6	7037	177	40.91	21	27	121	–							
Street, G.B.	1922-23	1922-23	1	2	1	11	7*	11.00	–	–	–	1							
Strudwick, H.	1909-10	1926	28	42	13	230	24	7.93	–	–	61	12							
Studd, C.T.	1882-83	1882-83	5	9	1	160	48	20.00	–	–	5	–	384	98	3	32.66	2-35	–	–
Studd, G.B.	1882-83	1882-83	4	7	0	31	9	4.42	–	–	8	–							
Subba Row, R.	1958	1961	13	22†	1	984	137	46.85	3	4	5	–	6	2	0	–	–	–	–
Such, P.M.	1993	1999	11	16	5	67	14*	6.09	–	–	4	–	3124	1242	37	33.56	6-67	2	–
Sugg, F.H.	1888	1888	2	2	0	55	31	27.50	–	–	–	–							
Sutcliffe, H.	1924	1935	54	84	9	4555	194	60.73	16	23	23	–							
Swann, G.P.	2008-09	2013-14	60	76	14	1370	85	22.09	–	5	54	–	15349	7642	255	29.96	6-65	17	3
Swetman, R.	1958-59	1959-60	11	17	2	254	65	16.93	–	1	24	2							
Tate, F.W.	1902	1902	1	2	1	9	5*	9.00	–	–	2	–	96	51	2	25.50	2-7	–	–
Tate, M.W.	1924	1935	39	52	5	1198	100*	25.48	1	5	11	–	12523	4055	155	26.16	6-42	7	1
Tattersall, R.	1950-51	1954	16	17†	7	50	10*	5.00	–	–	8	–	4228	1513	58	26.08	7-52	4	1
Tavaré, C.J.	1980	1989	31	56	2	1755	149	32.50	2	12	20	–	30	11	0	–	–	–	–
Taylor, J.P.	1992-93	1994	2	4†	2	34	17*	17.00	–	–	2	–	288†	156	3	52.00	1-18	–	–
Taylor, J.W.A.	2012	2012	2	3	0	48	34	16.00	–	–	2	–							
Taylor, K.	1959	1964	3	5	0	57	24	11.40	–	–	1	–							
Taylor, L.B.	1985	1985	2	1	1	1	1*	–	–	–	1	–							
Taylor, R.W.	1970-71	1983-84	57	83	12	1156	97	16.28	–	3	167	7							
Tennyson, Hon. L.H.	1913-14	1921	9	12	1	345	74*	31.36	–	4	6	–							
Terry, V.P.	1984	1984	2	3	0	16	8	5.33	–	–	2	–							
Thomas, J.G.	1985-86	1986	5	10	4	83	31*	13.83	–	–	–	–	774	504	10	50.40	4-70	–	–
Thompson, G.J.	1909	1909-10	6	10	1	273	63	30.33	–	2	5	–	1367	638	23	27.73	4-50	–	–
Thomson, N.I.	1964-65	1964-65	5	4	1	69	39	23.00	–	–	3	–	1488	568	9	63.11	2-55	–	–
Thorpe, G.P.	1993	2005	100	179†	28	6744	200*	44.66	16	39	105	–	138	37	0	–	–	–	–
Titmus, F.J.	1955	1974-75	53	76	11	1449	84*	22.29	–	10	35	5	15118	4931	153	32.22	7-79	7	–
Tolchard, R.W.	1976-77	1976-77	4	7	2	129	67	25.80	–	1	5	–							
Townsend, C.L.	1899	1899	2	3†	0	51	38	17.00	–	–	–	–	140	75	3	25.00	3-50	–	–
Townsend, D.C.H.	1934-35	1934-35	3	6	0	77	36	12.83	–	–	1	–	6	9	0	–	–	–	–
Townsend, L.F.	1929-30	1933-34	4	6	0	97	40	16.16	–	–	2	–	399	205	6	34.16	2-22	–	–

INDIVIDUAL CAREER RECORDS – ENGLAND continued

						BATTING AND FIELDING									BOWLING				
	First Test	Last Test	Tests	Inns	NO	Runs	HS	Avge	100	50	Ct	St	Balls	Runs	Wkts	Avge	BB	5wI	10wM
Tredwell, J.C.	2009–10	2009–10	1	1†		37	37	37.00	–	–	1	–	390	181	6	30.16	4-82	–	–
Tremlett, C.T.	2007	2013–14	12	15	4	113	25*	10.27	–	–	4	–	2902	1431	53	27.00	6-48	2	–
Tremlett, M.F.	1947–48	1947–48	3	5	2	20	18*	6.66	–	–	–	–	492	226	4	56.50	2-98	–	–
Trescothick, M.E.	2000	2006	76	143†	10	5825	219	43.79	14	29	95	–	300	155	1	155.00	1-34	–	–
Trott, A.E. ‡	1898–99	1898–99	2	4	0	23	16	5.75	–	–	–	–	474	198	17	11.64	5-49	1	–
Trott, I.J.L.	2009	2013–14	49	87	6	3763	226	46.45	9	18	29	–	702	398	5	79.60	1-5	–	–
Trueman, F.S.	1952	1965	67	85	14	981	39*	13.81	–	–	64	–	15178	6625	307	21.57	8-31	17	3
Tudor, A.J.	1998–99	2002–03	10	16	4	229	99*	19.08	–	1	3	–	1512	963	28	34.39	5-44	1	–
Tufnell, N.C.	1909–10	1909–10	1	1	0	14	14	14.00	–	–	1	1	–						
Tufnell, P.C.R.	1990–91	2001	42	59	29	153	22*	5.10	–	–	12	–	11288†	4560	121	37.68	7-47	5	2
Turnbull, M.J.L.	1929–30	1936	9	13	2	224	61	20.36	–	1	1	–							
Tyldesley, G.E.	1921	1928–29	14	20	2	990	122	55.00	3	6	2	–	2	2	0	–	–	–	–
Tyldesley, J.T.	1898–99	1909	31	55	1	1661	138	30.75	4	9	16	–							
Tyldesley, R.K.	1924	1930	7	7	1	47	29	7.83	–	1	1	–	1615	619	19	32.57	3-50	–	–
Tylecote, E.F.S.	1882–83	1886	6	9	1	152	66	19.00	–	1	5	5							
Tyler, E.J.	1895–96	1895–96	1	1†	0	0	0	0.00	–	–	–	–	145†	65	4	16.25	3-49	–	–
Tyson, F.H.	1954	1958–59	17	24	3	230	37*	10.95	–	–	4	–	3452	1411	76	18.56	7-27	4	1
Udal, S.D.	2005–06	2005–06	4	7	1	109	33*	18.16	–	–	1	–	596	344	8	43.00	4-14	–	–
Ulyett, G.	1876–77	1890	25	39	0	949	149	24.33	1	7	19	–	2627	1020	50	20.40	7-36	1	–
Underwood, D.L.	1966	1981–82	86	116	35	937	45*	11.56	–	–	44	–	21862†	7674	297	25.83	8-51	17	6
Valentine, B.H.	1933–34	1938–39	7	9	2	454	136	64.85	2	1	2	–							
Vaughan, M.P.	1999–2000	2008	82	147	9	5719	197	41.44	18	18	44	–	978	561	6	93.50	2-71	–	–
Verity, H.	1931	1939	40	44	12	669	66*	20.90	–	3	30	–	11173†	3510	144	24.37	8-43	5	2
Vernon, G.F.	1882–83	1882–83	1	2	2	14	11*	14.00	–	–	–	–							
Vine, J.	1911–12	1911–12	2	3	2	46	36	46.00	–	–	–	–							
Voce, W.	1929–30	1946–47	27	38	15	308	66	13.39	–	1	15	–	6360†	2733	98	27.88	7-70	3	2
Waddington, A.	1920–21	1920–21	2	4	0	16	7	4.00	–	–	1	–	276†	119	1	119.00	1-35	–	–
Wainwright, E.	1893	1897–98	5	9	0	132	49	14.66	–	–	2	–	127	73	0	–	–	–	–
Walker, P.M.	1960	1960	3	4	0	128	52	32.00	–	1	5	–	78†	34	0	–	–	–	–
Walters, C.F.	1933	1934	11	18	3	784	102	52.26	1	7	6	–							
Ward, Alan	1969	1976	5	6	3	40	21	8.00	–	–	3	–	761	453	14	32.35	4-61	–	–
Ward, Albert	1893	1894–95	7	13	0	487	117	37.46	1	3	1	–							
Ward, I.J.	2001	2001	5	9†	1	129	39	16.12	–	–	1	–							
Wardle, J.H.	1947–48	1957	28	41†	8	653	66	19.78	–	2	12	–	6597†	2080	102	20.39	7-36	5	1
Warner, P.F.	1898–99	1912	15	28	2	622	132*	23.92	1	3	3	–							

INDIVIDUAL CAREER RECORDS – ENGLAND *continued*

	First Test	Last Test	Tests	BATTING AND FIELDING									BOWLING						
				Inns	NO	Runs	HS	Avge	100	50	Ct	St	Balls	Runs	Wkts	Avge	BB	5wI	10wM
Warr, J.J.	1950-51	1950-51	2	4	0	4	4	1.00	–	–	–	–	584	281	1	281.00	1-76	–	–
Warren, A.	1905	1905	1	1	0	7	7	7.00	–	–	1	–	236	113	6	18.83	5-57	1	–
Washbrook, C.	1937	1956	37	66	6	2569	195	42.81	6	12	12	–	36	33	1	33.00	1-25	–	–
Watkin, S.L.	1991	1993	3	5	2	25	13	5.00	–	–	1	–	534	305	11	27.72	4-65	–	–
Watkins, A.J.	1948	1952	15	24†	4	810	137*	40.50	2	4	17	–	1364†	554	11	50.36	3-20	–	–
Watkinson, M.	1995	1995-96	4	6	1	167	82*	33.40	–	1	1	–	672	348	10	34.80	3-64	–	–
Watson, W.	1951	1958-59	23	37†	3	879	116	25.85	2	3	8	–	–						
Webbe, A.J.	1878-79	1878-79	1	2	0	4	4	2.00	–	–	2	–	–						
Wellard, A.W.	1937	1938	2	4	0	47	38	11.75	–	–	2	–	456	237	7	33.85	4-81	–	–
Wells, A.P.	1995	1995	1	2	1	3	3*	3.00	–	–	2	–	–						
Wharton, A.	1949	1949	1	2†	0	20	13	10.00	–	–	–	–	–						
Whitaker, J.J.	1986-87	1986-87	1	1	0	11	11	11.00	–	–	1	–	–						
White, C.	1994	2002-03	30	50	7	1052	121	24.46	1	5	14	–	3959	2220	59	37.62	5-32	3	–
White, D.W.	1961-62	1961-62	2	2†	0	0	0	0.00	–	–	–	–	220	119	4	29.75	3-65	–	–
White, J.C.	1921	1930-31	15	22	9	239	29	18.38	–	–	6	–	4801†	1581	49	32.26	8-126	3	1
Whysall, W.W.	1924-25	1930	4	7	0	209	76	29.85	–	2	7	–	16	9	0	–	–	–	–
Wilkinson, L.L.	1938-39	1938-39	3	2	1	3	2	3.00	–	–	–	–	573	271	7	38.71	2-12	–	–
Willey, P.	1976	1986	26	50	6	1184	102*	26.90	2	5	3	–	1091	456	7	65.14	2-73	–	–
Williams, N.F.	1990	1990	1	1	0	38	38	38.00	–	–	–	–	246	148	2	74.00	2-148	–	–
Willis, R.G.D.	1970-71	1984	90	128	55	840	28*	11.50	–	–	39	–	17357	8190	325	25.20	8-43	16	–
Wilson, C.E.M.	1898-99	1898-99	2	4	1	42	18	14.00	–	–	–	–	–						
Wilson, D.	1963-64	1970-71	6	7†	1	75	42	12.50	–	–	1	–	1472†	466	11	42.36	2-17	–	–
Wilson, E.R.	1920-21	1920-21	1	2	0	10	5	5.00	–	–	–	–	123	36	3	12.00	2-28	–	–
Woakes, C.R.	2013	2014	4	5	3	75	26*	37.50	–	–	2	–	570	313	6	52.16	3-30	–	–
Wood, A.	1938	1939	4	5	1	80	53	20.00	–	1	10	1	–						
Wood, B.	1972	1978	12	21	0	454	90	21.61	–	2	6	–	98	50	0	–	–	–	–
Wood, G.E.C.	1924	1924	3	2	0	6	6	3.50	–	–	5	1	–						
Wood, H.	1888	1891-92	4	4	1	204	134*	68.00	1	1	2	1	–						
Wood, R.	1886-87	1886-87	1	2†	0	6	6	3.00	–	–	–	–	–						
Woods, S.M.J. ‡	1895-96	1895-96	3	4†	0	122	53	30.50	–	1	4	–	195†	129	5	25.80	3-28	–	–
Woolley, F.E.	1909	1934	64	98†	7	3283	154	36.07	5	23	64	–	6495†	2815	83	33.91	7-76	4	1
Woolmer, R.A.	1975	1981	19	34	2	1059	149	33.09	3	2	10	–	546	299	4	74.75	1-8	–	–
Worthington, T.S.	1929-30	1936-37	9	11	0	321	128	29.18	1	1	8	–	633	316	8	39.50	2-19	–	–
Wright, C.W.	1895-96	1895-96	3	4	0	125	71	31.25	–	1	–	–	–						
Wright, D.V.P.	1938	1950-51	34	39	13	289	45	11.11	–	–	10	–	8135	4224	108	39.11	7-105	6	1
Wyatt, R.E.S.	1927-28	1936-37	40	64	6	1839	149	31.70	2	12	16	–	1395	642	18	35.66	3-4	–	–
Wynyard, E.G.	1896	1905-06	3	6	0	72	30	12.00	–	–	–	–	24	17	0	–	–	–	–

INDIVIDUAL CAREER RECORDS – ENGLAND continued

	First Test	Last Test	Tests	Inns	NO	Runs	HS	Avge	100	50	Ct	St	Balls	Runs	Wkts	Avge	BB	5wI	10wM
						BATTING AND FIELDING									*BOWLING*				
Yardley, N.W.D.	1938-39	1950	20	34	2	812	99	25.37	–	4	14	–	1662	707	21	33.66	3-67	–	–
Young, H.I.	1899	1899	2	2	0	43	43	21.50	–	–	1	–	556†	262	12	21.83	4-30	–	–
Young, J.A.	1947	1949	8	10	5	28	10*	5.60	–	–	5	–	2368†	757	17	44.52	3-65	–	–
Young, R.A.	1907-08	1907-08	2	4	0	27	13	6.75	–	–	6	–	–						

INDIVIDUAL CAREER RECORDS – AUSTRALIA

	First Test	Last Test	Tests	Inns	NO	Runs	HS	Avge	100	50	Ct	St	Balls	Runs	Wkts	Avge	BB	5wI	10wM
						BATTING AND FIELDING									*BOWLING*				
a'Beckett, E.L.	1928-29	1931-32	4	7	0	143	41	20.42	–	–	4	–	1062	317	3	105.66	1-41	–	–
Agar, A.C.	2013	2013	2	4†	0	130	98	32.50	–	1	–	–	504†	248	2	124.00	2-82	–	–
Alderman, T.M.	1981	1990-91	41	53	22	203	26*	6.54	–	–	27	–	10181	4616	170	27.15	6-47	14	1
Alexander, G.	1880	1884-85	2	4	0	52	33	13.00	–	–	2	–	168	93	2	46.50	2-69	–	–
Alexander, H.H.	1932-33	1932-33	1	2	1	17	17*	17.00	–	–	–	–	276	154	1	154.00	1-129	–	–
Allan, F.E.	1878-79	1878-79	1	1	0	5	5	5.00	–	–	–	–	180†	80	4	20.00	2-30	–	–
Allan, P.J.	1965-66	1965-66	1	–	–	–	–	–	–	–	–	–	192	83	2	41.50	2-58	–	–
Allen, R.C.	1886-87	1886-87	1	2	0	44	30	22.00	–	–	2	–	–						
Andrews, T.J.E.	1921	1926	16	23	1	592	94	26.90	–	4	12	–	156	116	1	116.00	1-23	–	–
Angel, J.	1992-93	1994-95	4	7†	1	35	11	5.83	–	–	1	–	748	463	10	46.30	3-54	–	–
Archer, K.A.	1950-51	1951-52	5	9	0	234	48	26.00	–	2	–	–	–						
Archer, R.G.	1952-53	1956-57	19	30	1	713	128	24.58	1	2	20	–	3576	1318	48	27.45	5-53	1	–
Armstrong, W.W.	1901-02	1921	50	84	10	2863	159*	38.68	6	8	44	–	8022	2923	87	33.59	6-35	3	–
Badcock, C.L.	1936-37	1938	7	12	1	160	118	14.54	1	1	3	–							
Bailey, G.J.	2013-14	2013-14	5	8	1	183	53	26.14	–	1	10	–							
Bannerman, A.C.	1878-79	1893	28	50	2	1108	94	23.08	–	8	21	–	292	163	4	40.75	3-111	–	–
Bannerman, C.	1876-77	1878-79	3	6	2	239	165*	59.75	1	–	–	–							
Bardsley, W.	1909	1926	41	66†	5	2469	193*	40.47	6	14	12	–							
Barnes, S.G.	1938	1948	13	19	2	1072	234	63.05	3	5	14	–	594	218	4	54.50	2-25	–	–
Barnett, B.A.	1938	1938	4	8†	1	195	57	27.85	–	1	3	2							
Barrett, J.E.	1890	1890	2	4†	1	80	67*	26.66	–	1	1	–							
Beard, G.R.	1979-80	1979-80	3	5	0	114	49	22.80	–	–	1	–	259	109	1	109.00	1-26	–	–
Beer, M.A.	2010-11	2011-12	2	3	1	6	2*	3.00	–	–	1	–	406†	178	3	59.33	2-56	–	–
Benaud, J.	1972-73	1972-73	3	5	0	223	142	44.60	1	–	–	–	24	12	2	6.00	2-12	–	–
Benaud, R.	1951-52	1963-64	63	97	7	2201	122	24.45	3	9	65	–	19108	6704	248	27.03	7-72	16	1
Bennett, M.J.	1984-85	1985	3	5	2	71	23	23.66	–	–	5	–	664†	325	6	54.16	3-79	–	–

INDIVIDUAL CAREER RECORDS – AUSTRALIA continued

	First Test	Last Test	Tests	BATTING AND FIELDING									BOWLING						
				Inns	NO	Runs	HS	Avge	100	50	Ct	St	Balls	Runs	Wkts	Avge	BB	5wI	10wM
Bevan, M.G.	1994-95	1997-98	18	30†	3	785	91	29.07	–	6	8	–	1285†	703	29	24.24	6-82	1	1
Bichel, A.J.	1996-97	2003-04	19	22	1	355	71	16.90	–	1	16	–	3337	1870	58	32.24	5-60	1	–
Bird, J.M.	2012-13	2013	3	4	3	7	6*	7.00	–	–	1	–	633	303	13	23.30	4-41	–	–
Blackham, J.M.	1876-77	1894-95	35	62	11	800	74	15.68	–	4	37	24	–	–	–	–	–	–	–
Blackie, D.D.	1928-29	1928-29	3	6†	4	24	11*	8.00	–	–	2	–	1260	444	14	31.71	6-94	1	–
Blewett, G.S.	1994-95	1999-2000	46	79	4	2552	214	34.02	4	15	45	–	1436	720	14	51.42	2-9	–	–
Bollinger, D.E.	2008-09	2010-11	12	14†	7	54	21	7.71	–	–	2	–	2401†	1296	50	25.92	5-28	2	–
Bonnor, G.J.	1880	1888	17	30	1	512	128	17.06	1	2	16	–	164	84	2	42.00	1-5	–	–
Boon, D.C.	1984-85	1995-96	107	190	20	7422	200	43.65	21	32	99	–	36	14	0	–	–	–	–
Booth, B.C.	1961	1965-66	29	48	6	1773	169	42.21	5	10	17	–	436	146	3	48.66	2-33	–	–
Border, A.R.	1978-79	1993-94	156	265†	44	11174	205	50.56	27	63	156	–	4009†	1525	39	39.10	7-46	2	1
Boyle, H.F.	1878-79	1884-85	12	16	4	153	36*	12.75	–	–	10	–	1743	641	32	20.03	6-42	1	–
Bracken, N.W.	2003-04	2005-06	5	6	2	70	37	17.50	–	–	2	–	1110†	505	12	42.08	4-48	–	–
Bradman, D.G.	1928-29	1948	52	80	10	6996	334	99.94	29	13	32	–	160	72	2	36.00	1-8	–	–
Bright, R.J.	1977	1986-87	25	39	8	445	33	14.35	–	–	13	–	5541†	2180	53	41.13	7-87	4	1
Bromley, E.H.	1932-33	1934	2	4†	0	38	26	9.50	–	–	2	–	60†	19	0	–	–	–	–
Brown, W.A.	1934	1948	22	35	1	1592	206*	46.82	4	9	14	–	–	–	–	–	–	–	–
Bruce, W.	1884-85	1894-95	14	26†	2	702	80	29.25	–	5	12	–	988†	440	12	36.66	3-88	–	–
Burge, P.J.P.	1954-55	1965-66	42	68	8	2290	181	38.16	4	12	23	–	–	–	–	–	–	–	–
Burke, J.W.	1950-51	1958-59	24	44	7	1280	189	34.59	3	5	18	–	814	230	8	28.75	4-37	–	–
Burn, E.J.K.	1890	1890	2	4	0	41	19	10.25	–	–	1	–	–	–	–	–	–	–	–
Burton, F.J.	1886-87	1887-88	2	4	2	4	2*	2.00	–	–	1	1	–	–	–	–	–	–	–
Callaway, S.T.	1891-92	1894-95	3	6	1	87	41	17.40	–	–	–	–	471	142	6	23.66	5-37	1	–
Callen, I.W.	1977-78	1977-78	1	2†	2	26	22*	–	–	–	–	–	440	191	6	31.83	3-83	–	–
Campbell, G.D.	1989	1989-90	4	4	0	10	6	2.50	–	–	1	–	951	503	13	38.69	3-79	–	–
Carkeek, W.	1912	1912	6	5†	2	16	6*	5.33	–	–	6	–	–	–	–	–	–	–	–
Carlson, P.H.	1978-79	1978-79	2	4	0	23	21	5.75	–	–	2	–	368	99	2	49.50	2-41	–	–
Carter, H.	1907-08	1921-22	28	47	9	873	72	22.97	–	4	44	21	–	–	–	–	–	–	–
Casson, B.	2008	2008	1	1	0	10	10	10.00	–	–	2	–	192†	129	3	43.00	3-86	–	–
Chappell, G.S.	1970-71	1983-84	87	151	19	7110	247*	53.86	24	31	122	–	5327	1913	47	40.70	5-61	1	–
Chappell, I.M.	1964-65	1979-80	75	136	10	5345	196	42.42	14	26	105	–	2873	1316	20	65.80	2-21	–	–
Chappell, T.M.	1981	1981	3	6	1	79	27	15.80	–	–	2	–	–	–	–	–	–	–	–
Charlton, P.C.	1890	1890	2	4	0	29	11	7.25	–	–	–	–	45	24	3	8.00	3-18	–	–
Chipperfield, A.G.	1934	1938	14	20	3	552	109	32.47	1	2	15	–	924	437	5	87.40	3-91	–	–
Clark, S.R.	2005-06	2009	24	26	7	248	39	13.05	–	–	4	–	5146	2243	94	23.86	5-32	2	–
Clark, W.M.	1977-78	1978-79	10	19	2	98	33	5.76	–	–	6	–	2793	1265	44	28.75	4-46	–	–
Clarke, M.J.	2004-05	2013-14	105	180	20	8240	329*	51.50	27	27	125	–	2387†	1152	31	37.16	6-9	2	–

229

INDIVIDUAL CAREER RECORDS – AUSTRALIA continued

	First Test	Last Test	Tests	Inns	NO	Runs	HS	BATTING AND FIELDING Avge	100	50	Ct	St	Balls	Runs	Wkts	BOWLING Avge	BB	5wI	10wM
Colley, D.J.	1972	1972	3	4	0	84	54	21.00	–	1	1	–	729	312	6	52.00	3-83	–	–
Collins, H.L.	1920-21	1926	19	31	1	1352	203	45.06	4	6	13	–	654†	252	4	63.00	2-47	–	–
Coningham, A.	1894-95	1894-95	1	2†	0	13	10	6.50	–	–	–	–	186†	76	2	38.00	2-17	–	–
Connolly, A.N.	1963-64	1970-71	29	45	20	260	37	10.40	–	–	17	–	7818	2981	102	29.22	6-47	4	–
Cook, S.H.	1997-98	1997-98	2	2†	2	3	3*	–	–	–	–	–	224	142	7	20.28	5-39	1	–
Cooper, B.B.	1876-77	1876-77	1	2	0	18	15	9.00	–	–	2	–	–	–	–	–	–	–	–
Cooper, W.H.	1881-82	1884-85	2	4	1	13	7	6.50	–	–	1	–	446	226	9	25.11	6-120	1	–
Copeland, T.A.	2011	2011	3	4	1	39	23*	13.00	–	–	2	–	648	227	6	37.83	2-24	–	–
Corling, G.E.	1964	1964	5	4	1	5	3	1.66	–	–	–	–	1159	447	12	37.25	4-60	–	–
Cosier, G.J.	1975-76	1978-79	18	32	1	897	168	28.93	2	3	14	–	899	341	5	68.20	2-26	–	–
Cottam, J.T.	1886-87	1886-87	1	2	0	4	3	2.00	–	–	1	–	–	–	–	–	–	–	–
Cotter, A.	1903-04	1911-12	21	37	2	457	45	13.05	–	–	8	–	4633	2549	89	28.64	7-148	7	–
Coulthard, G.	1881-82	1881-82	1	1	1	6	6*	–	–	–	–	–	–	–	–	–	–	–	–
Cowan, E.J.M.	2011-12	2013	18	32†	0	1001	136	31.28	1	6	24	–	–	–	–	–	–	–	–
Cowper, R.M.	1964	1968	27	46†	2	2061	307	46.84	5	10	21	–	3005	1139	36	31.63	4-48	–	–
Craig, I.D.	1952-53	1957-58	11	18	1	358	53	19.88	–	2	2	–	–	–	–	–	–	–	–
Crawford, W.P.A.	1956	1956-57	4	5	2	53	34	17.66	–	–	1	–	437	107	7	15.28	3-28	–	–
Cullen, D.J.	2005-06	2005-06	1	–	–	–	–	–	–	–	–	–	84	54	1	54.00	1-25	–	–
Cummins, P.J.	2011-12	2011-12	1	2	1	15	13*	15.00	–	–	1	–	264	117	7	16.71	6-79	1	–
Dale, A.C.	1997-98	1998-99	2	3†	0	6	5	2.00	–	–	–	–	348	187	6	31.16	3-71	–	–
Darling, J.	1894-95	1905	34	60†	2	1657	178	28.56	3	8	27	–	–	–	–	–	–	–	–
Darling, L.S.	1932-33	1936-37	12	18†	1	474	85	27.88	–	3	8	–	162	65	0	–	–	–	–
Darling, W.M.	1977-78	1979-80	14	27	1	697	91	26.80	–	6	5	–	–	–	–	–	–	–	–
Davidson, A.K.	1953	1962-63	44	61†	7	1328	80	24.59	–	5	42	–	11587†	3819	186	20.53	7-93	14	2
Davis, I.C.	1973-74	1977	15	27	1	692	105	26.61	1	4	9	–	150	70	0	–	–	–	–
Davis, S.P.	1985-86	1985-86	1	1	0	0	0	0.00	–	–	–	–	–	–	–	–	–	–	–
de Courcy, J.H.	1953	1953	3	6	2	81	41	16.20	–	–	3	–	–	–	–	–	–	–	–
Dell, A.R.	1970-71	1973-74	2	2	2	6	3*	–	–	–	–	–	559†	160	6	26.66	3-65	–	–
Dodemaide, A.I.C.	1987-88	1992	10	15	6	202	50	22.44	–	1	6	–	2184	953	34	28.02	6-58	1	–
Doherty, X.J.	2010-11	2012-13	4	7†	3	51	18*	12.75	–	–	2	–	918†	548	7	78.28	3-131	–	–
Donnan, H.	1891-92	1896	5	10	1	75	15	8.33	–	–	2	–	54	22	0	–	–	–	–
Doolan, A.J.	2013-14	2013-14	3	6	0	186	89	31.00	–	1	3	–	–	–	–	–	–	–	–
Dooland, B.	1946-47	1947-48	3	5	1	76	29	19.00	–	–	3	–	880	419	9	46.55	4-69	–	–
Duff, R.A.	1901-02	1905	22	40	3	1317	146	35.59	2	6	14	–	180	85	4	21.25	2-43	–	–
Duncan, J.R.F.	1970-71	1970-71	1	1	0	3	3	3.00	–	–	–	–	112	30	0	–	–	–	–
Dyer, G.C.	1986-87	1987-88	6	6	0	131	60	21.83	–	1	22	2	–	–	–	–	–	–	–

INDIVIDUAL CAREER RECORDS – AUSTRALIA *continued*

	First Test	Last Test	Tests	Inns	NO	Runs	HS	Avge	100	50	Ct	St	Balls	Runs	Wkts	Avge	BB	5wI	10wM
Dymock, G.	1973–74	1979–80	21	32†	7	236	31*	9.44	–	–	1	–	5545†	2116	78	27.12	7-67	5	1
Dyson, J.	1977–78	1984–85	30	58	7	1359	127*	26.64	2	5	10	–	–	–	–	–	–	–	–
Eady, C.J.	1896	1901–02	2	4	1	20	10*	6.66	–	–	2	–	223	112	7	16.00	3-30	–	–
Eastwood, K.H.	1970–71	1970–71	1	2†	0	5	5	2.50	–	–	–	–	40†	21	1	21.00	1-21	–	–
Ebeling, H.I.	1934	1934	1	2	0	43	41	21.50	–	–	1	–	186	89	3	29.66	3-74	–	–
Edwards, J.D.	1888	1888	3	6	1	48	26	9.60	–	–	1	–	–	–	–	–	–	–	–
Edwards, R.	1972	1975	20	32	3	1171	170*	40.37	2	9	7	–	12	20	0	–	–	–	–
Edwards, W.J.	1974–75	1974–75	3	6†	0	68	30	11.33	–	–	–	–	–	–	–	–	–	–	–
Elliott, M.T.G.	1996–97	2004	21	36†	1	1172	199	33.48	3	4	14	–	12†	4	0	–	–	–	–
Emery, P.A.	1994–95	1994–95	1	1†	1	8	8*	–	–	–	5	1							
Emery, S.H.	1912	1912	4	2	0	6	5	3.00	–	–	2	–	462	249	5	49.80	2-46	–	–
Evans, E.	1881–82	1886	6	10	2	82	33	10.25	–	–	5	–	1237	332	7	47.42	3-64	–	–
Fairfax, A.G.	1928–29	1930–31	10	12	4	410	65	51.25	–	4	15	–	1520	645	21	30.71	4-31	–	–
Faulkner, J.P.	2013	2013	1	2	0	45	23	22.50	–	–	–	–	166†	98	6	16.33	4-51	–	–
Favell, L.E.	1954–55	1960–61	19	31	3	757	101	27.03	1	5	9	–	–	–	–	–	–	–	–
Ferris, J.J. ‡	1886–87	1890	8	16†	4	98	20*	8.16	–	–	4	–	2030†	684	48	14.25	5-26	4	–
Fingleton, J.H.W.	1931–32	1938	18	29	1	1189	136	42.46	5	3	13	–	–	–	–	–	–	–	–
Fleetwood-Smith, L.O.	1935–36	1938	10	11	5	54	16*	9.00	–	–	–	–	3093†	1570	42	37.38	6-110	2	1
Fleming, D.W.	1994–95	2000–01	20	19	3	305	71*	19.06	–	2	9	–	4129	1942	75	25.89	5-30	3	–
Francis, B.C.	1972	1972	3	5	0	52	27	10.40	–	–	1	–	–	–	–	–	–	–	–
Freeman, E.W.	1967–68	1969–70	11	18	1	345	76	19.16	–	2	5	–	2183	1128	34	33.17	4-52	–	–
Freer, F.A.W.	1946–47	1946–47	1	1	1	28	28*	–	–	–	–	–	160	74	3	24.66	2-49	–	–
Gannon, J.B.	1977–78	1977–78	3	5	4	3	3*	3.00	–	–	3	–	726†	361	11	32.81	4-77	–	–
Garrett, T.W.	1876–77	1887–88	19	33	6	339	51*	12.55	–	1	7	–	2728	970	36	26.94	6-78	2	–
Gaunt, R.A.	1957–58	1963–64	3	4†	2	6	3	3.00	–	–	1	–	716	310	7	44.28	3-53	–	–
Gehrs, D.R.A.	1903–04	1910–11	6	11	0	221	67	20.09	–	2	6	–	6	4	0	–	–	–	–
George, P.R.	2010–11	2010–11	1	2	0	2	2	1.00	–	–	–	–	168	77	2	38.50	2-48	–	–
Giffen, G.	1881–82	1896	31	53	0	1238	161	23.35	1	6	24	–	6391	2791	103	27.09	7-117	7	1
Giffen, W.F.	1886–87	1891–92	3	6	0	11	3	1.83	–	–	1	–	–	–	–	–	–	–	–
Gilbert, D.R.	1985	1986–87	9	12	4	57	15	7.12	–	–	–	–	1647	843	16	52.68	3-48	–	–
Gilchrist, A.C.	1999–2000	2007–08	96	137†	20	5570	204*	47.60	17	26	379	37	–	–	–	–	–	–	–
Gillespie, J.N.	1996–97	2005–06	71	93	28	1218	201*	18.73	1	2	27	–	14234	6770	259	26.13	7-37	8	–
Gilmour, G.J.	1973–74	1976–77	15	22†	1	483	101	23.00	1	3	8	–	2661†	1406	54	26.03	6-85	3	–
Gleeson, J.W.	1967–68	1972	29	46	8	395	45	10.39	–	–	17	–	8857	3367	93	36.20	5-61	3	–
Graham, H.	1893	1896	6	10	0	301	107	30.10	2	–	3	–	–	–	–	–	–	–	–

INDIVIDUAL CAREER RECORDS – AUSTRALIA continued

	First Test	Last Test	Tests	Inns	NO	Runs	HS	Avge	100	50	Ct	St	Balls	Runs	Wkts	Avge	BB	5wI	10wM
						BATTING AND FIELDING									BOWLING				
Gregory, D.W.	1876-77	1878-79	3	5	2	60	43	20.00	-	-	1	-	20	9	0	-	-	-	-
Gregory, E.J.	1876-77	1876-77	1	2	0	11	11	5.50	-	-	1	-	-	-	-	-	-	-	-
Gregory, J.M.	1920-21	1928-29	24	34†	3	1146	119	36.96	2	7	37	-	5582	2648	85	31.15	7-69	4	-
Gregory, R.G.	1936-37	1936-37	2	3	0	153	80	51.00	-	2	1	-	24	14	0	-	-	-	-
Gregory, S.E.	1890	1912	58	100	7	2282	201	24.53	4	8	25	-	30	33	0	-	-	-	-
Grimmett, C.V.	1924-25	1935-36	37	50	10	557	50	13.92	-	1	17	-	14513	5231	216	24.21	7-40	21	7
Groube, T.U.	1880	1880	1	2	0	11	11	5.50	-	-	-	-	-	-	-	-	-	-	-
Grout, A.T.W.	1957-58	1965-66	51	67	8	890	74	15.08	-	3	163	24	-	-	-	-	-	-	-
Guest, C.E.J.	1962-63	1962-63	1	1	0	11	11	11.00	-	-	-	-	144	59	0	-	-	-	-
Haddin, B.J.	2008	2013-14	57	96	10	3032	169	35.25	4	17	228	5	-	-	-	-	-	-	-
Hamence, R.A.	1946-47	1947-48	3	4	1	81	30*	27.00	-	-	1	-	-	-	-	-	-	-	-
Hammond, J.R.	1972-73	1972-73	5	5	2	28	19	9.33	-	-	2	-	1031	488	15	32.53	4-38	-	-
Harris, R.J.	2009-10	2013-14	24	35	10	483	68*	19.32	-	2	11	-	4980	2324	103	22.56	7-117	5	-
Harry, J.	1894-95	1894-95	1	2	0	8	6	4.00	-	-	1	-	-	-	-	-	-	-	-
Hartigan, M.J.	1907-08	1907-08	2	4	0	170	116	42.50	1	-	1	-	12	7	0	-	-	-	-
Hartkopf, A.E.V.	1924-25	1924-25	1	2	0	80	80	40.00	-	1	-	-	240	134	1	134.00	1-120	-	-
Harvey, M.R.	1946-47	1946-47	1	2	0	43	31	21.50	-	-	-	-	-	-	-	-	-	-	-
Harvey, R.N.	1947-48	1962-63	79	137†	10	6149	205	48.41	21	24	64	-	414	120	3	40.00	1-8	-	-
Hassett, A.L.	1938	1953	43	69	3	3073	198*	46.56	10	11	30	-	111	78	0	-	-	-	-
Hastings, J.W.	2012-13	2012-13	1	2	0	52	32	26.00	-	-	1	-	234	153	1	153.00	1-51	-	-
Hauritz, N.M.	2004-05	2010-11	17	24	7	426	75	25.05	-	2	3	-	4200	2204	63	34.98	5-53	2	-
Hawke, N.J.N.	1962-63	1968	27	37	15	365	45*	16.59	-	-	9	-	6974	2677	91	29.41	7-105	6	1
Hayden, M.L.	1993-94	2008-09	103	184†	14	8625	380	50.73	30	29	128	-	54	40	0	-	-	-	-
Hazlitt, G.R.	1907-08	1912	9	12	4	89	34*	11.12	-	-	4	-	1563	623	23	27.08	7-25	1	-
Healy, I.A.	1988-89	1999-2000	119	182	23	4356	161*	27.39	4	22	366	29	-	-	-	-	-	-	-
Hendry, H.S.T.L.	1921	1928-29	11	18	1	335	112	20.93	1	2	10	-	1706	640	16	40.00	3-36	-	-
Henriques, M.C.	2012-13	2012-13	3	6	1	156	81*	31.20	-	1	1	-	318	155	2	77.50	1-48	-	-
Hibbert, P.A.	1977-78	1977-78	1	2†	0	15	13	7.50	-	-	1	-	-	-	-	-	-	-	-
Higgs, J.D.	1977-78	1980-81	22	36	16	111	16	5.55	-	-	3	-	4752	2057	66	31.16	7-143	2	-
Hilditch, A.M.J.	1978-79	1985-86	18	34	0	1073	119	31.55	2	6	13	-	-	-	-	-	-	-	-
Hilfenhaus, B.W.	2008-09	2012-13	27	38	12	355	56*	13.65	-	1	7	-	6078	2822	99	28.50	5-75	2	-
Hill, C.	1896	1911-12	49	89†	2	3412	191	39.21	7	19	33	-	-	-	-	-	-	-	-
Hill, J.C.	1953	1954-55	3	6	3	21	8*	7.00	-	-	2	-	606	273	8	34.12	3-35	-	-
Hoare, D.E.	1960-61	1960-61	1	2	0	35	35	17.50	-	-	2	-	232	156	2	78.00	2-68	-	-
Hodge, B.J.	2005-06	2008	6	11	2	503	203*	55.88	1	2	9	-	12	8	0	-	-	-	-
Hodges, J.R.	1876-77	1876-77	2	4†	1	10	8	3.33	-	-	-	-	136†	84	6	14.00	2-7	-	-
Hogan, T.G.	1982-83	1983-84	7	12	1	205	42*	18.63	-	-	2	-	1436†	706	15	47.06	5-66	1	-

INDIVIDUAL CAREER RECORDS – AUSTRALIA *continued*

	First Test	Last Test	Tests	Inns	NO	Runs	HS	Avge	100	50	Ct	St	Balls	Runs	Wkts	Avge	BB	5wI	10wM
Hogg, G.B.	1996–97	2007–08	7	10†	3	186	79	26.57	–	1	1	–	1524†	933	17	54.88	2-40	–	–
Hogg, R.M.	1978–79	1984–85	38	58	13	439	52	9.75	–	1	7	–	7633	3503	123	28.47	6-74	6	2
Hohns, T.V.	1988–89	1989	7	7†	1	136	40	22.66	–	–	3	–	1528	580	17	34.11	3-59	–	–
Hole, G.B.	1950–51	1954–55	18	33	2	789	66	25.45	–	6	21	–	398	126	3	42.00	1-9	–	–
Holland, R.G.	1984–85	1985–86	11	15	4	35	10	3.18	–	–	5	–	2889	1352	34	39.76	6-54	3	2
Hookes, D.W.	1976–77	1985–86	23	41†	3	1306	143*	34.36	1	8	12	–	96†	41	1	41.00	1-4	–	–
Hopkins, A.J.Y.	1901–02	1909	20	33	2	509	43	16.41	–	1	11	–	1327	696	26	26.76	4-81	–	–
Horan, T.P.	1876–77	1884–85	15	27	2	471	124	18.84	1	1	6	–	373	143	11	13.00	6-40	1	–
Hordern, H.V.	1910–11	1911–12	7	13	2	254	50	23.09	–	1	6	–	2148	1075	46	23.36	7-90	5	2
Hornibrook, P.M.	1928–29	1930	6	7†	1	60	26	10.00	–	–	7	–	1579†	664	17	39.05	7-92	1	–
Howell, W.P.	1897–98	1903–04	18	27†	6	158	35	7.52	–	–	12	–	3892	1407	49	28.71	5-81	1	–
Hughes, K.J.	1977	1984–85	70	124	6	4415	213	37.41	9	22	50	–	85	28	0	–	–	–	–
Hughes, M.G.	1985–86	1993–94	53	70	8	1032	72*	16.64	–	2	23	–	12285	6017	212	28.38	8-87	7	1
Hughes, P.J.	2008–09	2013	26	49†	0	1535	160	32.65	3	7	15	–	–	–	–	–	–	–	–
Hunt, W.A.	1931–32	1931–32	1	1†	0	0	0	0.00	–	–	1	–	96†	39	0	–	–	–	–
Hurst, A.G.	1973–74	1979–80	12	20	3	102	26	6.00	–	–	3	–	3054	1200	43	27.90	5-28	2	–
Hurwood, A.	1930–31	1930–31	2	2	0	5	5	2.50	–	–	2	–	517	170	11	15.45	4-22	–	–
Hussey, M.E.K.	2005–06	2012–13	79	137†	16	6235	195	51.52	19	29	85	–	588	306	7	43.71	1-0	–	–
Inverarity, R.J.	1968	1972	6	11	1	174	56	17.40	–	1	4	–	372†	93	4	23.25	3-26	–	–
Iredale, F.A.	1894–95	1899	14	23	1	807	140	36.68	2	4	16	–	12	3	0	–	–	–	–
Ironmonger, H.	1928–29	1932–33	14	21†	5	42	12	2.62	–	–	3	–	4695†	1330	74	17.97	7-23	4	2
Iverson, J.B.	1950–51	1950–51	5	7	3	3	1*	0.75	–	–	2	–	1108	320	21	15.23	6-27	1	–
Jackson, A.	1928–29	1930–31	8	11	1	474	164	47.40	1	2	7	–	–						
Jaques, P.A.	2005–06	2008	11	19†	0	902	150	47.47	3	6	7	–	–						
Jarman, B.N.	1959–60	1968–69	19	30	3	400	78	14.81	–	2	50	4	–						
Jarvis, A.H.	1884–85	1894–95	11	21	3	303	82	16.83	–	1	9	9	–						
Jenner, T.J.	1970–71	1975–76	9	14	5	208	74	23.11	–	1	5	–	1881	749	24	31.20	5-90	1	–
Jennings, C.B.	1912	1912	6	8	2	107	32	17.83	–	–	5	–	–						
Johnson, I.W.G.	1945–46	1956–57	45	66	12	1000	77	18.51	–	6	30	–	8780	3182	109	29.19	7-44	3	–
Johnson, L.J.	1947–48	1947–48	1	1	0	25	25*	–	–	–	2	–	282	74	6	12.33	3-8	–	–
Johnson, M.G.	2007–08	2013–14	59	88†	14	1637	123*	22.12	1	8	22	–	13227†	7240	264	27.42	8-61	12	3
Johnston, W.A.	1947–48	1954–55	40	49†	25	273	29	11.37	–	–	16	–	11048†	3826	160	23.91	6-44	7	–
Jones, D.M.	1983–84	1992	52	89	11	3631	216	46.55	11	14	34	–	198	64	1	64.00	1-5	–	–
Jones, E.	1894–95	1902–03	19	26	1	126	20	5.04	–	–	21	–	3754	1857	64	29.01	7-88	3	1
Jones, S.P.	1881–82	1887–88	12	24	4	428	87	21.40	–	1	12	–	262	112	6	18.66	4-47	–	–

233

INDIVIDUAL CAREER RECORDS – AUSTRALIA continued

	First Test	Last Test	Tests	Inns	NO	Runs	HS	Avge	100	50	Ct	St	Balls	Runs	Wkts	Avge	BB	5wI	10wM
				BATTING AND FIELDING									BOWLING						
Joslin, L.R.	1967-68	1967-68	1	2†	0	9	7	4.50	–	–	–	–	–	–	–	–	–	–	–
Julian, B.P.	1993	1995-96	7	9	1	128	56*	16.00	–	1	4	–	1098†	599	15	39.93	4-36	–	–
Kasprowicz, M.S.	1996-97	2005-06	38	54	12	445	25	10.59	–	–	16	–	7140	3716	113	32.88	7-36	4	–
Katich, S.M.	2001	2010-11	56	99†	6	4188	157	45.03	10	25	39	–	1039†	635	21	30.23	6-65	1	–
Kelleway, C.	1910-11	1928-29	26	42	4	1422	147	37.42	3	6	24	–	4363	1683	52	32.36	5-33	1	–
Kelly, J.J.	1896	1905	36	56	17	664	46*	17.02	–	–	43	20	–						
Kelly, T.J.D.	1876-77	1878-79	2	3	0	64	35	21.33	–	–	1	–							
Kendall, T.K.	1876-77	1876-77	2	4†	1	39	17*	13.00	–	–	2	–	563†	215	14	15.35	7-55	1	–
Kent, M.F.	1981	1981	3	6	0	171	54	28.50	–	2	6	–							
Kerr, R.B.	1985-86	1985-86	2	4	0	31	17	7.75	–	–	1	–							
Khawaja, U.T.	2010-11	2013	9	17†	2	377	65	25.13	–	2	5	–							
Kippax, A.F.	1924-25	1934	22	34	1	1192	146	36.12	2	8	13	–	72	19	0	–	–	–	–
Kline, L.F.	1957-58	1960-61	13	16†	9	58	15*	8.28	–	–	9	–	2373†	776	34	22.82	7-75	1	–
Krejza, J.J.	2008-09	2008-09	2	4	1	71	32	23.66	–	–	4	–	743	562	13	43.23	8-215	1	1
Laird, B.M.	1979-80	1982-83	21	40	2	1341	92	35.28	–	11	16	–	18	12	0	–	–	–	–
Langer, J.L.	1992-93	2006-07	105	182†	12	7696	250	45.27	23	30	73	–	6	3	0	–	–	–	–
Langley, G.R.A.	1951-52	1956-57	26	37	12	374	53	14.96	–	1	83	15							
Laughlin, T.J.	1977-78	1978-79	3	5†	0	87	35	17.40	–	–	3	–	516	262	6	43.66	5-101	1	–
Laver, F.J.	1899	1909	15	23	6	196	45	11.52	–	–	8	–	2361	964	37	26.05	8-31	2	–
Law, S.G.	1995-96	1995-96	1	1	1	54	54*	–	–	1	1	–	18	9	0	–	–	–	–
Lawry, W.M.	1961	1970-71	67	123†	12	5234	210	47.15	13	27	30	–	14†	6	0	–	–	–	–
Lawson, G.F.	1980-81	1989-90	46	68	12	894	74	15.96	–	4	10	–	11118	5501	180	30.56	8-112	11	2
Lee, B.	1999-2000	2008-09	76	90	18	1451	64	20.15	–	5	23	–	16531	9554	310	30.81	5-30	10	–
Lee, P.K.	1931-32	1932-33	2	3	0	57	42	19.00	–	–	1	–	436	212	5	42.40	4-111	–	–
Lehmann, D.S.	1997-98	2004-05	27	42†	2	1798	177	44.95	5	10	11	–	974†	412	15	27.46	3-42	–	–
Lillee, D.K.	1970-71	1983-84	70	90	24	905	73*	13.71	–	1	23	–	18467	8493	355	23.92	7-83	23	7
Lindwall, R.R.	1945-46	1959-60	61	84	13	1502	118	21.15	2	5	26	–	13650	5251	228	23.03	7-38	12	–
Love, H.S.B.	1932-33	1932-33	1	2	0	8	5	4.00	–	–	3	–							
Love, M.L.	2002-03	2003	5	8	3	233	100*	46.60	1	1	7	–							
Loxton, S.J.E.	1947-48	1950-51	12	15	0	554	101	36.93	1	3	7	–	906	349	8	43.62	3-55	–	–
Lyon, N.M.	2011	2013-14	33	41	21	323	40*	16.15	–	–	14	–	7351	3695	112	32.99	7-94	5	1
Lyons, J.J.	1886-87	1897-98	14	27	0	731	134	27.07	1	3	3	–	316	149	6	24.83	5-30	1	–
McAlister, P.A.	1903-04	1909	8	16	1	252	41	16.80	–	–	10	–							
Macartney, C.G.	1907-08	1926	35	55	4	2131	170	41.78	7	9	17	–	3561†	1240	45	27.55	7-58	2	1
McCabe, S.J.	1930	1938	39	62	5	2748	232	48.21	6	13	41	–	3746	1543	36	42.86	4-13	–	–

INDIVIDUAL CAREER RECORDS – AUSTRALIA *continued*

BATTING AND FIELDING / BOWLING

	First Test	Last Test	Tests	Inns	NO	Runs	HS	Avge	100	50	Ct	St	Balls	Runs	Wkts	Avge	BB	5wI	10wM
McCool, C.L.	1945-46	1949-50	14	17	4	459	104*	35.30	1	1	14	—	2504	958	36	26.61	5-41	3	—
McCormick, E.L.	1935-36	1938	12	14†	5	54	17*	6.00	—	—	8	—	2107	1079	36	29.97	4-101	—	—
McCosker, R.B.	1974-75	1979-80	25	46	5	1622	127	39.56	4	9	21	—	—						
McDermott, C.J.	1984-85	1995-96	71	90	13	940	42*	12.20	—	1	19	—	16586	8332	291	28.63	8-97	14	2
McDonald, A.B.	2008-09	2008-09	4	6	1	107	68	21.40	—	2	2	—	732	300	9	33.33	3-25	—	—
McDonald, C.C.	1951-52	1961	47	83	4	3107	170	39.32	5	17	14	—	8	3	0	—	—	—	—
McDonald, E.A.	1920-21	1921-22	11	12	5	116	36	16.57	—	2	3	—	2885	1431	43	33.27	5-32	2	—
McDonnell, P.S.	1880	1888	19	34	1	955	147	28.93	3	2	6	—	52	53	0	—	—	—	—
McGain, B.E.	2008-09	2008-09	1	2	0	2	2	1.00	—	—	—	—	108	149	0	—	—	—	—
MacGill, S.C.G.	1997-98	2008	44	47	11	349	43	9.69	—	1	16	—	11237	6038	208	29.02	8-108	12	2
McGrath, G.D.	1993-94	2006-07	124	138	51	641	61	7.36	—	1	38	—	29248	12186	563	21.64	8-24	29	3
McIlwraith, J.	1886	1886	1	2	0	9	7	4.50	—	—	1	—	—						
McIntyre, P.E.	1994-95	1996-97	2	4	1	22	16	7.33	—	—	—	—	393	194	5	38.80	3-103	—	—
McKay, C.J.	2009-10	2009-10	1	1	0	10	10	10.00	—	—	1	—	168	101	1	101.00	1-56	—	—
Mackay, K.D.	1956	1962-63	37	52†	7	1507	89	33.48	—	13	16	—	5792	1721	50	34.42	6-42	2	—
McKenzie, G.D.	1961	1970-71	60	89	12	945	76	12.27	—	2	34	—	17681	7328	246	29.78	8-71	16	3
McKibbin, T.R.	1894-95	1897-98	5	8†	2	88	28*	14.66	—	—	4	—	1032	496	17	29.17	3-35	—	—
McLaren, J.W.	1911-12	1911-12	1	2	2	0	0*	—	—	—	—	—	144	70	1	70.00	1-23	—	—
Maclean, J.A.	1978-79	1978-79	4	8	1	79	33*	11.28	—	—	18	1	—						
McLeod, C.E.	1894-95	1905	17	29	5	573	112	23.87	1	4	9	—	3374	1325	33	40.15	5-65	2	—
McLeod, R.W.	1891-92	1893	6	11†	0	146	31	13.27	—	—	3	—	1089	382	12	31.83	5-53	1	—
McShane, P.G.	1884-85	1887-88	3	6†	1	26	12*	5.20	—	—	2	1	108†	48	1	48.00	1-39	—	—
Maddocks, L.V.	1954-55	1956-57	7	12	2	177	69	17.70	—	1	19	1	—						
Maguire, J.N.	1983-84	1983-84	3	5	1	28	15*	7.00	—	—	2	—	616	323	10	32.30	4-57	—	—
Mailey, A.A.	1920-21	1926	21	29	9	222	46*	11.10	—	—	14	—	6119	3358	99	33.91	9-121	6	2
Mallett, A.A.	1968	1980	38	50	13	430	43*	11.62	—	—	30	—	9990	3940	132	29.84	8-59	6	1
Malone, M.F.	1977	1977	1	1	0	46	46	46.00	—	—	—	—	342	77	6	12.83	5-63	1	—
Mann, A.L.	1977-78	1977-78	4	8†	0	189	105	23.62	1	—	2	—	552	316	4	79.00	3-12	—	—
Manou, G.A.	2009	2009	1	2	1	21	13*	21.00	—	—	3	—	—						
Marr, A.P.	1884-85	1884-85	1	2	0	5	5	2.50	—	—	—	—	48	14	0	—	—	—	—
Marsh, G.R.	1985-86	1991-92	50	93	7	2854	138	33.18	4	15	38	—	—						
Marsh, R.W.	1970-71	1983-84	96	150†	13	3633	132	26.51	3	16	343	12	72	54	0	—	—	—	—
Marsh, S.E.	2011	2013-14	9	15†	0	493	148	32.86	2	1	6	—	—						
Martin, J.W.	1960-61	1966-67	8	13†	1	214	55	17.83	—	—	5	—	1846†	832	17	48.94	3-56	—	—
Martyn, D.R.	1992-93	2006-07	67	109	14	4406	165	46.37	13	23	36	—	348	168	2	84.00	1-0	—	—
Massie, H.H.	1881-82	1884-85	9	16	0	249	55	15.56	—	1	5	—	—						
Massie, R.A.L.	1972	1972-73	6	8†	1	78	42	11.14	—	—	1	—	1739	647	31	20.87	8-53	2	1
Matthews, C.D.	1986-87	1988-89	3	5†	0	54	32	10.80	—	—	1	—	570†	313	6	52.16	3-95	—	—

INDIVIDUAL CAREER RECORDS – AUSTRALIA *continued*

	First Test	Last Test	Tests	Inns	NO	Runs	HS	Avge	100	50	Ct	St	Balls	Runs	Wkts	Avge	BB	5wI	10wM
							BATTING AND FIELDING									*BOWLING*			
Matthews, G.R.J.	1983–84	1992–93	33	53†	8	1849	130	41.08	4	12	17	—	6271	2942	61	48.22	5-103	2	1
Matthews, T.J.	1911–12	1912	8	10	1	153	53	17.00	—	1	7	—	1081	419	16	26.18	4-29	—	—
Maxwell, G.J.	2012–13	2012–13	2	4	0	39	13	9.75	—	—	2	—	246	193	7	27.57	4-127	—	—
May, T.B.A.	1987–88	1994–95	24	28	12	225	42*	14.06	—	—	6	—	6577	2606	75	34.74	5-9	3	—
Mayne, E.R.	1912	1921–22	4	4	1	64	25*	21.33	—	—	2	—	6	1	0	—	—	—	—
Mayne, L.C.	1964–65	1969–70	6	11†	3	76	13	9.50	—	—	3	—	1251	628	19	33.05	4-43	—	—
Meckiff, I.	1957–58	1963–64	18	20	7	154	45*	11.84	—	—	9	—	3734†	1423	45	31.62	6-38	2	—
Meuleman, K.D.	1945–46	1945–46	1	1	0	0	0	0.00	—	—	1	—							
Midwinter, W.E. ‡	1876–77	1886–87	8	14	1	174	37	13.38	—	—	5	—	949	333	14	23.78	5-78	1	—
Miller, C.R.	1998–99	2000–01	18	24	3	174	43	8.28	—	—	6	—	4091	1805	69	26.15	5-32	3	1
Miller, K.R.	1945–46	1956–57	55	87	7	2958	147	36.97	7	13	38	—	10461	3906	170	22.97	7-60	7	1
Minnett, R.B.	1911–12	1912	9	15	1	391	90	26.06	—	3	—	—	589	290	11	26.36	4-34	—	—
Misson, F.M.	1960–61	1961	5	5	3	38	25*	19.00	—	—	6	—	1197	616	16	38.50	4-58	—	—
Moody, T.M.	1989–90	1992	8	14	0	456	106	32.57	2	3	9	—	432	147	2	73.50	1-17	—	—
Moroney, J.	1949–50	1951–52	7	12	1	383	118	34.81	2	1	—	—							
Morris, A.R.	1946–47	1954–55	46	79†	3	3533	206	46.48	12	12	15	—	111†	50	2	25.00	1-5	—	—
Morris, S.	1884–85	1884–85	1	1	0	14	10*	14.00	—	—	—	—	136	73	2	36.50	2-73	—	—
Moses, H.	1886–87	1894–95	6	10†	0	198	33	19.80	—	1	1	—							
Moss, J.K.	1978–79	1978–79	1	2†	1	60	38*	60.00	—	—	—	—							
Moule, W.H.	1880	1880	1	2	0	40	34	20.00	—	—	1	—	51	23	3	7.66	3-23	—	—
Muller, S.A.	1999–2000	1999–2000	2	2	2	6	6*	—	—	—	2	—	348	258	7	36.85	3-68	—	—
Murdoch, W.L. ‡	1876–77	1890	18	33	5	896	211	32.00	2	1	14	—							
Musgrove, H.A.	1884–85	1884–85	1	2	0	13	9	6.50	—	—	—	—							
Nagel, L.E.	1932–33	1932–33	1	2	0	21	21*	21.00	—	—	—	—	262	110	2	55.00	2-110	—	—
Nash, L.J.	1931–32	1936–37	2	2	0	30	17	15.00	—	—	6	—	311	126	10	12.60	4-18	—	—
Nicholson, M.J.	1998–99	1998–99	1	2	0	14	9	7.00	—	—	—	—	150	115	4	28.75	3-56	—	—
Nitschke, H.C.	1931–32	1931–32	2	2†	0	53	47	26.50	—	—	3	—							
Noble, M.A.	1897–98	1909	42	73	7	1997	133	30.25	1	16	26	—	7159	3025	121	25.00	7-17	9	2
Noblet, G.	1949–50	1952–53	3	4	1	22	13*	7.33	—	—	1	—	774	183	7	26.14	3-21	—	—
North, M.J.	2008–09	2010–11	21	35†	2	1171	128	35.48	5	4	17	—	1258	591	14	42.21	6-55	1	—
Nothling, O.E.	1928–29	1928–29	1	2	0	52	44	26.00	—	—	—	—	276	72	0	—	—	—	—
O'Brien, L.P.J.	1932–33	1936–37	5	8†	0	211	61	26.37	—	2	3	—							
O'Connor, J.D.A.	1907–08	1909	4	8†	1	86	20	12.28	—	—	3	—	692	340	13	26.15	5-40	1	—
O'Donnell, S.P.	1985	1985–86	6	10	3	206	48	29.42	—	—	4	—	940	504	6	84.00	3-37	—	—
Ogilvie, A.D.	1977–78	1977–78	5	10	0	178	47	17.80	—	—	5	—							
O'Keeffe, K.J.	1970–71	1977	24	34	9	644	85	25.76	—	1	15	—	5384	2018	53	38.07	5-101	1	—

INDIVIDUAL CAREER RECORDS – AUSTRALIA continued

	First Test	Last Test	Tests	Inns	NO	Runs	HS	Avge	100	50	Ct	St	Balls	Runs	Wkts	Avge	BB	5wI	10wM
Oldfield, W.A.S.	1920–21	1936–37	54	80	17	1427	65*	22.65	–	4	78	52	–	–	–	–	–	–	–
O'Neill, N.C.L.	1958–59	1964–65	42	69	8	2779	181	45.55	6	15	21	–	1392	667	17	39.23	4-41	–	–
O'Reilly, W.J.	1931–32	1945–46	27	39†	7	410	56*	12.81	–	1	7	–	10024	3254	144	22.59	7-54	11	3
Oxenham, R.K.	1928–29	1931–32	7	10	0	151	48	15.10	–	–	4	–	1802	522	14	37.28	4-39	–	–
Paine, T.D.	2010	2010–11	4	8	0	287	92	35.87	–	2	16	1	–	–	–	–	–	–	–
Palmer, G.E.	1880	1886	17	25	4	296	48	14.09	–	–	13	–	4517	1678	78	21.51	7-65	6	2
Park, R.L.	1920–21	1920–21	1	1	0	0	0	0.00	–	–	–	–	6	9	0	–	–	–	–
Pascoe, L.S.	1977	1981–82	14	19	9	106	30*	10.60	–	–	2	–	3403	1668	64	26.06	5-59	1	–
Pattinson, J.L.	2011–12	2013–14	13	18†	7	331	42	30.09	–	1	1	–	2550	1381	51	27.07	5-27	3	–
Pellew, C.E.	1920–21	1921–22	10	14	1	484	116	37.23	2	1	4	–	78	34	0	–	–	–	–
Phillips, W.B.	1983–84	1985–86	27	48†	2	1485	159	32.28	2	7	52	–	–	–	–	–	–	–	–
Phillips, W.N.	1991–92	1991–92	1	2	0	22	14	11.00	–	–	–	–	–	–	–	–	–	–	–
Philpott, P.I.	1964–65	1965–66	8	10	1	93	22	10.33	–	–	5	–	2262	1000	26	38.46	5-90	1	–
Ponsford, W.H.	1924–25	1934	29	48	4	2122	266	48.22	7	6	21	–	–	–	–	–	–	–	–
Ponting, R.T.	1995–96	2012–13	168	287	29	13378	257	51.85	41	62	196	–	587	276	5	55.20	1-0	–	–
Pope, R.J.	1884–85	1884–85	1	2	0	3	3	1.50	–	–	–	–	–	–	–	–	–	–	–
Quiney, R.J.	2012–13	2012–13	2	3†	0	9	9	3.00	–	–	5	–	150	29	0	–	–	–	–
Rackemann, C.G.	1982–83	1990–91	12	14	4	53	15*	5.30	–	–	2	–	2719	1137	39	29.15	6-86	3	1
Ransford, V.S.	1907–08	1911–12	20	38†	6	1211	143*	37.84	1	7	10	–	43†	28	1	28.00	1-9	–	–
Redpath, I.R.	1963–64	1975–76	66	120	11	4737	171	43.45	8	31	83	–	64	41	0	–	–	–	–
Reedman, J.C.	1894–95	1894–95	1	2	0	21	17	10.50	–	–	1	–	57	24	1	24.00	1-12	–	–
Reid, B.A.	1985–86	1992–93	27	34†	14	93	13	4.65	–	–	5	–	6244†	2784	113	24.63	7-51	5	2
Reiffel, P.R.	1991–92	1997–98	35	50	14	955	79*	26.52	–	6	15	–	6403	2804	104	26.96	6-71	5	–
Renneberg, D.A.	1966–67	1967–68	8	13	7	22	9	3.66	–	–	2	–	1598	830	23	36.08	5-39	2	–
Richardson, A.J.	1924–25	1926	9	13	0	403	100	31.00	1	2	1	–	1812	521	12	43.41	2-20	–	–
Richardson, V.Y.	1924–25	1935–36	19	30	0	706	138	23.53	1	1	24	–	–	–	–	–	–	–	–
Rigg, K.E.	1930–31	1936–37	8	12	0	401	127	33.41	1	1	5	–	–	–	–	–	–	–	–
Ring, D.T.	1947–48	1953	13	21	2	426	67	22.42	–	4	5	–	3024	1305	35	37.28	6-72	2	–
Ritchie, G.M.	1982–83	1986–87	30	53	5	1690	146	35.20	3	7	14	–	6	10	0	–	–	–	–
Rixon, S.J.	1977–78	1984–85	13	24	3	394	54	18.76	–	2	42	5	–	–	–	–	–	–	–
Robertson, G.R.	1997–98	1998–99	4	7	0	140	57	20.00	–	1	1	–	898	515	13	39.61	4-72	–	–
Robertson, W.R.	1884–85	1884–85	1	2	0	2	2	1.00	–	–	–	–	44	24	0	–	–	–	–
Robinson, R.D.	1977	1977	3	6	0	100	34	16.66	–	–	4	–	–	–	–	–	–	–	–
Robinson, R.H.	1936–37	1936–37	1	2	0	5	3	2.50	–	–	1	–	–	–	–	–	–	–	–
Rogers, C.J.L.	2007–08	2013–14	14	27†	0	1030	119	38.14	4	5	9	–	–	–	–	–	–	–	–

INDIVIDUAL CAREER RECORDS – AUSTRALIA *continued*

	First Test	Last Test	Tests	BATTING AND FIELDING									BOWLING						
				Inns	NO	Runs	HS	Avge	100	50	Ct	St	Balls	Runs	Wkts	Avge	BB	5wI	10wM
Rorke, G.F.	1958–59	1959–60	4	4†	2	9	7	4.50	–	–	1	–	703	203	10	20.30	3-23	–	–
Rutherford, J.W.	1956–57	1956–57	1	1	0	30	30	30.00	–	–	–	–	36	15	1	15.00	1-11	–	–
Ryder, J.	1920–21	1928–29	20	32	5	1394	201*	51.62	3	9	17	–	1897	743	17	43.70	2-20	–	–
Saggers, R.A.	1948	1949–50	6	5	2	30	14	10.00	–	–	16	8	–	–	–	–	–	–	–
Saunders, J.V.	1901–02	1907–08	14	23†	6	39	11*	2.29	–	–	5	–	3565†	1796	79	22.73	7-34	6	–
Scott, H.J.H.	1884	1886	8	14	1	359	102	27.61	1	1	8	–	28	26	0	–	–	–	–
Sellers, R.H.D.	1964–65	1964–65	1	1	0	0	0	0.00	–	–	1	–	30	17	0	–	–	–	–
Serjeant, C.S.	1977	1977–78	12	23	1	522	124	23.72	1	2	13	–	–	–	–	–	–	–	–
Sheahan, A.P.	1967–68	1973–74	31	53	6	1594	127	33.91	2	7	17	–	–	–	–	–	–	–	–
Shepherd, B.K.	1962–63	1964–65	9	14†	2	502	96	41.83	–	5	2	–	26	9	0	–	–	–	–
Siddle, P.M.	2008–09	2013–14	53	76	11	926	51	14.24	–	2	16	–	11223	5522	188	29.37	6-54	8	–
Sievers, M.W.	1936–37	1936–37	3	6	1	67	25*	13.40	–	–	4	–	602	161	9	17.88	5-21	1	–
Simpson, R.B.	1957–58	1977–78	62	111	7	4869	311	46.81	10	27	110	–	6881	3001	71	42.26	5-57	2	–
Sincock, D.J.	1964–65	1965–66	3	4	1	80	29	26.66	–	–	2	–	724†	410	8	51.25	3-67	–	–
Slater, K.N.	1958–59	1958–59	1	1	0	1	1*	–	–	–	–	–	256	101	2	50.50	2-40	–	–
Slater, M.J.	1993	2001	74	131	7	5312	219	42.83	14	21	33	–	25	10	1	10.00	1-4	–	–
Sleep, P.R.	1978–79	1989–90	14	21	1	483	90	24.15	–	3	4	–	2982	1397	31	45.06	5-72	1	–
Slight, J.	1880	1880	1	2	0	11	11	5.50	–	–	–	–	–	–	–	–	–	–	–
Smith, D.B.M.	1912	1912	2	3	1	30	24*	15.00	–	–	–	–	–	–	–	–	–	–	–
Smith, S.B.	1983–84	1983–84	3	5	0	41	12	8.20	–	–	1	–	–	–	–	–	–	–	–
Smith, S.P.D.	2010	2013–14	20	38	4	1361	138*	40.02	4	6	16	–	822	527	11	47.90	3-18	–	–
Spofforth, F.R.	1876–77	1886–87	18	29	6	217	50	9.43	–	1	11	–	4185	1731	94	18.41	7-44	7	4
Stackpole, K.R.	1965–66	1973–74	43	80	5	2807	207	37.42	7	14	47	–	2321	1001	15	66.73	2-33	–	–
Starc, M.A.	2011–12	2013	12	20†	6	431	99	30.78	–	3	4	–	2450†	1378	41	33.60	6-154	2	–
Stevens, G.B.	1959–60	1959–60	4	7	0	112	28	16.00	–	–	2	–	–	–	–	–	–	–	–
Symonds, A.	2003–04	2008–09	26	41	5	1462	162*	40.61	2	10	22	–	2094	896	24	37.33	3-50	–	–
Taber, H.B.	1966–67	1969–70	16	27	5	353	48	16.04	–	–	56	4	–	–	–	–	–	–	–
Tait, S.W.	2005	2007–08	3	5	2	20	8	6.66	–	–	1	–	414	302	5	60.40	3-97	–	–
Tallon, D.	1945–46	1953	21	26	3	394	92	17.13	–	2	50	8	–	–	–	–	–	–	–
Taylor, J.M.	1920–21	1926	20	28	0	997	108	35.60	1	8	11	–	114	45	1	45.00	1-25	–	–
Taylor, M.A.	1988–89	1998–99	104	186†	13	7525	334*	43.49	19	40	157	–	42	26	1	26.00	1-11	–	–
Taylor, P.L.	1986–87	1991–92	13	19†	1	431	87	26.93	–	2	10	–	2227	1068	27	39.55	6-78	1	–
Thomas, G.	1964–65	1965–66	8	12	1	325	61	29.54	–	3	3	–	–	–	–	–	–	–	–
Thoms, G.R.	1951–52	1951–52	1	2	0	44	28	22.00	–	–	–	–	–	–	–	–	–	–	–
Thomson, A.L.	1970–71	1970–71	4	5	4	22	12*	22.00	–	–	–	–	1519	654	12	54.50	3-79	–	–
Thomson, J.R.	1972–73	1985	51	73	20	679	49	12.81	–	–	20	–	10535	5601	200	28.00	6-46	8	–

INDIVIDUAL CAREER RECORDS – AUSTRALIA continued

BATTING AND FIELDING / BOWLING

	First Test	Last Test	Tests	Inns	NO	Runs	HS	Avge	100	50	Ct	St	Balls	Runs	Wkts	Avge	BB	5wI	10wM
Thomson, N.F.D.	1876-77	1876-77	2	4	0	67	41	16.75	–	–	3	–	112	31	1	31.00	1-14	–	–
Thurlow, H.M.	1931-32	1931-32	1	1	0	0	0	0.00	–	–	–	–	234	86	0	–	–	–	–
Toohey, P.M.	1977-78	1979-80	15	29	1	893	122	31.89	1	7	9	–	2	4	0	–	–	–	–
Toshack, E.R.H.	1945-46	1948	12	11	6	73	20*	14.60	–	–	4	–	3140†	989	47	21.04	6-29	4	1
Travers, J.P.F.	1901-02	1901-02	1	2†	0	10	9	5.00	–	–	1	–	48†	14	1	14.00	1-14	–	–
Tribe, G.E.	1946-47	1946-47	3	3†	1	35	25*	17.50	–	–	–	–	760†	330	2	165.00	2-48	–	–
Trott, A.E. ‡	1894-95	1894-95	3	5	3	205	85*	102.50	–	2	4	–	474	192	9	21.33	8-43	1	–
Trott, G.H.S.	1888	1897-98	24	42	0	921	143	21.92	1	4	21	–	1891	1019	29	35.13	4-71	1	–
Trumble, H.	1890	1903-04	32	57	14	851	70	19.79	–	4	45	–	8099	3072	141	21.78	8-65	9	3
Trumble, J.W.	1884-85	1886	7	13	1	243	59	20.25	–	1	3	–	600	222	10	22.20	3-29	–	–
Trumper, V.T.	1899	1911-12	48	89	8	3163	214*	39.04	8	13	31	–	546	317	8	39.62	3-60	–	–
Turner, A.	1975	1976-77	14	27†	1	768	136	29.53	3	3	15	–	–	–	–	–	–	–	–
Turner, C.T.B.	1886-87	1894-95	17	32	4	323	29	11.53	–	–	8	–	5179	1670	101	16.53	7-43	11	2
Veivers, T.R.	1963-64	1966-67	21	30†	4	813	88	31.26	–	7	7	–	4191	1375	33	41.66	4-68	–	–
Veletta, M.R.J.	1987-88	1989-90	8	11	0	207	39	18.81	–	–	12	–	–	–	–	–	–	–	–
Wade, M.S.	2011-12	2012-13	12	22†	4	623	106	34.61	2	3	33	3	6	0	0	–	–	–	–
Waite, M.G.	1938	1938	2	3	0	11	8	3.66	–	–	1	–	552	190	1	190.00	1-150	–	–
Walker, M.H.N.	1972-73	1977	34	43	13	586	78*	19.53	–	1	12	–	10094	3792	138	27.47	8-143	6	–
Wall, T.W.	1928-29	1934	18	24	5	121	20	6.36	–	–	11	–	4812	2010	56	35.89	5-14	3	–
Walters, F.H.	1884-85	1884-85	1	2	0	12	7	6.00	–	–	2	–	–	–	–	–	–	–	–
Walters, K.D.	1965-66	1980-81	74	125	14	5357	250	48.26	15	33	43	–	3295	1425	49	29.08	5-66	1	–
Ward, F.A.	1936-37	1938	4	8	2	36	18	6.00	–	–	1	–	1268	574	11	52.18	6-102	1	–
Warne, S.K.	1991-92	2006-07	145	199	17	3154	99	17.32	–	12	125	–	40704	17995	708	25.41	8-71	37	10
Warner, D.A.	2011-12	2013-14	30	56†	3	2467	180	46.54	8	12	24	–	294	218	4	54.50	2-45	–	–
Watkins, J.R.	1972-73	1972-73	1	2	1	39	36	39.00	–	–	1	–	48	21	0	–	–	–	–
Watson, G.D.	1966-67	1972	5	9	0	97	50	10.77	–	1	1	–	552	254	6	42.33	2-67	–	–
Watson, S.R.	2004-05	2013-14	52	97	3	3408	176	36.25	4	22	35	–	4813	2205	69	31.95	6-33	3	–
Watson, W.J.	1954-55	1954-55	4	7	1	106	30	17.66	–	–	2	–	6	5	0	–	–	–	–
Waugh, M.E.	1990-91	2002-03	128	209	17	8029	153*	41.81	20	47	181	–	4853	2429	59	41.16	5-40	1	–
Waugh, S.R.	1985-86	2003-04	168	260	46	10927	200	51.06	32	50	112	–	7805	3445	92	37.44	5-28	3	–
Wellham, D.M.	1981	1986-87	6	11	1	257	103	23.36	1	–	5	–	–	–	–	–	–	–	–
Wessels, K.C. ‡	1982-83	1985-86	24	42†	1	1761	179	42.95	4	9	18	–	90	42	0	–	–	–	–
Whatmore, D.F.	1978-79	1979-80	7	13	0	293	77	22.53	–	2	13	–	30	11	0	–	–	–	–
White, C.L.	2008-09	2008-09	4	7	2	146	46	29.20	–	–	1	–	558	342	5	68.40	2-71	–	–
Whitney, M.R.	1981	1992-93	12	19	8	68	13	6.18	–	–	2	–	2672†	1325	39	33.97	7-27	2	1
Whitty, W.J.	1909	1912	14	19	7	161	39*	13.41	–	–	4	–	3357†	1373	65	21.12	6-17	3	–

INDIVIDUAL CAREER RECORDS – AUSTRALIA continued

	First Test	Last Test	Tests	Inns	NO	Runs	HS	Avge	100	50	Ct	St	Balls	Runs	Wkts	Avge	BB	5wI	10wM
								BATTING AND FIELDING								*BOWLING*			
Wiener, J.M.	1979–80	1979–80	6	11	0	281	93	25.54	–	2	4	–	78	41	0	–	–	–	–
Williams, B.A.	2003–04	2003–04	4	6	3	23	10*	7.66	–	–	4	–	852	406	9	45.11	4-53	–	–
Wilson, J.W.	1956–57	1956–57	1	–	–	–	–	–	–	–	–	–	216†	64	1	64.00	1-25	–	–
Wilson, P.	1997–98	1997–98	1	2	2	0	0*	–	–	–	–	–	72	50	0	–	–	–	–
Wood, G.M.	1977–78	1988–89	59	112†	6	3374	172	31.83	9	13	41	–	–						
Woodcock, A.J.	1973–74	1973–74	1	1	0	27	27	27.00	–	–	1	–	–						
Woodfull, W.M.	1926	1934	35	54	4	2300	161	46.00	7	13	7	–	–						
Woods, S.M.J. ‡	1888	1888	3	6	0	32	18	5.33	–	–	1	–	217	121	5	24.20	2-35	–	–
Woolley, R.D.	1982–83	1983–84	2	2	0	21	13	10.50	–	–	7	–	–						
Worrall, J.	1884–85	1899	11	22	3	478	76	25.15	–	5	13	–	255	127	1	127.00	1-97	–	–
Wright, K.J.	1978–79	1979–80	10	18	5	219	55*	16.84	–	1	31	4	–						
Yallop, G.N.	1975–76	1984–85	39	70†	3	2756	268	41.13	8	9	23	–	192†	116	1	116.00	1-21	–	–
Yardley, B.	1977–78	1982–83	33	54	4	978	74	19.56	–	4	31	–	8909	3986	126	31.63	7-98	6	1
Young, S.	1997	1997	1	2†	1	4	4*	4.00	–	–	–	–	48	13	0	–	–	–	–
Zoehrer, T.J.	1985–86	1986–87	10	14	2	246	52*	20.50	–	1	18	1	–						

INDIVIDUAL CAREER RECORDS – SOUTH AFRICA

	First Test	Last Test	Tests	Inns	NO	Runs	HS	Avge	100	50	Ct	St	Balls	Runs	Wkts	Avge	BB	5wI	10wM
								BATTING AND FIELDING								*BOWLING*			
Abbott, K.J.	2012–13	2013–14	2	3	0	23	13	7.66	–	–	1	–	424	197	12	16.41	7-29	1	–
Ackerman, H.D.	1997–98	1997–98	4	8	0	161	57	20.12	–	1	1	–	–						
Adams, P.R.	1995–96	2003–04	45	55	15	360	35	9.00	–	–	29	–	8850†	4405	134	32.87	7-128	4	1
Adcock, N.A.T.	1953–54	1961–62	26	39	12	146	24	5.40	–	–	4	–	6391	2195	104	21.10	6-43	5	–
Amla, H.M.	2004–05	2014	79	137	12	6415	311*	51.32	22	27	63	–	54	37	0	–	–	–	–
Anderson, J.H.	1902–03	1902–03	1	2	0	43	32	21.50	–	–	1	–	–						
Ashley, W.H.	1888–89	1888–89	1	2†	0	1	1	0.50	–	–	–	–	173†	95	7	13.57	7-95	1	–
Bacher, A.	1965	1969–70	12	22	1	679	73	32.33	–	6	10	–	–						
Bacher, A.M.	1996–97	1999–2000	19	33	1	833	96	26.03	–	5	11	–	6	4	0	–	–	–	–
Balaskas, X.C.	1930–31	1938–39	9	13	1	174	122*	14.50	1	–	5	–	1572	806	22	36.63	5-49	1	–
Barlow, E.J.	1961–62	1969–70	30	57	2	2516	201	45.74	6	15	35	–	3021	1362	40	34.05	5-85	1	–
Baumgartner, H.V.	1913–14	1913–14	1	2	0	19	16	9.50	–	–	–	–	166†	99	2	49.50	2-99	–	–
Beaumont, R.	1912	1913–14	5	9	0	70	31	7.77	–	–	2	–	6	0	0	–	–	–	–
Begbie, D.W.	1948–49	1949–50	5	7	0	138	48	19.71	–	–	2	–	160	130	1	130.00	1-38	–	–

INDIVIDUAL CAREER RECORDS – SOUTH AFRICA continued

				BATTING AND FIELDING									BOWLING						
	First Test	Last Test	Tests	Inns	NO	Runs	HS	Avge	100	50	Ct	St	Balls	Runs	Wkts	Avge	BB	5wI	10wM
Bell, A.J.	1929	1935	16	23	12	69	26*	6.27	–	–	6	–	3342	1567	48	32.64	6-99	4	–
Bisset, M.	1898-99	1909-10	3	6	2	103	35	25.75	–	–	2	1	–						
Bissett, G.F.	1927-28	1927-28	4	4	2	38	23	19.00	–	–	–	–	989	469	25	18.76	7-29	2	–
Blanckenberg, J.M.	1913-14	1924	18	30	7	455	59	19.78	–	2	9	–	3888	1817	60	30.28	6-76	4	–
Bland, K.C.	1961-62	1966-67	21	39	5	1669	144*	49.08	3	9	10	–	394	125	2	62.50	2-16	–	–
Bock, E.G.	1935-36	1935-36	1	2	2	11	9*	–	–	–	–	–	138	91	0	–	–	–	–
Boje, N.	1999-2000	2006	43	62†	10	1312	85	25.23	–	4	18	–	8620†	4265	100	42.65	5-62	3	–
Bond, G.E.	1938-39	1938-39	1	1	0	0	0	0.00	–	–	–	–	16	16	0	–	–	–	–
Bosch, T.	1991-92	1991-92	1	2	1	5	5*	–	–	–	–	–	237	104	3	34.66	2-61	–	–
Botha, J.	2005-06	2010-11	5	6	2	83	25	20.75	–	–	3	–	1017	573	17	33.70	4-56	–	–
Botten, J.T.	1965	1965	3	6	0	65	33	10.83	–	–	1	–	828	337	8	42.12	2-56	–	–
Boucher, M.V. ‡	1997-98	2011-12	146	204	24	5498	125	30.54	5	35	530	23	8	6	1	6.00	1-6	–	–
Brann, W.H.	1922-23	1922-23	3	5	0	71	50	14.20	–	1	2	–	–						
Briscoe, A.W.	1935-36	1938-39	2	3	0	33	16	11.00	–	–	1	–	–						
Bromfield, H.D.	1961-62	1965	9	12	7	59	21	11.80	–	–	13	–	1810	599	17	35.23	5-88	1	–
Brown, L.S.	1931-32	1931-32	2	3	1	17	8	5.66	–	–	–	–	318	189	3	63.00	1-30	–	–
Burger, C.G.D.	1957-58	1957-58	2	4	1	62	37*	20.66	–	–	1	–	–						
Burke, S.F.	1961-62	1964-65	2	4	1	42	20	14.00	–	–	–	–	660	257	11	23.36	6-128	2	1
Buys, I.D.	1922-23	1922-23	1	2†	1	4	4*	4.00	–	–	–	–	144†	52	0	–	–	–	–
Cameron, H.B.	1927-28	1935	26	45	4	1239	90	30.21	–	10	39	12	–						
Campbell, T.	1909-10	1912	5	9	3	90	48	15.00	–	–	7	1	–						
Carlstein, P.R.	1957-58	1963-64	8	14	1	190	42	14.61	–	–	3	–	–						
Carter, C.P.	1912	1924	10	15	5	181	45	18.10	–	–	2	–	1475†	694	28	24.78	6-50	2	–
Catterall, R.H.	1922-23	1930-31	24	43	2	1555	120	37.92	3	11	12	–	342	162	7	23.14	3-15	–	–
Chapman, H.W.	1913-14	1921-22	2	4	1	39	17	13.00	–	–	1	–	126	104	1	104.00	1-51	–	–
Cheetham, J.E.	1948-49	1955	24	43	6	883	89	23.86	–	5	13	–	6	2	0	–	–	–	–
Chevalier, G.A.	1969-70	1969-70	1	2	1	0	0*	0.00	–	–	1	–	253†	100	5	20.00	3-68	–	–
Christy, J.A.J.	1929	1931-32	10	18	0	618	103	34.33	1	5	3	–	138	92	2	46.00	1-15	–	–
Chubb, G.W.A.	1951	1951	5	9	3	63	15*	10.50	–	–	–	–	1425	577	21	27.47	6-51	2	–
Cochran, J.A.K.	1930-31	1930-31	1	1	0	4	4	4.00	–	–	–	–	138	47	0	–	–	–	–
Coen, S.K.	1927-28	1927-28	2	4	2	101	41*	50.50	–	1	1	–	12	7	0	–	–	–	–
Commaille, J.M.M.	1909-10	1927-28	12	22	1	355	47	16.90	–	–	1	–	–						
Commins, J.B.	1994-95	1994-95	3	6	1	125	45	25.00	–	–	2	–	–						
Conyngham, D.P.	1922-23	1922-23	1	2	2	6	3*	–	–	–	1	–	366	103	2	51.50	1-40	–	–
Cook, F.J.	1895-96	1895-96	1	2	0	7	7	3.50	–	–	–	–	–						
Cook, S.J.	1992-93	1993	3	6	0	107	43	17.83	–	–	–	–	–						
Cooper, A.H.C.	1913-14	1913-14	1	2	0	6	6	3.00	–	–	1	–	–						

INDIVIDUAL CAREER RECORDS – SOUTH AFRICA *continued*

	First Test	Last Test	Tests	Inns	NO	Runs	HS	Avge	100	50	Ct	St	Balls	Runs	Wkts	Avge	BB	5wI	10wM
						BATTING AND FIELDING										*BOWLING*			
Cox, J.L.	1913–14	1913–14	3	6	1	17	12*	3.40	–	–	1	–	576	245	4	61.25	2-74	–	–
Cripps, G.	1891–92	1891–92	1	2	0	21	18	10.50	–	–	–	–	15	23	0	–	–	–	–
Crisp, R.J.	1935	1935–36	9	13	2	123	35	10.25	–	–	3	–	1429	747	20	37.35	5-99	1	–
Cronje, W.J.	1991–2000	1999–2000	68	111	9	3714	135	36.41	6	23	33	–	3800	1288	43	29.95	3-14	–	–
Cullinan, D.J.	1992–93	2000–01	70	115	12	4554	275*	44.21	14	20	67	–	120	71	2	35.50	1-10	–	–
Curnow, S.H.	1930–31	1931–32	7	14	0	168	47	12.00	–	–	5	–	–						
Dalton, E.L.	1929	1938–39	15	24	2	698	117	31.72	2	3	5	–	864	490	12	40.83	4-59	–	–
Davies, E.Q.	1935–36	1938–39	5	8†	3	9	3	1.80	–	–	–	–	768	481	7	68.71	4-75	–	–
Dawson, A.C.	2003	2003	2	1	0	10	10	10.00	–	–	–	–	252	117	5	23.40	2-20	–	–
Dawson, O.C.	1947	1948–49	9	15	1	293	55	20.92	–	1	10	–	1294	578	10	57.80	2-57	–	–
Deane, H.G.	1924	1930–31	17	27	2	628	93	25.12	–	3	8	–	–						
de Bruyn, Z.	2004–05	2004–05	3	5	1	155	83	38.75	–	1	–	–	216	92	3	30.66	2-32	–	–
de Kock, Q.	2013–14	2014	4	7†	0	246	81	35.14	–	2	19	1	–						
de Lange, M.	2011–12	2011–12	2	2	0	9	9	4.50	–	–	1	–	448	277	9	30.77	7-81	1	–
de Villiers, A.B.	2004–05	2014	95	159	16	7296	278*	51.02	19	36	177	3	204	104	2	52.00	2-49	–	–
de Villiers, P.S.	1993–94	1997–98	18	26	7	359	67*	18.89	–	2	11	–	4805	2063	85	24.27	6-23	5	2
de Wet, F.	2009–10	2009–10	2	2	0	20	20	10.00	–	–	1	–	426	186	6	31.00	4-55	–	–
Dippenaar, H.H.	1999–2000	2006–07	38	62	5	1718	177*	30.14	3	7	27	–	12	1	0	–	–	–	–
Dixon, C.D.	1913–14	1913–14	1	2	0	0	0	0.00	–	–	1	–	240	118	3	39.33	2-62	–	–
Donald, A.A.	1991–92	2001–02	72	94	33	652	37	10.68	–	–	18	–	15519	7344	330	22.25	8-71	20	3
Dower, R.R.	1898–99	1898–99	1	2	0	9	9	4.50	–	–	2	–	–						
Draper, R.G.	1949–50	1949–50	2	3	0	25	15	8.33	–	–	–	–	–						
Duckworth, C.A.R.	1956–57	1956–57	2	4	0	28	13	7.00	–	–	3	–	–						
Dumbrill, R.	1965	1966–67	5	10	0	153	36	15.30	–	–	3	–	816	336	9	37.33	4-30	–	–
Duminy, J.P.	1927–28	1929	3	6†	0	30	12	5.00	–	–	2	–	60†	39	1	39.00	1-17	–	–
Duminy, J.-P.	2008–09	2014	27	43†	8	1280	166	36.57	4	6	19	–	2118	1259	32	39.34	4-73	–	–
Dunell, O.R.	1888–89	1888–89	2	4	2	42	26*	14.00	–	–	1	–	–						
du Plessis, F.	2012–13	2014	17	28	4	1262	137	52.58	3	6	10	–	78	69	0	–	–	–	–
du Preez, J.H.	1966–67	1966–67	2	2	0	0	0	0.00	–	–	2	–	144	51	3	17.00	2-22	–	–
du Toit, J.F.	1891–92	1891–92	1	2	0	2	2*	–	–	–	1	–	85†	47	1	47.00	1-47	–	–
Dyer, D.V.	1947	1947	3	6	0	96	62	16.00	–	1	–	–	–						
Eksteen, C.E.	1993	1999–2000	7	11	2	91	22	10.11	–	–	5	–	1536†	494	8	61.75	3-12	–	–
Elgar, D.	2012–13	2014	12	19†	0	536	103*	31.52	2	2	10	–	307†	223	3	74.33	1-3	–	–
Elgie, M.K.	1961–62	1961–62	3	6	0	75	56	12.50	–	1	4	–	66†	46	0	–	–	–	–
Elworthy, S.	1998	2002–03	4	5	1	72	48	18.00	–	–	1	–	867	444	13	34.15	4-66	–	–
Endean, W.R.	1951	1957–58	28	52	4	1630	162*	33.95	3	8	41	–	–						

INDIVIDUAL CAREER RECORDS – SOUTH AFRICA *continued*

	First Test	Last Test	Tests	Inns	NO	Runs	HS	Avge	100	50	Ct	St	Balls	Runs	Wkts	Avge	BB	5wI	10wM
								BATTING AND FIELDING								BOWLING			
Farrer, W.S.	1961–62	1963–64	6	10	2	221	40	27.62	–	–	2	–	–	–	–	–	–	–	–
Faulkner, G.A.	1905–06	1924	25	47	4	1754	204	40.79	4	8	20	–	4227	2180	82	26.58	7-84	4	–
Fellows-Smith, J.P.	1960	1960	4	8	2	166	35	27.66	–	–	2	–	114	61	0	–	–	–	–
Fichardt, C.G.	1891–92	1895–96	2	4	0	15	10	3.75	–	–	2	–	–	–	–	–	–	–	–
Finlason, C.E.	1888–89	1888–89	1	2	0	6	6	3.00	–	–	–	–	12	7	0	–	–	–	–
Floquet, C.E.	1909–10	1909–10	1	2	1	12	11*	12.00	–	–	1	–	48	24	0	–	–	–	–
Francis, H.H.	1898–99	1898–99	2	4	0	39	29	9.75	–	–	1	–	–	–	–	–	–	–	–
Francois, C.M.	1922–23	1922–23	5	9	1	252	72	31.50	–	1	5	–	684	225	6	37.50	3-23	–	–
Frank, C.N.	1921–22	1921–22	3	6	0	236	152	39.33	1	–	–	–	–	–	–	–	–	–	–
Frank, W.H.B.	1895–96	1895–96	1	2	0	7	5	3.50	–	–	–	–	58	52	1	52.00	1-52	–	–
Fuller, E.R.H.	1952–53	1957–58	7	9	1	64	17	8.00	–	–	3	–	1898	668	22	30.36	5-66	1	–
Fullerton, G.M.	1947	1951	7	13	0	325	88	25.00	–	3	10	2	–	–	–	–	–	–	–
Funston, K.J.	1952–53	1957–58	18	33	1	824	92	25.75	–	5	7	–	–	–	–	–	–	–	–
Gamsy, D.	1969–70	1969–70	2	3	1	39	30*	19.50	–	–	5	–	6	4	0	–	–	–	–
Gibbs, H.H.	1996–97	2007–08	90	154	7	6167	228	41.95	14	26	94	–	–	–	–	–	–	–	–
Gleeson, R.A.	1895–96	1895–96	1	2	1	4	3	4.00	–	–	2	–	–	–	–	–	–	–	–
Glover, G.K.	1895–96	1895–96	1	2	1	21	18*	21.00	–	–	–	–	65	28	1	28.00	1-28	–	–
Goddard, T.L.	1955	1969–70	41	78†	5	2516	112	34.46	1	18	48	–	11736†	3226	123	26.22	6-53	5	–
Gordon, N.	1938–39	1938–39	5	6	2	8	7*	2.00	–	–	1	–	1966	807	20	40.35	5-103	2	–
Graham, R.	1898–99	1898–99	2	4	0	6	4	1.50	–	–	2	–	240	127	3	42.33	2-22	–	–
Grieveson, R.E.	1938–39	1938–39	2	2	0	114	75	57.00	–	1	7	3	–	–	–	–	–	–	–
Griffin, G.M.	1960	1960	2	4	0	25	14	6.25	–	–	–	–	432	192	8	24.00	4-87	–	–
Hall, A.E.	1922–23	1930–31	7	8†	2	11	5	1.83	–	–	4	–	2361†	886	40	22.15	7-63	3	1
Hall, A.J.	2001–02	2006–07	21	33	4	760	163	26.20	1	3	16	–	3001	1617	45	35.93	3-1	–	–
Hall, G.G.	1964–65	1964–65	1	1	0	0	0	0.00	–	–	–	–	186	94	1	94.00	1-94	–	–
Halliwell, E.A.	1891–92	1902–03	8	15	0	188	57	12.53	–	1	10	2	–	–	–	–	–	–	–
Halse, C.G.	1963–64	1963–64	3	3	3	30	19*	–	–	–	1	–	587	260	6	43.33	3-50	–	–
Hands, P.A.M.	1913–14	1924	7	12	0	300	83	25.00	–	2	3	–	37	18	0	–	–	–	–
Hands, R.H.M.	1913–14	1913–14	1	2	0	7	7	3.50	–	–	–	–	–	–	–	–	–	–	–
Hanley, M.A.	1948–49	1948–49	1	1	0	0	0	0.00	–	–	–	–	232	88	1	88.00	1-57	–	–
Harris, P.L.	2006–07	2010–11	37	48	5	460	46	10.69	–	1	16	–	8809†	3901	103	37.87	6-127	3	–
Harris, T.A.	1947	1948–49	3	5	1	100	60	25.00	–	1	1	–	–	–	–	–	–	–	–
Hartigan, G.P.D.	1912	1913–14	5	10	0	114	51	11.40	–	1	1	–	252	141	1	141.00	1-72	–	–
Harvey, R.L.	1935–36	1935–36	2	4	0	51	28	12.75	–	–	–	–	–	–	–	–	–	–	–
Hathorn, C.M.H.	1902–03	1910–11	12	20	1	325	102	17.10	1	–	5	–	–	–	–	–	–	–	–
Hayward, M.	1999–2000	2004	16	17	8	66	14	7.33	–	–	4	–	2821	1609	54	29.79	5-56	1	–

INDIVIDUAL CAREER RECORDS – SOUTH AFRICA *continued*

	First Test	Last Test	Tests	BATTING AND FIELDING									BOWLING						
				Inns	NO	Runs	HS	Avge	100	50	Ct	St	Balls	Runs	Wkts	Avge	BB	5wI	10wM
Hearne, F. ‡	1891–92	1895–96	4	8	0	121	30	15.12	–	–	2	–	62	40	2	20.00	2-40	–	–
Hearne, G.A.L.	1922–23	1924	3	5	0	59	28	11.80	–	–	3	–	–	–	–	–	–	–	–
Heine, P.S.	1955	1961–62	14	24	3	209	31	9.95	–	–	8	–	3890	1455	58	25.08	6-58	4	–
Henderson, C.W.	2001–02	2002–03	7	7	3	65	30	9.28	–	–	2	–	1962†	928	22	42.18	4-116	–	–
Henry, O.	1992–93	1992–93	3	3†	0	53	34	17.66	–	–	2	–	427†	189	3	63.00	2-56	–	–
Hime, C.F.W.	1895–96	1895–96	1	2	0	8	8	4.00	–	–	–	–	55	31	1	31.00	1-20	–	–
Hudson, A.C.	1991–92	1997–98	35	63	3	2007	163	33.45	4	13	36	–	–	–	–	–	–	–	–
Hutchinson, P.	1888–89	1888–89	2	4	0	14	11	3.50	–	–	3	–	–	–	–	–	–	–	–
Imran Tahir	2011–12	2014	15	16	7	109	29*	12.11	–	–	7	–	3199	1887	40	47.17	5-32	1	–
Ironside, D.E.J.	1953–54	1953–54	3	4	2	37	13	18.50	–	–	1	–	986	275	15	18.33	5-51	1	–
Irvine, B.L.	1969–70	1969–70	4	7†	0	353	102	50.42	1	2	2	–	–	–	–	–	–	–	–
Jack, S.D.	1994–95	1994–95	2	2	0	7	7	3.50	–	–	1	–	462	196	8	24.50	4-69	–	–
Johnson, C.L.	1895–96	1895–96	1	2	0	10	7	5.00	–	–	1	–	140	57	0	–	–	–	–
Kallis, J.H. ‡	1995–96	2013–14	165	278	39	13206	224	55.25	45	58	196	–	20172	9497	291	32.63	6-54	5	–
Keith, H.J.	1952–53	1956–57	8	16†	1	318	73	21.20	–	2	9	–	108†	63	0	–	–	–	–
Kemp, J.M.	2000–01	2005–06	4	6	0	80	55	13.33	–	1	3	–	479	222	9	24.66	3-33	–	–
Kempis, G.A.	1888–89	1888–89	1	2	0	0	0*	0.00	–	–	–	–	168†	76	4	19.00	3-53	–	–
Khan, I.	2008–09	2008–09	1	1†	0	20	20	20.00	–	–	1	–	–	–	–	–	–	–	–
Kirsten, G.	1993–94	2003–04	101	176†	15	7289	275	45.27	21	34	83	–	349	142	2	71.00	1-0	–	–
Kirsten, P.N.	1991–92	1994	12	22	2	626	104	31.30	1	4	8	–	54	30	0	–	–	–	–
Kleinveldt, R.K.	2012–13	2012–13	4	5	2	27	17*	9.00	–	–	2	–	667	422	10	42.20	3-65	–	–
Klusener, L.	1996–97	2004	49	69†	11	1906	174	32.86	4	8	34	–	6887	3033	80	37.91	8-64	1	–
Kotze, J.J.	1902–03	1907	3	5	2	2	2	0.40	–	–	3	–	413	243	6	40.50	3-64	–	–
Kuiper, A.P.	1991–92	1991–92	1	2	0	34	34	17.00	–	–	1	–	–	–	–	–	–	–	–
Kuys, F.	1898–99	1898–99	1	2	0	26	26	13.00	–	–	–	–	60	31	2	15.50	2-31	–	–
Lance, H.R.	1961–62	1969–70	13	22	1	591	70	28.14	–	5	7	–	948	479	12	39.91	3-30	–	–
Langeveldt, C.K.	2004–05	2005–06	6	4	2	16	10	8.00	–	–	2	–	999	593	16	37.06	5-46	1	–
Langton, A.C.B.	1935	1938–39	15	23	4	298	73*	15.68	–	2	8	–	4199	1827	40	45.67	5-58	1	–
Lawrence, G.B.	1961–62	1961–62	5	8	0	141	43	17.62	–	–	2	–	1334	512	28	18.28	8-53	2	–
le Roux, F.L.	1913–14	1913–14	1	2	0	1	1	0.50	–	–	–	–	54	24	0	–	–	–	–
Lewis, P.T.	1913–14	1913–14	1	2	0	0	0	0.00	–	–	–	–	–	–	–	–	–	–	–
Liebenberg, G.F.J.	1997–98	1998	5	8	0	104	45	13.00	–	–	1	–	–	–	–	–	–	–	–
Lindsay, D.T.	1963–64	1969–70	19	31	1	1130	182	37.66	3	5	57	2	–	–	–	–	–	–	–
Lindsay, J.D.	1947	1947	3	5	2	21	9*	7.00	–	–	4	1	–	–	–	–	–	–	–

INDIVIDUAL CAREER RECORDS – SOUTH AFRICA *continued*

	First Test	Last Test	Tests	BATTING AND FIELDING									BOWLING						
				Inns	NO	Runs	HS	Avge	100	50	Ct	St	Balls	Runs	Wkts	Avge	BB	5wI	10wM
Lindsay, N.V.	1921–22	1921–22	1	2	0	35	29	17.50	–	–	1	–	18	20	0	–	–	–	–
Ling, W.V.S.	1921–22	1922–23	6	10	0	168	38	16.80	–	–	1	–	–	–	–	–	–	–	–
Llewellyn, C.B.	1895–96	1912	15	28†	1	544	90	20.14	–	4	7	–	2292†	1421	48	29.60	6-92	4	1
Lundie, E.B.	1913–14	1913–14	1	2	1	1	1	1.00	–	–	–	–	286	107	4	26.75	4-101	–	–
Macaulay, M.J.	1964–65	1964–65	1	2	0	33	21	16.50	–	–	–	–	276†	73	2	36.50	1-10	–	–
McCarthy, C.N.	1948–49	1951	15	24	15	28	5	3.11	–	–	6	–	3499	1510	36	41.94	6-43	2	–
McGlew, D.J.	1951	1961–62	34	64	6	2440	255*	42.06	7	10	18	–	32	23	0	–	–	–	–
McKenzie, N.D.	2000	2008–09	58	94	7	3253	226	37.39	5	16	54	–	90	68	0	–	–	–	–
McKinnon, A.H.	1960	1966–67	8	13	7	107	27	17.83	–	–	1	–	2546†	925	26	35.57	4-128	–	–
McLaren, R.	2009–10	2013–14	2	3†	1	47	33*	23.50	–	–	–	–	264	162	3	54.00	2-72	–	–
McLean, R.A.	1951	1964–65	40	73	3	2120	142	30.28	5	10	23	–	4	–	0	–	–	–	–
McMillan, B.M.	1992–93	1998	38	62	12	1968	113	39.36	3	13	49	–	6048	2537	75	33.82	4-65	2	–
McMillan, Q.	1929	1931–32	13	21	4	306	50*	18.00	–	1	8	–	2021	1243	36	34.52	5-66	1	–
Mann, N.B.F.	1947	1951	19	31	2	400	52	13.33	–	1	3	–	5796†	1920	58	33.10	6-59	2	–
Mansell, P.N.F.	1951	1955	13	22	2	355	90	17.75	–	2	15	–	1506	736	11	66.90	3-58	–	–
Markham, L.A.	1948–49	1948–49	3	1	0	20	20	20.00	–	–	–	–	104	72	1	72.00	1-34	–	–
Marx, W.F.E.	1921–22	1921–22	3	6†	0	125	36	20.83	–	–	4	–	228	144	4	36.00	3-85	–	–
Matthews, C.R.	1992–93	1995–96	18	25	6	348	62*	18.31	–	1	4	–	3980	1502	52	28.88	5-42	2	–
Meintjes, D.J.	1922–23	1922–23	2	3	0	43	21	14.33	–	–	3	–	246	115	6	19.16	3-38	–	–
Melle, M.G.	1952–53	1952–53	7	12	4	68	17	8.50	–	–	4	–	1667	851	26	32.73	6-71	2	–
Melville, A.	1938–39	1948–49	11	19	2	894	189	52.58	4	3	8	–	–	–	–	–	–	–	–
Middleton, J.	1895–96	1902–03	6	12	5	52	22	7.42	–	3	1	–	1064†	442	24	18.41	5-51	2	–
Mills, C.H.	1891–92	1891–92	1	2	0	25	21	12.50	–	–	1	–	140	83	2	41.50	2-83	–	–
Milton, W.H.	1888–89	1891–92	3	6	0	68	21	11.33	–	–	2	–	79	48	2	24.00	1-5	–	–
Mitchell, B.	1929	1948–49	42	80	9	3471	189*	48.88	8	21	56	–	2525	1380	27	51.11	5-87	1	–
Mitchell, F. ‡	1912	1912	3	6	1	28	12	4.66	–	–	–	–	–	–	–	–	–	–	–
Morkel, D.P.B.	1927–28	1931–32	16	28	1	663	88	24.55	–	4	13	–	1704	821	18	45.61	4-93	–	–
Morkel, J.A.	2008–09	2008–09	1	1†	0	58	58	58.00	–	1	–	–	192	132	1	132.00	1-44	–	–
Morkel, M.	2006–07	2014	59	70†	11	706	40	11.96	–	–	14	–	11580	6101	204	29.90	6-23	6	–
Murray, A.R.A.	1952–53	1953–54	10	14	1	289	109	22.23	1	1	3	–	2374	710	18	39.44	4-169	–	–
Nel, A.	2001–02	2008	36	42	8	337	34	9.91	–	–	16	–	7630	3919	123	31.86	6-32	3	1
Nel, J.D.	1949–50	1957–58	6	11	0	150	38	13.63	–	–	1	–	–	–	–	–	–	–	–
Newberry, C.	1913–14	1913–14	4	8	0	62	16	7.75	–	–	3	–	558	268	11	24.36	4-72	–	–
Newson, E.S.	1930–31	1938–39	3	5	1	30	16	7.50	–	–	3	–	874	265	4	66.25	2-58	–	–
Ngam, M.	2000–01	2000–01	3	1	1	0	0*	–	–	–	1	–	392	189	11	17.18	3-26	–	–
Nicholson, F.	1935–36	1935–36	4	8	1	76	29	10.85	–	–	3	–	–	–	–	–	–	–	–

INDIVIDUAL CAREER RECORDS – SOUTH AFRICA continued

	First Test	Last Test	Tests	Inns	NO	Runs	HS	Avge	100	50	Ct	St	Balls	Runs	Wkts	Avge	BB	5wI	10wM
						BATTING AND FIELDING									*BOWLING*				
Nicolson, J.F.W.	1927–28	1927–28	3	5†	0	179	78	35.80	–	1	–	–	24	17	0	–	–	–	–
Norton, N.O.	1909–10	1909–10	1	2	0	9	7	4.50	–	–	–	–	90	47	4	11.75	4-47	–	–
Nourse, A.D.	1935	1951	34	62	7	2960	231	53.81	9	14	12	–	20	9	0	–	–	–	–
Nourse, A.W.	1902–03	1924	45	83†	8	2234	111	29.78	1	15	43	–	3234†	1553	41	37.87	4-25	–	–
Ntini, M.	1997–98	2009–10	101	116	45	699	32*	9.84	–	–	25	–	20834	11242	390	28.82	7-37	18	4
Nupen, E.P.	1921–22	1935–36	17	31	7	348	69	14.50	–	2	9	–	4159	1788	50	35.76	6-46	5	1
Ochse, A.E.	1888–89	1888–89	2	4	0	16	8	4.00	–	–	–	–	–	–	–	–	–	–	–
Ochse, A.L.	1927–28	1929	3	4	1	11	4*	3.66	–	–	1	–	649	362	10	36.20	4-79	–	–
O'Linn, S.	1960	1961–62	7	12†	1	297	98	27.00	–	2	4	–	–	–	–	–	–	–	–
Ontong, J.L.	2001–02	2004–05	2	4	1	57	32	19.00	–	–	1	–	185	133	1	133.00	1-79	–	–
Owen-Smith, H.G.O.	1929	1929	5	8	2	252	129	42.00	1	1	4	–	156	113	0	–	–	–	–
Palm, A.W.	1927–28	1927–28	1	2	0	15	13	7.50	–	–	1	–	–	–	–	–	–	–	–
Parker, G.M.	1924	1924	2	4	2	3	2*	1.50	–	–	–	–	366	273	8	34.12	6-152	1	–
Parkin, D.C.	1891–92	1891–92	1	2	0	6	6	3.00	–	–	1	–	130	82	3	27.33	3-82	–	–
Parnell, W.D.	2009–10	2013–14	4	3†	0	44	22	14.66	–	–	1	–	357†	258	7	36.85	2-17	–	–
Partridge, J.T.	1963–64	1964–65	11	12	5	73	13*	10.42	–	–	6	–	3684	1373	44	31.20	7-91	3	–
Pearse, C.O.C.	1910–11	1910–11	3	6	0	55	31	9.16	–	–	1	–	144	106	3	35.33	3-56	–	–
Pegler, S.J.	1909–10	1924	16	28	5	356	35*	15.47	–	–	5	–	2989	1572	47	33.44	7-65	2	–
Petersen, A.N.	2009–10	2014	33	60	3	2007	182	35.83	5	8	26	–	114	62	1	62.00	1-2	–	–
Peterson, R.J.	2003	2013–14	15	20†	4	464	84	27.29	–	3	9	–	2515†	1416	38	37.26	5-33	1	–
Philander, V.D.	2011–12	2014	26	34	9	684	74	27.36	–	4	8	–	5267	2481	115	21.57	6-44	9	2
Piedt, D.L.	2014	2014	1	1	0	13	13	13.00	–	–	2	–	294	152	8	19.00	4-62	–	–
Pithey, A.J.	1956–57	1964–65	17	27	1	819	154	31.50	1	4	3	–	12	5	0	–	–	–	–
Pithey, D.B.	1963–64	1966–67	8	12	1	138	55	12.54	–	1	6	–	1424	577	12	48.08	6-58	1	–
Plimsoll, J.B.	1947	1947	1	2	1	16	8*	16.00	–	–	–	–	237†	143	3	47.66	3-128	–	–
Pollock, P.M.	1961–62	1969–70	28	41	13	607	75*	21.67	–	2	9	–	6522	2806	116	24.18	6-38	9	1
Pollock, R.G.	1963–64	1969–70	23	41†	4	2256	274	60.97	7	11	17	–	414	204	4	51.00	2-50	–	–
Pollock, S.M.	1995–96	2007–08	108	156	39	3781	111	32.31	2	16	72	–	24353	9733	421	23.11	7-87	16	1
Poore, R.M.	1895–96	1895–96	3	6	0	76	20	12.66	–	–	3	–	9	4	1	4.00	1-4	–	–
Pothecary, J.E.	1960	1960	3	4	0	26	12	6.50	–	–	2	–	828	354	9	39.33	4-58	–	–
Powell, A.W.	1898–99	1898–99	1	2	0	16	11	8.00	–	–	2	–	20	10	1	10.00	1-10	–	–
Pretorius, D.	2001–02	2003	4	4	1	22	9	7.33	–	–	–	–	570	430	6	71.66	4-115	–	–
Prince, A.G.	2001–02	2011–12	66	104†	16	3665	162*	41.64	11	11	47	–	96	47	1	47.00	1-2	–	–
Prince, C.F.H.	1898–99	1898–99	1	2	0	6	5	3.00	–	–	–	–	–	–	–	–	–	–	–
Pringle, M.W.	1991–92	1995–96	4	6	2	67	33	16.75	–	–	–	–	652	270	5	54.00	2-62	–	–

INDIVIDUAL CAREER RECORDS – SOUTH AFRICA *continued*

	First Test	Last Test	Tests	Inns	NO	Runs	HS	Avge	100	50	Ct	St	Balls	Runs	Wkts	Avge	BB	5wI	10wM
								BATTING AND FIELDING								BOWLING			
Procter, M.J.	1966–67	1969–70	7	10	1	226	48	25.11	–	–	4	–	1514	616	41	15.02	6-73	1	–
Prommitz, H.L.E.	1927–28	1927–28	2	4	0	14	5	3.50	–	–	2	–	528	161	8	20.12	5-58	1	–
Quinn, N.A.	1929	1931–32	12	18†	3	90	28	6.00	–	–	1	–	2922†	1145	35	32.71	6-92	1	–
Reid, N.	1921–22	1921–22	1	2	0	17	11	8.50	–	–	–	–	126	63	2	31.50	2-63	–	–
Rhodes, J.N.	1992–93	2000	52	80	9	2532	117	35.66	3	17	34	–	12	5	0	–	–	–	–
Richards, A.R.	1895–96	1895–96	1	2	0	6	6	3.00	–	–	–	–							
Richards, B.A.	1969–70	1969–70	4	7	0	508	140	72.57	2	2	3	–	72	26	1	26.00	1-12	–	–
Richards, W.H.M.	1888–89	1888–89	1	2	0	4	4	2.00	–	–	–	–							
Richardson, D.J	1991–92	1997–98	42	64	8	1359	109	24.26	1	8	150	2							
Robertson, J.B.	1935–36	1935–36	3	6	1	51	17	10.20	–	–	2	–	738	321	6	53.50	3-143	–	–
Rose-Innes, A.	1888–89	1888–89	2	4	0	14	13	3.50	–	–	2	–	128†	89	5	17.80	5-43	1	–
Routledge, T.W.	1891–92	1895–96	4	8	0	72	24	9.00	–	–	2	–							
Rowan, A.M.B.	1947	1951	15	23	6	290	41	17.05	–	–	7	–	5193	2084	54	38.59	5-68	4	–
Rowan, E.A.B.	1935	1951	26	50	5	1965	236	43.66	3	12	14	–	19	7	0	–	–	–	–
Rowe, G.A.	1895–96	1902–03	5	9	3	26	13*	4.33	–	–	4	–	998†	456	15	30.40	5-115	1	–
Rudolph, J.A.	2003	2012–13	48	83†	9	2622	222*	35.43	6	11	29	–	664	432	4	108.00	1-1	–	–
Rushmere, M.W.	1991–92	1991–92	1	2	0	6	3	3.00	–	–	–	–							
Samuelson, S.V.	1909–10	1909–10	1	2	0	22	15	11.00	–	–	1	–	108	64	0	–	–	–	–
Schultz, B.N.	1992–93	1997–98	9	8†	2	9	6	1.50	–	–	2	–	1733†	749	37	20.24	5-48	2	–
Schwarz, R.O.	1905–06	1912	20	35	8	374	61	13.85	–	1	18	–	2639	1417	55	25.76	6-47	2	–
Seccull, A.W.	1895–96	1895–96	1	2	1	23	17*	23.00	–	–	1	–	60	37	2	18.50	2-37	–	–
Seymour, M.A.	1963–64	1969–70	7	10	3	84	36	12.00	–	–	2	–	1458	588	9	65.33	3-80	–	–
Shalders, W.A.	1898–99	1907	12	23	1	355	42	16.13	–	–	3	–	48	6	1	6.00	1-6	–	–
Shepstone, G.H.	1895–96	1898–99	2	4	0	38	21	9.50	–	–	2	–	115	47	0	–	–	–	–
Sherwell, P.W.	1905–06	1910–11	13	22	4	427	115	23.72	1	1	20	16							
Siedle, I.J.	1927–28	1935–36	18	34	4	977	141	28.73	1	5	7	–							
Sinclair, J.H.	1895–96	1910–11	25	47	1	1069	106	23.23	3	3	9	–	3598	1996	63	31.68	6-26	1	–
Smith, C.J.E.	1902–03	1902–03	3	6	1	106	45	21.20	–	–	2	–							
Smith, F.W.	1888–89	1895–96	3	6	1	45	12	9.00	–	–	2	–							
Smith, G.C. ‡	2001–02	2013–14	116	203†	13	9253	277	48.70	27	38	166	–	1418	885	8	110.62	2-145	–	–
Smith, VI.	1947	1957–58	9	16	6	39	11*	3.90	–	–	3	–	1655	769	12	64.08	4-143	–	–
Snell, R.P.	1991–92	1994–95	5	8	1	95	48	13.57	–	–	1	–	1025	538	19	28.31	4-74	–	–
Snooke, S.D.	1907	1907	1	1	0	0	0	0.00	–	–	2	–							
Snooke, S.J.	1905–06	1922–23	26	46	1	1008	103	22.40	1	5	24	–	1620	702	35	20.05	8-70	1	1
Solomon, W.R.T.	1898–99	1898–99	1	2	0	4	2	2.00	–	–	1	–							

INDIVIDUAL CAREER RECORDS – SOUTH AFRICA continued

	First Test	Last Test	Tests	BATTING AND FIELDING									BOWLING						
				Inns	NO	Runs	HS	Avge	100	50	Ct	St	Balls	Runs	Wkts	Avge	BB	5wI	10wM
Stewart, R.B.	1888–89	1888–89	1	2	0	13	9	6.50	–	–	2	–	–	–	–	–	–	–	–
Steyn, D.W.	2004–05	2014	75	95	21	1056	76	14.27	–	1	19	–	15975	8644	383	22.56	7-51	24	5
Steyn, P.J.R.	1994–95	1994–95	3	6	0	127	46	21.16	–	–	–	–	–	–	–	–	–	–	–
Stricker, L.A.	1909–10	1912	13	24	0	344	48	14.33	–	–	3	–	174	105	1	105.00	1-36	–	–
Strydom, P.C.	1999–2000	1999–2000	2	3	0	35	30	11.66	–	–	1	–	36†	27	0	–	–	–	–
Susskind, M.J.	1924	1924	5	8	0	268	65	33.50	–	4	1	–	–	–	–	–	–	–	–
Symcox, P.L.	1993	1998–99	20	27	1	741	108	28.50	1	4	5	–	3561	1603	37	43.32	4-69	–	–
Taberer, H.M.	1902–03	1902–03	1	1	0	2	2	2.00	–	–	–	–	60	48	1	48.00	1-25	–	–
Tancred, A.B.	1888–89	1888–89	2	4	1	87	29	29.00	–	–	2	–	–	–	–	–	–	–	–
Tancred, L.J.	1902–03	1913–14	14	26	1	530	97	21.20	–	2	3	–	–	–	–	–	–	–	–
Tancred, V.M.	1898–99	1898–99	1	2	0	25	18	12.50	–	–	1	–	–	–	–	–	–	–	–
Tapscott, G.L.	1913–14	1913–14	1	2	0	5	4	2.50	–	–	–	–	–	–	–	–	–	–	–
Tapscott, L.E.	1922–23	1922–23	2	3	1	58	50*	29.00	–	1	–	–	12	2	0	–	–	–	–
Tayfield, H.J.	1949–50	1960	37	60	9	862	75	16.90	–	2	26	–	13568	4405	170	25.91	9-113	14	2
Taylor, A.I.	1956–57	1956–57	1	2	0	18	12	9.00	–	–	–	–	–	–	–	–	–	–	–
Taylor, D.	1913–14	1913–14	2	4†	0	85	36	21.25	–	–	–	–	–	–	–	–	–	–	–
Taylor, H.W.	1912	1931–32	42	76	4	2936	176	40.77	7	17	19	–	342	156	5	31.20	3-15	–	–
Terbrugge, D.J.	1998–99	2003–04	7	8	5	16	4*	5.33	–	–	4	–	1012	517	20	25.85	5-46	1	–
Theunissen, N.H.C.D.	1888–89	1888–89	1	2	1	2	2*	2.00	–	–	–	–	80	51	0	–	–	–	–
Thornton, G.	1902–03	1902–03	1†	1	0	1	1*	–	–	–	1	–	24†	20	1	20.00	1-20	–	–
Tomlinson, D.S.	1935	1935	1	1	0	9	9	9.00	–	–	–	–	60	38	0	–	–	–	–
Traicos, A.J. ‡	1969–70	1969–70	3	4	2	8	5*	4.00	–	–	4	–	470	207	4	51.75	2-70	–	–
Trimborn, P.H.J.	1966–67	1969–70	4	4	2	13	11*	6.50	–	–	7	–	747	257	11	23.36	3-12	–	–
Tsolekile, T.L.	2004–05	2004–05	3	5	0	47	22	9.40	–	–	6	–	–	–	–	–	–	–	–
Tsotsobe, L.L.	2010	2010–11	5	5	2	19	8*	6.33	–	–	1	–	870†	448	9	49.77	3-43	–	–
Tuckett, L.	1947	1948–49	9	14	3	131	40*	11.90	–	–	9	–	2104	980	19	51.57	5-68	2	–
Tuckett, L.R.	1913–14	1913–14	1	2	1	0	0*	0.00	–	–	2	–	120	69	2	–	–	–	–
Twentyman-Jones, P.S.	1902–03	1902–03	1	2	0	0	0	0.00	–	–	–	–	–	–	–	–	–	–	–
van der Bijl, P.G.V.	1938–39	1938–39	5	9	0	460	125	51.11	1	2	1	–	–	–	–	–	–	–	–
van der Merwe, E.A.	1929	1935–36	2	4	1	27	19	9.00	–	–	3	–	–	–	–	–	–	–	–
van der Merwe, P.L.	1963–64	1966–67	15	23	2	533	76	25.38	–	3	11	–	79†	22	1	22.00	1-6	–	–
van Jaarsveld, M.	2002–03	2004–05	9	15	2	397	73	30.53	–	3	11	–	42	28	0	–	–	–	–
van Ryneveld, C.B.	1951	1957–58	19	33	6	724	83	26.81	–	3	14	–	1554	671	17	39.47	4-67	–	–
Varnals, G.D.	1964–65	1964–65	3	6	0	97	23	16.16	–	–	5	–	12	2	0	–	–	–	–
Viljoen, K.G.	1930–31	1948–49	27	50	2	1365	124	28.43	2	9	5	–	48	23	0	–	–	–	–
Vincent, C.L.	1927–28	1935	25	38†	12	526	60	20.23	–	2	27	–	5851†	2631	84	31.32	6-51	3	–

INDIVIDUAL CAREER RECORDS – SOUTH AFRICA *continued*

	First Test	Last Test	Tests	Inns	NO	Runs	HS	Avge	100	50	Ct	St	Balls	Runs	Wkts	Avge	BB	5wl	10wM
						BATTING AND FIELDING							BOWLING						
Vincent, C.H.	1888–89	1891–92	3	6†	0	26	9	4.33	–	–	1	–	369†	193	4	48.25	3-88	–	–
Vogler, A.E.E.	1905–06	1910–11	15	26	6	340	65	17.00	–	2	20	–	2764	1455	64	22.73	7-94	5	1
Wade, H.F.	1935	1935–36	10	18	2	327	40*	20.43	–	–	4	–	–						
Wade, W.W.	1938–39	1949–50	11	19	1	511	125	28.38	1	3	15	2	–						
Waite, J.H.B.	1951	1964–65	50	86	7	2405	134	30.44	4	16	124	17	–						
Walter, K.A.	1961–62	1961–62	2	3	0	11	10	3.66	–	–	3	–	495	197	6	32.83	4-63	–	–
Ward, T.A.	1912	1924	23	42	9	459	64	13.90	–	2	19	13	–						
Watkins, J.C.	1949–50	1956–57	15	27	1	612	92	23.53	–	3	12	–	2805	816	29	28.13	4-22	–	–
Wesley, C.	1960	1960	3	5†	0	49	35	9.80	–	–	1	–	–						
Wessels, K.C. ‡	1991–92	1994	16	29†	2	1027	118	38.03	2	6	12	–	–						
Westcott, R.J.	1953–54	1957–58	5	9	0	166	62	18.44	–	1	–	–	32	22	0	–	–	–	–
White, G.C.	1905–06	1912	17	31	2	872	147	30.06	2	4	10	–	498	301	9	33.44	4-47	–	–
Willoughby, C.M. ...	2003	2003	2	–†	–	8	5	2.00	–	–	–	–	300†	125	1	125.00	1-47	–	–
Willoughby, J.T.	1895–96	1895–96	2	4	0	8	5	2.00	–	–	–	–	275	159	6	26.50	2-37	–	–
Wimble, C.S.	1891–92	1891–92	1	2	0	0	0	0.00	–	–	–	–	–						
Winslow, P.L.	1949–50	1955	5	9	0	186	108	20.66	1	–	1	–	–						
Wynne, O.E.	1948–49	1949–50	6	12	0	219	50	18.25	–	1	3	–	–						
Zondeki, M.	2003	2008–09	6	5	0	82	59	16.40	–	1	1	–	780	480	19	25.26	6-39	1	–
Zulch, J.W.	1909–10	1921–22	16	32	2	983	150	32.76	2	4	4	–	24	28	0	–	–	–	–

INDIVIDUAL CAREER RECORDS – WEST INDIES

	First Test	Last Test	Tests	Inns	NO	Runs	HS	Avge	100	50	Ct	St	Balls	Runs	Wkts	Avge	BB	5wl	10wM
						BATTING AND FIELDING							BOWLING						
Achong, E.E.	1929–30	1934–35	6	11†	1	81	22	8.10	–	–	6	–	918†	378	8	47.25	2-64	–	–
Adams, J.C.	1991–92	2000–01	54	90†	17	3012	208*	41.26	6	14	48	5	2853†	1336	27	49.48	5-17	1	–
Alexander, F.C.M. ...	1957	1960–61	25	38	6	961	108	30.03	1	7	85	5	–						
Ali, Imtiaz	1975–76	1975–76	1	1	0	1	1*	–	–	–	–	–	204	89	2	44.50	2-37	–	–
Ali, Inshan	1970–71	1976–77	12	18†	1	172	25	10.75	–	–	7	–	3718†	1621	34	47.67	5-59	1	–
Allan, D.W.	1961–62	1966	5	7	1	75	40*	12.50	–	–	15	3	–						
Allen, I.B.A.	1991	1991	2	2	2	5	4*	–	–	–	1	–	282	180	5	36.00	2-69	–	–
Ambrose, C.E.L.	1987–88	2000	98	145†	29	1439	53	12.40	–	1	18	–	22103	8501	405	20.99	8-45	22	3
Arthurton, K.L.T. ...	1988	1995	33	50†	5	1382	157*	30.71	2	8	22	–	473†	183	1	183.00	1-17	–	–
Asgarali, N.S.	1957	1957	2	4	0	62	29	15.50	–	–	–	–	–						

INDIVIDUAL CAREER RECORDS – WEST INDIES *continued*

	First Test	Last Test	Tests	Inns	NO	Runs	HS	Avge	100	50	Ct	St	Balls	Runs	Wkts	Avge	BB	5wI	10wM
															BOWLING				
				BATTING AND FIELDING															
Atkinson, D.S.	1948-49	1957-58	22	35	6	922	219	31.79	1	5	11	–	5201	1647	47	35.04	7-53	3	1
Atkinson, E.S.	1957-58	1958-59	8	9	1	126	37	15.75	–	–	2	–	1634	589	25	23.56	5-42	1	–
Austin, Richard A.	1977-78	1977-78	2	2	0	22	20	11.00	–	–	2	–	6	5	0	–	–	–	–
Austin, Ryan A.	2009	2009	2	4	0	39	19	9.75	–	–	3	–	326	155	3	51.66	1-29	–	–
Bacchus, S.F.A.F.	1977-78	1981-82	19	30	0	782	250	26.06	1	3	17	–	6	3	0	–	–	–	–
Baichan, L.	1974-75	1975-76	3	6†	2	184	105*	46.00	1	–	2	–	–	–	–	–	–	–	–
Baker, L.S.	2008-09	2009	4	6†	4	23	17	11.50	–	–	1	–	660	395	5	79.00	2-39	–	–
Banks, O.A.C.	2002-03	2005	10	16	1	318	50*	26.50	–	1	6	–	2401	1367	28	48.82	4-87	–	–
Baptiste, E.A.E.	1983-84	1989-90	10	11	1	233	87*	23.30	–	1	2	–	1362	563	15	35.18	3-31	–	–
Barath, A.B.	2009-10	2012	15	28	0	657	104	23.46	1	4	13	–	6	3	0	–	–	–	–
Barrett, A.G.	1970-71	1974-75	6	7	1	40	19	6.66	–	–	13	–	1612	603	13	46.38	3-43	–	–
Barrow, I.M.	1929-30	1939	11	19	2	276	105	16.23	1	1	17	5	–	–	–	–	–	–	–
Bartlett, E.L.	1928	1930-31	5	8	1	131	84	18.71	–	1	2	–	–	–	–	–	–	–	–
Baugh, C.S.	2002-03	2011-12	21	36	2	610	68	17.94	–	3	43	5	–	–	–	–	–	–	–
Benjamin, K.C.G.	1991-92	1997-98	26	36	8	222	43*	7.92	–	–	2	–	5132	2785	92	30.27	6-66	4	1
Benjamin, W.K.M.	1987-88	1994-95	21	26	3	470	85	18.80	–	2	12	–	3694	1648	61	27.01	4-46	6	–
Benn, S.J.	2007-08	2014	22	33†	3	463	42	15.43	–	2	13	–	6194†	2813	79	35.60	6-81	6	–
Bernard, D.E.	2002-03	2009	3	6	1	202	69	40.40	–	3	–	–	258	185	4	46.25	2-30	–	–
Bess, B.J.	2010	2010	1	2	1	11	11*	11.00	–	–	–	–	78	92	1	92.00	1-65	–	–
Best, C.A.	1985-86	1990-91	8	13	1	342	164	28.50	1	–	8	–	30	21	0	–	–	–	–
Best, T.L.	2002-03	2013-14	25	38	6	401	95	12.53	–	–	6	–	3716	2291	57	40.19	6-40	2	–
Betancourt, N.	1929-30	1929-30	1	2	0	52	39	26.00	–	–	–	–	–	–	–	–	–	–	–
Binns, A.P.	1952-53	1955-56	5	8	1	64	27	9.14	–	1	14	3	–	–	–	–	–	–	–
Birkett, L.S.	1930-31	1930-31	4	8	0	136	64	13.00	–	1	4	–	126	71	1	71.00	1-16	–	–
Bishoo, D.	2011	2011-12	11	19†	8	143	26	13.00	–	–	8	–	3046	1582	40	39.55	5-90	1	–
Bishop, I.R.	1988-89	1997-98	43	63	11	632	48	12.15	–	–	8	–	8407	3909	161	24.27	6-40	6	–
Black, M.I.	2000-01	2001-02	6	11	3	21	6	2.62	–	–	1	–	954	597	12	49.75	4-83	–	–
Blackwood, J.	2014	2014	3	4	0	147	66*	49.00	–	2	1	–	120	69	2	34.50	2-14	–	–
Boyce, K.D.	1970-71	1975-76	21	30	3	657	95*	24.33	–	4	5	–	3501	1801	60	30.01	6-77	2	1
Bradshaw, I.D.R.	2005-06	2006	5	8†	1	96	33	13.71	–	–	3	–	1021†	540	9	60.00	3-73	–	–
Brathwaite, K.C.	2011	2014	14	27	2	956	212	38.24	2	6	7	–	46	50	1	50.00	1-43	–	–
Bravo, D.J.	2004	2010-11	40	71	4	2200	113	31.42	3	13	41	–	6466	3426	86	39.83	6-55	2	–
Bravo, D.M.	2010-11	2014	32	57†	0	2311	218	43.60	6	9	31	–	6†	2	0	–	–	–	–
Breese, G.R.	2002-03	2002-03	1	2	0	5	5	2.50	–	–	–	–	188	135	2	67.50	2-108	–	–
Browne, C.O.	1994-95	2004-05	20	30	6	387	68	16.12	–	1	79	2	–	–	–	–	–	–	–
Browne, C.R.	1928	1929-30	4	8	1	176	70*	25.14	–	1	1	–	840	288	6	48.00	2-72	–	–
Butcher, B.F.	1958-59	1969	44	78	6	3104	209*	43.11	7	16	15	–	256	90	5	18.00	5-34	1	–

INDIVIDUAL CAREER RECORDS – WEST INDIES *continued*

	First Test	Last Test	Tests	Inns	NO	Runs	HS	Avge	100	50	Ct	St	Balls	Runs	Wkts	Avge	BB	5wI	10wM
						BATTING AND FIELDING										BOWLING			
Butler, L.S.	1954–55	1954–55	1	1	1	16	16	16.00	–	–	–	–	240	151	2	75.50	2-151	–	–
Butts, C.G.	1984–85	1987–88	7	8	1	108	38	15.42	–	–	2	–	1554	595	10	59.50	4-73	–	–
Bynoe, M.R.	1958–59	1966–67	4	6	0	111	48	18.50	–	–	4	–	30†	5	1	5.00	1-5	–	–
Camacho, G.S.	1967–68	1970–71	11	22	0	640	87	29.09	–	4	4	–	18	12	0	–	–	–	–
Cameron, F.J.	1948–49	1948–49	5	7	1	151	75*	25.16	–	1	–	–	786	278	3	92.66	2-74	–	–
Cameron, J.H.	1939	1939	2	3	0	6	5	2.00	–	–	–	–	232	88	3	29.33	3-66	–	–
Campbell, S.L.	1994–95	2001–02	52	93	4	2882	208	32.38	4	18	47	–	–	–	–	–	–	–	–
Carew, G.M.	1934–35	1948–49	4	7	1	170	107	28.33	1	–	1	–	18†	2	0	–	–	–	–
Carew, M.C.	1963	1971–72	19	36†	3	1127	109	34.15	1	5	13	–	1174	437	8	54.62	1-11	–	–
Challenor, G.	1928	1928	3	6	0	101	46	16.83	–	–	–	–	–	–	–	–	–	–	–
Chanderpaul, S.	1993–94	2014	158	269†	49	11684	203*	53.10	30	65	65	–	1740	883	9	98.11	1-2	–	–
Chang, H.S.	1978–79	1978–79	4	2†	0	8	6	4.00	–	–	4	–	–	–	–	–	–	–	–
Chattergoon, S.	2007–08	2008–09	4	7†	0	127	46	18.14	–	–	6	1	–	–	–	–	–	–	–
Christiani, C.M.	1934–35	1934–35	4	7	3	896	107	26.35	–	4	6	2	234	108	3	36.00	3-52	–	–
Clarke, C.B.	1939	1939	3	4	1	3	2	1.00	–	–	2	–	456	261	6	43.50	3-59	–	–
Clarke, S.T.	1977–78	1981–82	11	16	5	172	35*	15.63	–	–	7	–	2477	1170	42	27.85	5-126	1	–
Collins, P.T.	1998–99	2006	32	47	7	235	24	5.87	–	–	6	–	6964†	3671	106	34.63	6-53	3	–
Collymore, C.D.	1998–99	2007	30	52	27	197	16*	7.88	–	–	6	–	6337	3004	93	32.30	7-57	4	1
Constantine, L.N.	1928	1939	18	33	0	635	90	19.24	–	4	28	–	3583	1746	58	30.10	5-75	2	–
Cottrell, S.S.	2013–14	2013–14	1	2	0	5	5	2.50	–	–	–	–	108†	72	1	72.00	1-72	–	–
Croft, C.E.H.	1976–77	1981–82	27	37	22	158	33	10.53	–	1	8	–	6165	2913	125	23.30	8-29	3	–
Cuffy, C.E.	1994–95	2002–03	15	23	9	58	15	4.14	–	–	5	–	3366	1455	43	33.83	4-82	–	–
Cummins, A.C.	1992–93	1994–95	5	6	1	98	50	19.60	–	1	1	–	618	342	8	42.75	4-54	–	–
Da Costa, O.C.	1929–30	1934–35	5	9	1	153	39	19.12	–	–	5	–	372	175	3	58.33	1-14	–	–
Daniel, W.W.	1975–76	1983–84	10	11	4	46	11	6.57	–	–	4	–	1754	910	36	25.27	5-39	1	–
Davis, B.A.	1964–65	1964–65	4	8	0	245	68	30.62	–	3	1	–	–	–	–	–	–	–	–
Davis, C.A.	1968–69	1972–73	15	29	5	1301	183	54.20	4	4	4	–	894	330	2	165.00	1-27	–	–
Davis, W.W.	1982–83	1987–88	15	17	4	202	77	15.53	–	1	10	–	2773	1472	45	32.71	4-19	–	–
de Caires, F.I.	1929–30	1929–30	3	6	0	232	80	38.66	–	2	1	–	12	9	0	–	–	–	–
Deonarine, N.	2004–05	2013–14	18	30†	2	725	82	25.89	1	5	16	–	1503	713	24	29.70	4-37	–	–
Depeiaza, C.C.	1954–55	1955–56	5	8	2	187	122	31.16	1	–	7	4	30	15	0	–	–	–	–
Dewdney, D.T.	1954–55	1957–58	9	12	5	17	5*	2.42	–	–	1	–	1641	807	21	38.42	5-21	1	–
Dhanraj, R.	1994–95	1995–96	4	4	0	17	9	4.25	–	–	1	–	1087	595	8	74.37	2-49	–	–
Dillon, M.	1996–97	2003–04	38	68	3	549	43	8.44	–	–	16	–	8704	4398	131	33.57	5-71	2	–
Dowe, U.G.	1970–71	1972–73	4	3	2	8	5*	8.00	–	–	3	–	1014	534	12	44.50	4-69	–	–

INDIVIDUAL CAREER RECORDS – WEST INDIES *continued*

	First Test	Last Test	Tests	Inns	NO	Runs	HS	Avge	100	50	Ct	St	Balls	Runs	Wkts	Avge	BB	5wI	10wM
						BATTING AND FIELDING									*BOWLING*				
Dowlin, T.M.	2009	2010	6	11	0	343	95	31.18	–	3	5	–	6	3	0	–	–	–	–
Drakes, V.C.	2002–03	2003–04	12	20	2	386	67	21.44	–	1	2	–	2617	1362	33	41.27	5-93	1	–
Dujon, P.J.L.	1981–82	1991	81	115	11	3322	139	31.94	5	16	267	5	–	–	–	–	–	–	–
Edwards, F.H.	2003	2012–13	55	88	28	394	30	6.56	–	–	10	–	9602	6249	165	37.87	7-87	12	1
Edwards, K.A.	2011	2014	17	32	1	986	121	31.80	2	8	15	–	24	19	0	–	–	–	–
Edwards, R.M.	1968–69	1968–69	5	8	1	65	22	9.28	–	–	–	–	1311	626	18	34.77	5-84	1	–
Ferguson, W.	1947–48	1953–54	8	10	3	200	75	28.57	–	2	11	–	2568	1165	34	34.26	6-92	3	1
Fernandes, M.P.	1928	1929–30	2	4	0	49	22	12.25	–	–	–	–	–	–	–	–	–	–	–
Findlay, T.M.	1969	1972–73	10	16	3	212	44*	16.30	–	–	19	2	–	–	–	–	–	–	–
Foster, M.L.C.	1969	1977–78	14	24	5	580	125	30.52	1	1	3	–	1776	600	9	66.66	2-41	–	–
Francis, G.N.	1928	1933	10	18	4	81	19*	5.78	–	–	7	–	1619	763	23	33.17	4-40	–	–
Frederick, M.C.	1953–54	1953–54	1	2	0	30	30	15.00	–	–	–	–	–	–	–	–	–	–	–
Fredericks, R.C.	1968–69	1976–77	59	109†	7	4334	169	42.49	8	26	62	–	1187†	548	7	78.28	1-12	–	–
Fudadin, A.B.	2012	2012	3	5†	1	122	55	30.50	–	1	4	–	30	11	0	–	–	–	–
Fuller, R.L.	1934–35	1934–35	1	1	0	1	1	1.00	–	–	–	–	48	12	0	–	–	–	–
Furlonge, H.A.	1954–55	1955–56	3	5	0	99	64	19.80	–	1	–	–	–	–	–	–	–	–	–
Gabriel, S.T.	2012	2014	9	11	3	18	13	2.25	–	–	7	–	1347	762	22	34.63	3-10	–	–
Ganga, D.	1998–99	2007–08	48	86	2	2160	135	25.71	3	9	30	–	186	106	1	106.00	1-20	–	–
Ganteaume, A.G.	1947–48	1947–48	1	1	0	112	112	112.00	1	–	–	–	–	–	–	–	–	–	–
Garner, J.	1976–77	1986–87	58	68	14	672	60	12.44	–	1	42	–	13169	5433	259	20.97	6-56	7	–
Garrick, L.V.	2000–01	2000–01	1	2	0	27	27	13.50	–	–	2	–	–	–	–	–	–	–	–
Gaskin, B.B.M.	1947–48	1947–48	2	3	0	17	10	5.66	–	–	1	–	474	158	2	79.00	1-15	–	–
Gayle, C.H.	1999–2000	2014	103	182†	11	7214	333	42.18	15	37	96	–	7109	3120	73	42.73	5-34	2	–
Gibbs, G.L.	1954–55	1954–55	1	2†	0	12	12	6.00	–	–	1	–	24†	7	0	–	–	–	–
Gibbs, L.R.	1957–58	1975–76	79	109	39	488	25	6.97	–	–	52	–	27115	8989	309	29.09	8-38	18	2
Gibson, O.D.	1995	1998–99	2	4	0	93	37	23.25	–	–	4	–	472	275	3	91.66	2-81	–	–
Gilchrist, R.	1957	1958–59	13	14	3	60	12	5.45	–	–	4	–	3227	1521	57	26.68	6-55	1	–
Goddard, J.D.C.	1947–48	1957	27	39†	11	859	83*	30.67	–	4	22	–	2931	1050	33	31.81	5-31	1	–
Gomes, H.A.	1976	1986–87	60	91†	11	3171	143	39.63	9	13	18	–	2401	930	15	62.00	2-20	–	–
Gomez, G.E.	1939	1953–54	29	46	5	1243	101	30.31	1	8	18	–	5236	1590	58	27.41	7-55	1	1
Grant, G.C.	1930–31	1934–35	12	22	6	413	71*	25.81	–	3	10	–	24	18	0	–	–	–	–
Grant, R.S.	1934–35	1939	7	11	1	220	77	22.00	–	1	13	–	986	353	11	32.09	3-68	1	–
Gray, A.H.	1986–87	1986–87	5	8	2	48	12*	8.00	–	–	6	–	888	377	22	17.13	4-39	–	–
Greenidge, A.E.	1977–78	1978–79	6	10	0	222	69	22.20	–	2	5	–	–	–	–	–	–	–	–
Greenidge, C.G.	1974–75	1990–91	108	185	16	7558	226	44.72	19	34	96	–	26	4	0	–	–	–	–

INDIVIDUAL CAREER RECORDS – WEST INDIES *continued*

	First Test	Last Test	Tests	Inns	NO	Runs	HS	Avge	100	50	Ct	St	Balls	Runs	Wkts	Avge	BB	5wI	10wM
								BATTING AND FIELDING								*BOWLING*			
Greenidge, G.A.	1971–72	1972–73	5	9	2	209	50	29.85	–	1	3	–	156	75	0	–	–	–	–
Grell, M.G.	1929–30	1929–30	1	2	0	34	21	17.00	–	–	1	–	30	17	0	–	–	–	–
Griffith, A.F.G.	1996–97	2000	14	27†	1	638	114	24.53	1	4	5	–	–	–	–	–	–	–	–
Griffith, C.C.	1959–60	1968–69	28	42	10	530	54	16.56	–	1	16	–	5631	2683	94	28.54	6-36	5	–
Griffith, H.C.	1928	1933	13	23	5	91	18	5.05	–	–	4	–	2663	1243	44	28.25	6-103	2	–
Guillen, S.C. ‡	1951–52	1951–52	5	6	2	104	54	26.00	–	1	9	2	–	–	–	–	–	–	–
Hall, W.W.	1958–59	1968–69	48	66	14	818	50*	15.73	–	2	11	–	10421	5066	192	26.38	7-69	9	1
Harper, R.A.	1983–84	1993–94	25	32	3	535	74	18.44	–	3	36	–	3615	1291	46	28.06	6-57	1	–
Haynes, D.L.	1977–78	1993–94	116	202	25	7487	184	42.29	18	39	65	–	18	8	1	8.00	1-2	–	–
Headley, G.A.	1929–30	1953–54	22	40	4	2190	270*	60.83	10	5	14	–	398	230	0	–	–	–	–
Headley, R.G.A.	1973	1973	2	4†	0	62	42	15.50	–	–	2	–	–	–	–	–	–	–	–
Hendriks, J.L.	1961–62	1969	20	32	8	447	64	18.62	–	2	42	5	–	–	–	–	–	–	–
Hinds, R.O.	2001–02	2009	15	25†	1	505	84	21.04	–	2	7	–	1743†	870	13	66.92	2-45	–	–
Hinds, W.W.	1999–2000	2005–06	45	80†	1	2608	213	33.01	5	14	32	–	1123	590	16	36.87	3-79	–	–
Hoad, E.L.G.	1928	1933	4	8	0	98	36	12.25	–	–	1	–	–	–	–	–	–	–	–
Holder, J.O.	2014	2014	1	2	0	90	52	45.00	–	1	1	–	120	50	2	25.00	2-26	–	–
Holder, R.I.C.	1996–97	1998–99	11	17	2	380	91	25.33	–	2	9	–	–	–	–	–	–	–	–
Holder, V.A.	1969	1978–79	40	59	11	682	42	14.20	–	–	16	–	9095	3627	109	33.27	6-28	3	–
Holding, M.A.	1975–76	1986–87	60	76	10	910	73	13.78	–	6	22	–	12680	5898	249	23.68	8-92	13	2
Holford, D.A.J.	1966	1976–77	24	39	5	768	105*	22.58	1	3	18	–	4816	2009	51	39.39	5-23	1	–
Holt, J.K.C.	1953–54	1958–59	17	31	2	1066	166	36.75	2	5	8	–	30	20	1	20.00	1-20	–	–
Hooper, C.L.	1987–88	2002–03	102	173	15	5762	233	36.46	13	27	115	–	13794	5635	114	49.42	5-26	4	–
Howard, A.B.	1971–72	1971–72	1	–†	–	–	–	–	–	–	1	–	372	140	2	70.00	2-140	–	–
Hunte, C.C.	1957–58	1966–67	44	78	6	3245	260	45.06	8	13	16	–	270	110	2	55.00	1-17	–	–
Hunte, E.A.C.	1929–30	1929–30	3	6	1	166	58	33.20	–	2	5	–	–	–	–	–	–	–	–
Hylton, L.G.	1934–35	1939	6	8	2	70	19	11.66	–	–	1	–	965	418	16	26.12	4-27	–	–
Jacobs, R.D.	1998–99	2004	65	112†	21	2577	118	28.31	3	14	207	12	–	–	–	–	–	–	–
Jaggernauth, A.S.	2008	2008	1	2†	1	0	0*	0.00	–	–	–	–	138	96	1	96.00	1-74	–	–
Johnson, H.H.H.	1947–48	1950	3	4	0	38	22	9.50	–	–	–	–	789	238	13	18.30	5-41	2	1
Johnson, L.R.	2014	2014	1	2†	0	107	66	53.50	–	1	1	–	24	9	0	–	–	–	–
Johnson, T.F.	1939	1939	1	1†	1	9	9*	–	–	–	1	–	240†	129	3	43.00	2-53	–	–
Jones, C.E.L.	1929–30	1934–35	4	7†	0	63	19	9.00	–	–	3	–	102†	11	0	–	–	–	–
Jones, P.E.W.	1947–48	1951–52	9	11	2	47	10*	5.22	–	–	4	–	1842	751	25	30.04	5-85	1	–
Joseph, D.R.E.	1998–99	1998–99	4	7	0	141	50	20.14	–	1	10	–	–	–	–	–	–	–	–
Joseph, S.C.	2004	2007	5	10	0	147	45	14.70	–	–	3	–	12	8	0	–	–	–	–

INDIVIDUAL CAREER RECORDS – WEST INDIES continued

	First Test	Last Test	Tests	Inns	NO	Runs	HS	Avge	100	50	Ct	St	Balls	Runs	Wkts	Avge	BB	5wI	10wM
								BATTING AND FIELDING								BOWLING			
Julien, B.D.	1973	1976–77	24	34	6	866	121	30.92	2	3	14	—	4542†	1868	50	37.36	5-57	1	—
Jumadeen, R.R.	1971–72	1978–79	12	14	10	84	56	21.00	—	1	4	—	3140†	1141	29	39.34	4-72	—	—
Kallicharran, A.I.	1971–72	1980–81	66	109†	10	4399	187	44.43	12	21	51	—	406	158	4	39.50	2-16	—	—
Kanhai, R.B.	1957	1973–74	79	137	6	6227	256	47.53	15	28	50	—	183	85	0	—	—	—	—
Kentish, E.S.M.	1947–48	1953–54	2	2	1	1	1*	1.00	—	—	1	—	540	178	8	22.25	5-49	1	—
King, C.L.	1976	1980	9	16	3	418	100*	32.15	1	2	5	—	582	282	3	94.00	1-30	—	—
King, F.M.	1952–53	1955–56	14	17	3	116	21	8.28	—	—	5	—	2869	1159	29	39.96	5-74	1	—
King, L.A.	1961–62	1967–68	2	4	0	41	20	10.25	—	—	2	—	476	154	9	17.11	5-46	1	—
King, R.D.	1998–99	2004–05	19	27	8	66	12*	3.47	—	—	2	—	3442	1733	53	32.69	5-51	1	—
Lambert, C.B.	1991	1998–99	5	9†	0	284	104	31.55	1	1	8	—	10	5	1	5.00	1-4	—	—
Lara, B.C. ‡	1990–91	2006–07	130	230†	6	11912	400*	53.17	34	48	164	—	60	28	0	—	1-1	—	—
Lashley, P.D.	1960–61	1966	4	7†	1	159	49	22.71	—	—	4	—	18	1	1	1.00	1-1	—	—
Lawson, J.J.C.	2002–03	2005–06	13	21	6	52	14	3.46	—	—	3	—	2364	1512	51	29.64	7-78	2	—
Legall, R.A.	1952–53	1952–53	4	5	0	50	23	10.00	—	—	8	1	—	—	—	—	—	—	—
Lewis, D.M.	1970–71	1970–71	3	5	2	259	88	86.33	—	3	8	—	—	—	—	—	—	—	—
Lewis, R.N.	1997–98	2007–08	5	10	0	89	40	8.90	—	—	8	—	883	456	4	114.00	2-42	—	—
Lloyd, C.H.	1966–67	1984–85	110	175†	14	7515	242*	46.67	19	39	90	—	1716	622	10	62.20	2-13	—	—
Logie, A.L.	1982–83	1991	52	78	9	2470	130	35.79	2	16	57	—	7	4	0	—	—	—	—
McGarrell, N.C.	2000–01	2001–02	4	6	2	61	33	15.25	—	—	2	—	1212†	453	17	26.64	4-23	—	—
McLean, N.A.M.	1997–98	2000–01	19	32†	2	368	46	12.26	—	—	5	—	3299	1873	44	42.56	3-53	—	—
McMorris, E.D.A.S.	1957–58	1966	13	21	0	564	125	26.85	1	3	5	—	—	—	—	—	—	—	—
McWatt, C.A.	1953–54	1954–55	6	9†	2	202	54	28.85	—	2	9	1	24	16	1	16.00	1-16	—	—
Madray, I.S.	1957–58	1957–58	2	3	0	3	2	1.00	—	—	2	—	210	108	0	—	—	—	—
Marshall, M.D.	1978–79	1991	81	107	11	1810	92	18.85	—	10	25	—	17584	7876	376	20.94	7-22	22	4
Marshall, N.E.	1954–55	1954–55	1	2	0	8	8	4.00	—	—	1	—	279	62	2	31.00	1-22	—	—
Marshall, R.E.	1951–52	1951–52	4	7	0	143	30	20.42	—	—	7	—	52	15	0	—	—	—	—
Marshall, X.M.	2005	2008–09	7	12	0	243	85	20.25	—	2	2	—	12	0	0	—	—	—	—
Martin, F.R.	1928	1930–31	9	18†	1	486	123*	28.58	1	—	2	—	1346†	619	3	77.37	3-91	—	—
Martindale, E.A.	1933	1939	10	14	3	58	22	5.27	—	—	5	—	1605	804	37	21.72	5-22	3	—
Mattis, E.H.	1980–81	1980–81	4	5	0	145	71	29.00	—	1	3	—	36	14	0	—	—	—	—
Mendonca, I.L.	1961–62	1961–62	2	2	0	81	78	40.50	—	1	8	2	—	—	—	—	—	—	—
Merry, C.A.	1933	1933	2	4	0	34	13	8.50	—	—	1	—	—	—	—	—	—	—	—
Miller, N.O.	2009	2009	1	2	0	5	5	2.50	—	—	—	—	132†	67	0	—	—	—	—
Miller, R.S.	1952–53	1952–53	1	1	0	23	23	23.00	—	—	—	—	96	28	0	—	—	—	—
Mohammed, D.	2003–04	2006–07	5	8†	1	225	52	32.14	—	1	1	—	1065†	668	13	51.38	3-98	—	—

INDIVIDUAL CAREER RECORDS – WEST INDIES *continued*

	First Test	Last Test	Tests	BATTING AND FIELDING Inns	NO	Runs	HS	Avge	100	50	Ct	St	BOWLING Balls	Runs	Wkts	Avge	BB	5wI	10wM
Morais, G.Gladstone	1929-30	1929-30	1	1†	1	12	12*		–	–	–	–	300†	189	1	189.00	1-139	–	–
Morton, R.S.	2005	2008	15	27	1	573	70*	22.03	–	4	20	–	66	50	0	–	–	–	–
Moseley, E.A.	1989-90	1989-90	2	4	0	35	26	8.75	–	–	1	–	522	261	6	43.50	2-70	–	–
Mudie, G.H.	1934-35	1934-35	1	1	0	5	5	5.00	–	–	–	–	174†	40	3	13.33	2-23	–	–
Murray, D.A.	1977-78	1981-82	19	31	3	601	84	21.46	–	3	57	5	–	–	–	–	–	–	–
Murray, D.L.	1963	1980	62	96	9	1993	91	22.90	–	11	181	8	–	–	–	–	–	–	–
Murray, J.R.	1992-93	2001-02	33	45	4	918	101*	22.39	1	3	99	3	–	–	–	–	–	–	–
Nagamootoo, M.V.	2000	2002-03	5	8†	1	185	68	26.42	–	1	2	–	1494	637	12	53.08	3-119	–	–
Nanan, R.	1980-81	1980-81	1	2	0	16	8	8.00	–	–	2	–	216	91	4	22.75	2-37	–	–
Narine, S.P.	2012	2013-14	6	7†	2	40	22*	8.00	–	–	2	–	1650	851	21	40.52	6-91	2	–
Nash, B.P.	2008-09	2011	21	33†	2	1103	114	33.42	2	8	6	–	492†	247	2	123.50	1-21	–	–
Neblett, J.M.	1934-35	1934-35	1	2	1	16	11*	16.00	–	–	–	–	216	75	1	75.00	1-44	–	–
Noreiga, J.M.	1970-71	1970-71	4	5	2	11	9	3.66	–	–	2	–	1322	493	17	29.00	9-95	1	–
Nunes, R.K.	1928	1929-30	4	8†	0	245	92	30.62	–	2	2	–	–	–	–	–	–	–	–
Nurse, S.M.	1959-60	1968-69	29	54	1	2523	258	47.60	6	10	21	–	42	7	0	–	–	–	–
Padmore, A.L.	1975-76	1976	2	2	1	8	8*	8.00	–	–	–	–	474	135	1	135.00	1-36	–	–
Pagon, D.J.	2004-05	2004-05	2	3	0	37	35	12.33	–	–	–	–	–	–	–	–	–	–	–
Pairaudeau, B.H.	1952-53	1957	13	21	0	454	115	21.61	1	3	6	–	6	3	0	–	–	–	–
Parchment, B.A.	2007-08	2008	2	4	0	55	20	13.75	–	–	1	–	–	–	–	–	–	–	–
Parry, D.R.	1977-78	1979-80	12	20	3	381	65	22.41	–	3	4	–	1909	936	23	40.69	5-15	1	–
Pascal, N.T.	2010	2010-11	2	2	0	12	10	6.00	–	–	1	–	102	59	0	–	–	–	–
Passailaigue, C.C.	1929-30	1929-30	1	2	1	46	44	46.00	–	–	–	–	12	15	0	–	–	–	–
Patterson, B.P.	1985-86	1992-93	28	38	16	145	21*	6.59	–	–	5	–	4829	2874	93	30.90	5-24	5	–
Payne, T.R.O.	1985-86	1985-86	1	1†	0	5	5	5.00	–	–	5	–	–	–	–	–	–	–	–
Permaul, V.	2012-13	2013-14	4	6	0	57	20	9.50	–	–	1	–	850	452	12	37.66	3-32	–	–
Perry, N.O.	1998-99	1999-2000	4	7	1	74	26	12.33	–	–	1	–	804	446	10	44.60	5-70	1	–
Phillip, N.	1977-78	1978-79	9	15	5	297	47	29.70	–	1	5	–	1820	1041	28	37.17	4-48	–	–
Phillips, O.J.	2009	2009	2	4†	0	160	94	40.00	–	1	1	–	–	–	–	–	–	–	–
Pierre, L.R.	1947-48	1947-48	1	–	–	–	–	–	–	–	–	–	42	28	0	–	–	–	–
Powell, D.B.L.	2002	2008-09	37	57	5	407	36*	7.82	–	–	8	–	7077	4068	85	47.85	5-25	1	–
Powell, K.O.A.	2011	2014	21	40†	1	1072	134	27.48	3	2	19	–	–	–	–	–	–	–	–
Powell, R.L.	1999-2000	2003-04	2	3	0	53	30	17.66	–	–	1	–	78	49	0	–	–	–	–
Rae, A.F.	1948-49	1952-53	15	24†	2	1016	109	46.18	4	4	10	–	–	–	–	–	–	–	–
Ragoonath, S.	1998-99	1998-99	2	4	1	13	9	4.33	–	–	–	–	–	–	–	–	–	–	–
Ramadhin, S.	1950	1960-61	43	58	14	361	44	8.20	–	–	9	–	13939	4579	158	28.98	7-49	10	1

INDIVIDUAL CAREER RECORDS – WEST INDIES continued

	First Test	Last Test	Tests	Inns	NO	Runs	HS	Avge	100	50	Ct	St	Balls	Runs	Wkts	Avge	BB	5wI	10wM
								BATTING AND FIELDING								BOWLING			
Ramdass, R.R.	2005	2005	1	2	0	26	23	13.00	–	–	2	6	–	–	–	–	–	–	–
Ramdin, D.	2005	2014	61	102	13	2419	166	27.17	4	11	178	6	–	–	–	–	–	–	–
Ramnarine, D.	1997–98	2001–02	12	21†	4	106	35*	6.23	–	–	8	–	3495	1383	45	30.73	5-78	1	–
Rampaul, R.	2009–10	2012–13	18	31†	8	335	40*	14.56	–	–	3	–	3440	1705	49	34.79	4-48	–	–
Reifer, F.L.	1996–97	2009	6	12†	0	111	29	9.25	–	1	6	–	–	–	–	–	–	–	–
Richards, D.M.	2009	2010	3	6	0	125	69	20.83	–	1	4	–	–	–	–	–	–	–	–
Richards, I.V.A.	1974–75	1991	121	182	12	8540	291	50.23	24	45	122	–	5170	1964	32	61.37	2-17	–	–
Richardson, R.B.	1983–84	1995	86	146	12	5949	194	44.39	16	27	90	–	66	18	0	–	–	–	–
Rickards, K.R.	1947–48	1951–52	2	3	0	104	67	34.66	–	1	–	–	–	–	–	–	–	–	–
Roach, C.A.	1928	1934–35	16	32	1	952	209	30.70	2	6	5	–	222	103	2	51.50	1-18	–	–
Roach, K.A.J.	2009	2014	28	44	8	329	41	9.13	–	–	8	–	5544	2884	111	25.98	6-48	6	1
Roberts, A.M.E.	1973–74	1983–84	47	62	11	762	68	14.94	–	3	9	–	11135	5174	202	25.61	7-54	11	2
Roberts, A.T.	1955–56	1955–56	1	2	0	28	28	14.00	–	–	–	–	–	–	–	–	–	–	–
Roberts, L.A.	1998–99	1998–99	1	1	0	0	0	0.00	–	–	–	–	–	–	–	–	–	–	–
Rodriguez, W.V.	1961–62	1967–68	5	7	0	96	50	13.71	–	1	3	–	573	374	7	53.42	3-51	–	–
Rose, F.A.	1996–97	2000	19	28	2	344	69	13.23	–	1	4	–	3124	1637	53	30.88	7-84	2	–
Rowe, L.G.	1971–72	1979–80	30	49	2	2047	302	43.55	7	7	17	–	86†	44	0	–	–	–	–
Russell, A.D.	2010–11	2010–11	1	1	0	2	2	2.00	–	–	1	–	138	104	1	104.00	1-73	–	–
St Hill, E.L.	1929–30	1929–30	2	4	0	18	12	4.50	–	–	–	–	558	221	3	73.66	2-110	–	–
St Hill, W.H.	1928	1929–30	3	6	0	117	38	19.50	–	1	1	–	12	9	0	–	–	–	–
Sammy, D.J.G.	2007	2013–14	38	63	2	1323	106	21.68	1	5	65	–	6215	3007	84	35.79	7-66	4	–
Samuels, M.N.	2000–01	2014	52	92	6	2983	260	34.68	5	20	23	–	3309	1850	34	54.41	4-13	–	–
Samuels, R.G.	1995–96	1996–97	6	12†	2	372	125	37.20	1	1	8	–	–	–	–	–	–	–	–
Sanford, A.	2001–02	2003–04	11	17	2	72	18*	4.80	–	–	4	–	2217	1316	30	43.86	4-132	–	–
Sarwan, R.R.	1999–2000	2011	87	154	8	5842	291	40.01	15	31	53	–	2022	1163	23	50.56	4-37	–	–
Scarlett, R.O.	1959–60	1959–60	3	4	1	54	29*	18.00	–	–	2	–	804	209	2	104.50	1-46	–	–
Scott, A.H.P.	1952–53	1952–53	1	1	0	5	5	5.00	–	–	–	–	264	140	0	–	–	–	–
Scott, O.C.	1928	1930–31	8	13	3	171	35	17.10	–	1	–	–	1405	925	22	42.04	5-266	1	–
Sealey, B.J.	1933	1933	1	2	0	41	29	20.50	–	–	1	–	30	10	1	10.00	1-10	–	–
Sealy, J.E.D.	1929–30	1939	11	19	2	478	92	28.11	–	3	6	1	156	94	3	31.33	2-7	–	–
Shepherd, J.N.	1969	1970–71	5	8	0	77	32	9.62	–	–	4	–	1445	479	19	25.21	5-104	1	–
Shillingford, G.C.	1969	1971–72	7	8†	1	57	25	8.14	–	–	2	–	1181	537	15	35.80	3-63	–	–
Shillingford, I.T.	1976–77	1977–78	4	7	0	218	120	31.14	1	–	1	–	–	–	–	–	–	–	–
Shillingford, S.	2010	2014	16	26	6	266	53*	13.30	–	1	9	–	4694	2419	70	34.55	6-49	6	2
Shivnarine, S.	1977–78	1978–79	8	14	1	379	63	29.15	–	4	6	–	336†	167	1	167.00	1-13	–	–
Simmons, L.M.P.	2008–09	2011–12	8	16	0	278	49	17.37	–	–	5	–	192	147	1	147.00	1-60	–	–
Simmons, P.V.	1987–88	1997–98	26	47	2	1002	110	22.26	1	4	26	–	624	257	4	64.25	2-34	–	–

INDIVIDUAL CAREER RECORDS – WEST INDIES *continued*

	First Test	Last Test	Tests	Inns	NO	Runs	HS	Avge	100	50	Ct	St	Balls	Runs	Wkts	Avge	BB	5wI	10wM
						BATTING AND FIELDING									BOWLING				
Singh, C.K.	1959–60	1959–60	2	3†	0	11	11	3.66	–	–	2	–	506†	166	5	33.20	2-28	–	–
Small, J.A.	1928	1929–30	3	6	0	79	52	13.16	–	1	3	–	366	184	3	61.33	2-67	–	–
Small, M.A.	1983–84	1984	2	1	1	3	3*	–	–	–	–	1	270	153	4	38.25	3-40	–	–
Smith, C.W.	1960–61	1961–62	5	10	1	222	55	24.66	–	1	4	–	–	–	–	–	–	–	–
Smith, D.R.	2003–04	2005–06	10	14	1	320	105*	24.61	1	1	9	–	651	344	7	49.14	3-71	–	–
Smith, D.S.	2002–03	2011	33	58†	2	1384	108	24.71	1	5	28	–	6	3	0	–	–	–	–
Smith, O.G.	1954–55	1958–59	26	42	3	1331	168	31.69	4	6	9	–	4431	1625	48	33.85	5-90	1	–
Sobers, G.S.	1953–54	1973–74	93	160†	21	8032	365*	57.78	26	30	109	–	21599†	7999	235	34.03	6-73	6	–
Solomon, J.S.	1958–59	1964–65	27	46	7	1326	100*	34.00	1	9	13	–	702	268	4	67.00	1-20	–	–
Stayers, S.C.	1961–62	1961–62	4	4	1	58	35*	19.33	–	–	20	–	636	364	9	40.44	3-65	–	–
Stollmeyer, J.B.	1939	1954–55	32	56	5	2159	160	42.33	4	12	20	–	990	507	13	39.00	3-32	–	–
Stollmeyer, V.H.	1939	1939	1	1	0	96	96	96.00	–	1	–	–	–	–	–	–	–	–	–
Stuart, C.E.L.	2000–01	2001–02	6	9	2	24	12*	3.42	–	–	2	–	1116	628	20	31.40	3-33	–	–
Taylor, J.E.	2003	2014	34	53	6	721	106	15.34	1	1	6	–	5994	3394	100	33.94	5-11	3	–
Taylor, J.O.	1957–58	1958–59	3	5	3	4	4*	2.00	–	–	–	–	672	273	10	27.30	5-109	1	–
Thompson, P.I.C.	1995–96	1996–97	2	3	1	17	10*	8.50	–	–	–	–	228	215	5	43.00	2-58	–	–
Tonge, G.C.	2009–10	2009–10	1	2	1	25	23*	25.00	–	–	–	–	168	113	1	113.00	1-28	–	–
Trim, J.	1947–48	1951–52	4	5	1	21	12	5.25	–	–	2	–	794	291	18	16.16	5-34	1	–
Valentine, A.L.	1950	1961–62	36	51	21	141	14	4.70	–	–	13	–	12953†	4215	139	30.32	8-104	8	2
Valentine, V.A.	1933	1933	2	4	1	35	19*	11.66	–	–	–	–	288	104	1	104.00	1-55	–	–
Walcott, C.L.	1947–48	1959–60	44	74	7	3798	220	56.68	15	14	53	11	1194	408	11	37.09	3-50	–	–
Walcott, L.A.	1929–30	1929–30	1	2	1	40	24	40.00	–	–	–	–	48	32	1	32.00	1-17	–	–
Wallace, P.A.	1997–98	1998–99	7	13	0	279	92	21.46	–	2	9	–	–	–	–	–	–	–	–
Walsh, C.A.	1984–85	2000–01	132	185	61	936	30*	7.54	–	–	29	–	30019	12688	519	24.44	7-37	22	3
Walton, C.A.K.	2009	2009	2	4	0	13	10	3.25	–	–	10	–	–	–	–	–	–	–	–
Washington, D.M.	2004–05	2004–05	1	1	0	7	7*	–	–	–	3	–	174	93	0	–	–	–	–
Watson, C.D.	1959–60	1961–62	7	6	1	12	5	2.40	–	–	1	–	1458	724	19	38.10	4-62	–	–
Weekes, E.D.	1947–48	1957–58	48	81	5	4455	207	58.61	15	19	49	–	122	77	1	77.00	1-8	–	–
Weekes, K.H.	1939	1939	2	3†	1	173	137	57.66	1	–	1	–	–	–	–	–	–	–	–
White, A.W.	1964–65	1964–65	2	4	1	71	57*	23.66	–	1	1	–	491	152	3	50.66	2-34	–	–
Wight, C.V.	1928	1929–30	2	4	1	67	23	22.33	–	1	–	–	30	6	0	–	–	–	–
Wight, G.L.	1952–53	1952–53	1	1	0	21	21	21.00	–	–	–	–	–	–	–	–	–	–	–
Wiles, C.A.	1933	1933	2	2	0	2	2	1.00	–	–	–	–	–	–	–	–	–	–	–
Willett, E.T.	1972–73	1974–75	5	8†	3	74	26	14.80	–	–	5	–	1326†	482	11	43.81	3-33	–	–
Williams, A.B.	1977–78	1978–79	7	12	0	469	111	39.08	2	1	5	–	–	–	–	–	–	–	–

INDIVIDUAL CAREER RECORDS – WEST INDIES continued

	First Test	Last Test	Tests	Inns	NO	Runs	HS	Avge	100	50	Ct	St	Balls	Runs	Wkts	Avge	BB	5wI	10wM
								BATTING AND FIELDING								BOWLING			
Williams, D.	1991-92	1997-98	11	19	1	242	65	13.44	–	1	40	2	–	–	–	–	–	–	–
Williams, E.A.V.	1939	1947-48	4	6	0	113	72	18.83	–	1	2	–	796	241	9	26.77	3-51	–	–
Williams, S.C.	1993-94	2001-02	31	52	3	1183	128	24.14	1	3	27	–	18	19	0	–	–	–	–
Wishart, K.L.	1934-35	1934-35	1	2†	0	52	52	26.00	–	1	–	–	–	–	–	–	–	–	–
Worrell, F.M.M.	1947-48	1963	51	87	9	3860	261	49.48	9	22	43	–	7141†	2672	59	38.72	7-70	2	–

INDIVIDUAL CAREER RECORDS – NEW ZEALAND

	First Test	Last Test	Tests	Inns	NO	Runs	HS	Avge	100	50	Ct	St	Balls	Runs	Wkts	Avge	BB	5wI	10wM
								BATTING AND FIELDING								BOWLING			
Adams, A.R.	2001-02	2001-02	1	2	0	18	11	9.00	–	–	1	–	190	105	6	17.50	3-44	–	–
Alabaster, J.C.	1955-56	1971-72	21	34	6	272	34	9.71	–	–	7	–	3992	1863	49	38.02	4-46	–	–
Allcott, C.F.W.	1929-30	1931-32	6	7†	2	113	33	22.60	–	–	3	–	1206†	541	6	90.16	2-102	–	–
Allott, G.I.	1995-96	1999	10	15	7	27	8*	3.37	–	–	2	–	2023†	1111	19	58.47	4-74	–	–
Anderson, C.J.	2013-14	2013-14	7	11†	1	327	116	32.70	1	1	4	–	720†	336	11	30.54	3-47	–	–
Anderson, R.W.	1976-77	1978	9	18	0	423	92	23.50	–	3	1	–	–	–	–	–	–	–	–
Anderson, W.M.	1945-46	1945-46	1	2†	0	5	4	2.50	–	–	1	–	–	–	–	–	–	–	–
Andrews, B.	1973-74	1973-74	2	3	2	22	17	22.00	–	–	1	–	256	154	2	77.00	2-40	–	–
Arnel, B.J.	2009-10	2011-12	6	12	4	45	8*	5.62	–	–	3	–	1008	566	9	62.88	4-95	–	–
Astle, N.J.	1995-96	2006-07	81	137	10	4702	222	37.02	11	24	70	–	5688	2143	51	42.01	3-27	–	–
Astle, T.D.	2012-13	2012-13	1	2	0	38	35	19.00	–	–	–	–	186	97	1	97.00	1-56	–	–
Badcock, F.T.	1929-30	1932-33	7	9	2	137	64	19.57	–	2	1	–	1608	610	15	38.12	4-80	–	–
Barber, R.T.	1955-56	1955-56	1	2	0	17	12	8.50	–	–	1	–	–	–	–	–	–	–	–
Bartlett, G.A.	1961-62	1967-68	10	18	1	263	40	15.47	–	–	8	–	1768	792	24	33.00	6-38	1	–
Barton, P.T.	1961-62	1962-63	7	14	0	285	109	20.35	1	1	4	–	–	–	–	–	–	–	–
Beard, D.D.	1951-52	1955-56	4	7	2	101	31	20.20	–	–	2	–	806	302	9	33.55	3-22	–	–
Beck, J.E.F.	1953-54	1955-56	8	15†	0	394	99	26.26	–	3	–	–	–	–	–	–	–	–	–
Bell, M.D.	1998-99	2007-08	18	32	2	729	107	24.30	2	3	19	–	–	–	–	–	–	–	–
Bell, W.	1953-54	1953-54	2	3	3	21	21*	–	–	–	1	–	491	235	2	117.50	1-54	–	–
Bennett, H.K.	2010-11	2010-11	1	1†	0	4	4	4.00	–	–	–	–	90	47	0	–	–	–	–
Bilby, G.P.	1965-66	1965-66	2	4	0	55	28	13.75	–	–	3	–	–	–	–	–	–	–	–
Blain, T.E.	1986	1993-94	11	20	3	456	78	26.82	–	2	19	2	–	–	–	–	–	–	–
Blair, R.W.	1952-53	1963-64	19	34	6	189	64*	6.75	–	–	5	–	3525	1515	43	35.23	4-85	–	–
Blunt, R.C.	1929-30	1931-32	9	13	1	330	96	27.50	–	1	5	–	936	472	12	39.33	3-17	–	–
Bolton, B.A.	1958-59	1958-59	2	3	0	59	33	19.66	–	–	1	–	–	–	–	–	–	–	–
Bond, S.E.	2001-02	2009-10	18	20	7	168	41*	12.92	–	–	8	–	3372	1922	87	22.09	6-51	5	1

INDIVIDUAL CAREER RECORDS – NEW ZEALAND continued

	First Test	Last Test	Tests	Inns	NO	Runs	HS	Avge	100	50	Ct	St	Balls	Runs	Wkts	Avge	BB	5wI	10wM
								BATTING AND FIELDING								BOWLING			
Boock, S.L.	1977-78	1988-89	30	41	8	207	37	6.27	–	–	14	–	6598†	2564	74	34.64	7-87	4	1
Boult, T.A.	2011-12	2014	25	34	17	285	52*	16.76	–	1	9	–	5074†	2498	91	27.45	6-40	3	1
Bracewell, B.P.	1978	1984-85	6	12	2	24	8	2.40	–	–	1	–	1036	585	14	41.78	3-110	–	–
Bracewell, D.A.J.	2011-12	2013-14	18	33	2	337	43	10.87	–	–	5	–	3184	1813	50	36.26	6-40	2	–
Bracewell, J.G.	1980-81	1990	41	60	11	1001	110	20.42	1	4	31	–	8403	3653	102	35.81	6-32	4	1
Bradburn, G.E.	1990-91	2000-01	7	10	2	105	30*	13.12	–	–	6	–	867	460	6	76.66	3-134	–	–
Bradburn, W.P.	1963-64	1963-64	2	4	0	62	32	15.50	–	–	2	–	–	–	–	–	–	–	–
Brown, V.R.	1985-86	1985-86	2	3†	1	51	36*	25.50	–	–	3	–	342	176	1	176.00	1-17	–	–
Brownlie, D.G.	2011-12	2013	14	25	1	711	109	29.62	1	4	17	–	66	52	1	52.00	1-13	–	–
Burgess, M.G.	1967-68	1980-81	50	92	6	2684	119*	31.20	5	14	34	–	498	212	6	35.33	3-23	–	–
Burke, C.	1945-46	1945-46	1	2	0	4	3	2.00	–	–	–	–	66	30	2	15.00	2-30	–	–
Burtt, T.B.	1946-47	1952-53	10	15	3	252	42	21.00	–	–	2	–	2593†	1170	33	35.45	6-162	3	–
Butler, I.G.	2001-02	2004-05	8	10	2	76	26	9.50	–	–	4	–	1368	884	24	36.83	6-46	1	–
Butterfield, L.A.	1945-46	1945-46	1	2	0	0	0	0.00	–	–	–	–	78	24	0	–	–	–	–
Cairns, B.L.	1973-74	1985-86	43	65	8	928	64	16.28	–	2	30	–	10628	4279	130	32.91	7-74	6	1
Cairns, C.L.	1989-90	2004	62	104	5	3320	158	33.53	5	22	14	–	11698	6410	218	29.40	7-27	13	1
Cameron, F.J.	1961-62	1965	19	30	20	116	27*	11.60	–	–	1	–	4570	1849	62	29.82	5-34	3	–
Cave, H.B.	1949	1958	19	31	5	229	22*	8.80	–	–	8	–	4074	1467	34	43.14	4-21	–	–
Chapple, M.E.	1952-53	1965-66	14	27	1	497	76	19.11	–	3	10	–	248†	84	1	84.00	1-24	–	–
Chatfield, E.J.	1974-75	1988-89	43	54	33	180	21*	8.57	–	–	7	–	10360	3958	123	32.17	6-73	3	–
Cleverley, D.C.	1931-32	1945-46	2	4†	3	19	10*	19.00	–	–	–	–	222	130	0	–	–	–	–
Collinge, R.O.	1964-65	1978	35	50	13	533	68*	14.40	–	2	10	–	7689†	3393	116	29.25	6-63	3	–
Colquhoun, I.A.	1954-55	1954-55	2	4	2	1	1*	0.50	–	–	4	–	–	–	–	–	–	–	–
Coney, J.V.	1973-74	1986-87	52	85	14	2668	174*	37.57	3	16	64	–	2835	966	27	35.77	3-28	–	–
Congdon, B.E.	1964-65	1978	61	114	7	3448	176	32.22	7	19	44	–	5620	2154	59	36.50	5-65	1	–
Cowie, J.	1937	1949	9	13	4	90	45	10.00	–	–	3	–	2028	969	45	21.53	6-40	4	–
Craig, M.D.	2014	2014	3	5†	3	128	67	64.00	–	1	2	–	702	490	12	40.83	4-91	–	–
Cresswell, G.F.	1949	1950-51	3	5†	3	14	12*	7.00	–	–	1	–	650	292	13	22.46	6-168	1	–
Cromb, I.B.	1931	1931-32	5	8	2	123	51*	20.50	–	1	1	–	960	442	8	55.25	3-113	–	–
Crowe, J.J.	1982-83	1989-90	39	65	4	1601	128	26.24	3	6	41	–	18	9	0	–	–	–	–
Crowe, M.D.	1981-82	1995-96	77	131	11	5444	299	45.36	17	18	71	–	1377	676	14	48.28	2-25	–	–
Cumming, C.D.	2004-05	2007-08	11	19	2	441	74	25.94	–	1	3	–	–	–	–	–	–	–	–
Cunis, R.S.	1963-64	1971-72	20	31	8	295	51	12.82	–	1	1	–	4250	1887	51	37.00	6-76	1	–
D'Arcy, J.W.	1958	1958	5	10	0	136	33	13.60	–	–	–	–	–	–	–	–	–	–	–
Davis, H.T.	1994	1997-98	5	7	4	20	8*	6.66	–	–	4	–	1010	499	17	29.35	5-63	1	–
de Groen, R.P.	1993-94	1994-95	5	10	4	45	26	7.50	–	–	–	–	1060	505	11	45.90	3-40	–	–

INDIVIDUAL CAREER RECORDS – NEW ZEALAND *continued*

	First Test	Last Test	Tests	Inns	NO	Runs	HS	Avge	100	50	Ct	St	Balls	Runs	Wkts	Avge	BB	5wI	10wM
						BATTING AND FIELDING										BOWLING			
Dempster, C.S.	1929-30	1932-33	10	15	4	723	136	65.72	2	5	2	—	5	10	0	—	—	—	—
Dempster, E.W.	1952-53	1953-54	5	8†	2	106	47	17.66	—	1	1	—	544†	219	2	109.50	1-24	—	—
Dick, A.E.	1961-62	1965	17	30	4	370	50*	14.23	—	1	47	4	—	—	—	—	—	—	—
Dickinson, G.R.	1929-30	1931-32	3	5	0	31	11	6.20	—	—	3	—	451	245	8	30.62	3-66	—	—
Donnelly, M.P.	1937	1949	7	12†	1	582	206	52.90	1	4	7	—	30†	20	0	—	—	—	—
Doull, S.B.	1992-93	1999-2000	32	50	11	570	46	14.61	—	—	16	—	6053	2872	98	29.30	7-65	6	—
Dowling, G.T.	1961-62	1971-72	39	77	3	2306	239	31.16	3	11	23	—	36	19	1	19.00	1-19	—	—
Drum, C.J.	2000-01	2001-02	5	5	2	10	4	3.33	—	—	4	—	806	482	16	30.12	3-36	—	—
Durning, J.A.	1932-33	1937	4	6	1	38	19	7.60	—	—	2	—	830	493	5	98.60	2-35	—	—
Edgar, B.A.	1978	1986	39	68†	4	1958	161	30.59	3	12	14	—	18	3	0	—	—	—	—
Edwards, G.N.	1976-77	1980-81	8	15	0	377	55	25.13	—	3	7	—	—	—	—	—	—	—	—
Elliott, G.D.	2007-08	2009-10	5	9	1	86	25	10.75	—	—	2	—	282	140	4	35.00	2-8	—	—
Emery, R.W.G.	1951-52	1951-52	2	4	0	46	28	11.50	—	—	—	—	46	52	2	26.00	2-52	—	—
Fisher, F.E.	1952-53	1952-53	1	2	0	23	14	11.50	—	—	—	—	204†	78	1	78.00	1-78	—	—
Fleming, S.P.	1993-94	2007-08	111	189†	10	7172	274*	40.06	9	46	171	—	6†	0	0	—	—	—	—
Flynn, D.R.	2008	2012-13	24	45†	5	1038	95	25.95	—	6	10	—	—	—	—	—	—	—	—
Foley, H.	1929-30	1929-30	1	2†	1	4	2	2.00	—	—	—	—	6†	0	0	—	—	—	—
Franklin, J.E.C.	2000-01	2012-13	31	46†	7	808	122*	20.71	1	2	12	—	4767†	2786	82	33.97	6-119	3	—
Franklin, T.J.	1983	1990-91	21	37	1	828	101	23.00	1	4	8	—	—	—	—	—	—	—	—
Freeman, D.L.	1932-33	1932-33	2	2	0	2	1	1.00	—	—	—	—	240	169	1	169.00	1-91	—	—
Fulton, P.G.	2005-06	2014	23	39	1	967	136	25.44	2	5	25	—	—	—	—	—	—	—	—
Gallichan, N.	1937	1937	1	2	0	32	30	16.00	—	—	—	—	264†	113	3	37.66	3-99	—	—
Gedye, S.G.	1963-64	1964-65	4	8	0	193	55	24.12	—	2	—	—	—	—	—	—	—	—	—
Germon, L.K.	1995-96	1996-97	12	21	3	382	55	21.22	—	1	27	2	—	—	—	—	—	—	—
Gillespie, M.R.	2007-08	2011-12	5	8	1	76	27	10.85	—	—	1	—	868	631	22	28.68	6-113	3	—
Gillespie, S.R.	1985-86	1985-86	1	1	0	28	28	28.00	—	—	—	—	162	79	1	79.00	1-79	—	—
Gray, E.J.	1983	1988-89	10	16	0	248	50	15.50	—	1	6	—	2076†	886	17	52.11	3-73	—	—
Greatbatch, M.J.	1987-88	1996-97	41	71†	5	2021	146*	30.62	3	10	27	—	6	0	0	—	—	—	—
Guillen, S.C. ‡	1955-56	1955-56	3	6	0	98	41	16.33	—	—	4	1	—	—	—	—	—	—	—
Guptill, M.J.	2008-09	2013	31	59	1	1718	189	29.62	2	12	33	—	332	258	5	51.60	3-37	—	—
Guy, J.W.	1955-56	1961-62	12	23†	2	440	102	20.95	1	3	2	—	—	—	—	—	—	—	—
Hadlee, D.R.	1969	1977-78	26	42	5	530	56	14.32	—	1	8	—	4883	2389	71	33.64	4-30	—	—
Hadlee, R.J.	1972-73	1990	86	134†	19	3124	151*	27.16	2	15	39	—	21918	9611	431	22.29	9-52	36	9
Hadlee, W.A.	1937	1950-51	11	19	1	543	116	30.16	1	2	6	—	—	—	—	—	—	—	—

INDIVIDUAL CAREER RECORDS – NEW ZEALAND *continued*

			BATTING AND FIELDING										BOWLING						
	First Test	Last Test	Tests	Inns	NO	Runs	HS	Avge	100	50	Ct	St	Balls	Runs	Wkts	Avge	BB	5wI	10wM
Harford, N.S.	1955–56	1958	8	15	0	229	93	15.26	–	2	–	–	–	–	–	–	–	–	–
Harford, R.I.	1967–68	1967–68	3	5†	2	7	6	2.33	–	–	11	1	–	–	–	–	–	–	–
Harris, C.Z.	1992–93	2002	23	42†	4	777	71	20.44	–	5	14	–	2560	1170	16	73.12	2-16	–	–
Harris, P.G.Z.	1955–56	1964–65	9	18	1	378	101	22.23	1	1	6	–	42	14	0	–	–	–	–
Harris, R.M.	1958–59	1958–59	2	3	0	31	13	10.33	–	–	–	–	–	–	–	–	–	–	–
Hart, M.N.	1993–94	1995–96	14	24†	4	353	45	17.65	–	1	9	–	3086†	1438	29	49.58	5-77	1	–
Hart, R.G.	2002	2003–04	11	19	3	260	57*	16.25	–	1	29	1	–	–	–	–	–	–	–
Hartland, B.R.	1991–92	1994	9	18	0	303	52	16.83	–	1	5	–	–	–	–	–	–	–	–
Haslam, M.J.	1992–93	1995–96	4	2†	1	4	3	4.00	–	–	2	–	493†	245	2	122.50	1-33	–	–
Hastings, B.F.	1968–69	1975–76	31	56	6	1510	117*	30.20	4	7	23	–	22	9	0	–	–	–	–
Hayes, J.A.	1950–51	1958	15	22	7	73	19	4.86	–	–	3	–	2675	1217	30	40.56	4-36	–	–
Henderson, M.	1929–30	1929–30	1	2†	1	8	6	8.00	–	–	1	–	90†	64	2	32.00	2-38	–	–
Hopkins, G.J.	2008	2010–11	4	7	1	71	15	11.83	–	–	9	–	–	–	–	–	–	–	–
Horne, M.J.	1996–97	2003	35	65	2	1788	157	28.38	4	5	17	–	66	26	0	–	–	–	–
Horne, P.A.	1986–87	1990–91	4	7†	0	71	27	10.14	–	–	3	–	–	–	–	–	–	–	–
Hough, K.W.	1958–59	1958–59	2	3	2	62	31*	62.00	–	–	1	–	462	175	6	29.16	3-79	–	–
How, J.M.	2005–06	2008–09	19	35	1	772	92	22.70	–	4	18	–	12	4	0	–	–	–	–
Howarth, G.P.	1974–75	1984–85	47	83	5	2531	147	32.44	6	11	29	–	614	271	3	90.33	1-13	–	–
Howarth, H.J.	1969	1976–77	30	42†	18	291	61	12.12	–	1	33	–	8833†	3178	86	36.95	5-34	2	–
Ingram, P.J.	2009–10	2009–10	2	4	0	61	42	15.25	–	–	–	–	–	–	–	–	–	–	–
James, K.C.	1929–30	1932–33	11	13	2	52	14	4.72	–	–	11	5	–	–	–	–	–	–	–
Jarvis, T.W.	1964–65	1972–73	13	22	1	625	182	29.76	1	2	3	–	12†	3	0	–	–	–	–
Jones, A.H.	1986–87	1994–95	39	74	8	2922	186	44.27	7	11	25	–	328	194	1	194.00	1-40	–	–
Jones, R.A.	2003–04	2003–04	1	2	0	23	16	11.50	–	–	–	–	–	–	–	–	–	–	–
Kennedy, R.J.	1995–96	1995–96	4	5	1	28	22	7.00	–	–	2	–	636	380	6	63.33	3-28	–	–
Kerr, J.L.	1931	1937	7	12	1	212	59	19.27	–	1	4	–	–	–	–	–	–	–	–
Kuggeleijn, C.M.	1988–89	1988–89	2	4	0	7	7	1.75	–	–	1	–	97	67	1	67.00	1-50	–	–
Larsen, G.R.	1994	1995–96	8	13	4	127	26*	14.11	–	–	5	–	1967	689	24	28.70	3-57	–	–
Latham, R.T.	1991–92	1992–93	4	7	0	219	119	31.28	1	–	5	–	18	6	0	–	–	–	–
Latham, T.W.M.	2013–14	2014	4	8†	0	317	83	39.62	–	3	3	–	–	–	–	–	–	–	–
Lees, W.K.	1976–77	1983	21	37	4	778	152	23.57	1	1	52	7	5	4	0	–	–	–	–
Leggat, I.B.	1953–54	1953–54	1	1	0	0	0	0.00	–	–	2	–	24	6	0	–	–	–	–
Leggat, J.G.	1951–52	1955–56	9	18	2	351	61	21.93	–	2	1	–	–	–	–	–	–	–	–
Lissette, A.F.	1955–56	1955–56	2	4	2	2	1*	1.00	–	–	1	–	288†	124	3	41.33	2-73	–	–

INDIVIDUAL CAREER RECORDS – NEW ZEALAND *continued*

	First Test	Last Test	Tests	BATTING AND FIELDING									BOWLING						
				Inns	NO	Runs	HS	Avge	100	50	Ct	St	Balls	Runs	Wkts	Avge	BB	5wI	10wM
Loveridge, G.R.	1995-96	1995-96	1	1	0	4	4*	–	–	–	–	–	12	5	0	–	–	–	–
Lowry, T.C.	1929-30	1931	7	8	0	223	80	27.87	–	2	8	–	–	–	–	–	–	–	–
McCullum, B.B.	2003-04	2014	87	151	8	5306	302	37.10	9	28	184	11	36	18	0	–	–	–	–
McEwan, P.E.	1979-80	1984-85	4	7	1	96	40*	16.00	–	–	5	–	36	13	0	–	–	–	–
MacGibbon, A.R.	1950-51	1958	26	46	5	814	66	19.85	–	3	13	–	5659	2160	70	30.85	5-64	1	–
McGirr, H.M.	1929-30	1929-30	2	1	0	51	51	51.00	–	1	–	–	180	115	1	115.00	1-65	–	–
McGregor, S.N.	1954-55	1964-65	25	47	2	892	111	19.82	1	3	9	–	–	–	–	–	–	–	–
McIntosh, T.G.	2008-09	2010-11	17	33†	2	854	136	27.54	2	4	10	–	–	–	–	–	–	–	–
McKay, A.J.	2010-11	2010-11	1	2	1	25	20*	25.00	–	–	–	–	186†	120	1	120.00	1-120	–	–
McLeod, E.G.	1929-30	1929-30	1	2†	1	18	16	18.00	–	–	–	–	12	5	0	–	–	–	–
McMahon, T.G.	1955-56	1955-56	5	7	4	7	4*	2.33	–	–	7	1	–	–	–	–	–	–	–
McMillan, C.D.	1997-98	2004-05	55	91	10	3116	142	38.46	6	19	22	–	2502	1257	28	44.89	3-48	–	–
McRae, D.A.N.	1945-46	1945-46	1	2†	0	8	8	4.00	–	–	1	–	84†	44	0	–	–	–	–
Marshall, H.J.H.	2000-01	2005-06	13	19	2	652	160	38.35	2	2	1	–	6	4	0	–	–	–	–
Marshall, J.A.H.	2004-05	2008	7	11	0	218	52	19.81	–	1	5	–	–	–	–	–	–	–	–
Martin, B.P.	2012-13	2013-14	5	6	1	74	41	14.80	–	–	–	–	1518†	646	12	53.83	4-43	–	–
Martin, C.S.	2000-01	2012-13	71	104	52	123	12*	2.36	–	–	14	–	14026	7878	233	33.81	6-26	10	1
Mason, M.J.	2003-04	2003-04	2	2	1	3	3	1.50	–	–	–	–	132	105	0	–	–	–	–
Matheson, A.M.	1929-30	1931	2	1	0	7	7	7.00	–	–	2	–	282	136	2	68.00	2-7	–	–
Meale, T.	1958	1958	2	4†	0	21	10	5.25	–	–	–	–	–	–	–	–	–	–	–
Merritt, W.E.	1929-30	1931	6	8	1	73	19	10.42	–	–	2	–	936	617	12	51.41	4-104	–	–
Meuli, E.M.	1952-53	1952-53	1	2	0	38	23	19.00	–	–	–	–	–	–	–	–	–	–	–
Milburn, B.D.	1968-69	1968-69	3	3	2	8	4*	8.00	–	–	6	2	–	–	–	–	–	–	–
Miller, L.S.M.	1952-53	1958	13	25†	0	346	47	13.84	–	–	1	–	2†	1	0	–	–	–	–
Mills, J.E.	1929-30	1932-33	7	10†	1	241	117	26.77	1	–	1	–	–	–	–	–	–	–	–
Mills, K.D.	2004	2008-09	19	30	5	289	57	11.56	–	1	4	–	2902	1453	44	33.02	4-16	–	–
Moir, A.M.	1950-51	1958-59	17	30	8	327	41*	14.86	–	–	2	–	2650	1418	28	50.64	6-155	2	–
Moloney, D.A.R.	1937	1937	3	6	0	156	64	26.00	–	1	3	–	12	9	0	–	–	–	–
Mooney, F.L.H.	1949	1953-54	14	22	2	343	46	17.15	–	–	22	8	8	0	0	–	–	–	–
Morgan, R.W.	1964-65	1971-72	20	34	1	734	97	22.24	–	5	12	–	1114	609	5	121.80	1-16	–	–
Morrison, B.D.	1962-63	1962-63	1	2†	0	10	10	5.00	–	–	1	–	186	129	2	64.50	2-129	–	–
Morrison, D.K.	1987-88	1996-97	48	71	26	379	42	8.42	–	–	14	–	10064	5549	160	34.68	7-89	10	–
Morrison, J.F.M.	1973-74	1981-82	17	29	0	656	117	22.62	1	3	9	–	264†	71	2	35.50	2-52	–	–
Motz, R.C.	1961-62	1969	32	56	3	612	60	11.54	–	3	9	–	7034	3148	100	31.48	6-63	5	–
Munro, C.	2012-13	2012-13	1	2†	0	15	15	7.50	–	–	–	–	108	40	2	20.00	2-40	–	–
Murray, B.A.G.	1967-68	1970-71	13	26	1	598	90	23.92	–	5	21	–	6	0	2	0.00	1-0	–	–
Murray, D.J.	1994-95	1994-95	8	16	1	303	52	20.20	–	1	6	–	–	–	–	–	–	–	–

INDIVIDUAL CAREER RECORDS – NEW ZEALAND continued

	First Test	Last Test	Tests	Inns	NO	Runs	HS	Avge	100	50	Ct	St	Balls	Runs	Wkts	Avge	BB	5wI	10wM
							BATTING AND FIELDING								BOWLING				
Nash, D.J.	1992–93	2001–02	32	45	14	729	89*	23.51	–	4	13	–	6196	2649	93	28.48	6-27	3	1
Neesham, J.D.S.	2013–14	2014	4	8†	1	448	137*	64.00	2	2	2	–	331	199	4	49.75	2-12	–	–
Newman, J.	1931–32	1932–33	3	4	0	33	19	8.25	–	–	2	–	425†	254	2	127.00	2-76	–	–
Nicol, R.J.	2011–12	2011–12	2	4	0	28	19	7.00	–	–	2	–	17	13	0	–	–	–	–
O'Brien, I.E.	2004–05	2009–10	22	34	5	219	31	7.55	–	–	7	–	4394	2429	73	33.27	6-75	1	–
O'Connor, S.B.	1997–98	2001–02	19	27†	9	103	20	5.72	–	–	6	–	3667†	1724	53	32.52	5-51	1	–
Oram, J.D.P.	2002–03	2009	33	59†	10	1780	133	36.32	5	6	15	–	4964	1983	60	33.05	4-41	–	–
O'Sullivan, D.R.	1972–73	1976–77	11	21	4	158	23*	9.29	–	–	2	–	2744†	1221	18	67.83	5-148	1	–
Overton, G.W.F.	1953–54	1953–54	3	6†	1	8	3*	1.60	–	–	1	–	729	258	9	28.66	3-65	–	–
Owens, M.B.	1992–93	1994	8	12	6	16	8*	2.66	–	–	3	–	1074	585	17	34.41	4-99	–	–
Page, M.L.	1929–30	1937	14	20	0	492	104	24.60	1	2	6	–	379	231	5	46.20	2-21	–	–
Papps, M.H.W.	2003–04	2007–08	8	16	1	246	86	16.40	–	2	11	–	–	–	–	–	–	–	–
Parker, J.M.	1972–73	1980–81	36	63	2	1498	121	24.55	3	5	30	–	40	24	1	24.00	1-24	–	–
Parker, N.M.	1976–77	1976–77	3	6	0	89	40	14.83	–	–	2	–	–	–	–	–	–	–	–
Parore, A.C.	1990	2001–02	78	128	19	2865	110	26.28	2	14	197	7	–	–	–	–	–	–	–
Patel, D.N.	1986–87	1996–97	37	66	8	1200	99	20.68	–	5	15	–	6594	3154	75	42.05	6-50	3	–
Patel, J.S.	2005–06	2012–13	19	30	7	276	27*	12.00	–	–	12	–	4723	2520	52	48.46	5-110	1	–
Petherick, P.J.	1976–77	1976–77	6	11	4	34	13	4.85	–	–	4	–	1305	685	16	42.81	3-90	–	–
Petrie, E.C.	1955–56	1965–66	14	25	5	258	55	12.90	–	1	25	–	–	–	–	–	–	–	–
Playle, W.R.	1958	1962–63	8	15	0	151	65	10.06	–	1	4	–	–	–	–	–	–	–	–
Pocock, B.A.	1993–94	1997–98	15	29	2	665	85	22.93	–	6	5	–	24	20	0	–	–	–	–
Pollard, V.	1964–65	1973	32	59	7	1266	116	24.34	2	7	19	–	4421	1853	40	46.32	3-3	–	–
Poore, M.B.	1952–53	1955–56	14	24	1	355	45	15.43	–	–	1	–	788	367	9	40.77	2-28	–	–
Priest, M.W.	1990	1998	3	4†	0	56	26	14.00	–	–	–	–	377†	158	3	52.66	2-42	–	–
Pringle, C.	1990–91	1994–95	14	21	4	175	30	10.29	–	–	3	–	2985	1389	30	46.30	7-52	1	1
Puna, N.	1965–66	1965–66	3	5	3	31	18*	15.50	–	–	1	–	480	240	4	60.00	2-40	–	–
Rabone, G.O.	1949	1954–55	12	20	2	562	107	31.22	1	2	5	–	1385	635	16	39.68	6-68	1	–
Redmond, A.J.	2008	2013–14	8	16	1	325	83	21.66	–	2	5	–	105	80	3	26.66	2-47	–	–
Redmond, R.E.	1972–73	1972–73	1	2†	0	163	107	81.50	1	1	–	–	–	–	–	–	–	–	–
Reid, J.F.	1978–79	1985–86	19	31†	3	1296	180	46.28	6	2	9	–	18	7	0	–	–	–	–
Reid, J.R.	1949	1965	58	108	5	3428	142	33.28	6	22	43	1	7725	2835	85	33.35	6-60	1	–
Richardson, M.H.	2000–01	2004–05	38	65†	3	2776	145	44.77	4	19	26	–	66†	21	1	21.00	1-16	–	–
Roberts, A.D.G.	1975–76	1976–77	7	12	1	254	84*	23.09	–	1	4	–	440	182	4	45.50	1-12	–	–
Roberts, A.W.	1929–30	1937	5	10	1	248	66*	27.55	–	3	4	–	459	209	7	29.85	4-101	–	–
Robertson, G.K.	1985–86	1985–86	1	1	0	12	12	12.00	–	–	–	–	144	91	1	91.00	1-91	–	–

INDIVIDUAL CAREER RECORDS – NEW ZEALAND continued

	First Test	Last Test	Tests	Inns	NO	Runs	HS	Avge	100	50	Ct	St	Balls	Runs	Wkts	Avge	BB	5wI	10wM
						BATTING AND FIELDING							BOWLING						
Rowe, C.G.	1945–46	1945–46	1	2	0	0	0	0.00	–	1	1	–	–	–	–	–	–	–	–
Rutherford, H.D.	2012–13	2014	14	25†	1	650	171	27.08	1	1	10	–	–	–	–	–	–	–	–
Rutherford, K.R.	1984–85	1994–95	56	99	8	2465	107*	27.08	3	18	32	–	256	161	1	161.00	1-38	–	–
Ryder, J.D.	2008–09	2011–12	18	33†	2	1269	201	40.93	3	6	12	–	492	280	5	56.00	2-7	–	–
Scott, R.H.	1946–47	1946–47	1	1	0	18	18	18.00	–	–	–	–	138	74	1	74.00	1-74	–	–
Scott, V.J.	1945–46	1951–52	10	17	1	458	84	28.62	–	3	7	–	18	14	0	–	–	–	–
Sewell, D.G.	1997–98	1997–98	1	1	1	1	1*	–	–	–	–	–	138†	90	0	–	–	–	–
Shrimpton, M.J.F.	1962–63	1973–74	10	19	0	265	46	13.94	–	–	2	–	257	158	5	31.60	3-35	–	–
Sinclair, B.W.	1962–63	1967–68	21	40	1	1148	138	29.43	3	3	8	–	60	32	2	16.00	2-32	–	–
Sinclair, I.M.	1955–56	1955–56	2	4†	1	25	18*	8.33	–	–	1	–	233	120	1	120.00	1-79	–	–
Sinclair, M.S.	1999–2000	2009–10	33	56	5	1635	214	32.05	3	4	31	–	42	14	0	–	–	–	–
Smith, F.B.	1946–47	1951–52	4	6	1	237	96	47.40	–	2	1	–							
Smith, H.D.	1932–33	1932–33	1	1	0	4	4	4.00	–	–	–	–	120	113	1	113.00	1-113	–	–
Smith, I.D.S.	1980–81	1991–92	63	88	17	1815	173	25.56	2	6	168	8	18	5	0	–	–	–	–
Snedden, C.A.	1946–47	1946–47	1	–	–	–	–	–	–	–	–	–	96	46	0	–	–	–	–
Snedden, M.C.	1980–81	1990	25	30†	8	327	33*	14.86	–	–	7	–	4775	2199	58	37.91	5-68	1	–
Sodhi, I.S.	2013–14	2014	8	11	1	193	58	19.30	–	1	3	–	1354	885	19	46.57	4-96	–	–
Southee, T.G.	2007–08	2014	34	56	6	917	77*	18.34	–	2	19	–	7105	3670	123	29.83	7-64	4	1
Sparling, J.T.	1958	1963–64	11	20	2	229	50	12.72	–	1	4	–	708	327	5	65.40	1-9	–	–
Spearman, C.M.	1995–96	2000–01	19	37	0	922	112	26.34	1	3	21	–							
Stead, G.R.	1998–99	1999–2000	5	8	0	278	78	34.75	–	2	2	–	6	1	0	–	–	–	–
Stirling, D.A.	1984–85	1986	6	9	2	108	26	15.42	–	–	1	–	902	601	13	46.23	4-88	–	–
Styris, S.B.	2002	2007–08	29	48	4	1586	170	36.04	5	6	23	–	1960	1015	20	50.75	3-28	–	–
Su'a, M.L.	1991–92	1994–95	13	18†	5	165	44	12.69	–	–	8	–	2843†	1377	36	38.25	5-73	2	–
Sutcliffe, B.	1946–47	1965	42	76†	8	2727	230*	40.10	5	15	20	–	538†	344	4	86.00	2-38	–	–
Taylor, B.R.	1964–65	1973	30	50†	6	898	124	20.40	2	2	10	–	6334	2953	111	26.60	7-74	4	–
Taylor, D.D.	1946–47	1955–56	3	5	0	159	77	31.80	–	1	2	–							
Taylor, L.R.P.L.	2007–08	2014	57	104	10	4365	217*	46.43	11	22	95	–	96	48	2	24.00	2-4	–	–
Thomson, K.	1967–68	1967–68	2	4	1	94	69	31.33	–	1	–	–	21	9	1	9.00	1-9	–	–
Thomson, S.A.	1989–90	1995–96	19	35	4	958	120*	30.90	1	5	7	–	1990	953	19	50.15	3-63	–	–
Tindill, E.W.T.	1937	1946–47	5	9†	1	73	37*	9.12	–	–	6	1							
Troup, G.B.	1976–77	1985–86	15	18	6	55	13*	4.58	–	–	2	–	3183†	1454	39	37.28	6-95	1	1
Truscott, P.B.	1964–65	1964–65	1	2	0	29	26	14.50	–	–	1	–							
Tuffey, D.R.	1999–2000	2009–10	26	36	10	427	80*	16.42	–	1	15	–	4877	2445	77	31.75	6-54	2	–
Turner, G.M.	1968–69	1982–83	41	73	6	2991	259	44.64	7	14	42	–	12	5	0	–	–	–	–
Twose, R.G.	1995–96	1999	16	27†	2	628	94	25.12	–	6	5	–	211	130	3	43.33	2-36	–	–

	First Test	Last Test	Tests	Inns	NO	Runs	HS	Avge	100	50	Ct	St	Balls	Runs	Wkts	Avge	BB	5wI	10wM
								BATTING AND FIELDING							*BOWLING*				
Vance, R.H.	1987–88	1989–90	4	7	0	207	68	29.57	–	1	1	–	–	–	–	–	–	–	–
van Wyk, C.F.K.	2011–12	2012–13	9	17	1	341	71	21.31	–	1	23	1	–	–	–	–	–	–	–
Vaughan, J.T.C.	1992–93	1996–97	6	12†	1	201	44	18.27	–	–	4	–	1040	450	11	40.90	4-27	–	–
Vettori, D.L. ‡	1996–97	2012	111	171†	22	4508	140	30.25	6	23	58	–	28508†	12281	359	34.20	7-87	20	3
Vincent, L.	2001–02	2007–08	23	40	1	1332	224	34.15	3	9	19	–	6	2	0	–	–	–	–
Vivian, G.E.	1964–65	1971–72	5	6†	0	110	43	18.33	–	–	3	–	198	107	1	107.00	1-14	–	–
Vivian, H.G.	1931	1937	7	10†	0	421	100	42.10	1	5	4	–	1311†	633	17	37.23	4-58	–	–
Wadsworth, K.J.	1969	1975–76	33	51	4	1010	80	21.48	–	5	92	4	–	–	–	–	–	–	–
Wagner, N.	2012	2014	15	22†	6	196	37	12.25	–	–	4	–	3274†	1864	55	33.89	5-64	1	–
Walker, B.G.K.	2000–01	2002	5	8	2	118	27*	19.66	–	–	5	–	669	399	5	79.80	2-92	–	–
Wallace, W.M.	1937	1952–53	13	21	0	439	66	20.90	–	5	5	–	6	5	0	–	–	–	–
Walmsley, K.P.	1994–95	2000–01	3	5	0	13	5	2.60	–	–	–	–	774	391	9	43.44	3-70	–	–
Ward, J.T.	1963–64	1967–68	8	12	6	75	35*	12.50	–	–	16	1	–	–	–	–	–	–	–
Watling, B.J.	2009–10	2014	24	41	6	1299	124	37.11	3	8	76	1	–	–	–	–	–	–	–
Watson, W.	1986	1993–94	15	18	6	60	11	5.00	–	–	4	–	3486	1387	40	34.67	6-78	1	–
Watt, L.	1954–55	1954–55	1	2	0	2	2	1.00	–	–	–	–	–	–	–	–	–	–	–
Webb, M.G.	1970–71	1973–74	3	2	0	12	12	6.00	–	–	–	–	732	471	4	117.75	2-114	–	–
Webb, P.N.	1979–80	1979–80	2	3	0	11	5	3.66	–	–	2	–	–	–	–	–	–	–	–
Weir, G.L.	1929–30	1937	11	16	2	416	74*	29.71	–	3	3	–	342	209	7	29.85	3-38	–	–
White, D.J.	1990–91	1990–91	2	4	0	31	18	7.75	–	–	3	–	3	5	0	–	–	–	–
Whitelaw, P.E.	1932–33	1932–33	2	4	2	64	30	32.00	–	–	–	–	–	–	–	–	–	–	–
Williamson, K.S.	2010–11	2014	34	62	3	2377	161*	40.28	7	13	30	–	1741	976	24	40.66	4-44	–	–
Wiseman, P.J.	1998	2004–05	25	34	8	366	36	14.07	–	–	11	–	5660	2903	61	47.59	5-82	2	–
Wright, J.G.	1977–78	1992–93	82	148†	7	5334	185	37.82	12	23	38	–	30	5	0	–	–	–	–
Young, B.A.	1993–94	1998–99	35	68	4	2034	267*	31.78	2	12	54	–	–	–	–	–	–	–	–
Young, R.A.	2010–11	2011–12	5	10	3	169	57	24.14	–	1	8	–	–	–	–	–	–	–	–
Yuile, B.W.	1962–63	1969–70	17	33	6	481	64	17.81	–	1	12	–	2897†	1213	34	35.67	4-43	–	–

INDIVIDUAL CAREER RECORDS – INDIA

	First Test	Last Test	Tests	Inns	NO	Runs	HS	Avge	100	50	Ct	St	Balls	Runs	Wkts	Avge	BB	5wI	10wM
								BATTING AND FIELDING							*BOWLING*				
Aaron, V.R.	2011–12	2014	3	6	2	18	9	4.50	–	–	1	–	522	379	8	47.37	3-97	–	–
Abid Ali, S.	1967–68	1974–75	29	53	3	1018	81	20.36	–	6	32	–	4164	1980	47	42.12	6-55	1	–
Adhikari, H.R.	1947–48	1958–59	21	36	8	872	114*	31.14	1	4	8	–	170	82	3	27.33	3-68	–	–

INDIVIDUAL CAREER RECORDS – INDIA *continued*

	First Test	Last Test	Tests	Inns	NO	Runs	HS	Avge	100	50	Ct	St	Balls	Runs	Wkts	Avge	BB	5wI	10wM
					BATTING AND FIELDING										BOWLING				
Agarkar, A.B.	1998–99	2005–06	26	39	5	571	109*	16.79	1	–	6	–	4857	2745	58	47.32	6-41	1	1
Amarnath, L.	1933–34	1952–53	24	40	4	878	118	24.38	–	4	13	–	4241	1481	45	32.91	5-96	2	–
Amarnath, M.	1969–70	1987–88	69	113	10	4378	138	42.50	11	24	47	–	3676	1782	32	55.68	4-63	–	–
Amarnath, S.	1975–76	1978–79	10	18†	0	550	124	30.55	1	3	4	–	11	5	1	5.00	1-5	–	–
Amar Singh, L.	1932	1936	7	14	1	292	51	22.46	–	1	3	–	2182	858	28	30.64	7-86	2	–
Amir Elahi ‡	1947–48	1947–48	1	2	0	17	13	8.50	–	–	–	–	–	–	–	–	–	–	–
Amre, P.K.	1992–93	1993	11	13	3	425	103	42.50	1	3	9	–	–	–	–	–	–	–	–
Ankola, S.A.	1989–90	1989–90	1	1	0	6	6	6.00	–	–	–	–	180	128	2	64.00	1-35	–	–
Apte, A.L.	1959	1959	1	2	0	15	8	7.50	–	–	–	–	–	3	0	–	–	–	–
Apte, M.L.	1952–53	1952–53	7	13	2	542	163*	49.27	1	3	2	–	6	3	0	–	–	–	–
Arshad Ayub	1987–88	1989–90	13	19	4	257	57	17.13	–	1	2	–	3663	1438	41	35.07	5-50	3	–
Arun, B.	1986–87	1986–87	2	2	1	4	2*	4.00	–	–	2	–	252	116	4	29.00	3-76	–	–
Arun Lal	1982–83	1988–89	16	29	1	729	93	26.03	–	6	13	–	16	7	0	–	–	–	–
Ashwin, R.	2011–12	2014	21	30	7	894	124	38.86	2	3	7	–	6330	3066	107	28.65	7-103	9	2
Azad, K.	1980–81	1983–84	7	12	0	135	24	11.25	–	–	3	–	750	373	3	124.33	2-84	–	–
Azharuddin, M.	1984–85	1999–2000	99	147	9	6215	199	45.03	22	21	105	–	13	16	0	–	–	–	–
Badani, H.K.	2001	2001	4	7†	1	94	38	15.66	–	–	6	–	48†	17	0	–	–	–	–
Badrinath, S.	2009–10	2009–10	2	3	0	63	56	21.00	–	1	2	–	–	–	–	–	–	–	–
Bahutule, S.V.	2000–01	2001	2	4†	1	39	21*	13.00	–	–	1	–	366	203	3	67.66	1-32	–	–
Baig, A.A.	1959	1966–67	10	18	0	428	112	23.77	1	2	6	–	18	15	0	–	–	–	–
Balaji, L.	2003–04	2004–05	8	9	0	51	31	5.66	–	–	1	–	1756	1004	27	37.18	5-76	1	–
Banerjee, S.A.	1948–49	1948–49	1	1	0	0	0	0.00	–	–	–	–	306	181	5	36.20	4-120	–	–
Banerjee, S.N.	1948–49	1948–49	1	2	0	13	8	6.50	–	–	3	–	273	127	5	25.40	4-54	–	–
Banerjee, S.T.	1991–92	1991–92	1	1	0	3	3	3.00	–	–	–	–	108	47	3	15.66	3-47	–	–
Bangar, S.B.	2001–02	2002–03	12	18	2	470	100*	29.37	1	3	4	–	762	343	7	49.00	2-23	–	–
Baqa Jilani, M.	1936	1936	1	2	1	16	12	16.00	–	–	–	–	90	55	0	–	–	–	–
Bedi, B.S.	1966–67	1979	67	101	28	656	50*	8.98	–	1	26	–	21364†	7637	266	28.71	7-98	14	1
Bhandari, P.	1954–55	1956–57	3	4	0	77	39	19.25	–	–	1	–	78	39	0	–	–	–	–
Bharadwaj, R.V.	1999–2000	1999–2000	3	3	0	28	22	9.33	–	–	3	–	247	107	1	107.00	1-26	–	–
Bhat, A.R.	1983–84	1983–84	2	3†	1	6	6	3.00	–	–	–	–	438†	151	4	37.75	2-65	–	–
Bhuvneshwar Kumar	2012–13	2014	11	16	2	343	63*	24.50	–	3	4	–	1661	847	28	30.25	6-82	2	–
Binny, R.M.H.	1979–80	1986–87	27	41	5	830	83*	23.05	–	5	11	–	2870	1534	47	32.63	6-56	2	–
Binny, S.T.R.	2014	2014	3	6	1	118	78	23.60	–	1	1	–	192	140	0	–	–	–	–
Borde, C.G.	1958–59	1969–70	55	97	11	3061	177*	35.59	5	18	37	–	5695	2417	52	46.48	5-88	1	–
Chandrasekhar, B.S.	1963–64	1979	58	80	39	167	22	4.07	–	–	25	–	15963	7199	242	29.74	8-79	16	2
Chauhan, C.P.S.	1969–70	1980–81	40	68	2	2084	97	31.57	–	16	38	–	174	106	2	53.00	1-4	–	–

| | | | | BATTING AND FIELDING | | | | | | | | | BOWLING | | | | | | |
	First Test	Last Test	Tests	Inns	NO	Runs	HS	Avge	100	50	Ct	St	Balls	Runs	Wkts	Avge	BB	5wI	10wM
Chauhan, R.K.	1992–93	1997–98	21	17	3	98	23	7.00	–	–	12	–	4749	1857	47	39.51	4-48	–	–
Chawla, P.P.	2005–06	2012–13	3	3†	0	6	4	2.00	–	–	1	–	492	270	7	38.57	4-69	–	–
Chopra, A.	2003–04	2004–05	10	19	0	437	60	23.00	–	2	15	–							
Chopra, N.	1999–2000	1999–2000	1	2	0	7	4	3.50	–	–	–	–	144	78	0	–	–	–	–
Chowdhury, N.R.	1948–49	1951–52	2	2	1	3	3*	3.00	–	–	–	–	516	205	1	205.00	1-130	–	–
Colah, S.H.M.	1932	1933–34	2	4	0	69	31	17.25	–	–	2	–							
Contractor, N.J.	1955–56	1961–62	31	52†	1	1611	108	31.58	1	11	18	–	186	80	1	80.00	1-9	–	–
Dahiya, V.	2000–01	2000–01	2	1	1	2	2*	–	–	–	6	1							
Dani, H.T.	1952–53	1952–53	1	–		–	–	–	–	–	1	–	60	19	1	19.00	1-9	–	–
Das, S.S.	2000–01	2001–02	23	40	2	1326	110	34.89	2	9	34	–	66	35	0	–	–	–	–
Dasgupta, D.	2001–02	2001–02	8	13	1	344	100	28.66	1	2	13	–							
Desai, R.B.	1958–59	1967–68	28	44	13	418	85	13.48	–	1	9	–	5597	2761	74	37.31	6-56	2	–
Dhawan, S.	2012–13	2014	10	17†	0	656	187	38.58	2	1	8	–	30	9	0	–	–	–	–
Dhoni, M.S.	2005–06	2014	88	140	15	4808	224	38.46	6	33	243	37	96	67	0	–	–	–	–
Dighe, S.S.	2000–01	2001	6	10	1	141	47	15.66	–	–	12	2							
Dilawar Hussain	1933–34	1936	3	6	0	254	59	42.33	–	3	6	1							
Divecha, R.V.	1951–52	1952–53	5	5	0	60	26	12.00	–	–	5	–	1044	361	11	32.81	3-102	–	–
Doshi, D.R.	1979–80	1983–84	33	38†	10	129	20	4.60	–	–	10	–	9322†	3502	114	30.71	6-102	6	–
Dravid, R. ‡	1996	2011–12	163	284	32	13265	270	52.63	36	63	209	–	120	39	1	39.00	1-18	–	–
Durani, S.A.	1959–60	1972–73	29	50†	2	1202	104	25.04	1	7	14	–	6446†	2657	75	35.42	6-73	3	1
Engineer, F.M.	1961–62	1974–75	46	87	3	2611	121	31.08	2	16	66	16							
Gadkari, C.V.	1952–53	1954–55	6	10	4	129	50*	21.50	–	1	6	–	102	45	0	–	–	–	–
Gaekwad, A.D.	1974–75	1984–85	40	70	4	1985	201	30.07	2	10	15	–	334	187	2	93.50	1-4	–	–
Gaekwad, D.K.	1952	1960–61	11	20	1	350	52	18.42	–	1	5	–	12	12	0	–	–	–	–
Gaekwad, H.G.	1952–53	1952–53	1	2†	0	22	14	11.00	–	–	–	–	222†	47	0	–	–	–	–
Gambhir, G.	2004–05	2014	56	100†	5	4046	206	42.58	9	21	38	–	12	4	0	–	–	–	–
Gandhi, D.J.	1999–2000	1999–2000	4	7	1	204	88	34.00	–	2	3	–							
Gandotra, A.	1969–70	1969–70	2	4†	0	54	18	13.50	–	–	1	–							
Ganesh, D.	1996–97	1996–97	4	7	3	25	8	6.25	–	–	–	–	461	287	5	57.40	2-28	–	–
Ganguly, S.C.	1996	2008–09	113	188†	17	7212	239	42.17	16	35	71	–	3117	1681	32	52.53	3-28	–	–
Gavaskar, S.M.	1970–71	1986–87	125	214	16	10122	236*	51.12	34	45	108	–	380	206	1	206.00	1-34	–	–
Ghavri, K.D.	1974–75	1980–81	39	57†	14	913	86	21.23	–	2	16	–	7036†	3656	109	33.54	5-33	4	–
Ghorpade, J.M.	1952–53	1959	8	15	0	229	41	15.26	–	1	4	–	150	131	0	–	–	–	–
Ghulam Ahmed	1948–49	1958–59	22	31	9	192	50	8.72	–	1	11	–	5650	2052	68	30.17	7-49	4	1
Gopalan, M.J.	1933–34	1933–34	1	2	1	18	11*	18.00	–	–	3	–	114	39	1	39.00	1-39	–	–

INDIVIDUAL CAREER RECORDS – INDIA *continued*

	First Test	Last Test	Tests	Inns	NO	Runs	HS	Avge	100	50	Ct	St	Balls	Runs	Wkts	Avge	BB	5wI	10wM
Gopinath, C.D.	1951–52	1959–60	8	12	1	242	50*	22.00	–	1	2	–	48	11	0	11.00	1-11	–	–
Guard, G.M.	1958–59	1959–60	2	2†	0	11	7	5.50	–	–	2	–	396†	182	3	60.66	2-69	–	–
Guha, S.	1967	1969–70	4	7	2	17	6	3.40	–	–	2	–	674	311	3	103.66	2-55	–	–
Gul Mohammad ‡	1946	1952–53	8	15†	0	166	34	11.06	–	–	3	–	77†	24	2	12.00	2-21	–	–
Gupte, B.P.	1960–61	1964–65	3	3	2	28	17*	28.00	–	–	–	–	678	349	3	116.33	1-54	–	–
Gupte, S.P.	1951–52	1961–62	36	42	13	183	21	6.31	–	–	14	–	11284	4403	149	29.55	9-102	12	1
Gursharan Singh	1989–90	1989–90	1	1	0	18	18	18.00	–	–	2	–	–					–	–
Hafeez, A.: see A.H. Kardar																			
Hanumant Singh	1963–64	1969–70	14	24	2	686	105	31.18	1	5	11	–	66	51	0	–	–	–	–
Harbhajan Singh	1997–98	2012–13	101	142	22	2202	115	18.35	2	9	42	–	28293	13372	413	32.37	8-84	25	5
Hardikar, M.S.	1958–59	1958–59	2	4	1	56	32*	18.66	–	–	3	–	108	55	1	55.00	1-9	–	–
Harvinder Singh	1997–98	2001	3	4	1	6	6	2.00	–	–	–	–	273	185	4	46.25	2-62	–	–
Hazare, V.S.	1946	1952–53	30	52	6	2192	164*	47.65	7	9	11	–	2840	1220	20	61.00	4-29	–	–
Hindlekar, D.D.	1936	1946	4	7	2	71	26	14.20	–	–	3	–						–	–
Hirwani, N.D.	1987–88	1996–97	17	22	12	54	17	5.40	–	–	5	–	4298	1987	66	30.10	8-61	4	1
Ibrahim, K.C.	1948–49	1948–49	4	8	0	169	85	21.12	–	1	–	–	–						
Indrajitsinhji, K.S.	1964–65	1969–70	4	7	1	51	23	8.50	–	–	6	3	–						
Irani, J.K.	1947–48	1947–48	2	3	2	3	2*	3.00	–	–	2	1	–						
Jadeja, A.	1992–93	1999–2000	15	24	2	576	96	26.18	–	4	5	–	3424†	1367	45	30.37	6-138	2	–
Jadeja, R.A.	2012–13	2014	12	19†	2	364	68	21.41	–	1	11	–	66	18	2	9.00	2-18	–	–
Jaffer, W.	1999–2000	2007–08	31	58	1	1944	212	34.10	5	11	27	–	606	255	4	63.75	4-60	–	–
Jahangir Khan, M.	1932	1936	4	7	0	39	13	5.57	–	–	4	–						–	–
Jai, L.P.	1933–34	1933–34	1	2	0	19	19	9.50	–	–	–	–	–						
Jaisimha, M.L.	1959	1970–71	39	71	4	2056	129	30.68	3	12	17	–	2097	829	9	92.11	2-54	–	–
Jamshedji, R.J.D.	1933–34	1933–34	1	2	0	5	4*	–	–	–	2	–	210†	137	3	45.66	3-137	–	–
Jayantilal, K.	1970–71	1970–71	1	2	1	5	5	5.00	–	–	–	–							
Johnson, D.J.	1996–97	1996–97	2	3	1	8	5	4.00	–	–	–	–	240	143	3	47.66	2-52	–	–
Joshi, P.G.	1951–52	1960–61	12	20	1	207	52*	10.89	–	1	18	9	–						
Joshi, S.B.	1996	2000–01	15	19†	2	352	92	20.70	–	1	7	–	3451†	1470	41	35.85	5-142	1	–
Kaif, M.	1999–2000	2006	13	22	3	624	148*	32.84	1	3	14	–	18	4	0	–	–	–	–
Kambli, V.G.	1992–93	1995–96	17	21†	1	1084	227	54.20	4	3	7	–	–					–	–
Kanitkar, H.H.	1999–2000	1999–2000	2	4†	0	74	45	18.50	–	1	–	–	6	2	0	–	–	–	–
Kanitkar, H.S.	1974–75	1974–75	2	4	0	111	65	27.75	–	1	–	–	–						
Kapil Dev	1978–79	1993–94	131	184	15	5248	163	31.05	8	27	64	–	27740	12867	434	29.64	9-83	23	2
Kapoor, A.R.	1994–95	1996–97	4	6	1	97	42	19.40	–	–	1	–	642	255	6	42.50	2-19	–	–

INDIVIDUAL CAREER RECORDS – INDIA continued

	First Test	Last Test	Tests	Inns	NO	Runs	HS	Avge	100	50	Ct	St	Balls	Runs	Wkts	Avge	BB	5wI	10wM
						BATTING AND FIELDING									*BOWLING*				
Kardar, A.H. ‡	1946	1946	3	5†	0	80	43	16.00	–	–	1	–	–	–	–	–	–	–	–
Karim, S.S.	2000-01	2000-01	1	1	0	15	15	15.00	–	–	1	5	–						
Karthik, K.D.	2004-05	2009-10	23	37	1	1000	129	27.77	1	7	51	5	–						
Kartik, M.	1999-2000	2004-05	8	10†	1	88	43	9.77	–	–	2	–	1932†	820	24	34.16	4-44	–	–
Kenny, R.B.	1958-59	1959-60	5	10	1	245	62	27.22	–	3	1	–							
Khan, Z.	2000-01	2013-14	92	127	24	1231	75	11.95	–	3	19	–	18785†	10247	311	32.94	7-87	11	1
Kirmani, S.M.H.	1975-76	1985-86	88	124	22	2759	102	27.04	2	12	160	38	19	13	1	13.00	1-9	–	–
Kishenchand, G.	1947-48	1952-53	5	10	4	89	44	8.90	–	–	1	–							
Kohli, V.	2011	2014	29	51	4	1855	119	39.46	6	9	28	–	144	70	0	–	–	–	–
Kripal Singh, A.G.	1955-56	1964-65	14	20	5	422	100*	28.13	1	2	4	–	1518	584	10	58.40	3-43	–	–
Krishnamurthy, P.	1970-71	1970-71	5	6	0	33	20	5.50	–	–	7	1							
Kulkarni, N.M.	1997	2000-01	3	2†	1	5	4	5.00	–	–	1	–	738†	332	2	166.00	1-70	–	–
Kulkarni, R.R.	1986-87	1986-87	3	2	0	2	2	1.00	–	–	1	–	366	227	5	45.40	3-85	–	–
Kulkarni, U.N.	1967-68	1967-68	4	8†	5	13	7	4.33	–	–	–	–	448†	238	5	47.60	2-37	–	–
Kumar, P.	2011	2011	6	10	0	149	40	14.90	–	–	2	–	1611	697	27	25.81	5-106	1	–
Kumar, V.V.	1960-61	1961-62	2	2	0	6	6	3.00	–	–	2	–	605	202	7	28.85	5-64	1	–
Kumble, A.	1990	2008-09	132	173	32	2506	110*	17.77	1	5	60	–	40850	18355	619	29.65	10-74	35	8
Kunderan, B.K.	1959-60	1967	18	34	4	981	192	32.70	2	3	23	7	24	13	0	–	–	–	–
Kuruvilla, A.	1996-97	1997-98	10	11	1	66	35*	6.60	–	–	–	–	1765	892	25	35.68	5-68	1	–
Lall Singh	1932	1932	1	2	0	44	29	22.00	–	–	1	–	–						
Lamba, R.	1986-87	1987-88	4	5	0	102	53	20.40	–	1	5	–	–						
Laxman, V.V.S.	1996-97	2011-12	134	225	34	8781	281	45.97	17	56	135	–	324	126	2	63.00	1-2	–	–
Madan Lal	1974	1986	39	62	16	1042	74	22.65	–	5	15	–	5997	2846	71	40.08	5-23	4	–
Maka, E.S.	1952-53	1952-53	2	1	1	2	2*	–	–	–	2	1							
Malhotra, A.O.	1981-82	1984-85	7	10	1	226	72*	25.11	–	1	2	–	18	3	0	–	–	–	–
Maninder Singh	1982-83	1992-93	35	38	12	99	15	3.80	–	–	9	–	8218†	3288	88	37.36	7-27	3	2
Manjrekar, S.V.	1987-88	1996-97	37	61	6	2043	218	37.14	4	9	25	–	17	15	0	–	–	–	–
Manjrekar, V.L.	1951-52	1964-65	55	92	10	3208	189*	39.12	7	15	19	2	204	44	1	44.00	1-16	–	–
Mankad, A.V.	1969-70	1977-78	22	42	3	991	97	25.41	–	6	12	–	41	43	0	–	–	–	–
Mankad, M.H.	1946	1958-59	44	72	5	2109	231	31.47	5	6	33	–	14686†	5236	162	32.32	8-52	8	2
Mantri, M.K.	1951-52	1954-55	4	8	1	67	39	9.57	–	–	8	1							
Meherhomji, K.R.	1936	1936	1	1	1	0	0*	–	–	–	1	–							
Mehra, V.L.	1955-56	1963-64	8	14	1	329	62	25.30	–	2	2	–	36	6	0	–	–	–	–
Merchant, V.M.	1933-34	1951-52	10	18	0	859	154	47.72	3	3	7	–	54	40	0	–	–	–	–
Mhambrey, P.L.	1996	1996	2	3	1	58	28	29.00	–	–	1	–	258	148	2	74.00	1-43	–	–
Milkha Singh, A.G.	1959-60	1961-62	4	6†	0	92	35	15.33	–	–	2	–	6	2	0	–	–	–	–

INDIVIDUAL CAREER RECORDS – INDIA *continued*

	First Test	Last Test	Tests	Inns	NO	Runs	HS	Avge	100	50	Ct	St	Balls	Runs	Wkts	Avge	BB	5wI	10wM
						BATTING AND FIELDING										*BOWLING*			
Mishra, A.	2008-09	2011	13	19	2	392	84	23.05	–	2	6	–	3497	1862	43	43.30	5-71	1	–
Mithun, A.	2010	2011	4	5	0	120	46	24.00	–	–	–	–	720	456	9	50.66	4-105	–	–
Modi, R.S.	1946	1952-53	10	17	1	736	112	46.00	1	6	3	–	30	14	0	–	–	–	–
Mohammed Shami	2013-14	2014	9	15	5	99	51*	9.90	–	–	1	–	1920	1162	32	36.31	5-47	1	–
Mohanty, D.S.	1997	1997-98	2	1	1	0	0*	–	–	–	–	–	430	239	4	59.75	4-78	–	–
Mongia, N.R.	1993-94	2000-01	44	68	8	1442	152	24.03	1	6	99	8							
More, K.S.	1986	1993	49	64	14	1285	73	25.70	–	7	110	20	12	12	0	–	–	–	–
Muddiah, V.M.	1959-60	1960-61	2	3	1	11	11	5.50	–	–	–	–	318	134	3	44.66	2-40	–	–
Mukund, A.	2011	2011	2	10†	0	211	62	21.10	–	1	5	–	12	14	0	–	–	–	–
Mushtaq Ali, S.	1933-34	1951-52	11	20	1	612	112	32.21	2	3	7	–	378†	202	3	67.33	1-45	–	–
Nadkarni, R.G.	1955-56	1967-68	41	67†	12	1414	122*	25.70	1	7	22	–	9165†	2559	88	29.07	6-43	4	1
Naik, S.S.	1974	1974-75	3	6	0	141	77	23.50	–	1	–	–	–	–	–	–	–	–	–
Naoomal Jaoomal	1932	1933-34	3	5	1	108	43	27.00	–	–	–	–	108	68	2	34.00	1-4	–	–
Narasimha Rao, M.V.	1978-79	1979-80	4	6	1	46	20*	9.20	–	–	8	–	463	227	3	75.66	2-46	–	–
Navle, J.G.	1932	1933-34	2	4	0	42	13	10.50	–	–	1	–	–	–	–	–	–	–	–
Nayak, S.V.	1982	1982	2	3†	1	19	11	9.50	–	–	1	–	231	132	1	132.00	1-16	–	–
Nayudu, C.K.	1932	1936	7	14	0	350	81	25.00	–	2	4	–	858	386	9	42.88	3-40	–	–
Nayudu, C.S.	1933-34	1951-52	11	19	3	147	36	9.18	–	–	3	–	522	359	2	179.50	1-19	–	–
Nazir Ali, S.	1932	1933-34	2	4	0	30	13	7.50	–	–	–	–	138	83	4	20.75	4-83	–	–
Nehra, A.	1998-99	2003-04	17	25	11	77	19	5.50	–	–	5	–	3447†	1866	44	42.40	4-72	–	–
Nissar, M.	1932	1936	6	11	3	55	14	6.87	–	–	2	–	1211	707	25	28.28	5-90	3	–
Nyalchand, S.	1952-53	1952-53	1	2†	1	7	6*	7.00	–	–	–	–	384†	97	3	32.33	3-97	–	–
Ojha, P.P.	2009-10	2013-14	24	27†	17	89	18*	8.90	–	–	10	–	7633†	3420	113	30.26	6-47	7	1
Pai, A.M.	1969-70	1969-70	1	2†	0	10	9	5.00	–	–	–	–	114	31	2	15.50	2-29	–	–
Palia, P.E.	1932	1936	2	4†	1	29	16	9.66	–	–	–	–	42†	13	0	–	–	–	–
Pandit, C.S.	1986	1991-92	5	8	1	171	39	24.42	–	–	14	2	–	–	–	–	–	–	–
Pankaj Singh	2014	2014	1	4	1	10	9	3.33	–	–	2	–	450	292	2	146.00	2-113	–	–
Parkar, G.A.	1982	1982	1	2	0	7	6	3.50	–	–	1	–	–	–	–	–	–	–	–
Parkar, R.D.	1972-73	1972-73	2	4	0	80	35	20.00	–	–	–	–	–	–	–	–	–	–	–
Parsana, D.D.	1978-79	1978-79	2	2†	0	1	1	0.50	–	–	3	–	120†	50	1	50.00	1-32	–	–
Patankar, C.T.	1955-56	1955-56	1	2	1	14	13	14.00	–	–	3	1	–	–	–	–	–	–	–
Pataudi, Nawab of, sen. ‡	1946	1946	3	5	0	55	22	11.00	–	–	–	–	–	–	–	–	–	–	–
Pataudi, Nawab of, jun.	1961-62	1974-75	46	83	3	2793	203*	34.91	6	16	27	–	132	88	1	88.00	1-10	–	–
Patel, B.P.	1974	1977-78	21	38	5	972	115*	29.45	1	5	17	–	–	–	–	–	–	–	–
Patel, J.M.	1954-55	1959-60	7	10	1	25	12	2.77	–	–	2	–	1725	637	29	21.96	9-69	2	1

INDIVIDUAL CAREER RECORDS – INDIA *continued*

	First Test	Last Test	Tests	BATTING AND FIELDING Inns	NO	Runs	HS	Avge	100	50	Ct	St	BOWLING Balls	Runs	Wkts	Avge	BB	5wI	10wM
Patel, M.M.	2005–06	2011	13	14	6	60	15*	7.50	–	–	6	–	2658	1349	35	38.54	4-25	–	–
Patel, P.A.	2002	2008	20	30†	7	683	69	29.69	–	4	41	8	–	–	–	–	–	–	–
Patel, R.G.M.	1988–89	1988–89	1	2†	0	0	0	0.00	–	–	1	–	84†	51	0	–	–	–	–
Pathan, I.K.	2003–04	2007–08	29	40†	5	1105	102	31.57	1	6	8	–	5884†	3226	100	32.26	7-59	7	2
Patiala, Yuvraj of	1933–34	1933–34	1	2	0	84	60	42.00	–	1	2	–	–	–	–	–	–	–	–
Patil, S.M.	1979–80	1984–85	29	47	4	1588	174	36.93	4	7	12	–	645	240	9	26.66	2-28	–	–
Patil, S.R.	1955–56	1955–56	1	1	1	14	14*	–	–	–	1	–	138	51	2	25.50	1-15	–	–
Phadkar, D.G.	1947–48	1958–59	31	45	7	1229	123	32.34	2	8	21	–	5994	2285	62	36.85	7-159	3	–
Powar, R.R.	2007	2007	2	2	0	13	7	6.50	–	–	–	–	252	118	6	19.66	3-33	–	–
Prabhakar, M.	1984–85	1995–96	39	58	9	1600	120	32.65	1	9	20	–	7475	3581	96	37.30	6-132	3	–
Prasad, B.K.V.	1996	2001	33	47	20	203	30*	7.51	–	–	6	–	7041	3360	96	35.00	6-33	7	1
Prasad, M.S.K.	1999–2000	1999–2000	6	10	1	106	19	11.77	–	–	15	–	–	–	–	–	–	–	–
Prasanna, E.A.S.	1961–62	1978–79	49	84	20	735	37	11.48	–	1	18	–	14353	5742	189	30.38	8-76	10	2
Pujara, C.A.	2010–11	2014	24	42	4	1872	206*	49.26	6	5	18	–	–	–	–	–	–	–	–
Punjabi, P.H.	1954–55	1954–55	5	10	0	164	33	16.40	–	–	5	–	–	–	–	–	–	–	–
Rahane, A.M.	2012–13	2014	10	19	2	678	118	39.88	2	4	5	–	–	–	–	–	–	–	–
Raina, S.K.	2010	2012	17	29†	2	768	120	28.44	1	7	22	–	921	532	13	40.92	2-1	–	–
Rai Singh, K.	1947–48	1947–48	1	2	0	26	24	13.00	–	–	–	–	–	–	–	–	–	–	–
Rajindernath, V.	1952–53	1952–53	1	–	–	–	–	–	–	–	–	4	–	–	–	–	–	–	–
Rajinder Pal	1963–64	1963–64	1	2	1	6	3*	6.00	–	–	–	–	78	22	0	–	–	–	–
Rajput, L.S.	1985	1985	2	4	0	105	61	26.25	–	1	1	–	–	–	–	–	–	–	–
Raju, S.L.V.	1989–90	2000–01	28	34	10	240	31	10.00	–	–	6	–	7602†	2857	93	30.72	6-12	5	1
Raman, W.V.	1987–88	1996–97	11	19†	1	448	96	24.88	–	4	6	–	348†	129	2	64.50	1-7	–	–
Ramaswami, C.	1936	1936	2	4†	1	170	60	56.66	–	1	1	–	–	–	–	–	–	–	–
Ramchand, G.S.	1952	1959–60	33	53	5	1180	109	24.58	2	5	20	–	4976	1899	41	46.31	6-49	1	–
Ramesh, S.	1998–99	2001	19	37†	1	1367	143	37.97	2	8	18	–	54	43	0	–	–	–	–
Ramji, L.	1933–34	1933–34	1	2	0	1	1	0.50	–	–	1	–	138	64	1	64.00	–	–	–
Rangachari, C.R.	1947–48	1948–49	4	6	3	8	8*	2.66	–	–	1	–	846	493	9	54.77	5-107	1	–
Rangnekar, K.M.	1947–48	1947–48	3	6†	0	33	18	5.50	–	–	–	–	–	–	–	–	–	–	–
Ranjane, V.B.	1958–59	1964–65	7	9	3	40	16	6.66	–	–	1	–	1265	649	19	34.15	4-72	–	–
Rathour, V.	1996	1996–97	6	10	0	131	44	13.10	–	1	–	–	–	–	–	–	–	–	–
Ratra, A.	2001–02	2002	6	10	1	163	115*	18.11	1	–	12	2	–	–	–	–	–	–	–
Razdan, V.	1989–90	1989–90	2	2	1	6	6*	6.00	–	–	–	–	240	141	5	28.20	5-79	1	–
Reddy, B.	1979	1979	4	5	1	38	21	9.50	–	–	9	2	–	–	–	–	–	–	–
Rege, M.R.	1948–49	1948–49	1	5	3	15	15	7.50	–	–	1	–	–	–	–	–	–	–	–
Roy, A.K.	1969–70	1969–70	4	7†	0	91	48	13.00	–	–	1	–	–	–	–	–	–	–	–

INDIVIDUAL CAREER RECORDS – INDIA *continued*

BATTING AND FIELDING / BOWLING

	First Test	Last Test	Tests	Inns	NO	Runs	HS	Avge	100	50	Ct	St	Balls	Runs	Wkts	Avge	BB	5wI	10wM
Roy, Pankaj	1951-52	1960-61	43	79	4	2442	173	32.56	5	9	16	–	104	66	1	66.00	1-6	–	–
Roy, Pranab	1981-82	1981-82	2	3	1	71	60*	35.50	–	1	1	–	–	–	–	–	–	–	–
Saha, W.P.	2009-10	2011-12	2	4	0	74	36	18.50	–	–	2	–	–	–	–	–	–	–	–
Sandhu, B.S.	1982-83	1983-84	8	11	4	214	71	30.57	–	2	1	–	1020	557	10	55.70	3-87	–	–
Sanghvi, R.L.	2000-01	2000-01	1	2†	0	2	2	1.00	–	–	–	–	74†	78	2	39.00	2-67	–	–
Sarandeep Singh	2000-01	2001-02	3	2	0	43	39*	43.00	–	–	1	–	678	340	10	34.00	4-136	–	–
Sardesai, D.N.	1961-62	1972-73	30	55	4	2001	212	39.23	5	9	4	–	59	45	0	–	–	–	–
Sarwate, C.T.	1946	1951-52	9	17	1	208	37	13.00	–	–	–	–	658	374	3	124.66	1-16	–	–
Saxena, R.C.	1967	1967	1	2	0	25	16	12.50	–	–	–	–	12	11	0	–	–	–	–
Sehwag, V. ‡	2001-02	2012-13	103	178	6	8503	319	49.43	23	31	90	–	3731	1894	40	47.35	5-104	1	–
Sekhar, T.A.	1982-83	1982-83	2	1	1	0	0*	–	–	–	–	–	204	129	0	–	–	–	–
Sen, P.K.	1947-48	1952-53	14	18	4	165	25	11.78	–	–	20	11	–	–	–	–	–	–	–
Sengupta, A.K.	1958-59	1958-59	1	2	0	9	8	4.50	–	–	1	–	–	–	–	–	–	–	–
Sharma, A.K.	1987-88	1987-88	1	2	0	53	30	26.50	–	–	1	–	24†	9	0	–	–	–	–
Sharma, C.	1984-85	1988-89	23	27	9	396	54	22.00	–	1	7	–	3470	2163	61	35.45	6-58	4	1
Sharma, G.	1984-85	1990-91	5	4	1	11	10*	3.66	–	–	2	–	1307	418	10	41.80	4-88	–	–
Sharma, I.	2007	2014	58	87	31	524	31*	9.35	–	–	12	–	11715	6542	178	36.75	7-74	6	1
Sharma, P.H.	1974-75	1976-77	5	10	0	187	54	18.70	–	1	1	–	24	8	0	–	–	–	–
Sharma, R.G.	2013-14	2014	7	12	2	489	177	48.90	2	1	8	–	244	152	1	152.00	1-26	–	–
Sharma, S.K.	1988-89	1990	2	3	1	56	38	28.00	–	–	1	–	414	247	6	41.16	3-37	–	–
Shastri, R.J.	1980-81	1992-93	80	121	14	3830	206	35.79	11	12	36	–	15751†	6185	151	40.96	5-75	2	–
Shinde, S.G.	1946	1952	7	11	5	85	14	14.16	–	–	1	–	1515	717	12	59.75	6-91	1	–
Shodhan, R.H.	1952-53	1952-53	3	4†	1	181	110	60.33	1	–	1	–	60†	26	0	–	–	–	–
Shukla, R.C.	1982-83	1982-83	1	–	–	–	–	–	–	–	1	–	294	152	2	76.00	2-82	–	–
Siddiqui, I.R.	2001-02	2001-02	1	2	1	29	24	29.00	–	–	1	–	114	48	1	48.00	1-32	–	–
Sidhu, N.S.	1983-84	1998-99	51	78	2	3202	201	42.13	9	15	9	–	6	9	0	–	–	–	–
Singh, Robin, jun.	1998-99	1998-99	1	1	0	0	0	0.00	–	–	–	–	240	176	3	58.66	2-74	–	–
Singh, R.P.	2005-06	2011	14	19	3	116	30	7.25	–	–	6	–	2534†	1682	40	42.05	5-59	1	–
Singh, R.R. (Robin)	1998-99	1998-99	1	2†	0	27	15	13.50	–	–	5	–	60	32	0	–	–	–	–
Singh, V.R.	2006	2007	5	6	2	47	29	11.75	–	–	1	–	669	427	8	53.37	3-48	–	–
Sivaramakrishnan, L.	1982-83	1985-86	9	9	1	130	25	16.25	–	–	9	–	2367	1145	26	44.03	6-64	3	–
Sohoni, S.W.	1946	1951-52	4	7	2	83	29*	16.60	–	–	2	–	532	202	2	101.00	1-16	–	–
Solkar, E.D.	1969-70	1976-77	27	48†	6	1068	102	25.42	1	6	53	–	2265†	1070	18	59.44	3-28	–	–
Sood, M.M.	1959-60	1959-60	1	2	0	3	3	1.50	–	–	–	–	–	–	–	–	–	–	–
Sreesanth, S.	2005-06	2011	27	40	13	281	35	10.40	–	–	5	–	5419	3271	87	37.59	5-40	3	–
Srikkanth, K.	1981-82	1991-92	43	72	3	2062	123	29.88	2	12	40	–	216	114	0	–	–	–	–

INDIVIDUAL CAREER RECORDS – INDIA *continued*

				BATTING AND FIELDING									BOWLING						
	First Test	Last Test	Tests	Inns	NO	Runs	HS	Avge	100	50	Ct	St	Balls	Runs	Wkts	Avge	BB	5wI	10wM
Srinath, J.	1991–92	2002–03	67	92	21	1009	76	14.21	–	4	22	–	15104	7196	236	30.49	8-86	10	1
Srinivasan, T.E.	1980–81	1980–81	1	2	0	48	29	24.00	–	–	–	–	–	–	–	–	–	–	–
Subramanya, V.	1964–65	1967–68	9	15	1	263	75	18.78	–	2	9	–	444	201	3	67.00	2-32	–	–
Sunderam, G.R.	1955–56	1955–56	2	1	1	3	3*	–	–	–	–	–	396	166	3	55.33	2-46	–	–
Surendranath	1958–59	1960–61	11	20	7	136	27	10.46	–	–	4	–	2602	1053	26	40.50	5-75	2	–
Surti, R.F.	1960–61	1969–70	26	48†	4	1263	99	28.70	–	9	26	–	3870†	1962	42	46.71	5-74	1	–
Swamy, V.N.	1955–56	1955–56	1	–	–	–	–	–	–	–	–	–	108	45	0	–	–	–	–
Tamhane, N.S.	1954–55	1960–61	21	27	5	225	54*	10.22	–	1	35	16	–	–	–	–	–	–	–
Tarapore, K.K.	1948–49	1948–49	1	1	0	2	2	2.00	–	–	–	–	114†	72	0	–	–	–	–
Tendulkar, S.R.	1989–90	2013–14	200	329	33	15921	248*	53.78	51	68	115	–	4240	2492	46	54.17	3-10	–	–
Umrigar, P.R.	1948–49	1961–62	59	94	8	3631	223	42.22	12	14	33	–	4725	1473	35	42.08	6-74	2	–
Unadkat, J.D.	2010–11	2010–11	1	2	1	2	1*	2.00	–	–	–	–	156†	101	0	–	–	–	–
Vengsarkar, D.B.	1975–76	1991–92	116	185	22	6868	166	42.13	17	35	78	–	47	36	0	–	–	–	–
Venkataraghavan, S.	1964–65	1983–84	57	76	12	748	64	11.68	–	2	44	–	14877	5634	156	36.11	8-72	3	1
Venkataramana, M.	1988–89	1988–89	1	2	2	0	0*	–	–	–	1	–	70	58	1	58.00	1-10	–	–
Vijay, M.	2008–09	2014	27	47	2	1706	167	36.29	4	6	24	–	66	35	1	35.00	1-12	–	–
Vinay Kumar, R.	2011–12	2011–12	1	2	0	11	6	5.50	–	–	–	–	78	73	1	73.00	1-73	–	–
Viswanath, G.R.	1969–70	1982–83	91	155	10	6080	222	41.93	14	35	63	–	70	46	1	46.00	1-11	–	–
Viswanath, S.	1985	1985	3	5	0	31	20	6.20	–	–	11	–							
Vizianagram, Maharajkumar of	1936	1936	3	6	2	33	19*	8.25	–	–	1	–							
Wadekar, A.L.	1966–67	1974	37	71†	3	2113	143	31.07	1	14	46	–	61†	55	0	–	–	–	–
Wassan, A.S.	1989–90	1990	4	5	1	94	53	23.50	–	1	1	–	712	504	10	50.40	4-108	–	–
Wazir Ali, S.	1932	1936	7	14	0	237	42	16.92	–	1	1	–	30	25	0	–	–	–	–
Yadav, N.S.	1979–80	1986–87	35	40	12	403	43	14.39	–	–	10	–	8360	3580	102	35.09	5-76	3	–
Yadav, U.T.	2011–12	2012–13	9	11	5	36	21	6.00	–	–	2	–	1485	1040	32	32.50	5-93	1	–
Yadav, V.	1992–93	1992–93	1	1	0	30	30	30.00	–	–	1	2	–	–	–	–	–	–	–
Yajurvindra Singh	1976–77	1979–80	4	7	1	109	43*	18.16	–	–	11	–	120	50	0	–	1-6	–	–
Yashpal Sharma	1979	1983–84	37	59	11	1606	140	33.45	2	9	16	–	30	17	1	17.00	1-6	–	–
Yograj Singh	1980–81	1980–81	1	2	1	10	6	5.00	–	–	–	–	90	63	1	63.00	1-63	–	–
Yohanman, T.	2001–02	2002–03	3	4	4	13	8*	–	–	–	1	–	486	256	5	51.20	2-56	–	–
Yuvraj Singh	2003–04	2012–13	40	62†	6	1900	169	33.92	3	11	31	–	931†	547	9	60.77	2-9	–	–

INDIVIDUAL CAREER RECORDS – PAKISTAN

BATTING AND FIELDING / BOWLING

	First Test	Last Test	Tests	Inns	NO	Runs	HS	Avge	100	50	Ct	St	Balls	Runs	Wkts	Avge	BB	5wI	10wM
Aamer Malik	1987-88	1994-95	14	19	3	565	117	35.31	2	3	15	1	156	89	1	89.00	1-0	–	–
Aamer Nazir	1992-93	1995-96	6	11	6	31	11	6.20	–	–	2	–	1057	597	20	29.85	5-46	1	–
Aamer Sohail	1992	1999-2000	47	83†	3	2823	205	35.28	5	13	36	–	2383†	1049	25	41.96	4-54	1	–
Aaqib Javed	1988-89	1998-99	22	27	7	101	28*	5.05	–	–	2	–	3918	1874	54	34.70	5-84	1	–
Abdul Kadir	1964-65	1964-65	4	8	0	272	95	34.00	–	2	–	1	–	–	–	–	–	–	–
Abdul Qadir	1977-78	1990-91	67	77	11	1029	61	15.59	–	3	15	–	17126	7742	236	32.80	9-56	15	5
Abdul Razzaq	1999-2000	2006-07	46	77	9	1946	134	28.61	3	7	15	–	7008	3694	100	36.94	5-35	1	–
Abdur Rauf	2009	2009-10	3	6	0	52	31	8.66	–	–	–	–	450	278	6	46.33	2-59	–	–
Abdur Rehman	2007-08	2014	22	31†	3	395	60	14.10	–	2	8	–	6892†	2910	99	29.39	6-25	2	–
Adnan Akmal	2010-11	2013-14	21	29	5	591	64	24.62	–	3	66	11	–	–	–	–	–	–	–
Afaq Hussain	1961-62	1964-65	2	4	4	66	35*	–	–	–	2	–	240	106	1	106.00	1-40	–	–
Aftab Baloch	1969-70	1974-75	2	3	1	97	60*	48.50	–	1	–	–	44	17	0	–	–	–	–
Aftab Gul	1968-69	1971	6	8	0	182	33	22.75	–	–	3	–	6	4	0	–	–	–	–
Agha Saadat Ali	1955-56	1955-56	1	1	1	8	8*	–	–	–	3	–	–	–	–	–	–	–	–
Agha Zahid	1974-75	1974-75	1	2	0	15	14	7.50	–	–	–	–	–	–	–	–	–	–	–
Ahmed Shehzad	2013-14	2014	5	10	0	359	147	35.90	1	2	3	–	48	28	0	–	–	–	–
Aizaz Cheema	2011	2012	7	5	5	1	1*	–	–	–	1	–	1200	638	20	31.90	4-24	–	–
Akram Raza	1989-90	1994-95	9	12	2	153	32	15.30	–	–	8	–	1526	732	13	56.30	3-46	–	–
Alimuddin	1954	1962	25	45	2	1091	109	25.37	2	7	8	–	84	75	1	75.00	1-17	–	–
Ali Naqvi	1997-98	1997-98	5	9	1	242	115	30.25	1	–	1	–	12	11	0	–	–	–	–
Ali Rizvi	1997-98	1997-98	1	–	–	–	–	–	–	–	–	–	111	72	2	36.00	2-72	–	–
Amir Elahi ‡	1952-53	1952-53	5	7	1	65	47	10.83	–	–	–	–	400	248	7	35.42	4-134	–	–
Anil Dalpat	1983-84	1984-85	9	12	1	167	52	15.18	–	1	22	3	–	–	–	–	–	–	–
Anwar Hussain	1952-53	1952-53	4	6	0	42	17	7.00	–	–	–	–	36	29	1	29.00	1-25	–	–
Anwar Khan	1978-79	1978-79	1	2	1	15	12	15.00	–	–	–	–	32	12	0	–	–	–	–
Arif Butt	1964-65	1964-65	3	5	0	59	20	11.80	–	–	–	–	666	288	14	20.57	6-89	1	–
Arshad Khan	1997-98	2004-05	9	8	2	31	9*	5.16	–	–	–	–	2538	960	32	30.00	5-38	1	–
Asad Shafiq	2010-11	2014	28	46	4	1548	130	36.85	4	9	24	–	138	53	2	26.50	2-31	–	–
Ashfaq Ahmed	1993-94	1993-94	1	2	1	1	1*	1.00	–	–	–	–	–	–	–	–	–	–	–
Ashraf Ali	1981-82	1987-88	8	8	3	229	65	45.80	–	2	17	5	–	–	–	–	–	–	–
Asif Iqbal	1964-65	1979-80	58	99	7	3575	175	38.85	11	12	36	–	3864	1502	53	28.33	5-48	2	–
Asif Masood	1968-69	1976-77	16	19	10	93	30*	10.33	–	–	5	–	3038	1568	38	41.26	5-111	1	–
Asif Mujtaba	1986-87	1996-97	25	41†	3	928	65*	24.42	–	8	19	–	666†	303	4	75.75	1-0	–	–
Asim Kamal	2003-04	2005-06	12	20†	1	717	99	37.73	–	8	10	–	–	–	–	–	–	–	–
Ata-ur-Rehman	1992	1996	13	15	6	76	19	8.44	–	–	2	–	1973	1071	31	34.54	4-50	–	–
Atif Rauf	1993-94	1993-94	1	2	0	25	16	12.50	–	–	–	–	–	–	–	–	–	–	–
Atiq-uz-Zaman	1999-2000	1999-2000	1	2	0	26	25	13.00	–	–	5	–	–	–	–	–	–	–	–
Azam Khan	1996-97	1996-97	1	1	0	14	14	14.00	–	–	–	–	–	–	–	–	–	–	–

INDIVIDUAL CAREER RECORDS – PAKISTAN continued

	First Test	Last Test	Tests	Inns	NO	Runs	HS	Avge	100	50	Ct	St	Balls	Runs	Wkts	Avge	BB	5wI	10wM
						BATTING AND FIELDING									BOWLING				
Azeem Hafeez	1983–84	1984–85	18	21†	5	134	24	8.37	–	–	1	–	4351†	2204	63	34.98	6-46	4	–
Azhar Ali	2010	2014	34	64	4	2305	157	38.41	5	15	29	–	150	100	1	100.00	1-4	–	–
Azhar Khan	1979–80	1979–80	1	1	0	14	14	14.00	–	–	–	–	18	2	1	2.00	1-1	–	–
Azhar Mahmood	1997–98	2001	21	34	4	900	136	30.00	3	1	14	–	3015	1402	39	35.94	4-50	–	–
Azmat Rana	1979–80	1979–80	1	1†	0	49	49	49.00	–	–	–	–	–				–		
Basit Ali	1992–93	1995–96	19	33	1	858	103	26.81	1	5	6	–	6	6	0	–	–	–	–
Bazid Khan	2004–05	2004–05	1	2	0	32	23	16.00	–	–	2	–	–				–		
Bilawal Bhatti	2013–14	2013–14	2	3	1	70	32	35.00	–	–	–	–	438	291	6	48.50	3-65	–	–
Danish Kaneria	2000–01	2010	61	84	33	360	29	7.05	–	–	18	–	17697	9082	261	34.79	7-77	15	2
D'Souza, A.	1958–59	1962	6	10	8	76	23*	38.00	–	–	3	–	1587	745	17	43.82	5-112	1	–
Ehsan Adil	2012–13	2012–13	1	2	0	21	12	10.50	–	–	–	–	73	54	2	27.00	2-54	–	–
Ehteshamuddin	1979–80	1982	5	3	1	2	2	1.00	–	–	2	–	940	375	16	23.43	5-47	1	–
Faisal Iqbal	2000–01	2009–10	26	44	2	1124	139	26.76	1	8	22	–	6	7	0	–	–	–	–
Farhan Adil	2003–04	2003–04	1	2	0	33	25	16.50	–	–	–	–	–				–		
Farooq Hamid	1964–65	1964–65	1	2	0	3	3	1.50	–	–	–	–	184	107	1	107.00	1-82	–	–
Farrukh Zaman	1976–77	1976–77	1	–	–	–	–	–	–	–	–	–	80†	15	0	–	–	–	–
Fawad Alam	2009	2009–10	3	6†	0	250	168	41.66	1	1	3	–	–				–		
Fazal Mahmood	1952–53	1962	34	50	6	620	60	14.09	–	1	11	–	9834	3434	139	24.70	7-42	13	4
Fazl-e-Akbar	1997–98	2003–04	5	8	4	52	25	13.00	–	–	2	–	882	511	11	46.45	3-85	–	–
Ghazali, M.E.Z.	1954	1954	2	4	0	32	18	8.00	–	–	–	–	48	18	0	–	–	–	–
Ghulam Abbas	1967	1967	1	2†	0	12	12	6.00	–	–	–	–	–				–		
Gul Mohammad ‡	1956–57	1956–57	1	2†	1	39	27*	39.00	–	–	–	–	–				–		
Hanif Mohammad	1952–53	1969–70	55	97	8	3915	337	43.98	12	15	40	–	206	95	1	95.00	1-1	–	–
Haroon Rashid	1976–77	1982–83	23	36	1	1217	153	34.77	3	5	16	–	8	3	0	–	–	–	–
Hasan Raza	1996–97	2005–06	7	10	1	235	68	26.11	–	2	5	–	6	1	0	–	–	–	–
Haseeb Ahsan	1957–58	1961–62	12	16	7	61	14	6.77	–	–	1	–	2835	1330	27	49.25	6-202	2	–
Humayun Farhat	2000–01	2000–01	1	2	0	54	28	27.00	–	–	–	–	–				–		
Iftikhar Anjum	2005–06	2005–06	1	1	1	9	9*	–	–	–	–	–	84	62	0	–	–	–	–
Ijaz Ahmed, sen.	1986–87	2000–01	60	92	4	3315	211	37.67	12	12	45	–	180†	77	2	38.50	1-9	–	–
Ijaz Ahmed, jun.	1995–96	1995–96	2	3	0	29	16	9.66	–	1	3	–	24	6	0	–	–	–	–
Ijaz Butt	1958–59	1962	8	16	2	279	58	19.92	–	1	5	–	–				–		

INDIVIDUAL CAREER RECORDS – PAKISTAN continued

	First Test	Last Test	Tests	BATTING AND FIELDING Inns	NO	Runs	HS	Avge	100	50	Ct	St	BOWLING Balls	Runs	Wkts	Avge	BB	5wI	10wM
Ijaz Faqih	1980–81	1987–88	5	8	1	183	105	26.14	1	–	–	–	534	299	4	74.75	1-38	–	–
Imran Farhat	2000–01	2012–13	40	77†	2	2400	128	32.00	3	14	40	–	427	284	3	94.66	2-69	–	–
Imran Khan	1971	1991–92	88	126	25	3807	136	37.69	6	18	28	–	19458	8258	362	22.81	8-58	23	6
Imran Nazir	1998–99	2002–03	8	13	0	427	131	32.84	2	1	4	–	–	0	0	–	–	–	–
Imtiaz Ahmed	1952–53	1962	41	72	1	2079	209	29.28	3	11	77	16	6	0	0	–	–	–	–
Intikhab Alam	1959–60	1976–77	47	77	10	1493	138	22.28	1	8	20	–	10474	4494	125	35.95	7-52	5	2
Inzamam-ul-Haq ‡	1992	2007–08	119	198	22	8829	329	50.16	25	46	81	–	9†	8	0	–	–	–	–
Iqbal Qasim	1976–77	1988–89	50	57†	15	549	56	13.07	–	1	42	–	13019†	4807	171	28.11	7-49	8	2
Irfan Fazil	1999–2000	1999–2000	1	2	1	4	3	4.00	–	–	2	–	48	65	2	32.50	1-30	–	–
Israr Ali	1952–53	1959–60	4	8†	1	33	10	4.71	–	–	1	–	318†	165	6	27.50	2-29	–	–
Jalaluddin	1982–83	1985–86	6	3	2	3	2	3.00	–	–	–	–	1197	537	11	48.81	3-77	–	–
Javed Akhtar	1962	1962	1	2	1	4	2*	4.00	–	–	–	–	96	52	0	–	–	–	–
Javed Burki	1960–61	1969–70	25	48	4	1341	140	30.47	3	4	7	–	42	23	0	–	–	–	–
Javed Miandad	1976–77	1993–94	124	189	21	8832	280*	52.57	23	43	93	1	1470	682	17	40.11	3-74	–	–
Junaid Khan	2011	2014	18	24	8	111	17	6.93	–	–	4	–	3946†	1874	65	28.83	5-38	5	–
Kabir Khan	1994	1994–95	4	5	2	24	10	8.00	–	–	1	–	655†	370	9	41.11	3-26	–	–
Kamran Akmal	2002–03	2010	53	92	6	2648	158*	30.79	6	12	184	22	–	–	–	–	–	–	–
Kardar, A.H. ‡	1952–53	1957–58	23	37†	3	847	93	24.91	–	5	15	–	2712†	954	21	45.42	3-35	–	–
Khalid Hasan	1954	1954	1	2	1	17	10	17.00	–	–	–	–	126	116	2	58.00	2-116	–	–
Khalid Ibadulla	1964–65	1967	4	8	0	253	166	31.62	1	1	3	–	336	99	1	99.00	1-42	–	–
Khalid Wazir	1954	1954	2	3	1	14	9*	7.00	–	–	–	–	–	–	–	–	–	–	–
Khan Mohammad	1952–53	1957–58	13	17	7	100	26*	10.00	–	–	4	–	3157	1292	54	23.92	6-21	4	–
Khurram Manzoor	2008–09	2014	16	30	1	817	146	28.17	1	7	8	–	–	–	–	–	–	–	–
Liaqat Ali	1974–75	1978	5	7	3	28	12	7.00	–	–	1	–	808†	359	6	59.83	3-80	–	–
Mahmood Hussain	1952–53	1962	27	39	6	336	35	10.18	–	–	5	–	5910	2628	68	38.64	6-67	2	–
Majid Khan	1964–65	1982–83	63	106	5	3931	167	38.92	8	19	70	–	3584	1456	27	53.92	4-45	–	–
Mansoor Akhtar	1980–81	1989–90	19	29	3	655	111	25.19	1	3	9	–	–	–	–	–	–	–	–
Manzoor Elahi	1984–85	1994–95	6	10	2	123	52	15.37	–	1	7	–	444	194	7	27.71	2-38	–	–
Maqsood Ahmed	1952–53	1955–56	16	27	1	507	99	19.50	–	2	13	–	462	191	3	63.66	2-12	–	–
Masood Anwar	1990–91	1990–91	1	2†	0	39	37	19.50	–	–	–	–	161†	102	3	34.00	2-59	–	–
Mathias, W.	1955–56	1962	21	36	3	783	77	23.72	–	3	22	–	24	20	0	–	–	–	–
Miran Bakhsh	1954–55	1954–55	2	3	2	1	1*	1.00	–	–	–	–	348	115	2	57.50	2-82	–	–
Misbah-ul-Haq	2000–01	2014	48	84	14	3285	161*	46.92	5	25	37	–	–	–	–	–	–	–	–
Mohammad Aamer	2009	2010	14	28†	6	278	30*	12.63	–	–	–	–	2867†	1484	51	29.09	6-84	3	–

INDIVIDUAL CAREER RECORDS – PAKISTAN *continued*

	First Test	Last Test	Tests	Inns	NO	Runs	HS	Avge	100	50	Ct	St	Balls	Runs	Wkts	Avge	BB	5wI	10wM
							BATTING AND FIELDING									BOWLING			
Mohammad Akram	1995-96	2000-01	9	15	6	24	10*	2.66	–	–	4	–	1477	859	17	50.52	5-138	1	1
Mohammad Asif	2004-05	2010	23	38†	13	141	29	5.64	–	–	3	–	5171	2583	106	24.36	6-41	7	1
Mohammad Aslam Khokhar	1954	1954	1	2	0	34	18	17.00	–	–	1	–	–						
Mohammad Ayub	2012	2012	1	2	0	47	25	23.50	–	–	1	–	–						
Mohammad Farooq	1960-61	1964-65	7	9	4	85	47	17.00	–	–	1	–	1422	682	21	32.47	4-70	–	–
Mohammad Hafeez	2003-04	2013-14	36	70	6	2174	196	33.96	5	9	26	–	2831	1190	35	34.00	4-16	–	–
Mohammad Hussain	1996-97	1998-99	2	3†	0	18	17	6.00	–	–	1	–	180†	87	3	29.00	2-66	–	–
Mohammad Ilyas	1964-65	1968-69	10	19	0	441	126	23.21	1	2	6	–	84	63	0	–	–	–	–
Mohammad Irfan	2012-13	2013-14	4	7	2	28	14	5.60	–	–	–	–	712†	389	10	38.90	3-44	–	–
Mohammad Khalil	2004-05	2004-05	2	4†	1	9	5	3.00	–	–	–	–	290†	200	0	–	–	–	–
Mohammad Munaf	1959-60	1961-62	4	7	1	63	19	12.60	–	–	–	–	769	341	11	31.00	4-42	–	–
Mohammad Nazir	1969-70	1983-84	14	18	10	144	29*	18.00	–	–	4	–	3262	1124	34	33.05	7-99	3	–
Mohammad Ramzan	1997-98	1997-98	1	2	0	36	29	18.00	–	–	1	–	–						
Mohammad Salman	2011	2011	2	4	0	25	13	6.25	–	–	2	1	–						
Mohammad Sami	2000-01	2012	36	56	14	487	49	11.59	–	–	7	–	7499	4483	85	52.74	5-36	2	–
Mohammad Talha	2008-09	2014	3	3	2	15	9*	7.50	–	–	–	–	608	368	9	40.88	3-65	–	–
Mohammad Wasim	1996-97	2000	18	28	2	783	192	30.11	2	2	22	2	–						
Mohammad Yousuf	1997-98	2010	90	156	12	7530	223	52.29	24	33	65	–	6	3	0	–	–	–	–
Mohammad Zahid	1996-97	2002-03	5	6	1	7	6*	1.40	–	–	4	–	792	502	15	33.46	7-66	1	1
Mohsin Kamal	1983-84	1994-95	9	11	7	37	13*	9.25	–	–	4	–	1348	822	24	34.25	4-116	1	–
Mohsin Khan	1977-78	1986-87	48	79	6	2709	200	37.10	7	9	34	–	86	30	0	–	–	–	–
Moin Khan	1990-91	2004-05	69	104	8	2741	137	28.55	4	15	128	20	–						
Mudassar Nazar	1976-77	1988-89	76	116	8	4114	231	38.09	10	17	48	–	5967	2532	66	38.36	6-32	1	–
Mufasir-ul-Haq	1964-65	1964-65	1	1	1	8	8*	–	–	–	1	–	222†	84	3	28.00	2-50	–	–
Munir Malik	1959-60	1962	3	4	1	7	4	2.33	–	–	1	–	684	358	9	39.77	5-128	1	–
Mushtaq Ahmed	1989-90	2003-04	52	72	16	656	59	11.71	–	2	23	–	12532	6100	185	32.97	7-56	10	3
Mushtaq Mohammad	1958-59	1978-79	57	100	7	3643	201	39.17	10	19	42	–	5260	2309	79	29.22	5-28	3	–
Nadeem Abbasi	1989-90	1989-90	3	2	0	46	36	23.00	–	–	6	–	–						
Nadeem Ghauri	1989-90	1989-90	1	1	0	0	0	0.00	–	–	–	–	48†	20	0	–	–	–	–
Nadeem Khan	1992-93	1998-99	2	3	1	34	25	17.00	–	–	1	–	432†	230	2	115.00	2-147	–	–
Nasim-ul-Ghani	1957-58	1972-73	29	50†	5	747	101	16.60	1	2	11	–	4406†	1959	52	37.67	6-67	2	–
Nasir Jamshed	2012-13	2012-13	2	4†	0	51	46	12.75	–	–	1	–	–						
Naushad Ali	1964-65	1964-65	6	11	0	156	39	14.18	–	–	9	–	–						
Naved Anjum	1989-90	1990-91	2	3	0	44	22	14.66	–	–	1	–	342	162	4	40.50	2-57	–	–
Naved Ashraf	1998-99	1999-2000	2	3	0	64	32	21.33	–	–	–	–	–						
Naved Latif	2001-02	2001-02	2	2	0	20	20	10.00	–	–	–	–	–						
Naved-ul-Hasan	2004-05	2006-07	9	15	3	239	42*	19.91	–	–	3	–	1565	1044	18	58.00	3-30	–	–

INDIVIDUAL CAREER RECORDS – PAKISTAN continued

	First Test	Last Test	Tests	Inns	NO	Runs	HS	Avge	100	50	Ct	St	Balls	Runs	Wkts	Avge	BB	5wI	10wM
													BATTING AND FIELDING → **BOWLING**						
Nazar Mohammad	1952–53	1952–53	5	8	1	277	124*	39.57	1	1	7	–	12	4	0	–	–	–	–
Niaz Ahmed	1967	1968–69	2	3	3	17	16*	–	–	–	1	–	294	94	3	31.33	2-72	–	–
Pervez Sajjad	1964–65	1972–73	19	20	11	123	24	13.66	–	–	9	–	4145†	1410	59	23.89	7-74	3	–
Qaiser Abbas	2000–01	2000–01	1	1†	0	2	2	2.00	–	–	–	–	96†	35	0	–	–	–	–
Qasim Umar	1983–84	1986–87	26	43	2	1502	210	36.63	3	5	15	–	6	0	0	–	–	–	–
Rahat Ali	2012–13	2013–14	6	11	5	70	35*	11.66	–	–	4	–	1366†	725	16	45.31	6-127	2	–
Rameez Raja	1983–84	1996–97	57	94	5	2833	122	31.83	2	22	34	–	–	–	–	–	–	–	–
Rashid Khan	1981–82	1984–85	4	6	3	155	59	51.66	–	1	2	–	738	360	8	45.00	3-129	–	–
Rashid Latif	1992	2003–04	37	57	9	1381	150	28.77	1	7	119	11	12	10	0	–	–	–	–
Rehman, S.F.	1957–58	1957–58	1	2	0	10	8	5.00	–	–	1	–	204	99	1	99.00	1-43	–	–
Riaz Afridi	2004–05	2004–05	1	1	0	9	9	9.00	–	–	–	–	186	87	2	43.50	2-42	–	–
Rizwan-uz-Zaman	1981–82	1988–89	11	19	1	345	60	19.16	–	3	4	–	132	46	4	11.50	3-26	–	–
Sadiq Mohammad	1969–70	1980–81	41	74†	2	2579	166	35.81	5	10	28	–	200	98	0	–	–	–	–
Saeed Ahmed	1957–58	1972–73	41	78	4	2991	172	40.41	5	16	13	–	1980	802	22	36.45	4-64	–	–
Saeed Ajmal	2009	2014	35	53	12	451	50	11.00	–	1	11	–	11592	5003	178	28.10	7-55	10	4
Saeed Anwar	1990–91	2001–02	55	91†	2	4052	188*	45.52	11	25	18	–	48†	23	0	–	–	–	–
Salahuddin	1964–65	1969–70	5	8	2	117	34*	19.50	–	–	3	–	546	187	7	26.71	2-36	–	–
Saleem Jaffar	1986–87	1991–92	14	14	6	42	10*	5.25	–	–	3	–	2531†	1139	36	31.63	5-40	1	–
Salim Altaf	1967	1978–79	21	31	12	276	53*	14.52	–	1	3	–	4001	1710	46	37.17	4-11	–	–
Salim Elahi	1995–96	2002–03	13	24	1	436	72	18.95	–	1	10	1	–	–	–	–	–	–	–
Salim Malik	1981–82	1998–99	103	154	22	5768	237	43.69	15	29	65	–	734	414	5	82.80	1-3	–	–
Salim Yousuf	1981–82	1990–91	32	44	5	1055	91*	27.05	–	5	91	13	–	–	–	–	–	–	–
Salman Butt	2003–04	2010	33	62†	0	1889	122	30.46	3	10	12	–	137	106	1	106.00	1-36	–	–
Saqlain Mushtaq	1995–96	2003–04	49	78	14	927	101*	14.48	1	2	15	–	14070	6206	208	29.83	8-164	13	3
Sarfraz Ahmed	2009–10	2014	8	16	1	488	103	32.53	1	4	18	2	–	–	–	–	–	–	–
Sarfraz Nawaz	1968–69	1983–84	55	72	13	1045	90	17.71	–	4	26	–	13951	5798	177	32.75	9-86	4	1
Shabbir Ahmed	2003–04	2005–06	10	15	5	88	24*	8.80	–	–	3	–	2576	1175	51	23.03	5-48	2	–
Shadab Kabir	1996	2001–02	5	7†	0	148	55	21.14	–	1	11	–	9	9	0	–	–	–	–
Shafiq Ahmed	1974	1980–81	6	10	1	99	27*	11.00	–	–	1	–	8	1	0	–	–	–	–
Shafqat Rana	1964–65	1969–70	5	7	0	221	95	31.57	–	2	5	–	36	9	1	9.00	1-2	–	–
Shahid Afridi	1998–99	2010	27	48	1	1716	156	36.51	5	8	10	–	3194	1709	48	35.60	5-52	1	–
Shahid Israr	1976–77	1976–77	1	1	1	7	7*	–	–	–	–	2	–	–	–	–	–	–	–
Shahid Mahboob	1989–90	1989–90	1	–	–	–	–	–	–	–	–	–	294	131	2	65.50	2-131	–	–
Shahid Mahmood	1962	1962	1	2†	0	25	16	12.50	–	–	–	–	36†	23	0	–	–	–	–

INDIVIDUAL CAREER RECORDS – PAKISTAN continued

	First Test	Last Test	Tests	BATTING AND FIELDING									BOWLING						
				Inns	NO	Runs	HS	Avge	100	50	Ct	St	Balls	Runs	Wkts	Avge	BB	5wI	10wM
Shahid Nazir	1996–97	2006–07	15	19	3	194	40	12.12	–	–	5	–	2234	1272	36	35.33	5-53	1	–
Shahid Saeed	1989–90	1989–90	1	1	0	12	12	12.00	–	–	–	–	90	43	0	–	–	–	–
Shakeel Ahmed, sen.	1992–93	1994–95	3	5	0	74	33	14.80	–	–	4	–	–	–	–	–	–	–	–
Shakeel Ahmed, jun.	1998–99	1998–99	1	1†	0	1	1	1.00	–	–	1	–	325†	139	4	34.75	4-91	–	–
Shan Masood	2013–14	2013–14	2	4†	0	96	75	24.00	–	1	2	–	–	–	–	–	–	–	–
Sharpe, D.A.	1959–60	1959–60	3	6	0	134	56	22.33	–	1	2	–	–	–	–	–	–	–	–
Shoaib Akhtar	1997–98	2007–08	46	67	13	544	47	10.07	–	–	12	–	8143	4574	178	25.69	6-11	12	2
Shoaib Malik	2001–02	2010	32	54	6	1606	148*	33.45	2	8	16	–	2245	1291	21	61.47	4-42	–	–
Shoaib Mohammad	1983–84	1995–96	45	68	7	2705	203*	44.34	7	13	22	–	396	170	5	34.00	2-8	–	–
Shujauddin	1954	1961–62	19	32	6	395	47	15.19	–	–	8	–	2313†	801	20	40.05	3-18	–	–
Sikander Bakht	1976–77	1982–83	26	35	12	146	22*	6.34	–	–	7	–	4870	2412	67	36.00	8-69	3	1
Sohail Khan	2008–09	2011	2	3	1	11	11	11.00	–	–	–	–	342	245	1	245.00	1-62	–	–
Sohail Tanvir	2007–08	2007–08	2	3†	0	17	13	5.66	–	–	2	–	504†	316	5	63.20	3-83	–	–
Tahir Naqqash	1981–82	1984–85	15	19	5	300	57	21.42	–	1	3	–	2800	1398	34	41.11	5-40	2	–
Talat Ali	1972–73	1978–79	10	18	2	370	61	23.12	–	2	4	–	20	7	0	–	–	–	–
Tanvir Ahmed	2010–11	2012–13	5	7	2	170	57	34.00	–	1	1	–	707	453	17	26.64	6-120	1	–
Taslim Arif	1979–80	1980–81	6	10	2	501	210*	62.62	1	2	6	3	30	28	1	28.00	1-28	–	–
Taufeeq Umar	2001–02	2012	43	81†	5	2943	236	38.72	7	14	47	–	78	44	0	–	–	–	–
Tauseef Ahmed	1979–80	1993–94	34	38	20	318	35*	17.66	–	–	9	–	7778	2950	93	31.72	6-45	3	–
Umar Akmal	2009–10	2011	16	30	2	1003	129	35.82	1	6	12	–	–	–	–	–	–	–	–
Umar Amin	2010	2010	4	8†	0	99	33	12.37	–	1	1	–	132	63	3	21.00	1-7	–	–
Umar Gul	2003–04	2012–13	47	67	9	577	65*	9.94	–	1	11	–	9599	5553	163	34.06	6-135	4	–
Wahab Riaz	2010	2014	8	11	3	91	27	11.37	–	–	1	–	1256†	744	23	32.34	5-63	1	–
Wajahatullah Wasti	1998–99	1999–2000	6	10	1	329	133	36.55	2	–	7	–	18	8	0	–	–	–	–
Waqar Hasan	1952–53	1959–60	21	35	1	1071	189	31.50	1	6	10	–	6	10	0	–	–	–	–
Waqar Younis	1989–90	2002–03	87	120	21	1010	45	10.20	–	–	18	–	16224	8788	373	23.56	7-76	22	5
Wasim Akram	1984–85	2001–02	104	147†	19	2898	257*	22.64	3	7	44	–	22627†	9779	414	23.62	7-119	25	5
Wasim Bari	1967	1983–84	81	112	26	1366	85	15.88	–	6	201	27	8	2	0	–	–	–	–
Wasim Raja	1972–73	1984–85	57	92†	14	2821	125	36.16	4	18	20	–	4082	1826	51	35.80	4-50	–	–
Wazir Mohammad	1952–53	1959–60	20	33	4	801	189	27.62	2	3	5	–	24	15	0	–	–	–	–
Yasir Ali	2003–04	2003–04	1	2	2	1	1*	–	–	–	–	–	120	55	2	27.50	1-12	–	–
Yasir Arafat	2007–08	2008–09	3	3	1	94	50*	47.00	–	1	–	–	627	438	9	48.66	5-161	1	–
Yasir Hameed	2003–04	2010	25	49	3	1491	170	32.41	2	8	20	–	78	72	0	–	–	–	–

	First Test	Last Test	Tests	Inns	NO	Runs	HS	Avge	100	50	Ct	St	Balls	Runs	Wkts	Avge	BB	5wI	10wM
				BATTING AND FIELDING									**BOWLING**						
Younis Ahmed	1969-70	1986-87	4	7†	1	177	62	29.50	—	1	—	—	6†	6	0	—	—	—	—
Younis Khan	1999-2000	2014	91	162	14	7610	313	51.41	24	28	101	—	804	491	9	54.55	2-23	—	—
Yousuf Youhana: see Mohammad Yousuf																			
Zaheer Abbas	1969-70	1985-86	78	124	11	5062	274	44.79	12	20	34	—	370	132	3	44.00	2-21	—	—
Zahid Fazal	1990-91	1995-96	9	16	0	288	78	18.00	—	1	5	—						—	—
Zahoor Elahi	1996-97	1996-97	2	3	0	30	22	10.00	—	—	1	—						—	—
Zakir Khan	1985-86	1989-90	2	2	2	9	9*	—	—	—	1	—	444	259	5	51.80	3-80	—	—
Zulfiqar Ahmed	1952-53	1956-57	9	10	4	200	63*	33.33	—	1	5	—	1285	366	20	18.30	6-42	2	1
Zulfiqar Babar	2013-14	2013-14	2	2	1	27	25*	27.00	—	—	—	—	494†	264	6	44.00	3-89	—	—
Zulqarnain	1985-86	1985-86	3	4	0	24	13	6.00	—	—	8	2						—	—

INDIVIDUAL CAREER RECORDS – SRI LANKA

	First Test	Last Test	Tests	Inns	NO	Runs	HS	Avge	100	50	Ct	St	Balls	Runs	Wkts	Avge	BB	5wI	10wM
				BATTING AND FIELDING									**BOWLING**						
Zulqarnain Haider	2010	2010	1	2	0	88	88	44.00	—	1	2	—						—	—
Ahangama, F.S.	1985	1985	3	3†	1	11	11	5.50	—	—	1	—	801	348	18	19.33	5-52	1	—
Amalean, K.N.	1985-86	1987-88	2	3	2	9	7*	9.00	—	—	1	—	244	156	7	22.28	4-97	—	—
Amerasinghe, A.M.J.G.	1983-84	1983-84	2	4	1	54	34	18.00	—	—	3	—	300†	150	3	50.00	2-73	—	—
Amerasinghe, M.K.D.I.	2007-08	2007-08	1	2	2	0	0*	—	—	—	—	—	150	105	1	105.00	1-62	—	—
Anurasiri, S.D.	1985-86	1997-98	18	22	5	91	24	5.35	—	—	4	—	3973†	1548	41	37.75	4-71	—	—
Arnold, R.P.	1996-97	2004	44	69†	4	1821	123	28.01	3	10	51	—	1334	598	11	54.36	3-76	—	—
Atapattu, M.S.	1990-91	2007-08	90	156	15	5502	249	39.02	16	17	58	—	48	24	1	24.00	1-9	—	—
Bandara, H.M.C.M.	1998	2005-06	8	11	3	124	43	15.50	—	—	4	—	1152	633	16	39.56	3-84	—	—
Bandaratilleke, M.R.C.N.	1998	2001-02	7	9	1	93	25	11.62	—	—	—	—	1722†	698	23	30.34	5-36	1	—
Chandana, U.D.U.	1998-99	2004-05	16	24	1	616	92	26.78	—	2	7	—	2685	1535	37	41.48	6-179	3	1
Chandimal, L.D.	2011-12	2014	14	24	3	934	116*	44.47	3	5	22	4						—	—
Dassanayake, P.B.	1993	1994-95	11	17	2	196	36	13.06	—	—	19	5						—	—
de Alwis, R.G.	1982-83	1987-88	11	19	0	152	28	8.00	—	—	21	2						—	—
de Mel, A.L.F.	1981-82	1986-87	17	28	5	326	34	14.17	—	—	9	—	3518	2180	59	36.94	6-109	3	—
de Saram, S.I.	1999-2000	1999-2000	4	5	0	117	39	23.40	—	—	1	—						—	—
de Silva, A.M.	1992-93	1993	3	3	0	10	9	3.33	—	—	4	1						—	—
de Silva, D.S.	1981-82	1984	12	22	3	406	61	21.36	—	2	5	—	3031	1347	37	36.40	5-59	1	—
de Silva, E.A.R.	1985	1990-91	10	16†	4	185	50	15.41	—	1	4	—	2328	1032	8	129.00	2-67	—	—

INDIVIDUAL CAREER RECORDS – SRI LANKA *continued*

				BATTING AND FIELDING									BOWLING						
	First Test	Last Test	Tests	Inns	NO	Runs	HS	Avge	100	50	Ct	St	Balls	Runs	Wkts	Avge	BB	5wI	10wM
de Silva, G.R.A.	1981–82	1982–83	4	7†	2	41	14	8.20	—	—	—	—	962†	385	7	55.00	2-38	—	—
de Silva, K.S.C.	1996–97	1998–99	8	12†	11	65	27	9.28	—	—	5	—	1585†	889	16	55.56	5-85	1	—
de Silva, P.A.	1984	2002	93	159	11	6361	267	42.97	20	22	43	—	2595	1208	29	41.65	3-30	—	—
de Silva, S.K.L.	1997–98	1997–98	3	4	2	36	20*	18.00	—	—	1	—							
de Silva, W.R.S.	2002	2007	3	2	1	10	5*	10.00	—	—	1	—	432†	209	11	19.00	4-35	—	—
Dharmasena, H.D.P.K.	1993	2003–04	31	51	7	868	62*	19.72	—	3	14	—	6939	2920	69	42.31	6-72	3	—
Dias, R.L.	1981–82	1986–87	20	36	1	1285	109	36.71	3	8	6	—	24	17	0	—	—	—	—
Dickwella, D.P.D.N.	2014	2014	3	5†	0	138	72	27.60	—	1	14	2							
Dilshan, T.M.	1999–2000	2012–13	87	145	11	5492	193	40.98	16	23	88	—	3385	1711	39	43.87	4-10	—	—
Dunusinghe, C.I.	1994–95	1995–96	5	10	0	160	91	16.00	—	1	13	2	—						
Eranga, R.M.S.	2011	2014	15	19	8	131	25*	11.90	—	—	5	—	3221	1712	50	34.24	4-49	—	—
Fernando, A.N.P.R.	2011–12	2014	8	12	3	52	17*	5.77	—	—	1	—	1468	1019	14	72.78	4-123	—	—
Fernando, C.R.D.	2000	2012	40	47	17	249	39*	8.30	—	—	10	—	6181	3784	100	37.84	5-42	3	—
Fernando, E.R.N.S.	1982–83	1983–84	5	10	0	112	46	11.20	—	1	—	—							
Fernando, K.A.D.M.	2003–04	2003–04	2	3	1	56	51*	28.00	—	1	—	—	126	107	1	107.00	1-29	—	—
Fernando, K.H.R.K.	2002–03	2002–03	2	4	0	38	24	9.50	—	—	1	—	234	108	4	27.00	3-63	—	—
Fernando, T.C.B.	2001–02	2002	9	8	3	132	45	26.40	—	—	4	—	1270	792	18	44.00	4-27	—	—
Gallage, I.S.	1999–2000	1999–2000	1	1	0	3	3	3.00	—	—	—	—	150	77	0	—	—		
Gamage, C.: see M.K.G.C.P. Lakshitha																			
Goonasekera, Y.	1982–83	1982–83	2	4†	0	48	23	12.00	—	—	6	—							
Goonatilleke, H.M.	1981–82	1982–83	5	10	2	177	56	22.12	—	1	10	3							
Gunawardene, D.A.	1998–99	2005–06	6	11†	0	181	43	16.45	—	—	2	—							
Guneratne, R.P.W.	1982–83	1982–83	1	2	2	0	0*	—	—	—	—	—	102	84	0	—	—		
Gurusinha, A.P.	1985–86	1996	41	70†	7	2452	143	38.92	7	8	33	—	1408	681	20	34.05	2-7	—	—
Hathurusinghe, U.C.	1990–91	1998–99	26	44	1	1274	83	29.62	—	8	7	—	1962	789	17	46.41	4-66	—	—
Herath, H.M.R.K.B.	1999	2014	57	81†	18	851	80*	13.50	—	1	15	—	16472†	7556	260	29.06	9-127	21	4
Hettiarachchi, D.	2000–01	2000–01	1	2	1	0	0*	0.00	—	—	—	—	162†	41	2	20.50	2-36	—	—
Jayasekera, R.S.A.	1981–82	1981–82	1	2	0	2	2	1.00	—	—	—	—							
Jayasuriya, S.T.	1990–91	2007–08	110	188†	14	6973	340	40.07	14	31	78	—	8188†	3366	98	34.34	5-34	2	—
Jayawardene, D.P.M.D.	1997	2014	149	252	15	11814	374	49.84	34	50	205	—	589	310	6	51.66	2-32	—	—
Jayawardene, H.A.P.W.	2000	2014	56	79	11	2075	154*	30.51	4	5	119	32	—						
Jeganathan, S.	1982–83	1982–83	2	4	0	19	8	4.75	—	—	—	—	30†	12	0	—	—	—	—
John, V.B.	1982–83	1984	6	10	5	53	27*	10.60	—	—	2	—	1281	614	28	21.92	5-60	2	—
Jurangpathy, B.R.	1985	1986–87	2	4	0	1	1	0.25	—	—	2	—	150	93	1	93.00	1-69	—	—

INDIVIDUAL CAREER RECORDS – SRI LANKA *continued*

	First Test	Last Test	Tests	Inns	NO	Runs	HS	Avge	100	50	Ct	St	Balls	Runs	Wkts	Avge	BB	5wI	10wM
				BATTING AND FIELDING									*BOWLING*						
Kalavitigoda, S.	2004–05	2004–05	1	2	0	8	7	4.00	–	–	2	–	–	–	–	–	–	–	–
Kalpage, R.S.	1993	1998–99	11	18†	2	294	63	18.37	–	2	10	–	1576	774	12	64.50	2-27	–	–
Kaluhalamulla, H.S.K.R.: see S. Randiv																			
Kaluperuma, L.W.S.	1981–82	1981–82	2	4	1	12	11*	4.00	–	–	2	–	162	93	0	–	–	–	–
Kaluperuma, S.M.S.	1983–84	1987–88	4	8	0	88	23	11.00	–	–	6	–	240	124	2	62.00	2-17	–	–
Kaluwitharana, R.S.	1992	2004–05	49	78	4	1933	132*	26.12	3	9	93	26	–	–	–	–	–	–	–
Kapugedera, C.K.	2006	2009	8	15	3	418	96	34.83	–	4	6	–	12	9	0	–	–	–	–
Karunaratne, F.D.M.	2012–13	2014	13	25†	2	701	85	30.47	–	4	10	–	12	5	0	–	–	–	–
Kulasekara, C.K.B.	2011–12	2011–12	1	2	0	22	15	11.00	–	–	–	–	168	80	1	80.00	1-65	–	–
Kulasekara, K.M.D.N.	2004–05	2014	21	28	1	391	64	14.48	–	1	8	–	3567	1794	48	37.37	4-21	–	–
Kuruppu, D.S.B.P.	1986–87	1991	4	7	1	320	201*	53.33	1	–	1	–	–	–	–	–	–	–	–
Kuruppuarachchi, A.K.	1985–86	1986–87	2	2	2	0	0*	–	–	–	–	–	272†	149	8	18.62	5-44	1	–
Labrooy, G.F.	1986–87	1990–91	9	14	3	158	70*	14.36	–	1	3	–	2158	1194	27	44.22	5-133	1	–
Lakmal, R.A.S.	2010–11	2014	21	28	11	115	18	6.76	–	–	4	–	3783	2100	43	48.83	4-78	–	–
Lakshitha, M.K.G.C.P.	2002	2002–03	2	3	0	42	40	14.00	–	–	1	–	288	158	5	31.60	2-33	–	–
Liyanage, D.K.	1992	2001	9	9†	0	69	23	7.66	–	–	1	–	1355	666	17	39.17	4-56	–	–
Lokuarachchi, K.S.	2003	2003–04	4	5	1	94	28*	23.50	–	–	1	–	594	295	5	59.00	2-47	–	–
Madugalle, R.S.	1981–82	1988	21	39	4	1029	103	29.40	1	7	9	–	84	38	0	–	–	–	–
Madurasinghe, M.A.W.R.	1988	1992	3	6†	1	24	11	4.80	–	–	–	–	396	172	3	57.33	3-60	–	–
Mahanama, R.S.	1985–86	1997–98	52	89	1	2576	225	29.27	4	11	56	–	36	30	0	–	–	–	–
Maharoof, M.F.	2004	2011	22	34	4	556	72	18.53	–	3	7	–	2940	1631	25	65.24	4-52	–	–
Malinga, S.L.	2004	2010	30	37	13	275	64	11.45	–	1	7	–	5209	3349	101	33.15	5-50	3	–
Mathews, A.D.	2009	2014	44	74	16	3054	160	52.65	4	18	22	–	2364	1174	19	61.78	4-44	–	–
Mendis, B.A.W.	2008	2014	19	19	6	213	78	16.38	–	1	2	–	4730	2434	70	34.77	6-99	4	1
Mendis, L.R.D.	1981–82	1988	24	43	1	1329	124	31.64	4	8	9	–	–	–	–	–	–	–	–
Mirando, M.T.T.	2003	2010–11	10	14†	3	94	15*	8.54	–	–	3	–	1668†	1040	28	37.14	5-83	1	–
Mubarak, J.	2002	2007–08	10	17†	1	254	48	15.87	–	–	13	–	84	50	0	–	–	–	–
Muralitharan, M.‡	1992	2010	132	162	56	1259	67	11.87	–	1	70	–	43715	18023	795	22.67	9-51	67	22
Nawaz, M.N.	2002	2002	1	2†	1	99	78*	99.00	–	1	–	–	–	–	–	–	–	–	–
Nissanka, R.A.P.	2003	2003	4	5	2	18	12*	6.00	–	–	–	–	587	366	10	36.60	5-64	1	–
Paranavitana, N.T.	2008–09	2012–13	32	60†	5	1792	111	32.58	2	11	27	–	102	86	1	86.00	1-26	–	–
Perera, A.S.A.	1998	2001	3	4	1	77	43*	25.66	–	–	1	–	408	180	1	180.00	1-104	–	–
Perera, M.D.K.	2013–14	2014	7	10	0	128	95	12.80	–	1	5	–	2179	1083	36	30.08	5-69	3	–
Perera, N.L.T.C.	2011	2012	6	10†	0	203	75	20.30	–	1	1	–	954	653	11	59.36	4-63	–	–
Perera, P.D.R.L.	1998–99	2002–03	8	9†	6	33	11*	11.00	–	–	2	–	1130†	661	17	38.88	3-40	–	–

INDIVIDUAL CAREER RECORDS – SRI LANKA *continued*

	First Test	Last Test	Tests	Inns	NO	Runs	HS	Avge	100	50	Ct	St	Balls	Runs	Wkts	Avge	BB	5wI	10wM
						BATTING AND FIELDING								*BOWLING*					
Pradeep, N.: see A.N.P.R. Fernando																			
Prasad, K.T.G.D.	2008	2014	15	21	1	338	47	16.90	–	–	5	–	2408	1596	33	48.36	5-50	1	–
Prasanna, S.	2011	2011	1	1	0	5	5	5.00	–	–	5	–	138	80	0	–	–	–	–
Pushpakumara, K.R.	1994	2001-02	23	31	12	166	44	8.73	–	–	10	–	3792	2242	58	38.65	7-116	4	–
Ramanayake, C.P.H.	1987-88	1993	18	24	9	143	34*	9.53	–	–	6	–	3654	1880	44	42.72	5-82	1	–
Ramyakumara, W.M.G.	2005	2005	2	3†	0	38	14	12.66	–	–	–	–	114†	66	2	33.00	2-49	–	–
Ranasinghe, A.N.	1981-82	1982-83	2	4	0	88	77	22.00	–	1	–	–	114†	69	1	69.00	1-23	–	–
Ranatunga, A.	1981-82	2000	93	155†	12	5105	135*	35.69	4	38	47	–	2373	1040	16	65.00	2-17	–	–
Ranatunga, D.	1989-90	1989-90	2	3	0	87	45	29.00	–	–	2	–							
Ranatunga, S.	1994	1996-97	9	17†	1	531	118	33.18	–	2	2	–							
Randiv, S.	2010	2012-13	12	17	1	147	39	9.18	–	2	1	–	3146	1613	43	37.51	5-82	1	–
Ratnayake, R.J.	1982-83	1991-92	23	36	6	433	56	14.43	–	2	9	–	4961	2563	73	35.10	6-66	5	–
Ratnayeke, J.R.	1981-82	1989-90	22	38†	6	807	93	25.21	–	5	1	–	3833	1972	56	35.21	8-83	4	–
Samarasekera, M.A.R.	1988	1991-92	4	7	0	118	57	16.85	–	1	3	–	192	104	3	34.66	2-38	–	–
Samaraweera, D.P.	1993-94	1994-95	7	14	0	211	42	15.07	–	–	5	–							
Samaraweera, T.T.	2001	2012-13	81	132	20	5462	231	48.76	14	30	45	–	1327	689	15	45.93	4-49	–	–
Sangakkara, K.C.	2000	2014	128	221†	17	11988	319	58.76	37	51	176	20	84	49	0	–	–	–	–
Senanayake, C.P.	1990-91	1990-91	3	5†	0	97	64	19.40	–	1	2	–							
Senanayake, S.M.S.M.	2013-14	2013-14	1	1	0	5	5	5.00	–	–	1	–	138	96	0	–	–	–	–
Silva, J.K.	2011-12	2014	14	26	0	954	139	36.69	1	6	20	1							
Silva, K.J.	1995-96	1997-98	7	4	1	6	6*	2.00	–	–	1	–	1533†	647	20	32.35	4-16	–	–
Silva, L.P.C.	2006-07	2007-08	11	17	1	537	152*	33.56	1	2	7	–	102	65	1	65.00	1-57	–	–
Silva, S.A.R.	1982-83	1988	9	16†	2	353	111	25.21	2	–	33	1							
Tharanga, W.U.	2005-06	2014	19	34†	1	1019	165	30.87	1	5	13	–	24	27	0	–	–	–	–
Thirimanne, H.D.R.L.	2011	2014	14	28†	4	610	155*	25.41	1	2	7	–							
Thushara, T.: see M.T.T. Mirando																			
Tillakaratne, H.P.	1989-90	2003-04	83	131†	25	4545	204*	42.87	11	20	122	2	76	25	0	–	–	–	–
Upashantha, K.E.A.	1998-99	2002	2	3	0	10	6	3.33	–	–	–	–	306	200	4	50.00	2-41	–	–
Vaas, W.P.U.J.C.	1994	2009	111	162†	35	3089	100*	24.32	1	13	31	–	23438†	10501	355	29.58	7-71	12	2
Vandort, M.G.	2001-02	2008-09	20	33†	2	1144	140	36.90	4	4	6	–							
Vithanage, K.D.K.	2012-13	2014	6	8†	2	245	103*	40.83	1	1	5	–	156	112	1	112.00	1-73	–	–
Warnapura, B.	1981-82	1982-83	4	8	0	96	38	12.00	–	–	2	–	90	46	0	–	–	–	–
Warnapura, B.S.M.	2007	2009	14	24†	1	821	120	35.69	2	7	14	–	54	40	0	–	–	–	–

INDIVIDUAL CAREER RECORDS – SRI LANKA *continued*

	First Test	Last Test	Tests	Inns	NO	Runs	HS	Avge	100	50	Ct	St	Balls	Runs	Wkts	Avge	BB	5wI	10wM
								BATTING AND FIELDING								*BOWLING*			
Warnaweera, K.P.J.	1985-86	1994	10	12†	3	39	20	4.33	–	–	–	–	2333	1021	32	31.90	4-25	–	–
Weerasinghe, C.D.U.S.	1985	1985	1	1	0	3	3	3.00	–	–	–	–	114	36	0	–	–	–	–
Welagedara, U.W.M.B.C.A.	2007-08	2014	21	30	6	218	48	9.08	–	–	5	–	3799†	2273	55	41.32	5-52	2	–
Wettimuny, M.D.	1982-83	1982-83	2	4	1	28	17	7.00	–	–	2	–		37	0	–	–	–	–
Wettimuny, S.	1981-82	1986-87	23	43	1	1221	190	29.07	2	6	10	–	24	37	0	–	–	–	–
Wickramasinghe, G.P.	1991-92	2000-01	40	64	5	555	51	9.40	–	1	18	–	7260	3559	85	41.87	6-60	3	–
Wickremasinghe, A.G.D.	1989-90	1992-93	3	3	1	17	13*	8.50	–	–	9	1							
Wijegunawardene, K.I.W.	1991	1991-92	2	4	1	14	6*	4.66	–	–	–	–	364	147	7	21.00	4-51	–	–
Wijekoon, G.: see W.M.G. Ramyakumara																			
Wijesuriya, R.G.C.E.	1981-82	1985-86	4	7	2	22	8	4.40	–	–	1	–	586†	294	1	294.00	1-68	–	–
Wijetunge, P.K.	1993	1993	1	2	0	10	10	5.00	–	–	–	–	312†	118	2	59.00	1-58	–	–
Zoysa, D.N.T.	1996-97	2004	30	40†	6	288	28*	8.47	–	–	4	–	4422†	2157	64	33.70	5-20	1	–

INDIVIDUAL CAREER RECORDS – ZIMBABWE

	First Test	Last Test	Tests	Inns	NO	Runs	HS	Avge	100	50	Ct	St	Balls	Runs	Wkts	Avge	BB	5wI	10wM
								BATTING AND FIELDING								*BOWLING*			
Arnott, K.J.	1992-93	1992-93	4	8	1	302	101*	43.14	1	1	4	–							
Blignaut, A.M.	2000-01	2005-06	19	36†	3	886	92	26.84	–	6	13	–	3173	1964	53	37.05	5-73	3	–
Brain, D.H.	1992-93	1994-95	9	13	3	115	28	10.45	–	–	1	–	1810†	915	30	30.50	5-42	1	–
Brandes, E.A.	1992-93	1999-2000	10	15	3	121	39	10.08	–	–	4	–	1996	951	26	36.57	3-45	–	–
Brent, G.B.	1999-2000	2001-02	4	6	0	35	25	5.83	–	–	1	–	818	314	7	44.85	3-21	–	–
Briant, G.A.	1992-93	1992-93	1	2	0	17	16	8.50	–	–	–	–							
Bruk-Jackson, G.K.	1993-94	1993-94	2	4	0	39	31	9.75	–	–	–	–							
Burmester, M.G.	1992-93	1992-93	3	4	2	54	30*	27.00	–	–	1	–	436	227	3	75.66	3-78	–	–
Butchart, I.P.	1994-95	1994-95	1	2	0	23	15	11.50	–	–	1	–	18	11	0	–	–	–	–
Campbell, A.D.R.	1992-93	2002-03	60	109†	4	2858	103	27.21	2	18	60	–	66	28	0	–	–	–	–
Carlisle, S.V.	1994-95	2005-06	37	66	6	1615	118	26.91	2	8	34	–							
Chakabva, R.W.	2011-12	2014	5	10	0	178	63	17.80	–	1	6	–							
Chatara, T.L.	2012-13	2014	5	10	1	63	22	7.00	–	–	–	–	1063	444	17	26.11	5-61	1	–
Chigumbura, E.	2004	2013	11	21	0	434	86	20.66	–	3	3	–	1353	779	16	48.68	5-54	1	–
Coventry, C.K.	2005-06	2005-06	2	4	0	88	37	22.00	–	–	3	–							
Cremer, A.G.	2004-05	2013	11	22	2	216	43	10.80	–	–	6	–	1616	1095	24	45.52	4-4	–	–
Crocker, G.J.	1992-93	1992-93	3	4†	1	69	33	23.00	–	–	–	–	456†	217	3	72.33	2-65	–	–

INDIVIDUAL CAREER RECORDS – ZIMBABWE *continued*

					BATTING AND FIELDING										BOWLING				
	First Test	Last Test	Tests	Inns	NO	Runs	HS	Avge	100	50	Ct	St	Balls	Runs	Wkts	Avge	BB	5wI	10wM
Dabengwa, K.M.	2005–06	2005–06	3	6†	0	90	35	15.00	–	–	1	–	438†	249	5	49.80	3-127	–	–
Dekker, M.H.	1993–94	1996–97	14	22†	1	333	68*	15.85	–	2	12	–	60†	15	0	–	–	–	–
Duffin, T.	2005–06	2005–06	2	4†	0	80	56	20.00	–	1	1	–	–						
Ebrahim, D.D.	2000–01	2005–06	29	55	1	1226	94	22.70	–	10	16	–	–						
Ervine, C.R.	2011	2012–13	4	8†	2	174	49	29.00	–	–	3	–	570	388	9	43.11	4-146	–	–
Ervine, S.M.	2003	2003–04	5	8†	0	261	86	32.62	–	3	7	–	54	35	0	–	–	–	–
Evans, C.N.	1996	2003–04	3	6	0	52	22	8.66	–	–	1	–	426	260	2	130.00	1-27	–	–
Ewing, G.M.	2003–04	2005–06	3	6	0	108	71	18.00	–	1	1	–							
Ferreira, N.R.	2005–06	2005–06	1	2†	0	21	16	10.50	–	–	–	–							
Flower, A.	1992–93	2002–03	63	112†	19	4794	232*	51.54	12	27	151	9	3	4	0	–	–	–	–
Flower, G.W.	1992–93	2003–04	67	123	6	3457	201*	29.54	6	15	43	–	3378†	1537	25	61.48	4-41	–	–
Friend, T.J.	2001	2003–04	13	19	4	447	81	29.80	–	3	2	–	2000	1090	25	43.60	5-31	1	–
Goodwin, M.W.	1997–98	2000	19	37	4	1414	166*	42.84	3	8	10	–	119	69	0	–	–	–	–
Gripper, T.R.	1999–2000	2003–04	20	38	1	809	112	21.86	1	5	14	–	793	509	6	84.83	2-91	–	–
Hondo, D.T.	2001–02	2004–05	9	15	6	83	19	9.22	–	–	5	–	1486	774	21	36.85	6-59	1	–
Houghton, D.L.	1992–93	1997–98	22	36	2	1464	266	43.05	4	4	17	–	5	0	0	–	–	–	–
Huckle, A.G.	1997–98	1998–99	8	14	3	74	28*	6.72	–	–	3	–	1568	872	25	34.88	6-109	2	1
James, W.R.	1993–94	1994–95	4	4	0	61	33	15.25	–	–	16	–							
Jarvis, K.M.	2011	2013	8	14	6	58	25*	7.25	–	–	3	–	1569	952	30	31.73	5-54	2	–
Jarvis, M.P.	1992–93	1994–95	5	3	1	4	2*	2.00	–	–	2	–	1273†	393	11	35.72	3-30	–	–
Johnson, N.C.	1998–99	2000	13	23†	1	532	107	24.18	1	4	12	–	1186	594	15	39.60	4-77	–	–
Lamb, G.A.	2011	2011	1	2	0	46	39	23.00	–	–	2	–	192	141	3	47.00	3-120	–	–
Lock, A.C.I.	1995–96	1995–96	1	2	1	8	8*	8.00	–	–	–	–	180	105	5	21.00	3-68	–	–
Madondo, T.N.	1997–98	2000–01	3	4	1	90	74*	30.00	–	1	1	–							
Mahwire, N.B.	2002–03	2005–06	10	17	6	147	50*	13.36	–	1	1	–	1287	915	18	50.83	4-92	–	–
Maregwede, A.	2004	2004	2	4	0	74	28	18.50	–	–	1	–							
Marillier, D.A.	2000–01	2001–02	5	7	1	185	73	30.83	–	2	2	–	616	322	11	29.27	4-57	–	–
Maruma, T.	2013	2013	1	2	0	20	10	10.00	–	–	1	–							
Masakadza, H.	2001	2014	26	52	2	1356	119	27.12	3	4	12	–	762	270	10	27.00	3-24	–	–
Masakadza, S.W.	2011–12	2013	4	7	1	88	24	14.66	–	–	2	–	865	410	14	29.28	4-32	–	–
Matambanadzo, E.Z.	1996–97	1999–2000	3	5	1	17	7	4.25	–	–	–	–	384	250	4	62.50	2-62	–	–

INDIVIDUAL CAREER RECORDS – ZIMBABWE continued

	First Test	Last Test	Tests	Inns	NO	Runs	HS	Avge	100	50	Ct	St	Balls	Runs	Wkts	Avge	BB	5wI	10wM
Matsikenyeri, S.	2003–04	2004–05	8	16	1	351	57	23.40	–	2	7	–	483	345	2	172.50	1-58	–	–
Mawoyo, T.M.K.	2011	2013	8	16	1	454	163*	30.26	1	3	6	–	–		–	–	–	–	–
Mhangwa, M.	1996–97	2000–01	15	25	8	34	8	2.00	–	–	2	–	2596	1006	32	31.43	3-23	–	–
Meth, K.O.	2013	2013	2	4	1	72	31*	24.00	–	–	–	–	324	98	4	24.50	2-41	–	–
Mpofu, C.B.	2004–05	2011–12	9	17	6	27	8	2.45	–	–	–	–	1448	889	20	44.45	4-92	–	–
Mupariwa, T.	2004	2004	1	2	1	15	14	15.00	–	–	–	–	204	136	0	–	–	–	–
Murphy, B.A.	1999–2000	2001–02	11	15	3	123	30	10.25	–	–	11	–	2153	1113	18	61.83	3-32	–	–
Mutendera, D.T.	2000–01	2000–01	1	2	0	10	10	5.00	–	–	–	–	84	29	0	–	–	–	–
Mutizwa, F.	2011–12	2011–12	1	2	0	24	18	12.00	–	–	–	–	–	–	–	–	–	–	–
Mutumbami, R.	2013	2014	5	10	1	195	43	21.66	–	–	14	2	–	–	–	–	–	–	–
Mwayenga, W.	2005–06	2005–06	1	2	1	15	14*	15.00	–	–	–	–	126	79	1	79.00	1-79	–	–
Ncube, N.	2011–12	2011–12	1	2	0	17	14	8.50	–	–	1	–	210	121	1	121.00	1-80	–	–
Nkala, M.L.	2000	2004–05	10	15	2	187	47	14.38	–	–	4	–	1452	727	11	66.09	3-82	–	–
Nyumbu, J.C.	2014	2014	1	2	0	15	13	7.50	–	–	–	–	321	181	5	36.20	5-157	1	–
Olonga, H.K.	1994–95	2002–03	30	45	11	184	24	5.41	–	–	10	–	4502	2620	68	38.52	5-70	2	–
Omarshah, A.H.	1992–93	1996	3	5†	0	122	62	24.40	–	1	–	–	186	125	1	125.00	1-46	–	1
Panyangara, T.	2004	2014	6	12	3	176	40*	19.55	–	–	–	–	1261	529	17	31.11	3-28	–	–
Peall, S.G.	1993–94	1994–95	4	6†	2	60	30	15.00	–	–	1	–	888	303	4	75.75	2-89	–	–
Price, R.W.	1999–2000	2012–13	22	38	8	261	36	8.70	–	–	4	–	6135†	2885	80	36.06	6-73	5	1
Pycroft, A.J.	1992–93	1992–93	3	5	0	152	60	30.40	–	1	2	–	–	–	–	–	–	–	–
Ranchod, U.	1992–93	1992–93	1	2	0	8	7	4.00	–	–	–	–	72	45	1	45.00	1-45	–	–
Rennie, G.J.	1997–98	2001–02	23	46†	1	1023	93	22.73	–	7	13	–	126†	84	1	84.00	1-40	–	–
Rennie, J.A.	1993–94	1997–98	4	6	1	62	22	12.40	–	–	1	–	724	293	3	97.66	2-22	–	–
Rogers, B.G.	2004–05	2004–05	4	8†	0	90	29	11.25	–	–	1	–	18	17	0	–	–	–	–
Sibanda, V.	2003–04	2014	13	26	0	571	93	21.96	–	2	16	–	–	–	–	–	–	–	–
Sikandar Raza	2013	2013	1	2	0	84	60	42.00	–	1	–	–	–	–	–	–	–	–	–
Strang, B.C.	1994–95	2001	26	45	9	465	53	12.91	–	1	11	–	5433†	2203	56	39.33	5-101	1	1
Strang, P.A.	1994–95	2001–02	24	41	10	839	106*	27.06	1	2	15	–	5720	2522	70	36.02	8-109	4	1
Streak, H.H.	1993–94	2005–06	65	107	18	1990	127*	22.35	1	11	17	–	13559	6079	216	28.14	6-73	7	–
Taibu, T.	2001	2011–12	28	54	3	1546	153	30.31	1	12	57	5	48	27	1	27.00	1-27	–	–
Taylor, B.R.M.	2004	2014	20	40	2	1358	171	35.73	4	7	19	–	42	38	0	–	–	–	–

INDIVIDUAL CAREER RECORDS – ZIMBABWE continued

	First Test	Last Test	Tests	BATTING AND FIELDING									BOWLING						
				Inns	NO	Runs	HS	Avge	100	50	Ct	St	Balls	Runs	Wkts	Avge	BB	5wI	10wM
Tiripano, D.T.	2014	2014	1	2	1	20	15*	20.00	–	–	1	–	156	65	2	32.50	2-65	–	–
Traicos, A.J. ‡	1992–93	1992–93	4	6	2	11	5	2.75	–	–	4	–	1141	562	14	40.14	5-86	1	–
Utseya, P.	2004	2013	4	8	1	107	45	15.28	–	–	2	–	753	410	10	41.00	3-60	–	–
Vermeulen, M.A.	2002–03	2014	9	18	0	449	118	24.94	1	2	6	–	6	5	0	–	–	–	–
Viljoen, D.P.	1997–98	2000–01	2	4†	0	57	38	14.25	–	–	1	–	105†	65	1	65.00	1-14	–	–
Vitori, B.V.	2011	2013	4	7†	2	52	19*	10.40	–	–	2	–	833†	464	12	38.66	5-61	1	–
Waller, A.C.	1996–97	1996–97	2	3	0	69	50	23.00	–	1	1	–	–	–	–	–	–	–	–
Waller, M.N.	2011–12	2013	8	16	1	386	72*	25.73	–	3	6	–	18	8	0	–	–	–	–
Watambwa, B.T.	2000–01	2001–02	6	8	5	11	4*	3.66	–	–	–	–	931	490	14	35.00	4-64	–	–
Whittall, A.R.	1996	1999–2000	10	18	3	114	17	7.60	–	–	8	–	1562	736	7	105.14	3-73	–	–
Whittall, G.J.	1993–94	2002–03	46	82	7	2207	203*	29.42	4	10	19	–	4686	2088	51	40.94	4-18	–	–
Williams, S.C.	2012–13	2014	2	4†	0	64	31	16.00	–	–	1	–	172†	113	2	56.50	2-95	–	–
Wishart, C.B.	1995–96	2005–06	27	50	1	1098	114	22.40	1	5	15	–	–	–	–	–	–	–	–

INDIVIDUAL CAREER RECORDS – BANGLADESH

	First Test	Last Test	Tests	BATTING AND FIELDING									BOWLING						
				Inns	NO	Runs	HS	Avge	100	50	Ct	St	Balls	Runs	Wkts	Avge	BB	5wI	10wM
Abdur Razzak	2005–06	2013–14	12	20†	6	245	43	17.50	–	–	4	–	2817†	1550	23	67.39	3-93	–	–
Abul Hasan	2012–13	2012–13	3	5†	3	165	113	82.50	1	–	3	–	528	371	3	123.66	2-80	–	–
Aftab Ahmed	2004–05	2009–10	16	31	3	582	82*	20.78	–	1	7	–	344	237	5	47.40	2-31	–	–
Akram Khan	2000–01	2003	8	16	0	259	44	16.18	–	–	3	–	–	–	–	–	–	–	–
Alamgir Kabir	2002	2003–04	3	5	1	8	4	2.00	–	–	–	–	261	221	0	–	–	–	–
Al-Amin Hossain	2013–14	2014	5	8	6	59	32*	29.50	–	–	–	–	832	438	6	73.00	3-80	–	–
Alok Kapali	2002	2005–06	17	34	1	584	85	17.69	–	2	5	–	1103	709	6	118.16	3-3	–	–
Al Sahariar	2000–01	2003	15	30	0	683	71	22.76	–	4	10	–	–	–	–	–	–	–	–
Aminul Islam	2000–01	2002–03	13	26	1	530	145	21.20	1	2	5	–	198	149	1	149.00	1-66	–	–
Anamul Haque	2012–13	2014	4	8	0	73	22	9.12	–	–	2	–	–	–	–	–	–	–	–
Anwar Hossain Monir	2003	2005	3	6	3	22	13	7.33	–	–	–	–	348	307	0	–	–	–	–
Anwar Hossain Piju	2002–03	2002–03	1	2	0	14	12	7.00	–	–	–	–	–	–	–	–	–	–	–
Ehsanul Haque	2002	2002	1	2	0	7	5	3.50	–	–	–	–	18	18	0	–	–	–	–
Elias Sunny	2011–12	2012–13	4	6†	1	38	20*	7.60	–	–	1	–	863†	518	12	43.16	6-94	1	–
Enamul Haque, sen.	2000–01	2003	10	19†	4	180	24*	12.00	–	–	1	–	2230†	1027	18	57.05	4-136	–	–
Enamul Haque, jun.	2003–04	2013	15	26	16	59	13	5.90	–	–	3	–	3549†	1787	44	40.61	7-95	3	1

INDIVIDUAL CAREER RECORDS – BANGLADESH continued

	First Test	Last Test	Tests	Inns	NO	Runs	HS	Avge	100	50	Ct	St	Balls	Runs	Wkts	Avge	BB	5wI	10wM
								BATTING AND FIELDING								BOWLING			
Fahim Muntasir	2001–02	2002	3	6	0	52	33	8.66	–	–	1	–	576	342	5	68.40	3-131	–	–
Faisal Hossain	2004	2004	1	2†	0	7	5	3.50	–	–	–	–	–	–	–	–	–	–	–
Habibul Bashar	2000–01	2007–08	50	99	1	3026	113	30.87	3	24	22	–	282	217	0	–	–	–	–
Hannan Sarkar	2002	2004–05	17	33	0	662	76	20.06	–	5	7	–	–	–	–	–	–	–	–
Hasibul Hossain	2000–01	2001–02	5	10	1	97	31	10.77	–	–	1	–	780	571	6	95.16	2-125	–	–
Imrul Kayes	2008–09	2014	18	36†	0	723	115	20.08	1	1	17	–	12	8	0	–	–	–	–
Jahurul Islam	2009–10	2013	7	14	1	347	48	26.69	–	–	7	–	–	–	–	–	–	–	–
Javed Omar	2000–01	2007	40	80	2	1720	119	22.05	1	8	10	–	6	12	0	–	–	–	–
Junaid Siddique	2007–08	2012–13	19	37†	0	969	106	26.18	1	7	11	–	18	11	0	–	–	–	–
Khaled Mahmud	2001–02	2003–04	12	23	1	266	45	12.09	–	–	2	–	1620	832	13	64.00	4-37	–	–
Khaled Mashud	2000–01	2007	44	84	10	1409	103*	19.04	1	3	78	9	–	–	–	–	–	–	–
Mahbubul Alam	2008–09	2008–09	4	7	3	5	2	1.25	–	–	–	–	587	314	5	62.80	2-62	–	–
Mahmudullah	2009	2014	20	38	2	1021	115	28.36	1	8	18	–	2816	1595	34	46.91	5-51	1	–
Manjural Islam	2000–01	2003–04	17	33†	11	81	21	3.68	–	–	4	–	2970†	1605	28	57.32	6-81	1	–
Manjural Islam Rana	2003–04	2004–05	6	11†	0	257	69	25.70	–	1	3	–	749†	401	5	80.20	3-84	–	–
Marshall Ayub	2013–14	2013–14	3	6	0	125	41	20.83	–	–	2	–	60	53	0	–	–	–	–
Mashrafe Mortaza	2001–02	2009	36	67	5	797	79	12.85	–	3	9	–	5990	3239	78	41.52	4-60	–	–
Mehrab Hossain, sen.	2000–01	2003	9	18	0	241	71	13.38	–	3	6	–	12	5	0	–	–	–	–
Mehrab Hossain, jun.	2007	2008–09	7	13†	0	243	83	20.25	–	1	2	–	407†	281	4	70.25	2-29	–	–
Mohammad Ashraful	2001–02	2013	61	119	5	2737	190	24.00	6	8	25	–	1733	1271	21	60.52	2-42	–	–
Mohammad Rafique	2000–01	2007–08	33	63†	6	1059	111	18.57	1	4	7	–	8744†	4076	100	40.76	6-77	7	–
Mohammad Salim	2003	2003	2	4	1	49	26	16.33	–	–	3	1	–	–	–	–	–	–	–
Mohammad Sharif	2000–01	2007	10	20	3	122	24*	7.17	–	–	5	–	1651	1106	14	79.00	4-98	–	–
Mominul Haque	2012–13	2014	9	17†	2	877	181	62.64	3	5	6	–	265†	167	1	167.00	1-10	–	–
Mushfiqur Rahim	2005	2014	40	75	5	2352	200	33.60	3	13	63	10	–	–	–	–	–	–	–
Mushfiqur Rahman	2000–01	2004–05	10	19	2	232	46*	13.64	–	–	6	–	1365	823	13	63.30	4-65	–	–
Naeem Islam	2008–09	2012–13	8	15	2	416	108	32.00	1	1	2	–	574	303	1	303.00	1-11	–	–
Nafees Iqbal	2004–05	2005–06	11	22	0	518	121	23.54	1	2	2	–	–	–	–	–	–	–	–
Naimur Rahman	2000–01	2002–03	8	15	1	210	48	15.00	–	–	4	–	1321	718	12	59.83	6-132	1	–
Nasir Hossain	2011–12	2014	16	27	1	958	100	36.84	1	6	10	–	861	413	8	51.52	3-52	–	–
Nazimuddin	2011–12	2012–13	3	6	0	125	78	20.83	–	1	1	–	–	–	–	–	–	–	–
Nazmul Hossain	2004–05	2011–12	2	4	2	16	8*	8.00	–	–	–	–	329	194	5	38.80	2-61	–	–

INDIVIDUAL CAREER RECORDS – BANGLADESH continued

	First Test	Last Test	Tests	BATTING AND FIELDING									BOWLING						
				Inns	NO	Runs	HS	Avge	100	50	Ct	St	Balls	Runs	Wkts	Avge	BB	5wI	10wM
Rafiqul Islam	2002-03	2002-03	1	2	0	7	6	3.50	–	–	–	–	–	–	–	–	–	–	–
Rajin Saleh	2003-04	2008-09	24	46	2	1141	89	25.93	–	7	15	–	438	268	2	134.00	1-9	–	–
Ranjan Das	2000-01	2000-01	1	2	0	2	2	1.00	–	–	1	–	132†	72	1	72.00	1-64	–	–
Raqibul Hasan	2008-09	2011-12	9	18	1	336	65	19.76	–	1	9	–	42	17	1	17.00	1-0	–	–
Robiul Islam	2010	2014	9	17	6	99	33	9.00	–	–	5	–	1860	992	25	39.68	6-71	2	–
Rubel Hossain	2009	2014	20	35	14	142	17	6.76	–	–	9	–	3366	2222	27	82.29	5-166	1	–
Sajidul Islam	2007-08	2013	3	6	0	18	6	3.00	–	–	–	–	330†	232	3	77.33	2-71	–	–
Sanwar Hossain	2001-02	2003-04	9	18	0	345	49	19.16	–	–	1	–	444	310	5	62.00	2-128	–	–
Shafiul Islam	2009-10	2014	7	14	1	173	53	13.30	–	1	2	–	1236	691	11	62.81	3-86	–	–
Shahadat Hossain	2005	2012-13	35	65	17	489	40	10.18	–	–	8	–	5180	3633	70	51.90	6-27	4	–
Shahriar Hossain	2000-01	2003-04	3	5	0	99	48	19.80	–	–	–	1	–						
Shahriar Nafees	2005-06	2013	24	48†	0	1267	138	26.39	1	7	19		–						
Shakib Al Hasan	2007	2013-14	34	65†	5	2278	144	37.96	2	16	14	–	8292†	4074	122	33.39	7-36	11	–
Shamsur Rahman	2013-14	2014	4	8	0	272	106	34.00	1	–	3	–	6	5	0	–	–	–	–
Shuvagata Hom	2014	2014	1	2	0	16	16	8.00	–	–	1	–	222	104	1	104.00	1-104	–	–
Sohag Gazi	2012-13	2013-14	10	16	1	325	101*	21.66	1	2	5	–	3151	1599	38	42.07	6-74	2	–
Suhrawadi Shuvo	2011-12	2011-12	1	2	0	15	15	7.50	–	–	–	–	297†	146	4	36.50	3-73	–	–
Syed Rasel	2005-06	2007	6	12†	4	37	19	4.62	–	–	–	–	879†	573	12	47.75	4-129	–	–
Taijul Islam	2014	2014	2	4†	0	18	12	4.50	–	–	1	–	588†	309	8	38.62	5-135	1	–
Talha Jubair	2002	2004-05	7	14	6	52	31	6.50	–	–	1	–	1090	771	14	55.07	3-135	–	–
Tamim Iqbal	2007-08	2014	34	66†	0	2435	151	36.89	4	16	9	–	30	27	0	–	–	–	–
Tapash Baisya	2002	2005	21	40	6	384	66	11.29	–	2	6	–	3376	2137	36	59.36	4-72	–	–
Tareq Aziz	2004	2004-05	3	6	4	22	10*	11.00	–	–	1	–	360	261	1	261.00	1-76	–	–
Tushar Imran	2002	2007	5	10	0	89	28	8.90	–	–	1	–	60	48	0	–	–	–	–
Ziaur Rahman	2013	2013	1	2	0	14	14	7.00	–	–	–	–	180	71	4	17.75	4-63	–	–

INDIVIDUAL CAREER RECORDS – ICC WORLD XI

	First Test	Last Test	Tests	BATTING AND FIELDING									BOWLING						
				Inns	NO	Runs	HS	Avge	100	50	Ct	St	Balls	Runs	Wkts	Avge	BB	5wI	10wM
Boucher, M.V. ‡	2005-06	2005-06	1	2	0	17	17	8.50	–	–	2	–	–						
Dravid, R. ‡	2005-06	2005-06	1	2	0	23	23	11.50	–	–	1	–	–						
Flintoff, A. ‡	2005-06	2005-06	1	2	0	50	35	25.00	–	–	–	–	204	107	7	15.28	4-59	–	–

BATTING AND FIELDING — BOWLING

	First Test	Last Test	Tests	Inns	NO	Runs	HS	Avge	100	50	Ct	St	Balls	Runs	Wkts	Avge	BB	5wI	10wM
Harmison, S.J. ‡	2005-06	2005-06	1	2	0	1	1	0.50	–	–	–	–	183	101	4	25.25	3-41	–	–
Inzamam-ul-Haq ‡	2005-06	2005-06	1	2	0	1	1	0.50	–	–	–	–							
Kallis, J.H. ‡	2005-06	2005-06	1	2	1	83	44	83.00	–	–	4	–	60	38	1	38.00	1-3	–	–
Lara, B.C. ‡	2005-06	2005-06	1	2†	0	41	36	20.50	–	–	2	–							
Muralitharan, M. ‡	2005-06	2005-06	1	2	0	2	2	1.00	–	–	2	–	324	157	5	31.40	3-55	–	–
Sehwag, V. ‡	2005-06	2005-06	1	2	0	83	76	41.50	–	1	1	–							
Smith, G.C. ‡	2005-06	2005-06	1	2†	0	12	12	6.00	–	–	3	–							
Vettori, D.L. ‡	2005-06	2005-06	1	2†	1	8	8*	8.00	–	–	–	–	162†	111	1	111.00	1-73	–	–

COMPLETE TEST RECORD FOR PLAYERS REPRESENTING TWO TEAMS

BATTING AND FIELDING — BOWLING

	First Test	Last Test	Tests	Inns	NO	Runs	HS	Avge	100	50	Ct	St	Balls	Runs	Wkts	Avge	BB	5wI	10wM
Amir Elahi (I/P)	1947-48	1952-53	6	9	1	82	47	10.25	–	–	–	–	400	248	7	35.42	4-134	–	–
Boucher, M.V. (SA/World)	1997-98	2011-12	147	206	24	5515	125	30.30	5	35	532	23	8	6	–	6.00	1-6	–	–
Dravid, R.S. (I/World)	1996	2011-12	164	286	32	13288	270	52.31	36	63	210	–	120	39	–	39.00	1-18	–	–
Ferris, J.J. (A/E)	1886-87	1891-92	9	17†	4	114	20*	8.76	–	–	4	–	2302†	775	61	12.70	7-37	6	1
Flintoff, A. (E/World)	1998	2009	79	130	9	3845	167	31.77	5	26	52	–	14951	7410	226	32.78	5-58	3	–
Guillen, S.C. (WI/NZ)	1951-52	1955-56	8	12	2	202	54	20.20	–	1	13	3							
Gul Mohammad (I/P)	1946	1956-57	9	17†	1	205	34	12.81	–	–	3	–	77†	24	2	12.00	2-21	–	–
Harmison, S.J. (E/World)	2002	2009	63	86	23	743	49*	11.79	–	–	7	–	13375	7192	226	31.82	7-12	8	1
Hearne, F. (E/SA)	1888-89	1895-96	6	10	–	168	30	16.80	–	–	3	–	62	40	2	20.00	2-40	–	–
Inzamam-ul-Haq (P/World)	1992	2007-08	120	200	22	8830	329	49.60	25	46	81	–	9†	8	0	–	–	–	–
Kallis, J.H. (SA/World)	1995-96	2013-14	166	280	40	13289	224	55.37	45	58	200	–	20232	9535	292	32.65	6-54	5	–
Kardar, A.H. (I/P)	1946	1957-58	26	42†	3	927	93	23.76	–	5	16	–	2712†	954	21	45.42	3-35	–	–
Lara, B.C. (WI/World)	1990-91	2006-07	131	232†	6	11953	400*	52.88	34	48	164	–	60	28	0	–	–	–	–
Midwinter, W.E. (E/A)	1876-77	1886-87	12	21	1	269	37	13.45	–	1	10	–	1725	605	24	25.20	5-78	1	–
Mitchell, F. (E/SA)	1898-99	1912	5	10	0	116	41	11.60	–	–	2	–							
Muralitharan, M. (SL/World)	1992	2010	133	164	56	1261	67	11.67	–	1	72	1	44039	18180	800	22.72	9-51	67	22
Murdoch, W.L. (A/E)	1876-77	1891-92	19	34	5	908	211	31.31	2	1	14	1							
Pataudi, Nawab of, sen. (E/I)	1932-33	1946	6	10	0	199	102	19.90	1	1	–	–							
Sehwag, V. (I/World)	2001-02	2012-13	104	180	6	8586	319	49.34	23	32	91	–	3731	1894	40	47.35	5-104	1	–
Smith, G.C. (SA/World)	2001-02	2013-14	117	205†	13	9265	277	48.25	27	38	169	–	1418	885	8	110.62	2-145	–	–
Traicos, A.J. (SA/Z)	1969-70	1992-93	7	10	4	19	5*	3.16	–	–	8	–	1611	769	18	42.72	5-86	1	–
Trott, A.E. (A/E)	1894-95	1898-99	5	9	3	228	85*	38.00	–	2	4	–	948	390	26	15.00	8-43	2	–
Vettori, D.L. (NZ/World)	1996-97	2012	112	173†	23	4516	140	30.10	6	23	58	–	28670†	12392	360	34.42	7-87	20	3
Wessels, K.C. (A/SA)	1982-83	1994	40	71†	3	2788	179	41.00	6	15	30	–	90	42	0	–	–	–	–
Woods, S.M.J. (A/E)	1888	1895-96	6	10	0	154	53	15.40	–	1	5	–	412	250	10	25.00	3-28	–	–

Index of player names

Every cricketer who appeared in official Test matches since 16 November, 2009, is listed alphabetically within his country's section of the index. The numbers that follow the cricketer's name are the reference numbers of the matches in which he played. Only the prefix of each match is listed, e.g. Test No. 2000/100 (E912, I452) – the 2,000th Test match, the 100th between England and India, England's 912th Test overall and India's 452nd – is shown here simply as 2000.

ENGLAND

ALI, Moeen Munir 2126, 2127, 2128, 2129, 2130, 2131, 2132
ANDERSON, James Michael 1942, 1943, 1944, 1945, 1958, 1959, 1968, 1969, 1970, 1971, 1982, 1983, 1984, 1985, 1986, 1994, 1996, 2000, 2001, 2002, 2003, 2031, 2032, 2033, 2038, 2039, 2043, 2044, 2049, 2050, 2051, 2061, 2062, 2063, 2064, 2079, 2080, 2081, 2088, 2089, 2090, 2091, 2092, 2093, 2094, 2103, 2104, 2105, 2106, 2107, 2126, 2127, 2128, 2129, 2130, 2131, 2132

BAIRSTOW, Jonathan Marc 2043, 2044, 2045, 2051, 2062, 2081, 2088, 2089, 2090, 2091, 2092, 2093, 2106, 2107
BALLANCE, Gary Simon 2107, 2126, 2127, 2128, 2129, 2130, 2131, 2132
BELL, Ian Ronald 1942, 1943, 1944, 1945, 1954, 1955, 1958, 1959, 1982, 1983, 1984, 1985, 1986, 1994, 1995, 1996, 2000, 2001, 2002, 2003, 2031, 2032, 2033, 2038, 2039, 2043, 2044, 2045, 2049, 2050, 2051, 2061, 2063, 2064, 2079, 2080, 2081, 2088, 2089, 2090, 2091, 2092, 2093, 2094, 2103, 2104, 2105, 2106, 2107, 2126, 2127, 2128, 2129, 2130, 2131, 2132
BOPARA, Ravinder Singh 2002, 2003, 2049
BORTHWICK, Scott George 2107
BRESNAN, Timothy Thomas 1954, 1955, 1958, 1985, 1986, 2001, 2002, 2003, 2039, 2043, 2044, 2045, 2049, 2050, 2061, 2064, 2091, 2092, 2093, 2105, 2106
BROAD, Stuart Christopher John 1942, 1943, 1944, 1945,

1954, 1955, 1968, 1969, 1970, 1971, 1982, 1983, 1994, 1995, 1996, 2000, 2001, 2002, 2003, 2031, 2032, 2033, 2038, 2043, 2044, 2049, 2050, 2051, 2061, 2062, 2079, 2080, 2081, 2088, 2089, 2090, 2091, 2092, 2093, 2094, 2103, 2104, 2105, 2106, 2107, 2126, 2127, 2128, 2129, 2130, 2131, 2132
BUTTLER, Joseph Charles 2130, 2131, 2132

CARBERRY, Michael Alexander 1954, 2103, 2104, 2105, 2106, 2107
COLLINGWOOD, Paul David 1942, 1943, 1944, 1945, 1954, 1955, 1968, 1969, 1970, 1971, 1982, 1983, 1984, 1985, 1986
COMPTON, Nicholas Richard Denis 2061, 2062, 2063, 2064, 2079, 2080, 2081, 2088, 2089
COOK, Alastair Nathan 1942, 1943, 1944, 1945, 1954, 1955, 1958, 1959, 1968, 1969, 1970, 1971, 1982, 1983, 1984, 1985, 1986, 1994, 1995, 1996, 2000, 2001, 2002, 2003, 2031, 2032, 2033, 2038, 2039, 2043, 2044, 2045, 2049, 2050, 2051, 2061, 2062, 2063, 2064, 2079, 2080, 2081, 2088, 2089, 2090, 2091, 2092, 2093, 2094, 2103, 2104, 2105, 2106, 2107, 2126, 2127, 2128, 2129, 2130, 2131, 2132

FINN, Steven Thomas 1954, 1955, 1958, 1959, 1968, 1969, 1970, 1971, 1982, 1983, 1984, 1995, 2039, 2045, 2050, 2051, 2063, 2079, 2080, 2081, 2088, 2089, 2090

JORDAN, Christopher James 2126, 2127, 2130, 2131, 2132

KERRIGAN, Simon Christopher 2094

MORGAN, Eoin Joseph Gerard 1958, 1959, 1968, 1969, 1970, 1971, 1994, 1995, 1996, 2000, 2001, 2002, 2003, 2031, 2032, 2033

ONIONS, Graham 1942, 1943, 1944, 2045

PANESAR, Mudhsuden Singh 2032, 2033, 2038, 2062, 2063, 2064, 2079, 2080, 2081, 2104, 2106
PATEL, Samit Rohit 2038, 2039, 2061, 2062, 2063
PIETERSEN, Kevin Peter 1942, 1943, 1944, 1945, 1954, 1955, 1958, 1959, 1968, 1969, 1970, 1971, 1982, 1983, 1984, 1985, 1986, 1994, 1995, 1996, 2000, 2001, 2002, 2003, 2031, 2032, 2033, 2038, 2039, 2043, 2044, 2045, 2049, 2050, 2061, 2062, 2063, 2064, 2079, 2080, 2090, 2091, 2092, 2093, 2094, 2103, 2104, 2105, 2106, 2107
PLUNKETT, Liam Edward 2126, 2127, 2128, 2129
PRIOR, Matthew James 1942, 1943, 1944, 1945, 1954, 1955, 1958, 1959, 1968, 1969, 1970, 1971, 1982, 1983, 1984, 1985, 1986, 1994, 1995, 1996, 2000, 2001, 2002, 2003, 2031, 2032, 2033, 2038, 2039, 2043, 2044, 2045, 2049, 2050, 2051, 2061, 2062, 2063, 2064, 2079, 2080, 2081, 2088, 2089, 2090, 2091, 2092, 2093, 2094, 2103, 2104, 2105, 2126, 2127, 2128, 2129

RANKIN, William Boyd 2107
ROBSON, Samuel David 2126, 2127, 2128, 2129, 2130, 2131, 2132
ROOT, Joseph Edward 2064, 2079, 2080, 2081, 2088, 2089, 2090,

2091, 2092, 2093, 2094, 2103,
2104, 2105, 2106, 2126, 2127,
2128, 2129, 2130, 2131, 2132

SHAHZAD, Ajmal 1959
SIDEBOTTOM, Ryan Jay 1945
STOKES, Benjamin Andrew 2104,
2105, 2106, 2107, 2128, 2129
STRAUSS, Andrew John 1942,
1943, 1944, 1945, 1958,
1959, 1968, 1969, 1970,
1971, 1982, 1983, 1984,
1985, 1986, 1994, 1995,
1996, 2000, 2001, 2002,
2003, 2031, 2032, 2033,
2038, 2039, 2043, 2044,
2045, 2049, 2050, 2051

SWANN, Graeme Peter 1942,
1943, 1944, 1945, 1954,
1955, 1958, 1959, 1968,
1969, 1970, 1971, 1982,
1983, 1984, 1985, 1986,
1994, 1995, 1996, 2000,
2001, 2002, 2003, 2031,
2032, 2033, 2038, 2039,
2043, 2044, 2045, 2049,
2051, 2061, 2062, 2063,
2064, 2088, 2089, 2090,
2091, 2092, 2093, 2094,
2103, 2104, 2105

TAYLOR, James William Arthur
2050, 2051
TREDWELL, James Cullum 1955

TREMLETT, Christopher Timothy
1984, 1985, 1986, 1994, 1995,
1996, 2000, 2031, 2103
TROTT, Ian Jonathan Leonard 1942,
1943, 1944, 1945, 1954, 1955,
1958, 1959, 1968, 1969, 1970,
1971, 1982, 1983, 1984, 1985,
1986, 1994, 1995, 1996, 2000,
2001, 2031, 2032, 2033, 2038,
2039, 2043, 2044, 2045, 2049,
2050, 2051, 2061, 2062, 2063,
2064, 2079, 2080, 2081, 2088,
2089, 2090, 2091, 2092, 2093,
2094, 2103

WOAKES, Christopher Roger 2094,
2130, 2131, 2132

AUSTRALIA

AGAR, Ashton Charles 2090, 2091

BAILEY, George John 2103, 2104,
2105, 2106, 2107
BEER, Michael Anthony 1986, 2041
BIRD, Jackson Munro 2068, 2069,
2093
BOLLINGER, Douglas Erwin 1940,
1941, 1946, 1947, 1948, 1956,
1957, 1963, 1964, 1972, 1983

CLARKE, Michael John 1939, 1940,
1941, 1946, 1947, 1948, 1956,
1957, 1963, 1964, 1972, 1973,
1982, 1983, 1984, 1985, 1986,
2005, 2006, 2007, 2018, 2019,
2020, 2021, 2027, 2028, 2029,
2030, 2040, 2041, 2042, 2056,
2057, 2058, 2067, 2068, 2069,
2075, 2076, 2077, 2090, 2091,
2092, 2093, 2094, 2103, 2104,
2105, 2106, 2107, 2120, 2121,
2122
COPELAND, Trent Aaron 2005,
2006, 2007
COWAN, Edward James McKenzie
2027, 2028, 2029, 2030, 2040,
2041, 2042, 2056, 2057, 2058,
2067, 2068, 2069, 2075, 2076,
2077, 2078, 2090
CUMMINS, Patrick James 2019

DOHERTY, Xavier John 1982, 1983,
2076, 2077
DOOLAN, Alexander James 2120,
2121, 2122

FAULKNER, James Peter 2094

GEORGE, Peter Robert 1973

HADDIN, Bradley James 1939,
1940, 1941, 1946, 1947,
1948, 1956, 1957, 1982,
1983, 1984, 1985, 1986,
2005, 2006, 2007, 2018,
2019, 2020, 2021, 2027,
2028, 2029, 2030, 2077,
2090, 2091, 2092, 2093,
2094, 2103, 2104, 2105,
2106, 2107, 2120, 2121, 2122

HARRIS, Ryan James 1956, 1957,
1983, 1984, 1985, 2005, 2006,
2018, 2029, 2030, 2040, 2042,
2091, 2092, 2093, 2094, 2103,
2104, 2105, 2106, 2107, 2120,
2121, 2122
HASTINGS, John Wayne 2058
HAURITZ, Nathan Michael 1939,
1940, 1941, 1946, 1947, 1948,
1956, 1957, 1972, 1973
HENRIQUES, Moises Constantino
2075, 2076, 2077
HILFENHAUS, Benjamin William
1939, 1963, 1964, 1972, 1973,
1982, 1984, 1985, 1986, 2027,
2028, 2029, 2030, 2040, 2041,
2042, 2056, 2057, 2067
HUGHES, Phillip Joel 1947, 1956,
1984, 1985, 1986, 2005, 2006,
2007, 2018, 2019, 2020, 2021,
2067, 2068, 2069, 2075, 2076,
2077, 2078, 2090, 2091
HUSSEY, Michael Edward Killeen
1939, 1940, 1941, 1946, 1947,
1948, 1956, 1957, 1963, 1964,
1972, 1973, 1982, 1983, 1984,
1985, 1986, 2005, 2006, 2007,
2018, 2019, 2020, 2021, 2027,
2028, 2029, 2030, 2040, 2041,
2042, 2056, 2057, 2058, 2067,
2068, 2069

JOHNSON, Mitchell Guy 1939, 1940,
1941, 1946, 1947, 1948, 1956,
1957, 1963, 1964, 1972, 1973,
1982, 1984, 1985, 1986, 2005,
2006, 2007, 2018, 2019, 2058,
2068, 2069, 2078, 2103, 2104,
2105, 2106, 2107, 2120, 2121,
2122

KATICH, Simon Mathew 1939, 1940,
1941, 1946, 1948, 1956, 1957,
1963, 1964, 1972, 1973, 1982,
1983
KHAWAJA, Usman Tariq 1986, 2005,
2006, 2019, 2020, 2021, 2091,
2092, 2093

LYON, Nathan Michael 2005, 2006,
2007, 2018, 2019, 2020, 2021,

2027, 2028, 2030, 2040, 2041,
2042, 2056, 2057, 2058, 2067,
2068, 2069, 2075, 2077, 2078,
2092, 2093, 2094, 2103, 2104,
2105, 2106, 2107, 2120, 2121,
2122

McKAY, Clinton James 1941
MARSH, Shaun Edward 2006, 2007,
2018, 2027, 2028, 2029, 2030,
2120, 2121
MAXWELL, Glenn James 2076, 2078

NORTH, Marcus James 1939, 1940,
1941, 1946, 1947, 1948, 1956,
1957, 1963, 1964, 1972, 1973,
1982, 1983

PAINE, Timothy David 1963, 1964,
1972, 1973
PATTINSON, James Lee 2020, 2021,
2027, 2028, 2041, 2056, 2057,
2075, 2076, 2078, 2090, 2091,
2122
PONTING, Ricky Thomas 1939,
1940, 1941, 1946, 1947, 1948,
1956, 1957, 1963, 1964, 1972,
1973, 1982, 1983, 1984, 1985,
2005, 2007, 2018, 2019, 2020,
2021, 2027, 2028, 2029, 2030,
2040, 2041, 2042, 2056, 2057,
2058

QUINEY, Robert John 2056, 2057

ROGERS, Christopher John Llewellyn
2090, 2091, 2092, 2093, 2094,
2103, 2104, 2105, 2106, 2107,
2120, 2121, 2122

SIDDLE, Peter Matthew 1939, 1940,
1946, 1947, 1948, 1982, 1983,
1984, 1985, 1986, 2007, 2018,
2019, 2020, 2021, 2027, 2028,
2029, 2030, 2040, 2056, 2057,
2067, 2068, 2069, 2075, 2076,
2077, 2078, 2090, 2091, 2092,
2093, 2094, 2103, 2104, 2105,
2106, 2107, 2120, 2121
SMITH, Steven Peter Devereux 1963,
1964, 1984, 1985, 1986, 2077,

2078, 2090, 2091, 2092, 2093, 2094, 2103, 2104, 2105, 2106, 2107, 2120, 2121, 2122
STARC, Mitchell Aaron 2020, 2021, 2029, 2042, 2058, 2067, 2069, 2075, 2077, 2090, 2092, 2094

WADE, Matthew Scott 2040, 2041, 2042, 2056, 2057,

2058, 2067, 2068, 2069, 2075, 2076, 2078
WARNER, David Andrew 2020, 2021, 2027, 2028, 2029, 2030, 2040, 2041, 2042, 2056, 2057, 2058, 2067, 2068, 2069, 2075, 2076, 2077, 2078, 2092, 2093, 2094, 2103, 2104, 2105, 2106, 2107, 2120, 2121, 2122

WATSON, Shane Robert 1939, 1940, 1941, 1946, 1947, 1948, 1957, 1963, 1964, 1972, 1973, 1982, 1983, 1984, 1985, 1986, 2005, 2006, 2007, 2018, 2019, 2040, 2041, 2042, 2058, 2067, 2068, 2075, 2076, 2078, 2090, 2091, 2092, 2093, 2094, 2103, 2104, 2105, 2106, 2107, 2122

SOUTH AFRICA

ABBOTT, Kyle John 2074, 2122
AMLA, Hashim Mahomed 1942, 1943, 1944, 1945, 1951, 1952, 1960, 1961, 1962, 1977, 1978, 1987, 1988, 1989, 2018, 2019, 2024, 2025, 2026, 2035, 2036, 2037, 2049, 2050, 2051, 2056, 2057, 2058, 2070, 2071, 2072, 2073, 2074, 2099, 2111, 2112, 2120, 2121, 2122, 2133, 2134, 2137

BOTHA, Johan 1962, 1977, 1978
BOUCHER, Mark Verdon 1942, 1943, 1944, 1945, 1951, 1960, 1961, 1962, 1977, 1978, 1987, 1988, 1989, 2018, 2019, 2024, 2025, 2026, 2035, 2036, 2037

DE KOCK, Quinton 2121, 2133, 2134, 2137
DE LANGE, Marchant 2025, 2037
DE VILLIERS, Abraham Benjamin 1942, 1943, 1944, 1945, 1951, 1952, 1960, 1961, 1962, 1977, 1978, 1987, 1988, 1989, 2018, 2019, 2024, 2025, 2026, 2035, 2036, 2037, 2049, 2050, 2051, 2056, 2057, 2058, 2070, 2071, 2072, 2073, 2074, 2099, 2100, 2111, 2112, 2120, 2121, 2122, 2133, 2134, 2137
DE WET, Friedel 1942, 1944
DUMINY, Jean-Paul 1942, 1943, 1944, 1945, 1951, 1952, 2037, 2049, 2050, 2051, 2056, 2099, 2100, 2111, 2112, 2120, 2121, 2122, 2133, 2134, 2137
DU PLESSIS, Francois 2057, 2058, 2070, 2071, 2072, 2073, 2074, 2099, 2100, 2111, 2112, 2120, 2121, 2122, 2133, 2134, 2137

ELGAR, Dean 2058, 2070, 2071, 2072, 2073, 2074, 2100, 2121, 2122, 2133, 2134, 2137

HARRIS, Paul Lee 1942, 1943, 1944, 1951, 1952, 1960, 1961, 1962, 1977, 1978, 1987, 1988, 1989

IMRAN TAHIR 2018, 2019, 2024, 2025, 2026, 2035, 2036, 2049, 2050, 2051, 2057, 2100, 2111, 2133, 2134

KALLIS, Jacques Henry 1942, 1943, 1944, 1945, 1951, 1952, 1960, 1961, 1962, 1977, 1978, 1987, 1988, 1989, 2018, 2019, 2024, 2025, 2026, 2035, 2036, 2049, 2050, 2051, 2056, 2057, 2058, 2070, 2071, 2072, 2073, 2099, 2100, 2111, 2112
KLEINVELDT, Rory Keith 2056, 2057, 2071, 2074

McLAREN, Ryan 1945, 2120
MORKEL, Morne 1942, 1943, 1944, 1945, 1951, 1952, 1960, 1961, 1962, 1977, 1978, 1987, 1988, 1989, 2018, 2019, 2024, 2025, 2026, 2035, 2036, 2037, 2049, 2050, 2051, 2056, 2057, 2058, 2070, 2071, 2072, 2073, 2099, 2100, 2111, 2112, 2120, 2121, 2122, 2133, 2134, 2137

NTINI, Makhaya 1942, 1943

PARNELL, Wayne Dillon 1945, 1951, 1952, 2121
PETERSEN, Alviro Nathan 1952, 1960, 1961, 1962, 1977, 1978, 1987, 1988, 1989, 2026, 2035, 2036, 2037, 2049, 2050, 2051, 2056, 2057, 2058, 2070, 2071, 2072, 2073, 2074, 2099, 2100,

2111, 2112, 2120, 2122, 2133, 2134, 2137
PETERSON, Robin John 2058, 2070, 2071, 2072, 2073, 2074, 2099, 2112, 2120
PHILANDER, Vernon Darryl 2018, 2019, 2024, 2026, 2035, 2036, 2037, 2049, 2050, 2051, 2056, 2058, 2070, 2072, 2073, 2074, 2099, 2100, 2111, 2112, 2120, 2121, 2122, 2133, 2134, 2137
PIEDT, Dane Lee-Roy 2137
PRINCE, Ashwell Gavin 1942, 1943, 1944, 1945, 1951, 1952, 1960, 1961, 1962, 1977, 1978, 1987, 1988, 1989, 2018, 2019, 2024, 2025

RUDOLPH, Jacobus Andries 2018, 2019, 2024, 2025, 2026, 2035, 2036, 2037, 2049, 2050, 2051, 2056, 2057

SMITH, Graeme Craig 1942, 1943, 1944, 1945, 1951, 1952, 1960, 1961, 1962, 1977, 1978, 1987, 1988, 1989, 2018, 2019, 2024, 2025, 2026, 2035, 2036, 2037, 2049, 2050, 2051, 2056, 2057, 2058, 2070, 2071, 2072, 2073, 2074, 2099, 2100, 2111, 2112, 2120, 2121, 2122
STEYN, Dale Willem 1943, 1944, 1945, 1951, 1952, 1960, 1961, 1962, 1977, 1978, 1987, 1988, 1989, 2018, 2019, 2024, 2025, 2026, 2035, 2036, 2037, 2049, 2050, 2051, 2056, 2057, 2058, 2070, 2071, 2072, 2073, 2074, 2099, 2100, 2111, 2112, 2120, 2121, 2122, 2133, 2134, 2137

TSOTSOBE, Lonwabo Lennox 1960, 1961, 1987, 1988, 1989

WEST INDIES

BARATH, Adrian Boris 1939, 1940, 1979, 1980, 1997, 1998, 1999, 2016, 2017, 2040, 2041, 2042, 2043, 2044, 2045
BAUGH, Carlton Seymour 1979, 1980, 1981, 1992, 1993, 1997, 1998, 1999, 2012, 2013, 2015, 2016, 2017, 2040, 2041, 2042

BENN, Sulieman Jamaal 1939, 1940, 1941, 1960, 1961, 1962, 1980, 1981, 2123, 2124, 2125, 2138, 2139
BESS, Brandon Jeremy 1962
BEST, Tino la Bertram 2045, 2053, 2059, 2060, 2084, 2085, 2101, 2102, 2108, 2109, 2110

BISHOO, Devendra 1992, 1993, 1997, 1998, 1999, 2012, 2013, 2015, 2016, 2017, 2040
BLACKWOOD, Jermaine 2124, 2138, 2139
BRATHWAITE, Kraigg Clairmonte 1993, 2012, 2013, 2015, 2016,

2017, 2040, 2041, 2042, 2110, 2124, 2125, 2138, 2139

BRAVO, Dwayne John 1939, 1940, 1941, 1960, 1961, 1962, 1979, 1980, 1981

BRAVO, Darren Michael 1979, 1980, 1981, 1992, 1993, 1997, 1998, 1999, 2012, 2013, 2015, 2016, 2017, 2040, 2041, 2042, 2043, 2044, 2045, 2059, 2060, 2084, 2085, 2101, 2102, 2108, 2109, 2123, 2124, 2125, 2138, 2139

CHANDERPAUL, Shivnarine 1939, 1940, 1960, 1961, 1962, 1979, 1980, 1981, 1992, 1997, 1998, 1999, 2012, 2013, 2015, 2016, 2040, 2041, 2042, 2043, 2044, 2052, 2053, 2059, 2060, 2084, 2085, 2101, 2102, 2108, 2109, 2110, 2123, 2124, 2125, 2138, 2139

COTTRELL, Sheldon Shane 2101

DEONARINE, Narsingh 1941, 1960, 1961, 1962, 2040, 2041, 2042, 2045, 2052, 2053, 2102, 2108, 2109, 2110

DOWLIN, Travis Montague 1939, 1941, 1960, 1961

EDWARDS, Fidel Henderson 1997, 1998, 1999, 2012, 2013, 2015, 2016, 2017, 2040, 2041, 2043, 2060

EDWARDS, Kirk Anton 1999, 2012, 2013, 2015, 2016, 2017, 2040, 2043, 2044, 2108, 2109, 2110, 2123, 2124, 2125, 2138, 2139

FUDADIN, Assad Badyr 2045, 2052, 2053

GABRIEL, Shannon Terry 2043, 2084, 2085, 2102, 2108, 2109, 2124, 2138, 2139

GAYLE, Christopher Henry 1939, 1940, 1941, 1960, 1961, 1962, 1979, 1980, 1981, 2052, 2053, 2059, 2060, 2084, 2085, 2101, 2102, 2123, 2124, 2125, 2138

HOLDER, Jason Omar 2125

JOHNSON, Leon Rayon 2139

NARINE, Sunil Philip 2045, 2052, 2053, 2059, 2060, 2110

NASH, Brendan Paul 1939, 1940, 1941, 1960, 1961, 1962, 1979, 1980, 1981, 1992, 1993, 1997

PASCAL, Nelon Troy 1960, 1981

PERMAUL, Veerasammy 2059, 2060, 2101, 2110

POWELL, Kieran Omar Akeem 1999, 2013, 2015, 2017, 2041, 2042, 2043, 2044, 2045, 2052, 2053, 2059, 2060, 2084, 2085, 2101, 2102, 2108, 2109, 2110, 2123

RAMDIN, Denesh 1939, 1940, 1941, 1960, 1961, 1962, 2043, 2044, 2045, 2052, 2053, 2059, 2060, 2084, 2085, 2101, 2102, 2108, 2109, 2110, 2123, 2124, 2125, 2138, 2139

RAMPAUL, Ravindranath 1939, 1940, 1941, 1960, 1961, 1992, 1993,

1997, 1998, 1999, 2012, 2015, 2017, 2042, 2044, 2045, 2052, 2059

RICHARDS, Dale Maurice 1962

ROACH, Kemar Andre Jamal 1939, 1940, 1941, 1961, 1962, 1979, 1980, 1981, 1992, 1993, 2013, 2016, 2040, 2041, 2042, 2043, 2044, 2052, 2053, 2084, 2085, 2123, 2124, 2125, 2138, 2139

RUSSELL, Andre Dwayne 1979

SAMMY, Darren Julius Garvey 1940, 1979, 1980, 1981, 1992, 1993, 1997, 1998, 1999, 2012, 2013, 2015, 2016, 2017, 2040, 2041, 2042, 2043, 2044, 2045, 2052, 2053, 2059, 2060, 2084, 2085, 2101, 2102, 2108, 2109, 2110

SAMUELS, Marlon Nathaniel 1993, 1998, 1999, 2012, 2013, 2015, 2016, 2017, 2043, 2044, 2045, 2052, 2053, 2059, 2060, 2084, 2085, 2101, 2102, 2108, 2109, 2110, 2123

SARWAN, Ramnaresh Ronnie 1940, 1941, 1992, 1993, 1997, 1998

SHILLINGFORD, Shane 1960, 1961, 1962, 1979, 1980, 2041, 2042, 2044, 2084, 2085, 2101, 2102, 2108, 2109, 2123, 2125

SIMMONS, Lendl Mark Platter 1992, 1993, 1997, 1998, 2012

SMITH, Devon Sheldon 1981, 1992

TAYLOR, Jerome Everton 1939, 2123, 2124, 2125, 2138, 2139

TONGE, Gavin Courtney 1941

NEW ZEALAND

ANDERSON, Corey James 2097, 2098, 2108, 2109, 2110, 2118, 2119

ARNEL, Brent John 1956, 1957, 1975, 1990, 1991, 2036

ASTLE, Todd Duncan 2066

BENNETT, Hamish Kyle 1974

BOND, Shane Edward 1936

BOULT, Trent Alexander 2021, 2034, 2035, 2053, 2054, 2055, 2065, 2066, 2070, 2071, 2079, 2080, 2081, 2088, 2089, 2097, 2098, 2108, 2109, 2110, 2118, 2119, 2123, 2124, 2125

BRACEWELL, Douglas Andrew John 2014, 2020, 2021, 2034, 2035, 2036, 2037, 2052, 2053, 2054, 2055, 2065, 2066, 2070, 2071, 2089, 2097, 2098

BROWNLIE, Dean Graham 2014, 2020, 2021, 2034, 2037, 2052, 2053, 2070, 2071, 2079, 2080, 2081, 2088, 2089

CRAIG, Mark Donald 2123, 2124, 2125

ELLIOTT, Grant David 1936, 1937

FLYNN, Daniel Raymond 1936, 1937, 1938, 2037, 2052, 2054, 2055, 2065, 2066, 2070, 2071

FRANKLIN, James Edward Charles 1991, 2054, 2055, 2065, 2070

FULTON, Peter Gordon 1936, 1937, 2079, 2080, 2081, 2088, 2089, 2097, 2098, 2108, 2109, 2110, 2118, 2119, 2123

GILLESPIE, Mark Raymond 2036, 2037

GUPTILL, Martin James 1936, 1937, 1938, 1953, 1956, 1957, 1975, 1976, 1990, 1991, 2014, 2020, 2021, 2034, 2035, 2036, 2037, 2052, 2053, 2054, 2055, 2065, 2066, 2070, 2071, 2089

HOPKINS, Gareth James 1974, 1975, 1976

INGRAM, Peter John 1953, 1956

LATHAM, Thomas William Maxwell 2119, 2123, 2124, 2125

McCULLUM, Brendon Barrie 1936, 1937, 1938, 1953, 1956, 1957, 1974, 1975, 1976, 1990, 1991,

2014, 2020, 2021, 2034, 2035, 2036, 2037, 2052, 2053, 2054, 2055, 2065, 2066, 2070, 2071, 2079, 2080, 2081, 2088, 2089, 2097, 2098, 2108, 2109, 2110, 2118, 2119, 2123, 2124, 2125

McINTOSH, Timothy Gavin 1936, 1937, 1938, 1953, 1956, 1957, 1974, 1975, 1976, 1990

McKAY, Andrew John 1976

MARTIN, Bruce Philip 2079, 2080, 2081, 2088, 2097

MARTIN, Christopher Stewart 1936, 1937, 1938, 1953, 1956, 1957, 1974, 1975, 1976, 1990, 1991, 2014, 2020, 2021, 2034, 2035, 2036, 2037, 2052, 2054, 2070

MUNRO, Colin 2071

NEESHAM, James Douglas Sheehan 2119, 2123, 2124, 2125

NICOL, Robert James 2035, 2036

O'BRIEN, Iain Edward 1936, 1937, 1938

PATEL, Jeetan Shashi 1953, 1957, 1974, 2014, 2054, 2055, 2065, 2066, 2070, 2071

REDMOND, Aaron James 2108
RUTHERFORD, Hamish
   Duncan 2079, 2080, 2081,
   2088, 2089, 2097, 2098, 2108,
   2109, 2110, 2118, 2119, 2124,
   2125
RYDER, Jesse Daniel 1974,
   1975, 1976, 1990, 1991, 2020,
   2021

SINCLAIR, Mathew Stuart 1957
SODHI, Inderbir Singh 2097, 2098,
   2108, 2109, 2110, 2118, 2123,
   2124
SOUTHEE, Timothy Grant 1938,
   1953, 1956, 1957, 1975, 1976,
   1990, 1991, 2020, 2021, 2034,
   2035, 2053, 2055, 2065, 2066,
   2079, 2080, 2081, 2088, 2089,
   2108, 2109, 2110, 2118, 2119,
   2123, 2124, 2125

TAYLOR, Luteru Ross Poutoa Lote
   1936, 1937, 1938, 1953, 1956,
   1957, 1974, 1975, 1976, 1990,
   1991, 2014, 2020, 2021, 2034,
   2035, 2036, 2037, 2052, 2053,
   2054, 2055, 2065, 2066, 2079,
   2080, 2081, 2088, 2089, 2097,
   2098, 2108, 2109, 2110, 2118,
   2123, 2124, 2125
TUFFEY, Daryl Raymond 1937, 1938,
   1953, 1956

VAN WYK, Cornelius Francois Kruger
   2035, 2036, 2037, 2052,
   2053, 2054, 2055, 2065,
   2066
VETTORI, Daniel Luca 1936, 1937,
   1938, 1953, 1956, 1957, 1974,
   1975, 1976, 1990, 1991, 2014,
   2020, 2034, 2035, 2036, 2037,
   2052

WAGNER, Neil 2052, 2053, 2071,
   2079, 2080, 2081, 2088, 2089,
   2098, 2108, 2109, 2110, 2118,
   2119, 2125
WATLING, Bradley-John 1938, 1953,
   1956, 1957, 1974, 2014, 2034,
   2053, 2070, 2071, 2079, 2080,
   2081, 2088, 2097, 2098, 2108,
   2109, 2110, 2118, 2119, 2123,
   2124, 2125
WILLIAMSON, Kane Stuart 1974,
   1975, 1976, 1990, 1991, 2014,
   2020, 2021, 2034, 2035, 2036,
   2037, 2052, 2053, 2054, 2055,
   2065, 2066, 2070, 2071, 2079,
   2080, 2081, 2088, 2089, 2097,
   2098, 2109, 2110, 2118, 2119,
   2123, 2124, 2125

YOUNG, Reece Alan 1990, 1991,
   2014, 2020, 2021

INDIA

AARON, Varun Raymond 2017, 2131,
   2132
ASHWIN, Ravichandran 2015, 2016,
   2017, 2027, 2028, 2030, 2054,
   2055, 2061, 2062, 2063, 2064,
   2075, 2076, 2077, 2078, 2101,
   2102, 2111, 2131, 2132

BADRINATH, Subramaniam 1951,
   1952
BHUVNESHWAR KUMAR 2075,
   2076, 2077, 2078, 2101, 2102,
   2128, 2129, 2130, 2131, 2132
BINNY, Stuart Terence Roger 2128,
   2129, 2132

CHAWLA, Piyush Pramod 2064

DHAWAN, Shikhar 2077, 2101, 2102,
   2111, 2112, 2118, 2119, 2128,
   2129, 2130
DHONI, Mahendra Singh 1933, 1934,
   1935, 1950, 1951, 1952, 1965,
   1966, 1967, 1972, 1973, 1974,
   1975, 1976, 1987, 1988, 1989,
   1997, 1998, 1999, 2000, 2001,
   2002, 2003, 2015, 2016, 2017,
   2027, 2028, 2029, 2054, 2055,
   2061, 2062, 2063, 2064, 2075,
   2076, 2077, 2078, 2101, 2102,
   2111, 2112, 2118, 2119, 2128,
   2129, 2130, 2131, 2132
DRAVID, Rahul 1933, 1934, 1935,
   1949, 1950, 1965, 1966, 1967,
   1972, 1973, 1974, 1975, 1976,
   1987, 1988, 1989, 1997, 1998,
   1999, 2000, 2001, 2002, 2003,
   2015, 2016, 2017, 2027, 2028,
   2029, 2030

GAMBHIR, Gautam 1933, 1934,
   1949, 1950, 1951, 1952, 1965,
   1972, 1974, 1975, 1976, 1987,
   1989, 2000, 2002, 2003, 2015,
   2016, 2017, 2027, 2028, 2029,
   2030, 2054, 2055, 2061, 2062,
   2063, 2064, 2131, 2132

HARBHAJAN SINGH 1933, 1934,
   1935, 1950, 1951, 1952, 1965,
   1966, 1972, 1973, 1974, 1975,
   1976, 1987, 1988, 1989, 1997,
   1998, 1999, 2000, 2001, 2062,
   2075, 2076

JADEJA, Ravindrasinh Anirudhsinh
   2064, 2075, 2076, 2077, 2078,
   2112, 2118, 2119, 2128, 2129,
   2130, 2131

KARTHIK, Krishankumar Dinesh
   1949
KOHLI, Virat 1997, 1998, 1999, 2017,
   2027, 2028, 2029, 2030, 2054,
   2055, 2061, 2062, 2063, 2064,
   2075, 2076, 2077, 2078, 2101,
   2102, 2111, 2112, 2118, 2119,
   2128, 2129, 2130, 2131, 2132
KUMAR, Praveenkumar 1997, 1998,
   1999, 2000, 2001, 2002

LAXMAN, Vangipurappu Venkata Sai
   1933, 1934, 1935, 1949, 1952,
   1965, 1966, 1967, 1972, 1974,
   1975, 1976, 1987, 1988, 1989,
   1997, 1998, 1999, 2000, 2001,
   2002, 2003, 2015, 2016, 2017,
   2027, 2028, 2029, 2030

MISHRA, Amit 1933, 1949, 1951,
   1952, 1967, 1997, 2002, 2003
MITHUN, Abhimanyu 1965, 1966,
   1967, 1998
MOHAMMED SHAMI 2101, 2102,
   2111, 2112, 2118, 2119, 2128,
   2129, 2130
MUKUND, Abhinav 1997, 1998,
   1999, 2000, 2001

OJHA, Pragyan Prayish 1934, 1935,
   1950, 1965, 1966, 1967, 1972,
   1973, 1974, 1975, 1976, 2015,
   2016, 2017, 2054, 2055, 2061,
   2062, 2063, 2064, 2077, 2078,
   2101, 2102

PANKAJ SINGH 2130, 2131
PATEL, Munaf Musa 1999
PUJARA, Cheteshwar Arvind
   1973, 1988, 1989, 2054,
   2055, 2061, 2062, 2063,
   2064, 2075, 2076, 2077,
   2078, 2101, 2102, 2111,
   2112, 2118, 2119, 2128,
   2129, 2130, 2131, 2132

RAHANE, Ajinkya Madhukar
   2078, 2111, 2112, 2118,
   2119, 2128, 2129, 2130, 2131,
   2132
RAINA, Suresh Kumar 1966,
   1967, 1972, 1973, 1974, 1975,
   1976, 1987, 1997, 1998, 1999,
   2000, 2001, 2002, 2003, 2054,
   2055

SAHA, Wriddhaman Prasanta 1951,
   2030
SEHWAG, Virender 1933, 1934, 1935,
   1949, 1950, 1951, 1952, 1965,
   1966, 1967, 1972, 1973, 1974,
   1975, 1976, 1987, 1988, 1989,
   2002, 2003, 2015, 2016, 2017,
   2027, 2028, 2029, 2030, 2054,
   2055, 2061, 2062, 2063, 2064,
   2075, 2076
SHARMA, Ishant 1933, 1949, 1950,
   1951, 1952, 1965, 1966, 1967,
   1972, 1976, 1987, 1988, 1989,
   1997, 1998, 1999, 2000, 2001,
   2002, 2003, 2015, 2016, 2017,
   2027, 2028, 2029, 2030, 2063,
   2064, 2075, 2076, 2077, 2078,
   2111, 2112, 2118, 2119, 2128,
   2129, 2132
SHARMA, Rohit Gurunath 2101,
   2102, 2111, 2112, 2118, 2119,
   2130
SINGH, Rudra Pratap 2003
SREESANTH, Shanthakumaran 1934,
   1935, 1949, 1973, 1974, 1975,
   1976, 1987, 1988, 1989, 2001,
   2002, 2003

TENDULKAR, Sachin Ramesh 1933, 1934, 1935, 1949, 1950, 1951, 1952, 1965, 1966, 1967, 1972, 1973, 1974, 1975, 1976, 1987, 1988, 1989, 2000, 2001, 2002, 2003, 2015, 2016, 2017, 2027, 2028, 2029, 2030, 2054, 2055, 2061, 2062, 2063, 2064, 2075, 2076, 2077, 2078, 2101, 2102

UNADKAT, Jaydev Dipakbhai 1987

VIJAY, Murali 1935, 1950, 1951, 1952, 1966, 1967, 1973, 1988, 1997, 1998, 1999, 2075, 2076, 2077, 2078, 2101, 2102, 2111, 2112, 2118, 2119, 2128, 2129, 2130, 2131, 2132
VINAY KUMAR, Ranganath 2029

YADAV, Umeshkumar Tilak 2015, 2016, 2027, 2028, 2029, 2030, 2054, 2055, 2061

YUVRAJ SINGH 1933, 1934, 1935, 1949, 1950, 1965, 2001, 2015, 2016, 2061, 2062, 2063

ZAHEER KHAN 1933, 1934, 1935, 1949, 1950, 1951, 1952, 1972, 1973, 1974, 1975, 1988, 1989, 2000, 2027, 2028, 2029, 2030, 2054, 2055, 2061, 2062, 2063, 2111, 2112, 2118, 2119

PAKISTAN

ABDUR RAUF 1946
ABDUR REHMAN 1977, 1978, 1990, 1991, 1992, 1993, 2010, 2011, 2022, 2023, 2031, 2032, 2033, 2046, 2047, 2095, 2096, 2115, 2135, 2136
ADNAN AKMAL 1977, 1978, 1990, 1991, 2008, 2009, 2010, 2011, 2022, 2023, 2031, 2032, 2033, 2046, 2047, 2048, 2095, 2096, 2099, 2100, 2113
AHMED SHEHZAD 2113, 2114, 2115, 2135, 2136
AIZAZ CHEEMA 2008, 2009, 2022, 2023, 2031, 2033, 2047
ASAD SHAFIQ 1978, 1990, 1991, 1992, 1993, 2009, 2010, 2011, 2022, 2023, 2031, 2032, 2033, 2046, 2047, 2048, 2072, 2073, 2074, 2095, 2096, 2099, 2100, 2113, 2114, 2115, 2135, 2136
AZHAR ALI 1963, 1964, 1968, 1969, 1970, 1971, 1977, 1978, 1990, 1991, 1992, 1993, 2008, 2009, 2010, 2011, 2022, 2023, 2031, 2032, 2033, 2046, 2047, 2048, 2072, 2073, 2074, 2095, 2096, 2099, 2100, 2115, 2135, 2136

BILAWAL BHATTI 2113, 2114

DANISH KANERIA 1937, 1938, 1947, 1948, 1963, 1964, 1968

EHSAN ADIL 2074

FAISAL IQBAL 1938, 1946, 1947
FAWAD ALAM 1936

IMRAN FARHAT 1936, 1937, 1938, 1946, 1947, 1948, 1963, 1964, 1968, 1969, 1970, 1971, 2074

JUNAID KHAN 2008, 2009, 2010, 2011, 2032, 2046, 2047, 2048, 2072, 2095, 2096, 2099, 2100, 2113, 2114, 2115, 2135, 2136

KAMRAN AKMAL 1936, 1937, 1938, 1946, 1947, 1963, 1964, 1968, 1970, 1971
KHURRAM MANZOOR 1936, 1948, 2095, 2096, 2099, 2100, 2113, 2114, 2115, 2135, 2136

MISBAH-UL-HAQ 1937, 1938, 1946, 1947, 1977, 1978, 1990, 1991, 1992, 1993, 2008, 2009, 2010, 2011, 2022, 2023, 2031, 2032, 2033, 2047, 2048, 2072, 2073, 2074, 2095, 2096, 2099, 2100, 2113, 2114, 2115, 2135, 2136
MOHAMMAD AAMER 1936, 1937, 1938, 1946, 1948, 1963, 1964, 1968, 1969, 1970, 1971
MOHAMMAD ASIF 1936, 1937, 1938, 1946, 1947, 1948, 1963, 1964, 1968, 1969, 1970, 1971
MOHAMMAD AYUB 2046
MOHAMMAD HAFEEZ 1977, 1978, 1990, 1991, 1992, 1993, 2008, 2009, 2010, 2011, 2022, 2023, 2031, 2032, 2033, 2046, 2047, 2048, 2072, 2073, 2074, 2095, 2096, 2113, 2114
MOHAMMAD IRFAN 2073, 2074, 2099, 2100
MOHAMMAD SALMAN 1992, 1993
MOHAMMAD SAMI 1947, 1978, 2048
MOHAMMAD TALHA 2115, 2135
MOHAMMAD YOUSUF 1936, 1937, 1938, 1946, 1947, 1948, 1970, 1971

NASIR JAMSHED 2072, 2073

RAHAT ALI 2072, 2074, 2095, 2096, 2113, 2114

SAEED AJMAL 1936, 1946, 1969, 1970, 1971, 1977, 1992, 1993, 2008, 2009, 2010, 2011, 2022, 2023, 2031, 2032, 2033, 2046, 2047, 2048, 2072, 2073, 2074,

2095, 2096, 2099, 2100, 2113, 2114, 2115, 2135, 2136
SALMAN BUTT 1937, 1938, 1946, 1947, 1948, 1963, 1964, 1968, 1969, 1970, 1971
SARFRAZ AHMED 1948, 2072, 2073, 2074, 2114, 2115, 2135, 2136
SHAHID AFRIDI 1963
SHAN MASOOD 2099, 2100
SHOAIB MALIK 1936, 1937, 1948, 1964, 1968, 1969
SOHAIL KHAN 2008

TANVIR AHMED 1978, 1990, 1991, 1993, 2073
TAUFEEQ UMAR 1977, 1978, 1990, 1991, 1992, 1993, 2008, 2009, 2010, 2011, 2022, 2023, 2031, 2032, 2033, 2046, 2047, 2048

UMAR AKMAL 1936, 1937, 1938, 1946, 1947, 1948, 1963, 1964, 1968, 1969, 1970, 1971, 1977, 1992, 1993, 2008
UMAR AMIN 1963, 1964, 1968, 1969
UMAR GUL 1936, 1937, 1938, 1947, 1948, 1963, 1964, 1968, 1969, 1977, 1978, 1990, 1991, 1992, 2009, 2010, 2011, 2022, 2023, 2031, 2032, 2033, 2046, 2048, 2072, 2073

WAHAB RIAZ 1970, 1971, 1977, 1990, 1991, 1992, 1993, 2136

YASIR HAMEED 1970, 1971
YOUNIS KHAN 1977, 1978, 1990, 1991, 2008, 2009, 2010, 2011, 2022, 2023, 2031, 2032, 2033, 2046, 2047, 2048, 2072, 2073, 2074, 2095, 2096, 2099, 2100, 2113, 2114, 2115, 2135, 2136

ZULFIQAR BABAR 2099, 2100
ZULQARNAIN HAIDER 1969

SRI LANKA

CHANDIMAL, Lokuge Dinesh 2025, 2026, 2038, 2048, 2069, 2082, 2083, 2113, 2114, 2115, 2116, 2117, 2127, 2133

DICKWELLA, Dickwella Patabandige Dilantha Niroshan 2134, 2135, 2136
DILSHAN, Tillekeratne Mudiyanselage 1933, 1934, 1935, 1965, 1966,

1967, 1979, 1980, 1981, 1994, 1995, 2005, 2006, 2007, 2009, 2010, 2011, 2024, 2025, 2026, 2038, 2039, 2046, 2047, 2066, 2067, 2068, 2069, 2082, 2083

ERANGA, Ranaweera Mudiyanselage
Shaminda 2007, 2065, 2066,
2067, 2068, 2082, 2083, 2113,
2114, 2115, 2116, 2126, 2127,
2133, 2135

FERNANDO, Aththachchi Nuwan
Pradeep Roshan 2009, 2046,
2047, 2069, 2114, 2117, 2126,
2127
FERNANDO, Congenige Randhi
Dilhara 1966, 1981, 1995, 1996,
2024, 2025, 2048

HERATH, Herath Mudiyanselage
Rangana Keerthi Bandara 1933,
1934, 1935, 1965, 1980, 1981,
1994, 1995, 1996, 2005, 2007,
2009, 2010, 2011, 2024, 2025,
2026, 2038, 2039, 2046, 2047,
2048, 2065, 2066, 2067, 2068,
2069, 2082, 2083, 2113, 2114,
2115, 2116, 2126, 2127, 2133,
2134, 2135, 2136

JAYAWARDENE, Denagamage
Proboth Mahela de Silva 1933,
1934, 1935, 1965, 1966, 1967,
1979, 1980, 1981, 1994, 1995,
1996, 2005, 2006, 2007, 2009,
2010, 2011, 2024, 2025, 2026,
2038, 2039, 2046, 2047, 2048,
2065, 2066, 2067, 2068, 2069,
2113, 2114, 2115, 2116, 2117,
2126, 2127, 2133, 2134, 2135,
2136
JAYAWARDENE, Hewasandatchige
Asiri Prasanna Wishvanath 1933,
1934, 1935, 1965, 1966, 1967,
1979, 1980, 1981, 1994, 1995,
1996, 2005, 2006, 2007, 2009,
2038, 2039, 2046, 2047, 2048,
2065, 2066, 2067, 2068, 2113,
2114, 2115, 2126

KALUHALAMULLA, Hewa
Kaluhalmullage Suraj Randiv see
RANDIV, Suraj
KARUNARATNE, Frank Dimuth
Madushanka 2065, 2067, 2068,
2069, 2082, 2083, 2113, 2114,
2115, 2116, 2117, 2126, 2127
KULASEKARA, Chamith Kosala
Bandara 2011

KULASEKARA, Kulasekara
Mudiyanselage Dinesh Nuwan
1935, 1980, 2046, 2047, 2048,
2065, 2066, 2067, 2082, 2083,
2126

LAKMAL, Ranasinghe Arachchige
Suranga 1980, 1981, 1994, 1995,
1996, 2005, 2006, 2007, 2009,
2010, 2038, 2039, 2069, 2083,
2113, 2114, 2115, 2116, 2117,
2133, 2134

MAHAROOF, Mohamed Farveez
1994, 1995
MALINGA, Separamadu Lasith 1965,
1967
MATHEWS, Angelo Davis 1933,
1934, 1935, 1965, 1966, 1967,
1979, 1980, 1981, 2005, 2006,
2007, 2009, 2010, 2011, 2024,
2025, 2026, 2039, 2046, 2047,
2048, 2065, 2066, 2067, 2068,
2069, 2082, 2083, 2113, 2114,
2115, 2116, 2117, 2126, 2127,
2133, 2134, 2135, 2136
MENDIS, Balapuwaduge Ajantha
Winslo 1934, 1966, 1967, 1979,
1980, 1981, 1994, 2082, 2117,
2134
MIRANDO, Magina Thilan
Thushara 1979
MURALITHARAN, Muttiah 1933,
1934, 1935, 1965

PARANAVITANA, Nishad Tharanga
1933, 1934, 1935, 1965, 1966,
1967, 1979, 1980, 1981, 1994,
1995, 1996, 2005, 2006, 2007,
2009, 2010, 2011, 2024, 2025,
2046, 2047, 2048, 2065, 2066
PERERA, Mahawaduge Dilruwan
Kamalaneth 2115, 2116, 2117,
2133, 2134, 2135, 2136
PERERA, Narangoda
Liyanaarachchilage Tissara
Chirantha 1994, 1996, 2024,
2025, 2026, 2048
PRADEEP, Nuwan see FERNANDO,
Aththachchi Nuwan Pradeep Roshan
PRASAD, Kariyawasam Tirana
Gamage Dammika 1933, 1966,
1979, 2010, 2011, 2026, 2039,
2068, 2069, 2127, 2135, 2136

PRASANNA, Seekkuge 2006

RANDIV, Suraj 1966, 1967, 1979,
2005, 2006, 2011, 2038, 2039,
2046, 2047, 2065, 2066

SAMARAWEERA, Thilan Thusara
1933, 1934, 1935, 1965, 1966,
1967, 1979, 1980, 1981, 1994,
1995, 1996, 2005, 2006, 2024,
2025, 2026, 2038, 2039, 2046,
2047, 2048, 2065, 2066, 2067,
2068, 2069
SANGAKKARA, Kumar
Chokshanada 1933, 1934,
1935, 1965, 1966, 1967, 1979,
1980, 1981, 1994, 1995, 1996,
2005, 2006, 2007, 2009, 2010,
2011, 2024, 2025, 2026, 2038,
2039, 2046, 2047, 2048, 2065,
2066, 2067, 2068, 2082, 2083,
2113, 2114, 2115, 2116, 2117,
2126, 2127, 2133, 2134, 2135,
2136
SENANAYAKE, Senanayake
Mudiyanselage Sachithra
Madhushanka 2113
SILVA, Jayan Kaushal 2010, 2011,
2024, 2113, 2114, 2115, 2116,
2117, 2126, 2127, 2133, 2134,
2135, 2136

THARANGA, Warushavithana
Upul 2133, 2134, 2135, 2136
THIRIMANNE, Hettige Don
Rumesh Lahiru 1996, 2007,
2009, 2010, 2026, 2038, 2039,
2069, 2082, 2083, 2126, 2127,
2133, 2136
THUSHARA, Thilan see MIRANDO,
Magina Thilan Thushara

VITHANAGE, Kasun Disi
Kithuruwan 2082, 2083, 2116,
2117, 2134, 2135

WELAGEDARA, Uda Walawwe
Mahim Bandaralage Chanaka
Asanka 1933, 1934, 1935, 1965,
1967, 1995, 1996, 2005, 2006,
2007, 2009, 2010, 2011, 2024,
2025, 2026, 2038, 2067, 2068,
2136

ZIMBABWE

CHAKABVA, Regis Wiriranai 2014,
2034, 2084, 2087, 2137
CHATARA, Tendai Larry 2084, 2085,
2095, 2096, 2137
CHIGUMBURA, Elton 2004, 2086,
2087, 2095, 2096
CREMER, Alexander Graeme 2034,
2084, 2085, 2086, 2087

ERVINE, Craig Richard 2004, 2008,
2084, 2085

JARVIS, Kyle Malcolm 2004, 2008,
2014, 2034, 2084, 2085, 2086, 2087

LAMB, Gregory Arthur 2008

MARUMA, Timycen 2086
MASAKADZA, Hamilton 2004,
2008, 2014, 2034, 2084, 2085,
2086, 2087, 2095, 2096,
2137
MASAKADZA, Shingirai Winston
2034, 2086, 2087, 2095
MAWOYO, Tinotenda Mbiri
Kanayi 2004, 2008, 2014,
2034, 2084, 2085, 2095,
2096
METH, Keegan Orry 2086, 2087

MPOFU, Christopher Bobby 2004,
2008, 2014
MUTIZWA, Forster 2034
MUTUMBAMI, Richmond 2086,
2087, 2095, 2096, 2137

NCUBE, Njabulo 2014
NYUMBU, John Curtis 2137

PANYANGARA, Tinashe 2095,
2096, 2137
PRICE, Raymond William 2004,
2008, 2014, 2084

SIBANDA, Vusimuzi 2004,
2008, 2014, 2084, 2085,
2086, 2087, 2095, 2096,
2137
SIKANDAR RAZA 2095

TAIBU, Tatenda 2004, 2008,
2014, 2034

TAYLOR, Brendan Ross Murray
2004, 2008, 2014, 2034, 2084,
2085, 2086, 2087, 2096, 2137
TIRIPANO, Donald Tatenda 2137

UTSEYA, Prosper 2085, 2095, 2096

VERMEULEN, Mark Andrew 2137

VITORI, Brian Vitalis 2004, 2008,
2034, 2096

WALLER, Malcolm Noel 2014, 2034,
2084, 2085, 2086, 2087, 2095,
2096
WILLIAMS, Sean Colin 2085,
2137

BANGLADESH

ABDUR RAZZAK 1954, 1955, 1959,
2004, 2097, 2098, 2117
ABUL HASAN 2060, 2082, 2083
AFTAB AHMED 1953, 1954
AL-AMIN HOSSAIN 2098, 2116,
2117, 2138, 2139
ANAMUL HAQUE 2082, 2097, 2098,
2139

ELIAS SUNNY 2012, 2022, 2023,
2082
ENAMUL HAQUE, jun. 2086

IMRUL KAYES 1949, 1950, 1953,
1954, 1955, 1958, 1959, 2004,
2012, 2013, 2117, 2138

JAHURUL ISLAM 1955, 1958, 1959,
2082, 2083, 2086, 2087
JUNAID SIDDIQUE 1950, 1953,
1954, 1955, 1958, 1959, 2059

MAHMUDULLAH 1949, 1950, 1953,
1954, 1955, 1958, 1959, 2004,
2022, 2023, 2059, 2060, 2082,
2083, 2086, 2117, 2138, 2139
MARSHALL AYUB 2097, 2098,
2116
MOHAMMAD ASHRAFUL 1949,
1950, 1953, 1958, 1959, 2004,
2022, 2082, 2083, 2086, 2087

MOMINUL HAQUE 2082, 2083,
2087, 2097, 2098, 2116, 2117,
2138, 2139
MUSHFIQUR RAHIM 1949, 1950,
1953, 1954, 1955, 1958, 1959,
2004, 2012, 2013, 2022, 2023,
2059, 2060, 2082, 2083, 2086,
2087, 2097, 2098, 2116, 2117,
2138, 2139

NAEEM ISLAM 1954, 1955, 2012,
2013, 2059, 2060
NASIR HOSSAIN 2012, 2013, 2022,
2023, 2059, 2060, 2082, 2083,
2086, 2087, 2097, 2098, 2116,
2117, 2138, 2139
NAZIMUDDIN 2022, 2023, 2060
NAZMUL HOSSAIN 2023

RAQIBUL HASAN 1949, 1950, 2012,
2013
ROBIUL ISLAM 1958, 2004, 2023,
2083, 2086, 2087, 2097, 2116,
2139
RUBEL HOSSAIN 1949, 1950,
1953, 1954, 1955, 1958, 2004,
2012, 2013, 2022, 2059, 2060,
2083, 2086, 2097, 2098, 2116,
2138

SAJIDUL ISLAM 2087

SHAFIUL ISLAM 1949, 1950, 1953,
1955, 1959, 2004, 2139
SHAHADAT HOSSAIN 1949,
1950, 1953, 1954, 1958, 1959,
2012, 2013, 2022, 2023, 2059,
2082
SHAHRIAR NAFEES 1949, 2004,
2012, 2013, 2022, 2023, 2059,
2060, 2086
SHAKIB AL HASAN 1949, 1950,
1953, 1954, 1955, 1958, 1959,
2004, 2012, 2013, 2022, 2023,
2059, 2060, 2086, 2087, 2097,
2098, 2116, 2117
SHAMSUR RAHMAN 2116, 2117,
2138, 2139
SHUVAGATA HOM 2138
SOHAG GAZI 2059, 2060, 2082,
2083, 2086, 2087, 2097, 2098,
2116, 2117
SUHRAWADI SHUVO 2013

TAIJUL ISLAM 2138, 2139
TAMIM IQBAL 1949, 1950,
1953, 1954, 1955, 1958,
1959, 2004, 2012, 2013,
2022, 2023, 2059, 2060, 2083,
2087, 2097, 2098, 2116, 2117,
2138, 2139

ZIAUR RAHMAN 2087